This richly illustrated volume is the first book in English to address itself to the problem of relating theology and architecture in the building of Presbyterian/Reformed churches. Its basic concern is that a church interested in proclaiming the gospel must also be interested in architecture, for year after year the architecture of the church proclaims a message that either augments the preached Word or conflicts with it.

In the first main division, a theologian and preacher discusses such matters as God's communication of Himself to His people, the relation of Word and Sacraments, the office of the laity or people of God, the relation of this office to the offices of minister, elder and deacon, and the place of the choir and organ in the praise of God by the congregation.

In the second main division, an experienced architect presents the practical and technical aspect of achieving theologically accurate church architecture. Here a large number of very helpful suggestions are made for both the architect and the people of the congregation, including the church building committee.

Throughout the book the many striking photographs and clear diagrams serve to illustrate particular points and general concepts. The photographs give impressive evidence that the Christian faith can find significant expression in the architectural forms and materials of today. The diagrams will be especially useful in understanding the more practical and technical aspects.

While addressed specifically to Presbyterian/Reformed churches, this volume will be found to be a valuable source-book for building committees and architects, students and scholars, of all the churches.

$20.00

serve University; his engineering through Case Institute of Technology; and his art through the Cleveland Institute of Art. His interest in the field of theology stems from an active membership in the Reformed Church in America, in which he has served as elder, deacon, Sunday School superintendent and teacher, and member of the denomination's Christian Action Commission.

CHRIST AND ARCHITECTURE

photography and layout by the authors   photo technology, John Orr

CHRIST AND ARCHITECTURE

building Presbyterian / Reformed churches

DONALD J. BRUGGINK   CARL H. DROPPERS

WILLIAM B. EERDMANS PUBLISHING COMPANY
GRAND RAPIDS   MICHIGAN

BRESCIA COLLEGE LIBRARY
OWENSBORO, KENTUCKY

The Scripture quotations in this publication are from the Revised Standard Version of the Bible, copyrighted 1946 and 1952 by the Division of Christian Education of the National Council of Churches, and used by permission. Exception p. 598.

Copyright © 1965 William B. Eerdmans Publishing Company. All rights reserved. Library of Congress Catalog Card No. 63-11498. Printed in the United States of America.

we dedicate this book to our parents

92084

Preface

It is to be hoped that this book will prove useful to students, helpful to architects, and stimulating to scholars in further research. It will, however, have failed its purpose if it does not communicate its concern for theologically accurate church architecture to the people of the congregation, including, of course, the people of the church building committee. Architects and theologians alike will remain frustrated in their attempts to build good churches unless the congregation is also concerned.

Christ and Architecture attempts to be very practical in meeting the needs of the Church. Having pursued questions of history and theology in words, it proceeds to give form to its ideas in pictures and diagrams. Often, after using a photograph to illustrate a given point, a sequence of photos of the same church will enable the reader to see the total architectural context. During these photographic tours the sequence of pictures is not interrupted with unrelated material in the text. Words must wait, when necessary, for the visual presentation of church architecture.

The intention of the sequence of pictures is to show a church in its wholeness, to convey the truth that good architecture embodies all of a building, and that snatches and pieces cannot be tacked on here and there. For great architecture, every element must be brought within the discipline of the total concept. It is not, however, the intention of this book to promote either these particular churches, or their particular styles. Therefore, having illustrated the issues, the book again returns to the use of words to describe the theological specifications, or, as they are hereafter called, the criteria, for Presbyterian/Reformed architecture. It is in words, and with criteria similar to those laid down here, that the church building committee should communicate with its architect. These criteria have been placed in capitals for the convenience of the reader.

We must acknowledge that while the photographs in this volume are of our own taking, they would be less than they are except for the expert photo technology of Mr. John Orr of Mt. Kisco, New York, who has captured the very best of every picture.

The assistance of many people in gathering the materials for this book is gratefully acknowledged: that of pastors, architects, organ builders, custodians, and many others who do not fit neatly into occupational descriptions. More particularly, we would like to thank the Reverend Dr. Howard G. Hageman, minister of the North Reformed Church, Newark, whose broad scholarship, which includes this subject, has been an initial and continuing stimulation; Dr. Louis H. Benes, who as editor of *The Church Herald* has long encouraged a better architecture for churches of the Reformed faith; Professor D. Dr. Oskar Söhngen, Vice President of the Evangelische Kirchenbautag, and an editor of *Kunst und Kirche*, Berlin, for his encouragement in the initial stages of this undertaking; Scott T. Ritenour, Executive Director of the Department of Church Building and Architecture of the NCCC, New York, for his assistance; the Reverend Reinhard Ring of the Deutsche Evangelisch-Reformierte Gemeinde, Frankfurt am Main, who in addition to furnishing us with information, and the talented guidance of his secretary, extended his warm hospitality as well. Appreciation must also be expressed to the Flentrop Orgelbouw for their gracious assistance; and to M. Marchand, Executive Secretary of the Bernische Synodalrat, for detailed information concerning the Swiss churches.

To Miss Mildred Schuppert, Librarian, Western Theological Seminary, we are indebted for her helpful assistance in research and detail; to Mrs. Harriet Bobeldyke, Mrs. Carolyn Heitmann, Miss Estella Karsten, and Mrs. Norma Sprick, secretaries who have handled reams of typescript and correspondence with unfailing good humor, we are also grateful, as we are to Mrs. Margaret James, who read proofs, and to Mr. William B. Eerdmans, Jr., Mr. Cornelius Lambregtse, and Mr. Calvin Bulthuis of the Wm. B. Eerdmans Publishing Company, whose assistance and understanding have been much appreciated. Those who have contributed most by way of endurance are undoubtedly our wives and children.

For our greatest assistance, however, we are indebted to Dr. G. A. J. ter Linden, Secretary of the Bouw- en Restauratie-Commissie der Nederlandse Hervormde Kerk, who not only provided us with a precise guide to the most important new churches in the Netherlands, and enabled us to gain entrance thereto, but who as secretary of the Commissie has played no small part in stimulating the architectural climate in the Netherlands, which has provided us with some of the finest examples of architecture for Reformed churches.

Donald J. Bruggink
Carl H. Droppers

Contents

Preface			vii
Chapter	1	THEOLOGICAL ARCHITECTURE	1
	2	THE WORD OF GOD	25
	3	CHRIST'S SACRAMENTS	125
	4	THE PEOPLE OF GOD	283
	5	CHOIROLATRY	387
	6	THE KING OF INSTRUMENTS	417
	7	HERESY IN THE SANCTUARY	445

Donald J. Bruggink

Foreword to Part II			487
Chapter	8	TEAMWORK IN CHURCH BUILDING	489
	9	ECONOMY IN CHURCH BUILDING	515
	10	EXPRESSION IN CHURCH BUILDING	555
	11	THE STRUCTURE OF THE CHURCH BUILDING	615
	12	THE SHAPE OF THE CHURCH BUILDING	637
	13	PROGRAMMING THE CHURCH BUILDING	655

Carl H. Droppers

Appendix	THE CHOICE OF AN ORGAN	681
Bibliography		691
Indexes		694

and the Reformed responded with an attempt to transform these inherited buildings into structures more suitable for biblical worship.

One should not surmise, however, that architecture became a theological concern only with the Reformation. In the Book of Exodus one finds chapter after chapter concerning the building of the tabernacle. Why should God be concerned with the architecture of the tabernacle, beyond the fact that it should be a good and careful piece of workmanship? There is a concern with architecture because the tabernacle and its arrangements are to tell the people something about God. The structure in which Israel is to worship is to be an aid to God's message. It is to be, in fact, a part of that message.

Scholars insist that the style of the tabernacle (and later the style of the temple) closely resembled that of the pagan architecture around Israel. At this period of time there was no separate style in which God was to be worshipped. But while style was a matter of indifference, architecture as a whole was not, for the plan of the tabernacle had a message.

The plan of the tabernacle must be understood in relation to God's great act of revelation in the history of his people Israel. The tabernacle, like most of Israel's worship, looks back to God's great act of deliverance from the bondage of Egypt. The furniture of Israel's worship was designed to call to the attention of the worshippers this mighty act of God. The laver of bronze would remind them of their escape through the Red Sea, the table of shewbread would by its presence speak of the God who fed them on manna in the wilderness. The lampstand and the table of incense would call to mind the pillars of fire and cloud by which they were led through the wilderness. In the Holy of Holies stood the Ark, the symbol of God's presence, which contained the Tables of the Law written on Mount Sinai. The Holy of Holies was to remind the people of God's giving of the Law, and just as the people were commanded not to touch the foot of the mountain when Moses went up to talk with God, so too the people had to stay outside of the Holy of

Holies. Only once a year could even the High Priest, representing the people of Israel (even as Moses had represented them) enter into God's presence. In short, the architecture spoke of God's love in his deliverance of Israel from the bondage of Egypt and his giving of the Law.

If these were worthy of architectural portrayal in the tabernacle, then are not God's deliverance of the Christian from the bondage of sin and his giving of redemption in Jesus Christ worthy of accurate architectural representation as well? It should really shame us as Christians, and especially those of us who claim to be "reformed according to the Word of God," that while Jewish congregations are still concerned about portraying in architecture the light of the Law given at Sinai, we so often give but a garbled account of the gospel in our architecture.

Beth Sholom Synagogue, Elkins Park, Pennsylvania (cf. pp. 596-603)
Frank Lloyd Wright, architect, and Rabbi Mortimer J. Cohen

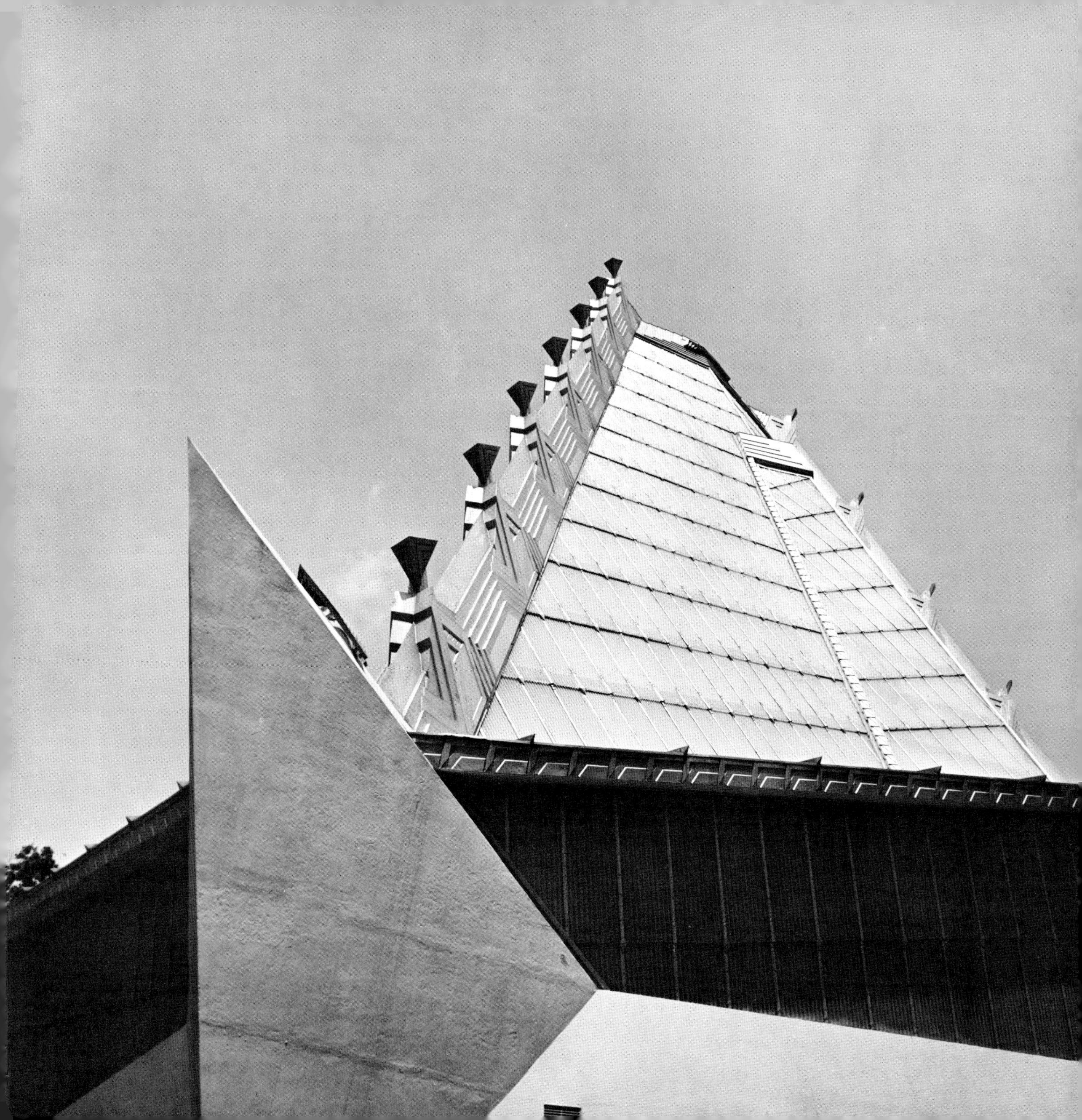

It is most unfortunate that many people understand the word architecture solely in terms of style. When a congregation is contemplating a building program and someone asks either minister or member about the architecture of the church, the immediate response is likely to be in terms of style: "We're thinking of Colonial, but may use modified Gothic, although some of the members want Modern." From what has already been said, it should be obvious that this book is not concerned with style as an end in itself; rather, it is concerned with architecture as the servant of the gospel. A church is a place where God's people gather together to worship him, and how they worship, as well as what they believe, is either reinforced or undermined by the architecture. Church architecture is therefore first and foremost a matter of theology rather than a matter of style. Thus the Protestant churches pictured in this volume are often of diverse style while nevertheless being good Reformed churches. Once it is possible to assess the worth of architecture for churches in terms of theology rather than style, one is able to appreciate both the superb old Swiss church in Kirchenthurnen and the more recent Gnadenkirche in Frankfurt am Main. The former is the careful work of Swiss craftsmen in a traditional Swiss style. As one studies carefully the architectural features it will commend itself as a fine Reformed church.

Kirchenthurnen, Switzerland

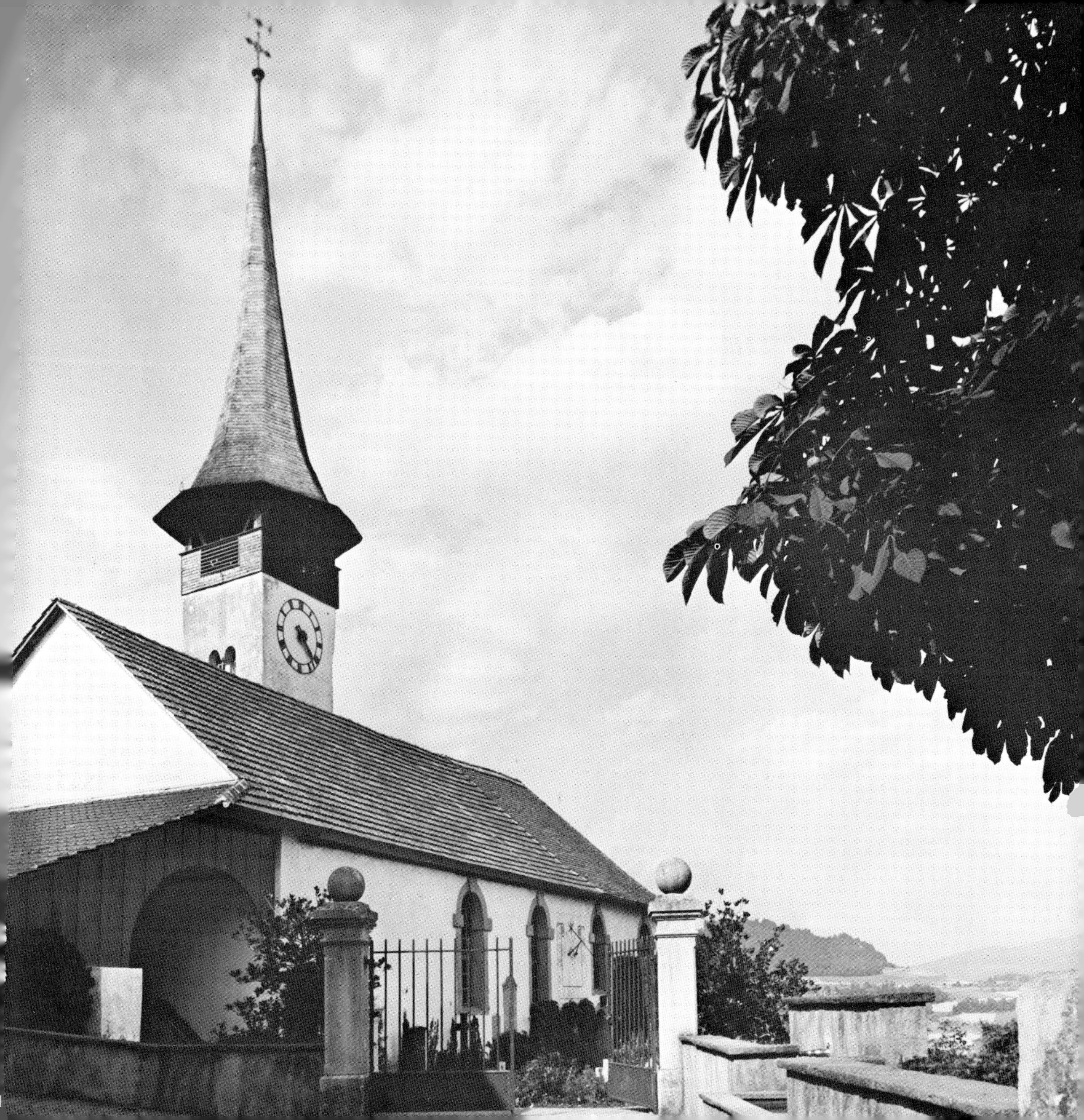

The present Lord's table stands before the baptismal font upon which is a wooden cover originally used as the Lord's table. It bears the inscription of its donor: "Benedicht Keusa, Kilchmeier, hat diesen Tisch verehret 1673."

Herr ich habe lieb
die Stätte deines Hauses
und den Ort
da deine Ehre wohnt
Ps. 26.8.
Kommet her zu mir
alle die ihr mühselig
und beladen seid
ich will euch erquicken
Matth. 11.28.

The pulpit with its sounding board, like the church itself, was built in 1673.

Der Herr ist
nahe allen die ihn
anrufen, allen,
die ihn mit Ernst
anrufen
Ps. 145,18.

Organ by Th. Kuhn of Mannedorf/Zürich

Hauptwerk

Principal	8
Rohrflöte	8
Octav	4
Spitzflöte	4
Nachthorn	2
Quinte	2⅔
Terz	1⅗
Mixtur 4–5 ranks	2
Schalmei	8

Rückpositiv

Gedackt	8
Principal	4
Rohrflöte	4
Flageolet	2
Larigot	1⅓
Scharf 3–5 ranks	1
Krummhorn	8

Pedal

Principalbass	16
Subbass	16
Principal	8
Bordun	8
Oktave	4
Zinke	8

The original organ by Samson Scherrer was built in 1773. In 1908 it fell victim to Romantic influences and a new organ was built into the principal case. Fortunately the casework of the original organ was spared, together with the pipes of the Rückpositiv. In 1954 the firm of Th. Kuhn undertook the task of building a new instrument with Classic voicing and tracker action, using the 1773 casework and Rückpositiv.

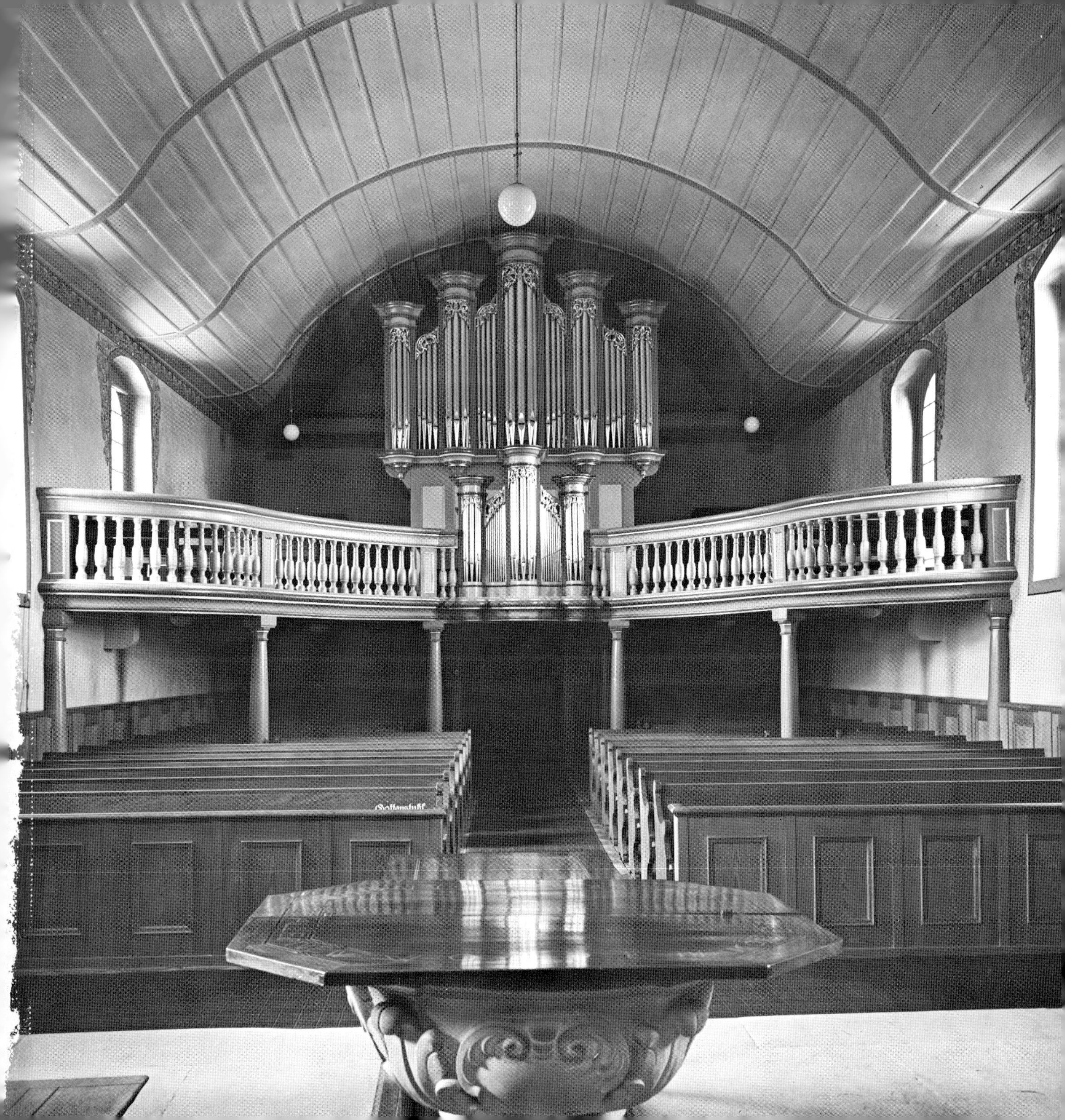

The history of the Gnadenkirche is altogether different from that of the church at Kirchenthurnen. The former belongs to a Reformed congregation dating back to the arrival of refugees from the Marian persecutions in England (1599). Before World War II this congregation (Deutsche Evanglisch-Reformierte Gemeinde) occupied a large Gothic church in the center of Frankfurt. This church, together with most of the center of the city, was destroyed in the bombing. In the midst of the shortages and extreme poverty of early postwar Germany the congregation found a bombed "greenhouse" on the edge of a large estate. The building was repaired and is still in use today by the northeast parish of this Reformed group. Despite its inauspicious beginnings and the demands imposed by the pre-existent structure, it still displays a sensible architectural arrangement that makes its character as a Reformed church unmistakable. These two churches, the one ancient and traditional in a quiet Swiss village, the other an emergency house of worship in a bombed greenhouse, have this in common architecturally: both make an accurate statement concerning the theology of the Reformation.

Grace Church (Gnadenkirche), Deutsche Evangelisch-Reformierte Gemeinde, Frankfurt am Main, West Germany

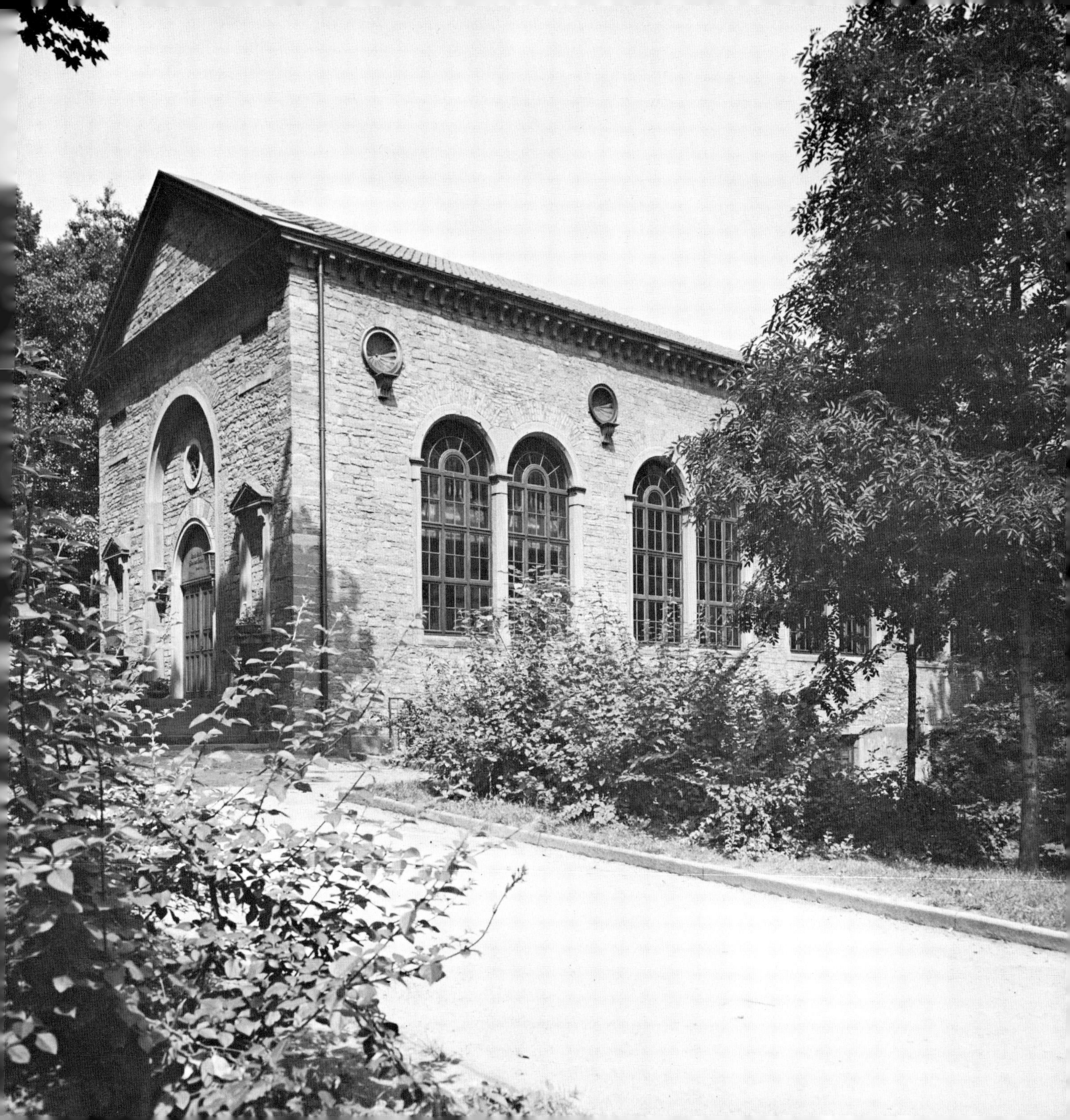

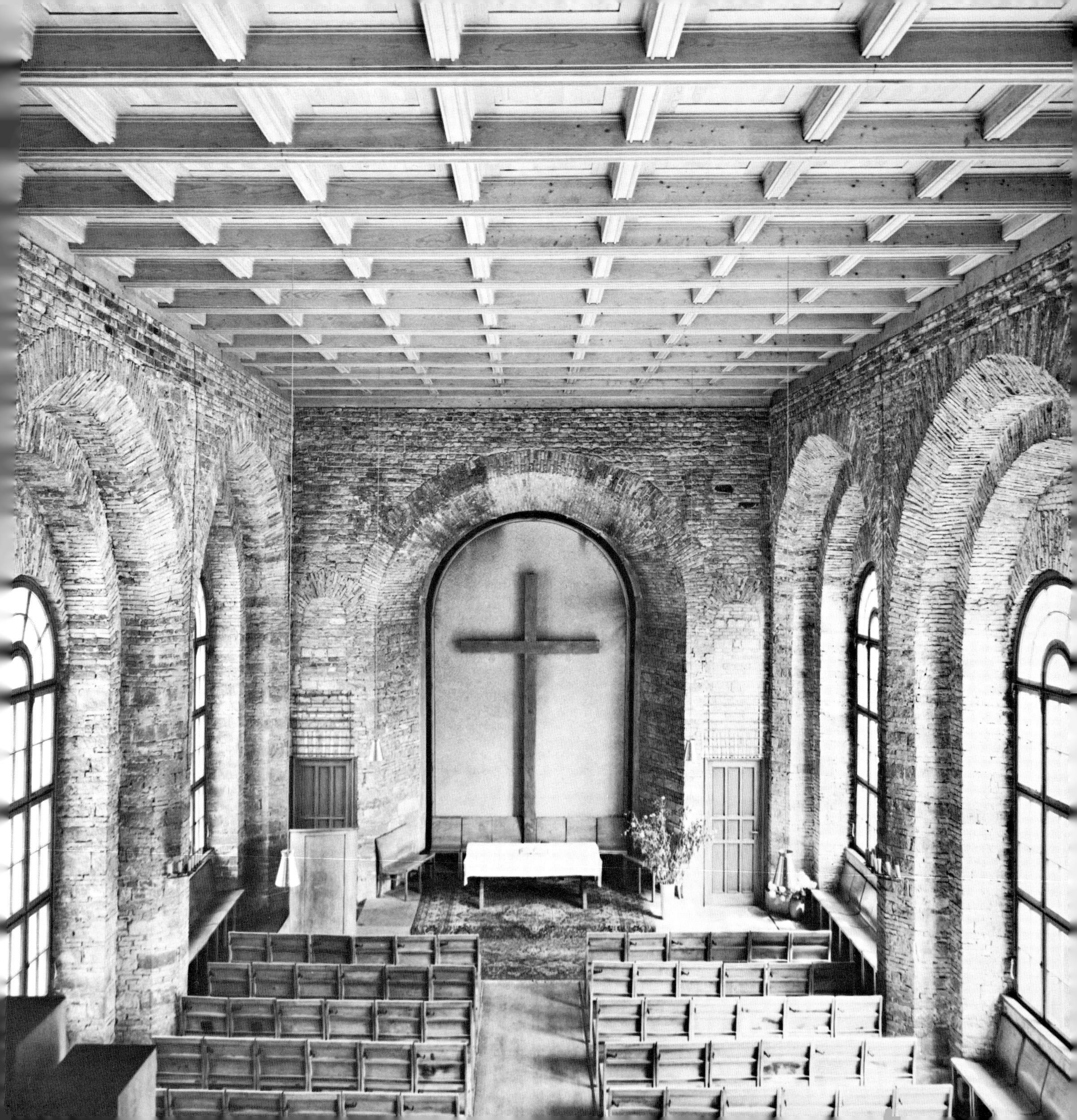

But if church architecture is really a matter of gospel, how does one explain the fact that in all too many Presbyterian/Reformed churches in America the relationship of architecture to theology seems never to have been considered? The answer involves historical circumstance and an architectural emphasis upon style while theologians remained silent concerning the nature of the Church in its relation to architecture.

In the United States, historical circumstance has conspired to throw together people of every religious and architectural background, who in turn employ architects of varied religious and architectural background. With a situation such as this, leading almost inevitably to the mongrelization of religious architecture, one would have expected the theologians to have rushed to the fore to provide guidance to ministers, building committees, and architects. Such, however, has not been the case. No great book concerning Presbyterian/Reformed architecture has ever been published in America, and within the last three decades, despite the tremendous amount of church building, there has not been published in English so much as a single book on Reformed church architecture.[1]

In a situation where theologians took scant interest in the theology of architecture, architects were left to concentrate entirely upon style. When the Gothic revival hit the United States the congregation in Litchfield, Connecticut, abandoned their fifty-year-old Colonial structure (which became the city auditorium) so that they might worship in a wooden Gothic structure. The strength of these stylistic fads becomes apparent when one learns that this abandoned Colonial church in Litchfield, now restored, stands as

---

[1] Credit, however, must be given to the Presbytery of Chicago for publishing the pamphlet, *The Architectural Setting for Reformed Worship* (1960), by the able church historians, James H. Nichols and Leonard J. Trinterud. This superb essay contains a brief but excellent historical survey of the relation of architecture to the Reformation. A number of articles by Howard G. Hageman constitute a small but excellent contribution to the literature defining the role of theology in church architecture.

one of the crowning achievements of New England Colonial church architecture, while the Gothic monstrosity that once replaced it has mercifully disappeared. The Gothic revival was followed by the Romanesque revival (see Chapter 5). Its stylistic reign was short, owing to the Columbian Exposition at Chicago in 1893, which led to such a rash of Classical churches that almost every city in the country still has at least one church that bears a rather ungainly resemblance to the Pantheon in Rome or the Parthenon in Athens.

Not only architects were caught up in this complete preoccupation with matters of style. When the Interdenominational Bureau of Church Architecture of the National Council of Churches was established, its infatuation was the same, and throughout the 1940s it had little more to offer Protestantism than the warmed-over medievalisms of the Anglo-Catholic ecclesiologists of a century before. (Fortunately, under the able leadership of Scott T. Ritenour, this situation has been corrected.)

In view of this stylistic mania, it is pointless to blame those ministers and building committees who have had all manner of heretical churches foisted upon them. The local church usually finds its energies exhausted with matters of size, location, and above all, financing. It would be an exceptional committee that could afford the time or talent to do much theological-architectural research into what the building should be. The architect, almost always lacking in formal theological training, often coming from a different religious background, and without any guide or program concerning the nature of a Presbyterian/Reformed church, can hardly be expected to become a theologian in order to design properly. If blame is to be placed anywhere, then the greatest portion must be given to the theologians, who for so long have allowed the church to proceed without guidance in matters of what its architecture should proclaim.

However, if the Presbyterian/Reformed churches of America suffer woefully from a lack of informed conversation between theologian and architect, they can make rapid and exciting gains through the assistance and example of their Reformed brethren in Europe. In Switzerland, Germany, and the Netherlands, theologians and architects have been in conversation since the First Congress for Protestant Church Architecture in Berlin in 1894. These discussions became increasingly fruitful in the years between the two World Wars, and following World War II the churches were able to capitalize on this mutual understanding in much of their new building. All of these continental Reformed groups now work with established sets of principles so that the architects may be assisted in their task of accurately expressing Reformed theology. The contrast in resources between the churches in this country, and, for example, the Nederlandse Hervormde Kerk is quite revealing. In addition to the books and articles published as the result of the aforementioned discussions between theologians and architects, there is also the official Kerkbouw en Restauratie Commissie, which stands ready to assist all churches in finding qualified architects, reviewing plans, and doing all it can to encourage proper theological expression in church architecture. The scene is not dominated by the Commissie, however, for there is also a private society that regularly publishes illustrated pamphlets evaluating the latest churches.[2] The whole matter is also brought before the public in magazine articles and through popular lectures carried by the state radio.

It may well be pointed out that the United States also has its conferences of church architects, its publications devoted exclusively to church building, and its ecclesiastical advisory bodies. But the significant thing that distinguishes these groups from their European counterparts is that in America theology is only a minor consideration while in Europe it is major.

---

[2] *The Prof. Dr. G. van der Leeuw-Stichting,* Ontmoetingscentrum voor kerk en kunst, Amsterdam.

The result is, as one knowledgeable European architect observed, that while American architects frequently offer brilliant solutions to structural problems, the general architectural impression is, from a theological viewpoint, one of chaos. Richard M. Bennett, writing on Protestant church architecture, observed that "Protestantism in America has no unity of faith and no architectural expression."[3]

The situation of the Presbyterian/Reformed churches in America is very much akin to that of the Church of England, so well described by Peter Hammond.[4] Like the Anglicans, we have simply not given enough thought to our theology in relation to church architecture. Unlike the Church of England, however, we are not imitating the "traditional" churches of an earlier age; rather, we are being tossed about on a shifting sea of eclectic borrowings. This situation will continue until we are willing to give some very serious thought to our understanding of the relationship between gospel and architecture. If the gospel and its proclamation are important, and if architecture can proclaim the gospel in a significant way, then we must consider with absolute seriousness its architectural proclamation.

Before proceeding into the heart of the discussion, it would perhaps be well to clarify a few matters of vocabulary.

East and West: The end of the church that contains the pulpit and/or

---

[3] Paul Thiry, Richard M. Bennett, & Henry L. Kamphoefer, *Churches and Temples* (New York: Reinhold Publishing Corp., 1954), p. 10P. This opinion was representative until late 1961. In that year the Lucerne International Joint Conference on Church Architecture and Church Building was sponsored by the Church Architectural Guild of America and the Department of Church Building and Architecture of the National Council of Churches of Christ, U. S. A. The insistence of the Europeans that church architecture is basically a matter of theology, and the acceptance of this dictum by a large number of the competent men at that conference, has made the above quotation not as completely true now as it was in 1954.

[4] *Liturgy and Architecture* (London: Barrie & Rockliff, 1960).

the Lord's table will, in accordance with common ecclesiastical practice, be referred to as the east end of the church, while the end at which one usually enters will be described as the west end. At one time these terms had geographical meaning, and for centuries churches were built with the altar at the east end. The divine light of Father and Son was by some "regarded as rising and enthroned in the East, like the sun in the natural firmament";[5] while others, with a particular understanding of Matthew 24:27, looked to the east for the return of Christ. With these principles in disuse, east no longer has geographical meaning in describing a church, but the term is still useful in describing the end at which the pulpit and/or Lord's table is located.

Presbyterian/Reformed: The term Presbyterian was originally applied by virtue of the fact that the Reformed of the Church of Scotland would not bow to an episcopal form of government, but insisted upon the presbyterian system which had been brought from Geneva by John Knox. Their valiant and victorious struggle stamped them with the name Presbyterian, albeit they were thoroughly Reformed in theology, even as the Reformed on the Continent were presbyterian in church government. Since the primary considerations of this volume in relation to architecture are theological, the theological designation, Reformed, will hereafter be used to describe the Presbyterian/Reformed in their common heritage of scriptural understanding.

Liturgy and Theology: Liturgy is a splendid New Testament word that carries a wealth of meaning, all of which is bound up with the idea of service to God. It is applied to the priests, the offerings, the vessels of the temple used in the service of God (Luke 1:23, Hebrews 9:21), the "sacrificial service" (Philippians 2:17), and the service of officers of the Church. That this word

---

[5] *Documents for Sacred Architecture* (Collegeville, Minnesota: The Liturgical Press, 1957), p. 19.

liturgy should come to be used of worship indicates the importance with which worship was rightly held as service! But the service of worship must be governed not by tradition, let alone by aesthetics, but by theology. Thus Conrad H. Massa has well said that for the Reformers "the liturgy of the Church was the working out of its theology in the activity of corporate worship."[6] Thus, there is a propriety in speaking, as does Hammond, of "liturgy and architecture," and meaning very much the same as "theology and architecture." Architecture, however, must also be liturgy (i.e., service to God) in working out the theology of a church in its physical structure. Just as liturgy is theology in action, so architecture is theology in material structure. Thus liturgy seems a word more appropriate to describe the role of architecture, rather than its underlying basis. Both architecture and liturgy must be determined by theology.

This volume is offered as a discussion of the most basic problems concerning the architectural expression of the Church of Jesus Christ reformed according to the Word of God. Compared to the thorough European investigations and studies, it will seem a very basic primer, which is what it is intended to be. It is a practical handbook for architects, building committees, and ministers, rather than a detailed discussion or history of Reformed architecture—although perhaps some day that necessary volume can be provided. The present volume, moreover, is not a theology textbook, although at crucial points theology must be discussed at some length to indicate the way in which architecture must go. In these instances Scripture, the Reformed Confessions, and the writings of John Calvin have frequently been cited: Scripture because it alone is the final court of appeal of the Reformed,

---

[6] "Architectural Implications of Recent Trends in Reformed Liturgy," *The Princeton Seminary Bulletin*, LIV, 3 (Feb. 1961), p. 49.

the Confessions to show the consensus of Reformed thinking concerning the Scriptures, and Calvin because of his tremendous influence as a biblical interpreter upon all subsequent Reformed theology. The attempt has been made to keep the book as compact as possible; it deals with the essentials of the theological/architectural problems, and condenses them to simply-stated criteria for architectural programming.

Discussions of the role of theology in church architecture are often hampered by the inability of many to visualize an architectural solution. This is to a large extent the result of the stereotyped churches (where the options seem to be limited to either a central pulpit or a split chancel) with which we are familiar. For this reason it is desirable both to discuss the theological principles of church architecture and to illustrate them in order that they may become meaningful options. Thus a large number of photographs and diagrams accompany the text to illustrate how the principles discussed have been handled in actual construction. Few American churches appear because in those rare instances where theology has played a correct role in the building of an American Reformed church, its architecture has been such that it has not received wide attention. However, the advanced efforts of the Reformed on the Continent have offered a wealth of illustrative material for this purpose. These efforts are shown not that they may be copied, or that their style may become normative, but rather that from them we may learn to express architecturally the fact that we are the Church of Jesus Christ reformed according to the Word of God.

2

The Word of God

Because church architecture expresses theology, it is imperative to ask the theological question: "How does God speak to his people?" The very fact that Christian worship is the subject of concern will give a basic answer: "God speaks to his people through Christ." It is when the next question is asked that a marked divergence within Christianity is revealed. For the next question must be, "How does Christ speak, or communicate himself, to his people?"

That God indeed does come to his people in Christ Jesus is the very essence of the Christian faith, and in this all Christians agree. But when one asks how Christ comes to his Church, then a sharp difference of opinion arises, one that cuts very deep theologically, and thus architecturally. To this question one very large segment of Christendom answers that Christ communicates himself to his people by way of the altar. This is the answer of the Roman Catholic Church: Christ communicates himself, and thus his grace, through the Mass. Architecturally, this doctrine is clearly stated in every Roman Catholic church, for invariably the altar stands in the focus of attention.

But is this the answer of the Reformed churches? Architecturally, one would suspect that it is, for in recent years the elevated Lord's table, built like an altar against the east wall, seems to have become very popular in Reformed churches. Is the answer of Rome concerning the altar also the Reformed answer, or is this an instance of allowing architectural style to govern the message, rather than demanding that the message govern the architecture?

An altar placed at the focal point of the church makes perfect sense within the context of Roman Catholicism. At the center of Roman theology, worship, and architecture stands the Mass, and the altar upon which the Mass is celebrated. Certainly the altar should hold the central position in a Roman church, for in the Mass, celebrated on the altar, Christ "offers Himself to God" in such a way as "to satisfy the justice of God for the sins committed against Him."[1] "The Mass is the Sacrifice . . . in which Christ, through the ministry of the priest, offers Himself to God in an unbloody manner under the appearances of bread and wine."[2] "In the Mass [Christ] applies to us the merits and satisfaction of His death on the cross."[3]

This central act of faith and worship affects the faithful both in life and in death. "The more fervently [the people] participate in the offering of the Mass, the more benefits they will receive from this precious sacrifice . . . ."[4]

---

[1] John A. O'Brien, *Understanding the Catholic Faith, An Official Edition of the Revised Baltimore Catechism No. 3* (Notre Dame, Indiana: Ave Maria Press, 1955), Q. 361, p. 212.
[2] *Ibid.*, Q. 357, p. 210.
[3] *Ibid.*, Q. 362, p. 213.
[4] Francis J. Connell, *New Baltimore Catechism No. 3, Official Revised Edition, 1949* (Benzinger Brothers, Inc.), p. 212.

Christ communicates himself bodily to his people from the altar, for through the Mass it is still possible for Christ to "associate intimately with men" and through the Mass he can indeed "be the intimate companion of everyone of His faithful followers."[5] When a loved one dies, the mass cards displayed at the funeral remind one of the Masses that are to be said on the altar to effect meritoriously the quicker release of the soul of the loved one from purgatory. Church architecture is theological, and the Roman Catholic Church says consistently and eloquently that the altar stands at the center of worship. "The Holy Eucharist is the very center of Catholic worship, and the heart of Catholic life."[6]

When in 1927 Karl Moser built the Church of St. Antony (St. Antoniuskirche) in Basel, it must have been a shocking structure to the conservative Swiss. Even today the uninformed tourist makes remarks about this "terribly modern church" with its exposed, unfinished concrete still showing the marks and even the grain of the forms, and this, inside as well as out, neither plastered nor painted, just plain concrete used in conjunction with steel and glass, simply and honestly. But it should be noted that the architectural theology of this church is the traditional theology of Rome: the altar remains at the focal point of the church.

---

[5] *Ibid.,* p. 204.
[6] *Ibid.,* p. 204.

28

The Church of St. Antony (St. Antoniuskirche), Basel, Switzerland
Karl Moser, architect

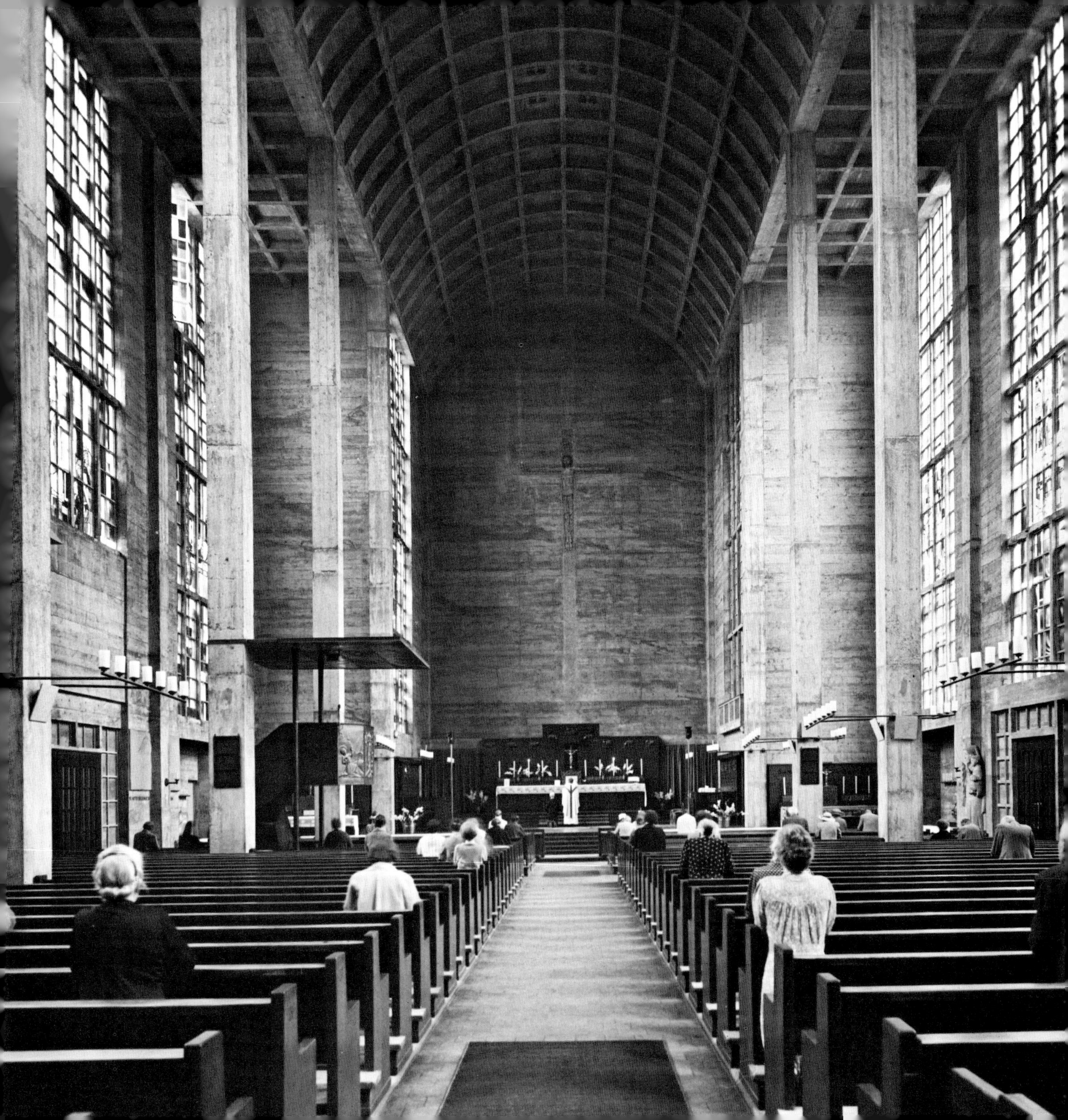

Anyone interested in church architecture will have noticed, however, that in recent Roman Catholic churches, especially in Europe, the altar has not been staying in its customary place, tight against the east wall. While remaining the focal point of the church, it has moved forward. The theological reason for this change in the position of the altar has come from the "liturgical movement," the most lively and biblically informed movement within the Church of Rome. The liturgical movement is the result of a combination of several movements of renewal within the Roman Church. The first of these was the Belgian liturgical movement begun in 1909 under Dom Lambert. Having a strong pastoral emphasis and a concern with the liturgy as "the great school of Christian living and spirituality," the movement sought through the liturgy "to share in the very life of Christ in his body the Church."[7] After World War I this movement coalesced with two others, one of which was predominantly theological, the other biblical. The first centered in the German abbey of Maria Laach; the second stemmed from the work of Pius Parsch and the Augustinian canons of Klosterneuburg, Austria. Combining with these groups in the early 1920s were the various Roman Catholic youth movements, of which the "Quickborn" circle in Germany was extremely influential.[8]

With astounding swiftness, some of the basic ideas of this liturgical movement combined with the modern movement in architecture, and through the person of Auguste Perret (an expert in reinforced-concrete construction who had never built a church) Notre-Dame du Raincy came into being. This spectacularly successful church of reinforced concrete and stained glass was both structurally honest and theologically bold.[9] The church was consecrated in 1923.

---

[7] Peter Hammond, *Liturgy & Architecture* (London, Barrie & Rockliff, 1960), p. 50.
[8] *Ibid.*, pp. 50ff.
[9] Ferdinand Pfammatter, *Betonkirchen* (Zurich: Benziger Verlag, 1948), pp. 32ff.

Aware of the relationship between theology, liturgy, and architecture, various societies were formed in which clergy, theologians, architects and artists sought to work out the basic principles of church architecture. One result was the document "Directives for the Shaping of the House of God, according to the Spirit of the Roman Liturgy,"[10] published by the German Liturgical Commission in 1946.

What, then, is the theological answer of the liturgical movement to the question of how Christ communicates with his people? Obviously, the answer cannot be a contradiction of accepted Roman teaching concerning transubstantiation. But the movement is intent upon recovering the "fullness" of the Mass, of making plain the fact that the Eucharist is not only an objective sacrifice, but also a supper. It is in doing this that the altar has come forward, and significant recoveries have been made theologically.

The altar is the table of the Lord from which the family of the Lord is nourished by his presence. Rudolf Schwarz, certainly one of the most gifted of Roman Catholic architects, emphasizes this fact again and again in his beautiful book *The Church Incarnate*.[11] The Mass is not something simply to be performed by the priest on behalf of the people while they sit passively, busy with their rosaries or perhaps their own thoughts. No, the liturgical movement seeks to recover the fact that the Lord's Supper is to be a dynamic celebration in which the people participate. The Church is the family of Christ, and this family must gather round his table for the sacred meal. But unless one is willing to settle for a buffet supper, using an altar tight against the wall for a sideboard, the traditional place of the altar is inappropriate. Nor is this sense of

---

[10] Available in English translation as *Documents for Sacred Architecture* (Collegeville, Minn.: Liturgical Press, 1957). This document strongly influenced the "Diocesan Building Directives" issued by the Liturgical Commission of the Roman Catholic diocese of Superior, Wisconsin in 1957, the text of which is published in *Liturgical Arts,* XXVI, pp. 7–9, 43–44.

[11] (Chicago: Henry Regnery Co., 1958). Cf. Rudolf Schwarz, *Kirchenbau* (Heidelberg: F. H. Kerle Verlag, 1960). Profusely illustrated.

the family relationship, and the participation by the people, stimulated if the priest celebrates with his back to Christ's family. Accordingly, the table has been moved forward, and the priest is able to officiate facing his people, from behind the table, as in the ancient Basilican position.

All Saints Church (Alleheiligenkirche), Basel, Switzerland
Hermann Baur, architect. Altar by Albert Schilling

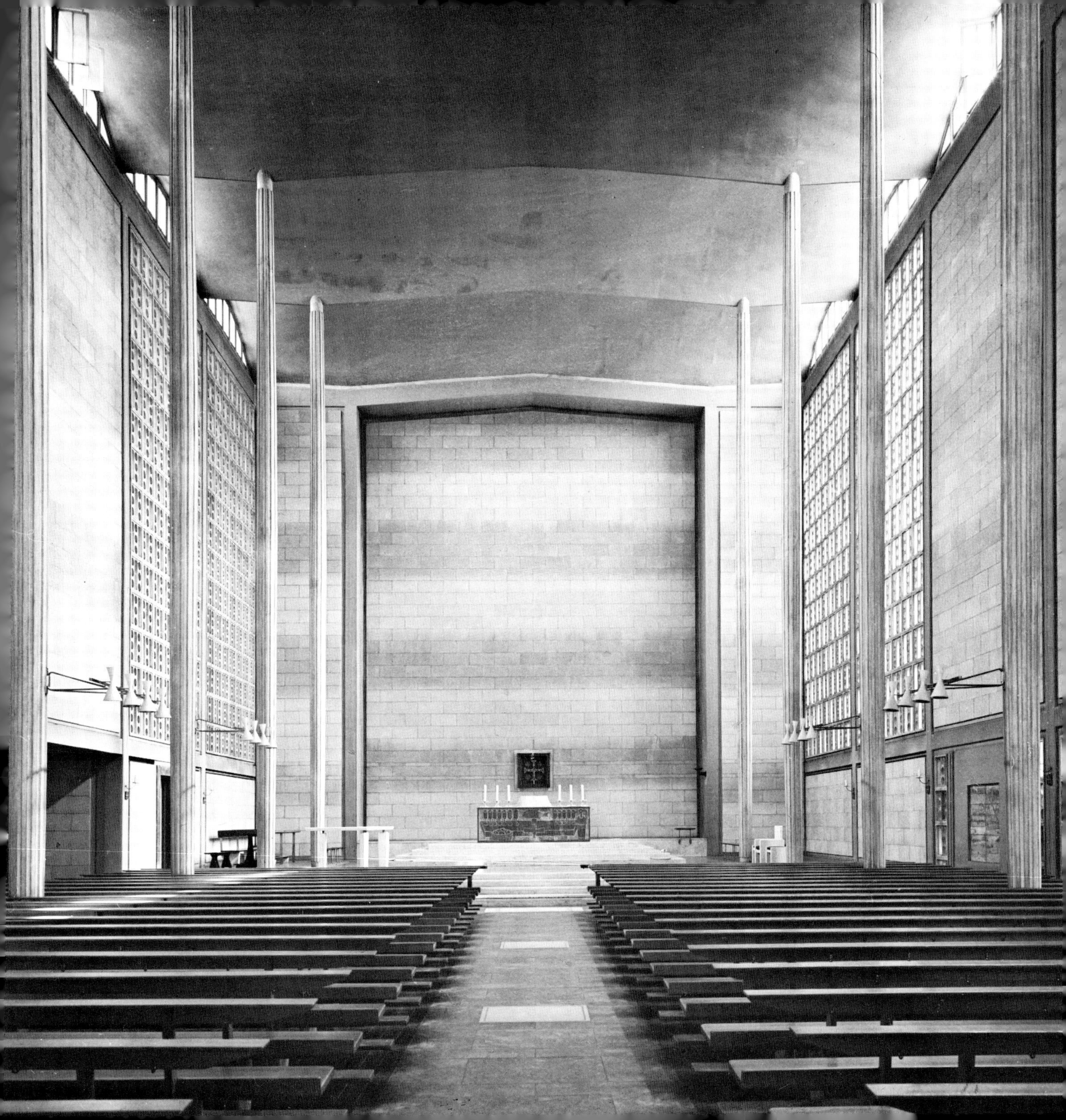

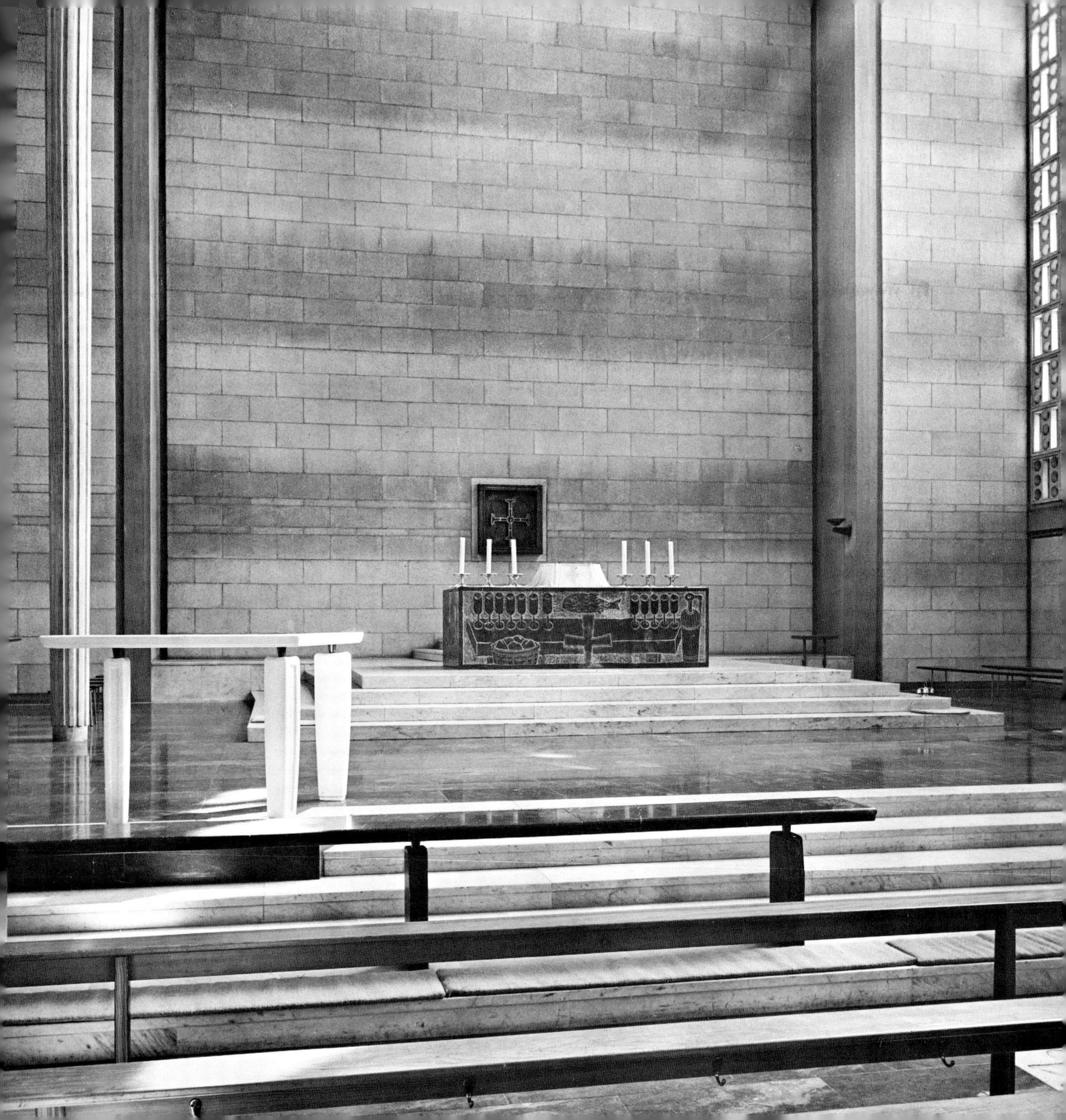

While the Roman Catholic Church is modifying the traditions of centuries in bringing forth the altar from the wall to make it more truly the Lord's table, all too many of the Reformed are building churches with split chancels and east-end altars. While within the Church of Rome tradition is being informed and transformed by the living Word of God, there are multitudes of Protestants who are allowing traditional styles to dictate architectural heresies.

In moving the altar closer to the people, the people in turn are being grouped more closely about the altar/table, which in some churches is placed on the long side of the room, the pews placed in a shallow arc about it. In other instances, a circular plan has been used in which the altar is in the very center of the building. Because theology and architecture go hand in hand, a theology which has again become aware of the Eucharist as a meal as well as a sacrifice demands an altar that is as well a table. This dual nature of the sacrament, as understood by Rome, is also translated into architecture through sculptured altars that are suggestive of tables.

A further result has occurred: the altar has been cleared of a lot of superfluous ornamentation. Again, this represents a return to the earlier practice of the Church, for in the early centuries nothing was allowed on the table except that which was used in the celebration of the Eucharist. Not until the twelfth century were the cross and candlesticks placed on the altar, and only in the sixteenth century did the altar crucifixes become obligatory. Under the influence of the liturgical movement many of the churches on the Continent are setting the candlesticks in the pavement around the altar and suspending the crucifix above and behind it, leaving the altar relatively free of ornamentation.

The Church of Brother Klaus (Bruderklausenkirche), Basel-Birsfelden, Switzerland. Hermann Baur, architect

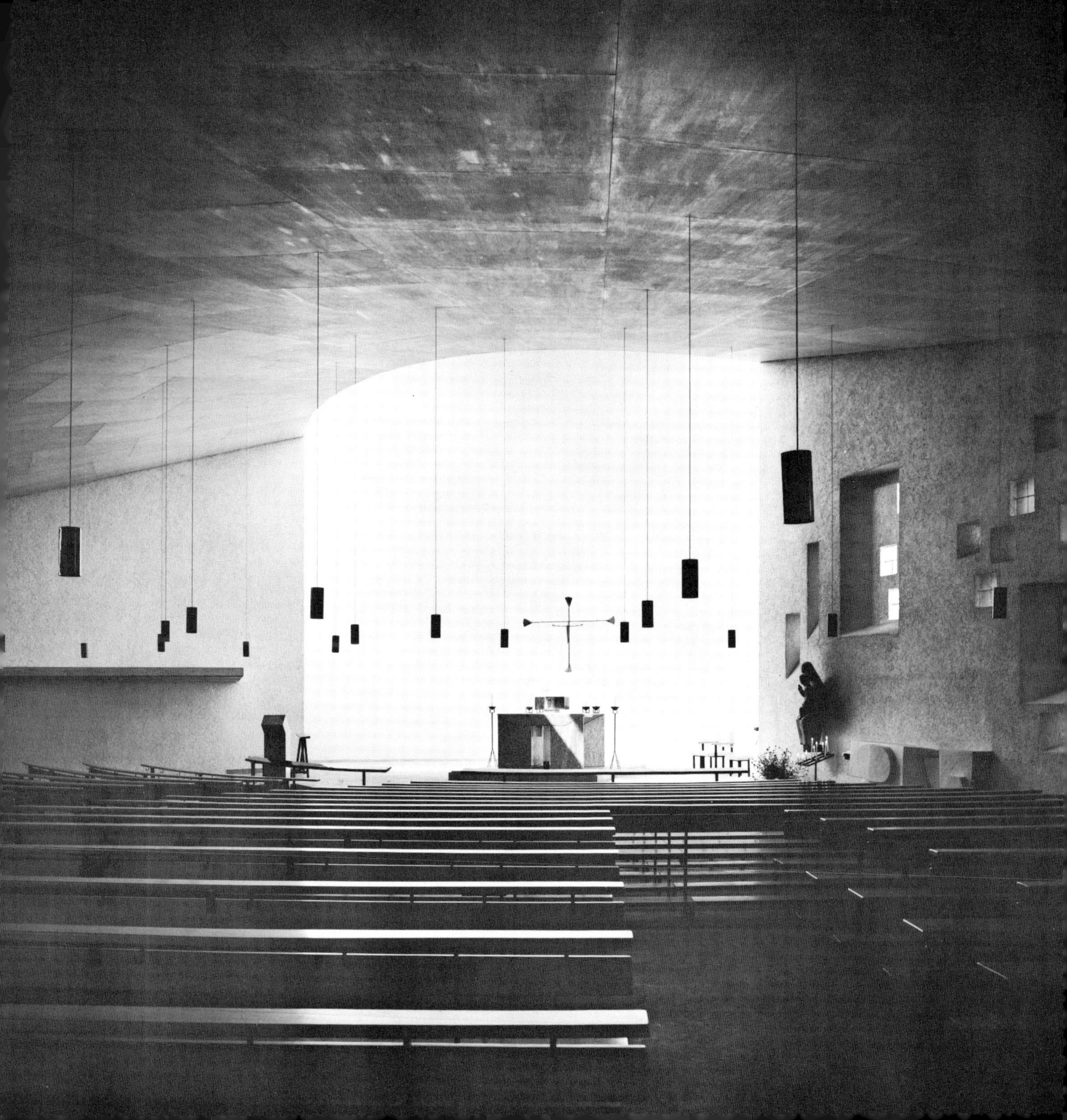

Brother Klaus, the name taken by so many Swiss Roman Catholic churches, refers to Niklaus von Flüe (1417–1489), a famous Swiss hermit, canonized in 1947.

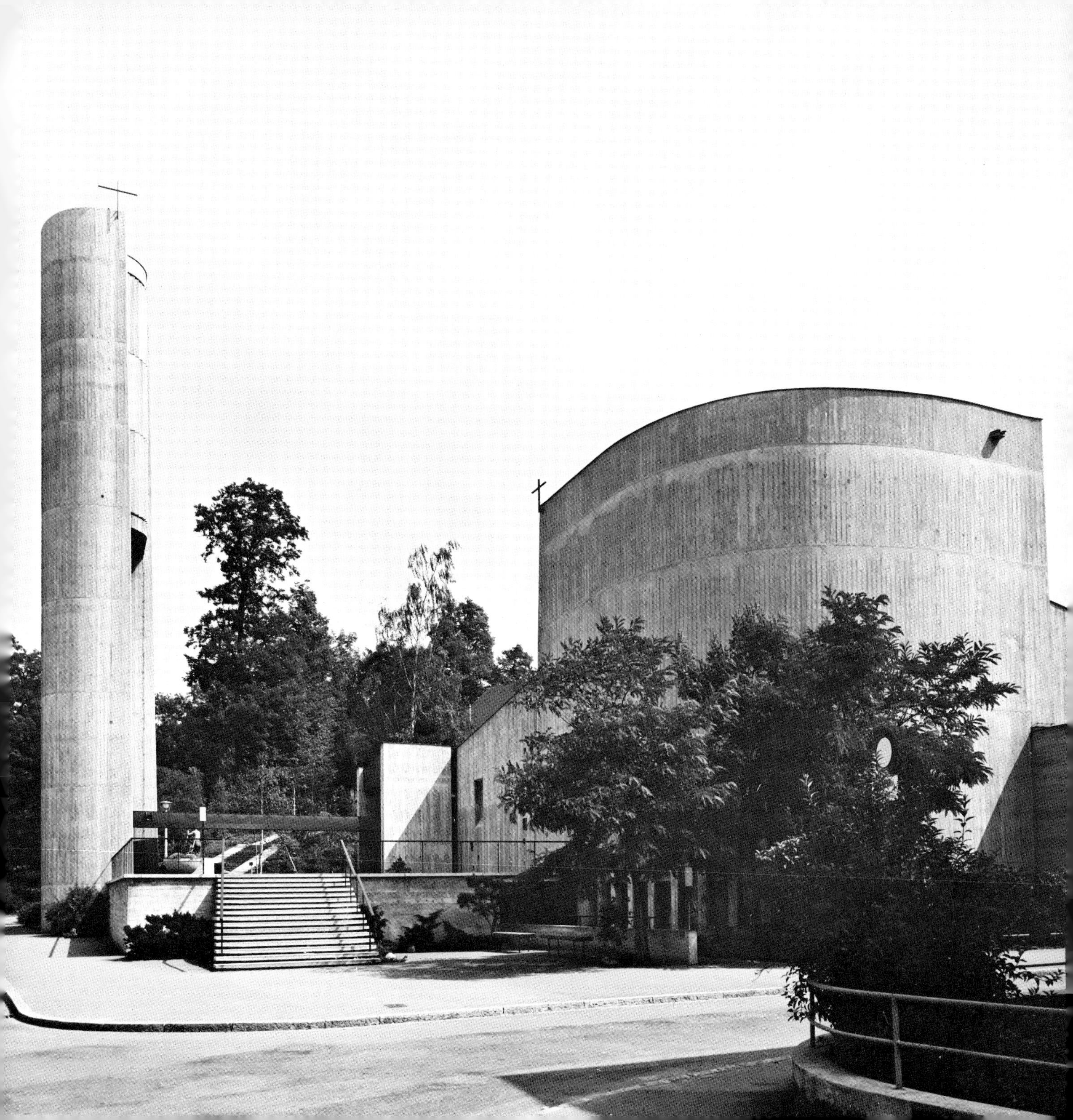

It is not a little disconcerting that while Rome is returning to a more biblical use of the Lord's table, all too many Reformed churches are busy decking out their tables with brass crosses and candlesticks, available in such weary profusion by makers of religious goods. There is no doubt that this cluttering of our tables is done not out of malice, but from lack of information. But does that not make it all the more tragic, that the heirs of the Reformation should through ignorance be contributing to an unbiblical confusion on the Lord's table, while our Roman brethren are in the light of Holy Scripture clearing theirs?

With the liturgical movement there has come this deepened understanding of the Church as the body of Christ, and therefore as an intimate community of brethren. That body has Christ as its head, and for the Roman Catholic the principal symbol of Christ in a church is the altar. Because there is but one Christ there is also to be but one altar within each church room. Thus the "Diocesan Building Directives" insist that the altar " 'ought not to be needlessly multiplied,' " and " 'where auxiliary altars are necessary . . . they should be placed out of view of the congregation.' "[12] The custom of putting one altar in each eucharistic room has always been practiced by Orthodox Christendom. While in many of even the modern churches in Europe there is still more than one altar visible, the auxiliary altars tend to be less conspicuous, and in the best churches are reduced to one.

In all of these instances in which the practice of Rome is being brought into closer conformity with the Scriptures, all Christians can rejoice. And not only for these elements of liturgy which find their outcome architecturally can one rejoice, but also for the accomplishment of a liturgy in the vernacular, the direction toward more frequent communion for the laity, possibly even

---

[12] Quoted by Hammond, *op. cit.*, p. 36. The text is published in the American periodical, *Liturgical Arts,* Vol. XXVI, pp. 7–9 and 43–44.

including the cup. As Reformed believers we can meet with even greater joy the increasing emphasis which is being put upon the reading and preaching of God's Word. On the other hand, it must be clearly understood that the basic Roman Catholic answer to our original question has not changed. To the question "How does Christ communicate himself to his people?" the answer is still, "Through the Mass." It is of course a wonderful improvement that for the first time in pontifical annals the Pontiff (Pius XII) has referred to the Eucharist as both "sacrifice and meal,"[13] but whether sacrifice or meal, in Roman theology it is still through the Mass that Christ communicates himself to his people. Rome simply cannot ever place predominant emphasis on preaching the Word, as do the Reformed, because for Rome Christ is not given in his very substance in preaching. In short, there is no transubstantiation in preaching, but only in the Mass.

The papacy, in the encyclical *Mediator Dei et Hominum*, published in 1947 with the express intention of circumscribing the liturgical movement, explicitly reaffirmed the objective nature of eucharistic worship, which is concerned with the sacrifice of the Cross renewed by the priest. " 'The sacrifice,' it declares, 'is really accomplished . . . ; it is in no way necessary that the people should ratify what has been done by the sacred minister.' "[14] The objective, transubstantive character of the Mass (i.e., its meritoriousness, irrespective of a congregation), is further reaffirmed by Pius XII in this same document when he declares:

> It is a false doctrine that would lead a priest to refuse to celebrate unless the faithful come to Communion; and it is still worse to ground this view—that the faithful must necessarily communicate together with the priest— on the sophisti-

---

[13] J.-D. Benoit, *Liturgical Renewal, Studies in Catholic and Protestant Developments on the Continent* (London: SCM Press Ltd., 1958), p. 72.
[14] *Ibid.*

cal contention that the Mass besides being a Sacrifice is also the banquet of a community of brethren; and that the general Communion of the faithful is to be regarded as the culminating point of the whole celebration."[15]

In order that the objective character of the sacrifice of the Mass would in no way be diminished, Pius XII described as erroneous the view "that the celebration of a single Mass attended piously by a hundred priests is the equivalent of a hundred Masses celebrated by a hundred priests."[16] The point is further driven home by the assertion that in view of its objective, transubstantive character, "one Mass cannot be equivalent to a hundred Masses, even if the hundred were each said by a priest on his own, and the single Mass were attended by an innumerable multitude."[17]

The above is not offered to suggest in any way that the theological advances of the liturgical movement are unreal—albeit they are undoubtedly in advance of the official thinking of certain sections of the hierarchy. Rather, it is quoted to indicate the complete and absolute seriousness with which Rome maintains the objective value of the transubstantiation of the Mass in which Christ, under the appearance of the bread and wine, comes in his actual body and blood, thus to communicate with and nourish his people. Pius XII, in *Mediator Dei*, reaffirms this objective value of the Mass in no uncertain terms. The liturgical movement does not deny the transubstantiation of the Mass, but wishes the active participation of the people in this Holy Mystery that they may more directly participate in its blessings. Not only for the Pope, but for the advanced theologians of the liturgical movement as well, it is not through the Word, but through the flesh of the Mass that Christ most fully communicates himself. That Christ gives himself in the

---

[15] *Ibid.,* p. 79.
[16] *Ibid.,* p. 80.
[17] *Ibid.*

Eucharist—this completely dominates and overshadows everything else. "Since at the Consecration in the Mass our divine Lord becomes present upon the altar, it is . . . Christ's throne on earth."[18] "The altar should appear with greatest prominence as the most sacred object, the very center and heart of the entire environment."[19] Similarly the American "Diocesan Building Directives" insist that the altar, as the principal symbol of Christ in his church, "must possess absolute prominence over all else contained by the church . . . it must be the unchallenged focal point of the building. . . ."[20]

How does Christ communicate himself to his people? The Roman answer is that Christ gives himself to the faithful in the Mass, and that answer is theologically and thus architecturally emphatic. Thus, in the magnificent Michaelskirche by Rudolf Schwarz in Frankfurt am Main, a church of magnificent aesthetic purity, one which with superb architectural logic embodies much of what is best in the liturgical movement, one nonetheless finds no pulpit.

---

[18] *Documents for Sacred Architecture*, p. 18.
[19] *Ibid.*, p. 19.
[20] Hammond, *op. cit.*, p. 36.

The Church of St. Michael (St. Michaelskirche), Frankfurt am Main
Rudolf Schwarz, architect

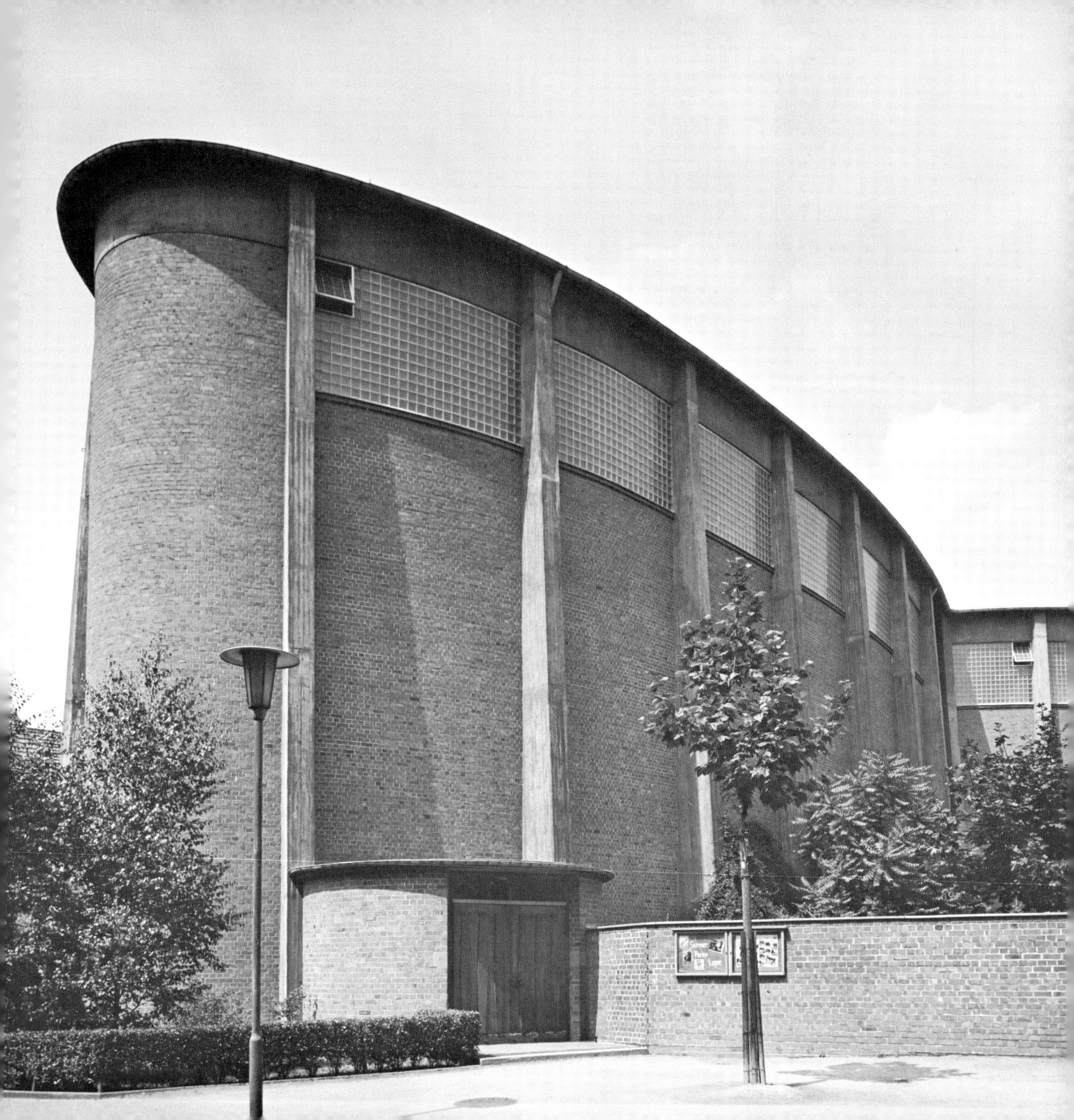

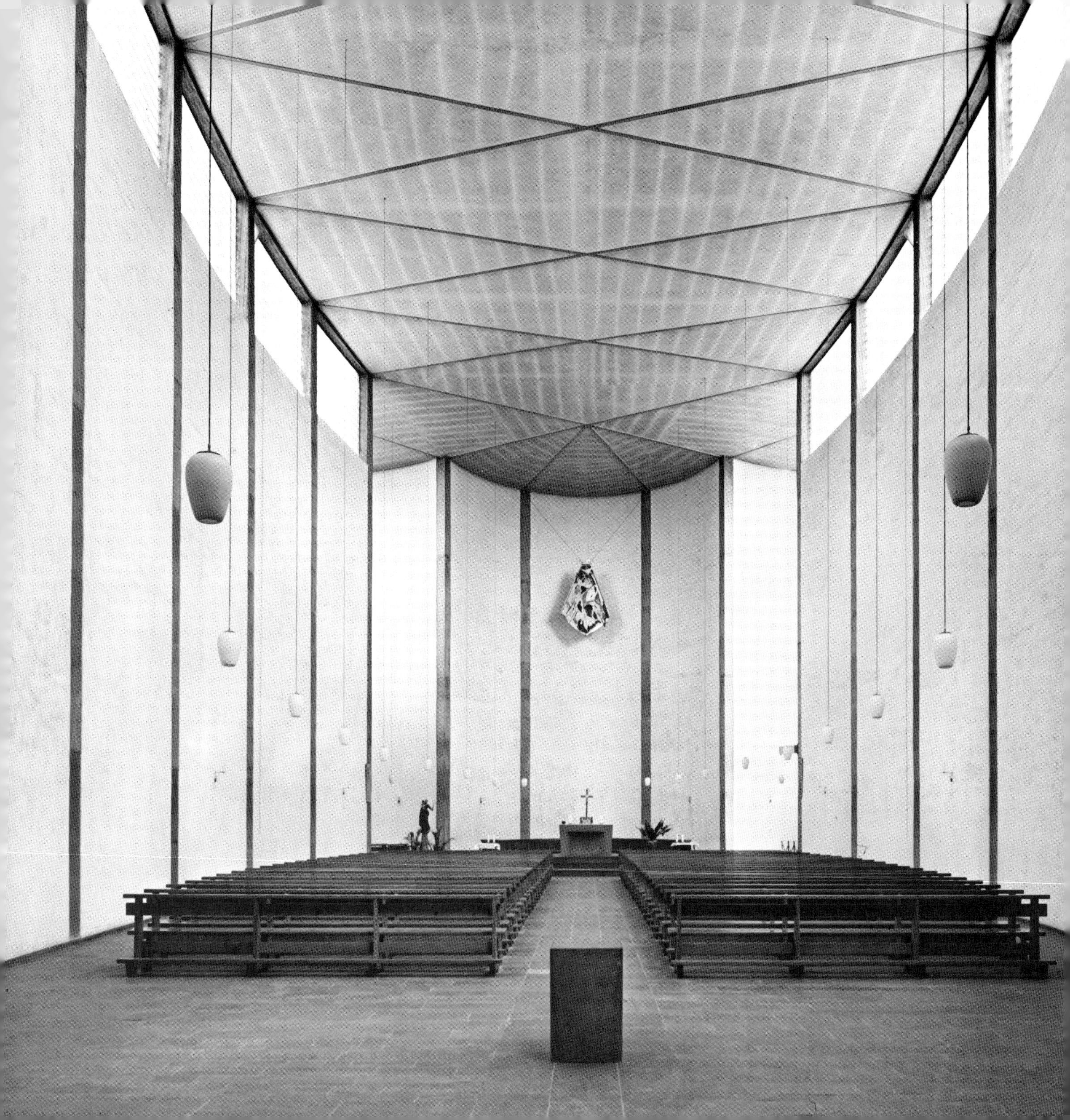

The "workday chapel" is partially visible north of the altar

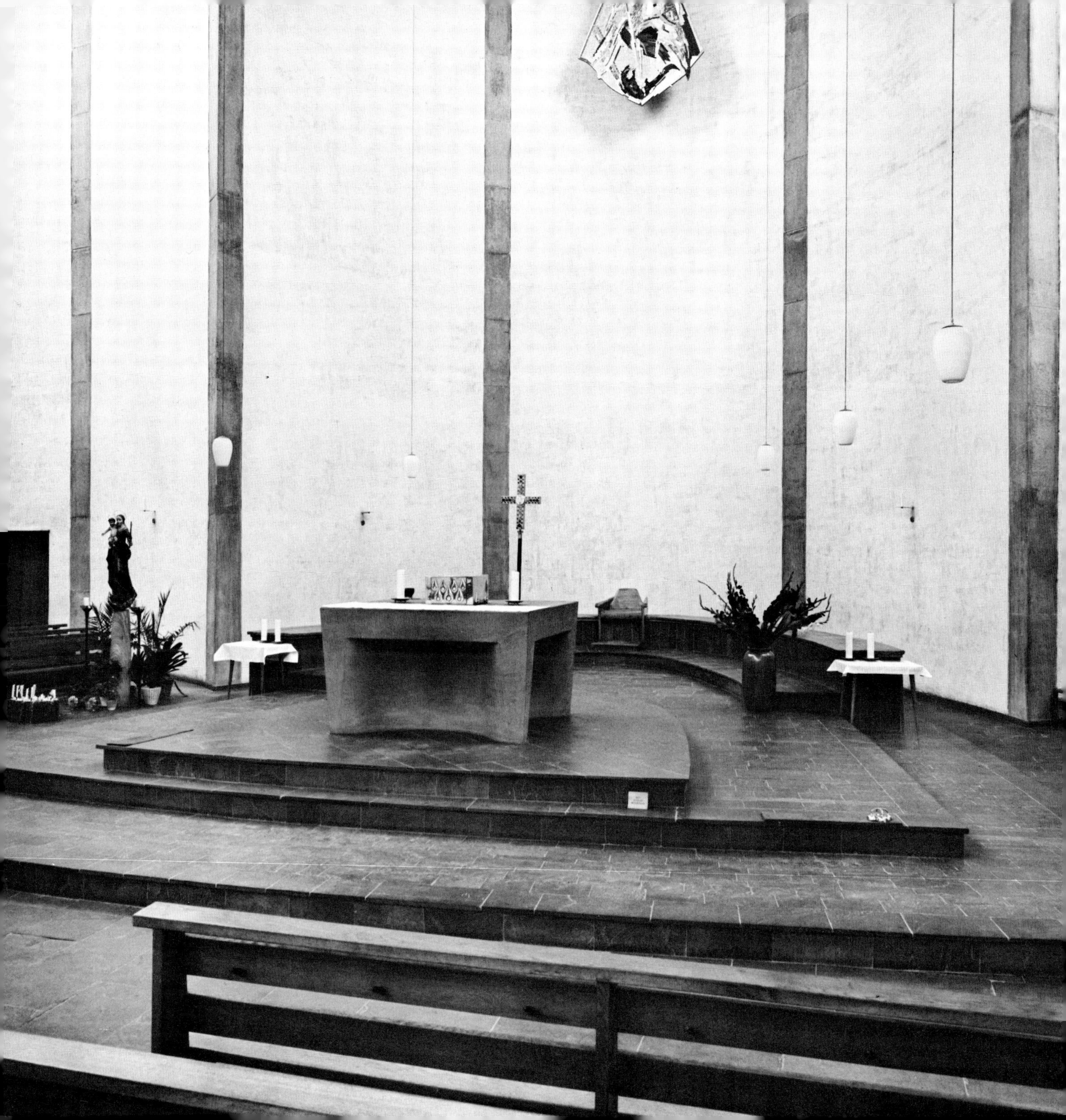

The organ and choir are located south of the altar

Organ by Förster & Nicolaus of Lich/Oberhessen

Hauptwerk		*Brustwerk*	
Quintade	16	Quintade	8
Prinzipal	8	Gedackt	4
Rohrflöte	8	Prinzipal	2
Oktave	4	Quinte	1 1/3
Nachthorn	4	Regal	8
Blockflöte	2	Scharf 3 ranks	
Mixtur 5 ranks			
Trompete	8		

Oberwerk		*Pedal*	
Gedackt	8	Subbass	16
Prinzipal	4	Oktavbass	8
Rohrflöte	4	Pommer	8
Nasard	2 2/3	Oktavbass	4
Waldflöte	2	Pedalmixtur 5 ranks	
Terz	1 3/5	Posaune	16
Sifflöte	1	Klarine	4
Zimbel 3–4 ranks			
Krumhorn	8		

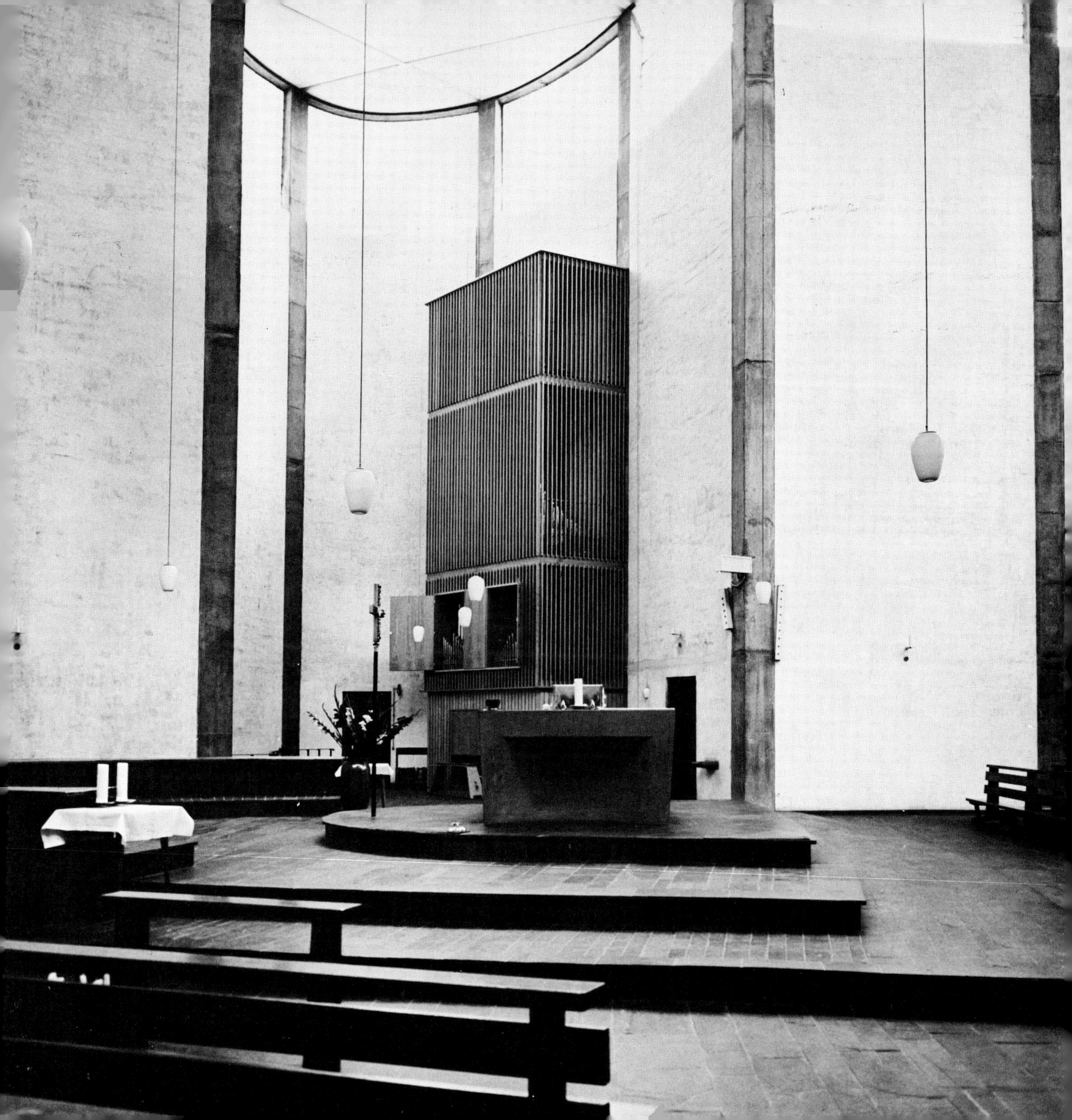

The baptismal font

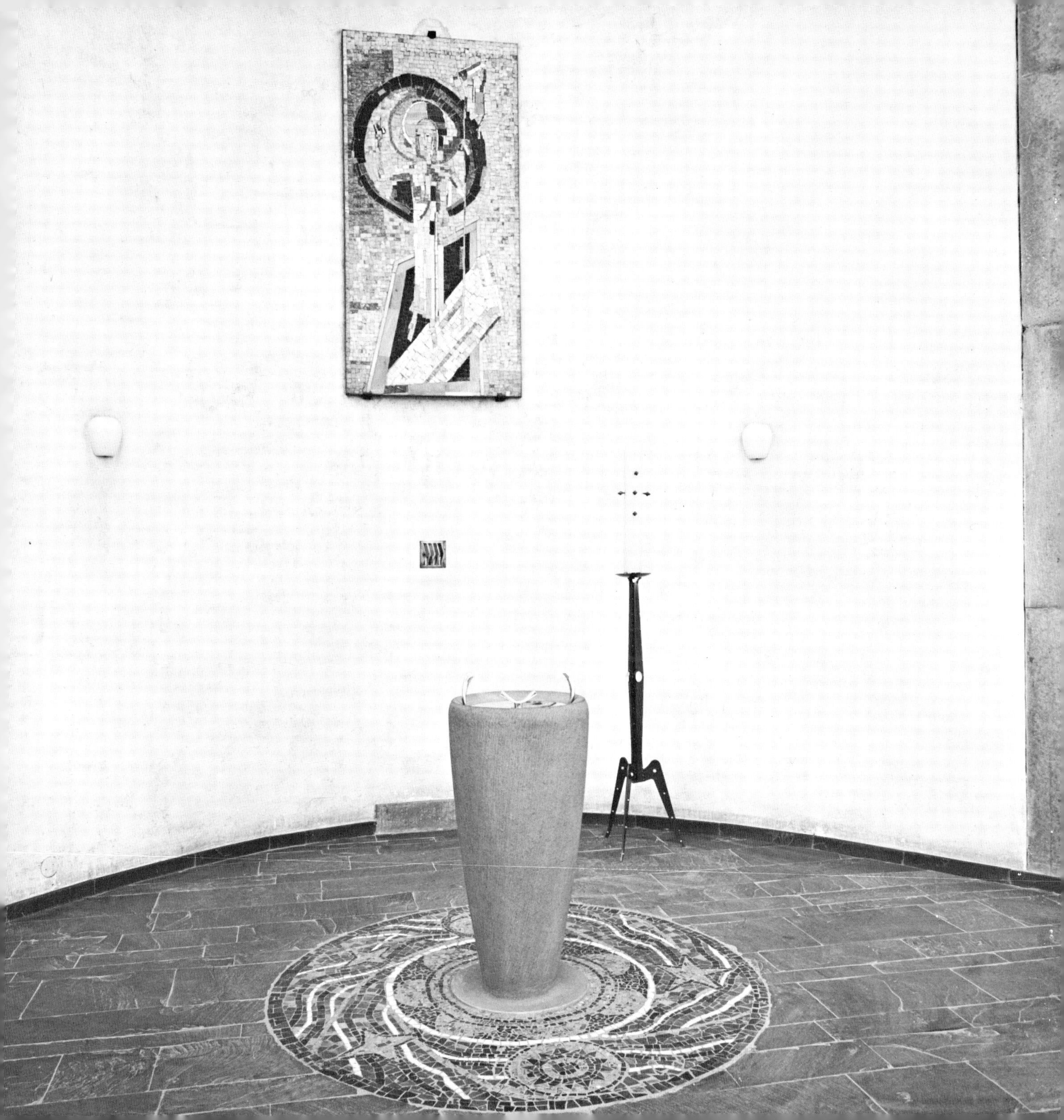

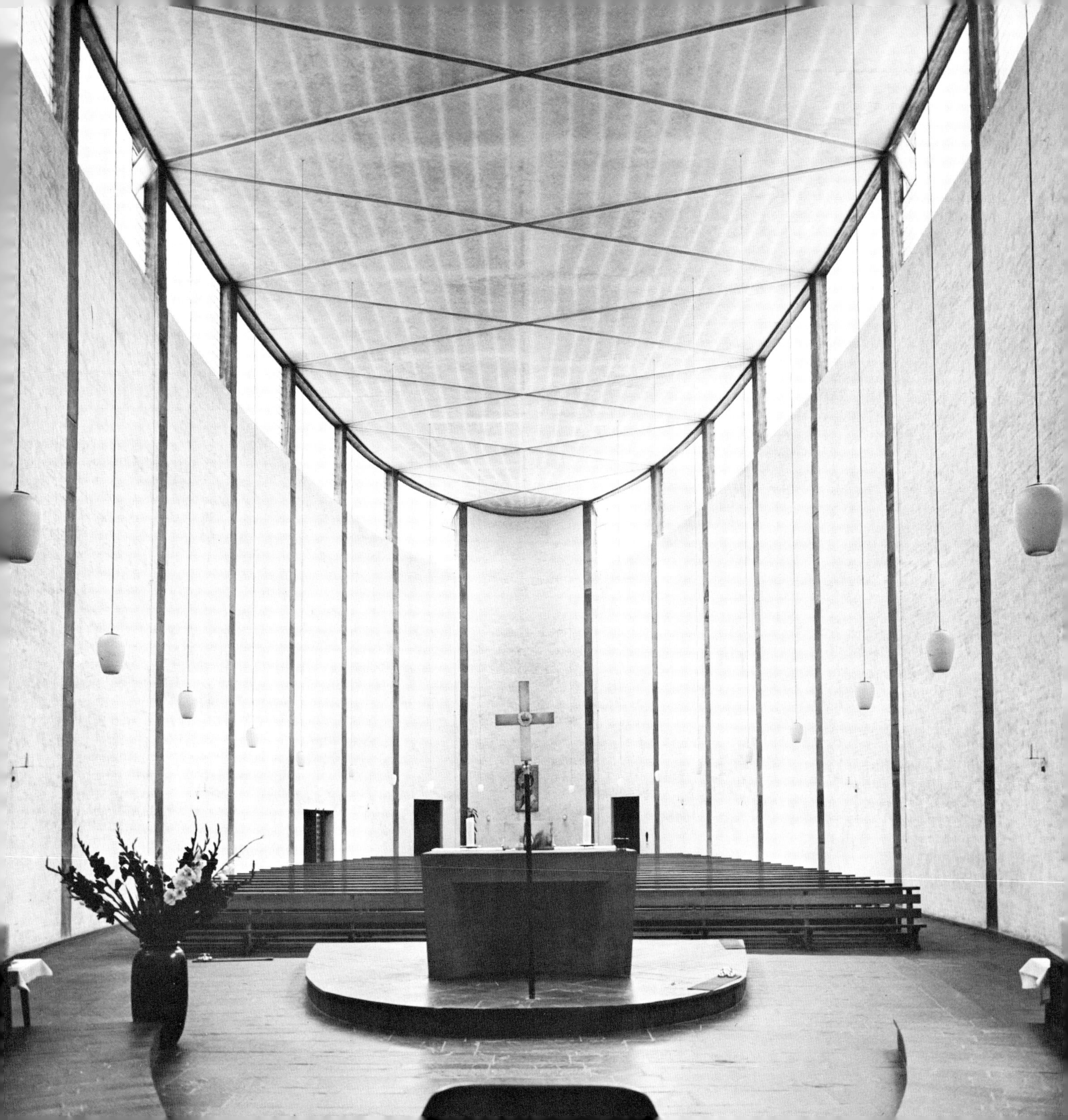

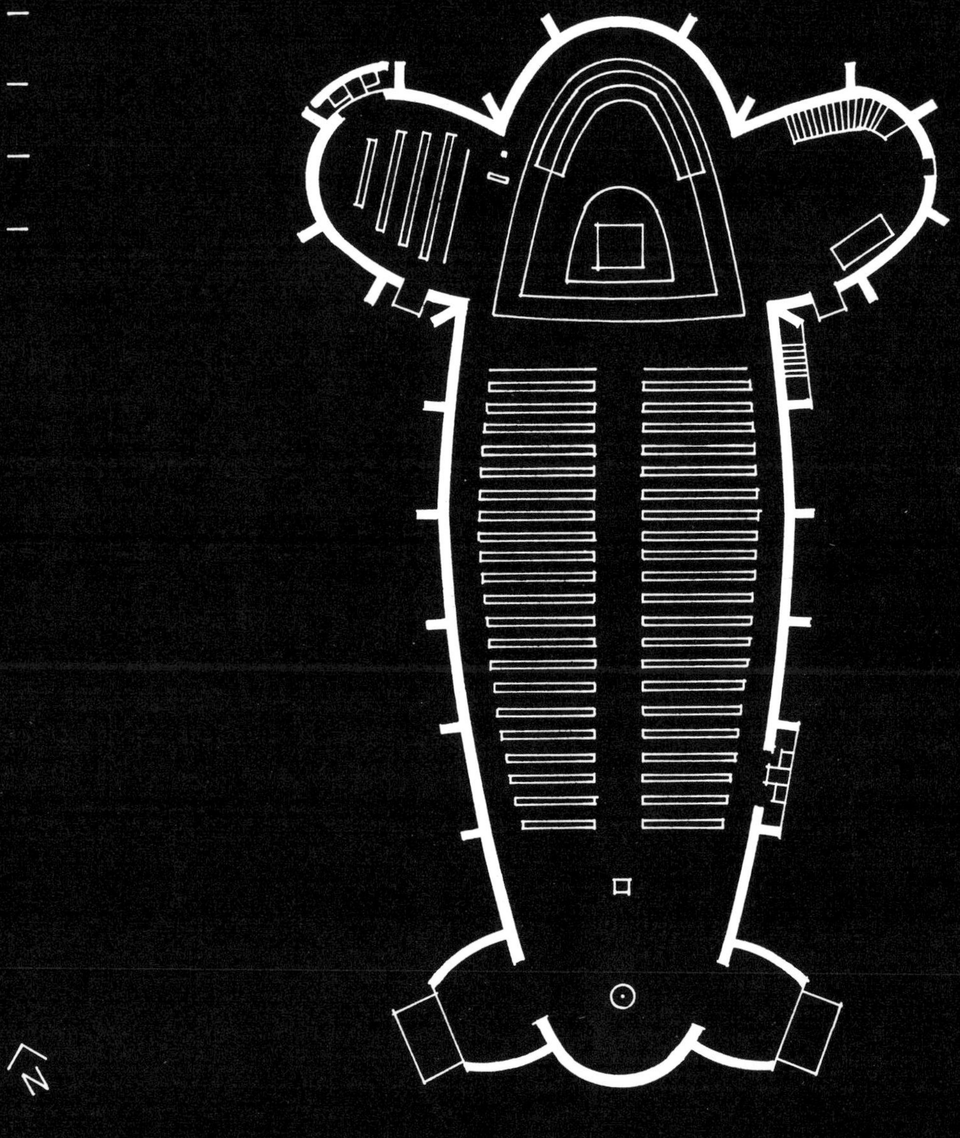

How does Christ communicate with his people? While architecturally and theologically the Roman Catholic answer is emphatic, one need not be a particularly perspicacious observer to note that the Reformed (in the United States, at least) have no clear architectural answer to this question. In fact, in many churches it is painfully apparent that either the question has not been asked, or else the answer is grossly in error. This confused gospel in architecture is all the more regrettable because of the clarity with which the gospel was understood by these churches as they were reformed according to the Word of God. The biblical insights of the Reformation remain valid and continue to be a necessity for the well-being of Christ's Church. It is therefore the responsibility of those churches which live in the Reformed tradition to proclaim this biblical message clearly not only in theology, but in architecture as well.

How does Christ communicate with his people? The answer of the Church of Jesus Christ reformed according to the Word of God is that Christ communicates himself to his Church through Word and Sacrament! This was the message Luther and Calvin found in God's Word; this remains the position of those churches which are reformed according to his Word. God communicates himself through Word and Sacrament.

One must never forget that Christ comes to us in not only his Word, but also in his Sacraments! The Sacraments must receive an emphasis fully commensurate with their God-given importance. They should in no way be neglected, as has all too frequently happened within the Reformed tradition. However, discussions of their rightful place must be put aside until the next chapter, for at this point it is necessary to witness to the power of the Word to communicate Christ to his Church.

To those within the Reformed tradition the importance of the Word will appear obvious enough, but it is a view to which many would take exception. While there is an element within the liturgical movement which also gives great place to the preaching of the Word, there are also those like Mauriac, who writes

> A good priest has nothing to say to me. I watch him, and that is enough for me. . . . The religious order that speaks best about God is that of the Benedictines because they never go into the pulpit. . . . How sorry I am for the Protestants, whose worship is nothing but words![21]

While strongly put, this position is perhaps not as exceptional as it might sound, for in the official catechism of Father Connell there is no reference in its index to either "Word of God" or "preaching" despite its 499 questions and answers which together with their amplifications cover some 320 pages of rather small print! Precisely because of an exaggerated preoccupation with the Eucharist (a predilection shared by many high churchmen outside the Roman and Orthodox fold) it is necessary to restate the place of the Word in communicating Christ.

Word of Communication

First, one must state quite emphatically that the biblical witness makes it unmistakably clear that God's Word speaks to man's understanding. God's Word addresses itself to men's minds. From the very first pages of Scripture one finds pictured a God who "commanded the man, saying . . ." (Genesis 2:16), and even when man disobeyed, "the Lord God called to the man, and said to him . . ." (Genesis 3:9). This portrayal of God's relationship to man is quite commensurate with the doctrine that God created man in his own image, and while to be made in the image of God is primarily a matter of being able to image God in love and righteousness, there is involved as well a necessary freedom and rationality, without which love and righteousness are impossible.

---

[21] *La Table ronde*, No. 12 (Dec. 1948), p. 1996, cited by J.-D. Benoit, *op. cit.*, p. 104.

The biblical depiction of God in rational communication with man continues through the call of Abraham and the promises given him: "Now the Lord said to Abram, 'Go from your country . . . and I will make of you a great nation . . .'" (Genesis 12:1-2). The deliverance of this incipient nation from Egypt constitutes the act of God around which all of Israel's worship revolves. The Scriptures are plain that the mighty acts of deliverance take place in order that "you shall know that I am the Lord your God, who has brought you out from under the burdens of the Egyptians" (Exodus 6:7). This emphasis upon knowing becomes virtually a theme of the Exodus. Nor is it simply a matter of knowing the power of God to deliver, for God gives the Law on Sinai, which of necessity must be rationally appropriated.

With the passing of the centuries, God continues to speak to Israel, first through judges, then through kings and prophets. There are rite and ritual to be constant reminders of her deliverance, that she might remember the deeds by which God has revealed himself and might obey the Law which he has given. But when Israel's rites become dead form, and the sacrifices become means by which the people somehow feel that they can control God and guarantee his blessings, then God sends the prophets to speak to Israel, and to remind her that the form of her ritual is valueless without its content. Thus Amos could cry out "'I hate, I despise your feasts, and I take no delight in your solemn assemblies. . . . But let justice roll down like waters and righteousness like an everflowing stream'" (5:21,24). Because rite and ritual, performed in abundance, have lost their meaning and effect, God's Word comes through Amos directed to Israel's understanding.

The prophets speak at God's command: "Now the word of the Lord came to me saying, . . . 'I appointed you a prophet to the nations. . . . Behold, I have put my words in your mouth'" (Jeremiah 1:4, 5, 9) and "thus says the Lord, the God of hosts: . . . 'behold, I am making my words in your mouth a fire . . .'" (5:14). As Jeremiah speaks of the new covenant which God is to make with his people, he proclaims that it shall be a time when " 'no longer shall each man teach his neighbor and each his brother, saying, "Know the Lord," for they shall all know me, from the least of them to the greatest, says the Lord . . .' " (31:34).

There is no need for further quotations from the prophets to indicate God's desire to speak to and communicate with his people. Nor, when we come to the New Testament, need there be an extended attempt to show that Jesus addressed himself to the understanding of men. He came to reveal God, and thus as he taught he could cry out " 'Hear and understand . . .' " (Matthew 15:10) and to his followers he could say "But blessed are your eyes, for they see, and your ears, for they hear" (Matthew 13:16). The content of the Gospels does not consist of the details of rite and ritual, but of the teachings of Jesus, which function not as ends in themselves, but as a means of revealing Christ.

Similarly, the apostles come preaching to men's minds. Peter preaches at Pentecost and 3,000 believe and are baptized. They are forbidden to preach by the authorities who murdered Jesus, but at the risk of their lives they continue. Stephen preaches before the Council, and for it they take his life. The apostles undertake arduous journeys that they may proclaim the gospel. Everywhere in the Epistles one finds this concern with the preaching of the Word. In the tenth chapter of Romans, Paul, extolling the righteousness offered by God and the promise that " 'every one who calls upon the name of the Lord will be saved' " (v. 13), is forced to ask

> But how are men to call upon him in whom they have not believed? And how are they to believe in him of whom they have never heard? And how are they to hear without a preacher? (v. 14). So faith comes from what is heard, and what is heard comes by the preaching of Christ (v. 17).

Let there be no mistake, the gospel is a message that comes to man's mind, to man's understanding! Paul, when dealing with a manifestation of tongues which he seems to acknowledge as a gift of the Spirit, is quick to emphasize the necessity of worshipping with one's mind:

> Therefore, he who speaks in a tongue should pray for the power to interpret. For if I pray in a tongue, my spirit prays but my mind is unfruitful. What am I to do? I will pray with the spirit and I will pray with the mind also; I will sing with the spirit and I will sing with the mind also. . . . I thank God that I speak in tongues more than you all; nevertheless in church I would rather speak five words with my mind, in order to instruct others, than ten thousand words in a tongue.   I Corinthians 14:13–19.

In the light of the biblical witness, is it not a bit strange that some would exalt the Eucharist at the expense of the Word? Those who insist that an understanding of God's message is only for the clergy and an elite group of the laity, while all of the people can participate in the Eucharist as a universal Christian activity,[22] are simply not correctly reflecting the Scriptures. God's message, in word as well as in ritual, whether in Old Testament or New, is everyone's business. The message of the gospel is everyone's business, for faith comes by the preaching of the Word, and is sustained by Word and Sacrament. Nor does it hurt to point out that while the New Testament Scriptures are full of references to the preaching of the Word and whole sections of that preaching, there is relatively little said about the Sacrament of the Lord's Supper. In the Gospels it receives three overt references, each an account of its institution (Mark 14:22ff., Matthew 26:26ff., and Luke 22:15ff.), and the references of John. There is no explicit mention of the Supper as such in Acts (although it may be inferred in a number of places), while in the Letters it is specifically mentioned only three times: I Corinthians 10:16ff., 11:20–34, 16:20, 22. Certainly, a simple count should not be allowed to derogate from

---

[22] Is this not what Dom Gregory Dix implies in his contrast between "theology" and "Liturgy"? *The Shape of the Liturgy* (Westminster: Dacre Press, 1945) p. 7.

the importance of the Supper, instituted by Christ himself, but it should lead us to ask some very searching questions of those who would exalt the Mass or Eucharist at the expense of the preaching of the Word.

The validity of the biblical emphasis upon the Word as the vehicle of God's communication with man was given ample historical display at the Reformation. The story need not be repeated, but with sizable segments of Protestantism apparently captivated by the concept of the Eucharist as the heart of Christian worship, it is time to reiterate that prior to the Reformation there were celebrations of the Mass in great number while the Church remained full of corruption and the people in ignorance. Only with the searching of the Word, and its fearless preaching, did the Church begin to be reformed from within.

While many of those who proclaimed the Word were excommunicated, the reform occasioned by the Word continued, so that large portions of Christendom (portions that would have been far greater had not the established order exterminated the Reformed whenever that was possible) received the clear message of the gospel with its power of salvation. Through preaching, common men became theologians according to their capacities, and rejoiced in their knowledge of God's love. Lest any man doubt the efficacy of the Word, the indirect benefits of the Reformation should also be noted, for the counter-Reformation brought an increase of preaching and teaching for Roman Catholics as well. And even today, four centuries later, the power of God to communicate to men through his Word is still in evidence by the strength not only of those Protestant congregations which have remained faithful to the Word, but also by the strength and vitality of the Roman Catholic Church where she exists in close proximity to, and maintains, a vital biblical witness.

Some may pity the Reformed because their religion is so much a preaching of the Word. Others may be certain that the salvation of Protestantism lies in more pomp and ritual, and many devout Christians, whose nurture and education have been centered around the Eucharist, may in sincerity and reverence seek to elevate this gift far above any other. But as those who have received the inheritance of the Reformation, we of all people are responsible for a continued witness to the biblical revelation that God speaks to men's minds. God has made men rational creatures, and he communicates with them on the highest plane. God speaks to man's understanding. God speaks, and man is responsible for his reply.

Word of Power

It would be a great mistake, however (albeit one often made by proponents of the Mass), to understand the biblical doctrine of the Word of God as one that involves "mere words" or a "bare intellectualism" or even one that limits God's Word to "historical knowledge."[23] For the biblical presentation of the Word, like Protestant doctrine, recognizes that God's Word is not merely a word of information or advice. The Bible reveals the Word of God as a powerful and effectual Word. While God speaks to man's understanding, it must also be understood that God's Word is a powerful Word, able to effect what it proclaims.

Thus in Genesis, even before God speaks to Adam, one reads that "God said, 'Let there be light'; and there was light" (1:3). The biblical doctrine of creation is that of creation by the Word of God. At the time of deliverance from Egypt, God tells Moses to announce to Pharaoh what will happen, and things happen as announced. Throughout the books of the prophets, we find the

---

[23] In Connell's Catechism, *op. cit.*, the one question that deals with the Word (Q. 23) asks: "Can we know God in any other way than by our natural reason?" to which the answer is given: "from the truths found in Sacred Scripture and in Tradition. . ." (p. 15). Later, in an appendix, the Bible is referred to as the chief source of "our historical knowledge of Jesus Christ, His life and teachings. . ." (p. 298).

Word of God coming to the prophets, and on the basis of that Word Elijah says there will be no rain, and there is none; that after three years it will come, and it comes. The Word of the Lord comes to Isaiah, and while the undefeated armies of Sennacherib threaten Jerusalem, Isaiah calmly assures King Hezekiah that the city has nothing to fear, and the army withdraws.

Word Made Flesh

But the Word of God which we find in the Old Testament, a Word which both speaks to the understanding and is also a powerful, effectual Word, is but the prelude of God's revelation, for in the fullness of time the Word is made flesh!

> And the Word became flesh and dwelt among us, full of grace and truth; we have beheld his glory, glory as of the only Son from the Father. . . . No one has ever seen God; the only Son, who is in the bosom of the Father, he has made him known. John 1:14, 18.

God's powerful, effectual Word assumes flesh and blood in the person of Jesus Christ. The Christ who stands at the heart of the Lord's Supper is the same Christ designated by Scripture as "the Word of God."

> In the beginning was the Word, and the Word was with God, and the Word was God. He was in the beginning with God; all things were made through him, and without him was not anything made that was made. In him was life, and the life was the light of men. John 1:1–4.

The Word was life and the light of men. God is a speaking God, a God whose speaking is also acting, and a God whose Word is his Son. It was not the Reformers, but the Apostles who first called the very Son of God the Word of God. In the face of the Gospel of John and its witness to Christ it is absurd to speak of the emphasis upon God's Word as "mere words" or "bare intellectualism," for in the Word made flesh God comes to us.

Let there be no mistake on this issue: the biblical witness is not merely that Christ came bringing words about God, but that he is God's Word. In Jesus' life and ministry we see the unique Word which is at once a Word addressed to our understanding and a Word that is act. Jesus, confronted with the paralytic, said "your sins are forgiven" (Matthew 9:1ff.). His speech, addressed to the understanding of men, seemed to the scribes to be blasphemy. But Jesus gives the proof of the power of his words by also saying "Rise, take up your bed and go home." Jesus, who is forgiveness, addresses words of forgiveness to the paralytic, and offers proof to all by healing the man with a Word.

Jesus exhibits the power of the Word by blessing the five loaves and two fish, and feeding the multitude of five thousand men (John 6:1ff.). Having given them the parable in miracle form, Jesus teaches in words what he is in fact and has so recently illustrated: "I am the bread of life! he who comes to me shall not hunger, and he who believes in me shall never thirst" (6:35)—words addressed to the understanding, Word which takes form in act, all to convey the truth of God as it is present to them, and to us, in Jesus Christ.

In this same Gospel there is the account of Lazarus, dead so long that after four days even his sisters were keenly aware that he had started to decompose. But because the death had taken place "that the Son of God [might] be glorified by means of it" (John 11:4) Jesus, having explicitly made the claim " 'I am the resurrection and the life . . .' " (11:25), "cried out with a loud voice, 'Lazarus, come out.' The dead man came out . . ." (11:43–44). Again, Christ who is himself the light and life of men speaks words to the understanding of Mary and to his disciples, and demonstrates by his effectual Word to Lazarus that which he is for all who accept him.

It is just this Word of God, who is also Son of God, who is offered to men in the preaching of the Word! It is because the Word who was in the beginning and who was with God and who was God and who made all things and who is both the life and light of men is offered from the pulpit that this preaching of the Word must not in any way be minimized! The question may well be asked how it can be that the Word of God made flesh in Jesus Christ can possibly come to us as Word of God through the instrumentality of some minister in the pulpit. At the same time it must be noted that this is precisely the same question as to how the Word of God made flesh can come to us in water, bread and wine through the instrumentality of some minister at font or table. The two problems are no different, and for both Scripture has an identical answer: whether Christ comes to us from pulpit, font, or table, he does so through the operation of the Holy Spirit.

Word, Spirit, and Union with Christ

God's Word is a Word to our understanding, and a Word of power which can join us to Christ through the operation of the Holy Spirit. If we fail to take full account of the role of the Holy Spirit in any doctrine of Word and Sacrament, we fall either into an enervated rationalism or a form of sacerdotal magic. The Holy Spirit is not to be omitted from any doctrine of Word or Sacrament.

When God addresses himself to men's minds in his Word, it is by the Holy Spirit that he opens our minds so that we may understand the Word. The work of the Holy Spirit includes an address to our understanding. Thus, Jesus, shortly before going out to Gethsemane and the Cross, tells his disciples of another Counselor, "even the Spirit of truth":

> "These things I have spoken to you, while I am still with you. But the Counselor, the Holy Spirit, whom the Father will send in my name, he will teach you all things," and bring to your remembrance all that I have said to you. John 14:25.

Apostolic recognition of the role of the Holy Spirit in the understanding of God's message is obvious in I Corinthians 2:12–13:

> Now we have received . . . the Spirit which is from God, that we might understand the gifts bestowed on us by God. And we impart this in words not taught by human wisdom but taught by the Spirit, interpreting spiritual truths to those who possess the Spirit.

It was upon this biblical basis that the Reformers insisted that only by the operation of the Holy Spirit could God's Word be understood unto salvation: "The heavenly doctrine proves to be useful and efficacious to us only so far as the Spirit both forms our minds to understand it and our hearts to submit to its yoke."[24]

Just as it is only through the work of the Holy Spirit that the Word can be understood, so it is the Holy Spirit who in his power makes the Word effectual. This is implicit in many passages from John. In the fourteenth chapter of the Gospel the promise of the Spirit of truth is immediately followed by a statement concerning the attendant keeping of Christ's commandments:

> And I will pray the Father, and he will give you another Counselor, to be with you forever, even the Spirit of truth. . . . He who has my commandments and keeps them, he it is who loves me. . . .　　　　John 14:16–17, 21.

Similarly, in the First Letter of John, the Christian is pointed to the effectual working of the Spirit in his own life for assurance: "We know that we have passed out of death into life, because we love the brethren. He who does not love remains in death" (I John 3:14). The very presence of the

---

[24] Calvin, *Commentary on Luke*, 24:45, *Corpus Reformatorum* 34:427, quoted by Ronald S. Wallace, *Calvin's Doctrine of the Word and Sacrament* (Grand Rapids: Wm. B. Eerdmans Publishing Co., 1953), p. 128.

Spirit is discerned by his effectual working within the Christian: ". . . if we love one another, God abides in us and his love is perfected in us. By this we know we abide in him and he in us, because he has given us of his own Spirit" (I John 4:12–13).

But it should also be made clear that the Bible does not allow us to see the fruits of faith as a joint action of Word and Spirit somehow strangely abstracted from Christ. For insofar as the Word of God is Christ, and the Holy Spirit is the Spirit of Christ, so the Christian is a Christian only in Christ. The foundation of Christian faith is that we have life and light in Christ, that in him we have salvation, newness of life, and life beyond death, even to the resurrection of the dead. This is to be had in Christ, and the biblical, the Reformed, doctrine of Word and Sacrament is that as the Holy Spirit of God works in each, we are joined to Christ.[25]

---

[25] Even though neither the doctrine of union with Christ nor the doctrine of the Holy Spirit receives much attention from many pulpits (due undoubtedly to a combination of rationalism on the one hand, which eliminated such "unreasonable" biblical teaching, and scholastic orthodoxy on the other, which by an exclusive preoccupation with forensic theories of the atonement all but eliminated these biblical doctrines through monumental neglect), both Holy Spirit and union with Christ are a part of the clear biblical witness. Their absence is in no small part the cause of subsequent theological aberrations. No important field of biblical revelation can long be neglected without necessitating serious distortions in other fields. For example, this neglect of the Holy Spirit long ago had a serious effect on Roman Catholic dogmatics. The whole understanding of the transubstantiation of the Mass would have been impossible with a healthy doctrine of the Spirit (for what would have been the purpose of a partial physical presence when the Holy Spirit assures us of union with Christ?). Nor is it any wonder that Protestantism has indeed been guilty of "mere words" and "excessive intellectualism" when, neglecting the role of the Spirit, and indeed the Word to which the Spirit bears witness, it has attempted a message of its own in rationalistic words. Nor is it any wonder that for many the Lord's Supper is reduced to a memorial service, for it can be no more if the Holy Spirit is absent.

> How do we receive those benefits which the Father bestowed on his only-begotten Son . . . that he might enrich poor and needy men? . . . To sum up, the Holy Spirit is the bond by which Christ effectually unites us to himself.[26]

Perhaps it would be well to bring this matter of union with Christ through the Holy Spirit into sharp focus in terms of more familiar doctrine, e.g., in terms of redemption, sanctification, and resurrection. The belief in the forgiveness of sin and reconciliation with God through Jesus Christ stands at the heart of our faith. But in the preaching of forgiveness and justification through faith, it occasionally escapes the hearer that in Scripture this forgiveness is premised upon union with Christ. And it is the Apostle Paul, whose writings were most heavily used by those who preached a purely forensic, or imputational justification, who emphasizes most clearly union with Christ. Thus, in Ephesians he states that God has "blessed us in Christ" (1:3), "he chose us in him" (1:4), "In him we have redemption through his blood, the forgiveness of our trespasses, according to the riches of his grace . . ." (1:7). "In him you also, who have heard the word of truth, the gospel of your salvation, and have believed in him, were sealed with the promised Holy Spirit . . ." (1:13). Note that the believer is "sealed" with the Holy Spirit in Christ, who is truth and salvation. It is "God, who is rich in mercy" who "made us alive together with Christ" (2:5). For the Gentiles who were "without God in the world . . . now in Christ . . . have been brought near in the blood of Christ" (2:12–13). We are indeed "members of his body" (5:30). John also witnesses "and we are in him who is true, in his

---

[26] John Calvin, *Institutes of the Christian Religion,* Vol. I, Library of Christian Classics, trans. Ford Lewis Battles, Copyright © 1960, W. L. Jenkins. Used by permission. (Philadelphia: Westminster Press, 1960), 3:1:1, p. 538. Henceforth, *Institutes.* For a brief discussion of the role of union with Christ in Calvin's theology see Edward A. Dowey, Jr., *The Knowledge of God in Calvin's Theology* (New York: Columbia University Press, 1952), pp. 197–204.

son Jesus Christ. This is the true God and eternal life" (I John 5:20). Reconciliation and forgiveness are understood in the Scriptures upon the premise of union with Christ.[27]

What is true of reconciliation is also true of the Christian life.[28] Christian living is not something that the Christian is to do at his own discretion, or by his own powers (were that possible, then Christ would not have needed to go to the cross). The Bible teaches that the Christlike life is to be lived, and inevitably will be lived, because of our being united with Christ, because we are "in him." John connects this matter of Christian life with Christ and the giving of his Spirit: "All who keep his commandments abide in him, and he in them. And by this we know that he abides in us, by the Spirit which he has given us" (I John 3:24).[29] Paul also connects our status of union with Christ to the inevitability of a Christlike life: "we who first hoped in Christ have been destined and appointed to live for the praise of his glory" (Ephesians

---

[27] For an extended treatment of the role of union with Christ in this phase of Calvin's theology see Paul van Buren, *Christ in Our Place* (Grand Rapids: Wm. B. Eerdmans Publishing Co., 1957) pp. 95–140.

[28] It is at this point that the forensic teaching of the Reformed scholastics suffered serious breakdown, giving painful point to the caricature of the Reformed as those who insisted upon right belief far more than upon right living. While justification could be explained in terms of legal imputation, this forensic method was devoid of power in the area of sanctification. Among certain small sects of English separatists the acceptance of a doctrine of imputed sanctification was followed by the practice "let us sin the more that grace may abound." These antinomian practices so horrified men like Richard Baxter that there was a theological rebound away not only from an imputed sanctification, but also from an imputed justification, and because the vital doctrine of union with Christ was lacking, the result was a form of justification by works (neonomianism, in the theological parlance of the day).

[29] For analysis of all the "in Christ" passages in John see Brooke Foss Westcott, *The Epistles of St. John* (London: Macmillan, 1886), pp. 174ff. For a full citation of the "in Christ" passages with brief comment see Gerhard Kittel, *Theologisches Wörterbuch zum Neuen Testament, Zweiter Band,* △—H (Stuttgart: Verlag Von W. Kohlhammer, 1935), pp. 537–539.

1:12). "For we are his workmanship, created in Christ for good works, which God prepared beforehand, that we should walk in them" (Ephesians 2:10). The actuality with which the Apostles understand this union with Christ comes to the fore when Paul uses the union of the Christian with Christ as an argument against fornication: "Do you not know that your bodies are members of Christ? Shall I therefore take the members of Christ and make them members of a prostitute? Never!" (I Corinthians 6:15).[30]

Just as our reconciliation with God and our Christian life depend upon our union with Christ, so also do our expectations of continued life in him, which includes our resurrection. Paul, when confronted by disbelief in personal resurrection on the part of some in the Church of Corinth, uses the audacious argument (solidly grounded on the premise of union with Christ) that if Christians are not raised from the dead, then neither could Christ have risen, for the one must inevitably follow from the other.

> But if there is no resurrection of the dead, then Christ has not been raised; . . . We are even found to be misrepresenting God, because we testified of God that he raised Christ, whom he did not raise if it is true that the dead are not raised. For if the dead are not raised, then Christ has not been raised. . . .
>
> But in fact Christ has been raised from the dead, the first fruits of those who have fallen asleep.   I Corinthians 15:12, 15, 16, 20.

Not only is the resurrection of the Christian seen as inevitable because of the resurrection of Christ (for are we not in union with him, a union as strong as the Holy Spirit of God who joins us to him?), but because of this union with Christ, Paul sees the Christian as even now joined to Christ as he sits at the right hand of God:

---

[30] For a more adequate view of the place of union with Christ in the life of a Christian see Ronald S. Wallace, *Calvin's Doctrine of the Christian Life* (Grand Rapids: Wm. B. Eerdmans Publishing Co., 1959).

> But God . . . even when we were dead through our trespasses, made us alive together with Christ . . . and raised us up with him, and made us sit with him in the heavenly places in Christ Jesus . . . .   Ephesians 2:4–6.

Writing to the Christians at Colossae, Paul, building upon his understanding of union with Christ, can assure them "For you have died, and your life is hid with Christ in God" (Colossians 3:3).

This is a crucial point upon which even the architecture of the church must turn, the point that all the benefits to which Christianity lays claim—redemption, forgiveness, a Christian life, and resurrection from the dead—are to be had in Christ, in being joined to him. This union with him takes place through the means of both Word and Sacrament, by the power of the Holy Spirit. As has been demonstrated above, this is biblical teaching, and it is Reformed doctrine:

> Yet a serious wrong is done to the Holy Spirit, unless we believe that it is through his incomprehensible power that we come to partake of Christ's flesh and blood.[31]
>
> But he unites himself to us by the Spirit alone. By the grace and the power of the same Spirit we are made his members, to keep us under himself and in turn to possess him.[32]
>
> . . . the secret power of the Spirit is the bond of our union with Christ.[33]

But perhaps the importance of this biblical truth can be best seen when contrasted with the Roman Catholic doctrine of the Mass. As was previously noted, the Mass is built upon the doctrine of transubstantiation (fixed as dogma by the Fourth Lateran Council in 1215), which holds that the bread and wine literally become the body and blood of Christ, only the "accidents"

---

[31] Calvin, *Institutes,* 4:17:33, p. 1405.
[32] *Ibid.,* 3:1:3, p. 541.
[33] *Ibid.,* 4:17:33, p. 1405.

of bread and wine remaining. This means not only the physical presence of Christ in the Mass, but also that in the Mass Christ "offers himself to God in an unbloody manner under the appearances of bread and wine."[34] Each sacrifice is of course considered meritorious, and thus Pius XII can well assert that a thousand masses said by a thousand priests each celebrating alone are of far more value than one Mass attended by an innumerable multitude of the faithful.[35] The Mass has objective validity because Christ is objectively there, and thus to partake of the Mass is to partake of Christ.

But so to partake of Christ physically present in the Mass is to partake of him in a very limited, partial way. For in partaking of the Mass one does not receive the fullness of Christ's merits (which would be completely adequate for salvation), but only a part. Father Connell's catechism assures the laity that "the more fervently they participate in the offering of the Mass, the more benefits they will receive from this precious sacrifice" and that "a boy who serves Mass or a person who sings in the choir will partake more abundantly of the fruits of the Holy Sacrifice, other things being equal, than one who merely assists as a member of the congregation."[36] Seemingly, while one partakes of Christ, one partakes of but a part, and the extent of participation depends upon the fervency and type of activity of the person involved. The encouragement of the Roman laity toward multiple Masses, both for themselves and for their dead, argues strongly that the participation is extremely partial, gaining but a portion of Christ's merits and satisfaction. And to multiple Masses must be added all the other means by which the laity obtain indulgence to lessen the extent of their unsatisfied sins and their consequent purgation in purgatory. It is in the Mass that Christ communicates himself to his people—but in a very partial way.

---

[34] O'Brien, *op. cit.*, Q. 357, p. 210.
[35] *Mediator Dei*, quoted by Benoit, *op. cit.*, p. 80.
[36] *Op. cit.*, p. 212.

A comparison at this point with the Reformed doctrine of Word and Sacraments is particularly revealing, for the Reformed position sees the Christian joined to the whole Christ and all his benefits, rather than engaging in the partial participation of the Mass. For it is not the flesh and blood of Christ hidden under the accidents of bread and wine that constitutes our union with him, but the Holy Spirit who joins us to the whole Christ.

> And there is no need of [transubstantiation] for us to enjoy a participation in [Christ's body], since the Lord bestows this benefit upon us through his Spirit so that we may be made one in body, spirit, and soul with him. The bond of this connection is therefore the Spirit of Christ, with whom we are joined in unity, and is like a channel through which all that Christ himself is and has is conveyed to us.[37]

Nor should it be overlooked that in being so joined to Christ we are united with him in his once-for-all sacrifice on the cross. Scripture states that this was a totally sufficent, once-for-all sacrifice which need never be repeated. Christ "appeared once for all . . . to put away sin by the sacrifice of himself" (Hebrews 9:26). This sacrifice was sufficient to atone for all sin, to redeem men completely. Through the actions of the Holy Spirit, we are united to the whole Christ and his whole forgiveness.

> . . . a serious wrong is done to the Holy Spirit unless we believe that it is through his incomprehensible power that we come to partake of Christ's flesh and blood. . . . It was of chief importance to know how the body of Christ, as once for all it was given for us, is made ours, and how we become partakers of the blood once shed. For that is to possess Christ entire, crucified, that we may enjoy all his benefits.[38]

---

[37] Calvin, *Institutes* 4:17:12, p. 1373.
[38] *Ibid.*, 4:17:33, p. 1405.

This is the source of joy that the Church of Jesus Christ, reformed according to the Word of God, is given to possess. In this faith there is no need for penance, indulgences, and the constant concern for the accumulation of works and merits, whether through prayers or participation in the Mass. Nor is there the uncertainty which betrays itself in every Mass for the dead in purgatory. The joy of the biblical faith is to know that through the Word and Sacrament the Holy Spirit has so united us to Christ by his incomprehensible power that Christ and all his benefits are ours: complete forgiveness by grace alone, the presence of the Spirit to help us "live in him, rooted and built up in him" (Colossians 2:6–7), with the knowledge that so far are we from the "wrath of God" (the fear of which plays such a prominent part of every Requiem) that our lives are already "hid with Christ in God" and that "when Christ who is our life appears, then you also will appear with him in glory" (Colossians 3:3–4).

It is the contention of this book that this joyful biblical faith, which is our Reformed faith, is eminently worthy of accurate architectural expression in our churches!

Thus in our architecture we must not exaggerate the importance of the Eucharist in relation to the Word, for by both Word and Sacrament we are bound to Christ by the Holy Spirit of God. Precisely by virtue of the power of the Holy Spirit must all false distinctions between Word and Sacraments be broken down. This false distinction has too long played its role among not only Roman Catholics but other high churchmen as well. Addleshaw, in his very helpful and able book, nonetheless quotes with obvious approval Archbishop Laud, who seemingly settled the matter for a great many people when he

> spoke of the altar as "the greatest place of God's residence upon earth"; he showed how it was much more important than the pulpit, "for there 'tis Hoc est corpus meum, 'This is my body'; but in the pulpit 'tis at most but Hoc est

verbum meum, 'this is my word.' And a greater reverence, no doubt, is due to the body than to the word of our Lord."[39]

A similar false distinction seems evident in the work of Dom Gregory Dix, when he distinguishes between the "Book on the lectern and the Bread and Cup on the table" as "the Liturgy of the Spirit and the Liturgy of the Body, centering upon the Word of God enounced and the Word of God made flesh."[40] It is precisely against such a distinction that the Reformed protest, for it is not a matter of the Spirit speaking to us through the Word while Christ communicates his body to us in the Eucharist, but rather it is in both Word and Sacrament that the Holy Spirit unites us with the whole Christ and all his benefits.

Howard Hageman has stated the point exceedingly well:

> In the act of Christian worship, Word and Sacrament belong together. Any attempt to set up an antithesis between them is completely false to the Biblical witness. They belong together not as successive or even complementary acts. They are aspects of a single whole. Word and Sacrament are only different media for the same reality, Christ's coming into the midst of his people.[41]

In their relationship to Christ there can be no thought of primacy of either Word or Sacrament. Both present Christ, and both present him in his fullness; through both, the Holy Spirit makes us partakers of Christ and all his benefits. In relationship to Christ there can be no primacy of the Eucharist, just as in relationship to Christ there can be no primacy of the Word.

But in considering man's ability to receive the Word and Sacraments, the Reformers spoke clearly and forcefully in making a valid distinction which

---

[39] G. W. O. Addleshaw & Frederick Etchells, *The Architectural Setting of Anglican Worship* (London: Faber & Faber Ltd., 1948), p. 138, quoting Laud's *Works,* VI, 59.
[40] Dix, *op. cit.,* p. 743.
[41] Howard G. Hageman, *Pulpit and Table* (Richmond: John Knox Press, 1962), p. 112.

sounded very much like a doctrine of the primacy of the Word. Neither Calvin nor Luther ever intended any slight to the Sacraments, nor any diminution of their dominical authority. But both, confronted with a Roman Mass that for centuries had remained an enigma to the common people and had been turned into a form of meritorious magic, were very clear on the fact which confronted them: that a Sacrament not informed by the vivifying Word was dead. Thus Calvin rightly insisted upon the indispensability of the Word: "Let us therefore learn that the chief part of the sacraments consists in the Word and without it they are absolute corruptions."[42] Calvin also quotes Augustine to the same effect:

> Let the word be added to the element and it will become a sacrament. For whence comes this great power of water that in touching the body it should cleanse the heart, unless the word makes it?[43]

This is a theme to which Calvin returns again and again. Having defined the sacraments in terms of "signs," Calvin looks back to the signs given by God in the Old Testament and finds that there as well God added his Word to make the signs meaningful:

> Indeed, it was known even from the beginning of the world that whenever God gave a sign to the holy patriarchs it was inseparably linked to doctrine, without which our senses would have been stunned in looking at the bare sign. Accordingly, when we hear the sacramental word mentioned, let us understand the promise, proclaimed in a clear voice by the minister, to lead the people by the hand wherever the sign tends and directs us.[44]

And as the sacraments are also seals, Calvin remarks that

---

[42] Calvin, *Commentary on Isaiah*, 6:8, quoted by Wallace, op. cit., p. 73.
[43] Augustine, *John's Gospel* LXXX. 3, quoted by Calvin, *Institutes*, 4:14:4.
[44] Calvin, *Institutes*, 4:14:4, pp. 1279–80.

> the seals which are attached to government documents and other public acts are nothing taken by themselves, for they would be attached in vain if the parchment had nothing written on it. Yet, when added to the writing, they do not on that account fail to confirm and seal what is written.[45]

In a similar fashion the Sacraments are seals when added to the Word.

Something remarkably like the indispensability of the Word is being proclaimed among the avant-garde of the liturgical movement. Fr. Roguet at the Assisi congress observed concerning the Sacraments that

> However clear, however free of superfluous matter the rites may be, they are still mysteries into which we can penetrate only by faith. And faith needs to be illumined and formed by the word.[46]

In a similar vein, Louis Bouyer "goes so far as to affirm that the bread of the Word of God is as necessary as the bread of the Eucharist—further, that the eucharistic bread would be of no avail if it were not accompanied by the bread of God's Word."[47] And is it possible that the action of the Second Vatican Council by which preaching has been made mandatory on all Sundays and holy days of obligation is at least a partial recognition that there may have been some truth in the assertion by Calvin that

> the right administering of the Sacrament cannot stand apart from the Word. For whatever benefit may come to us from the Supper requires the Word: whether we are to be confirmed in faith, or exercised in confession, or aroused

---

[45] *Ibid.*, 4:14:5, p. 1280.

[46] *La Maison-Dieu,* Nos. 47, 48, 1956, IV, p. 152, quoted by Benoit, *op. cit.,* p. 100.

[47] *La Maison-Dieu,* No. 39, 1954, IV, p. 52, quoted by Benoit, *op. cit.,* p. 94, who further remarks that "Such is the present state—in a few outstanding personalities, it is true, rather than in the general body of church members—of the biblical revival in the Roman Catholic Church."

to duty, there is need of preaching. Therefore, nothing more preposterous could happen in the Supper than for it to be turned into a silent action . . . ."[48]

In this judgment the Reformers must be sustained. The Sacraments communicate Christ to us as fully as the Word, but the Word is indispensable to the Sacraments, and this indispensability of the Word must be stated as clearly in our architecture as in our theology.

In applying this theology to architecture, the two should be joined by a brief statement in which the gifts of the theologian and architect may be brought to bear upon this single problem. Upon the foundation that has thus far been laid, let us establish the first criteria of architecture for Reformed churches:

TO SET FORTH THE GOD-ORDAINED MEANS BY WHICH CHRIST COMES TO HIS PEOPLE, THE REFORMED MUST GIVE VISUAL EXPRESSION TO THE IMPORTANCE OF BOTH WORD AND SACRAMENTS.

BECAUSE THE WORD IS INDISPENSABLE, THE PULPIT, AS THE ARCHITECTURAL MANIFESTATION OF THE WORD, MUST MAKE ITS INDISPENSABILITY ARCHITECTURALLY CLEAR.

Very obviously, this means that there can be no thought of building

---

[48] *Institutes,* 4:17:39, p. 1416. It should be noted, however, that even among the most advanced proponents of the liturgical movement there would be none who would take the Reformed position that the Sacrament can bring us no more of Christ than the Word alone: "Hence, any man is deceived who thinks anything more is conferred upon him through the sacraments than what is offered by God's Word and received by him in true faith." "From this something else follows: assurance of salvation does not depend upon participation in the sacrament, as if justification consisted in it. For we know that justification is lodged in Christ alone, and that it is communicated to us no less by the preaching of the gospel than by the seal of the sacrament, and without the latter can stand unimpaired." *Ibid.,* 4:14:14, p. 1290.

churches in which an altar, or even a table (much less a worship center) is given the architectural focus while the pulpit is relegated to a strictly secondary role. Much less is it possible to omit the pulpit altogether![49] But enough of what should not be done. What are the ways in which the first criteria are to be given architectural expression?

At the time of the Reformation these principles were both understood and applied (albeit in reaction to the Mass the Lord's table often received less attention than it deserved). Thus in Saint-Pierre in Geneva, the high altar, separated from the people and containing the relics of the saints, was torn down, as were the rood screen and choir stalls, which signified a separation of clergy and people. The pulpit was moved from the side of the nave (the second pillar on the right) to the crossing (where it was placed on the first pillar on the left). More important than the position of the pulpit was the positioning of the people around it, for it now became the focal point for the congregation. When seats began to be used, they formed an amphitheater around the pulpit, seats being placed in the apse, as well as in the crossing (an arrangement which continues to exist in many former Swiss cathedrals, including the Basel Munster).[50] While the pulpit formed the focal point, the Lord's Supper was celebrated at a simple communion table which "in order to avoid misconceptions, . . . was set up only when the Holy Communion

---

[49] As, for example, when the primary emphasis is placed upon the Eucharist. Thus Peter Hammond (*op. cit.,* p. 118) can refer to the church at Crownhill, England, as "one of the most satisfactory buildings for liturgy completed in this country since the war" even though "there is no pulpit; a lectern serves both for the proclamation and the exposition of the word."

[50] André Biéler, *Liturgie et Architecture,* (Geneva: Labor et Fides, 1961) pp. 72ff., with diagrams on p. 77.

was celebrated."[51] St. Bavo Church (officially, Grote Kerk, Hervormd) in Haarlem, is illustrative of another Reformed solution to the problem. Again the high altar in the apse was destroyed. And again, the pulpit was made the focus of the church around which was grouped the seating. The former choir was used as a room for the celebration of the Lord's Supper (avondmaalsruimte) in which long tables were set up at which the congregation could sit together at the Supper.

---

[51] André Biéler, "Liturgy and Architecture," *Lucerne International Joint Conference on Church Architecture and Church Building* (New York: mimeographed & copyrighted by the Dept. of Church Building & Architecture of the NCCC, 1962), p. 56. The radical rearrangement of their churches by the Reformers makes it apparent how little truth there is in the often repeated claim that these men were not concerned about symbols. It was because they were so keenly aware of the symbolic power of the old arrangements that these were so completely altered. While it is true that the Reformed refused to develop an elaborate system of symbols, they nonetheless used what inevitably would have symbolic value with theological accuracy. It may be true that this was not all done with conscious consideration of symbolic implications, but what was done for the practical needs of the congregation was done that they might worship in a manner conforming to their theology, and that is the desire of this book for the Reformed churches of today.

The carved pulpit is post-Reformation, dating from 1679, while the Gothic sounding board dates back to 1432.

St. Bavo Church (officially, The Great Church—Grote Kerk), Hervormd, Haarlem, The Netherlands

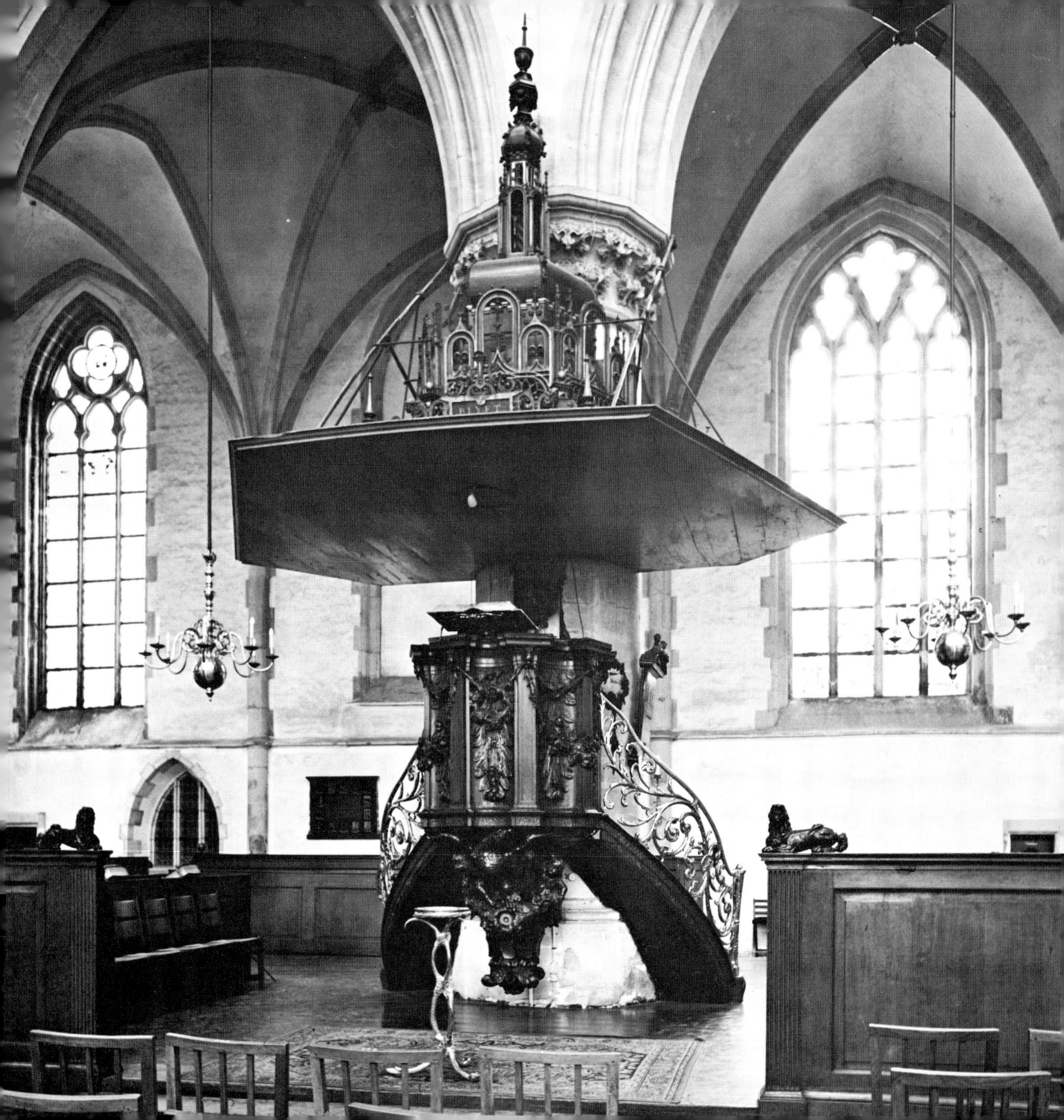

The organ was built by Christian Müller between 1735 and 1738. It has been used by both Handel and Mozart (who was allowed to play on it although only ten years old). Altered in 1868, it was returned to its original tonal design by Marcussen.

Hoofdwerk		Bovenwerk		Rugpositief	
Praestant	16	Quintadena	16	Praestant	8
Bourdon	16	Praestant	8	Quintadena	8
Octaaf	8	Quintadena	8	Holpijp	8
Roerfluit	8	Baarpijp	8	Octaaf	4
Viola de Gamba	8	Octaaf	4	Fluit douce	4
Roerquint	6	Flagfluit	4	Speelfluit	3
Octaaf	4	Nasard	3	Super Octaaf	2
Gemshoorn	4	Nachthoorn	2	Sesquialter 2, 3, 4 ranks	
Quint-praestant	3	Flageolet	1½	Cornet 4 ranks	
Woudfluit	2	Sesquialter 2 ranks		Mixtuur 6–8 ranks	
Tertiaan 2 ranks		Mixtuur 4, 5, 6 ranks		Cymbaal 3 ranks	
Mixtuur 4–10 ranks		Cymbaal 3 ranks		Fagot	16
Scherp 6, 7, 8 ranks		Schalmei	8	Trompet	8
Trompet	16	Dolceaan	8	Trechterregaal	8
Trompet	8	Vox Humana	8		
Hautbois	8				
Trompet	4	Pedaal		Pedaal	
		Principaal	32	Ruischquint 3 ranks	
		Praestant	16	Mixtuur 6–10 ranks	
		Subbas	16	Bazuin	32
		Roerquint	12	Bazuin	16
		Octaaf	8	Trompet	8
		Holfluit	2	Trompet	4
				Cink	2

While looking toward the west, the organ overshadows everything else, but it is to be noted that the chairs and pews are so placed that the real focus of attention is the pulpit. Immediately to each side of the pulpit are the pews with desks supporting the massive Bibles of the elders and deacons.

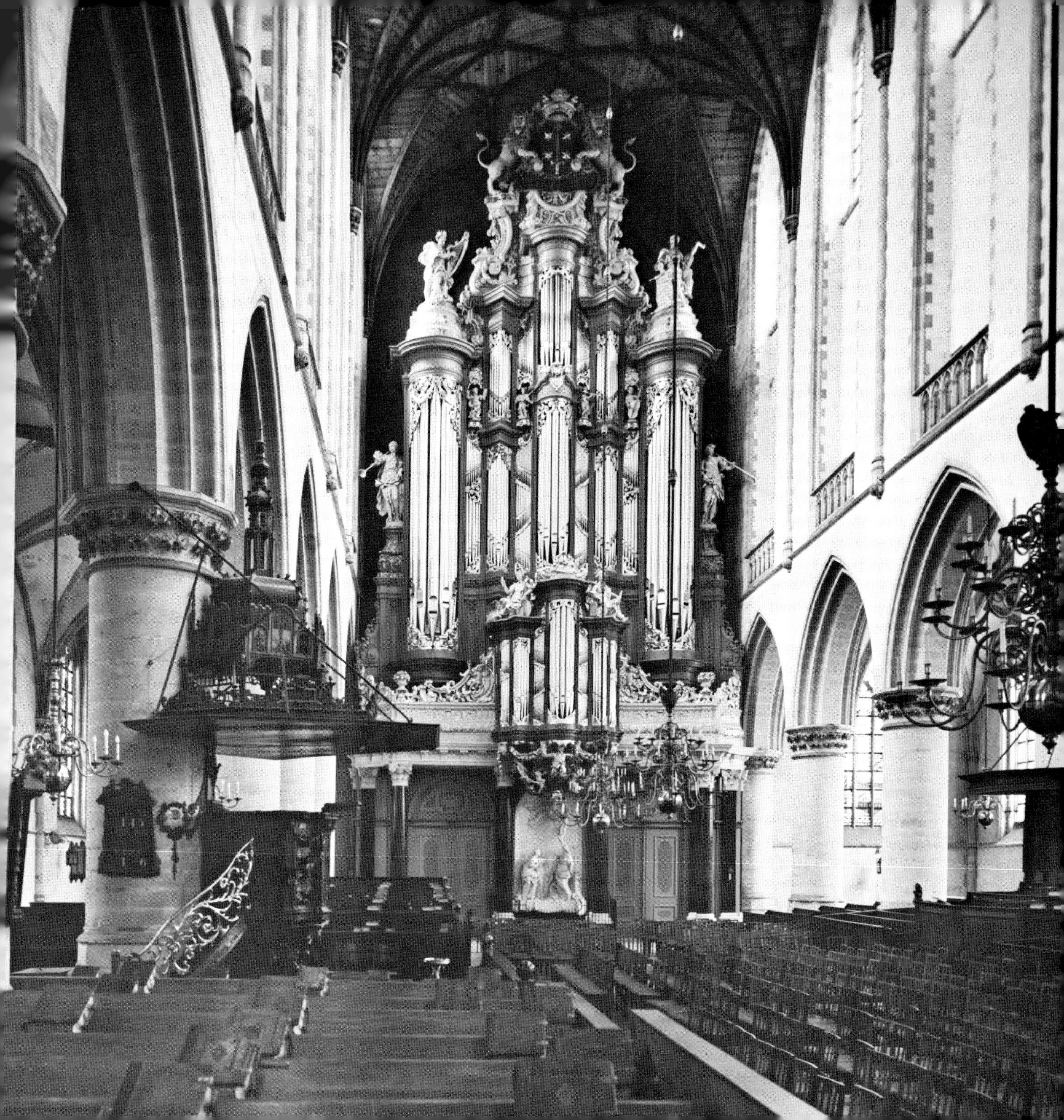

At the time of the Reformation the choir screen was left intact to separate the two "rooms": the nave for preaching, and the choir for the Lord's Supper.

The copper screen (1509–1517) is by Jan Fierens of Malines. The ribbed cedar vault was constructed in the 15th and 16th centuries.

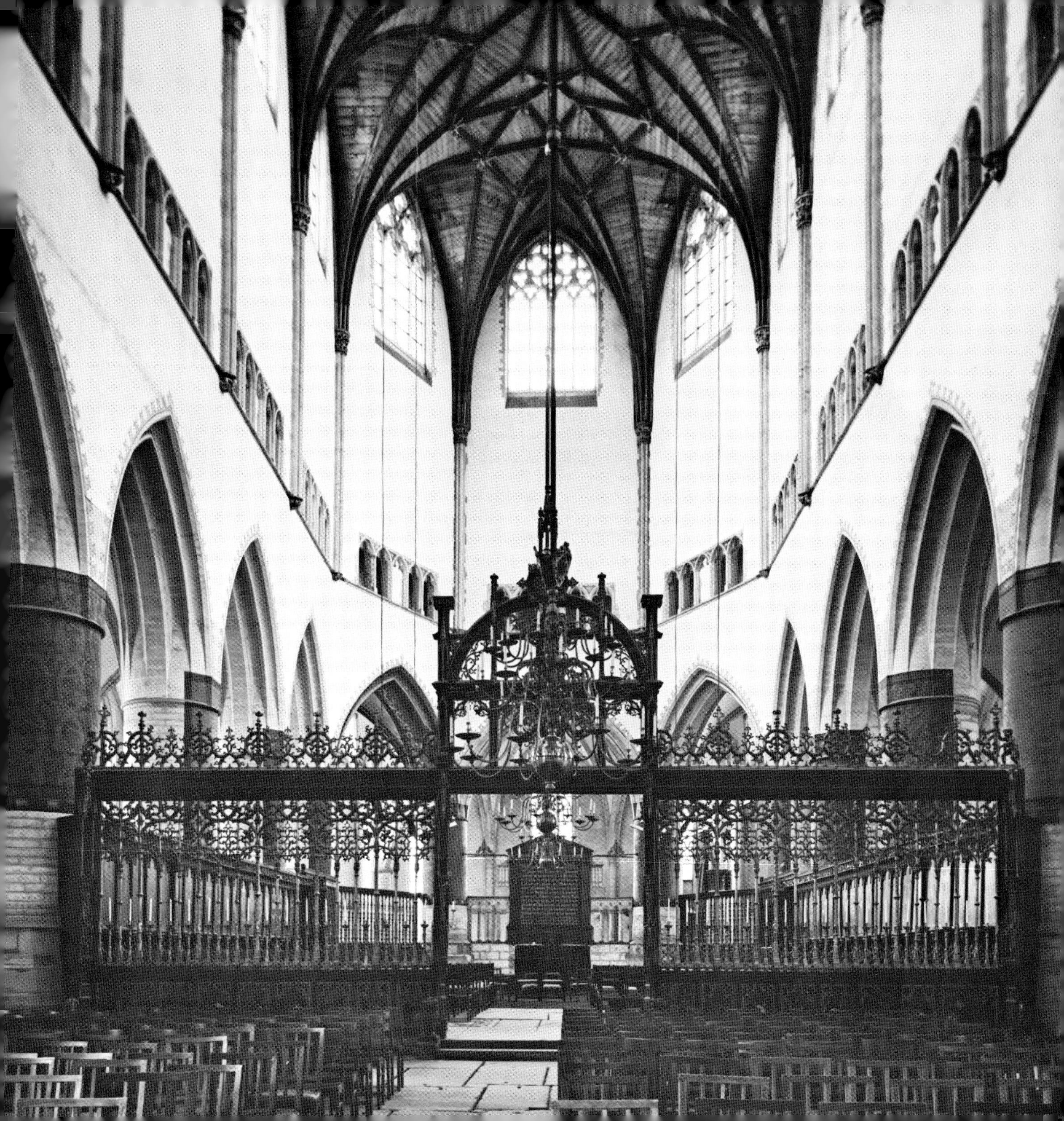

At the east end of St. Bavo Church, in the apse near where the high altar once stood, a tablet was erected bearing the words of institution of the Lord's Supper, written in the language of the people. Within the choir and apse long tables are set up at which the people may sit to partake of the Supper.

D'Heer Christus Hemelsch brood — Geeft 'tleven door sijn dood

Ick hebt vanden Heere ontfanghen dat ick u ghegevē hebbe. Want de Heer Jesus inder nacht doe hy verradē wert nā dat Broot dāctē en brack het en seyde: Nemet etet dat is mij Lijf dat voor u gebrokē wert. Sulcx doet tot mijner gedachtenisse. Desgelijckē oocx dē drinckebeker na dē Avontmael en seyde: dese drinckebeker is dat nieuwe Testamēt in mijnē Bloede. Sulcx doet so dickwils als ghy het drinckē sult tot mijnē ghedachtenisse. Wāt so dicwils als ghy van desen Broode etē sult en vā desē drinckebeker drinckē so verkōdiget dē doot des Heeren tot dat hy coemt.

Dē drickbeker der danckegginghe dien wy danckleggēde drincken is die niet die gemeynscap des Bloets Christi: het broot dat wij brekē is dat niet die gemeyscap des Lichaems Christi.

The Church of Saint-Pierre in Geneva, and St. Bavo Church in Haarlem represent the two most common solutions to the problem of how to conduct Reformed worship in buildings originally designed for the Roman Mass. The Lutherans frequently reached the same solution as that represented by St. Bavo Church. The screen and rood-loft were retained, and in effect two separate rooms, the nave for preaching and the apse for the Lord's Supper, were put into use. Word and Sacrament each had its own church.[52] The solutions were similar in England and in Scotland,[53] and governing them all was the desire that the Word of God be heard.[54]

The impact that these Reformation decisions had was evidenced when it was necessary to build new churches. When the Nieuwe Kerk was built in The Hague, The Netherlands, in 1649–55, it was a church built for preaching,[55] with no evidence of the forms of Roman worship. When the great fire of London destroyed much of the city, the new churches of Sir Christopher Wren were not influenced by Medieval Roman Catholic forms, but were "auditory churches," so called and so built that the preached word could be clearly heard.[56] While this auditory principle was dominant, the other aspect of the Reformed solution in using different parts of the church for different purposes was also felt in that while the number of rooms was now reduced to one, the Lord's Table was often put behind the pulpit, as if it were in a sepa-

---

[52] Addleshaw & Etchells, *op. cit.*, p. 45. See, e.g., the floor plan of the Grosse Kirche, Emden. Willy Weyres & Otto Bartning, *Kirchen, Handbuch für den Kirchenbau* (Münich: Callwey, 1959), p. 240.

[53] George Hay, *The Architecture of Scottish Post-Reformation Churches, 1560–1843* (Oxford: Clarendon Press, 1957), pp. 21ff.

[54] See Addleshaw & Etchells, *op. cit.*, p. 245f, for Martin Bucer's correspondence of 1577 with the Church of England concerning this matter.

[55] Weyres & Bartning, *op. cit.*, p. 243.

[56] Part of Wren's letter to a friend in 1708 in which he discusses the principles of "The Auditory Church" can also be found in an appendix of Addleshaw & Etchells, *op. cit.*, pp. 247–50.

rate room.[57] Both in the reorganization of existing churches at the Reformation and in the later building of auditory churches, the Word was preached in the midst of the people, while its indispensability was everywhere in evidence through the care taken that the people might hear the Word proclaimed. It was this necessity to hear, so that the Word might be appropriated by the hearer, that determined the relationship of people and pulpit. This arrangement continued to be the norm until the Romantic age and the neohistorical revival.[58]

But what is to be our contemporary expression of the importance of Word and Sacraments? The place of the Sacraments must wait until the next chapter, while consideration is here given to the pulpit and the expression of the indispensability of the Word.

One of the most obvious means to declare architecturally the indispensability of the Word would be to put the pulpit in the focal point of the church, pre-empting the spot previously reserved for the altar. This position is not new or novel, nor is it some aberration of the Reformation. Rather, there is every reason to believe that it is the most ancient position of the pulpit. In the first formal church buildings, the basilicas of the third century, the shape of the building was usually a rectangle with a semi-circular apse on the short east end. The floor of this apse was raised several steps above the floor of the nave, and in its center was the bishop's chair, from which he preached (in the early days of the Church there was one bishop for each church). Surrounding the bishop were his presbyters, and in front of the raised area, between the

---

[57] Addleshaw & Etchells, *op. cit.,* pp. 56ff. This was the original arrangement of old St. Paul's (1766) in New York, where the pulpit stood in front of the table, much to the mystification of those who think of the split chancel and central altar as true and traditional Anglican architecture.

[58] Otto H. Senn, "Church Building and Liturgy in the Protestant Church," *Lucerne International Joint Conference on Church Architecture and Church Building* (New York: mimeographed & copyrighted by the Dept. of Church Building & Architecture, NCCC, 1962), p. 6.

bishop and the congregation, was the Lord's Table around which the deacons were grouped.[59] To this same point an interesting quote from Ruskin may be cited:

> The Scotch congregations [with their central pulpits] are perfectly right, and have restored the real arrangement of the primitive churches. The chevalier Bunsen informed me lately, that, in all the early basilicas he has examined the lateral pulpits are of more recent date than the rest of the building; that he knows of none placed in the position which they now occupy, both in the basilicas and gothic churches, before the ninth century; and that there can be no doubt that the bishop always preached or exhorted, in the primitive times, from his throne in the centre of the apse, the altar being always set at the centre of the church. . . . His Excellency found by experiment in Santa Maria Maggiore, the largest of the Roman basilicas, that the voice could be heard more plainly from the centre of the apse than from any other spot in the whole church. . . .[60]

To exalt the place of preaching by giving it the central position in the church is thus a practice that goes back to the basilicas of the early centuries. The pulpit was moved to the side only with the ascendancy of the doctrine of the Mass in later centuries. While the Reformation often left the pulpit on a pillar in the nave, the seating was then so arranged as to make it the focal point of worship.

In small churches the simple expedients of placing the pulpit in a central position (a fortunately familiar practice) against an uncluttered background (an exceedingly rare practice seldom found in the United States) are sufficient to give the proclamation of the Word an adequate architectural statement. It

---

[59] Victor Fiddes, *The Architectural Requirements of Protestant Worship* (Toronto: The Ryerson Press, 1961), p. 28.

[60] A. L. Drummond, *The Church Architecture of Protestantism* (Edinburgh: T. & T. Clark, 1934), p. 206.

should be added that the pulpit should be of good workmanship, and of such shape, decoration and material as is in keeping with its place within the church as a whole. This almost always means that it should be designed by the architect who designs the building. Here of all places a congregation should not try to save money by purchasing some stock item from a religious supplier. It is undoubtedly very true that sermons can be good in spite of a cheap and awkward pulpit, just as it is true that one's wife may be a wonderful woman even if dressed in rags, but both speak rather eloquently of the respective concern and regard of congregation and husband. The proclamation of the Word deserves a pulpit which both by its position and by its design and workmanship declares the importance which the congregation attaches to the Word.

When one considers the visual statement of the Word in any church seating more than two hundred, the problems become very much more difficult. As the seats are placed farther and farther from the pulpit, it visually becomes smaller and smaller, and thus less commanding. While this situation cannot be corrected simply by getting larger and larger ministers (although sometimes more active ministers do help), it is possible to get larger and larger pulpits! The pulpits of the sixteenth through eighteenth centuries, with their commanding height, generous decoration, and elaborate sounding boards, were a far cry from the little reading desks with which we are so familiar. Within the last century the size of our pulpits has become so diminutive that when one is seated in the midst of the congregation there is real difficulty in seeing the minister at all, let alone the pulpit. Many churches have attempted to overcome this difficulty by the peculiarly perverse expedient of sloping the floor. This solution is perverse because it is exceedingly expensive and allows the continued use of the diminutive pulpit. While sloping the floor at great cost does make it easier to see above the heads of the people in front, it does nothing to give the necessary visual significance to the preaching of the Word, and frequently accomplishes the opposite.

The need for this expensive solution could be obviated by the very thing which is also so necessary in a large church for an effective visual statement of the Word: a high pulpit. It is, after all, the angle of vision between the man in the pew and the minister that assures easy vision, and to provide that proper angle it is much less expensive to lift the minister and his pulpit than to adjust the pews of the entire congregation! The high pulpit will also give visual expression to the importance of the Word, which a sloping floor, no matter how expensive, cannot do.

However, in the attempt to achieve an unmistakable visual statement concerning the indispensability of the Word, by far the most exciting architectural opportunities lie in the sounding board!

The Church of the Cross (Kruiskerk), Hervormd, Amstelveen, The Netherlands. Prof. M. F. Duintjer, architect

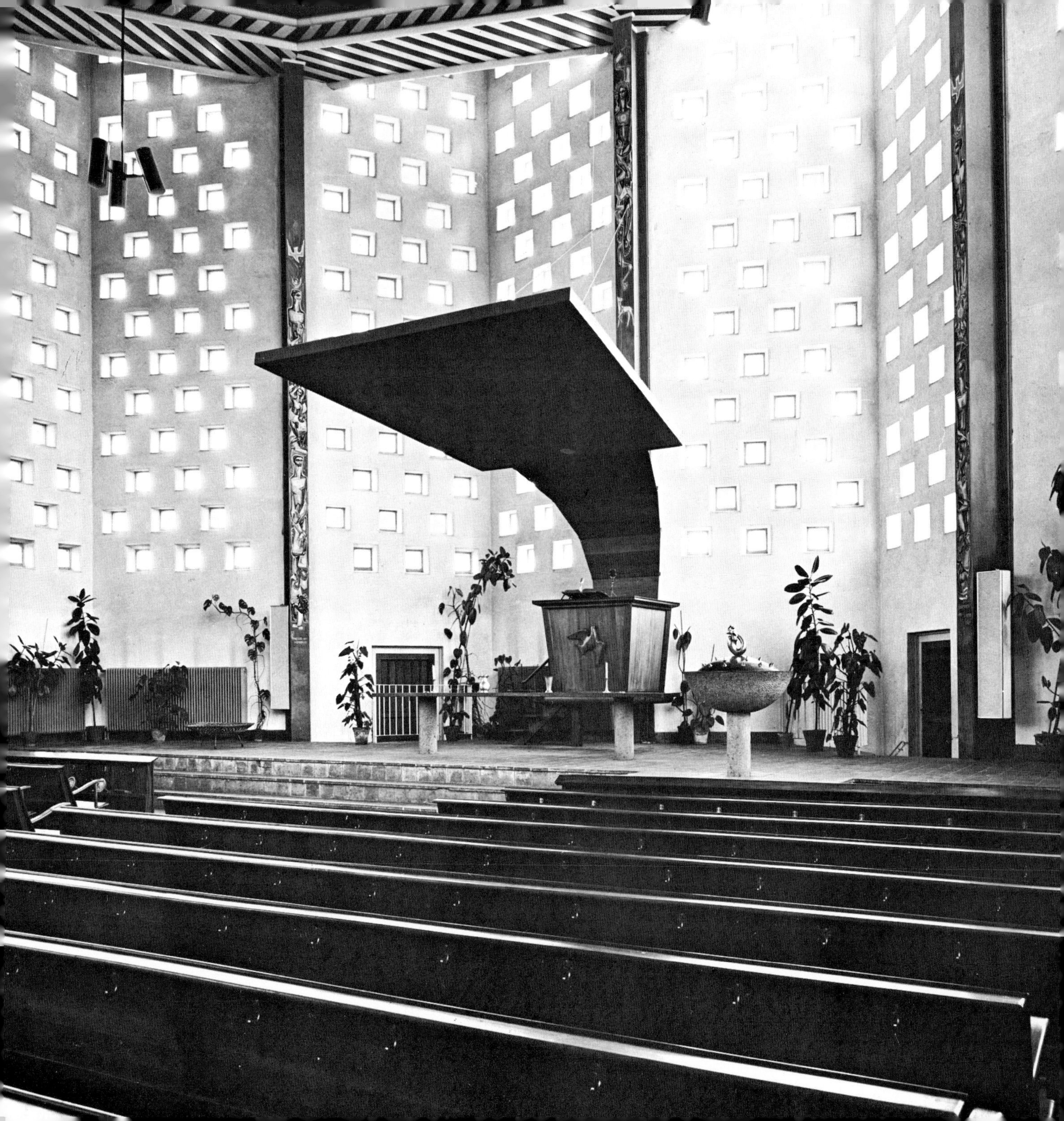

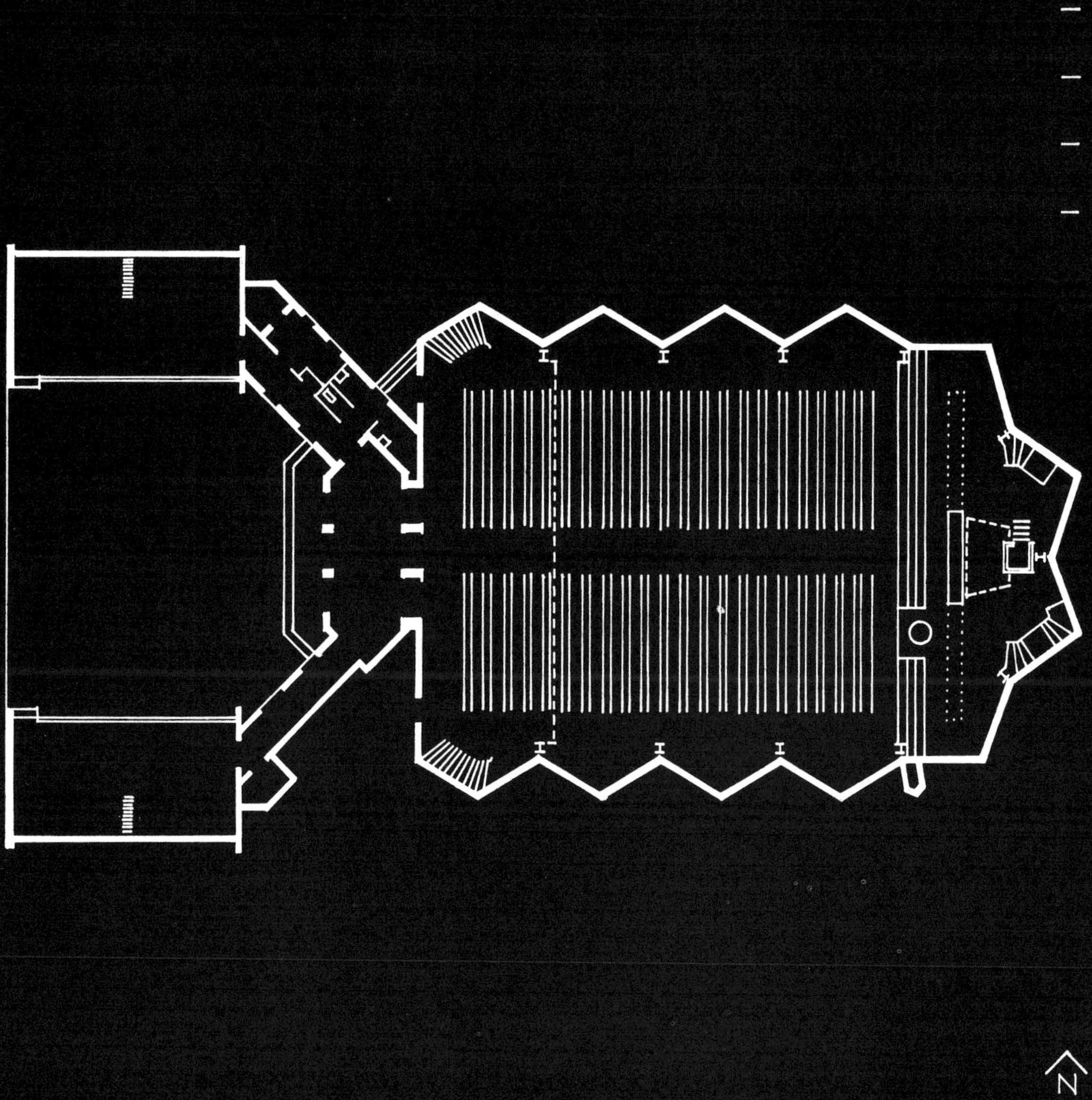
N

The Church of the Cross is sited so that there is an uninterrupted view of five blocks down a long pool. The church itself is placed in a large park even though The Netherlands has the highest population density of any nation on earth, and might justify many other uses for the land besides that of beautifying the community.

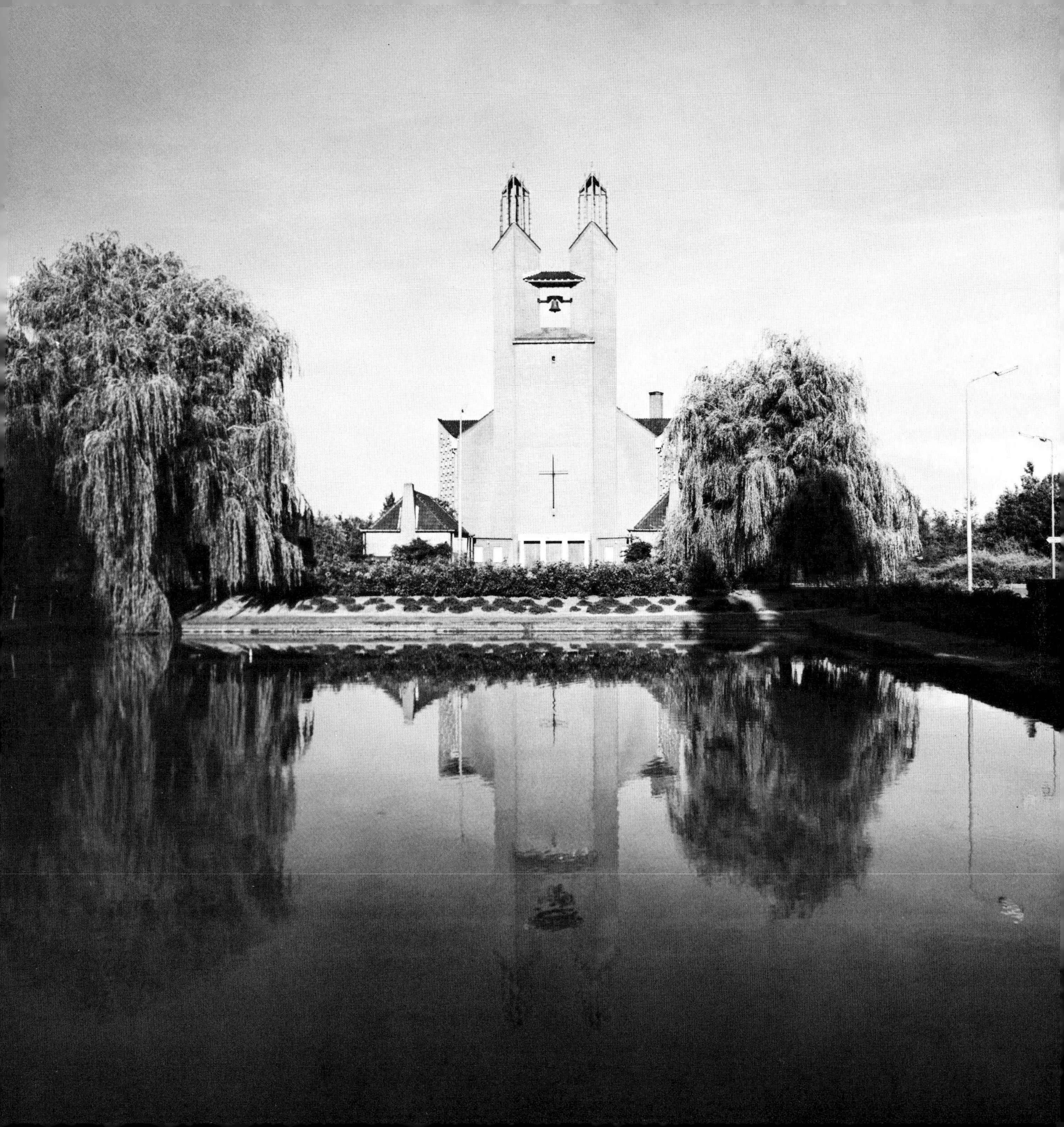

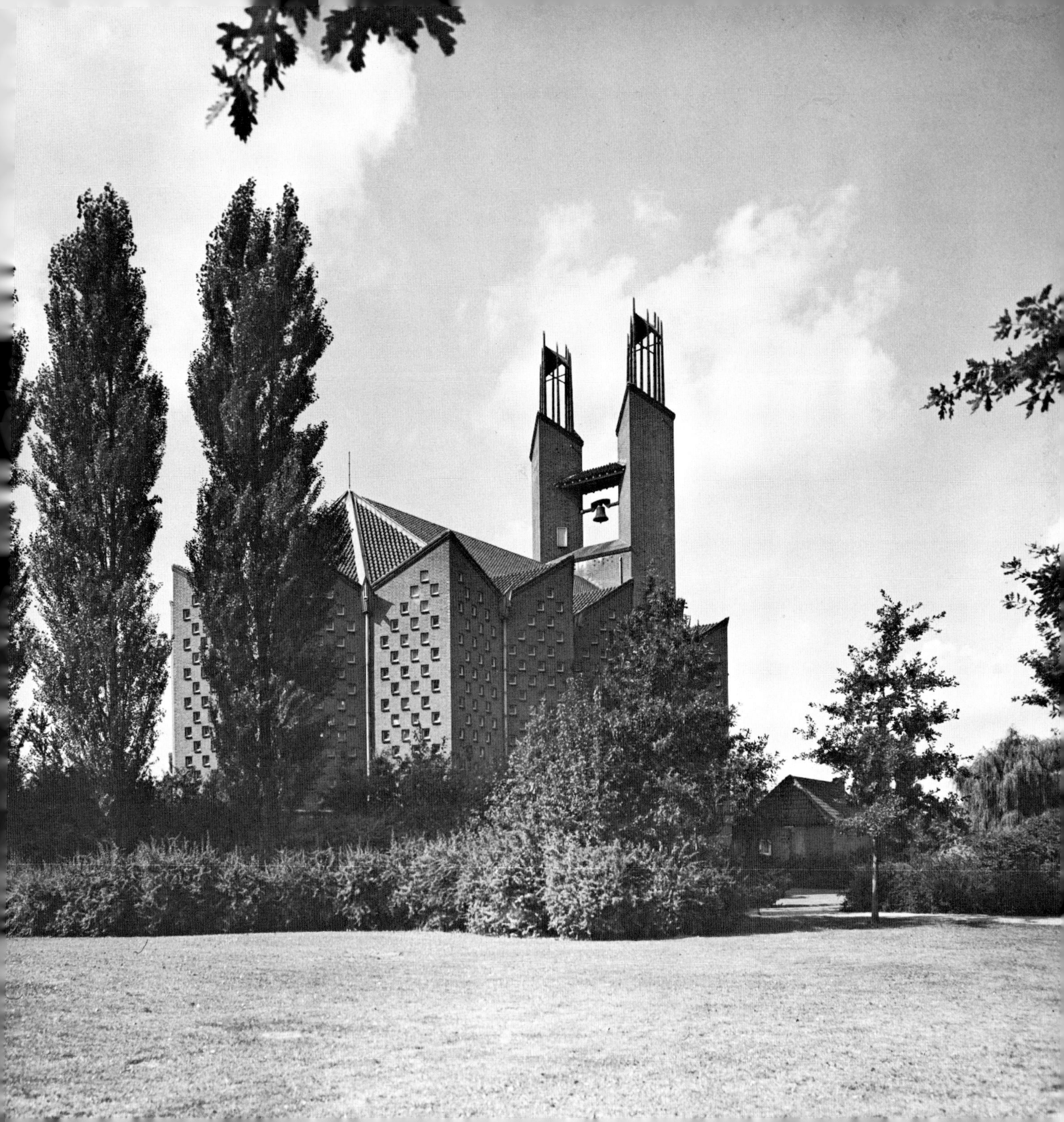

"Jesus Christ is Lord"

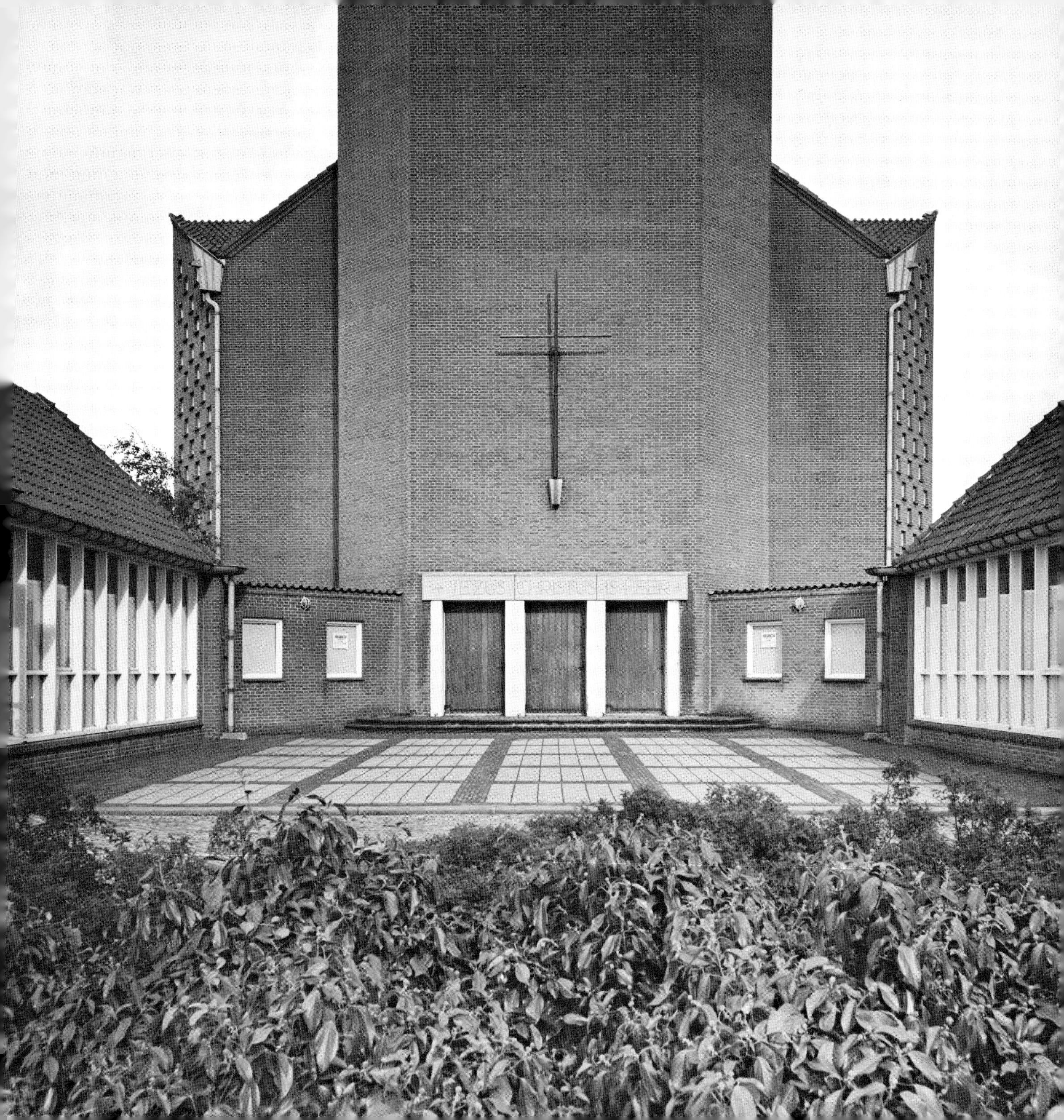
JEZUS CHRISTUS IS HEER

The pulpit appropriately bears the symbol of the Holy Spirit

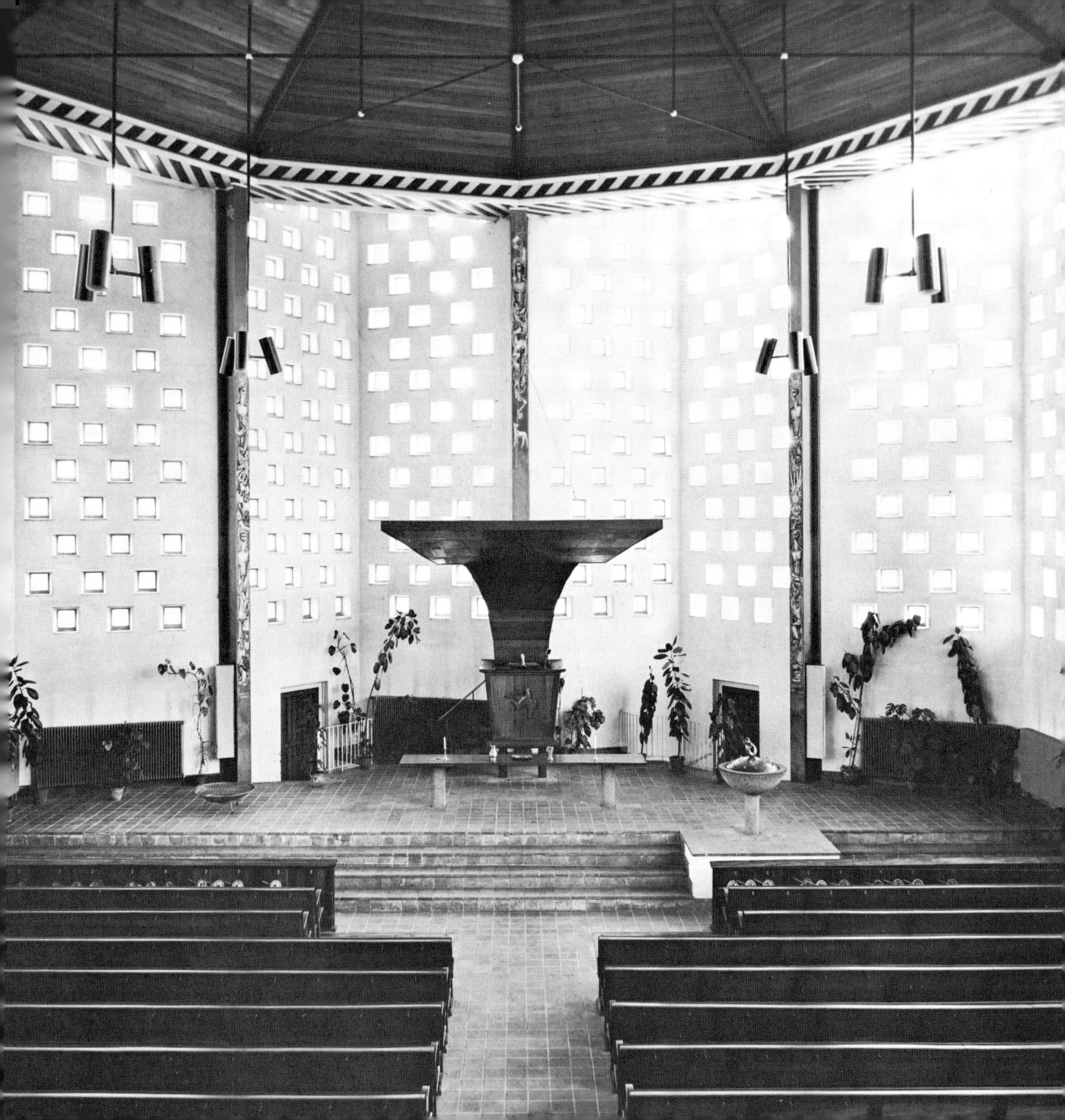

Organ by D. A. Flentrop of Zaandam

Hoofdwerk		Positief		Pedaal	
Prestant	8	Holpijp	8	Prestant	16
Roerfluit	8	Prestant	4	Octaaf	8
Octaaf	4	Roerfluit	4	Octaaf	4
Spitsquint	2⅔	Octaaf	2	Fluit	2
Vlakfluit	2	Quint	1⅓	Mixtuur 2–4 ranks	
Mixtuur 4–5 ranks	1⅓	Scherp 4–5 ranks	⅔	Bazuin	16
Trompet	8	Regaal	8		

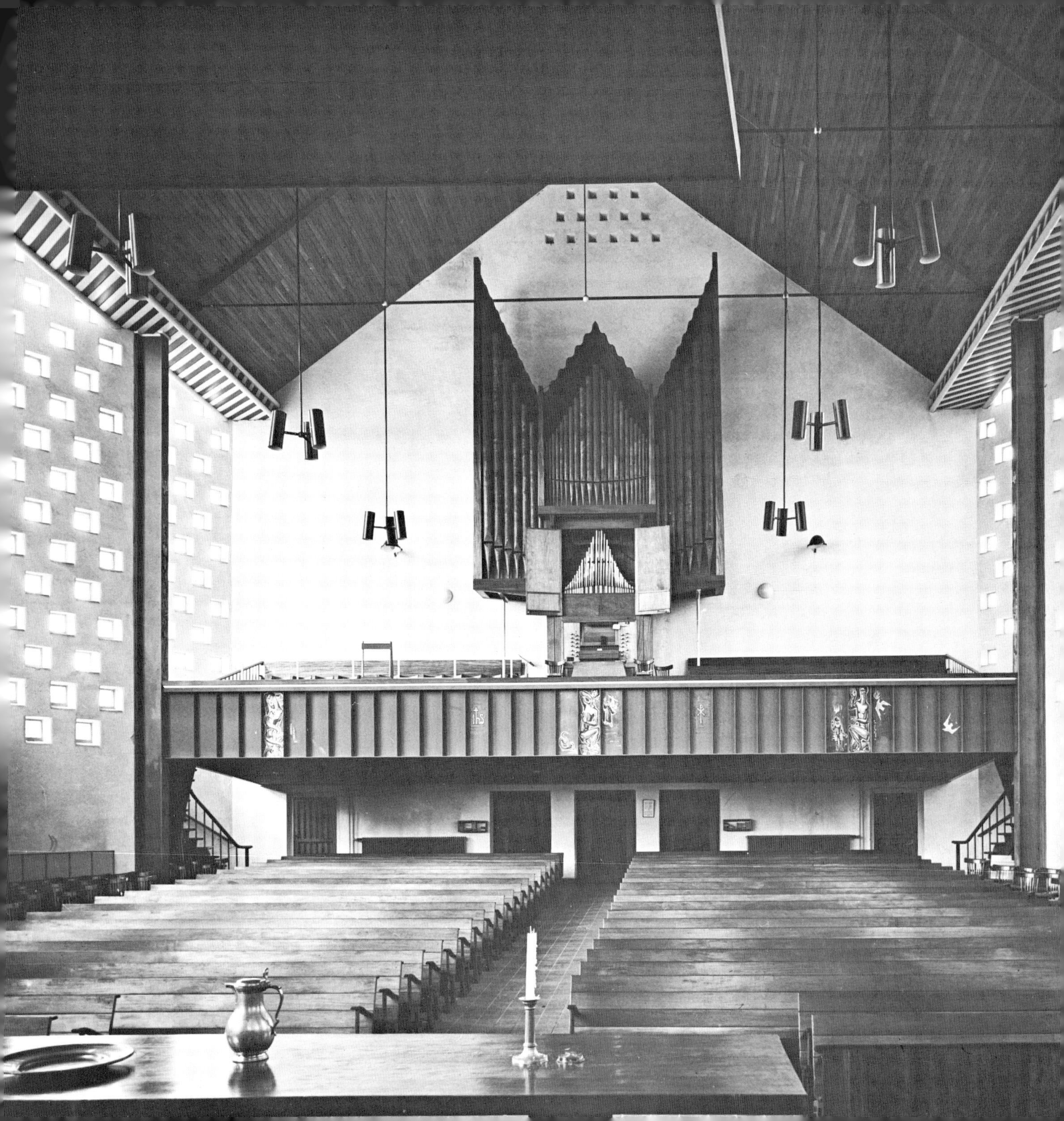

The sounding board originated in the large Medieval churches where under ceilings of up to a hundred feet in height, it was an absolute necessity if the preacher was to be heard. With the Reformed emphasis upon preaching, sounding boards remained a necessity, and have continued to be used in Europe in even the newest churches. The sounding board was also long used in America, but its demise began about the time that it became fashionable to display the choir and/or organ behind the minister—in which case the sounding board would simply have been an obstruction to this visual treat. It was this same period that saw the pulpit reduced to a reading desk on a low platform, where, with choir in the background, and often a proscenium arch overhead, the service could be performed. Much the same fate overtook many of the pulpits in Scotland. George Hay describes the church in Ceres, Fife, where "the sounding board of the pulpit was destroyed when an organ was given pride of place and upon the top of the latter the carved dove finial now perches disconsolately."[61]

Nevertheless, the disfavor accorded the sounding board in the last century in no way calls into question its basic merits. These merits include the most obvious one of offering splendid architectural opportunities visually to emphasize the Word in even the largest churches. Its original purpose also remains a merit: it is a definite aid to the speaker. Having gotten rid of the sounding board in the name of progress, our churches have instead turned to electrical sound amplification to perform its function. A few of these installations have admirable acoustical properties, but in most churches they leave much to be desired, frequently distorting the voice, often being too loud or too soft, with dead spots, areas of conflict, and occasionally a case of ear-shattering feedback. On the other hand, the sounding board, once it is built, has no parts to wear out, never suffers from weak tubes or a failure

---

[61] *Op. cit.,* pp. 133–34.

of current, is always in operating order, and will not howl, hiss, pop, or shriek. It must, of course, be acoustically well designed if it is to have more than a symbolic purpose, but with such design, it can send the minister's voice to the farthest reaches of the church free from distortion.

When there is a desire to give adequate visual emphasis to the pulpit, the place of the Bible within the pulpit should not be overlooked. The pulpit has its importance only as the place where God's Word is proclaimed, and while a Bible must remain of limited size, the pulpit Bible nonetheless should be placed so that at least its front edge can be seen by all. To this end the architect will also need to know the size of the pulpit Bible so that the board upon which it rests can be designed to fit it. The tendency found in so many modern American pulpits (copied undoubtedly from the speaker's stands they so closely resemble) to place the Bible out of sight below the rim of the pulpit may be very handy for keeping the minister's notes and manuscript out of view, but it should be avoided. Thus, another criterion of architecture for Reformed churches is:

BECAUSE THE PULPIT DERIVES ITS IMPORTANCE FROM THE PREACHING OF THE WORD, THE BIBLE SHOULD BE VISIBLE IN THE PULPIT.

However, it should be noted that these criteria (page 80) for architecture for Reformed churches specify neither high pulpits nor sounding boards. Neither should it be supposed that a central pulpit is required, apt as that solution may be. For just as there is no one fitting style in which to build a church, neither is there one perfect arrangement or floor plan. As Peter Hammond so ably points out, "loyalty to a theological and liturgical programme is compatible with the greatest possible flexibility of plan. . . . What is essential is that every specific solution should spring from, and be informed by, an adequate theological programme."[62] This holds true whether the "theological programme" be Anglican or Reformed, and just as a church must insist that her building express the theology of the Church as set forth by her theologians, so too a church must recognize that it is the province of the architect to create the forms to embody those principles.

In exploring the architectural possibilities for giving expression to our first criteria we began with a central pulpit, and for larger churches gave it height, and a sounding board. The Church of the Cross (Kruiskerk), Amstelveen, uses all three of these devices. Although the Church of the Resurrection (Opstandingskerk), Amsterdam-West, does not give much height to its pulpit and has it well off to the side, it nonetheless is completely faithful to its task of proclaiming week by week through its architecture that the Word of God is indispensable.

---

[62] Hammond, *op. cit.*, p. 83.

The Church of the Resurrection (Opstandingskerk), Hervormd, Amsterdam-West. Prof. M. F. Duintjer, architect

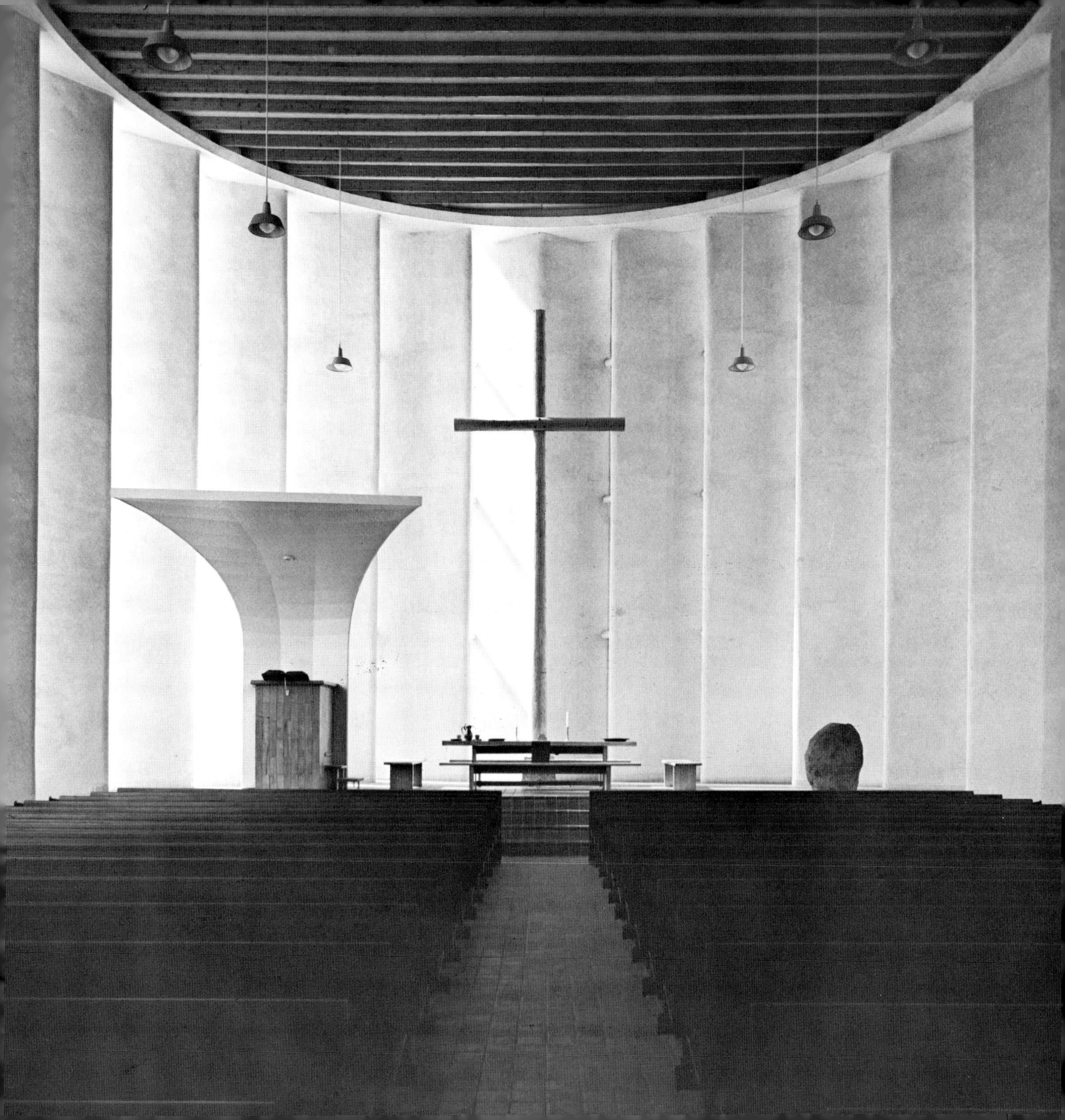

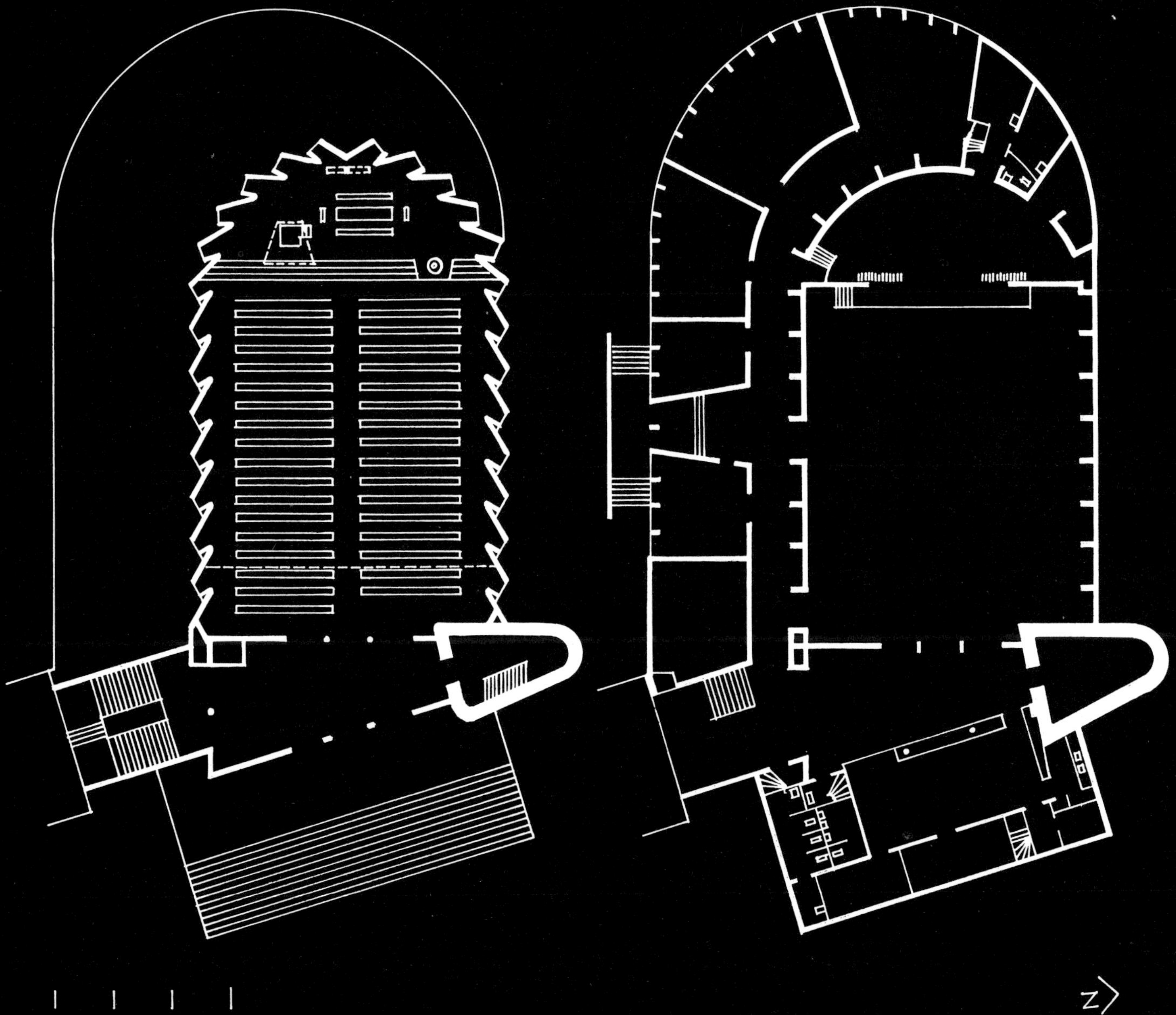

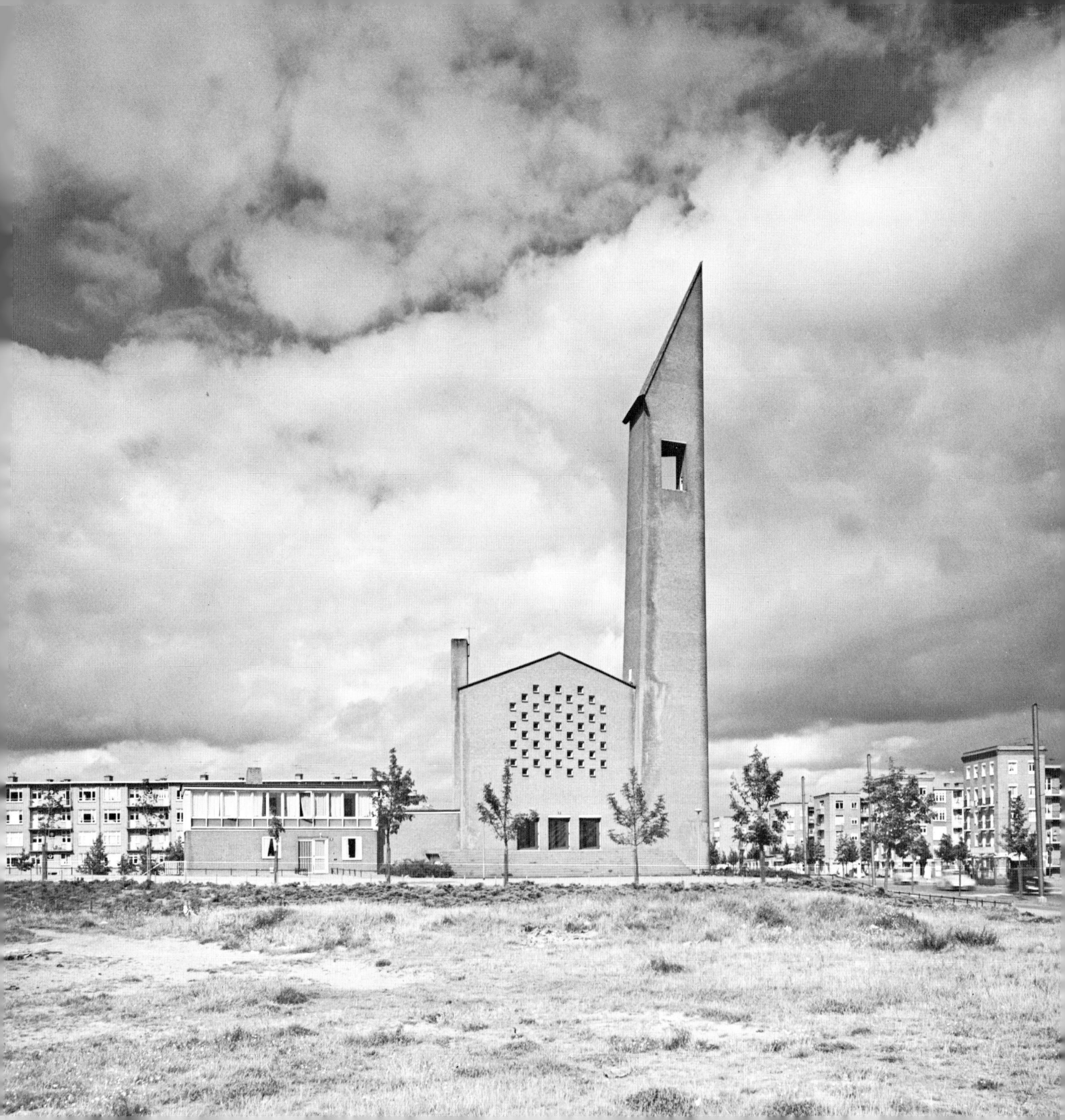

"The Lord is truly risen!" — *mural in the narthex*

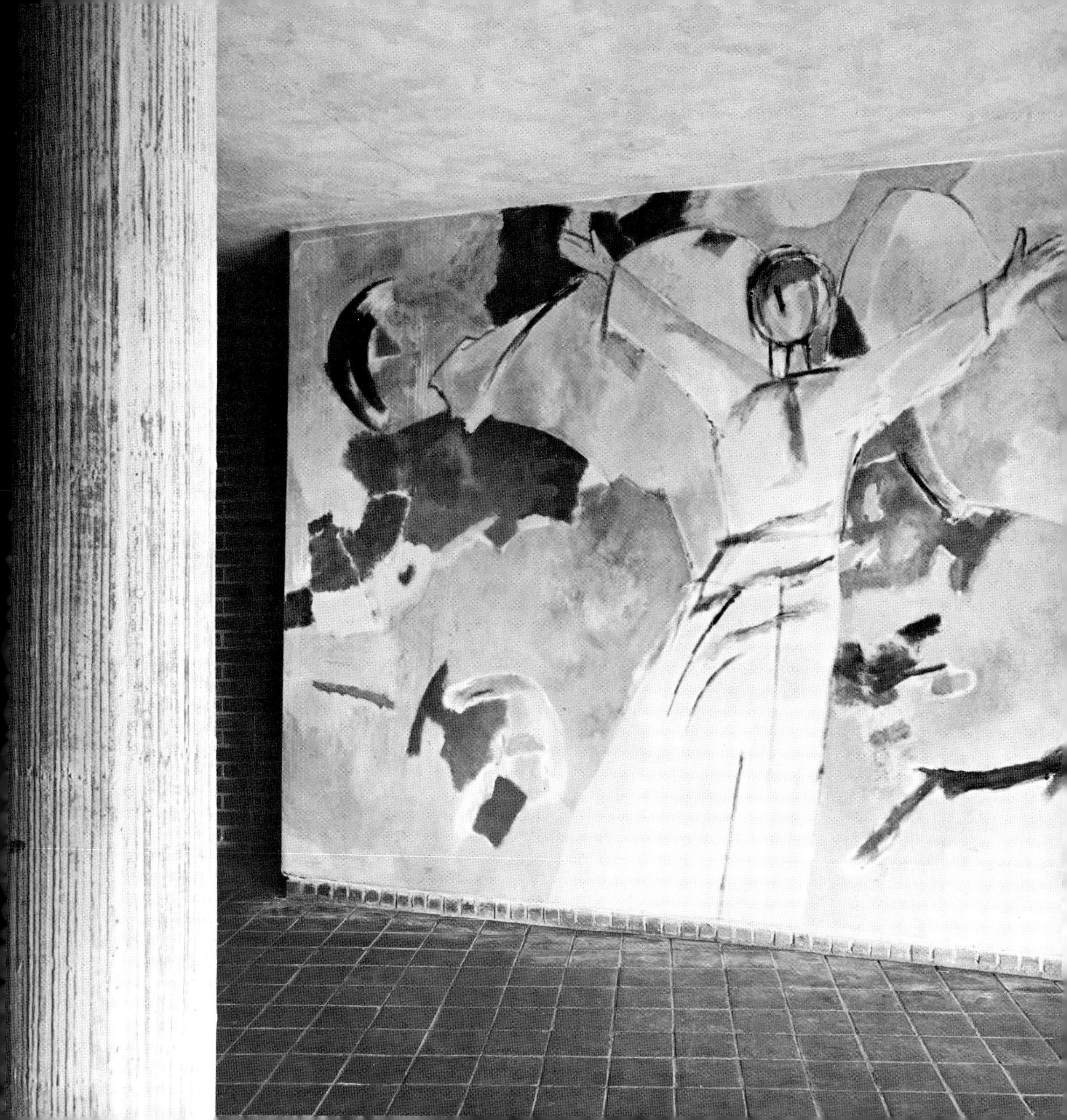

Within this simple interior of great theological significance, the whole room is full of life and excitement as the movement of the sun constantly varies the illumination of the sanctuary.

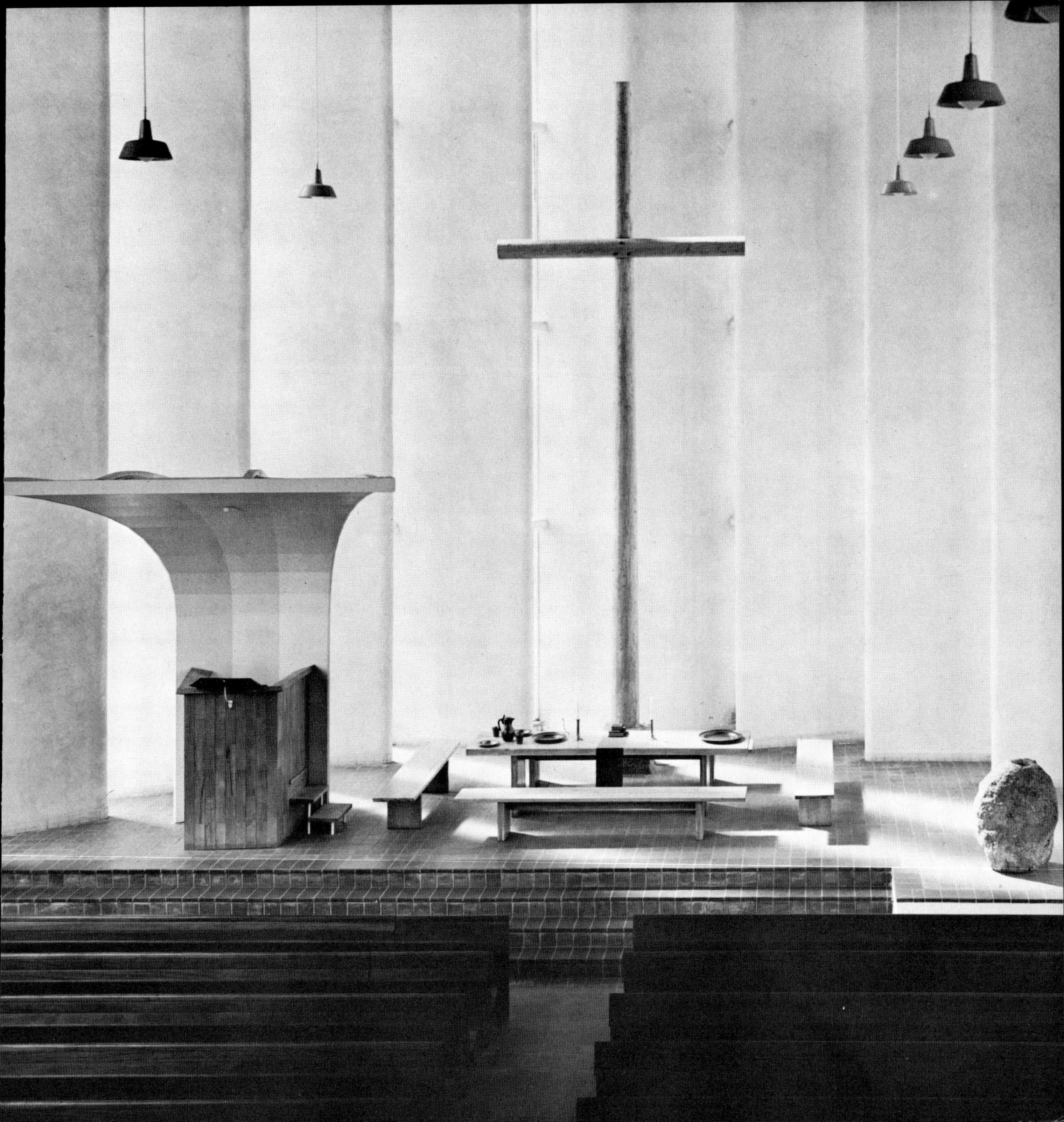

While obviously not intended as a concert instrument, this small positiv of exquisite tonal quality is nonetheless adequate both for the music of the worship service and for leading the congregation of up to 450 persons in hymns of praise.

Positiv by D. A. Flentrop of Zaandam

Holpijp   8
Prestant   4
Roerfluit   4
Gemshoorn   2
Sesquialter 2 ranks
Cymbel 1–2 ranks

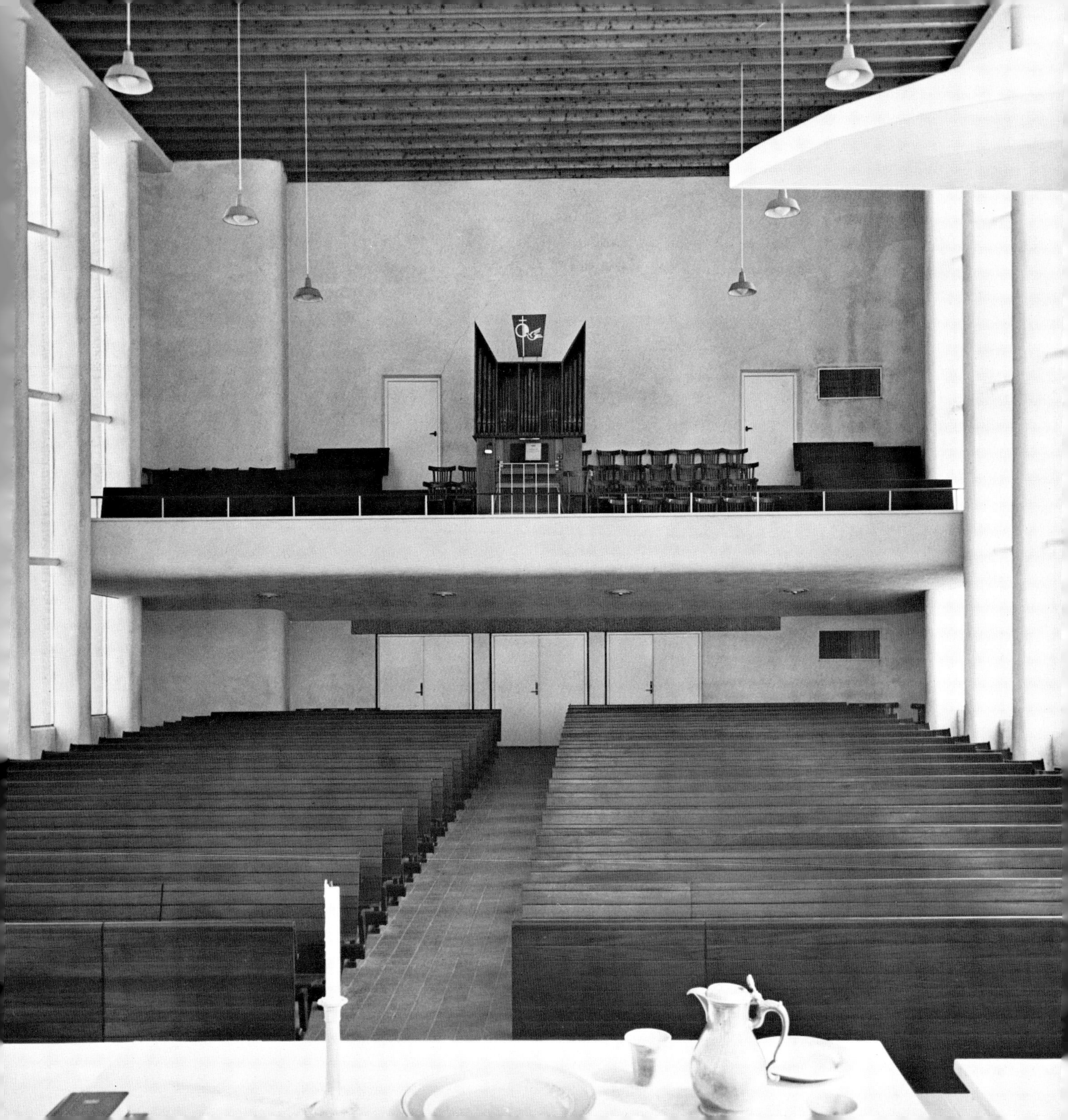

Surrounding a large assembly hall directly under the sanctuary are a number of bright and cheerful rooms used for the church school and for youth and fellowship activities, which are means whereby the church can reach out into the community.

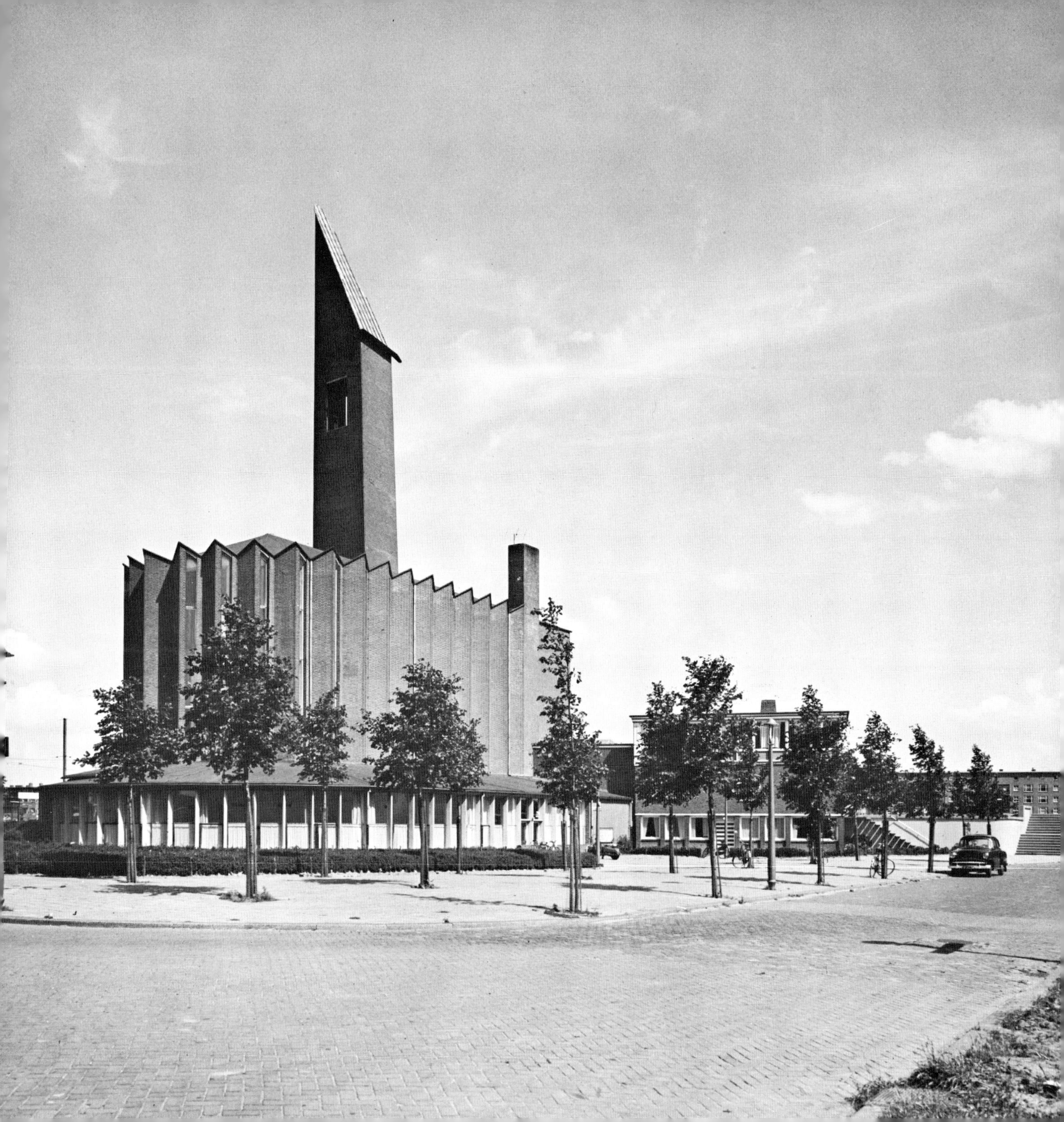

3

Christ's Sacraments

While upon entering some Reformed churches one might see Roman doctrine in the form of an exalted central altar, more often one sees a very rationalistic faith! Whether one likes it or not, architecture speaks. When little or no thought has been given to the matter, it sometimes speaks a message in contradiction to what is believed. All too many Reformed churches portray in their architecture that they are rationalistic, proud churches which are so confident of their reason and their preaching that they have no need of the Sacraments Christ ordained.

When one enters a church in which the communion table cannot be seen from the pews, there is certainly no visual indication that the Sacraments are considered of much importance. Visually, the implication is that they are of no account, whatever the church's real feeling may be. Or, if the table is placed at the foot of the center aisle, on the same level as the pews, covered with the morning's floral display and offering plates, does this really show a great deal more respect for the Sacrament? And if many of our Reformed churches have dealt carelessly with the Lord's table, what has been the fate of the baptismal font? In almost all cases it can barely be seen in an empty church (let alone when the congregation is present!), peeping above the backs of the pews, visually insignificant in comparison with the flags, pianos, lectern, organ and choir. If it calls attention to itself at all it is usually by its very ugliness, often rendered in a style and material completely alien to the rest of the church.

How is one to account for this lack of respect for the Sacraments? It could at one point have been explained in terms of pietism, where more and more the Supper was limited to the spiritually elite while the majority within the church felt themselves quite unworthy of partaking. This, however true at one time, would hardly constitute an explanation for today. On the other hand, rationalism was offended by the Sacraments. What Howard Hageman has to say about the frequency of celebration in the eighteenth century also has its implications for the visual display given the Sacraments:

> Though for very different reasons, both pietism and rationalism discouraged frequent celebrations of the Eucharist. Infrequent communions were the rule in pietism because of the awesomeness of the occasion; in rationalism because of the embarrassment of irrationality. But the result was the same. . . . Calvin's vision of Word and Sacrament was completely lost by either party as the pulpit came to obscure the Table.[1]

We still live in an age in which man, despite the blows he has suffered, retains a high degree of self-confidence. Hence it is perhaps not surprising that the Sacraments, with all the humility they require, should be relegated to unimportant places in our churches. But if unintentionally we have allowed the

---

[1] *Op. cit.,* pp. 54–55.

pride of our reason (which has been so much a part of all our lives since the Enlightenment) to be built into our churches, then it is well when we build a new church to build it as one "reformed according to the Word of God," and not as one that witnesses to our self-confidence.

But before attempting to state a criterion for the visual presentation of the Sacraments let us first ask: what is their nature and purpose? That the Sacraments are not to be understood as in any way superior to the Word by some transubstantial offering of the physical presence of Christ under the "accidents" of bread and wine was made clear in the previous chapter. The Sacraments are not superior to the Word. On the other hand, one must not allow a proper recognition of the Word to derogate the Sacraments. Calvin states the Reformed position clearly:

> Therefore, let it be regarded as a settled principle that the sacraments have the same office as the Word of God: to offer and set forth Christ to us, and in him the treasures of heavenly grace.[2]

But, of course, if the Sacraments have the same office as the Word of God, and if both join us to Christ through the power of the Holy Spirit, then for what purpose are the Sacraments added to the Word? Calvin's opening sentence in defining the Sacraments speaks to this very point: "We have in the sacraments another aid to our faith related to the preaching of the gospel."[3]

Now let it be said immediately that a satisfactory understanding of the place of the Sacraments is impossible apart from humility. Without humility questions arise as to how the Sacraments can add to a faith already existent through the Word. Calvin encountered similar questions in Geneva:

> Some say that our faith cannot be made better if it is already good, for it is not faith unless it leans unshaken, firm, and steadfast upon God's mercy. It would

---
[2] *Institutes*, 4:14:17, p. 1292.
[3] *Ibid.*, 4:14:1, p. 1276.

have been better for them to pray with the apostles that the Lord increase their faith (Luke 17:5) than confidently to pretend such perfection of faith as no one of the children of men ever attained in this life.[4]

Such questions betray a pride in one's own capacity which the Reformers did not share. The object of the Sacraments is the same as that of the Word: Christ. Through both, the Holy Spirit joins us to him and all his benefits. But because of "our dull capacity, and to lead us by the hand as tutors lead children," the Sacraments have been given to us.[5]

> But as our faith is slight and feeble unless it be propped on all sides and sustained by every means, it trembles, wavers, totters, and at last gives way. Here our merciful Lord, according to his infinite kindness, so tempers himself to our capacity that he condescends to lead us to himself even by these earthly elements, and to set before us in the flesh a mirror of spiritual blessings.[6]

The Sacraments are not needed because the Word is inadequate, but because we are inadequate.

But in what way do the Sacraments strengthen faith? The Westminster Larger Catechism in Question 162 explains a Sacrament as a "holy ordinance instituted . . . to signify, seal, and exhibit . . . the benefits of his mediation; to strengthen and increase . . . faith . . . ." The Heidelberg Catechism states that Sacraments are "visible, holy signs and seals instituted by God . . . that he may the more fully disclose and seal to us the promise of the gospel . . ." (Question 66). However, to speak of the Sacraments as signs and seals without a keen awareness as to the biblical implications of these words is to miss their weighty content.

The function of the Sacraments as signs can best be understood in

---

[4] *Ibid.*, 4:14:7, pp. 1282–83.
[5] *Ibid.*, 4:14:6, p. 1281.
[6] *Ibid.*, 4:14:3, p. 1278.

terms of the signs of Jesus' ministry. Jesus came preaching and teaching. Surely these words should have been enough to bring men unto him. But in the life of Jesus one sees the marvelous condescension of God, for added to Jesus' words were the signs of his ministry. Thus when the disciples of John the Baptist come to ask whether he is the Messiah, or whether they must look for another, Jesus points them to his signs: "Go and tell John what you hear and see: the blind receive their sight and the lame walk, lepers are cleansed and the deaf hear, and the dead are raised up, and the poor have good news preached to them" (Matthew 11:4–6). In the Gospel of John these signs are clearly used by Jesus as a means of revealing himself. At the marriage feast of Cana Jesus turns the water meant "for the Jewish rites of purification" (John 2:6)—the ritual ablutions of the old covenant—into the wine of the new covenant. Because of the superiority of the wine of the new covenant over the water of the old, John can say that "This, the first of his signs Jesus did at Cana in Galilee, and manifested his glory . . ." (John 2:11). An even clearer example is found in the feeding of the five thousand (John 6). Having demonstrated his power by the sign of the miraculous feeding of the multitude, Jesus goes on to proclaim in words, "I am the bread of life." Jesus demonstrates by sign what he proclaims by word.

One should not miss the relationship between these events of Jesus' ministry, these signs by which he attests to the truth of his Word, and the signs of the Sacraments. Here a certain little book by Oscar Cullmann, *Early Christian Worship*,[7] should be required reading for all those who fail to give adequate place to the Sacraments. For Cullmann sees in the Gospel of John at least eleven such attempts (of which two examples have just been given) to relate the signs of Jesus' ministry to the signs of the Sacraments. For example, Cullmann's exegesis indicates that John wished the early Church

---

[7] (London: SCM Press Ltd., 1953).

to connect the wine of the miracle at Cana with the wine of the Lord's Supper. As Christians celebrated the Supper, its significance was to be augmented by this message and sign from the ministry of Jesus—in this Supper Christians partake of the wine of the new covenant of Christ in whom alone is true purification. So, too, in the bread of the Sacrament we are reminded of Christ who is the bread of life—and this is so clearly delineated in John 6, and in the liturgies for the Lord's Supper, that no further comment is needed. Cullmann goes so far as to say that "clearly the sacraments mean the same for the Church as the miracles of the historical Jesus for his contemporaries."[8]

In an attempt to clarify the role of the Sacraments to the Church today one might suggest that even as the miracles of Jesus' ministry were to strengthen the faith of those who heard his words, so the Sacraments of Jesus' present ministry are to strengthen the faith of those who hear the Word. Read the Gospels without the miracles and one has something of an indication of the Church without the Sacraments, for as the miracles were the signs of his ministry, so the Sacraments are the signs of his present ministry.

The word seal, which is so glibly used of the Sacraments, also takes on force and power when one returns to Scripture for its content. The literal meaning of the seal was the same as its contemporary usage, and by transmitting its impression to wax it was used to seal letters, documents, doors, or money bags. This literal usage, however, gave birth to a wide range of metaphorical usage. For example, the seal was used literally to secure the lion's den in Daniel 6:17, and the sepulcher of Christ, Matthew 27:66, but in Romans 15:28 Paul speaks of bringing the collection to Jerusalem, and thereby "sealing to them this fruit." Paul is speaking not of the literal sealing

---

[8] *Ibid.,* pp. 37–119.

of the money bags, which would have been done months before at the source of the collection, but is speaking metaphorically of "the setting of the seal on an accomplished work."[9] The Sacraments are a setting of God's seal upon us in a redemption accomplished in Christ.

Another biblical usage of the word seal is in the sealing up of a book "because it is finished and nothing more is to be added; so vision and prophecy are sealed up, Daniel 9:24, 12:4, 9 . . . ."[10] This usage is also applicable to the Sacraments, for they seal unto us the finished work of Christ to which nothing more is to be added.

A third usage of the term seal is the familiar one of giving confirmation or attestation to a document. Our usual experience with the seal in this fashion is on a diploma or legal papers. The seal is to offer the strongest possible attestation of the truth involved. It is in this sense that the Bible uses the term seal not only to refer to royal letters (Esther 8:8, 10) and legal documents (Jeremiah 32:10, 11, 14, 44), but also to the "seal of circumcision" (Romans 4:11) as it is the attestation of Abraham's faith. The word seal is used in this same sense to describe God's attestation of his Son (John 6:27). Paul uses the term in connection with the action of the Holy Spirit when he speaks of Christians as having been "sealed with the promised Holy Spirit" (Ephesians 1:13), and of "the Holy Spirit of God, in whom you were sealed for the day of redemption" (Ephesians 4:30). In II Corinthians 1:22 Paul speaks of God as having "put his seal upon us and given us his Spirit in our hearts as a guarantee." Not only do these passages represent the strength with which the Scriptures use this word seal by connecting it with the Holy Spirit who does the sealing, but New Testament scholars

---

[9] A. G. Herbert, "Seal," *A Theological Word Book of the Bible,* ed. by Alan Richardson (New York: The Macmillan Co., 1953), p. 222.
[10] *Ibid.*

generally understand these passages as also having reference to Baptism. Exegetically this is entirely justified on the basis of the close relation between the water of baptism and the giving of the Spirit (John 3:5, 4:10–15, 7:38, 19:34, Acts 10:47, Ephesians 5:26, I Peter 3:20, I John 5;6–8, Revelation 7:17; cf. John 7:37–38, Revelation 21:6, 22:1, 17). Baptism is the sign and seal of engrafting into Christ, while the Holy Spirit effects the reality.

In achieving a strong biblical emphasis upon the Sacraments and their Christ-given role in the confirmation of faith, one must not become involved in a confusion of the sign and the thing signified. In short, there is no room for a doctrine of baptismal regeneration. The Sacraments are not a means by which man controls God, but are God's signs and seals to strengthen the Christian in his faith. Baptismal regeneration stands this relationship on its head in asserting that the Sacraments affect God. Baptism is not to inform God that we are his, but to assure us that we belong to God. Baptism is the sign to assure us of the reality which has taken place for us in Christ and is communicated by the Holy Spirit. As Calvin points out, "If the Spirit be lacking, the sacraments can accomplish nothing more in our minds than the splendor of the sun shining upon blind eyes . . ." for "the sacraments properly fulfill their office only when the Spirit, that inward teacher, comes to them . . . ."[11] Even as the Holy Spirit is necessary for the effectual preaching of the Word, so the Holy Spirit is necessary for a proper celebration of the Sacraments. And the work of the Holy Spirit, in both Word and Sacraments, is to unite us with Christ and all his benefits. In short: "Christ is the matter or (if you prefer) the substance of all the sacraments; for in him they have all their firmness, and they do not promise anything apart from him."[12] True, the Sacraments are nothing apart from Christ, but they have their

---

[11] *Institutes,* 4:14:9, p. 1284.
[12] *Ibid.,* 4:14:16, p. 1291.

function and validity precisely in being signs and seals to Christ's people of their relationship to him.

As has already been indicated, it is evident that all too many congregations are so confident of themselves and their ability to hear the Word that they do not feel the need of Christ's Sacraments to strengthen their faith. In such situations, the Sacraments will play a small part in architecture. Such confidence, however, is more fitting to Rationalists, Deists, or Unitarians than it is to those who are truly "reformed according to the Word of God." If, however, the Christian takes seriously what the Bible has to say about the power of sin and the necessity of being joined to Christ, then the Sacraments which minister to the weakness of our faith and join us to Christ and all his benefits will of necessity play a visually prominent part in our architecture.

Christ's Sacrament of Baptism

. . . the sign of the prophet Jonah. For as Jonah was three days and three nights in the belly of the whale, so will the Son of man be three days and three nights in the heart of the earth.
Matthew 12:39–40.
Do you not know that all of us who have been baptized into Christ Jesus were baptized into his death? We were buried therefore with him by baptism into death, so that as Christ was raised from the dead by the glory of the Father, we too might walk in newness of life. *Romans 6:3–4.*

Baptismal font, The Church of the Cross (Kruiskerk), Hervormd, Amstelveen Font, Ben Guntenaar. Prof. M. F. Duintjer, architect

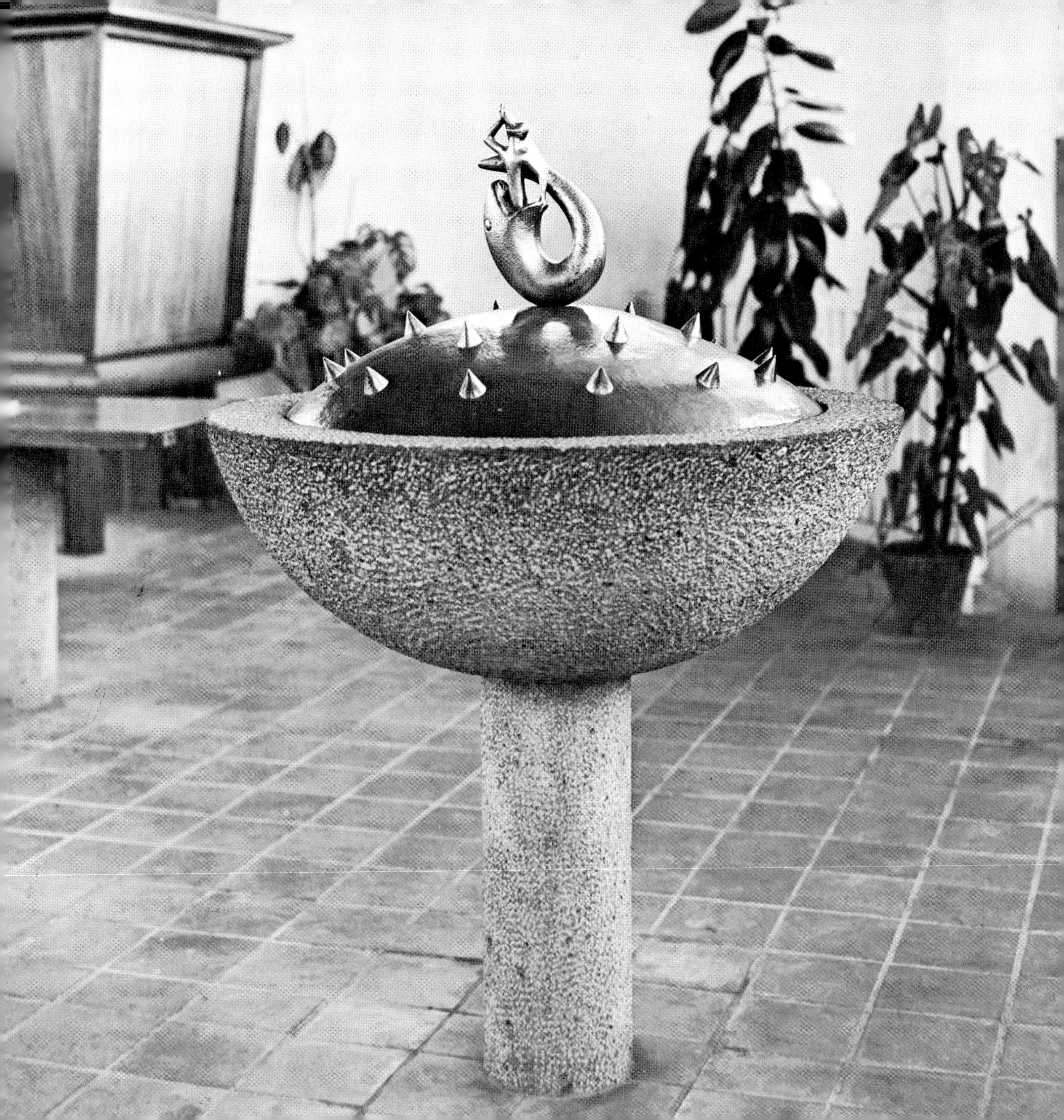

Baptism as Entrance into Christ

The whole message of Baptism is Jesus Christ. That is also the message of the cross. That is the message of the gospel. But in Baptism there is the visible, tangible sign of water to which God has attached his promise that I "am as certainly washed with his blood and Spirit from the uncleanness of my soul and from all my sins, as I am washed externally with water . . . ."[13] That I in faith have been baptized signifies that I too participate in the benefits of Christ, that even as the water of Baptism touches me, so Christ has cleansed me by his blood in his one sacrifice on the cross.

Calvin, however, in his first sentence on Baptism, reminds us immediately that Baptism is not a purely personal thing, but that because we are baptized into Christ, we are also baptized into the body of Christ, the Church:

> Baptism is the sign of the initiation by which we are received into the fellowship of the church, in order that, engrafted in Christ, we may be reckoned among God's children.[14]

So too the Belgic Confession: it is Baptism "by which we are received into the Church of God and separated from all other people . . ." (Article XXXIV). Because Baptism is the sign of our entrance in the Church, the body of Christ, it has long been the custom of Roman Catholics to put the baptismal font near the door where one enters the church. The Bishops of Germany give the following "Directives for the Building of a Church":

> In the sacrament of baptism we are born anew as children of God and we are incorporated into the Church, the Mystical Body of Christ. . . . The baptismal

---

[13] *The Heidelberg Catechism, 400th Anniversary Edition, 1563–1963,* trans. Allen O. Miller and M. Eugene Osterhaven (Boston: United Church Press, 1962), Answer 69, p. 68.

[14] *Institutes,* 4:15:1, p. 1303.

> font, which should be of imposing design and proportions, should be located in its own distinct area near to the entrance of the church.[15]

Thus one is always reminded that entry into the Church is through baptism. This symbolism is carried to its ultimate in a church built for the Oxford Mission in Calcutta at Barisal in Eastern Bengal,

> where the church is approached through a narthex containing a large tank, which stretches across its entire width. All unbaptized persons must remain to the west of this tank until they pass through it at their baptism. Those who are baptized enter the church through doors placed to the east of the narthex, and opening directly into the room for the eucharistic assembly.[16]

While it is true that we are baptized into Christ, this doctrine is subject to the perversion of baptismal regeneration, in which the sign is confused with the thing signified, thus making the power of God wait for the performance of the outward sign.[17] When in the Medieval Church the efficacy of the rite came to be placed in its performance, there was no longer any need to place Baptism within the context of the living congregation, and so along with the doctrine of baptismal regeneration there grew up the practice of private baptisms attended only by the family and friends. Despite the position of the font near the door, the Sacrament of Baptism ceased to have a real relationship to the living Church.

The Reformers, while holding that Baptism indeed was the sign and

---

[15] *Documents for Sacred Architecture*, pp. 21–22.
[16] Hammond, *op. cit.*, p. 46.
[17] For the Cambridge Ecclesiologists (to whom we owe the plethora of deep-chanceled pseudo-Gothic churches in England and America) "A font had to be near the church door . . . as symbolizing that Baptism is the way into membership of the Body of Christ. . . . Their sense of order was disturbed by an infant being allowed into the holiest part of the church before it was even baptized." Addleshaw & Etchells, *op. cit.*, p. 207.

seal of entrance into the body of Christ, wished to put the Sacrament into its true relationship to the living congregation. This was especially necessary in reference to infant baptism, for once baptismal regeneration was denied, the biblical teaching of the covenant had to be emphasized, the baptism of infants being based precisely upon their relationship to this covenant community. Therefore, the Reformers moved the font to the front of the church where Baptism was performed in the midst of the covenant people of God, or, as the Scots phrased it, "in the face of the congregation." This example was followed among all the Reformed on the Continent, and in Scotland, where the Westminster divines (1645) "reaffirmed the traditional Reformed attitude to baptism, by declaring, 'Nor is it [Baptism] to be administered in private places or privately, but in the place of public worship, and in the face of the congregation, where the people may most conveniently see and hear . . . .' "[18] The Reformation saw that Baptism, as the sign and seal of entrance into the body of Christ, most appropriately takes place in reference to the living Church rather than to the church structure. Therefore any architectural criterion must take into account that

AS THE SIGN AND SEAL OF BEING BAPTIZED INTO CHRIST, BAPTISM IS TO BE PERFORMED IN THE FACE OF THE CONGREGATION, WHERE THEY, THE BODY OF CHRIST, MAY BOTH SEE AND HEAR.

Historically, precisely this was done by the simple expedient of either moving the font from the door to the pulpit and/or table (as was done in Geneva, in placing it near the pulpit), or by placing a basin upon the Lord's Table.[19] This latter custom is still followed in many of the churches of

---

[18] Hay, *op. cit.,* pp. 188–89.
[19] W. D. Maxwell, *John Knox's Genevan Service Book 1556* (Edinburgh: Oliver & Boyd, 1931), pp. 115–16.

Switzerland, and is commended by no less a personage than Karl Barth.[20] This usage, in a superb setting, is found in the chaste surroundings of the Bullinger Church.

---

[20] Karl Barth, "Protestantism and Architecture," *Theology Today,* XIX, No. 2 (July 1962), p. 272. Barth, to make his Christological point, suggested that not only font and table, but pulpit as well, be combined into one piece of furniture. Since the completion of the photographs for this book, prof. M. F. Duintjer has produced a pulpit-font-table for the Thomaskerk (Hervormd), Zeist, The Netherlands. Periodical of the Prof. Dr. G. van der Leeuw-Stichting, Amsterdam: May, 1963, pp. 1030–1042. In this country, St. Paul's African Methodist Episcopal Church, Cleveland, Ohio (Raymond P. Chaty and Carl H. Droppers, architects), does precisely this to emphasize the unity of Word and Sacraments in Christ (p. 505).

The Lord's table equipped for service as font, with silver baptismal bowl, napkin, and liturgy.

The Bullinger Church (Bullingerkirche), Reformed, Zurich, Switzerland
Bros. Pfister, architects

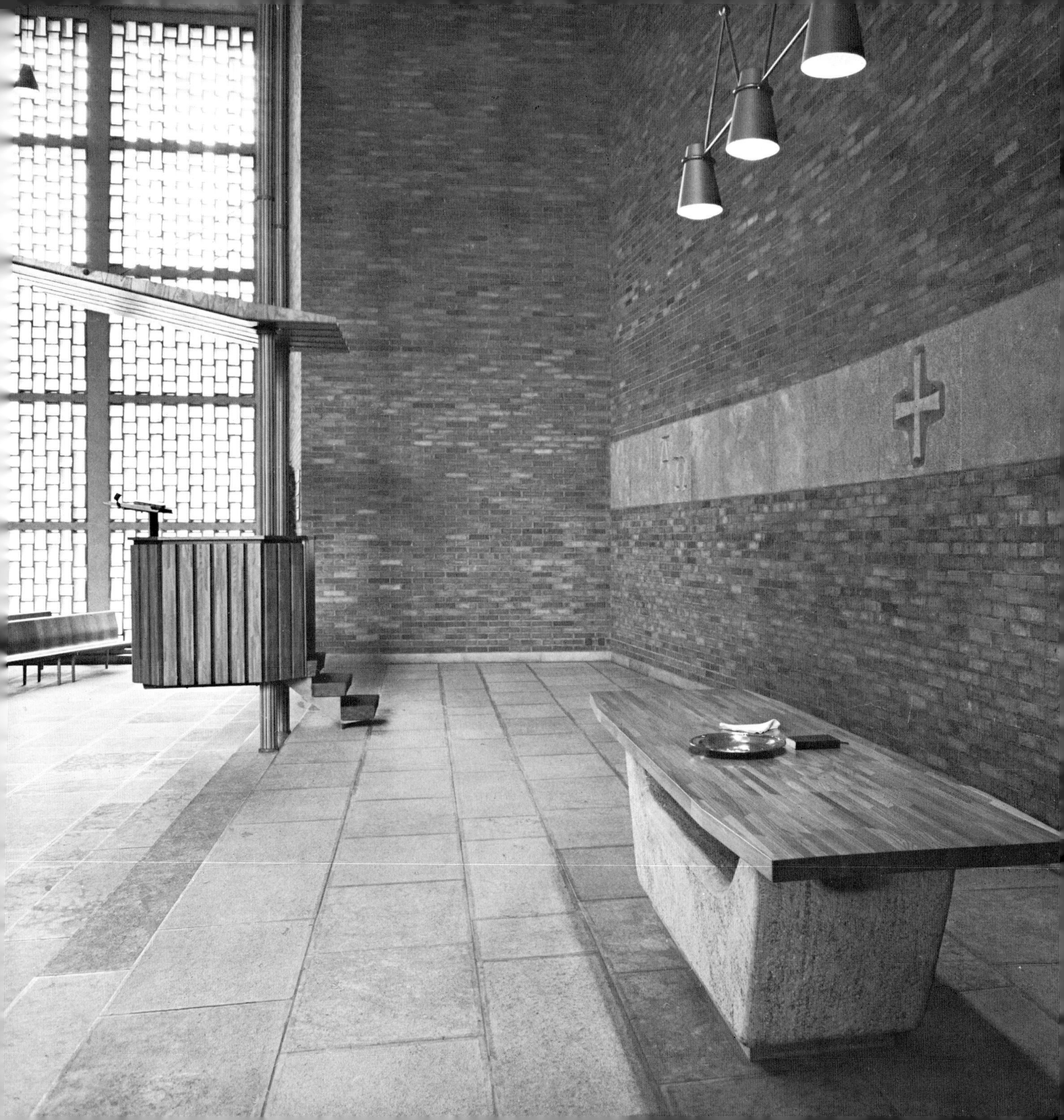

With a tremendous expanse of east wall, the architects have used restraint, limiting their symbolism to a narrow band of stone upon which an Alpha and Omega have been carved behind the pulpit, while behind the table are cross, chalice, and dove. This restraint enables the means by which Christ communicates himself to his people, his Word and Sacraments, to present themselves visually with great emphasis.

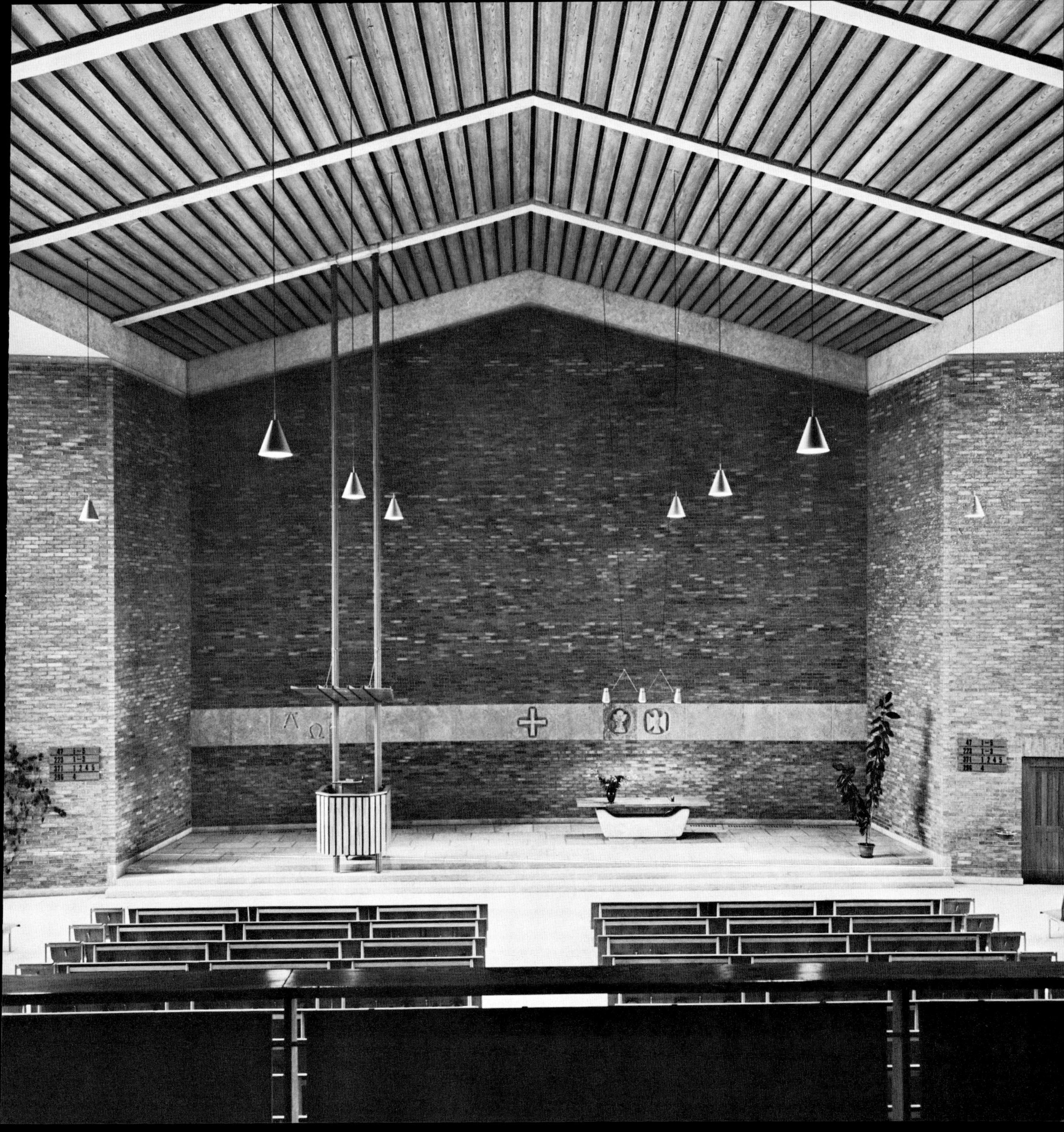

An interesting variant of the table/font idea appears in the Swiss Reformed Church in Boningen near Interlaken, where the table, which also serves as the font, rests on a pedestal shaped like a font, thus giving a constant visual appearance of font and table. An historical precedent for such a font/table has already been noted in the church at Kirchenthurnen, where in 1673 such an arrangement was in use (cf. pp. 9, 13).

The Church (Kirche Bonigen), Reformed, Bonigen near Interlaken, Switzerland
Ernst & Ulrich Indermühle, architects

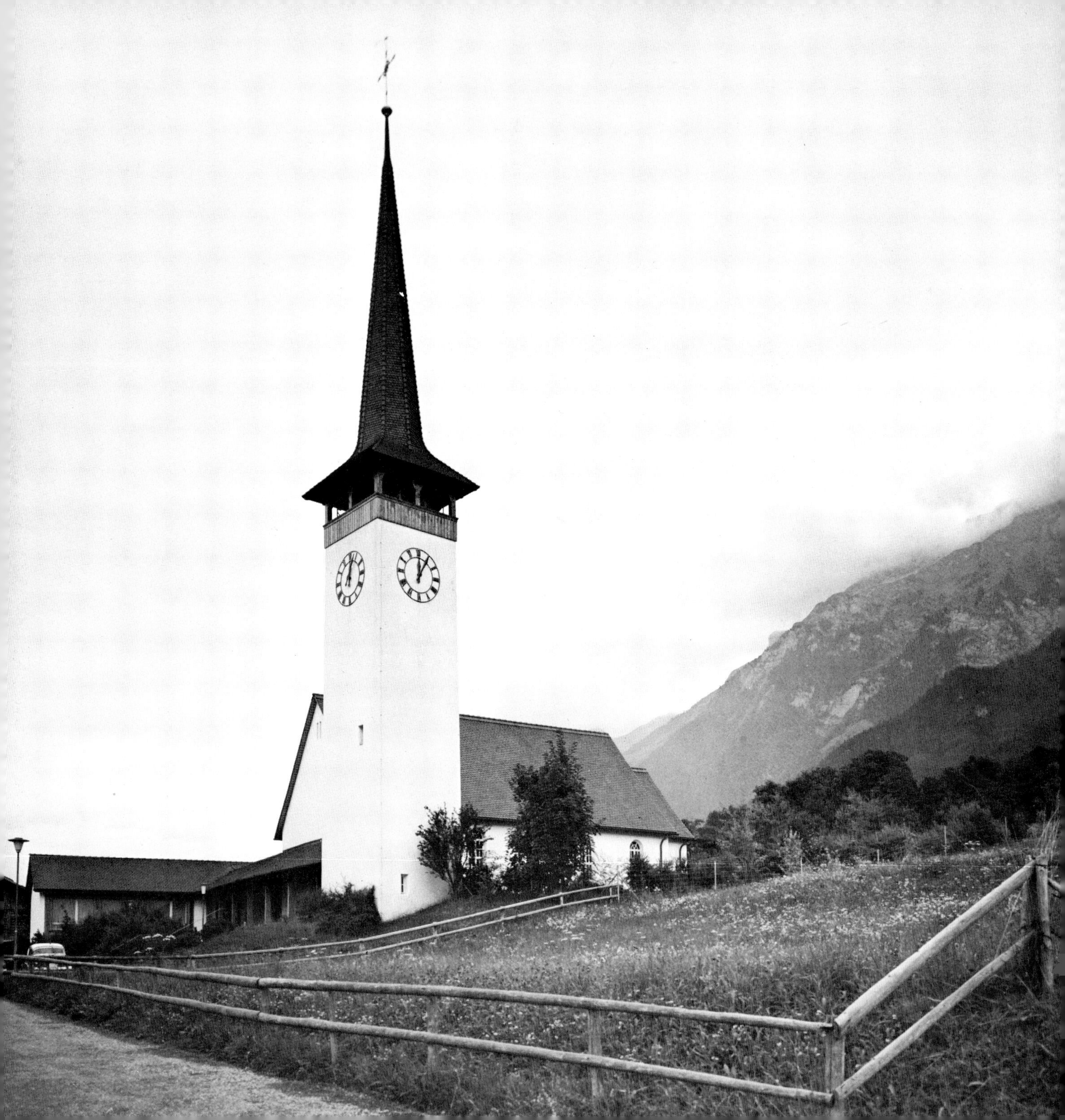

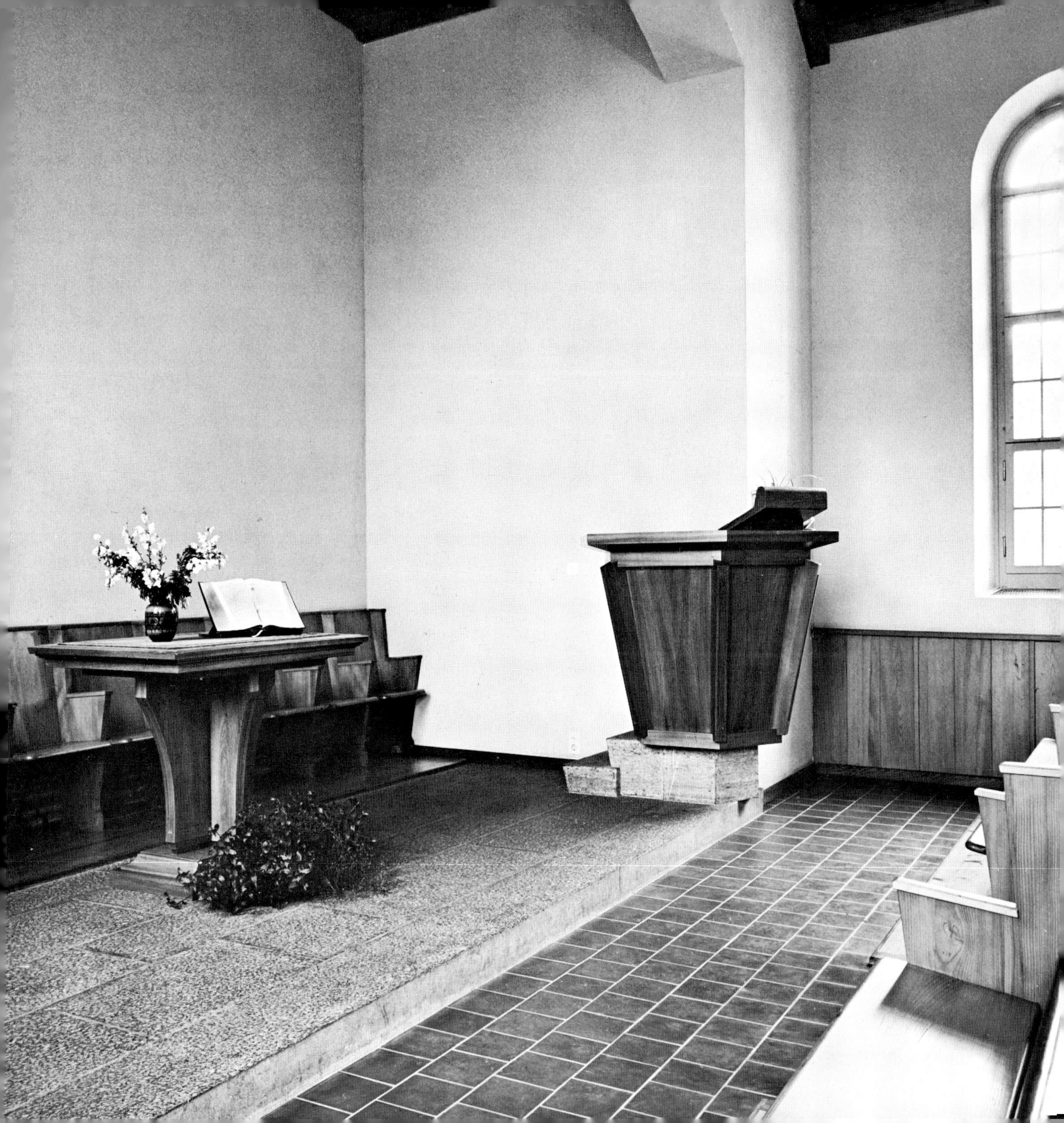

Among the Scots the normal practice was to "bracket the basin to the pulpit" the basin being either of silver or pewter, usually held in a wrought-iron bracket.[21] It should be very clear, however, that the Reformers, whether through the use of a font clamped to their pulpit or a bowl on the table, meant no disrespect to the Sacrament. Quite the opposite! It was their contention that the Sacrament of Baptism, as God's sign and seal of entry into the body of Christ, was so important that it had to be performed in its proper setting, and the font was brought from the door of the church to the pulpit or table because the Reformers knew the Church to be God's gathered people, rather than the building in which the Church worshipped. Therefore they held it most natural that this symbol of entry into the Church be performed in the midst of the Church, i.e., the gathered congregation of worshippers, who in the words of the Apostle Paul are themselves the body of Christ. In short, the Reformers saw clearly that the Church of Christ was the people, not the building, and that Baptism constituted an entry into the congregation, not the building, and for that reason insisted that Baptism be in the face of the congregation.[22]

Having said this, and stoutly maintaining that the Reformers were right in their preference for putting their symbol in relationship to the real body of Christ, it must be added that the church building as a whole also constitutes a symbol. Therefore when the font, as the symbol of Baptism, can be put into a proper relationship to the building as the symbol of the Church, such sym-

---

[21] Hay, *op. cit.,* p. 189.

[22] Indicative of the complete divorce between theology and church architecture in the United States (until very recently) is the following by Elbert M. Conover, former head of the Interdenominational Bureau of Church Architecture: "Let us hope that the custom of parading babies before the Sunday morning congregation will be eliminated, and that the chapel may be used for this service on Sunday afternoons or at other times . . . ." *The Church Building Guide* (New York: The Interdenominational Bureau of Church Architecture, 1946), p. 83. The same advice is found in *Building for Worship* by the same author and publisher, 1945, p. 42.

bolism is certainly to be desired, providing that Baptism still takes place in visible and audible relationship to the living body of Christ, the assembled congregation. A splendid church which achieves both symbols at once in a highly successful way is the Ark.

For CHRIST also died for sins once for all, the righteous for the unrighteous, that he might bring us to God, being put to death in the flesh but made alive in the spirit;

> *in which he went and preached to the spirits in prison, who formerly did not obey, when God's patience waited in the days of NOAH, during the building of the ARK, in which a few, that is, eight persons, were saved through water.*

BAPTISM, which corresponds to this, now saves you, not as a removal of dirt from the body but as an answer to God for a clear conscience through the resurrection of Jesus Christ. . . . I Peter 3:18–21 (Capitals mine.)

The Ark (De Ark), Hervormd, Amsterdam-Slotervaart, The Netherlands
P. Zanstra, architect

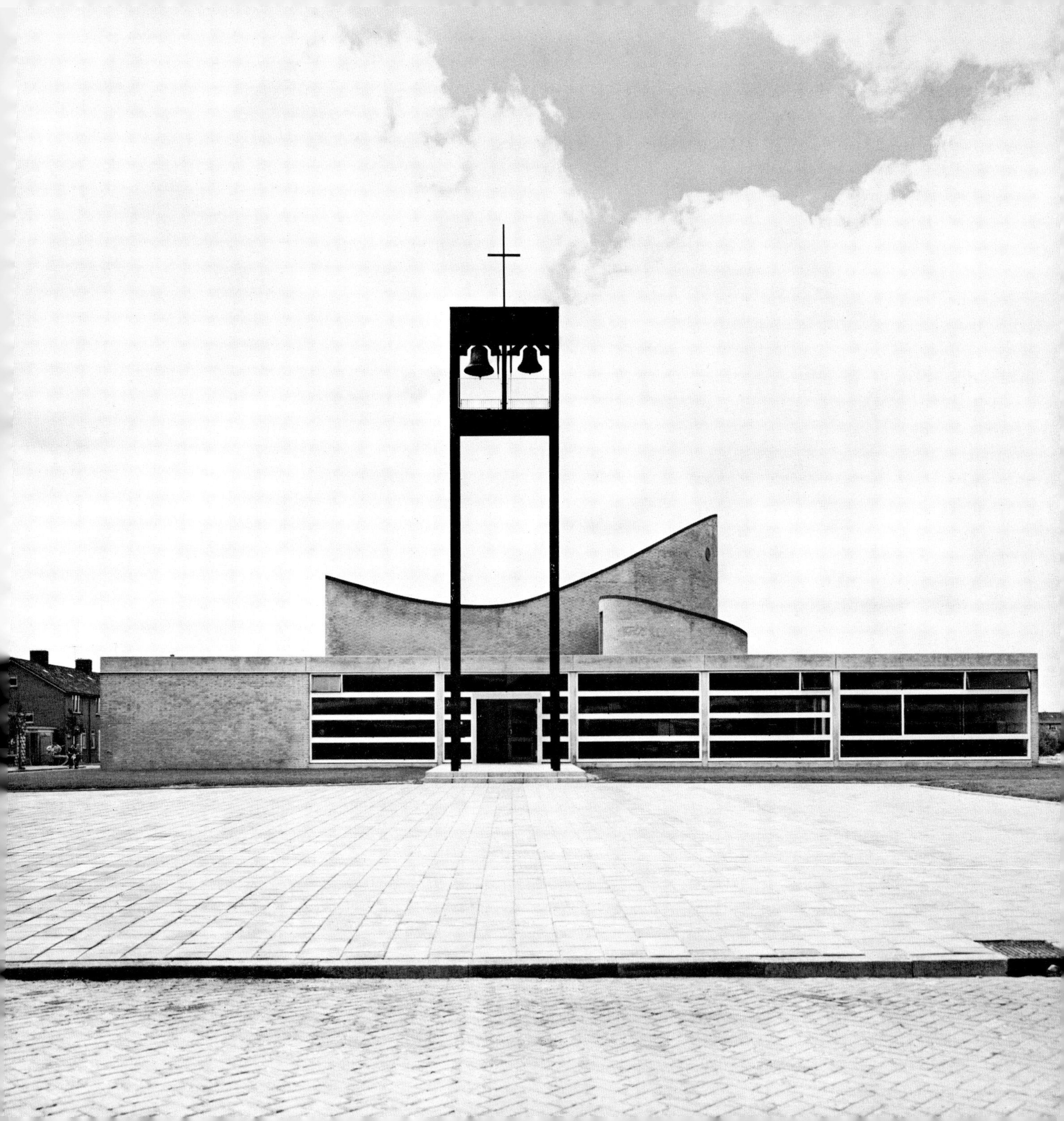

The Ark offers itself as a safe conveyance of the Lord to the people of Slotervaart, a busy, apartment-filled suburb of Amsterdam.

As in Noah's Ark everything had to find a place, here too, seemingly everything necessary to a church home had to find a place under one roof. Within the large square of this church house the architect has included not only the sanctuary of the Ark,[1] but around it all of the rooms necessary for the church to express man-to-man relationships. This living the Christlike life in relationship to others, this horizontal relationship, is clearly expressed by the strong horizontal lines of the window framing. For those on the outside, the large expanse of window area makes the work of the people of God open and inviting. Within this Ark are contained a study for the minister,[2] administration[3] and consistory rooms,[4] places to catechize,[5] club rooms,[5] hobby rooms,[6] a fellowship hall for 200,[7] complete with an ample stage,[8] a kitchen,[9] a room for coats,[10] the washrooms,[11] and the Diakonia (which serves as clinic, health instruction center, administrative center for those who express the love of the Church in going out to care for the sick—in short, any of the work of the Deaconess.[12] All of these man-to-man activities are under the same roof, accessible from the open traffic area surrounding the Ark.

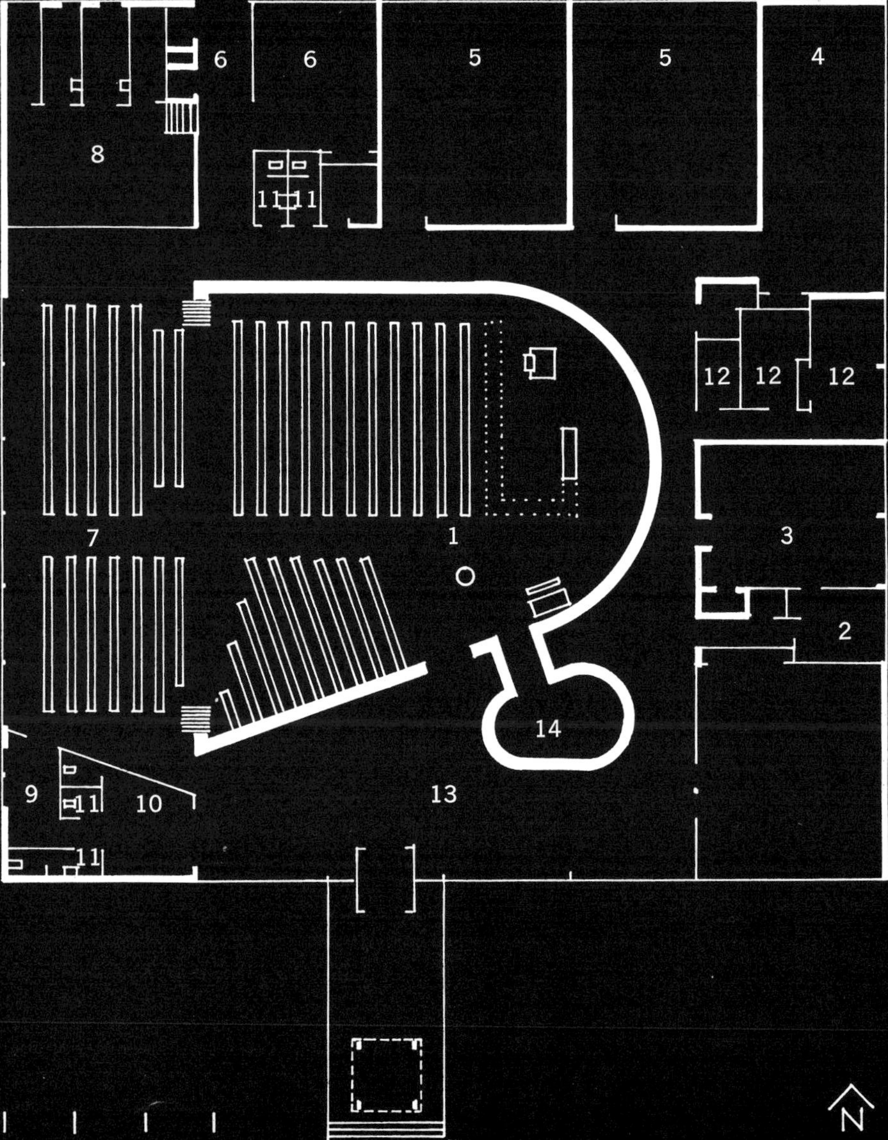
6
6
5
5
4
8
11
11
12
12
12
7
1
3
2
14
9
11
10
13
11
N

But while this is certainly a well-equipped congregational house ministering to the needs of men, it is equally the house of God! For in the very midst of all this activity stands the sanctuary. Upon entering the first, glass-enclosed church building, one finds oneself in a spacious narthex,[13] equipped with tables and often coffee . . . .

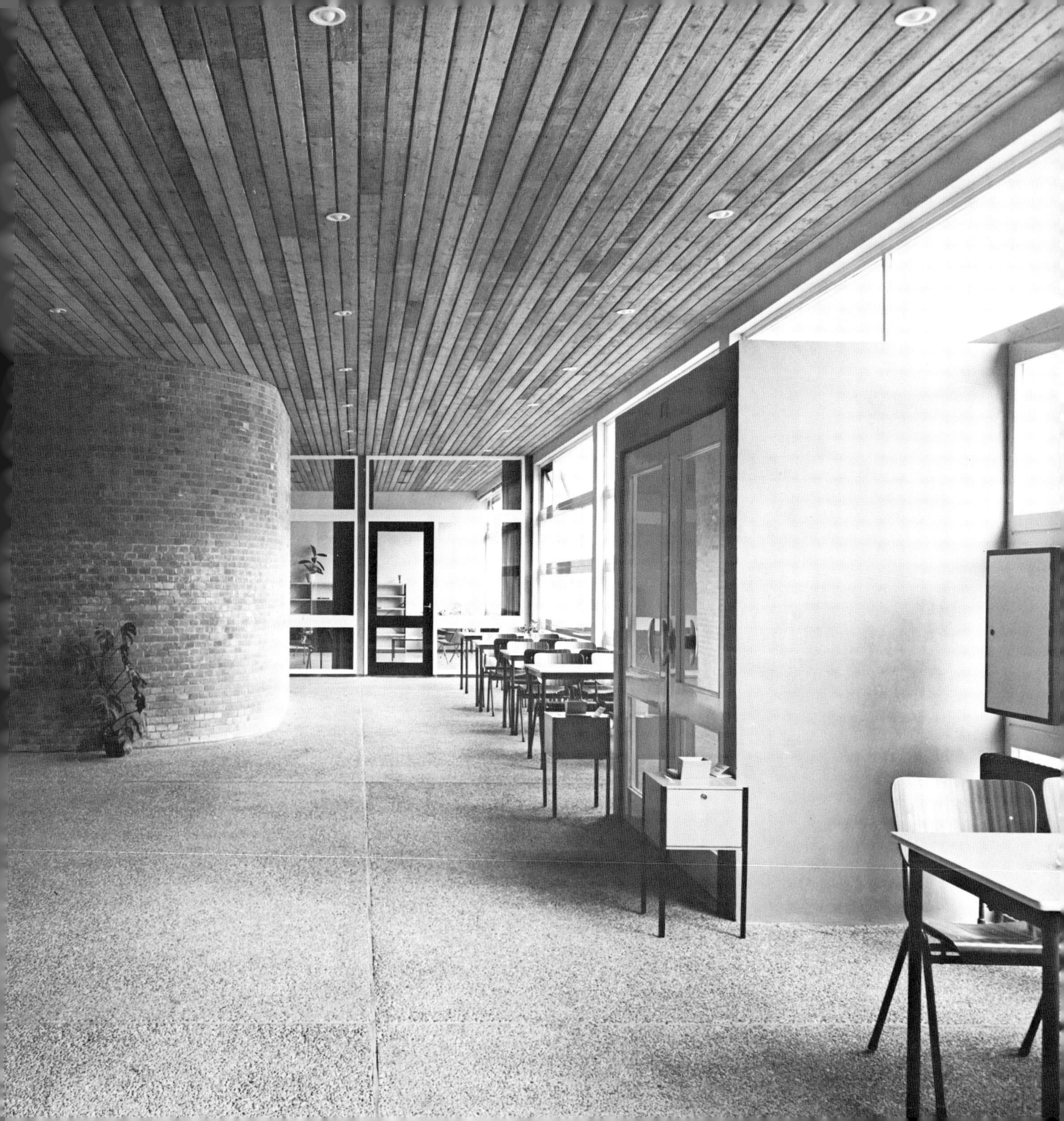

but one is also confronted with a solid wall, of the same brick as that used on the exterior, pierced with a single door, beyond which is an immediate confrontation with the challenge or comfort of the baptismal font (cf. I Peter 3:18–21).

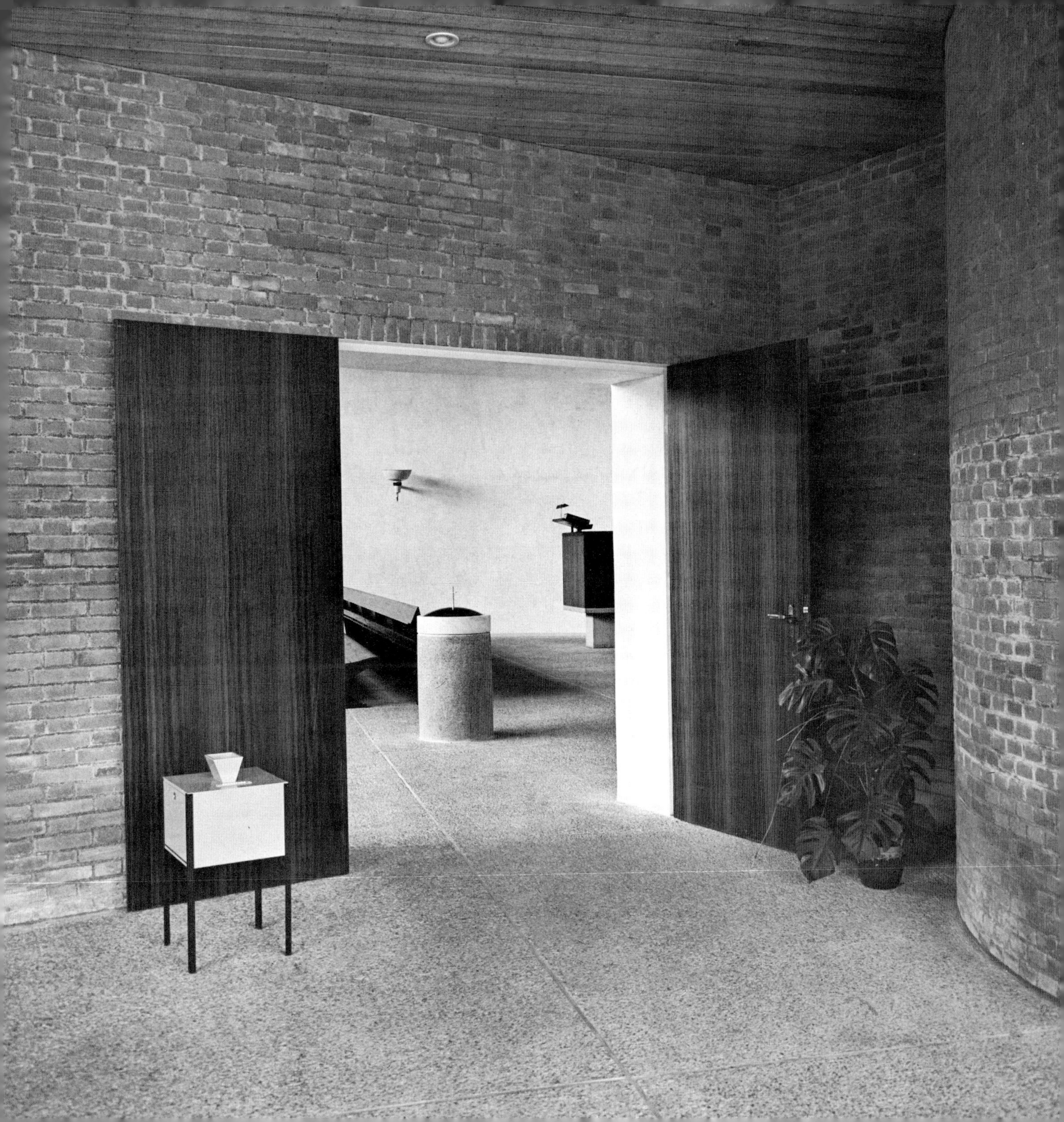

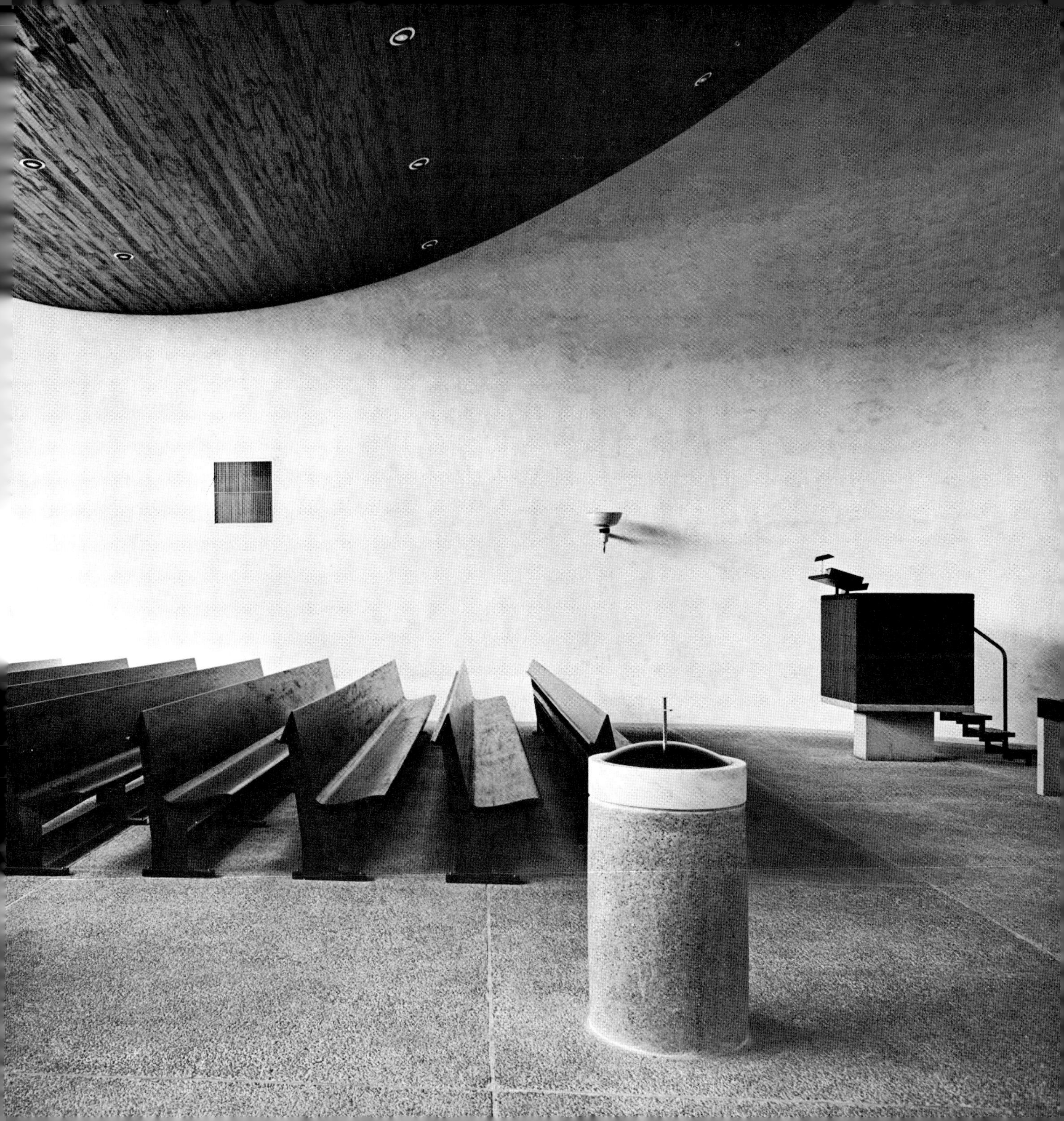

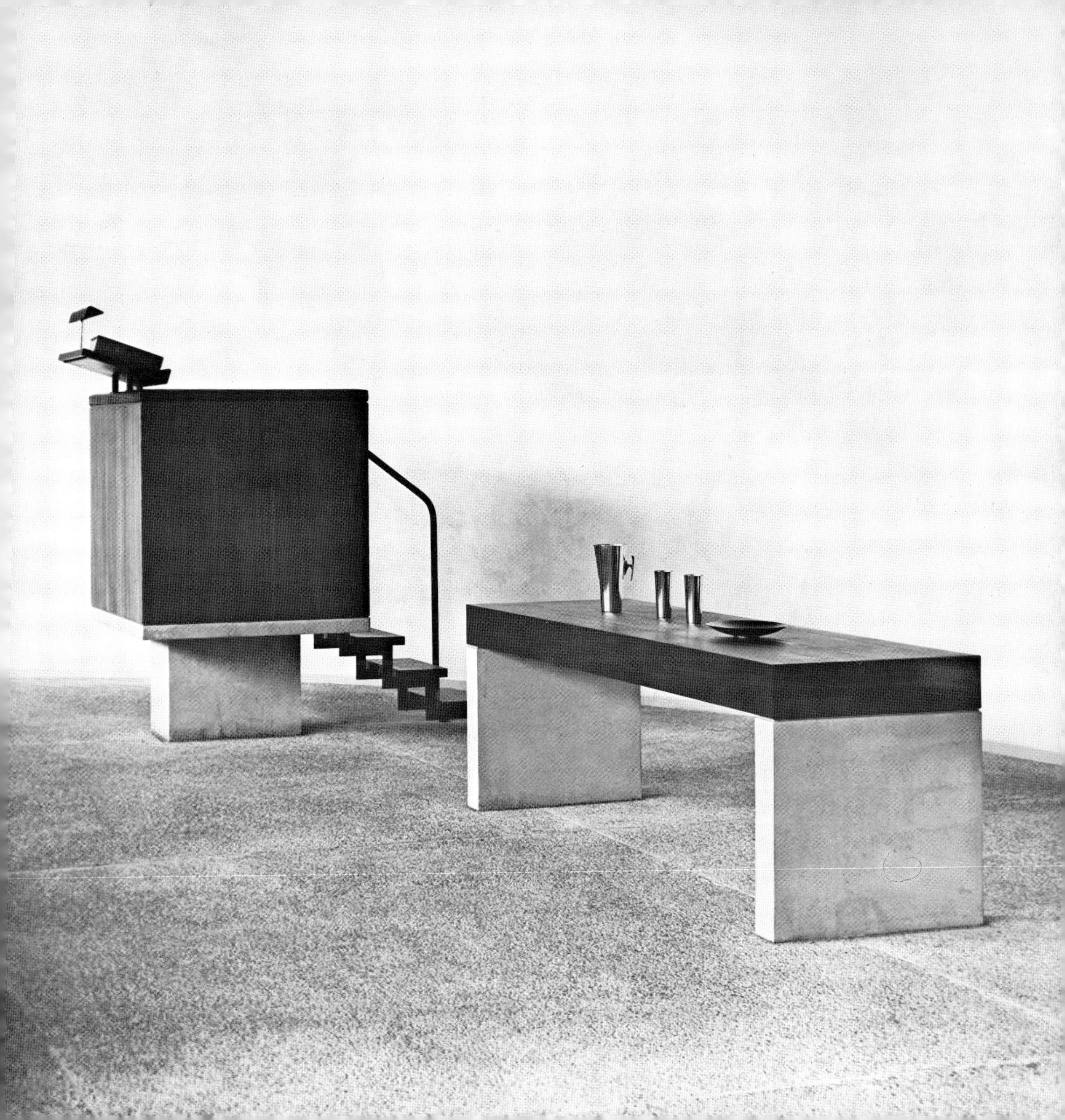

Positiv (temporary) by L. Verschueren of Heijthuijsen

Bourdon   8–4
Principal   4–2

The font is integrally related to the Lord's table and the pulpit, all of which are on exactly the same level as the congregation, for it was the intention of the architect that the total sanctuary, or church room, should be the liturgical center! This means, unfortunately, that when the sanctuary is filled, it is impossible to see either table or font, but perhaps the intimacy of this sanctuary (seating for 231, with additional seating for 190 in the fellowship room adjoining), together with the forceful confrontation of the font when entering and the active participation at the Lord's table by each member (the table is extended so that it will seat 44 when the Supper is served), indicates that the congregation and architect have in this instance chosen rightly.

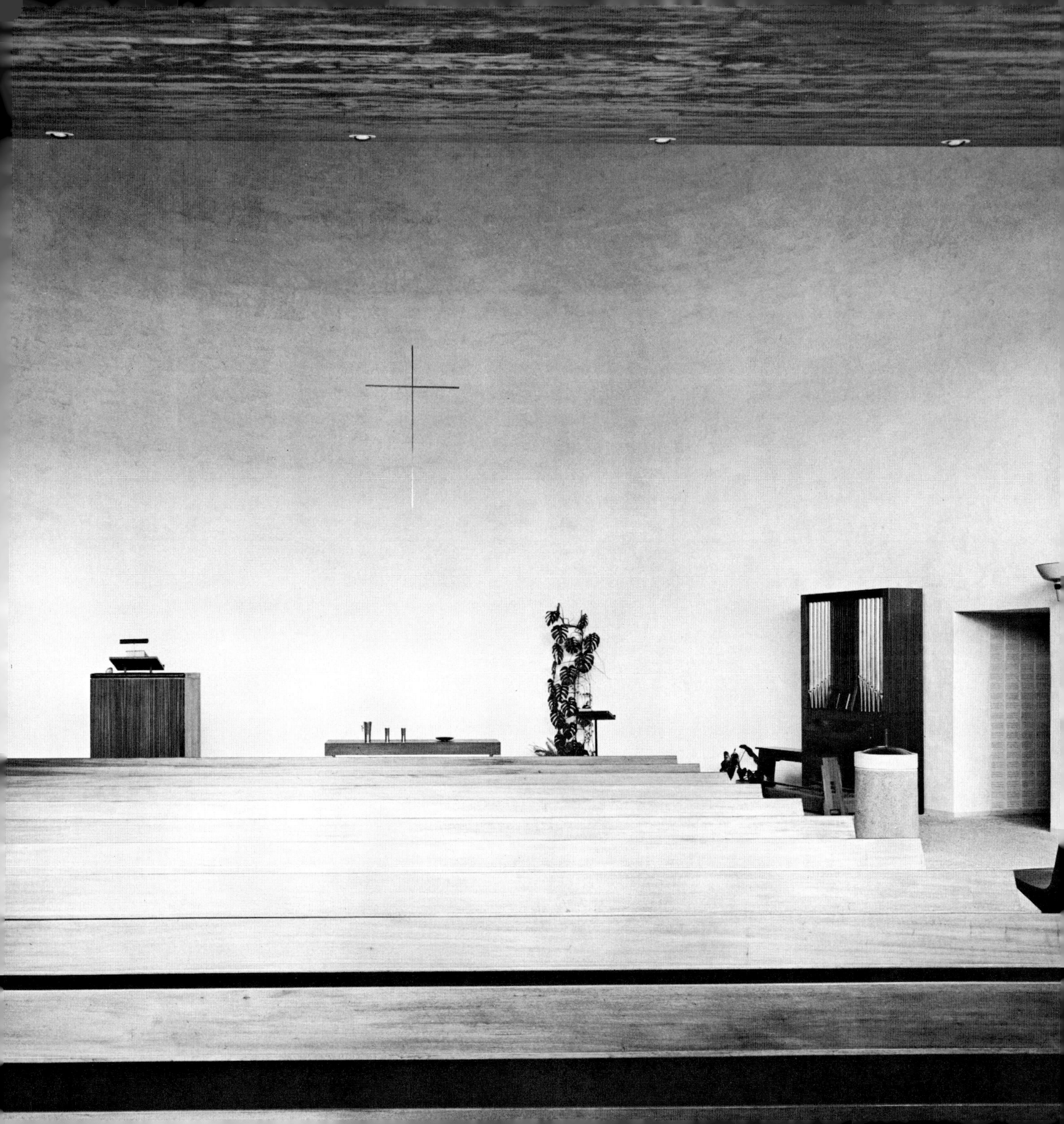

In addition to being a house of God each Sunday, and a house of God in which men minister in love to the needs of men each day of the week, provision is also made for the private worship of God throughout the week. There has been provided a prayer chapel,[14] *which among the Calvinists of the Netherlands was the first to be built.*

Because it is the first, considerably more thought has gone into it than into the casually regarded prayer chapels in our own country. It can be entered only through the sanctuary. Only in relationship to Baptism, the Lord's Supper, and the preaching of the Word can one pray aright. There is no implication here that the prayer chapel is for those who don't need the formal ministration of Word and Sacrament, or that it is really possible to worship God in complete independence of his covenant people. The prayer chapel rightly exists in relationship to the sanctuary, and can be entered only through it. The architectural expression of theological truth is excellent.

Because it is the first, there are some who are acutely aware that fruitful prayer is not something that can come spontaneously, but that even the Lord's people (as the disciples) must be taught how to pray. Dr. W. G. Overbosch, one of the leaders in the realm of architectural-theological relationships in the Netherlands, pointed out in his radio broadcast, "Het Geladen Schip," that with empty minds as with empty hands the devil soon finds something to do. The emptiness of the prayer chapel, which should be filled with meaningful prayer, has rather unsuccessfully been filled with a gigantic plant placed by the custodian. Instruction in, and the development of, meaningful and purposeful prayer will be more difficult.

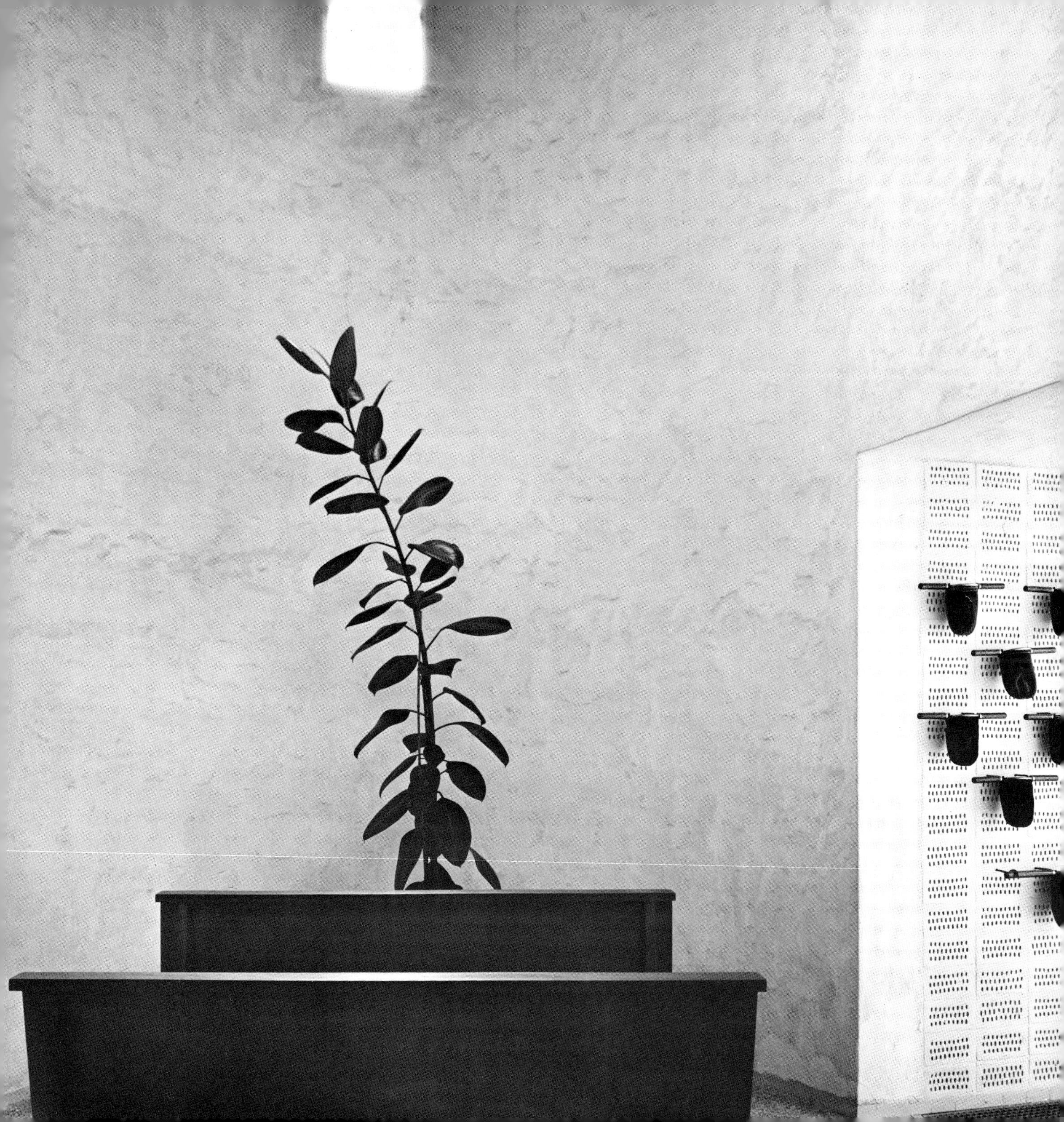

This is a superb church. The space within the sanctuary has been well handled, conveying a sense of security and peace, while at the same time the sweeping line of the ceiling at once makes the sanctuary alive with upward movement and expectation.

As one leaves either a service of worship, or the private worship of the prayer chapel, one must pass the baptismal font to return to the world, being reminded that one nonetheless returns to the world in Christ.

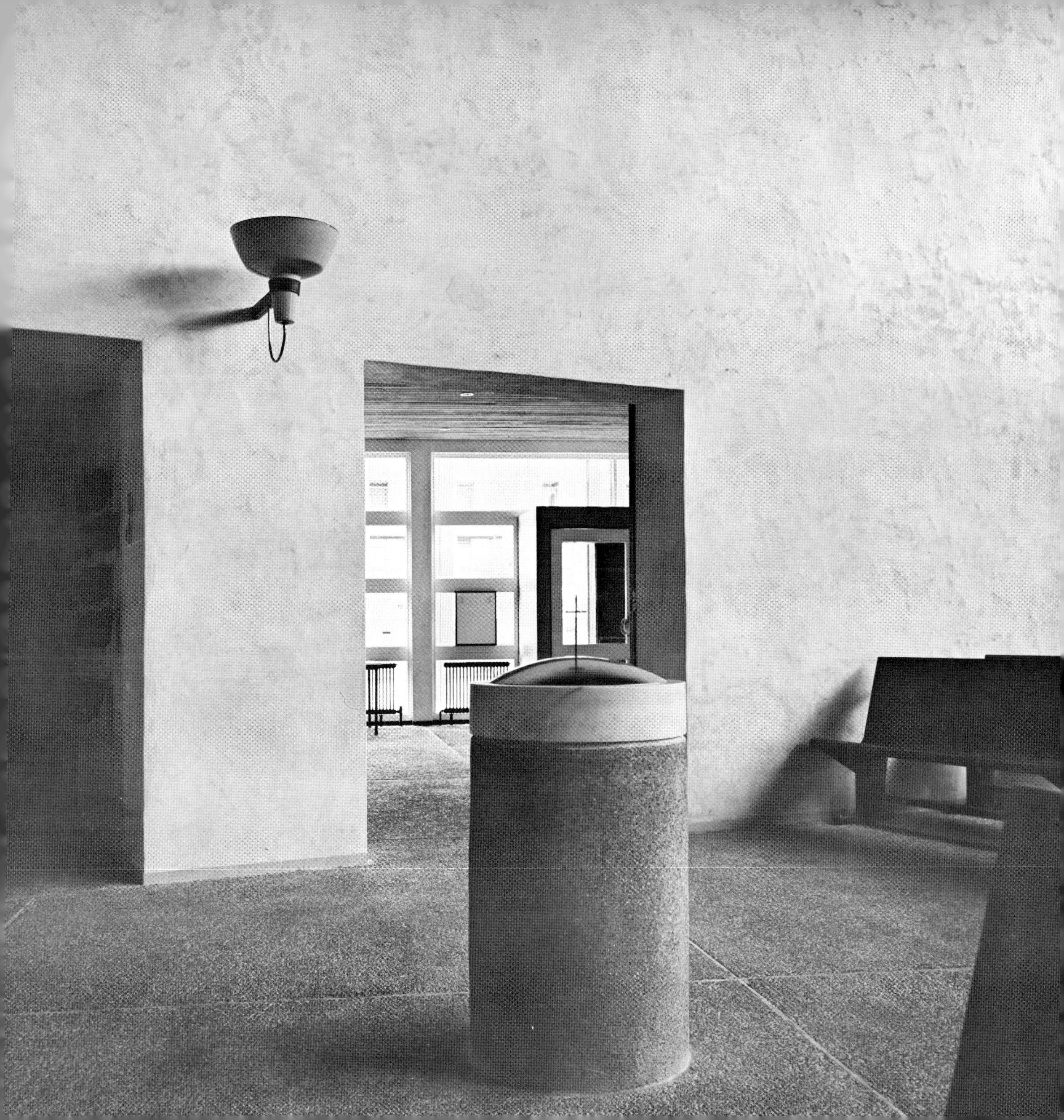

Baptism: A Continuing Participation in Christ's Atoning Work

The first criterion for an architectural statement of the Sacrament of Baptism was that AS THE SIGN AND SEAL OF BEING BAPTIZED INTO CHRIST, BAPTISM IS TO BE PERFORMED IN THE FACE OF THE CONGREGATION, WHERE THE BODY OF CHRIST MAY BOTH SEE AND HEAR. To that end, bracketing the font to the pulpit, or placing a bowl on the communion table, were both satisfactory ways of placing the action of baptism in the right place. But it is very obvious that this constitutes a rather weak architectural statement by virtue of the relatively small form of the bowl used either on the table or in a bracket. The permanent nature of Baptism, together with the living relationship into which it engrafts the Christian, would seem to require a stronger architectural affirmation.

Baptism is even more than entrance into Christ; it includes a continual participation in Christ's atoning work. The distinction between the Reformed doctrine and that of Rome should be carefully noted, for the latter teaches that Baptism takes away all punishment due original sin and "all actual sins committed before baptism."[23] Just as the Roman doctrine of the Mass meant a partial participation in Christ, so their doctrine of Baptism again means a partial participation limited to his forgiveness of pre-baptismal sins, together with an infusion of sanctifying grace. The Reformed, however, understand the Scriptures to teach that Baptism is baptism into the whole Christ and all his benefits, including his once-for-all death on the cross. Calvin states this biblical teaching without ambiguity:

> But we must realize that at whatever time we are baptized, we are once for all washed and purged for our whole life. Therefore, as often as we fall away, we

---

[23] Connell, *op. cit.*, Q. 422, p. 238. Cf. questions 175a, 308a, 397b, and 380.

ought to recall the memory of our baptism and fortify our mind with it, that we may always be sure and confident of the forgiveness of sins.[24]

All of our sins are forgiven in Christ. There is no sin for which we in any degree whatsoever earn forgiveness. This is all of grace; it comes completely from God. We have forgiveness only in Christ, and it is into Christ—the whole Christ—that we are baptized. We cannot leave Baptism behind us at the door of the church. Baptism must be continually before us, for as Calvin observes,

> there is no doubt that all pious folk throughout life, whenever they are troubled by a consciousness of their faults, may venture to remind themselves of their baptism, that from it they may be confirmed in assurance of that sole and perpetual cleansing which we have in Christ's blood.[25]

In view of this truth the following can be added to the criteria concerning Baptism:

BAPTISM INVOLVES CONTINUING PARTICIPATION IN THE ATONING WORK OF CHRIST; THEREFORE THE FONT SHOULD STAND EMPHATICALLY BEFORE THE CONGREGATION AS A CONTINUING REMINDER OF THIS REDEMPTIVE RELATIONSHIP TO CHRIST.

If nothing else, this new criterion would mean that while the table or pulpit bracket represents an adequate place for performing the Sacrament of Baptism, it is inadequate as a continuing visual reminder of that Sacrament. The same criticism would be true for the majority of fonts used in America. While their size might be adequate for a small church, most of them are placed on the floor in the front of the church, well off to the side, usually just peeping above the tops of the pews (when the church is without its congregation—at

---

[24] *Institutes*, 4:15:3, p. 1305.
[25] *Ibid.*, 4:15:4, p. 1307.

which times even the slight symbolism of an inch or two of font is wasted). Even when visible, the font is usually of considerably less visual importance than the hymn boards, let alone the piano or the flags. The font speaks to us of our baptism into Christ and our continued dependence upon his redeeming work; therefore let us at least elevate the baptismal font to a level where it can be seen! The magnificent font in the Church of the Cross (Kruiskerk) in Amstelveen is not wasted by being out of sight, but is raised four full steps above the level of the nave so that its base stands on a pavement level with the height of the backs of the pews. From that height it can be a constant reminder to the congregation of their new life in Christ into whom they have been baptized (see pp. 95, 105, 135).

Once elevated to the place where it can be seen, the size of the font and its quality become more important. To achieve proper quality and size it will be necessary to have fonts designed by architects and artists, rather than the usual marble bird-baths or wooden "Gothic" creations from religious supply houses. It will also mean that the font will have to bear a real visual relationship to the pulpit and the table. The architect will have to address himself either to working with such forms, sizes and materials as to suggest by comparison their relatively equal importance, or else to working with different forms and materials so that he can perhaps avoid the necessity of any similarity of size.[26] Either solution is acceptable. It is only the hesitant compromise that is unacceptable, for then the usual result is to leave the font with a suggested relationship to the table (whether by similarity of material or form) but

---

[26] This has been rather skillfully done in the Immanuëlkerk (Gereformeerd), Delft, the Netherlands. There the relative sizes are completely different (the table being of concrete and extremely long, making it impossible to imitate in the font without building a swimming pool). Therefore the architects switched to steel (commensurate with the exposed roof members) for the base, on which is mounted a large polished-brass bowl. To compensate further for the great difference in size, the table is behind the pulpit, while the font is well in front of it (pp. 255–63ff.).

of such lesser magnitude as visually to cast into question the importance of Baptism. Because Baptism is a once-for-all event in which we are given the sign and seal that we participate in the atoning work of Christ which is completely adequate for our salvation, the baptismal font should stand visible before God's people in a dignified way, for it speaks of their redemption in Christ which is life.

The Church of St. Mark offers a splendid example of how in using the same materials and size the importance of the Sacraments has been equated to the point where the font holds its place with the Lord's table and the pulpit.

The Church of St. Mark (St. Markuskirche), Reformed, Bern, Switzerland
Karl Müller & Henry Daxelhofer, architects. Font, table and pulpit by Max Fueter

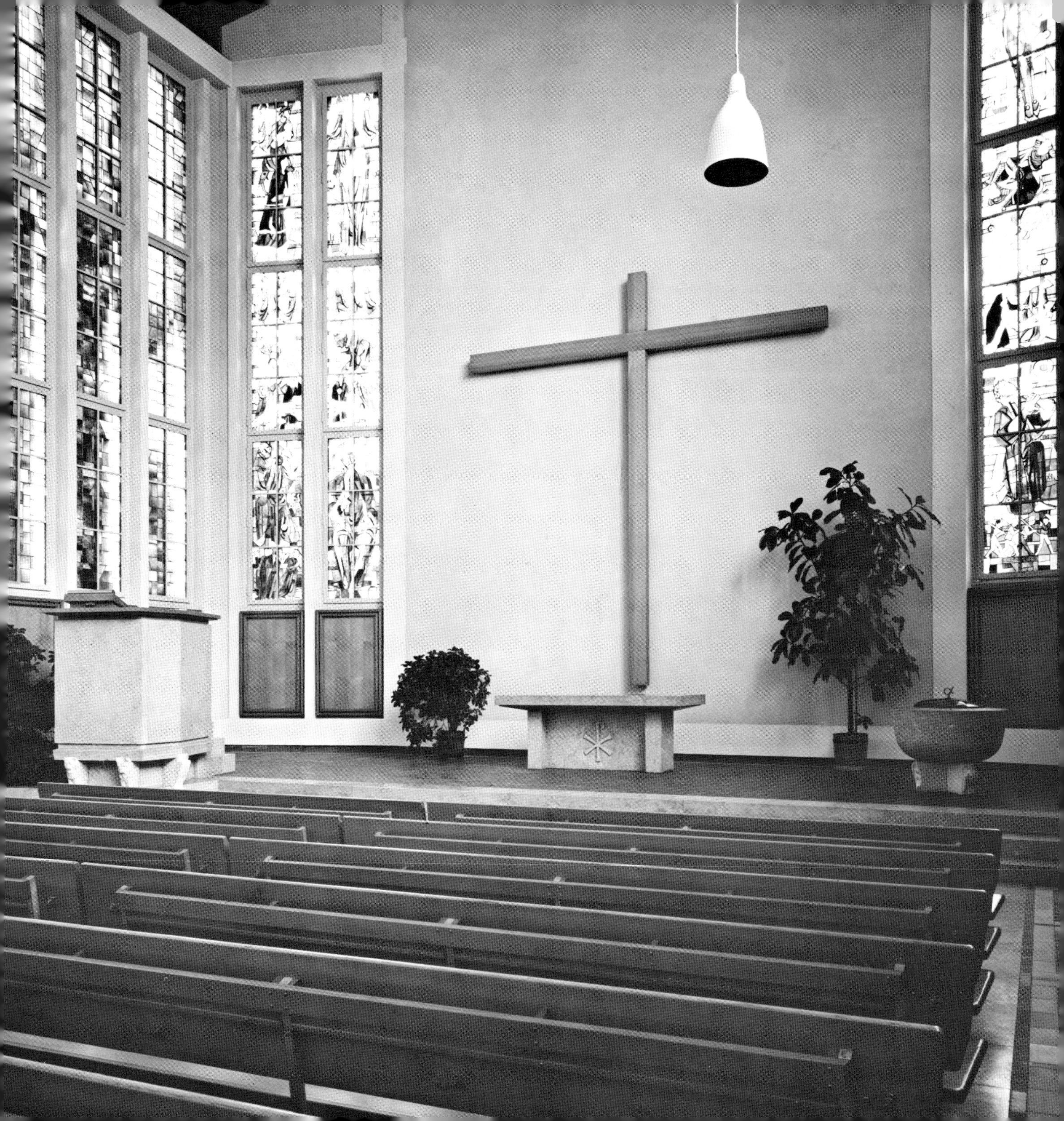

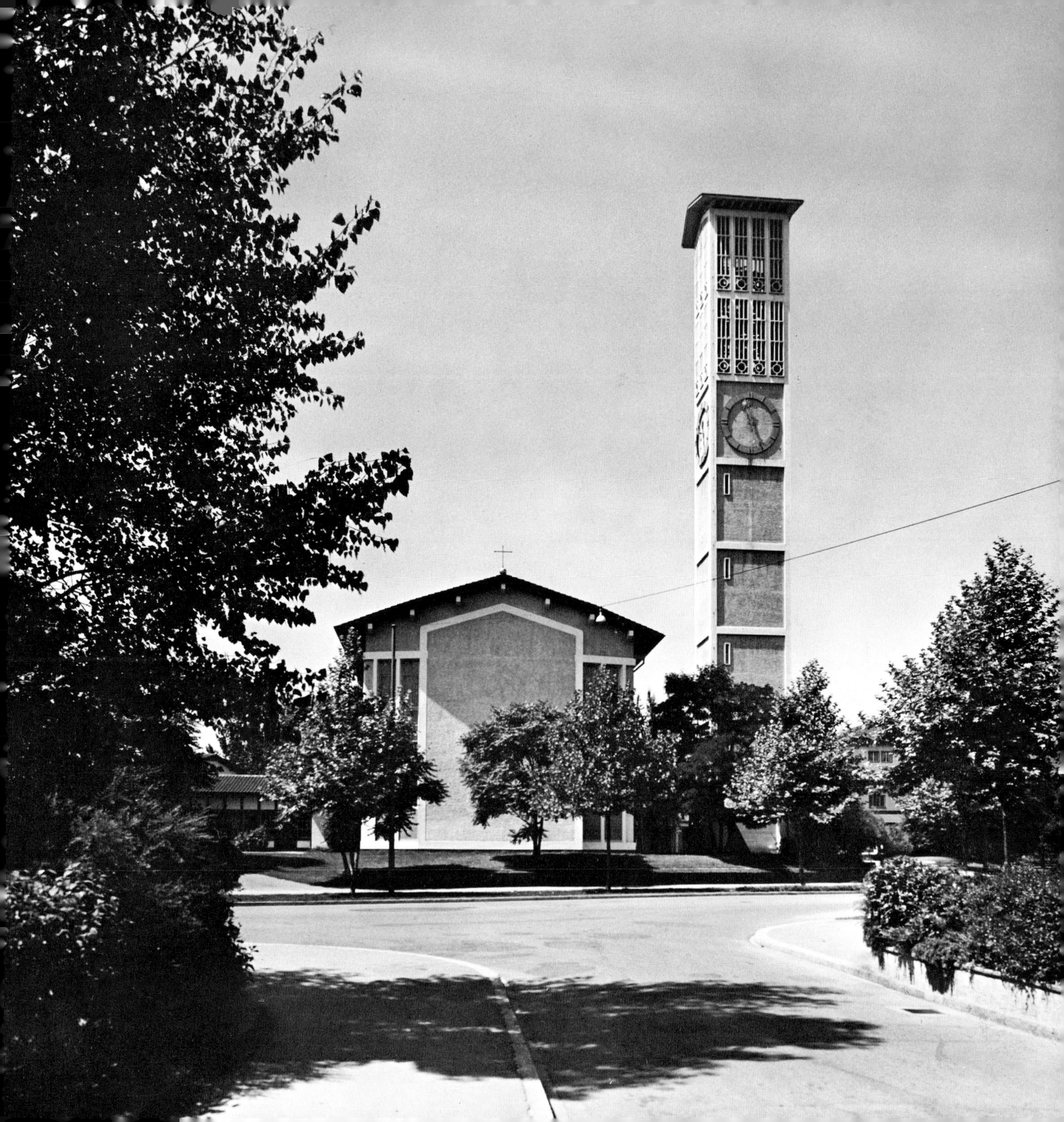

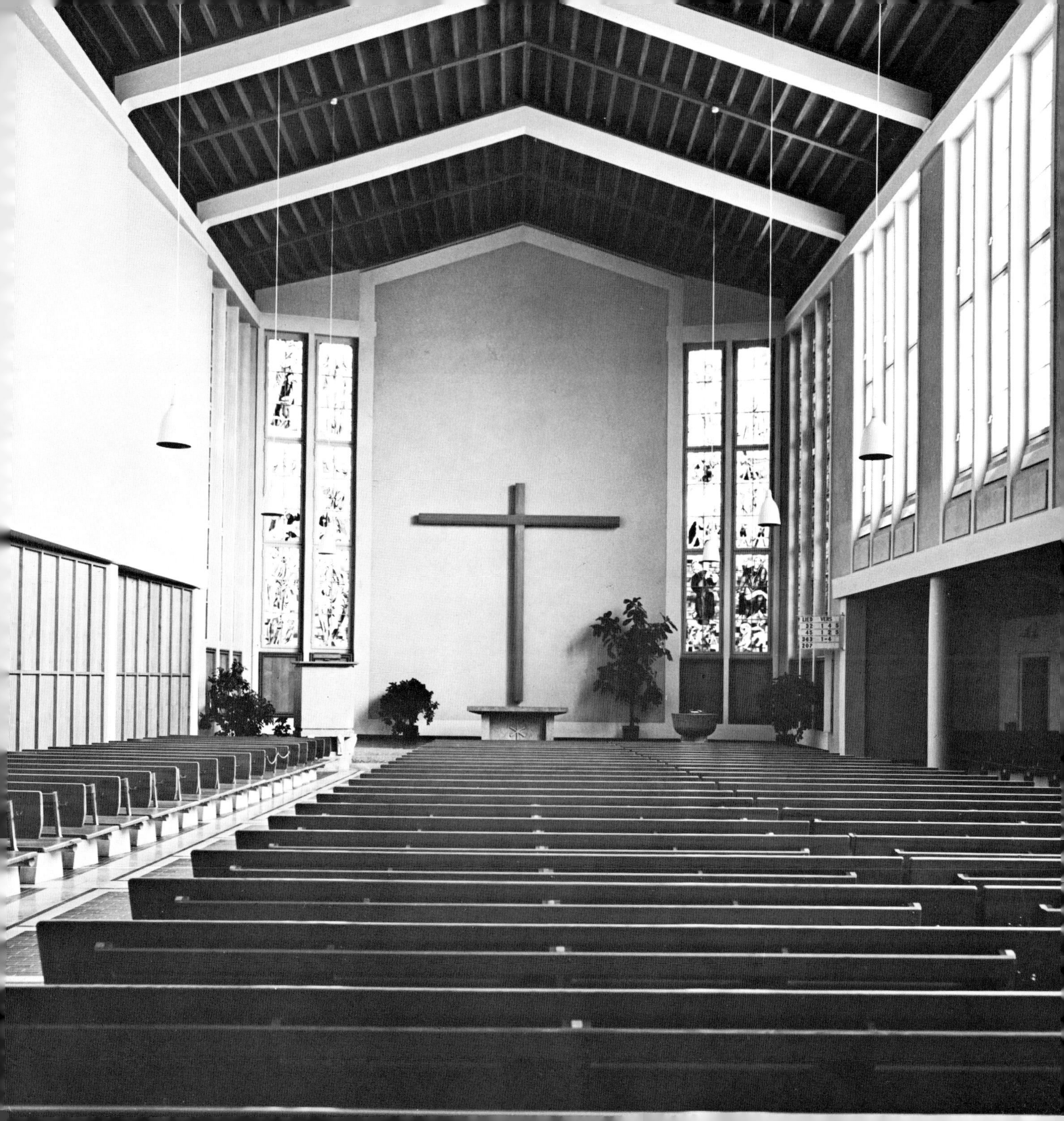

Organ by Goll & Cie of Lucerne

Hauptwerk

Bourdon	16
Principal	8
Rohrflöte	8
Oktav	4
Hohlflöte	4
Oktav	2
Mixtur	2
Zinke	8

Oberwerk

Principal	8
Hohlflöte	8
Salicional	8
Oktav	4
Nachthorn	4
Waldflöte	2
Quinte	2⅔
Terz	1⅗
Scharf 4–6 ranks	1⅓
Trompete	8
Clairon	4

Positiv

Suavial	8
Gedackt	8
Principal	4
Rohrflöte	4
Oktav	2
Flagelot	2
Quinte	2⅔
Larigot	1⅓
Mixtur 4–5 ranks	1
Krummhorn	8

Pedal

Principalbass	16
Subbass	16
Principal	8
Spitzflöte	8
Oktav	4
Mixtur 5 ranks	4
Posaune	16
Trompete	8

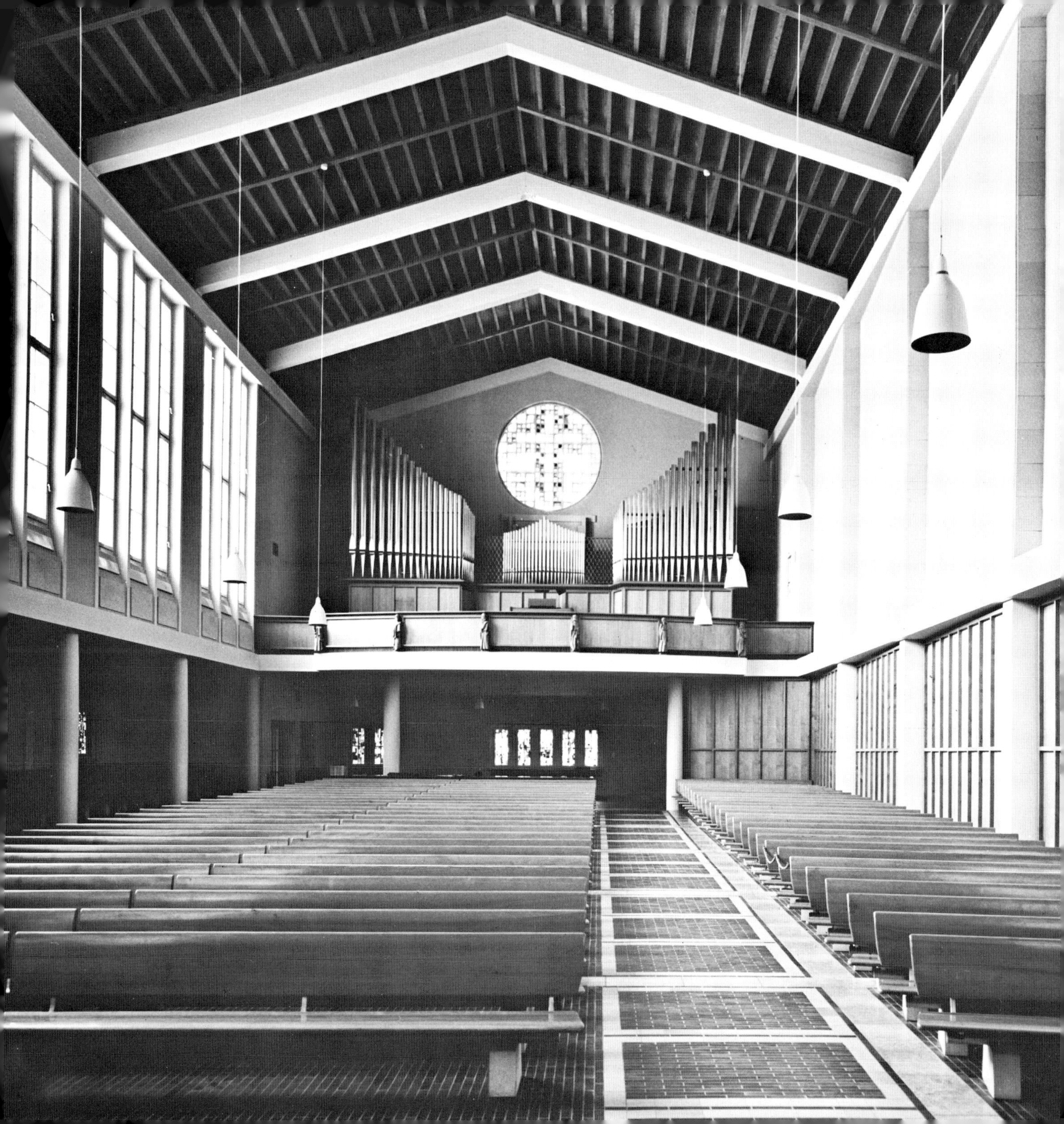

Baptism: A Continuing Participation in Christ's Resurrection to Newness of Life

The assertion is often made that Christianity must be more concerned with the here and the now, rather than that which will happen after death. With this every student of Scripture will agree. This concern with the life of the Christian here and now also necessitates a greater place in the architecture of the church for the baptismal font, for it is the symbol and the reminder that we have been bapized into Christ, into his resurrection unto newness of life.

> How can we who died to sin still live in it? Do you not know that all of us who have been baptized into Christ Jesus were baptized into his death? We were buried therefore with him by baptism into death, so that as Christ was raised from the dead by the glory of the Father, we too might walk in newness of life. Romans 6:2–4.

If a congregation is concerned about the conduct of its members, if it wants to have the teachings of Scripture applied to everyday life, then certainly it should have a prominent baptismal font that can be readily seen, for as the above verses remind us, when one is baptized into Christ, one also joins him in his death to sin. Commenting on the above passage from Romans, Calvin observes:

> By these words he not only exhorts us to follow Christ as if he had said that we are admonished through baptism to die to our desires by an example of Christ's death . . . . But he also takes hold of something far higher, namely, that through baptism Christ makes us sharers in his death, that we may be engrafted in it.[27]

In this union with Christ, our lives become ever more like his. More of the peace, righteousness, and love which were his find expression in our lives. To

---

[27] *Institutes*, 4:15:5, p. 1307.

live a life contrary to his is to put in question our union with him. If the members of a congregation would prefer not to be reminded that they are in Christ, then it would undoubtedly be good strategy to hide the baptismal font somewhere behind a row of pews. In such a position its presence is not likely to be felt, nor are people likely to be reminded of their relationship to Christ as members baptized into him. If the pulpit is obvious, and nothing else, then perhaps we might get the feeling that we may listen to the lecture but do as we wish with it. But add the font and we are told by it that we are not our own to say yes or no as we wish, but we belong to our Lord Jesus Christ into whom we have been baptized.

BAPTISM CONSTITUTES CONTINUING PARTICIPATION IN THE RESURRECTED CHRIST; THEREFORE THE FONT SHOULD STAND EMPHATICALLY BEFORE THE CONGREGATION AS A CONTINUING REMINDER THAT THEY HAVE BEEN RAISED TO NEWNESS OF LIFE IN CHRIST.

The Church of Gümligen offers a fine example of a recent church in a style sympathetic to, and yet not bound by, the past. While the church fits in beautifully with its surroundings, its liturgical center leaves no doubt as to its Reformed nature.

The Church (Kirche Gümligen), Reformed, Gümligen near Bern, Switzerland
Max Böhm, architect

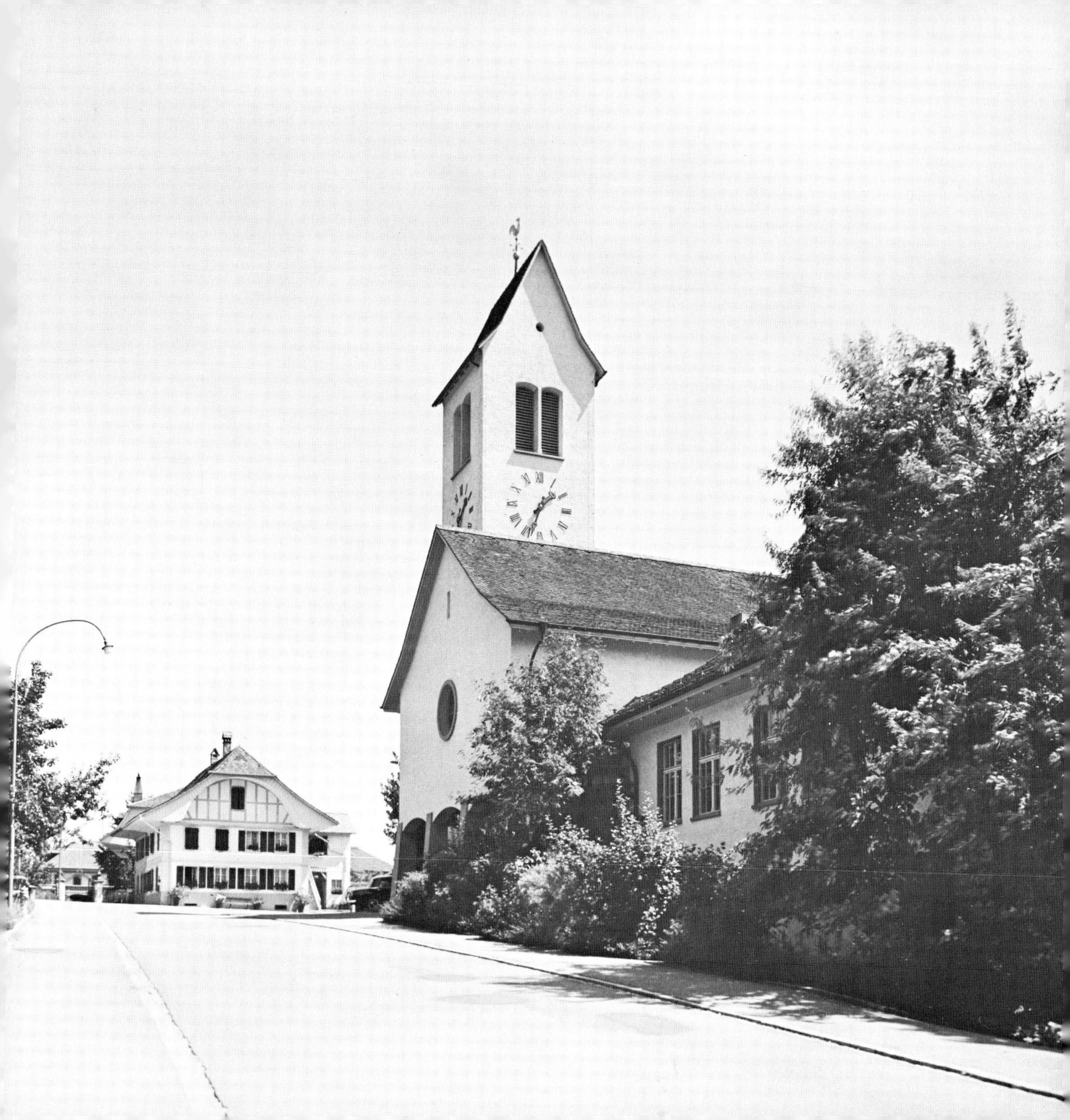

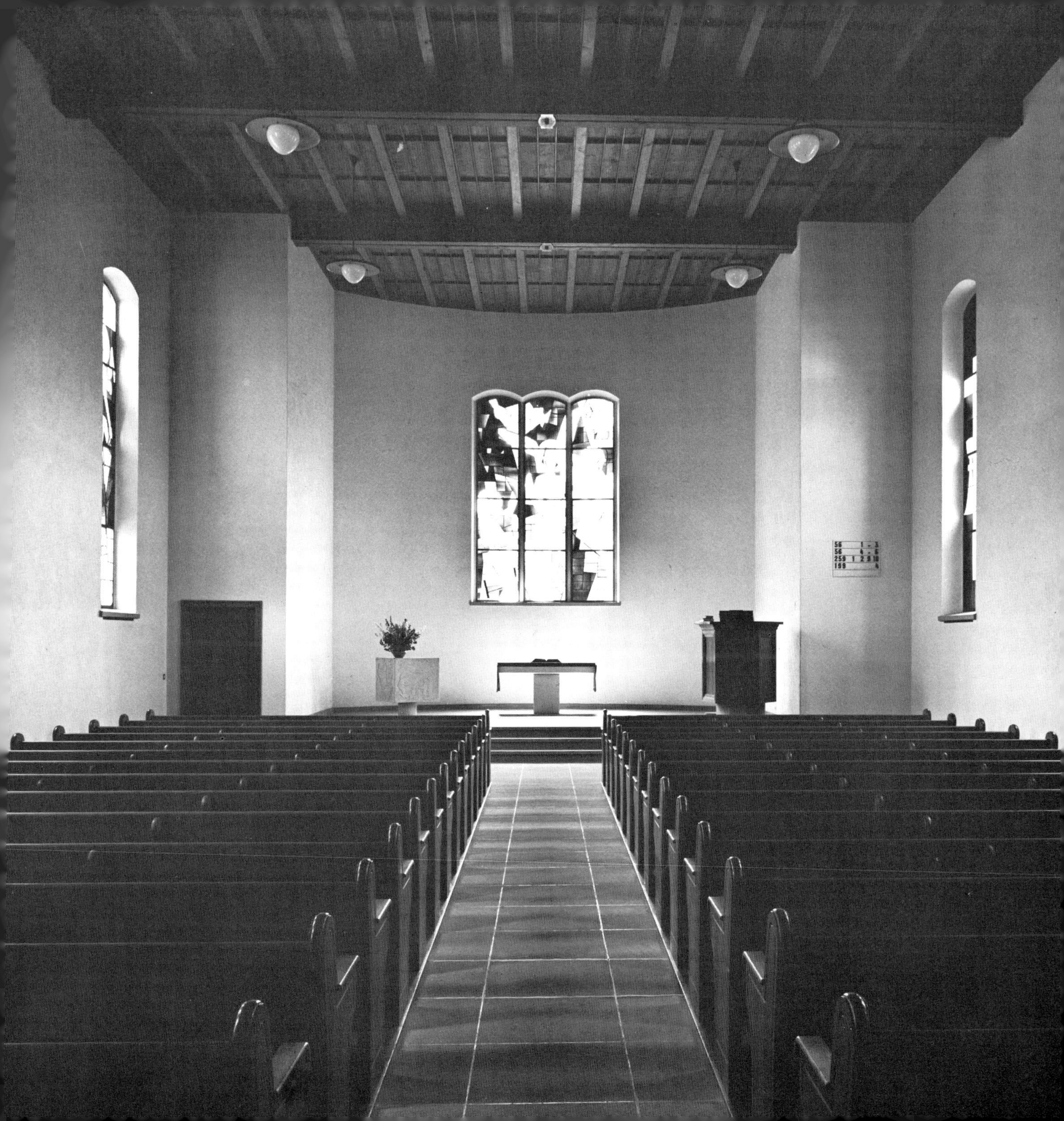
56 1 - 3
56 4 - 6

The font and the table are made of the same material, and in size are very nicely balanced. The font carries rich carving on all four sides, the first depicting Noah's Ark (I Peter 3:18–21); the second the children of Israel passing through the Red Sea on dry ground (I Corinthians 10:1–5); side three (shown in photograph) presents the Egyptians being engulfed in the returning waters of the sea (here Calvin offers an interesting comment: "Baptism indeed promises to us the drowning of our Pharaoh [Exodus 14:28] and the mortification of our sin, but not so that it no longer exists or gives us trouble, but only that it may not overcome us," Institutes 4:15:11); side four presents the rock from which flow fountains of living water (I Corinthians 10:4, Exodus 17:6, and John 4:13–14, 7:37–38).

Font by Max Fueter

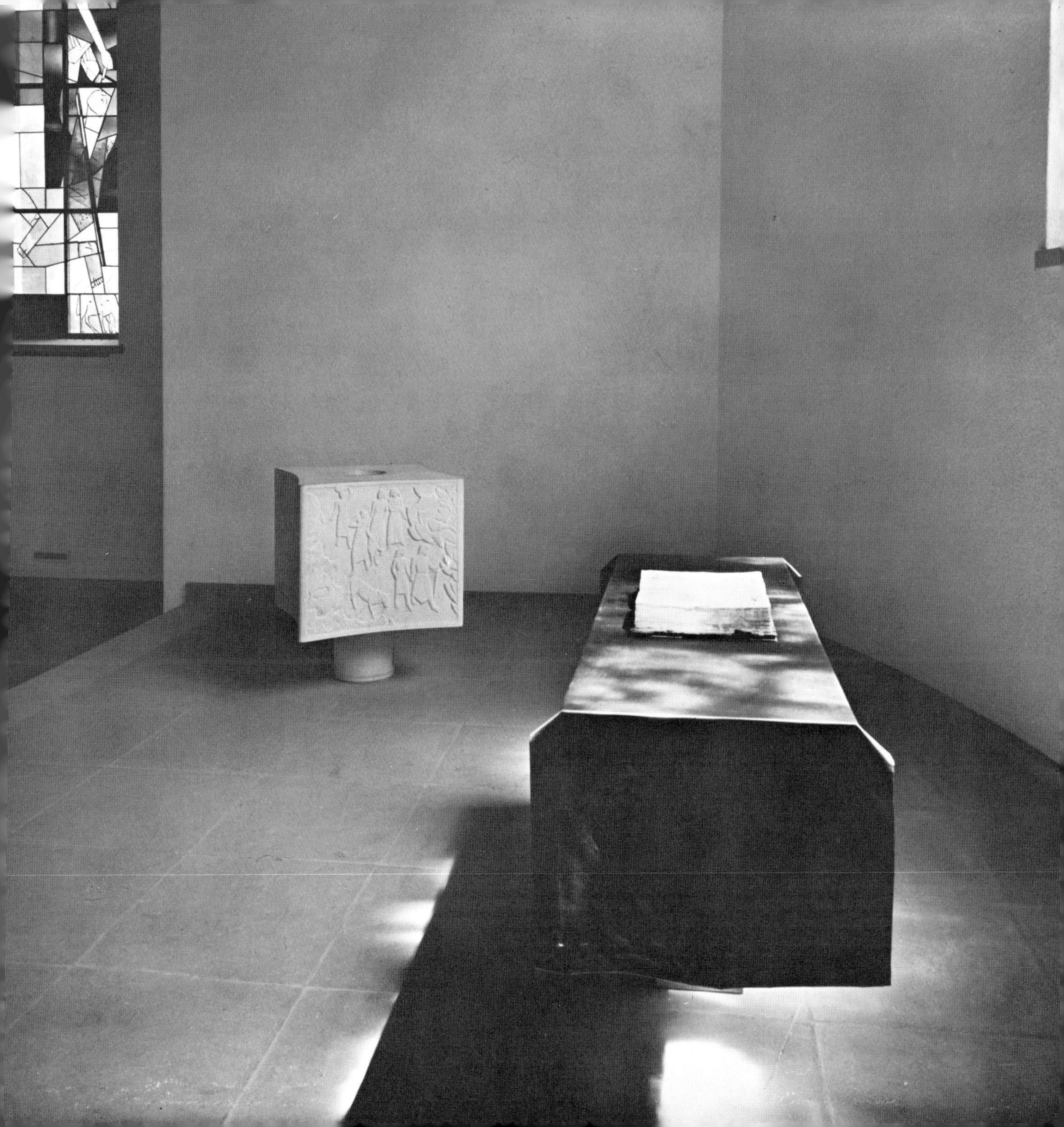

Parma Park Reformed Church, Cleveland, Ohio
Raymond P. Chaty & Carl H. Droppers, architects. Harry M. Huston, contractor
Donald J. Bruggink, theological consultant

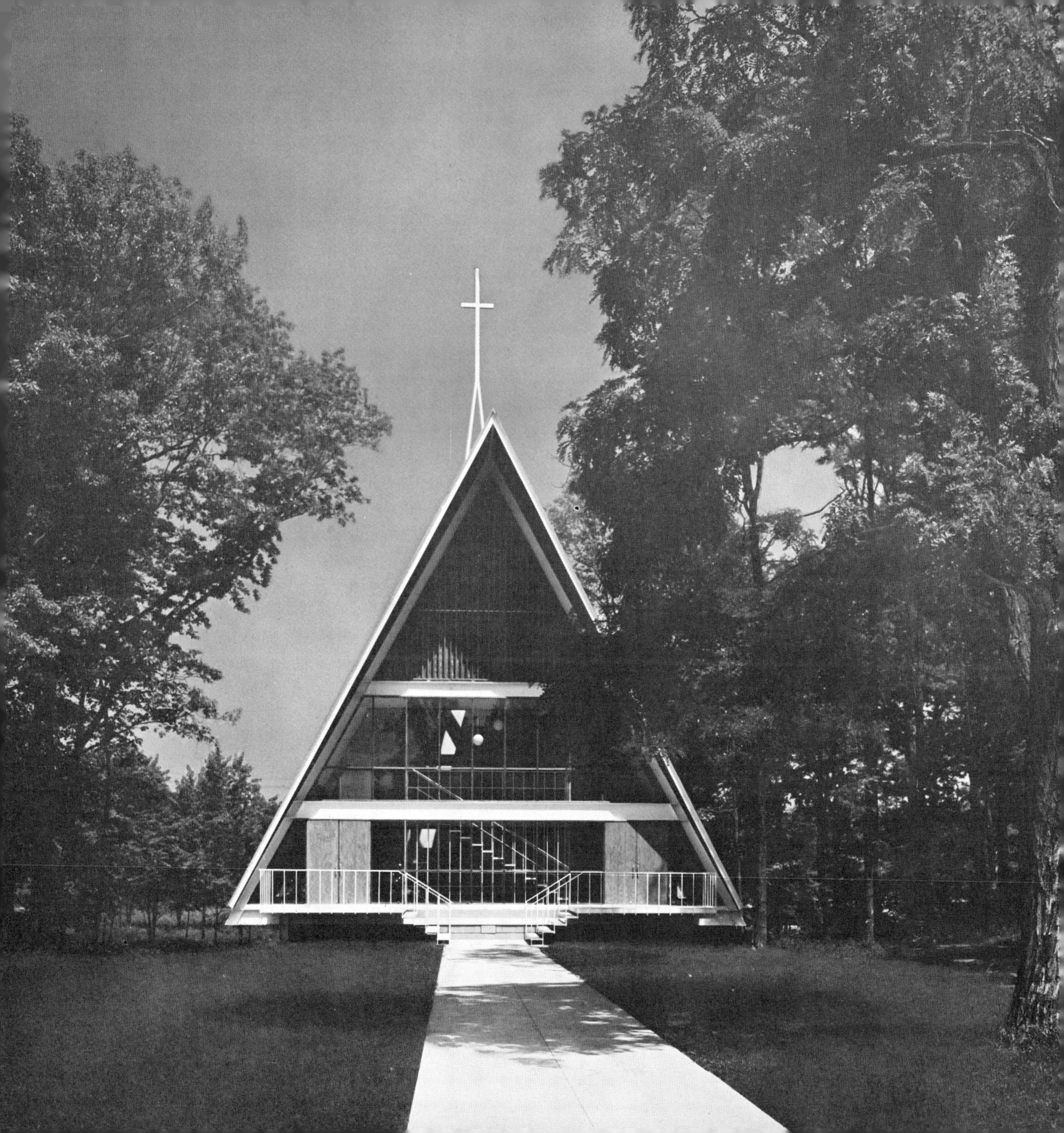

The spacious narthex contains the delightfully detailed stairs leading both to the choir-organ balcony, and down to the multi-purpose rooms on ground level. The sense of spaciousness in both narthex and nave is enhanced by the glass wall separating the two.

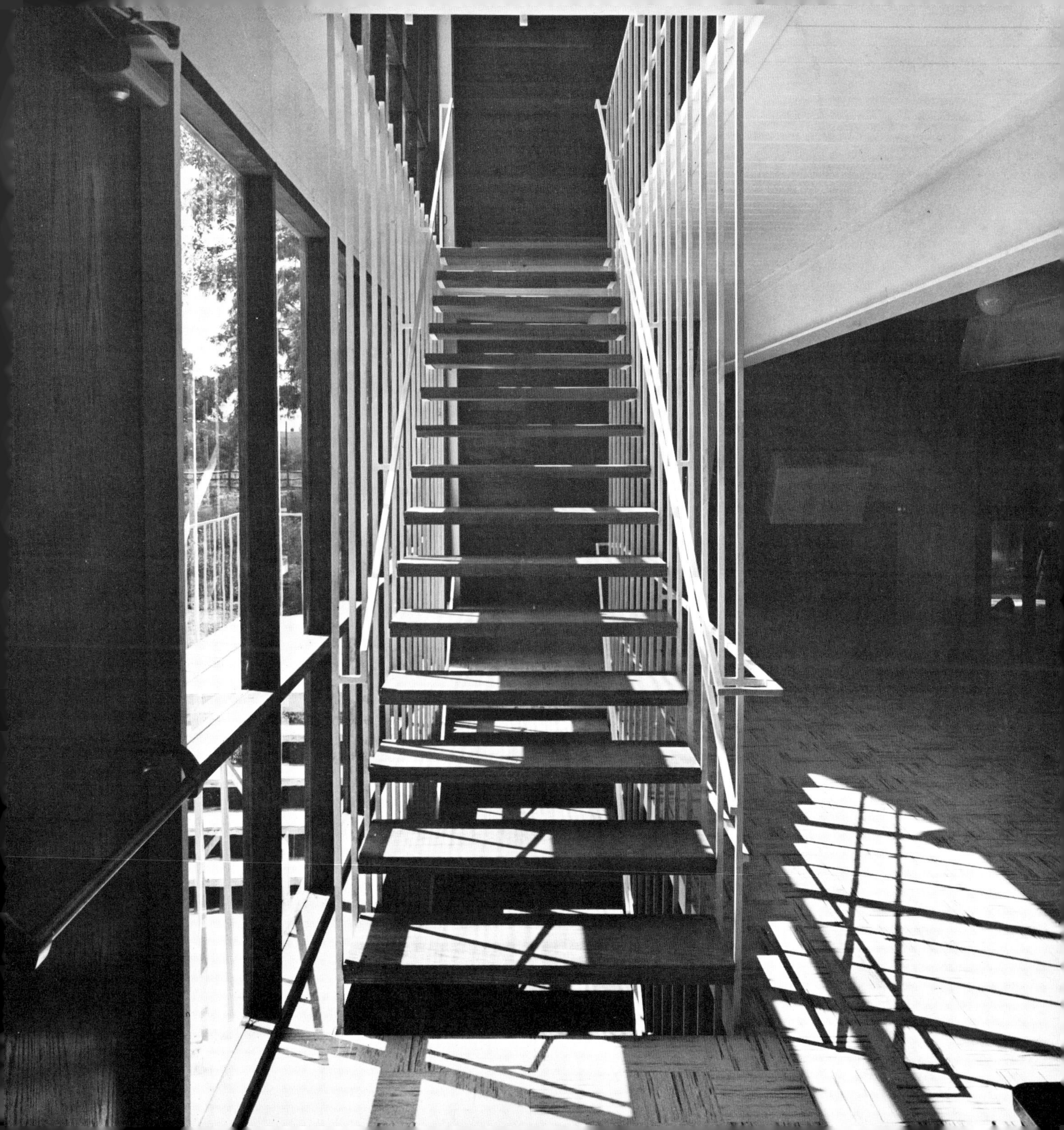

The east end of the church (geographical north) is approached by a drive from the street. The lower level contains educational and multi-purpose rooms, the second the sanctuary and a multi-purpose room, the third the pastor's study, and above that an equipment level for exhaust fan and future air conditioner.

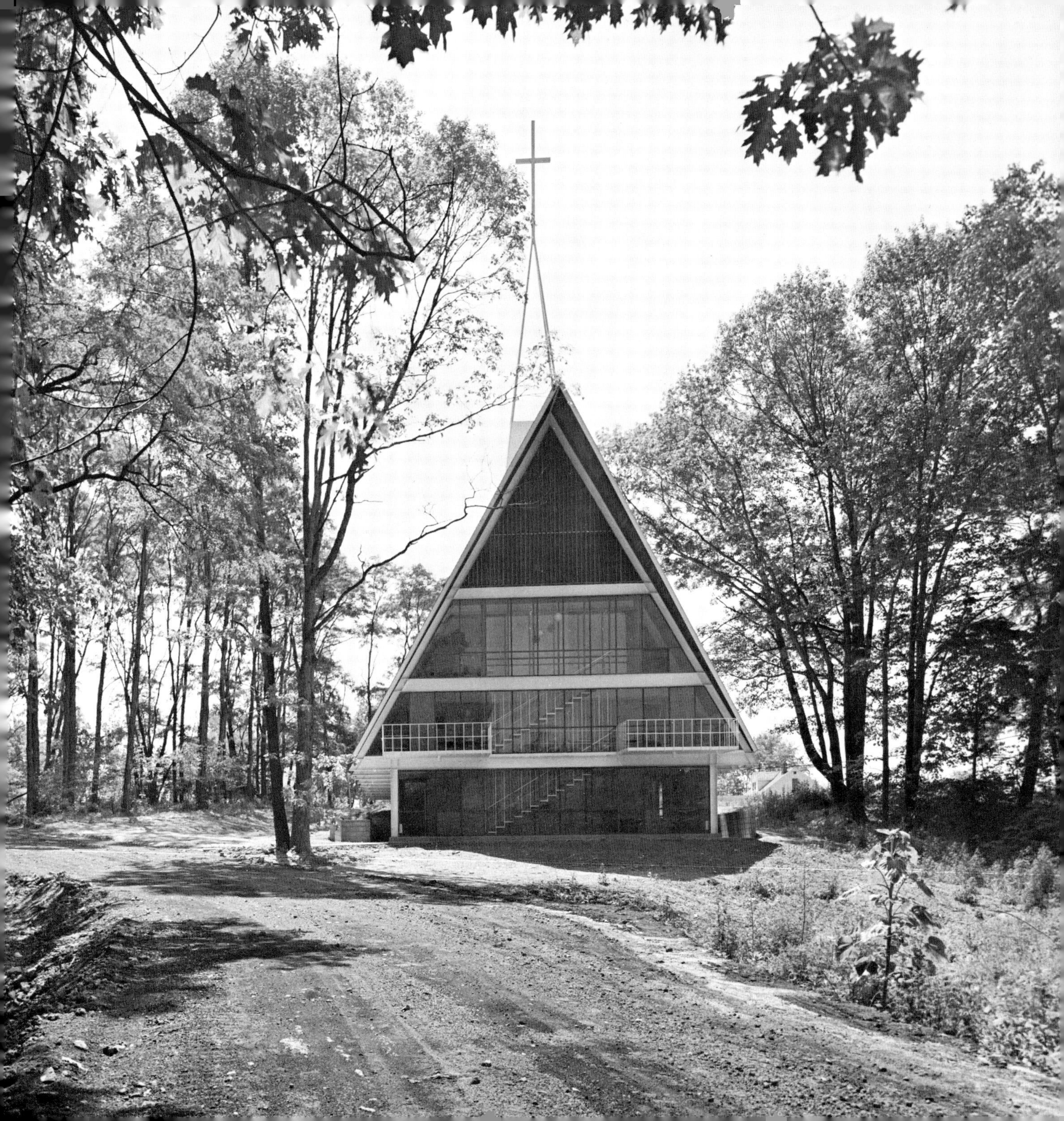

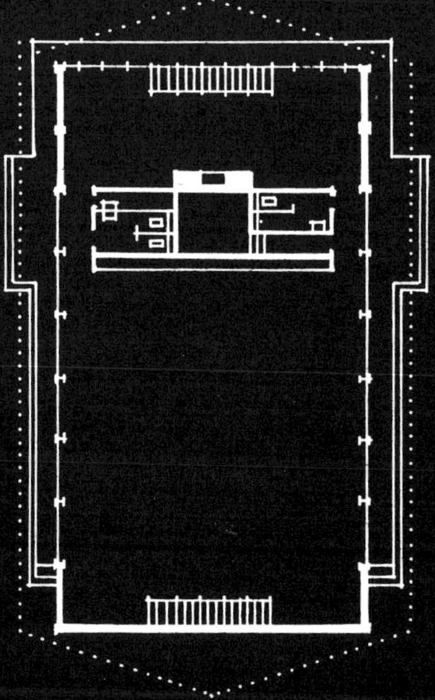
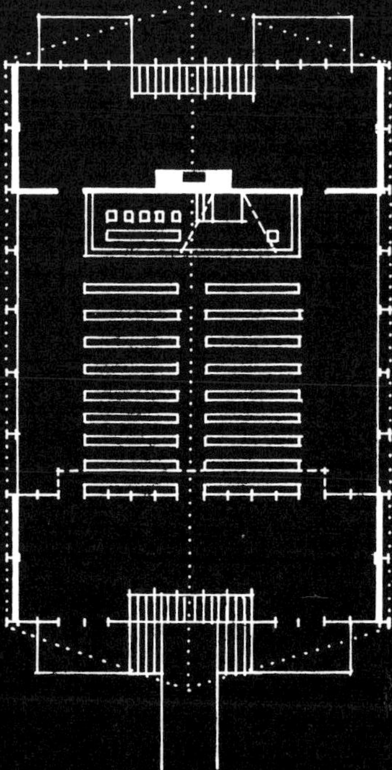

The Christ-ordained means of grace: table, pulpit, font

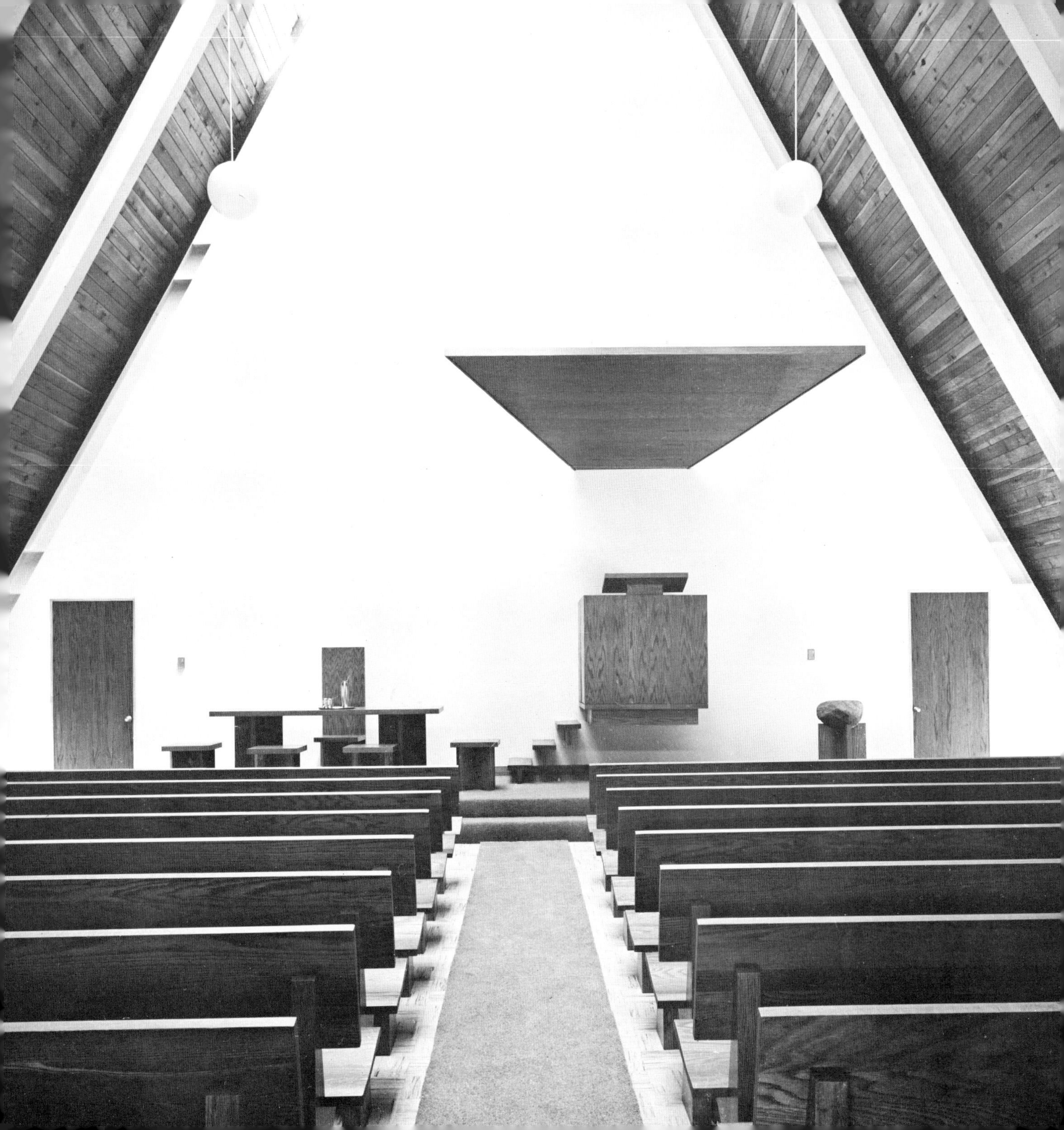

A stock pew was altered to the architect's specifications by placing a shelf for hymnals, liturgies and Bibles under the seat, thus adding to the serenity of the church by eliminating the usually cluttered and disordered book racks. The shelf is also drilled to receive the communion glasses of those who partake of the communion in their pews.

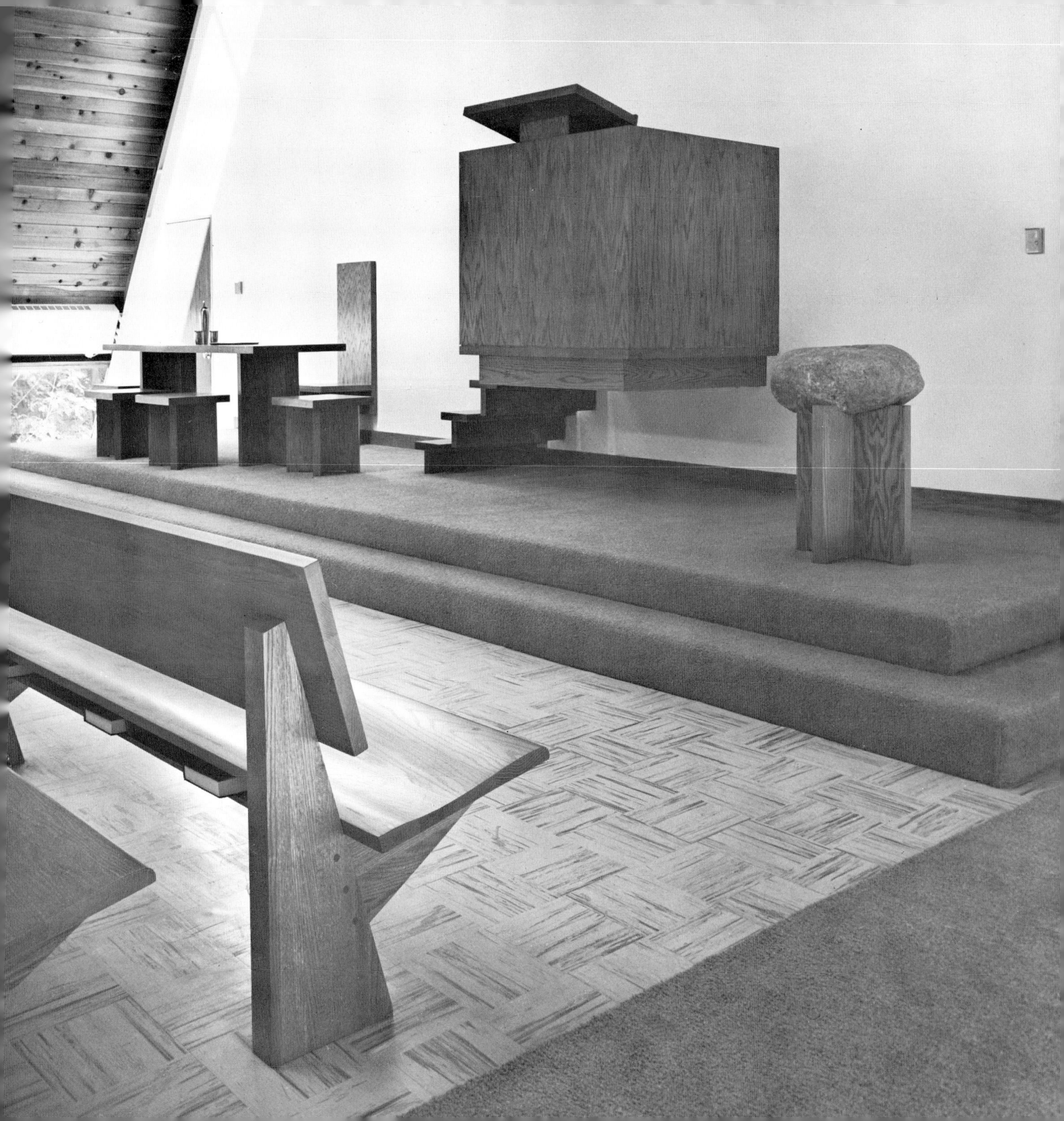

Working within a very limited budget, the architects designed all of the liturgical furniture so that it could be made from solid-core doors. While the cost was but a fraction of stock catalog furniture, its design nonetheless insures the necessary impact demanded for a strong statement of Word and Sacraments.

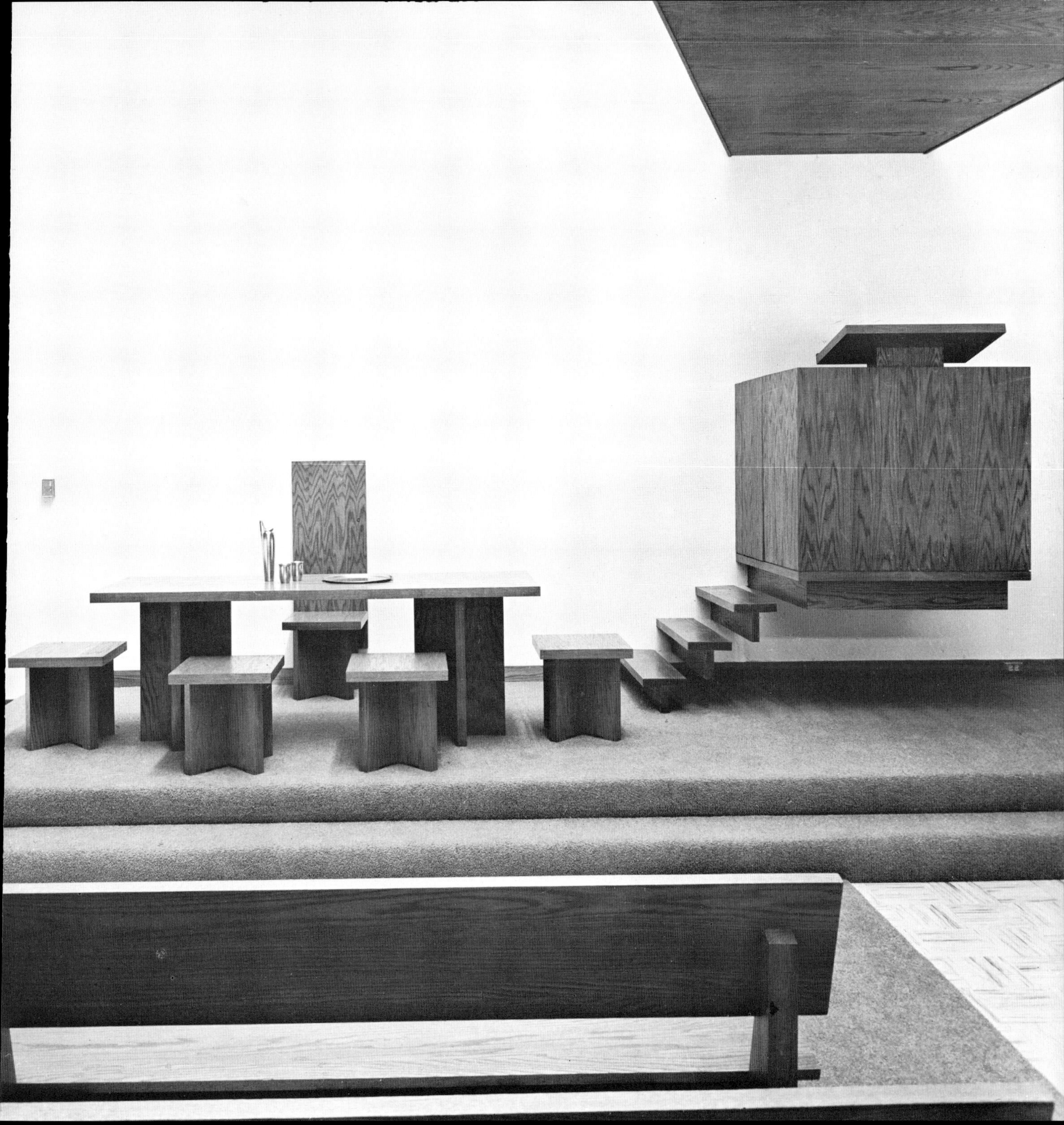

> *I want you to know, Brethren, that our fathers were all under the cloud, and all passed through the sea, and all were baptized into Moses in the cloud and in the sea, and all ate the same supernatural food and all drank the same supernatural drink. For they drank from the supernatural Rock which followed them, and the Rock was Christ.*
>
> *I Corinthians 10:1–4.*

The sacramental inference of the above verses is pronounced: baptism by cloud and sea marking deliverance from Egypt parallels baptism by water marking deliverance from sin. The supernatural food (manna) and drink (water from the rock) in the sojourn in the wilderness parallels the bread and wine of the Lord's Supper which strengthens us in the sojourn of this life as we journey toward the Promised Rest. Paul says that the Rock from which poured forth strength and sustenance for the sojourn in the wilderness was Christ, the same Christ who in the water of Baptism offers his strength, his cleansing, that we may stand before the Father. Paul is saying that we enter the Promised Rest by the strength of Christ, even as Israel entered the Promised Land.

Nor should the context of Paul's words be overlooked. His concern is to warn the Corinthians that they must not suppose that their Baptism will save them regardless of their lives. All Israel was baptized, "Nevertheless with most of them God was not pleased; for they were overthrown in the wilderness" (I Corinthians 10:5). It is possible, says Paul, to deny our Baptism by the way we live. If we are truly baptized into Christ, then having died to sin and having been raised up in him unto newness of life, our lives will show it in their conformity to Christ.

Baptismal font by Raymond P. Chaty & Carl H. Droppers

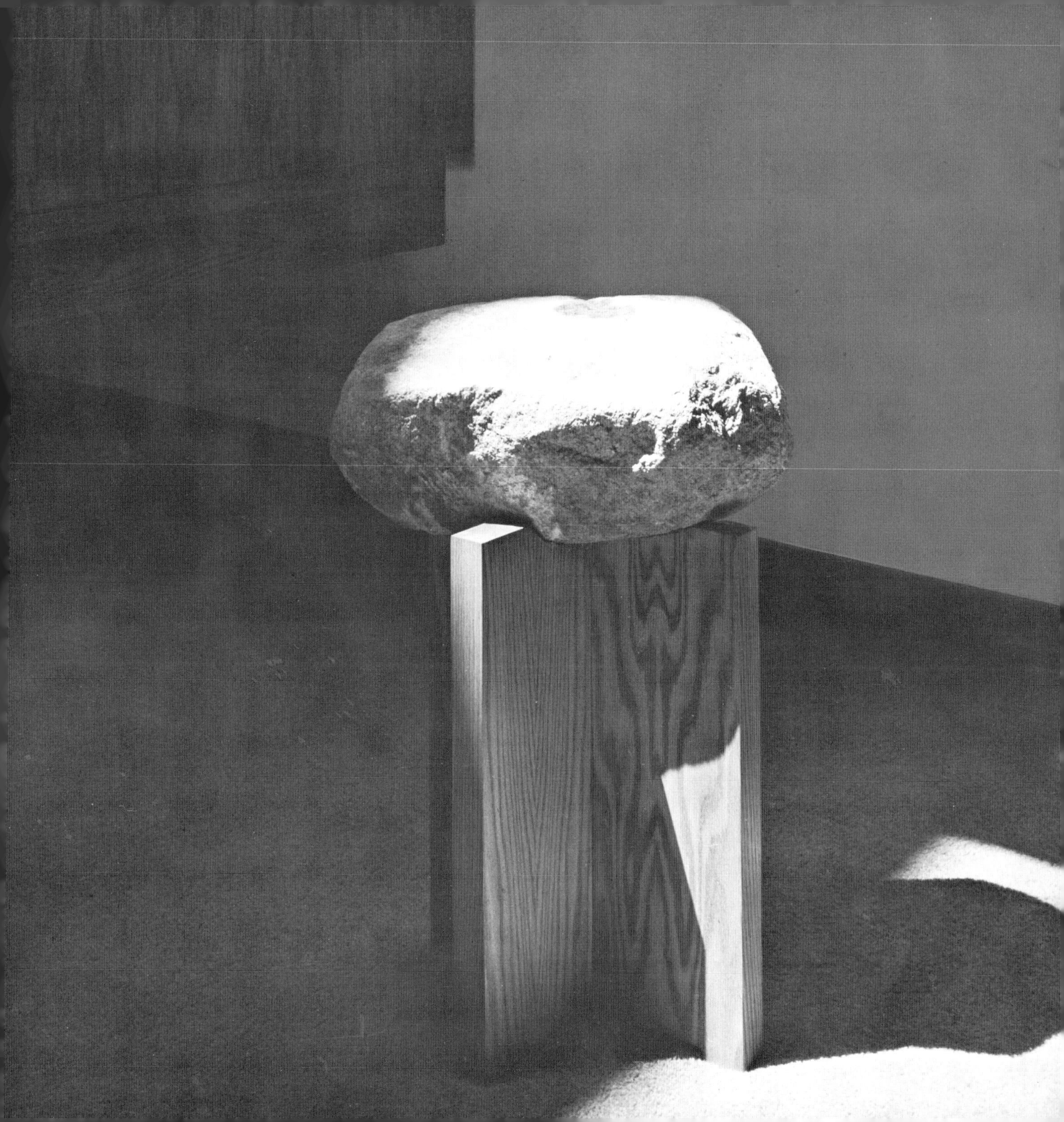

The Lord's Supper

God's mercy causes great difficulties to man's understanding—undoubtedly because true mercy is so difficult for man. For what is harder for man to understand and accept than the fact that God at great pain, suffering, and death won a full and final victory over death and sin on the cross, and yet while God has won, he also waits! God waits, and in the meantime man's life is filled with pain and sin and death, and men question the wisdom of God's waiting. Why should God wait if he has already won the victory? God has won, but God also waits, and he waits because he is merciful. God waits that the gospel may be proclaimed and his house may be filled (Luke 14:23).

The Table of the Last Supper

During this period of waiting in which the Christian often suffers, God, through the Holy Supper, points us back to the Last Supper, to the Christ who willingly suffered that he might establish a new covenant with mankind, a covenant established at the cost of his blood. Thus the Lord's Supper ever points us back to the Last Supper, whence, having instituted this very Supper of the new covenant, Christ went to Gethsemane and then to Golgotha. The tables in our churches are to remind us of the table of the Last Supper.

The Table of the Present Lord

But during this period of waiting, while the crucified Christ, who is also the victorious risen Christ, is ascended, the Sacraments have been given the Church. Just as miraculous signs attended our Lord's Word in the days of his flesh, so now when he is at the right hand of the Father, the Sacraments have been given that signs may still be joined to his Word. And because of this time of mercy, this time of waiting, it is also fitting that two Sacraments have been given. For while both of these Sacraments are signs and seals by which the Holy Spirit unites us with Christ, nonetheless each has a different emphasis. Baptism speaks most forcefully of the once-for-all victory of Christ, and our participation in that victory. The total sufficiency of Christ's victory is reflected in the "onceness" of Baptism. Neither needs to be repeated.

But God waits. Although righteous before God in Christ, our lives here are still involved in sin, and while our baptism assures us that the victory has been won in Christ, our lives are often far from victorious. Because God does not crush sin, but still waits that men may have opportunity to repent and join the family of God, sin, uncrushed, is still a reality even in the life of the Christian. Thus the Lord's Supper is given for our repeated use to assure us that while the glory of Christ is yet hidden, he has nonetheless won the victory, and we are in him, have forgiveness in him, and participate in all his benefits. As Christians we are living in this world, but already living as well in the new creation, and are given the Lord's Supper to assure us that we are in him and participate in all his blessings. Even as on the first Easter the risen Lord ate with his disciples, first at Emmaus and then at Jerusalem (Luke 24:13–53), to assure them of his living presence, so the Church, with Pentecost added to Easter, may be assured of his continued presence in the eating of the Lord's Supper.[28] The tables in our churches are also to remind us of the tables at Emmaus and Jerusalem and the ascended Lord who is still present at his table in the Spirit.

In thinking of the Lord's Supper we must be careful not to think exclusively in terms of the "Last Supper." Nor has full justice been done to the biblical witness when Easter and Pentecost, by which we are assured of his continued presence with us in the Supper, have been added. To the once-for-

---

[28] For a stimulating discussion of the Sacraments consult T. F. Torrance, *Conflict and Agreement in the Church, Vol. 2, The Ministry and the Sacraments of the Gospel* (London: Lutterworth Press, 1960), pp. 213ff.

all events and the continued presence of Christ must be added his words: "This do till I come." The resurrection, ascension and coming again make this Supper of the crucified Christ a Messianic Meal.

The Table of the Messianic Meal

In their expectation of the Messiah the Jews spoke of his reign in terms with which they were familiar. Thus the coming of the Messiah was described as a great feast at which the Messiah would be the host. It was at once a symbol of satisfaction, of fulfillment, and of honor (e.g. Isaiah 25:6–9). In his earthly ministry, Jesus often used this same figure to allude to himself as the Messiah and to teach that God would welcome people of all nations to this Messianic banquet (the parable of Luke 14:15–24 repeats the emphasis of the prophecy of Isaiah 25:6–9, that the Messianic banquet will be for all peoples). In the book of Revelation, the symbol is again repeated: "And the angel said to me, 'Write this: Blessed are those who are invited to the marriage supper of the Lamb' " (19:9). In the life of the early Church the Lord's Supper was not confined to a backward look, but it was also the Lord's Supper in that it looked to the future, for the Lord's Supper was already a foretaste of that great Messianic Meal when Christ would come again. The tables in our churches are to remind us of the table of the Messianic feast when the Lord will return and make all things new.

It is thus that the Lord's Supper constitutes such an effective instrument of the Spirit, for in the midst of our Christian lives with all of their need for forgiveness and strength, we are assured that we are joined to the Christ who lived and died in our place, and will come again to make full manifestation of his victory over sin and death. The Supper is both of remembrance and of anticipation, and between his ascension and coming again, it offers us the certainty of God's promise joined to a physical sign.

Godly souls can gather great assurance and delight from this Sacrament; in it they have a witness of our growth into one body with Christ such that whatever is his may be called ours. . . . This is the wonderful exchange which . . . he has made with us; that, becoming Son of man with us, he has made us sons of God with him; that, by his descent to earth, he has prepared an ascent to heaven for us; that, by taking on our mortality, he has conferred his immortality upon us; that, accepting our weakness, he has strengthened us by his power; that, receiving our poverty unto himself, he has transferred his wealth to us; that, taking the weight of our iniquity upon himself . . . he has clothed us with his righteousness.[29]

The Table of a United Family

The Lord's Supper points us backward to the once-for-all saving acts of Christ. The Lord's Supper points us forward to the full manifestation of his victory when he comes again. But in so joining us to the Christ who was, and is, and is to come, the Sacrament of the Lord's Supper bears powerful witness to our union with Christ, and thus union with one another in his body, the Church. As Paul says, "The bread which we break, is it not a participation in the body of Christ? Because there is one bread, we who are many are one body, for we all partake of the same bread" (I Corinthians 10:17). Paul's intention should not escape us, the "one bread" who makes the many "one body" is Christ Jesus (John 6:35). But it is the bread of the Sacrament which forcefully reminds us that as we all partake of the one bread, Christ Jesus, we are indeed members of one body. (Here it is unfortunate that in the name of sanitation the bread at too many Lord's Suppers in the United States shows a terrible fragmentation. The symbol would be less strained if we passed from one to another a portion of bread, as is frequently done in the Church of Scotland.)

---

[29] *Institutes*, 4:17:2, pp. 1361–62.

For those whose roots belong in the Scottish portion of the Reformation this emphasis of the Lord's Supper upon unity in Christ should be especially strong. Prof. James S. McEwen, in an excellent book on John Knox, *The Faith of John Knox*,[30] points out that Knox perhaps stressed this aspect of the Supper more than any of the other Reformers. While even Calvin (perhaps in reaction to certain fanatics who cared nothing for church order or decency) could counsel the persecuted Huguenots to forego celebrating the Sacraments until they had an opportunity to organize their Church, Knox, at every opportunity in his 1555–56 visit to Scotland, gathered together a few of the faithful and administered the Lord's Supper for the establishment of the Church.[31] Already in 1550, Knox could describe the Lord's Supper in these terms:

> The Lord Jesus, by earthly and visible things set before us, lifteth us up to heavenly and invisible things—He prepares His spiritual banquet—He witnesses that He Himself was the living bread—He sets forth the bread and wine to eat and drink—He giveth unto us Himself—and all this He does through the power of the Holy Ghost. . . . Herewith, also, the Lord Jesus gathers us unto one visible body, so that we be members one of another, and make altogether one body, whereof Jesus Christ is the only Head.[32]

It is by the visible Sacrament that the body of Christ visible is set forth. The unity of Christ's Church—which if important on a denominational level is even more important in the relation of one Church member to another within a congregation—cannot be a purely "spiritual" unity any more than the Sacraments can be purely "spiritual" or than was Christ purely "spiritual." Even as Christ was flesh and blood and the signs and seals of the Sacraments are real bread and wine, so the unity of Christ's Church must have visible expression in the flesh and blood of this world. The tangible elements of the

---

[30] (Richmond: John Knox Press, 1961).
[31] *Ibid.*, pp. 55ff.
[32] *Ibid.*, p. 56, quoting from Knox's *Works*, III, pp. 73ff.

Sacrament should impress upon the Church Christ's demand for the tangible unity of his people, even as it should impress us with the reality of our connection with the Lord of the Last Supper who gave himself for us, and the reality of our connection with the Lord who rules over all and is coming again to make his victory known to all—the Lord in whose name we partake of this Supper until he comes.

Before proceeding to the architectural statement of the Supper, something should be said about the question of the frequency with which the Lord's Supper should be celebrated. New Testament scholarship generally regards the Supper in the early Church to have been celebrated weekly. And it is well known that Calvin desired a weekly Communion in Geneva. Even more important in this regard is the fact that Calvin's Strassburg liturgy contained only one order of service for the Lord's Day, and this order was climaxed with the celebration of the Lord's Supper. On those Sundays when it was not celebrated there was simply a rubric to indicate the point at which the service might be terminated.[33] That Calvin never achieved his weekly Lord's Supper at Geneva was the result not so much of a Zwinglian influence based upon a devalued Sacrament, but upon the attitude of magistrates and people alike which had been inherited from Rome, where despite daily Masses the communion of the people was often only once a year, and where Communion on even a monthly basis was considered "frequent."[34] However, when discussing frequency of celebration today—whether in relation to the New Testament or the Reformation Church—the whole context of worship must be considered. That is to say, there is every indication that the New Testament Church did not limit its weekly assemblies to a strict sixty minutes. The situation then was similar to some of the mission areas today where Christians

---

[33] *Institutes,* 4:17:43, p. 1421, and Hageman, *op. cit.,* pp. 25f.
[34] *Institutes,* 4:17:43, p. 1421, footnote 39.

meet for the greater part of the Lord's Day to worship. In Reformation Geneva, at St. Peter's, there were on Sunday sermons at daybreak, 9 a.m. and 3 p.m., in addition to the catechizing of the young at noon, not to mention further mandatory sermons on Monday, Wednesday, and Friday.[35] The point is simply this, that historically, the practice of, or desire for, a weekly celebration of the Lord's Supper was in the midst of an ample diet of the proclamation of the Word. As the consideration of a more adequate use of the Supper grows, it should not be divorced from the total problem of a generally more ample diet of worship.

While the problem of frequency is well outside the scope of this book, it serves to point up the fact that if celebration at present is limited to a mere four times per year then the architectural symbolism by which the attention of the congregation is directed to the Sacrament on the remaining forty-eight Sundays should be both emphatic and accurate. If, on the other hand, celebration is frequent but the architectural accouterments of the Sacrament are misleading, then there is simply error compounded. Thus, whether the Lord's Supper is to be celebrated frequently or rarely, it is imperative that the architectural statement be accurate.

The Lord's Supper as a means by which the Holy Spirit joins us to Christ was discussed above. Its concrete relationships with the Christ of the Last Supper whose blood was shed and body was broken for us, as well as with the same Christ whose victory will be manifest when he comes again, and with whom in the meantime we are joined together in one body—these three aspects of the Supper have been briefly considered. In all three aspects of the Supper, it is clear that it is just that: a supper. The Last Supper to which we look back and at which Christ instituted this Sacrament was conducted at a table. The symbol of the great Messianic Meal when Christ

---

[35] T. H. L. Parker, *The Oracles of God* (London: Lutterworth Press, 1947), p. 33.

returns again involves the symbol of the table. Our oneness in Christ, which is symbolized in the bread and wine of which we partake, again involves the symbolism of a table, even as the table is appropriate for the family of Christ. This aspect of the Lord's Supper has not been lost on those scholars of the liturgical movement who, while bound to the traditional interpretation of the Mass as a sacrifice, have nonetheless seen the biblical emphasis upon the meal, and as a result have emphasized this aspect of the Eucharist. This emphasis has been so strong that in church after church on the Continent the altars are more and more assuming the shape of tables, even to the extent of standing upon four legs like a table. The writers of the liturgical movement persistently emphasize the altar as the table of the family of God. This is good biblical doctrine, and it is to the shame of the Reformed that while the Christian brethren who are most tightly bound by tradition are recapturing this biblical teaching of the family of God and expressing it in their architecture, so many of the children of the Reformation are setting up altars appropriate only for a high Roman doctrine of the Mass as the re-sacrifice of Christ.[36] But it is this Roman doctrine of the re-sacrifice of Christ which is absolutely repudiated by all of the Reformers. There is no need for an altar. An altar in fact is either totally incongruous, or a denial of the sufficiency of Christ's once-for-all sacrifice.[37] Calvin succinctly sums up the matter by observing that Christ has "given us a Table at which to

---

[36] The criticism which Q. 80 of the Heidelberg Catechism levels at this doctrine remains valid.

[37] It is true, of course, that in response to God's grace we are to live lives of gratitude, so that Paul can appeal to us "by the mercies of God, to present your bodies as a living sacrifice, holy and acceptable to God . . ." (Romans 12:1). But an altar is in no sense appropriate for such lives of gratitude. The Lord's Supper is **not a means by which we do something on God's behalf** (any more than preaching is for God's edification). The Lord's Supper is given for man's benefit, that he may be assured of his participation in Christ and all his benefits.

feast, not an altar upon which to offer a victim; he has not consecrated priests to offer sacrifice, but ministers to distribute the sacred banquet."[38] If any architectural criterion is to be stated with regard to the Sacrament of the Lord's Supper, the very minimum statement would be this:

FOR THE CELEBRATION OF THE LORD'S SUPPER, THE TABLE SHOULD LOOK LIKE A TABLE!

This seems so terribly self-evident that some word of explanation would seem to be required concerning the plethora of altarlike tables found in churches of Reformed persuasion. Certainly there cannot be so many devotees of the doctrine of the Mass in our midst! One would rather suspect that the pope of "style" which required copies of the forms of other ages and beliefs is responsible. To show just how foreign are the beliefs that produced the forms which "style" dictates for use, it would perhaps be well to consider briefly the rise and use of the altar form. By the third century the Church, which had suffered much persecution and had learned to value the gift of steadfastness, was doing honor to those who had given their lives for the Faith. It became the custom to show honor by holding the sacramental meal on the tombs of the martyrs whether in catacomb or cemetery.[39] With the building of churches on the sites of martyrdoms, the remains were moved into the churches and placed in stone coffins "which by the high Middle Ages had everywhere in the West replaced the wooden communion tables. Every altar was thus a coffin, and without the body, or parts of the body, of a

---

[38] *Institutes*, 4:18:12, p. 1440.
[39] Nichols & Trinterud, *op. cit.*, pp. 9, 10. No church of Reformed persuasion planning to build should be without a few dozen copies of this magnificent little pamphlet. It should be made required reading not only for the building committee but also for those who would criticize on the basis of "accepted usage" or "style."

martyr, it was incomplete, as is the case with Roman altars to this day."[40] The form of these stone coffin boxes also perfectly matched the rising doctrine of the Mass as a sacrifice—for indeed, was not the Eucharist being performed upon an altar?

The Reformers were perfectly aware of the incongruity of this situation, and as a result the stone altars were torn down and replaced, for there was to be no re-sacrificing of Christ, or worship of saintly relics in the Church of Jesus Christ reformed according to the Word of God. This was equally true in England, where, during the reign of Edward VI, Hooper "in one of his Lent sermons before the court in 1550 had expressed a wish that the magistrates might be pleased 'to turn the altars into tables according to the first institution of Christ.' "[41] In the summer of that same year, Ridley "in his injunctions for the diocese of London . . . exhorts curates, churchwardens and questmen . . . 'to erect and set up the Lord's Board, after the form of an honest table, decently covered.' "[42] The 1552 Prayer Book dropped the term "altar" and speaks of "the table," "the Lord's table," or "God's board."[43] Interestingly enough, in a civil suit in 1845 a stone altar was torn down at the order of the judge, "and on the grounds of this judgment stone altars have in subsequent cases been declared illegal in the Church of England."[44] The situation in England has been especially singled out because of its association in the minds of so many people with "traditional English Gothic" and all of its Medieval accouterments, including coffin altars, despite the fact that this "traditional Gothic" is the product of Romanticism, the Victorian

---

[40] *Ibid.*, p. 10.
[41] Hooper, *Early Writings*, Parker Society, p. 488, quoted by Addleshaw & Etchells, *op. cit.*, p. 25.
[42] Addleshaw & Etchells, *op. cit.*, p. 26.
[43] *Ibid.*, p. 27.
[44] *Ibid.*, p. 135.

age, and the high-church Cambridge Ecclesiologists. More must be said on this subject in a subsequent chapter. For the present let it suffice to say that so far are coffin altars removed from the Reformation that the Church of England had little to do with them until after the 1850s. Everywhere throughout the Reformation Church it was recognized that Christ gave us "a Table at which to feast, not an altar upon which to offer a victim . . ."[45]

If a table is for a supper and is to be used as a table, and not as a coffin for relics or as an altar for sacrifice, then it should also have the accouterments of a table. This would mean a second criterion for the table:

ONLY THOSE ARTICLES WHICH ARE COMMENSURATE WITH THE CELEBRATION OF THE LORD'S SUPPER SHOULD BE PLACED UPON THE TABLE.

To accept this criterion means that there will be no need to spend several hundred dollars for expensive brocade coverings and hangings (the proper Roman Catholic term is antependium), for a real table need have only such covering (if any) as a table would ordinarily have when not in use. At most a white cloth would be used, but even that would probably be reserved for times when the Supper is actually celebrated.

This criterion also requires decisions as to whether flowers, offering plates, candles, and the cross constitute "articles commensurate with the celebration of the Lord's Supper." What about the beautiful flowers which grace our churches each Sunday, are they to be placed on the table? It is rather hard to believe that they were there for the Last Supper, and it certainly does no honor to the table to use it week after week as a convenient flower stand. Another place should be found to mount the flowers. The consideration should be whether or not flowers are commensurate with the

---

[45] *Institutes*, 4:18:12, p. 1440.

celebration of the Lord's Supper. Since this is highly questionable, it seems inappropriate to place them on the table.

Then there is the problem of the offering plates. These are not articles commensurate with the celebration of the Lord's Supper, and to place them on the table is to invite confusion as to whether the Supper speaks entirely of God's gracious gift to man in Christ, or whether it speaks of man giving something to God. The latter idea is frequently used by those who feel that there is something to be gained in maintaining the use of the term altar in preference to the Lord's table. "It is an altar," they say, "because we offer ourselves in sacrifice to God in response to his love for us." It is because this gratitude is such a biblical intention, and one enjoined by the Reformation catechisms, that this idea falls on receptive ears. But it must be clearly distinguished that our gratitude for God's love is to be our response to Word and Sacraments, and is not, per se, a part of the Supper. To bring in this admittedly fine sentiment and very Christian response at this particular point is ultimately to bring confusion into the meaning of the Supper.

Nor should the issue be confused by the fact that in the early Church it was customary for the people to bring the bread and wine for the Supper, which at informal gatherings for worship were simply produced at the proper time, but which in larger formal services (which necessitated a more structured worship) were brought forward in what is now known liturgically as the offering. The practice obviously arose from necessity, and long continued as a practical solution to the particular liturgical problem. This in no way justifies, however, the confusion of grace and gratitude in the midst of the Supper. The content of the Supper must be decided on the basis of Scripture, not on an interpretation of tradition, no matter how venerable. Whether one looks to Maundy Thursday, to Easter, or the Lord's return, the content of the Supper is pure grace. It is to this grace of God that we must respond in gratitude. But the response is not a part of the Sacrament! Let us have the humility to celebrate the Sacraments as they were given to us by the Lord: looking back to his once-for-all sacrifice for us, looking ahead to the time when he will come again, and finding assurance and strength for our present lives in the knowledge that we are one with him and his Church. If our practice each Sunday is not to lead us into a misunderstanding of the nature of the Supper, then it is mandatory that another spot be found for the offering plates.[46]

In comparison with the question of the offering plates, the matter of the candles, and even that of the cross, is somewhat easier. Originally candles were used for utilitarian purposes, for light. Their usage became fixed during the Middle Ages so that according to Roman tradition seven candlesticks are used on the altar when a bishop pontificates, six are used for solemn and high Masses, and two for a low Mass. Seemingly, most Protestant churches celebrate a perpetual low Mass! Candles are, in fact, completely meaningless for Protestants, and unless there is a specific desire to clutter the Lord's table with the superfluous, and thereby confuse the fact that the table does have real theological significance, it would be better if the candles were entirely omitted.

And what of the cross itself? Surely no one could find objection to the use of this universal Christian symbol of the death of Christ. But what are the implications? In present Roman Catholic practice a crucifix is required either on, behind, or above the altar—the visible representation of the Christ who is daily re-sacrificed on the altar. But the doctrine of the Mass was rejected at the Reformation because it was contrary to the biblical evidence. Statues were similarly rejected as being temptations to misunderstanding and misdirected emphasis. It is maintained, however, that the plain cross without

---

[46] It must be further recognized that almsgiving is not to be associated with the traditional offertory of the Canon of the Mass, but that it was first given liturgical status in Cranmer's Book of Common Prayer of 1549. See G. A. Michell, *Landmarks in Liturgy* (London: Darton, Longman & Todd, 1961), pp. 63ff.

the crucifix is a satisfactory witness to our biblical belief that Christ's once-for-all sacrifice is complete. But does this attempt to justify the brass cross approach the problem from the right direction? Does not the issue become much clearer in the light of the criterion (p. 214), that "only those articles which are commensurate with the celebration of the Lord's Supper should be placed upon the table"? In brief, should one not ask whether the symbol of the cross is a part of the Christ-ordained plan of the Sacrament of the Lord's Supper? Does not the symbolism of that Sacrament consist particularly in the bread and wine? Because they speak so eloquently of the broken body and shed blood of Christ, should not the symbol of the cross be reserved for other use, rather than intruding it on the Lord's table?

Nor can one appeal to the early Church to defend the usage of such things as even candles and crosses, for these practices were relatively late:

> The ancient church had permitted nothing on the Lord's Table save the actual cloth and vessels of the sacrament, and the Gospels, and these only for the sacred meal. But from the Carolingian period [8th and 9th centuries] the coffin-altar began to acquire bric-a-brac; the cross, candlesticks, the 'tabernacle' for the consecrated elements, and containers for miraculous relics of the saints.[47]

Quite interestingly, one hears of Protestants adding candles and crosses to their "altars" because they wish to become more "traditional" while the informed theologians of the Roman Catholic liturgical movement, guided by a historical, rather than a sentimental tradition, are returning to a purer usage of the Lord's table. Many of the altars of recent European Roman Catholic churches have provided a separate place for the tabernacle, while the crucifix is often in abstract form and suspended, and the candles are often set on the pavement.

---

[47] Nichols & Trinterud, op. cit., p. 10.

As those who stand in the Reformed tradition we can be proud that at the time of the Reformation the usage of the table was returned to much of its original purity, with candles, crosses, and certainly crucifixes, completely disallowed. In Zwingli's service even the communion vessels of silver and gold were replaced by wooden cups and plates.[48] Within the Church of England at the time of the Reformation "nothing but a carpet or covering was ordered by Canon LXXXII to be put on the altar; and generally speaking nothing else was put on when there was no Communion service."[49] It is interesting to note that, while for many people the Episcopal Church is synonymous with a deep chancel and an altar bearing cross and candles, Canon Addleshaw maintains in the conclusion of his excellent volume that:

> The altar should . . . look like a table, and not like a dresser or sideboard, or a stand for flowers or candles. Its ornaments should be determined by its nature as the table of the Lord, and not primarily by aesthetic considerations or the need of something to hold the attenion of the congregation during the service and to make convenient focus for their devotions. Whatever ornaments are used they should therefore help to bring out this character of the altar as a table, and this is best done when they are kept to a minimum.[50]

Should not we who claim to be reformed according to the Word of God, and who are proud that we are ever willing to be so reformed, be true to God's Word, and return to the pure celebration of the Sacrament, expressing this architecturally by limiting the accessories of the table to those articles which are commensurate to the celebration of the Lord's Supper?

---

[48] Hageman, *op. cit.*, p. 210.
[49] Addleshaw & Etchells, *op. cit.*, p. 168.
[50] *Ibid.*, p. 226.

The Lord's table

Zorgvliet Church (Zorgvlietkerk), Hervormd, The Hague, The Netherlands. M. Kuyper & ir. C. Westerduin, architects

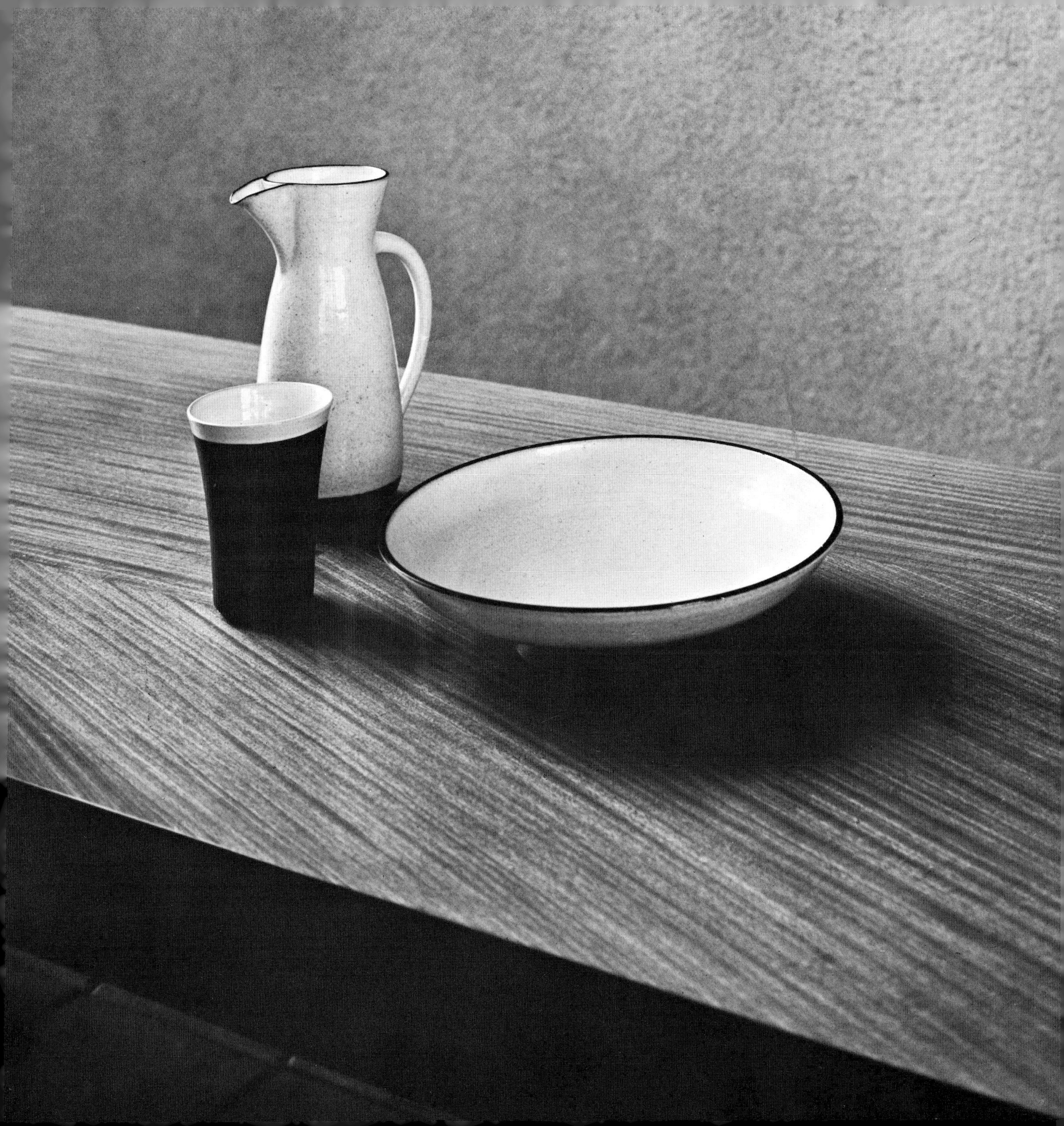

Although it has certainly been implied in what has already been said, it should nonetheless be explicitly stated as a further criterion that

THE LORD'S TABLE SHOULD BE ACCESSIBLE AND VISIBLE.

If the table is to symbolize the Supper, then it must be able to be seen, and while this sounds so desperately elementary as to be insulting, prevailing customs in the furnishing of churches indicates that perhaps the point should nevertheless be stated. In the vast majority of American churches there are apparently only two options: a central east-wall altar, or a little communion table on the floor in front of the pulpit, glimpsed only as one walks down the center aisle, or, lacking such an aisle, best ascertained as the source of support for the flowers, or the point upon which the deacons converge with the offering plates.

The very infrequency with which most churches celebrate the Sacrament makes visibility all the more essential, for without the weekly observance of the early Church the visual symbol of the table must serve to remind us of the promises and assurance of the Sacrament. If we cannot actually partake of the Sacrament, at least the visible presence of the table will remind us of Christ's dying in our place, so joining us to himself that we are as surely one with him as when we touch and taste the bread and wine, and that this same Christ is coming again to make manifest his victory. This is a message which week by week should be visibly before Christ's people.

At the same time, the table should be visible so that it can be used during the whole service—and not just during the Lord's Supper. In the Reformation church at Strasbourg in both the French and German congregations, the entire service, excepting only the sermon, was taken by the minister from the table.[51] Theologically, taking much of the service from the com-

---

[51] Maxwell, *op. cit.*, pp. 36ff. It is Maxwell's opinion that it was the necessity to be heard that took the service away from the table and into the pulpit.

munion table can be justified on the basis that our praise and our prayers are accepted by God only in Christ, and that the table reminds us of our union with him. However, it must also be remembered that Baptism likewise speaks of our union with Christ, and that the Holy Spirit also works through the preaching of the Word to join men to Christ. Theologically, one can offer praise or prayer from baptismal font or pulpit as well as from the table. Richard Paquier, however, has an observation on this matter that has such a pointed thrust that many ministers may wish to go to the table to pray, for Paquier wishes to make the communion table the place of prayer because prayers from the pulpit so easily become a kind of preaching to God.[52]

The table must, however, be more than visible—it must also be accessible! It must never be fenced off as the private preserve of the clergy as in pre-Reformation times. It is true that many Reformation churches kept their chancel screens intact, using them as walls and doors for the separate room in which the Lord's Supper was held. But in those instances the doors were not to keep out the people, but rather to reserve the Lord's Supper for those who partook, while children, unworthy adults, and hungry dogs were kept out.[53] None of these groups now present such difficulties at the Supper that fences or screens are needed in order to keep them from the table. And since it is not our custom to kneel for Communion, there is no reason whatsoever to use rails. A rail implies a separation of the table from the laity, and in view of the message of the Lord's Supper that we are all one in Christ, the contradiction of the rail is hardly appropriate.

What are the practical means of achieving both accessibility and visibility for the Lord's Table? One solution to the problem that is very popular today, especially among Roman Catholics and Episcopalians, was suggested by Mar-

---

[52] Massa, *op. cit.*, p. 54.
[53] Addleshaw & Etchells, *op. cit.*, p. 41.

tin Bucer (upon the supposition that it was the common plan of the most ancient churches—for which there is no evidence). This is that churches be built round, with the clergy officiating from the middle.[54] Rudolph Schwarz looked upon the circle as the ideal theoretical form of the church for the celebration of the Eucharist, although because of other considerations he never built such a church. The advantages are clear: the entire family of God surrounds the table. People face one another as in an ordinary family meal, instead of looking at the backs of heads, as if attending a spectator sport. People can gather around the table in a position for fellowship and mutual understanding and love, with Christ in their very midst.[55] In this country most of the round churches have been built by the Church of Rome, and this is quite fitting since this type of structure is at its best when the Eucharist stands at the heart of the service. When one attempts such a plan for Reformed worship, however, the difficulties become obvious. As the congregation gathers around the table, they also gather around the minister, who must then preach to the people while they are seated on three or four sides of him. More will be said in the following chapter about the resulting difficulties in communication. Nonetheless, an admirable attempt has been made to solve this problem with a variant of the circular plan, the form of a Greek cross, in the Church of Christ, Düren.

---

[54] *Ibid.*, p. 246, quoting Bucer's *Scripta Anglicana*, Basel, 1577, p. 457.
[55] Schwarz, *op. cit.*, pp. 35ff.

The Church of Christ (Christuskirche), Reformed, Düren, (Rhld.) Germany
Dr. Hentrich & Hans Heuser, architects

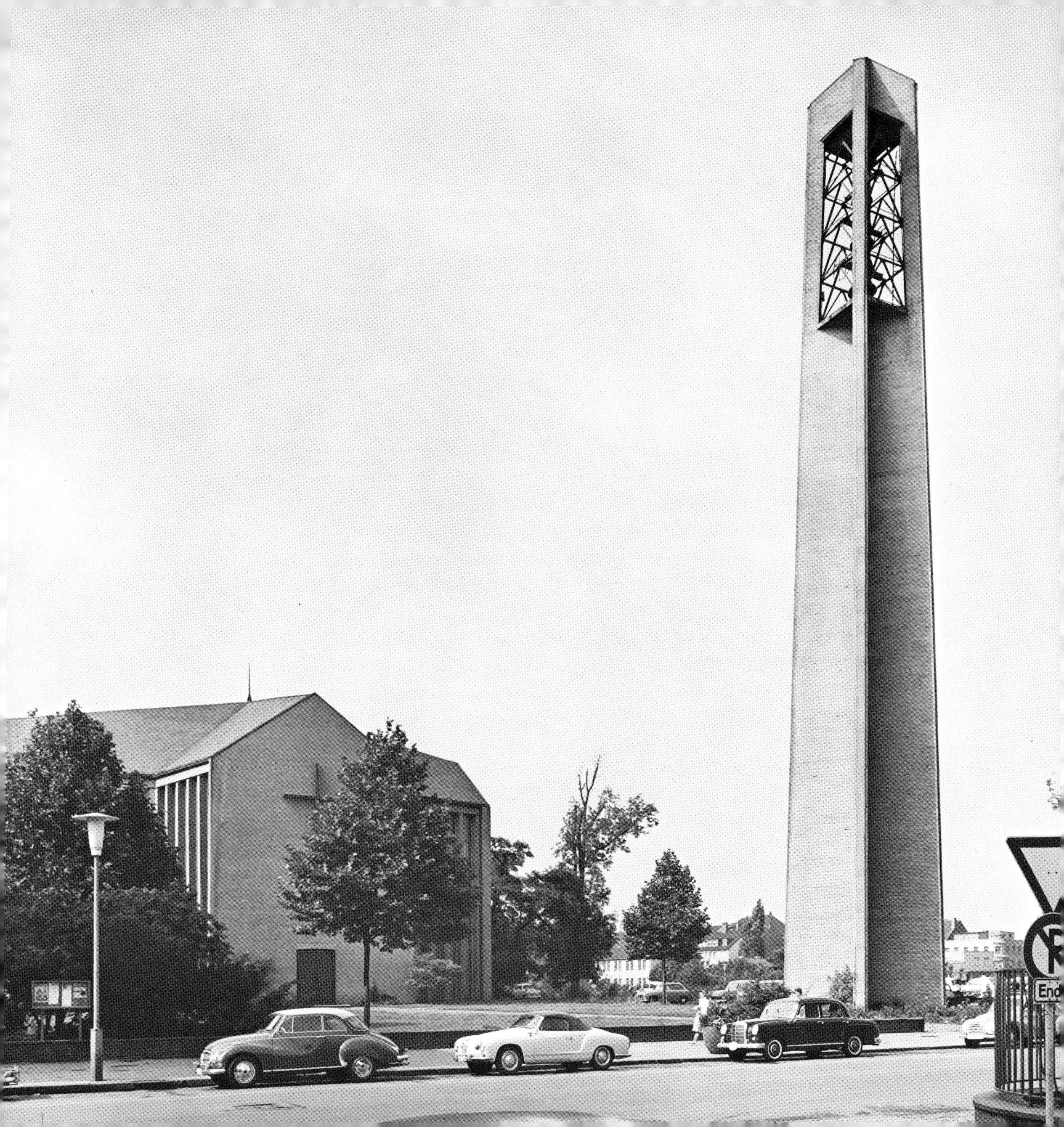

Entering the doors of this church to fellowship with Christ, one is reminded that one comes to Christ through the four Evangelists.

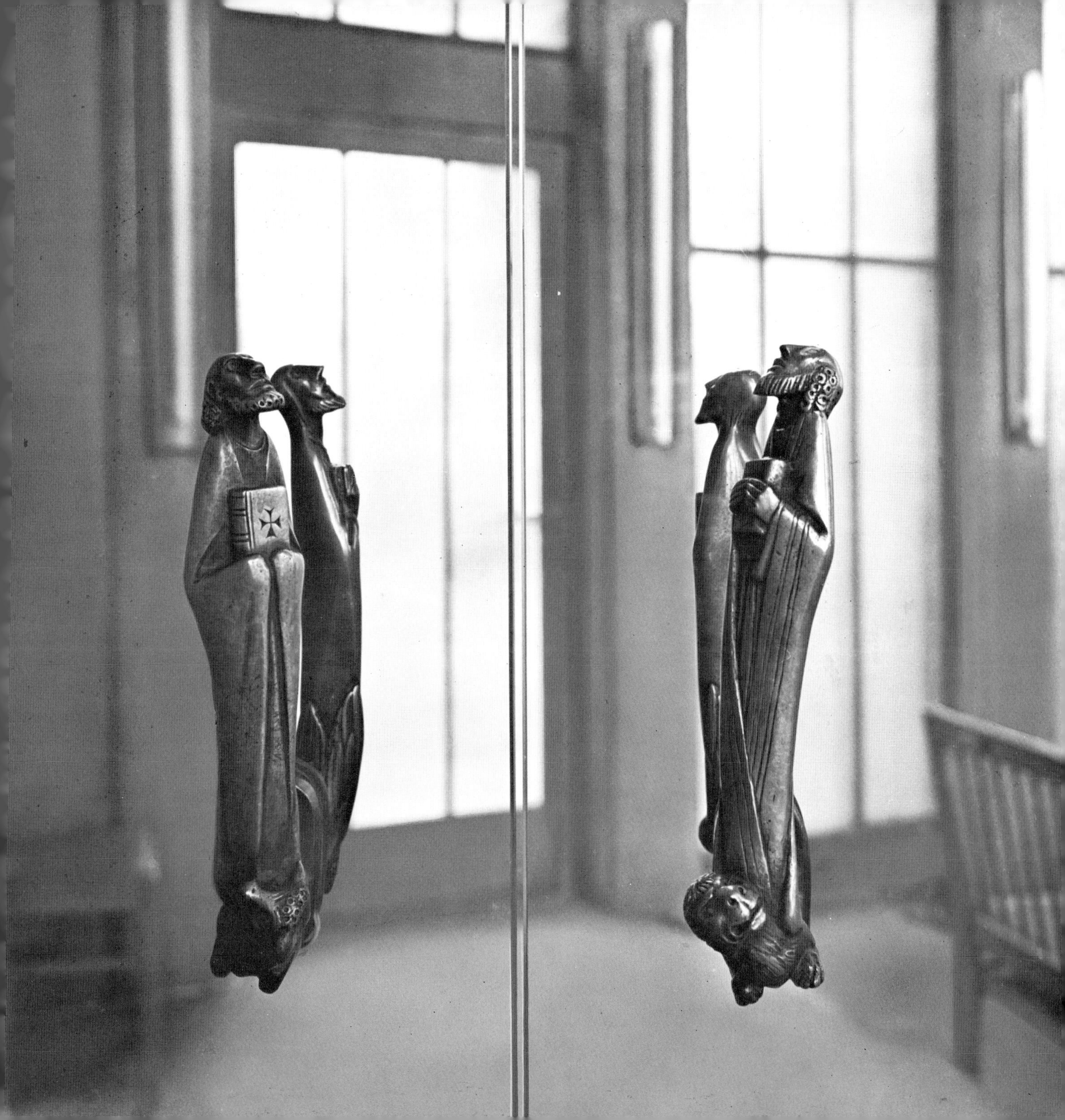

Organ by Willi Peter of Cologne—Mulheim

Positiv

Holzgedeckt	8
Flute douce	8
Quintade	8
Praestant	4
Rohrflöte	4
Oktave	2
Larigot	1⅓
Sesquialtera	2⅔, 1⅗
Scharf 4–5 ranks	1
Doppelkegelregal	8

Hauptwerk

Quintade	16
Prinzipal	8
Rohrgedeckt	8
Oktave	4
Blockflöte	4
Nasat	2⅔
Superoktave	2
Flachflöte	2
Mixtur 5–8 ranks	2
Scharfzimbel 3 ranks	⅓
Fagott	16
Trompete	8

Schwellwerk

Gedacktpommer	16
Holzprinzipal	8
Spitzflöte	8
Kleinprinzipal	4
Nachthorn	4
Querpfeife	2
Sifflöte	1
Obertöne	1⅓, ⅘, 4/7
Scharfmixtur 5–8 ranks	1⅓
Krummhorn	8
Trompete	4

Pedal

Prinzipalbass	16
Subbass	16
Oktavbass	8
Spitzgedeckt	8
Oktavbass	4
Holzflöte	4
Gemshorn	2
Hintersatz 6 ranks	4
Lieblich Posaune	32
Posaune	8
Basstrompete	8
Rohrschalmei	4

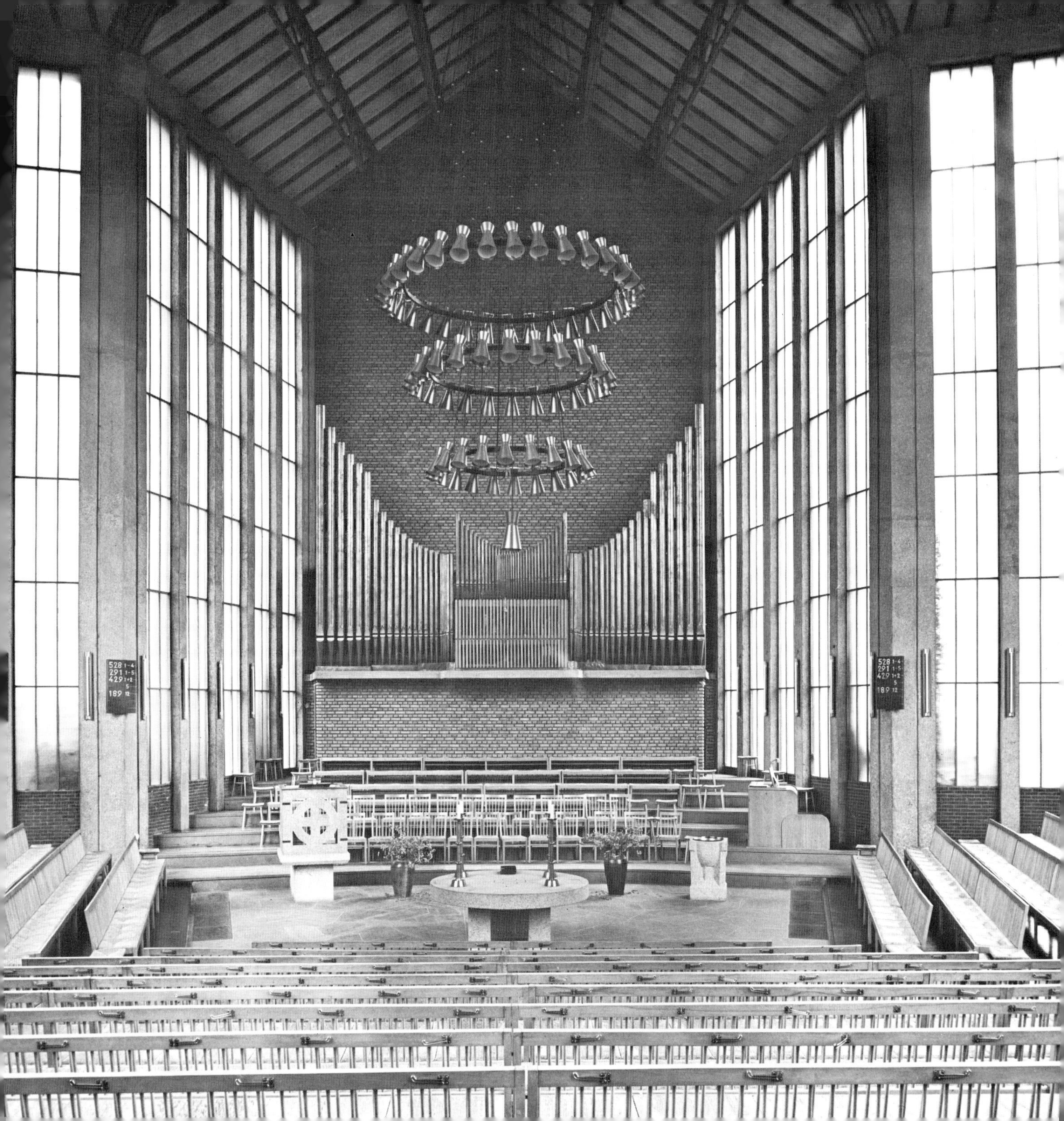
528 1-4
291 1-5
429 1+2
5
189 12

To effect visibility and accessibility, the simplest expedient is that of elevating the table while being careful not to create any barriers between the table and the people of God. Broad steps should be provided to invite easy access. Churches already illustrated in this volume that have used this simple expedient range from the ancient church at Kirchenthurnen (pp. 9–11) to the emergency post-war Grace Church (Gnadenkirche) at Frankfurt a/M (p. 17), The Bullinger Church (pp. 141–43), The Reformed Church at Bonigen (p. 145), the Church of St. Mark (Markuskirche) (pp. 173, 177), the Reformed Church, Gümligen (pp. 185, 187), and the two magnificent churches by Prof. Duintjer, The Church of the Cross (Kruiskerk), Amstelveen (pp. 95, 105) and The Church of the Resurrection (Opstandingskerk), Amsterdam-West (pp. 111, 119). As is quite obvious from these illustrations, the larger the church, the higher must be the elevation of the Lord's table. In not one of the churches illustrated does the visibility given the table detract from the importance of the pulpit. The architects in every case (albeit some more effectively than others) display the Reformed character of these churches by also emphasizing the preaching of the Word. Surely this simple expedient should be more widely used in our Reformed churches in America, that the table may not only be accessible, but also visible.

The criteria concerning the communion table have carried us this far: The Lord's table must look like a table and not an altar. The table must have the accouterments of a table and a supper, and not those of an altar, flower pedestal, or resting place for the offering plates. And this tablelike table, attired as a table, should be both accessible and visible. Would it now be possible in those congregations which are really willing to be Reformed, to go one step farther and return to the practice of physically using the communion table as a table? Would it be possible to return to the ancient practice of the early Church, as well as of most of the Reformed churches in prior centuries, in actually having the congregation of God gather around the table, there to partake? As a fourth criterion for the table let it be suggested that whenever possible

THE LORD'S TABLE SHOULD BE DESIGNED TO BE ACTUALLY USED AS A TABLE WITH THE COMMUNICANTS SEATED AROUND IT.

The participation of the Lord's people at the table is a practice to which exceptions can be found even in the early years of the Reformation. For example, taking Communion in the pews can be traced back to the Reformation church in Zurich, where under the leadership of Ulrich Zwingli a low doctrine of the Sacrament prevailed.[56] The practice was later followed by English nonconformists, for whom it meant obviating the necessity of kneeling to receive Communion. However, the practice for almost all other Reformed churches, both on the Continent and in Scotland, was to use the table as a table. George Hay gives specific examples of Scottish churches in which provision was made for long communion tables at which the people could sit.[57] This usage continued in the Scottish churches until the 19th century, when population pressures in many city churches made going forward to sit at table impractical for lack of space. These difficulties notwithstanding, the abandonment of the table for the convenience of partaking in the pews was roundly condemned by the General Assembly.[58] As space became more and more of a problem, one innovation was the folding communion pew, where there was provided "at the front of the church a block of seats with hinged backs and movable benches to each alternate row. These were so designed

---

[56] For a detailed and sympathetic treatment of Zwingli's liturgy, see Bard Thompson, ed., *Liturgies of the Western Church* (Cleveland: The World Publishing Co. [Living Age Books], 1961), pp. 141–156.

[57] Hay, *op. cit.,* pp. 33, 64, 85, 87, 90, 118, 124, 131, 132, 133, 181, and especially 126.

[58] *Ibid.,* p. 183.

that by the adjustment of a few bolts a number of long tables and flanking benches was quickly achieved."[59] (Interestingly enough, and as evidence of the widespread usage of the Lord's table as a table, there is a very similar arrangement in the St. Thomas Reformed Church in Charlotte Amalie, St. Thomas, the Virgin Islands, a church built in 1848.) However, while in Scotland the use of the table was almost completely lost in the 19th century, on the Continent, and especially in the Netherlands, the practice of using the Lord's table as such has continued in a very large number of churches and is now finding increasing favor.

Theologically, this usage of the table is very appropriate. The table speaks to us of our sustenance by the Lord, and of our union with Christ and therefore with the other members of the body of Christ. "So we, though many, are one body in Christ, and individually members one of another" (Romans 12:5). In Christ we are members of the same family, "sons of God," and may cry "Abba! Father!" (Romans 8:14,15). Thus it is fitting that as a family we should gather together about a table. Nichols and Trinterud observe that

> No other major Christian rite so stresses the sense of the church as the body of Christ as the Reformed communion. The gathering about the table as the new family of Christ speaks unforgettably of the company of the disciples at the beginning of Christian history and the Messianic Banquet at its end, while the passing of Christ's gifts from hand to hand declares that every believer is truly a minister of his fellows.[60]

This talk of "gathering about the table" need not be purely metaphorical, as it unfortunately is in almost all of our American churches. The Reformed

---

[59] *Ibid.,* pp. 182–83, see fig. 58. Examples of such an arrangement still exist at Dunfermline North Kirk, Tingwall, and Torphichen.
[60] *Op. cit.,* p. 15.

brethren in the Netherlands offer many examples of how literal participation at the Lord's table is effected. In The Church of the Cross (Kruiskerk), Amstelveen (pp. 95, 105), the table is extended for communion across the entire front of the church. In a similar fashion, in the Ark, in Slotervaart, the table is extended (pp. 153, 157–63) until it will seat forty-four. In the very small rural Reformed Church in Bant, in the Northeast Polder, the table is of such size that it can be used with very minor extensions.

A superb little church, built within an extremely small budget which was entirely the responsibility of the pioneers on this new land. The church fits in beautifully with the prevailing polder architecture of high, red-tiled roofs.

The Reformed Church (Hervormd), Bant, N. O. P., The Netherlands
Prof. ir. C. Wegener Sleeswijk & S. J. S. Wichers, architects

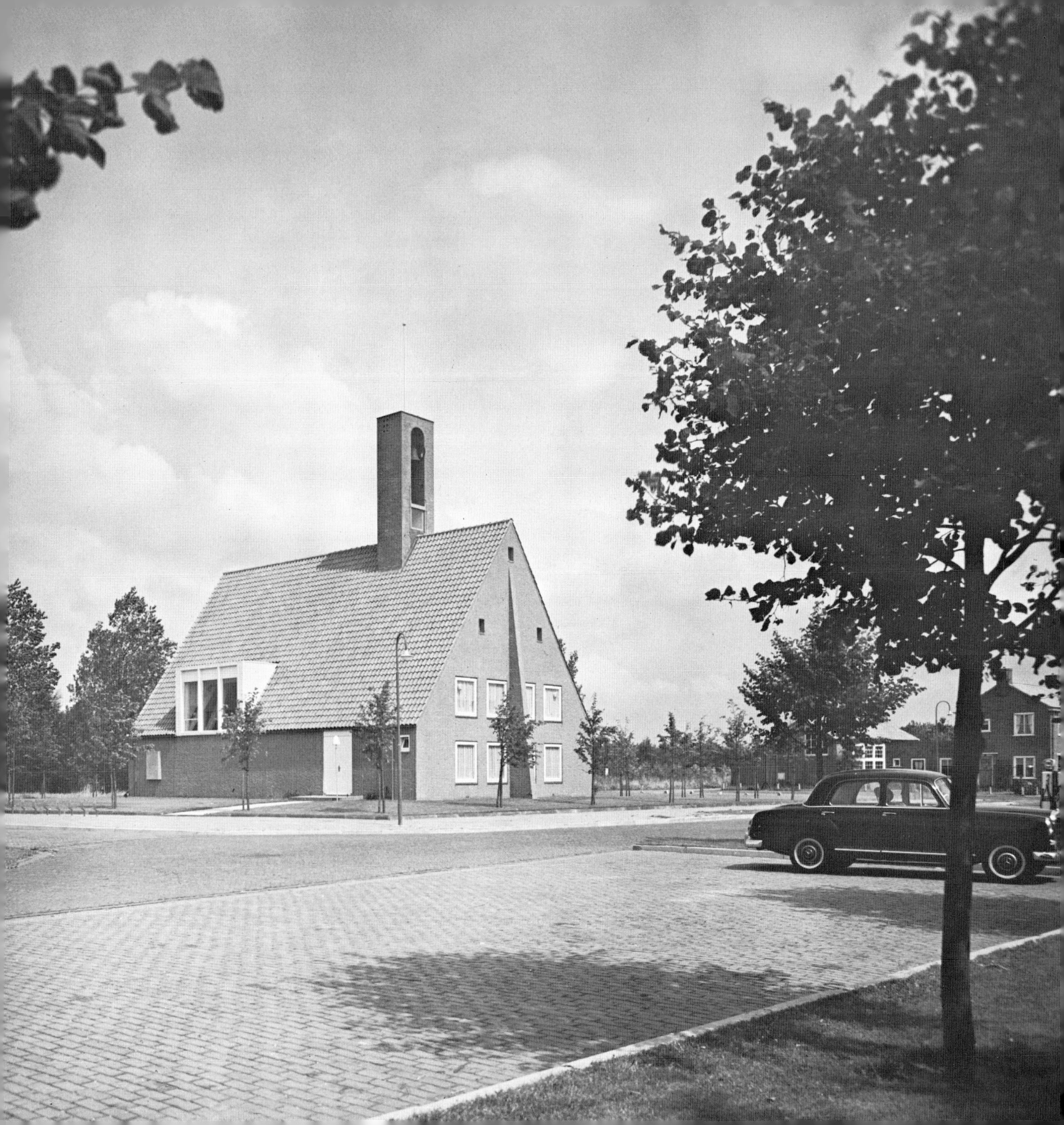

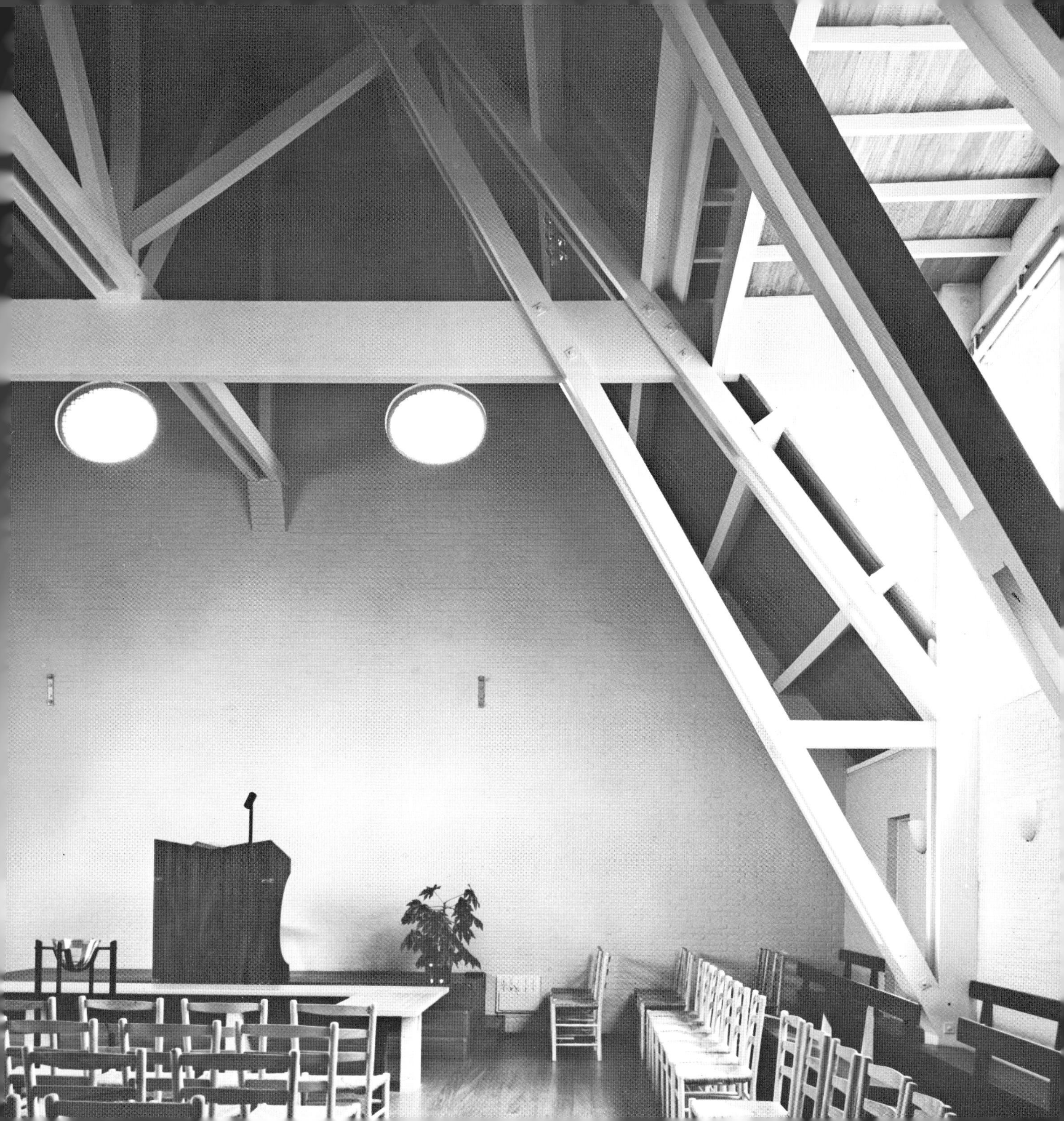

While the church and congregation are small, in a straightforward, simple way there is a clear and uninterrupted statement of the indispensability of the Word and the importance of the two Sacraments.

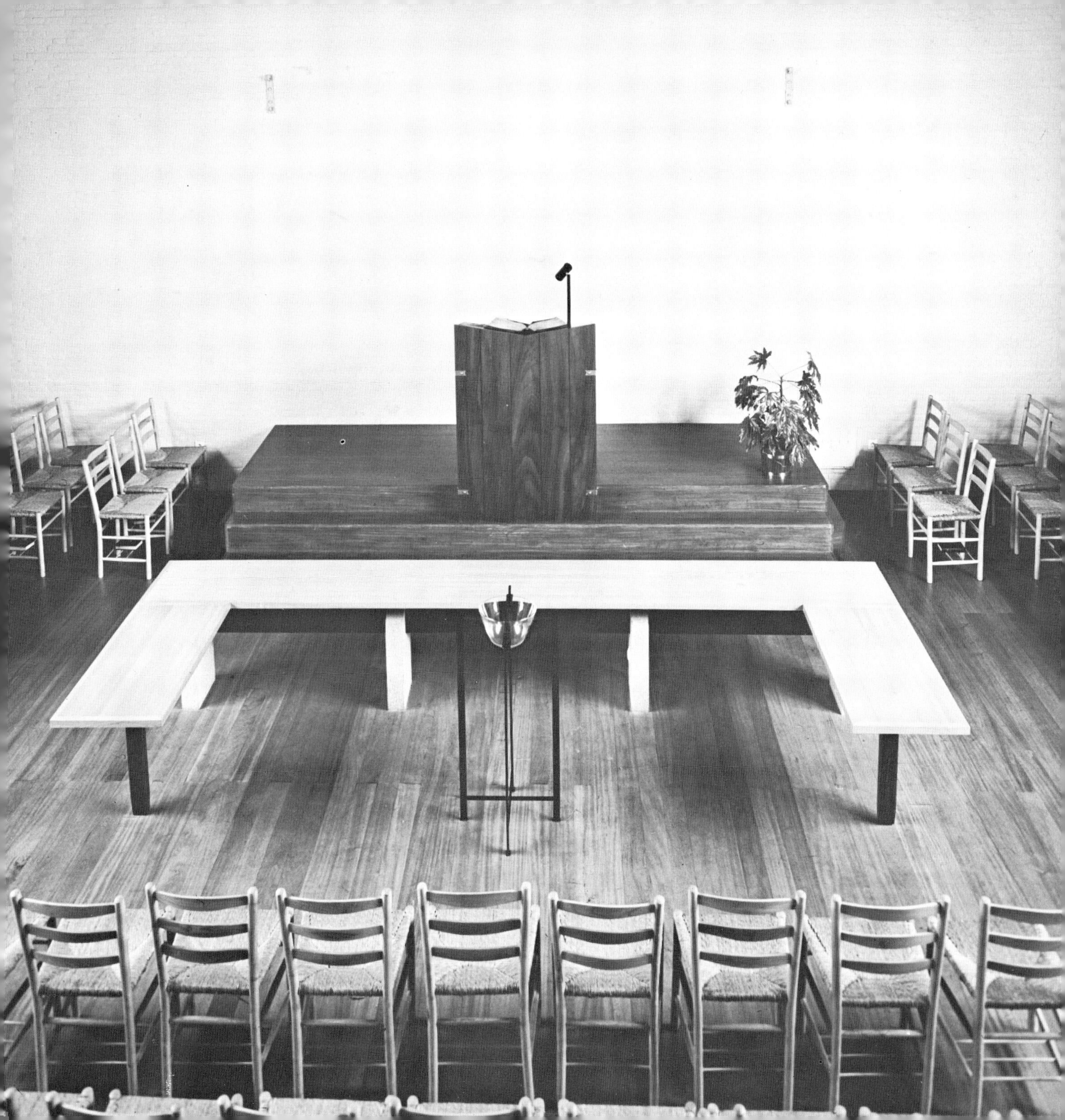

Positiv by Ahrend & Brunzema of Loga by Leer (Ostfriesland)

Gedackt   8
Praestant   4
Rohrflöte   4
Oktave   2
Scharf 2 ranks

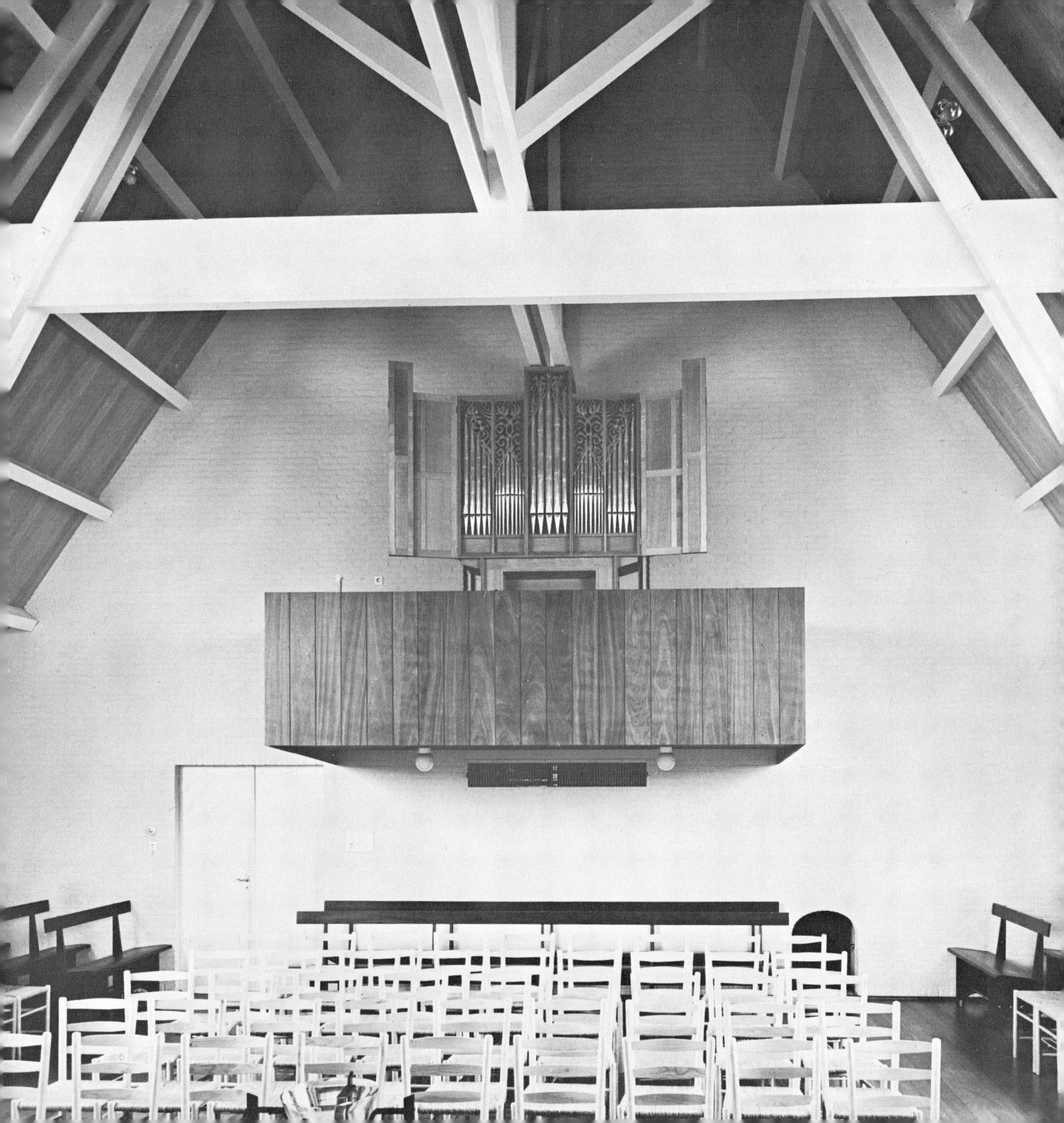

While the situation in Scotland in the early nineteenth century drove real tables out of their city churches, the Dutch, even in some of the newest city churches, are seeking to retain a table at which Christ's family may sit to partake.

Positiv (temporary) by Van Vulpen of Utrecht

Prestant	4
Holpijp	8
Roerfluit	4
Octaaf	2
Mixtuur 2 ranks	

The most striking feature of this church is the great Lord's Table at which a large number of the congregation can be accommodated at one time. Photo looking from the midst of the table toward the organ balcony at the west end of the church.

The Wilhelmina Church (Wilhelminakerk), Hervormd, The Hague, The Netherlands. Prof. ir. H. T. Zwiers, architect

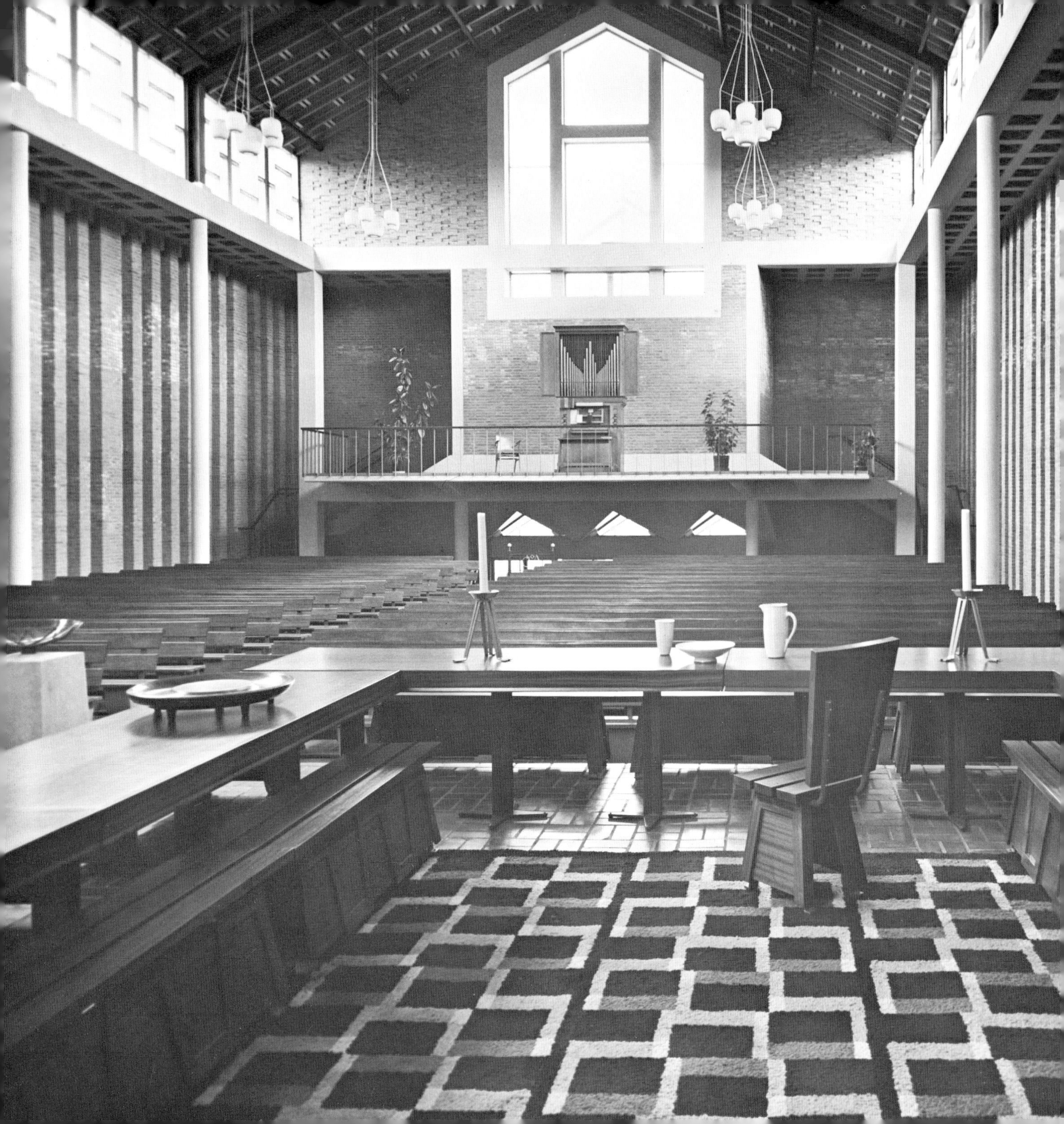

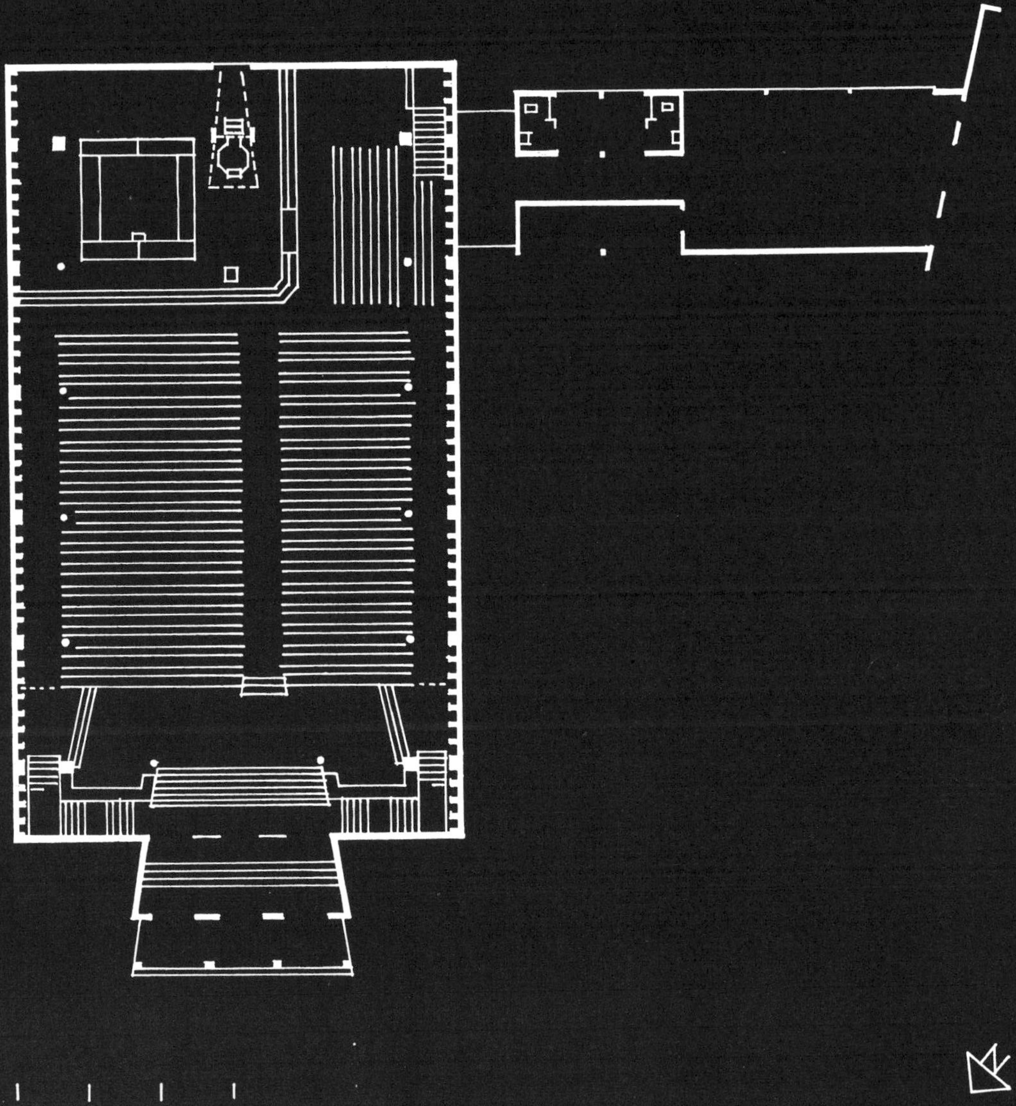

Font, pulpit and table

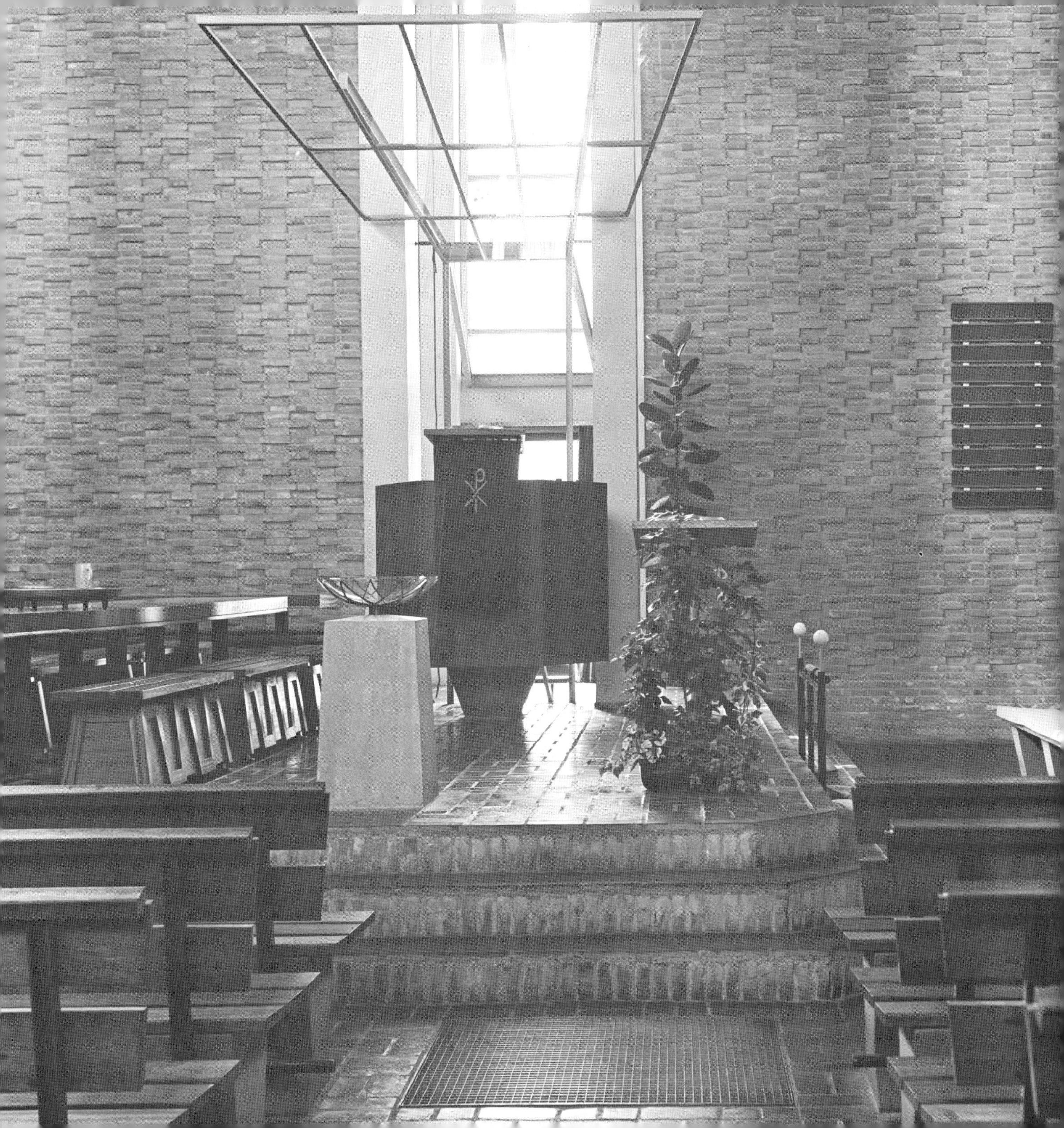

Both pulpit and lectern can be oriented toward the seats to the south which are used for weddings and other occasions when the number of people may be small. Thus there is a small chapel within the larger church which is completely usable as a part of the main sanctuary during regular worship services.

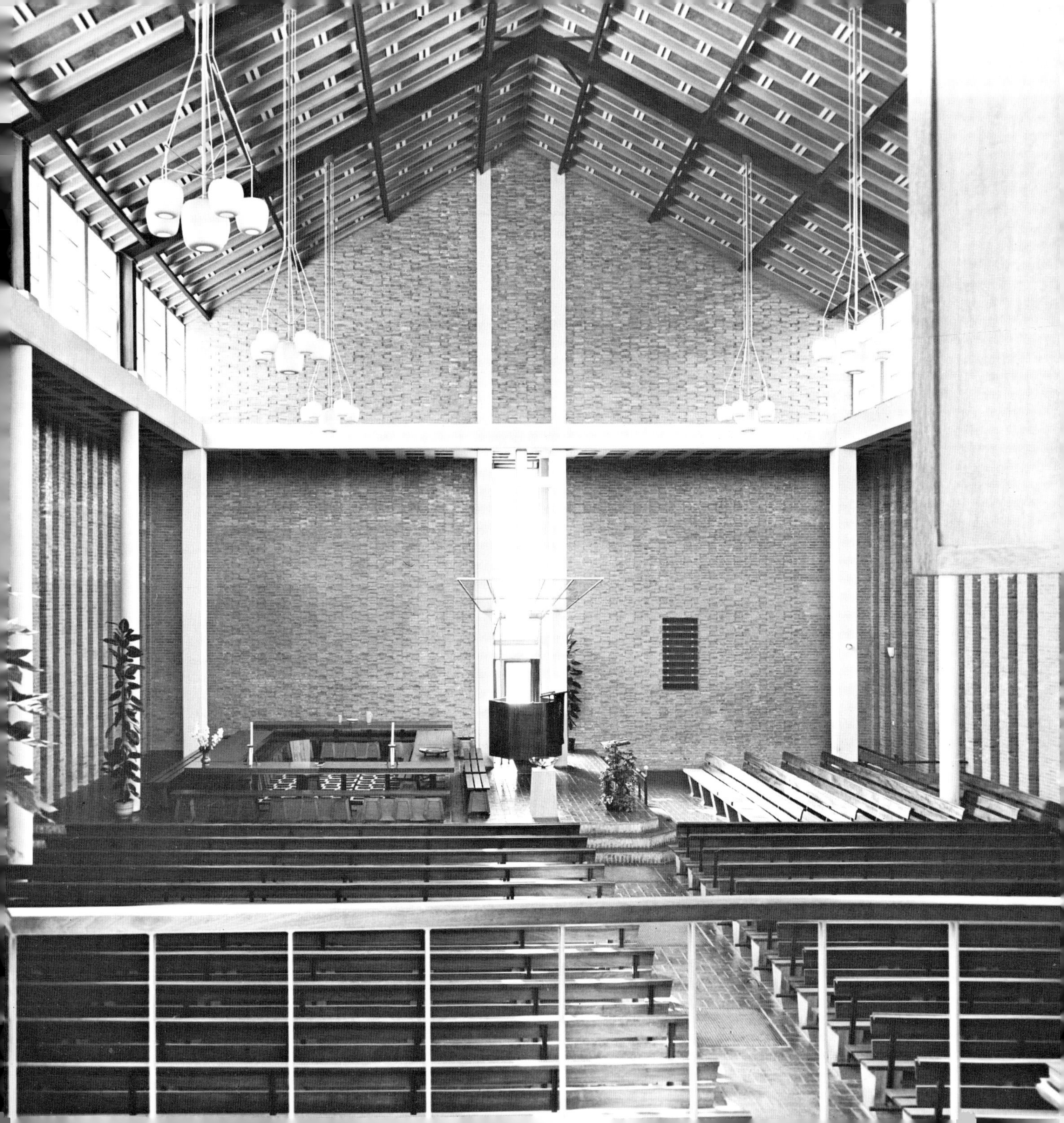

The glass sounding board as seen from the far side of the table

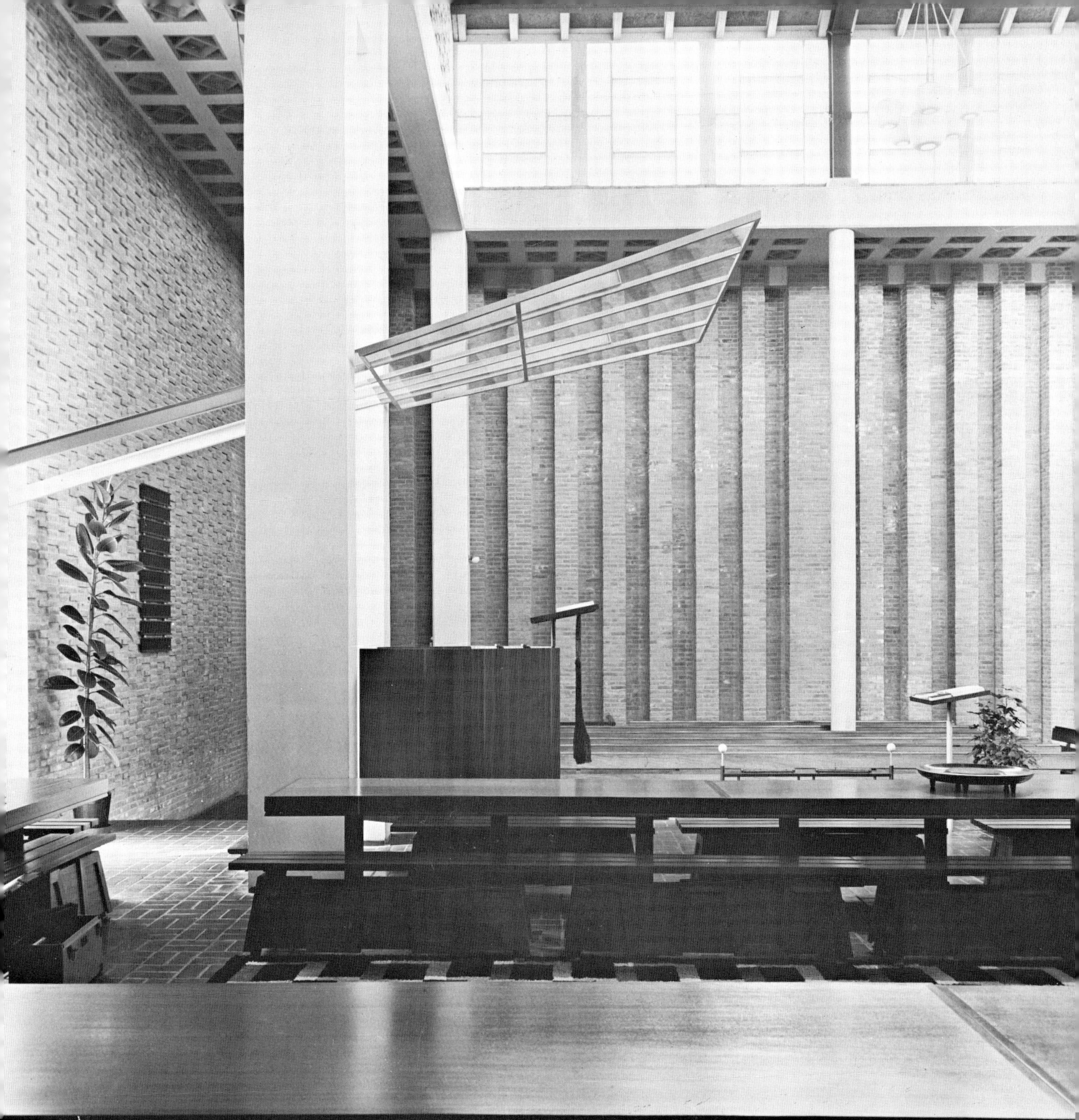

The possibility should also be considered of going to a separate room for the celebration of the Lord's Supper. This custom, as was earlier noted, began when the Reformers made very practical use of the choirs in the large Roman churches they inherited.[61] Few congregations today would be interested in a communion room so entirely separate that the table would be out of sight when the Supper was not being celebrated. But the ingenuity of the Dutch in creating new churches for Reformed worship seemingly knows no bounds, for they have given us at once "separate" rooms and very visible and accessible tables as well.

Something of this concept of a separate room is apparent in the Wilhelminakerk (pp. 241–49), where, although the table is completely within the main room of the church, the square formed by the table, with the added touch of a rug within the square, definitely imparts the feeling of a separate room despite the absence of walls.

This concept has been carried a step further in the wonderful Immanuel Church, in Delft. While the table is placed behind the pulpit, even as the pulpit is placed behind the baptismal font, the size and shape of each is such that, while standing in suitable theological progression, they neither hide nor compete with one another (even with a pulpit directly in front of it, hiding a table large enough to seat seventy people is rather difficult). If the form and material used for the font is not immediately apparent, it becomes a more integral part of the total church after one has considered the ceiling/roof structure. On the exterior, the building bears the "chi rho" (Christ-King) above the entrance, while at the peak of the roof, the weather vane assumes the form of a fish, a reminder of the early Christian symbol (the Greek acrostic which spelled fish was derived from "Jesus Christ, God's Son, Savior"). With the exception of these meaningful symbols, those who think

---

[61] E.g., St. Bavo Church, Haarlem (pp. 87, 89ff).

of churches in terms of "style" will find little of comfort, but the exterior houses a congregation whose architecture marks them indelibly as a part of the Church of Jesus Christ reformed according to the Word of God.

Immanuel Church (Immanuëlkerk), Gereformeerd, Delft, The Netherlands
Prof. F. A. Eschauzier, Frits Eschauzier, Fons van den Berg, & Paul de Vletter, architects

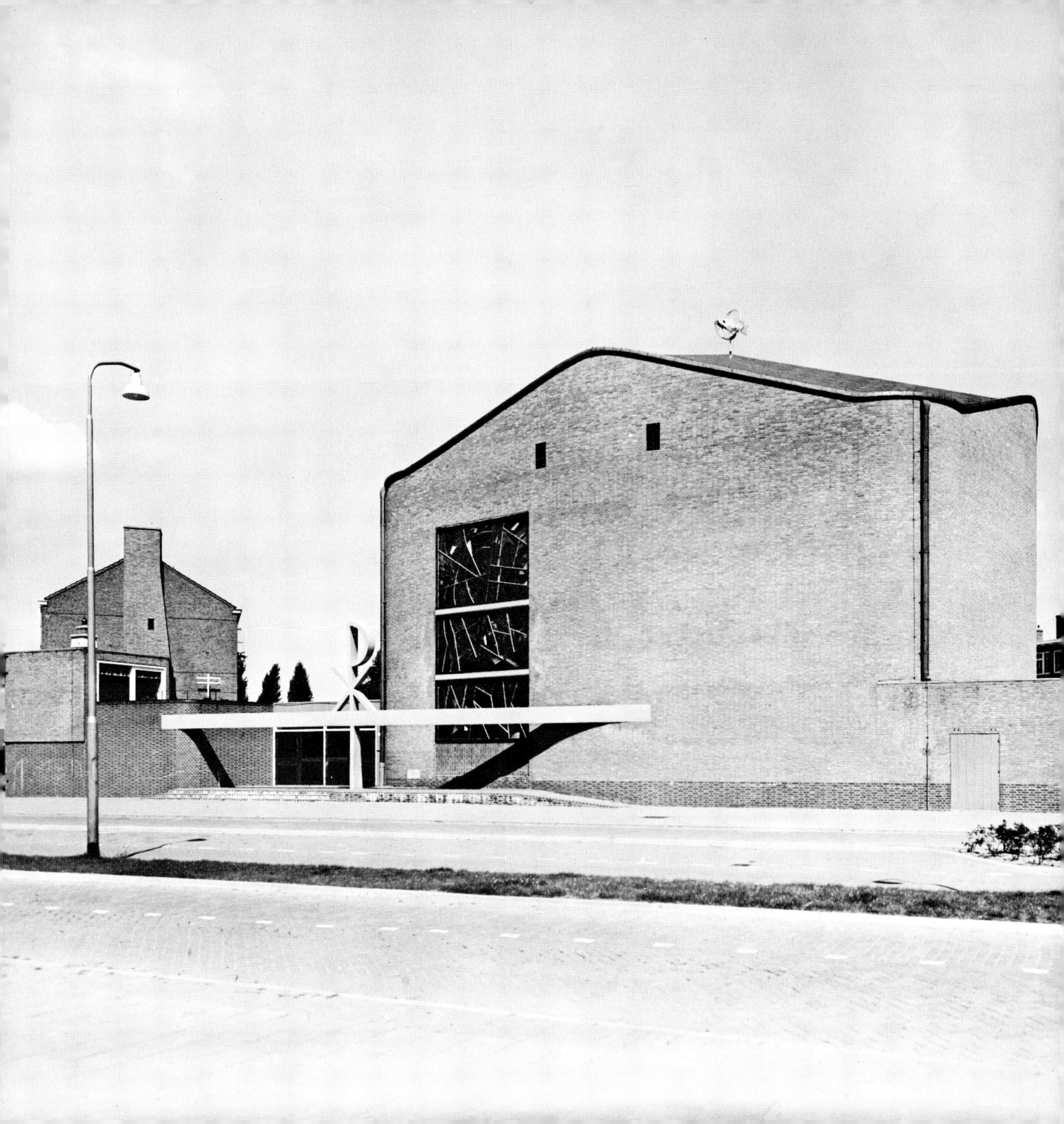

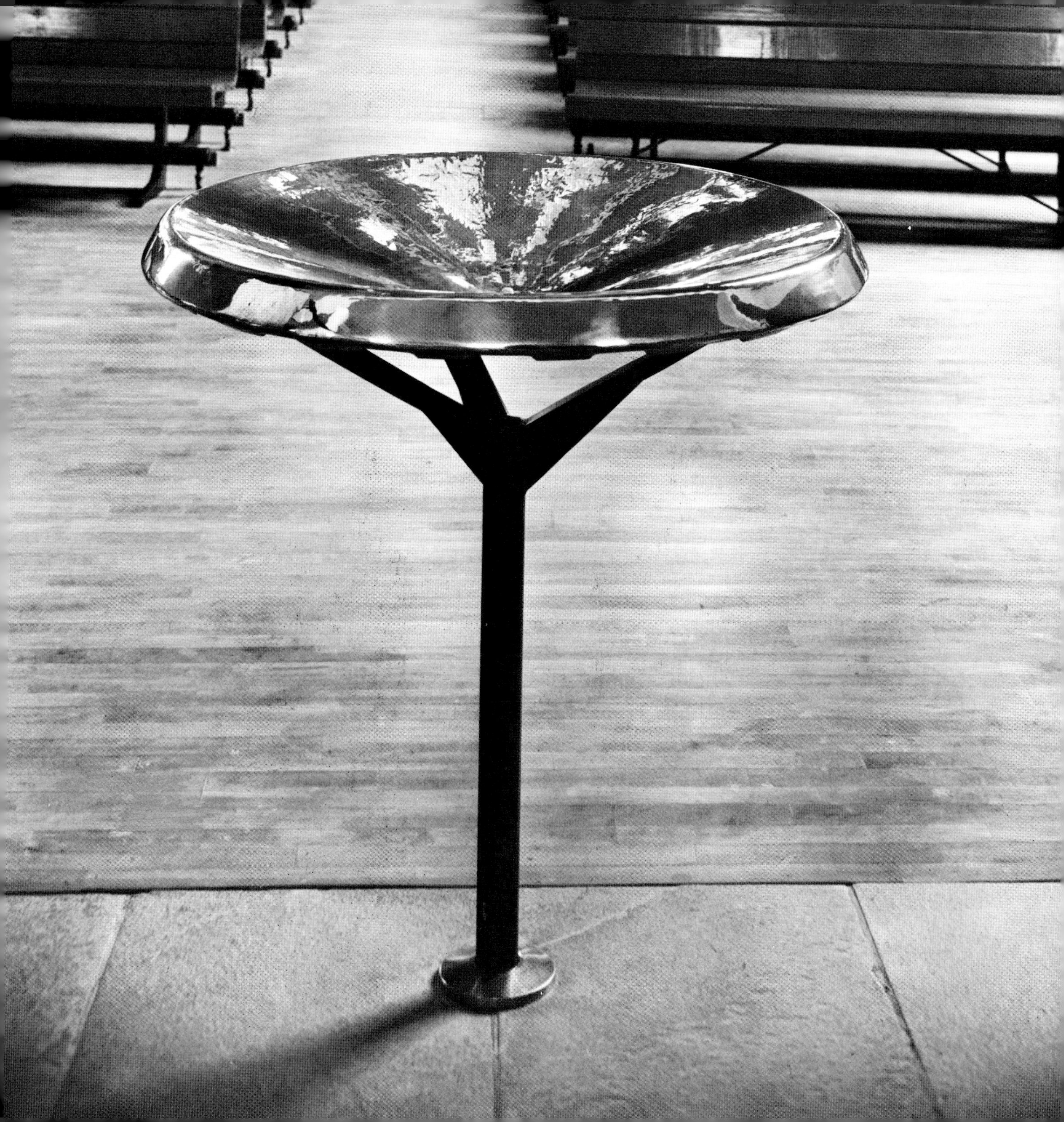

Table, pulpit, and font, without any applied symbols, are in themselves forceful symbols of Christ's relationship to his people.

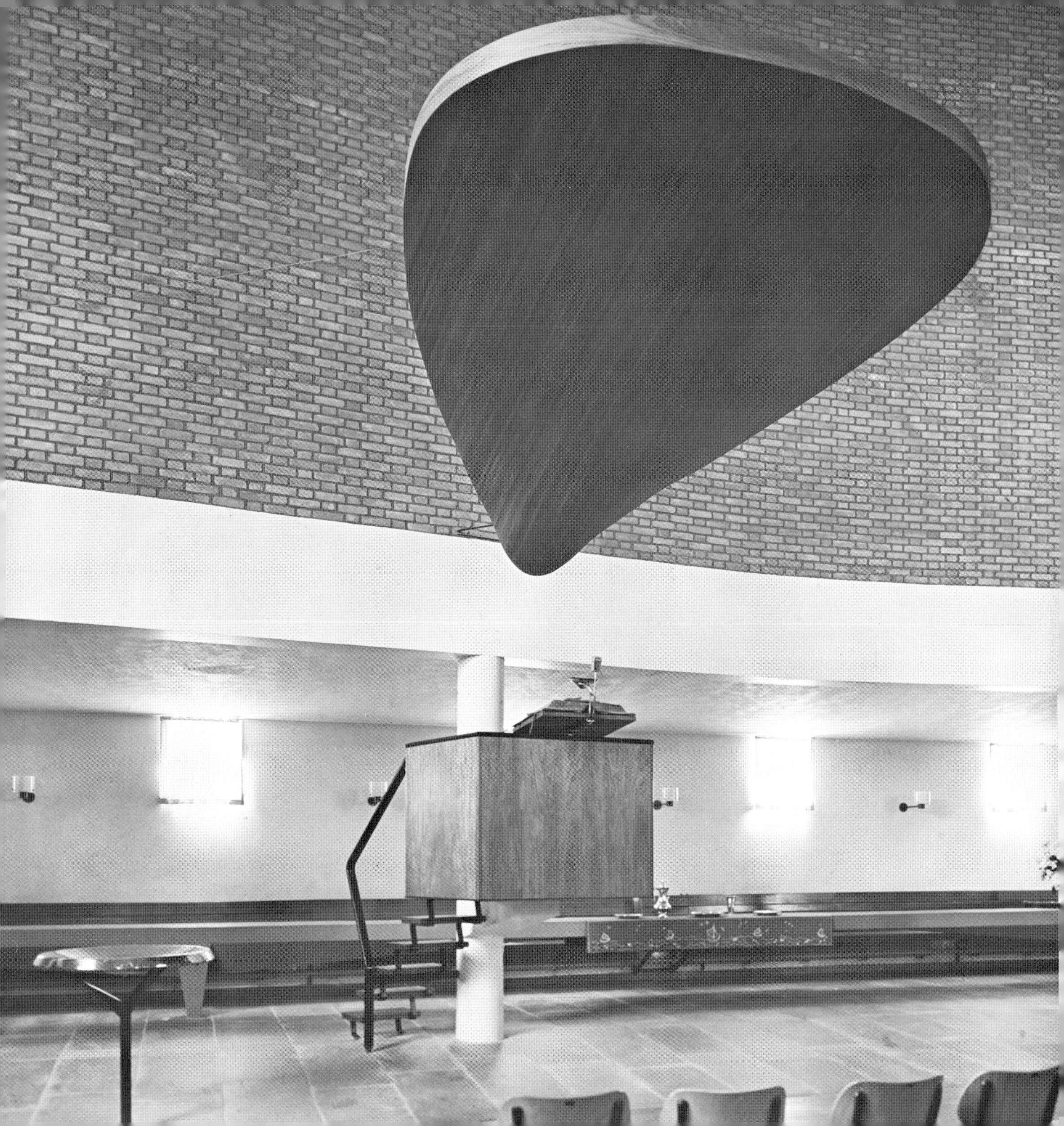

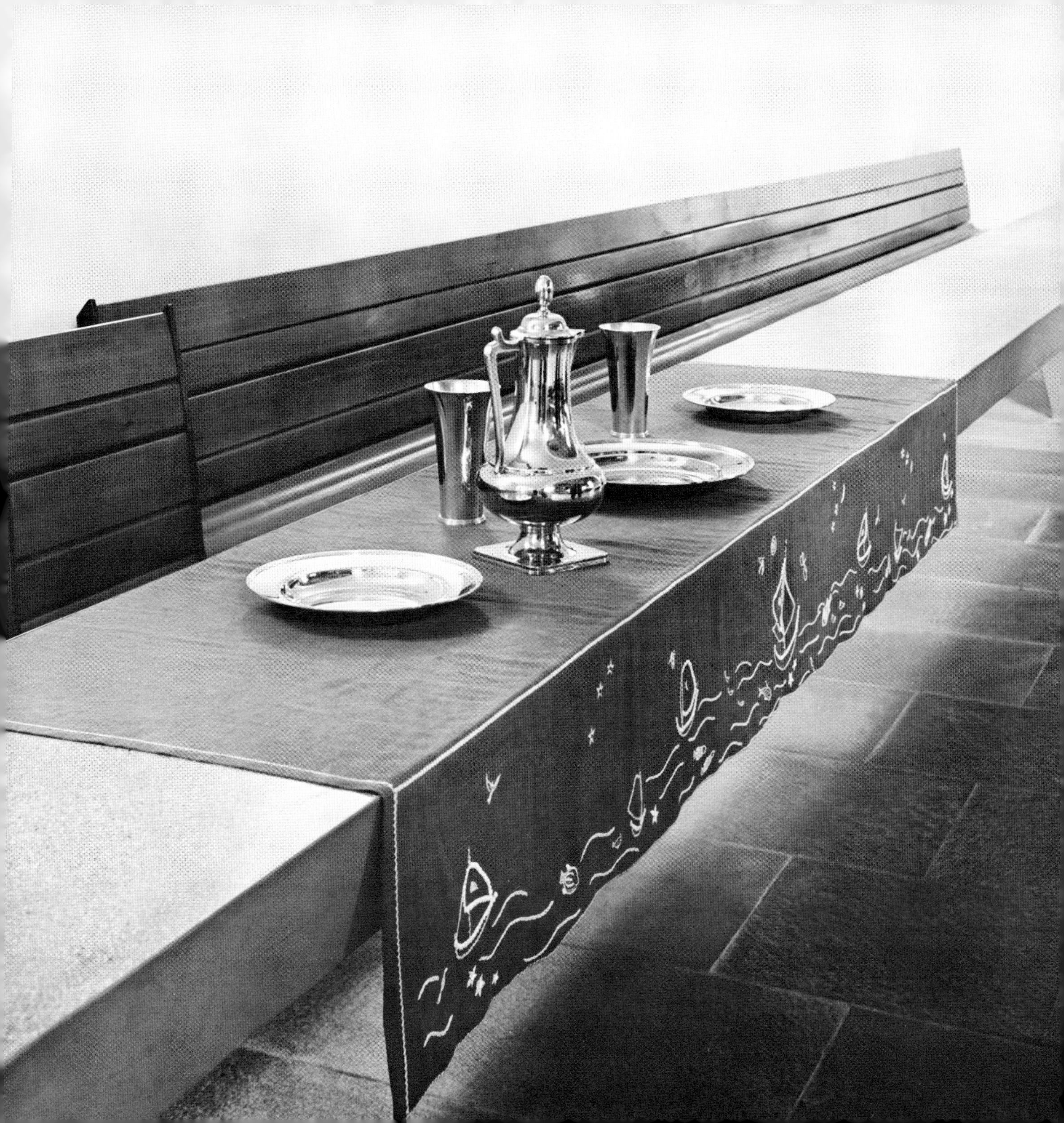

For the celebration of the Lord's Supper, the table, forty-five feet long and seating seventy, is covered with white table linen.

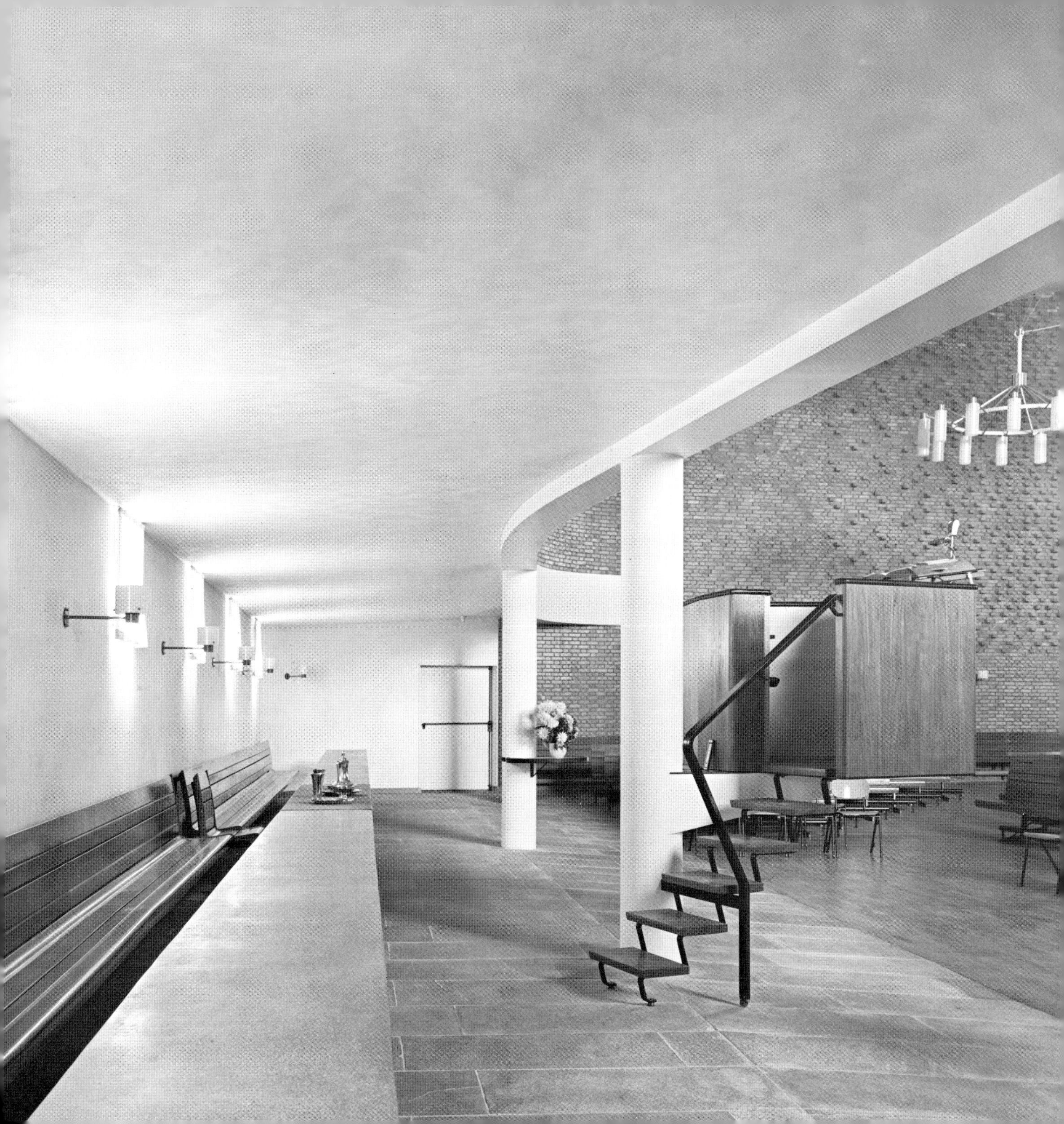

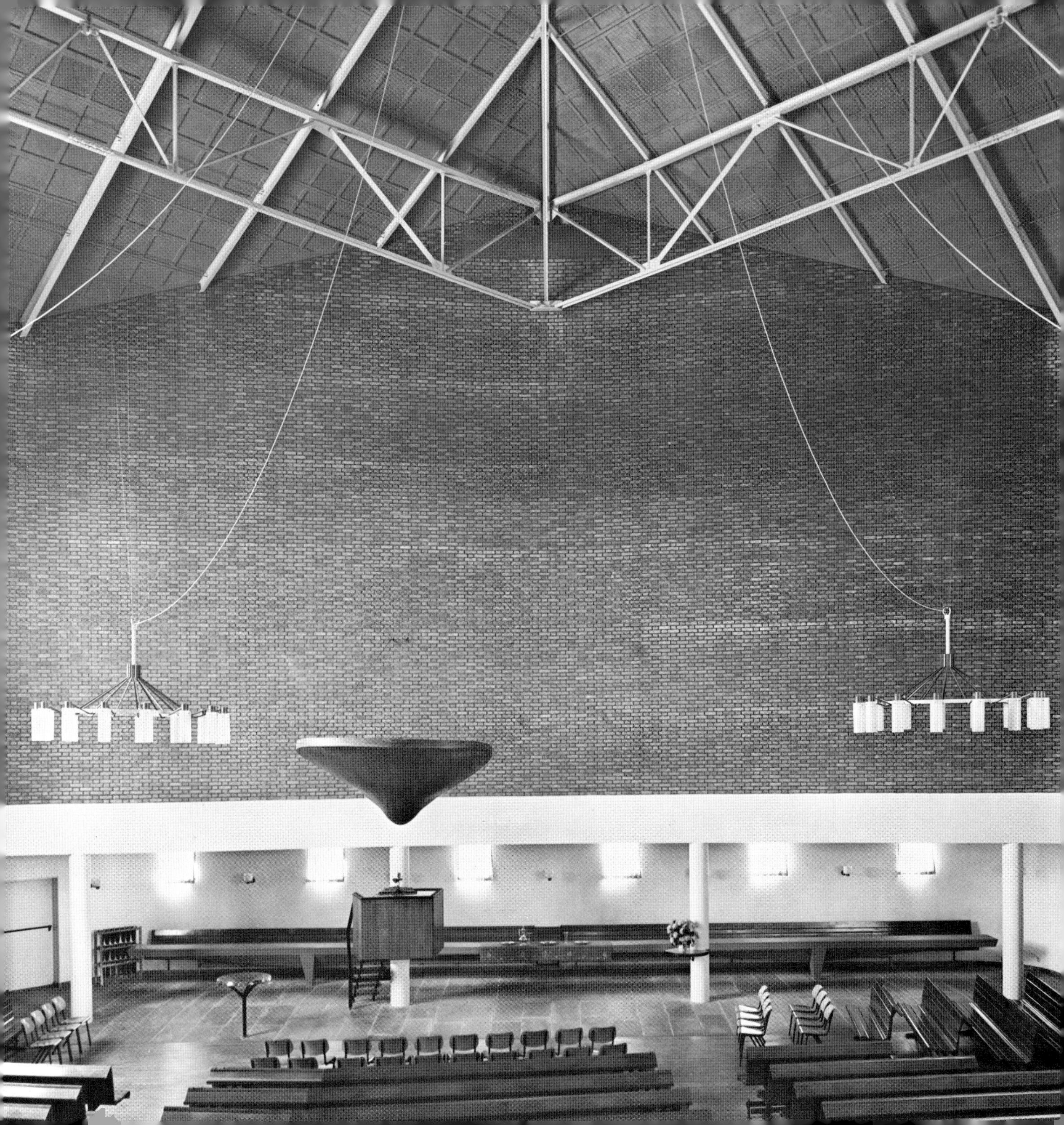

The concept of a separate communion room has been carried one step further by Architect K. L. Sijmons Dzn. of Zanstra, Giesen and Sijmons, in the Church of the Advent, in Loosduinen, a suburb of The Hague. Whether or not there are many architects able to design a separate communion room that stands in such significant relationship to the sanctuary is of course as problematical as to whether or not there are many congregations willing to spend the extra money needed for this separate room. But because the architectural environment in this country seems all too often limited to a choice between warmed-over Medieval Gothic with a split chancel and east-wall altar, or a nearly invisible little table down on the floor underneath the pulpit, flowers, and offering plates, thorough consideration of the fruitful work of these Dutch architects and theologians is certainly in order. In the meantime we await the design of a church such as that suggested by Prof. Carl H. Droppers, in which the separate communion room will be placed on a level six or eight feet above that of the congregation, with at least one table set near enough to the edge of this room so that its purpose is evident. And perhaps this communion room can be so designed that while part of the congregation considers its participation in the Supper by the singing of hymns and the reading of Scripture, others ascend to the upper room to partake in faith of Christ.[62]

---

[62] The *Book of Common Order* of the Scottish Reformation ordered that "the whole history of Christ's passion" be read during the Lord's Supper. W. D. Maxwell, *Concerning Worship* (London: Oxford University Press, 1948), p. 20.

The Church of the Advent (Adventskerk), Hervormd, The Hague-Loosduinen
The architectural firm of Zanstra, Giesen, & Sijmons, with design and execution by K. L. Sijmons Dzn., architect

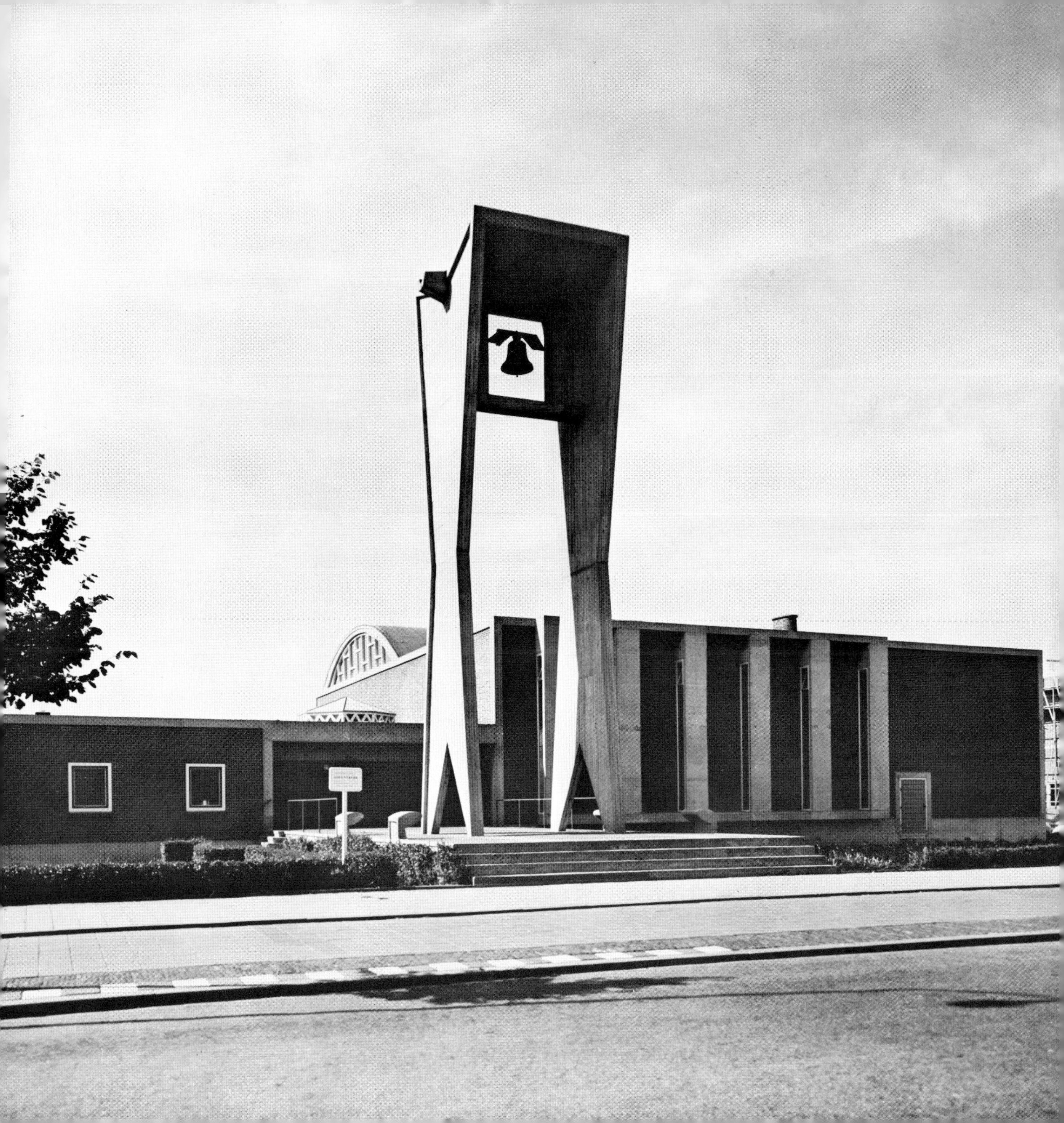

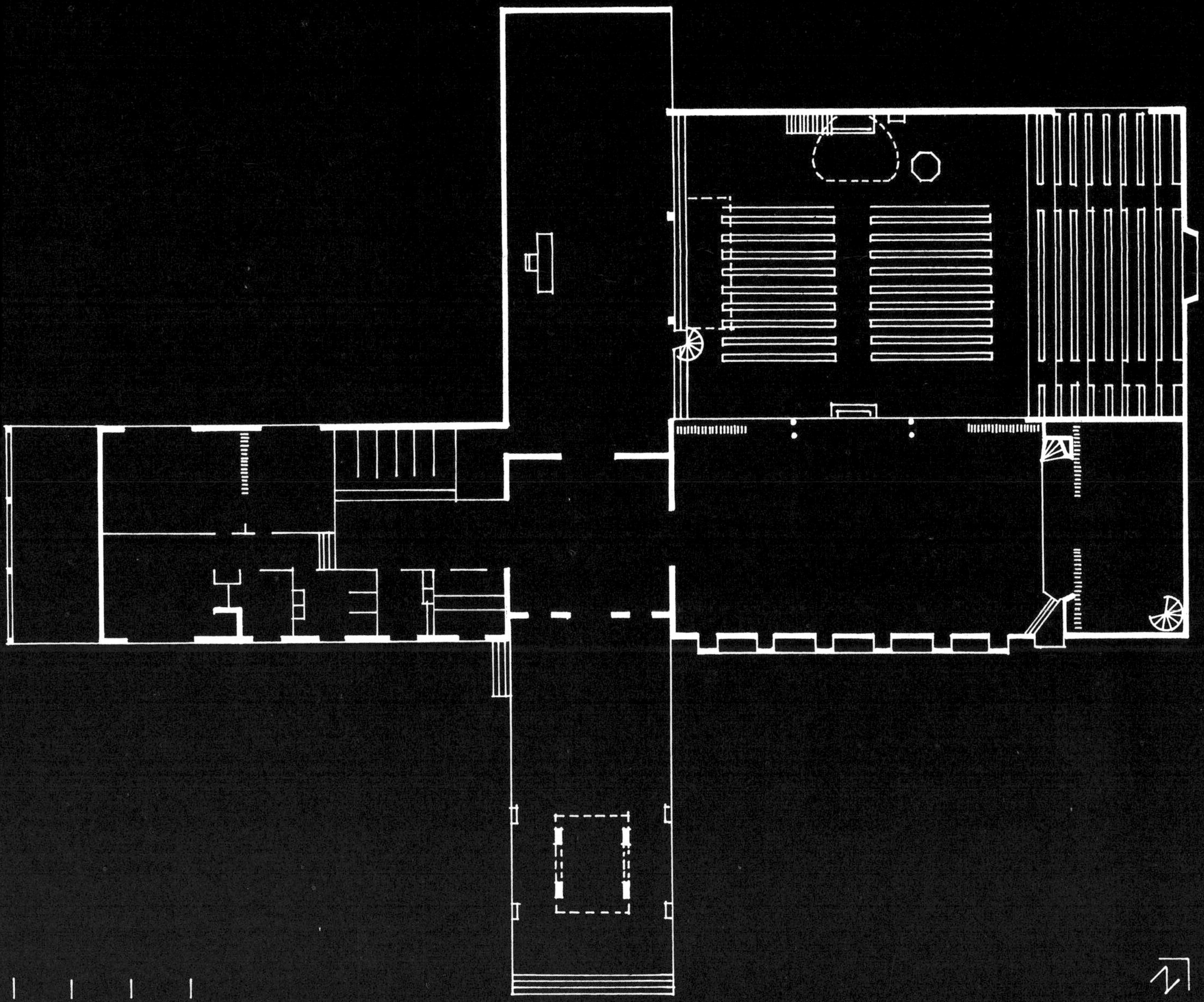

Organ by W. van Leeuwen of Leiderdorp

Hoofdwerk

Prestant	8
Roerfluit	8
Octaaf	4
Sesquialter 3 ranks	
Mixtuur 4–6 ranks	

Borstwerk

Spitsgedekt	8
Speelfluit	4
Prestant	2
Nasard	1½
Schalmei	8

Pedaal

Subbas	16
Prestant	8
Roerfluit	8
Octaaf	4
Mixtuur 4–5 ranks	

With all of its wonderful aspects, The Church of the Advent also has a very standard—and very useful—feature of Dutch churches: an overflow room which while it is usually used for services, can also be shut off from the sanctuary for the double purpose of reducing the seating capacity of the main church room (in this case 432), and providing meeting space for other than distinctly worship purposes. So skillfully is this space designed in this church, as in many others, that it is not nearly so much "overflow" space as a part of the sanctuary that can be temporarily set aside for other purposes. The savings achieved in such double usage more than compensates for the generous expenditure of space in providing a separate communion room (avondmaalsruimte).

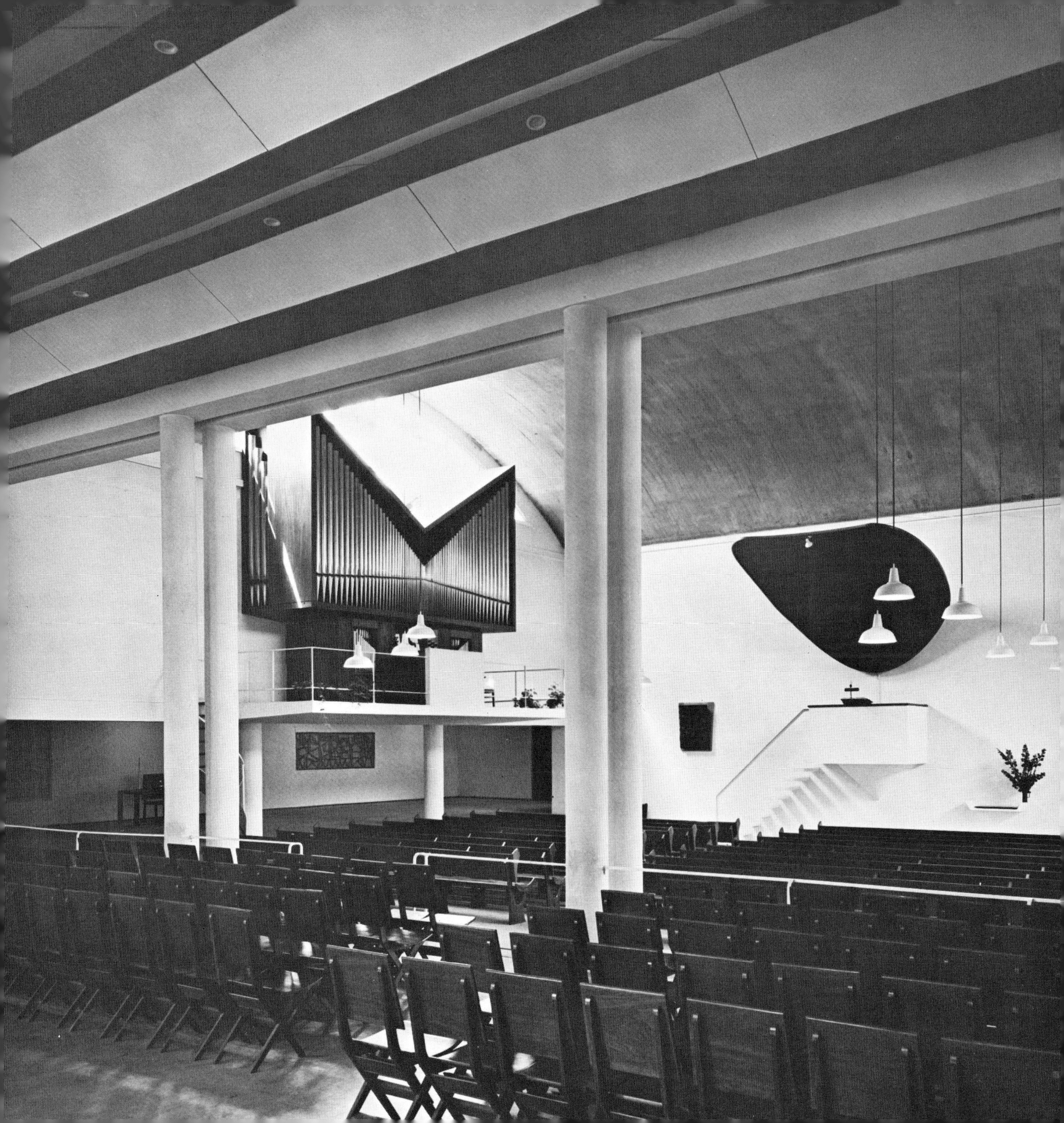

The pulpit is at once a positive and elegant statement, and near it is a special shelf, in view of the entire congregation, where the offerings are to be placed.

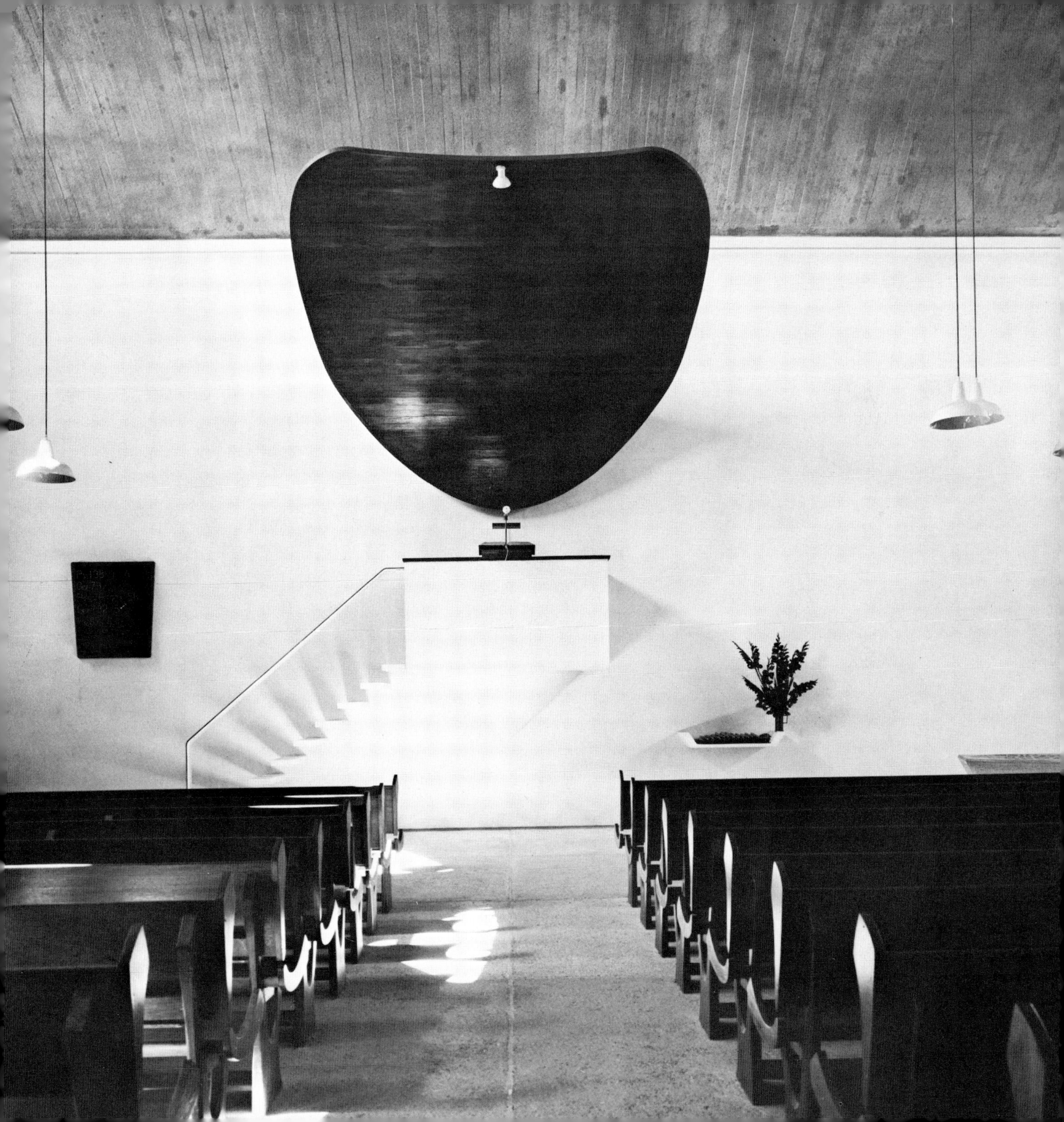

The shelf for the "zakjes" also doubles as a proper place to offer the beauty of the flowers.

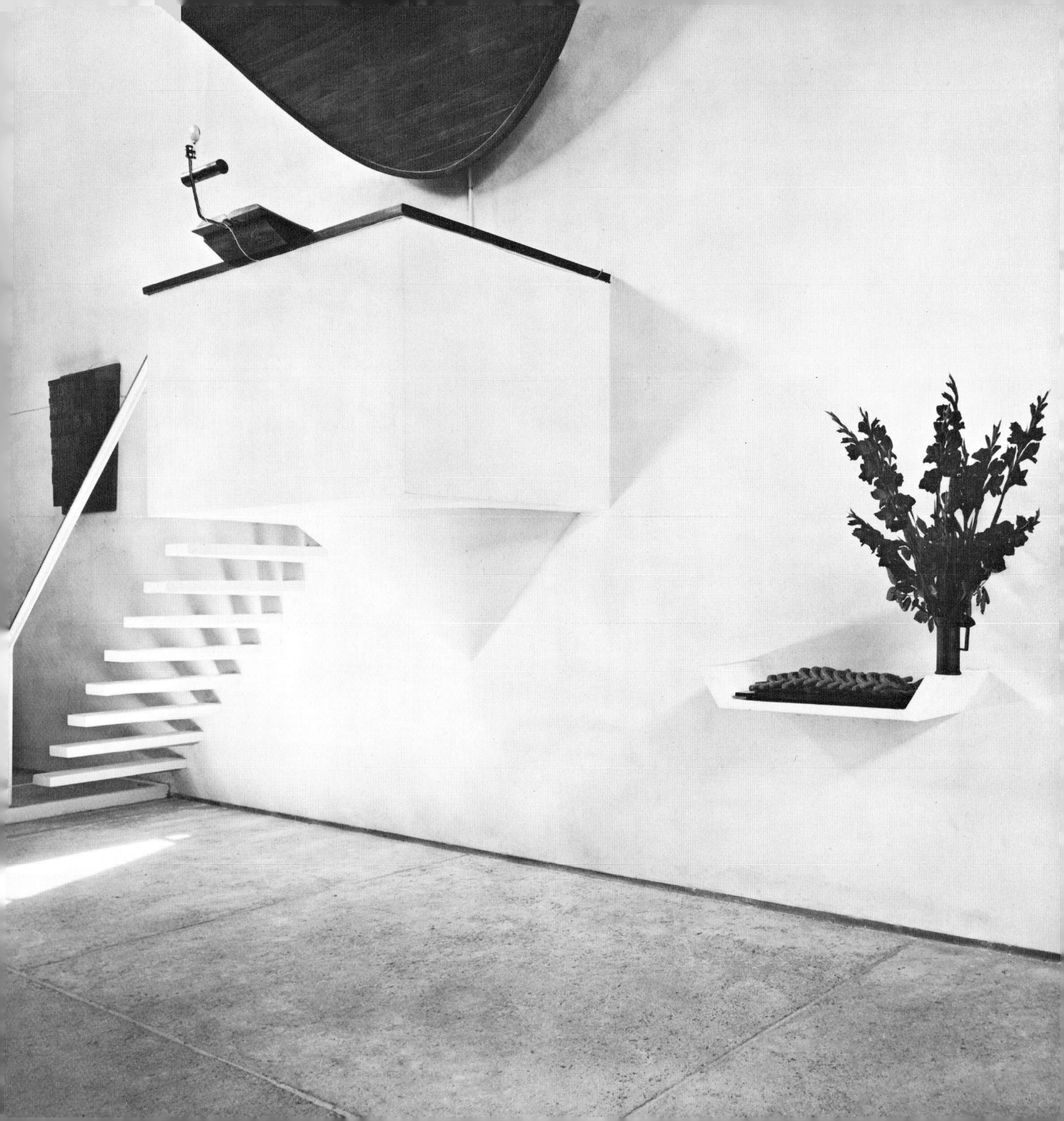

The massive stone baptismal font is an adequate statement even in a church that devotes an entire room to the Lord's Supper. It is five feet across, with a shallow bowl capable of sending the sound of splashing water throughout the entire church. It is well liked by everyone but the sexton, who must fill it with three pails of hot water and two of cold water for every service of Baptism.

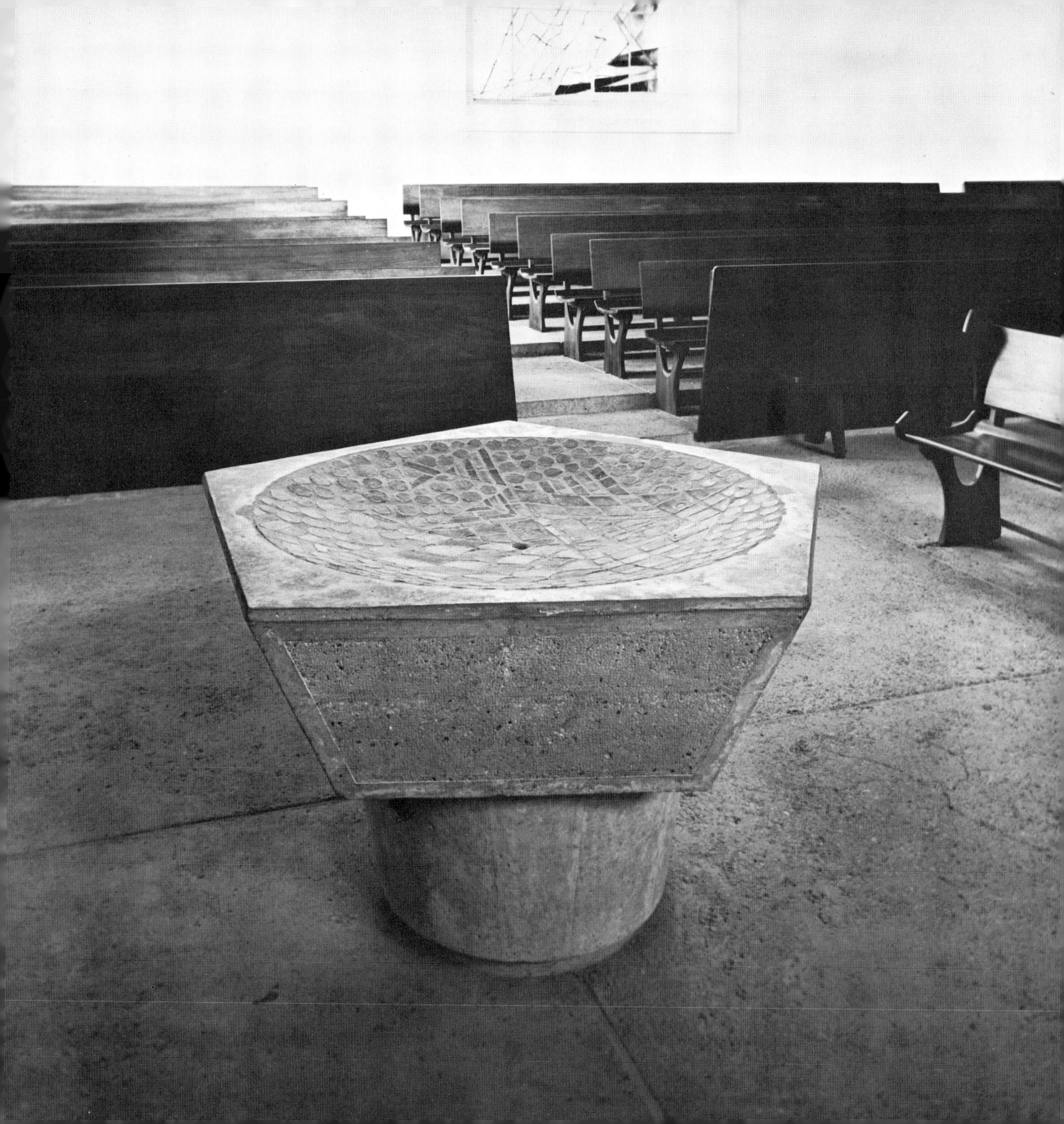

Visible at all times from the sanctuary, the Communion room is reserved entirely for communion usage. Between celebrations of the Lord's Supper, a single table and chair occupy the room as symbols of the supper. To celebrate the supper the room is filled with tables.

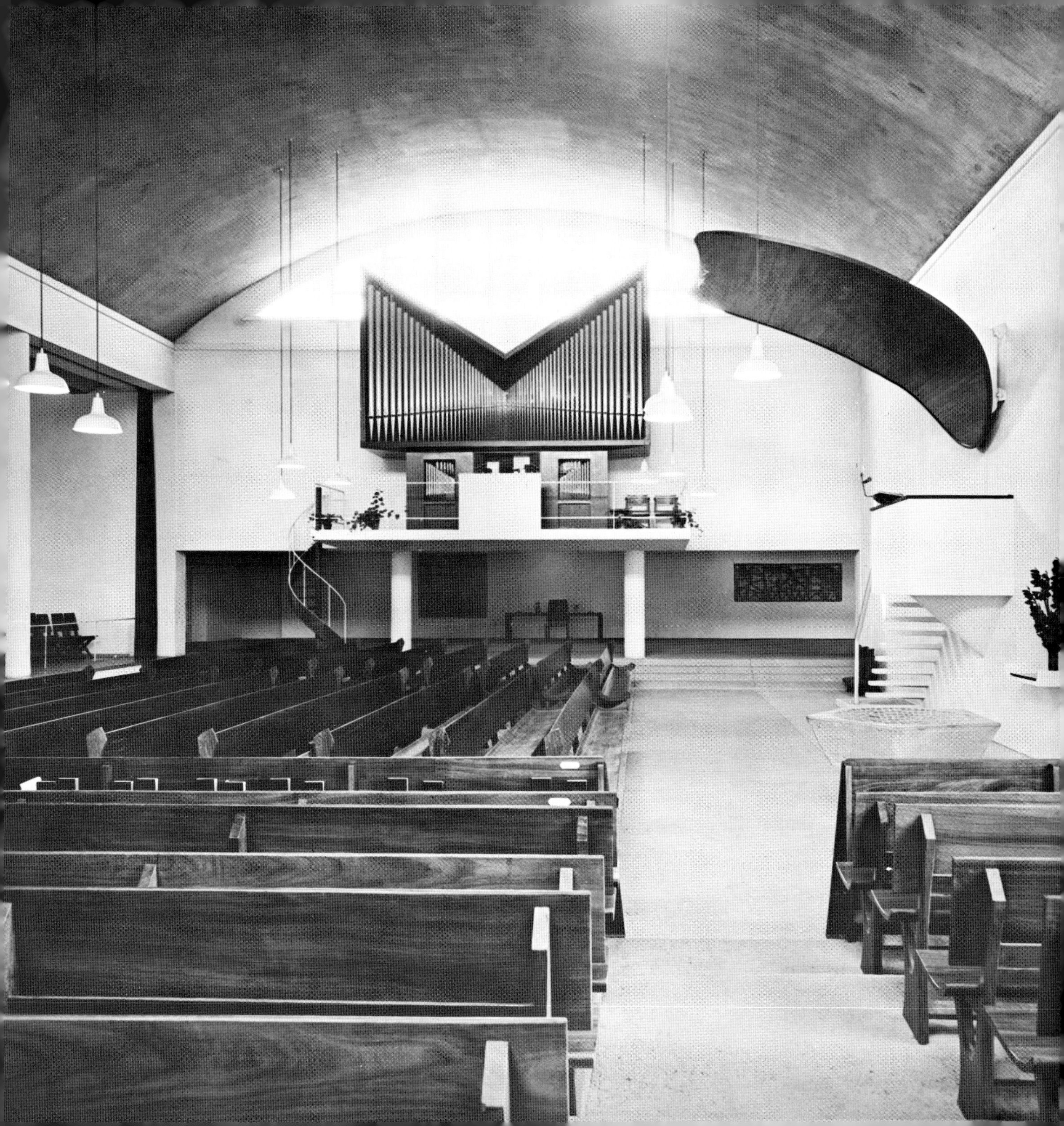

The Communion room

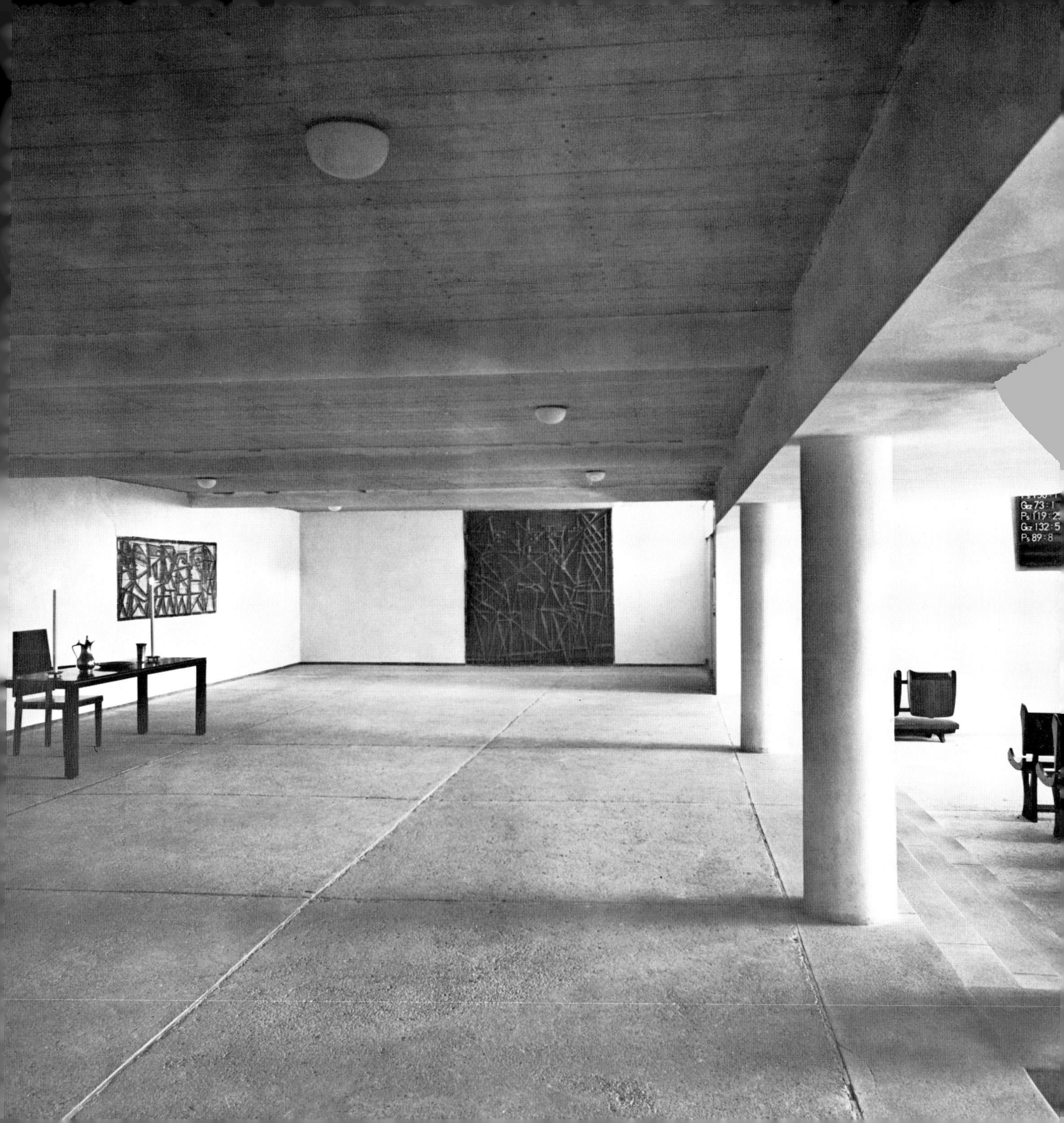
Gez 73 : 1
Ps 119 : 2
Gez 132 : 5
Ps 89 : 8

The Four Evangelists, who also have their place within the room for the Lord's Supper.

Ceramic mural by Dirk Hubers

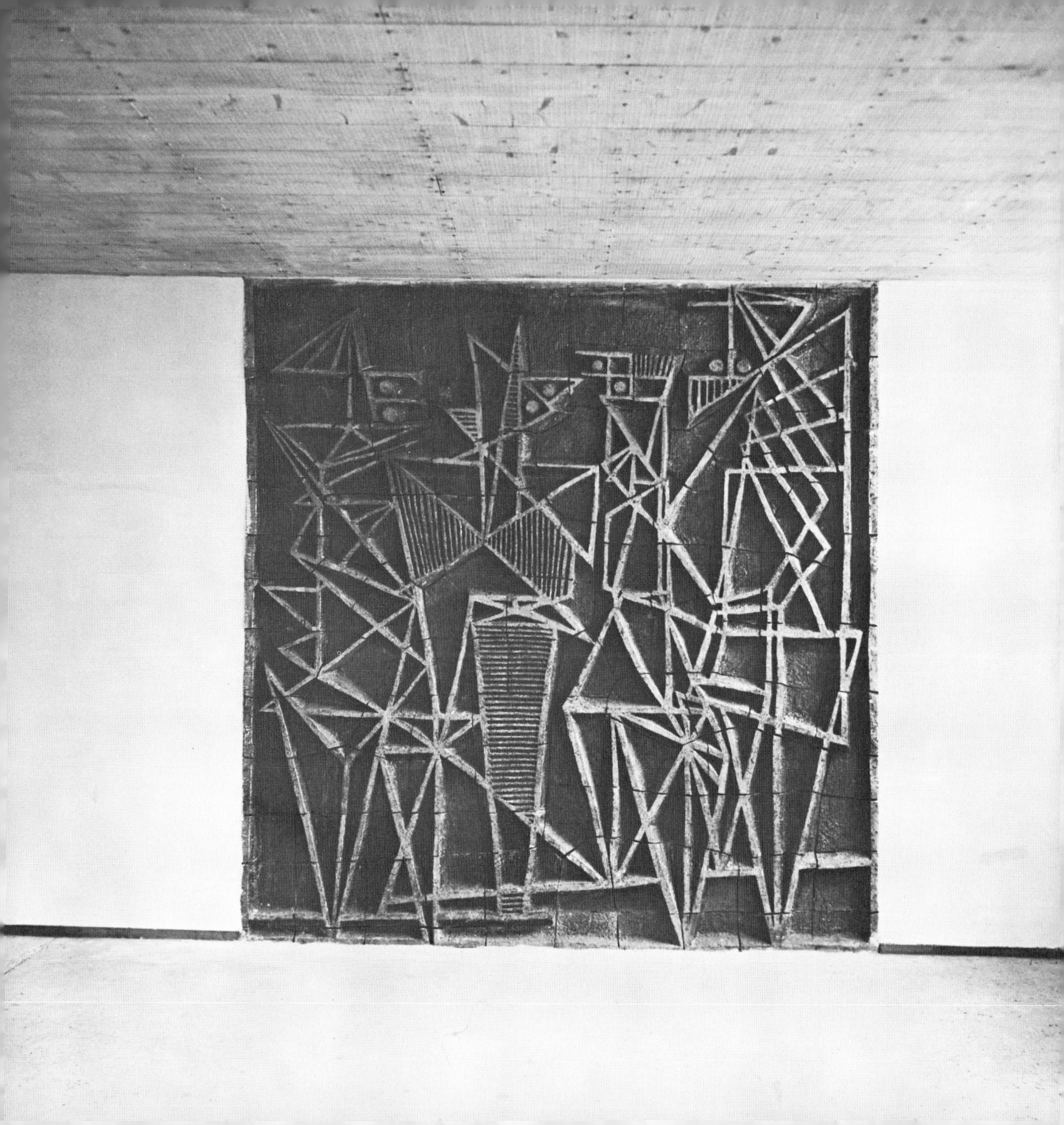

4

The People of God

The use of the word laity has been often derogated by those who would exalt the place of the laity over against the clergy. But this antagonism to the term fails to consider its Greek root, λαός, or people. When within the context of the Church the laity is spoken of, it is nothing less exalted than the whole people of God. While it is of course true that one of the finest of dictionaries insists that the laity are "the great body of the people of a religious faith as distinguished from its clergy," the same volume also informs one that the word acquired this meaning by way of Greek to Latin to Old French to Middle English,[1] and on its way was inescapably influenced by the Medieval concept of the Church with its orders. But those who are

---

[1] *Webster's Third New International Dictionary, Unabridged* (Springfield, Mass.: G. & C. Merriam Co., 1961), *in loco*.

willing to be reformed according to the Word of God must allow reformation of their vocabularies as well, and as the New Testament uses the term within the context of the Church, the λαός are the people of God, and the clergy, rather than being apart from these people (much less above them!), are but a group within this whole.² When the New Testament speaks of a "priesthood" among the Christians it uses the term to describe all believers (e.g. I Peter 2:9)! The Reformers enunciate the doctrine of the priesthood of all believers, and maintain the special offices of minister, deacon, and elder by including them within this priesthood.

The laity (including ministers, deacons, and elders) are the people who are also known as the Church. The English word church is used to translate the Greek word ἐκκλησία, which literally means "the called out" (ἔκκλητοι) and originally (4th & 5th cent. B.C.) was used to refer to the people of a Greek city state who were called out, or gathered together, by the proclamation of the herald to conduct the business of the city state.

The men who translated the Old Testament into Greek often used this Greek word, ἐκκλησία, as an equivalent of the Hebrew word, qahal, קָהָל, meaning an assembly, convocation, or congregation. The New Testament writers took it over with a governing genitive, either stated or implied, to indicate that this was the people or congregation gathered by Christ, called out to be his own.

Thus the Church in the New Testament sense is never the building, but the people, the called-out, gathered people of God, the laity. The building derives its name of church from the people it houses. Thus the Church is housed in churches.

Perhaps it seems strange that the discussion of the architecture of the

---

[2] W. F. Arndt & F. W. Gingrich, *A Greek-English Lexicon of the New Testament* (Cambridge: University Press, 1957), *in loco*.

building started with Word and Sacraments, rather than with the Church, the called-out people of God. This is not an oversight or convenience, but a theological approach to the matter, for it must be noticed that the Church is not a voluntary society that comes together of its own volition to satisfy its own ends. Rather, the Church, as one is reminded by the very derivation of its name, is a group that is "called out" of this world to belong to Christ. Just as in the Greek city states the herald ($κῆρυξ$) of the state called forth the people from their homes to the public gathering, so the heralds of God call out his people unto himself. Thus Paul proudly speaks of himself as a $κῆρυξ$ (I Timothy 2:7), a herald, and the message of the gospel is itself called the $κήρυγμα$.

This truth must be asserted in our architecture, for the Church today is still composed of those who have been called by Christ, and that calling takes place through the Word, of which the pulpit is both place and symbol of proclamation. The Church is still built around the preaching of the Word, and nourished by the Sacraments, and it is therefore not at all inappropriate that in our architecture we should put first things first, and give primary expression to pulpit, font, and table. It is Christ who through his Word and Sacraments gathers the people of God, and therefore one does not design around the congregation but around the symbols of Christ's presence. To begin in any other way is to deny the sovereignty of God and to deny God's initiative in the Incarnation through which he calls men out of this world to be a people unto himself.[3] Any architecture worthy of scriptural teaching must start with the Christ who calls men unto himself through the Word and Sacraments.[4]

---

[3] This thought is given emphasis by Richard Paquier in *Traite' de Liturgique,* 1954. See the article by Conrad H. Massa, *op. cit.,* pp. 50ff.

[4] But if it is bad theology to design first around the congregation, it is far worse to design around the aesthetic inclinations of the congregation, thus making "style" rather than Christ the point at which one begins.

But while one does not begin with the congregation, their theological status as the called-out people of God must be taken into consideration in the architecture of the building which is to house them. At the time of the Reformation the place of the people of God was assumed very naturally, and thus very accurately. When the pulpit assumed its proper place in worship the people very naturally grouped themselves about it, and on whatever side of the pulpit they might find themselves, they faced it so as to hear God's Word proclaimed. The eastward direction of Roman Catholic architecture was ignored as the people orientated themselves around the Word and Sacraments.[5]

It would perhaps be unnecessary to recall these simple things which our forefathers in the faith did so naturally, were it not for "the 'revolutionary' repudiation of the prevailing conception of the church, which was transferred to the church building" in the nineteenth century.[6] This "revolution," which took place under the influence of "romantic and neo-historical ideas," radically altered the concept of the people of God gathered about the Word.

> The congregation no longer converges on the centre, but faces the raised chancel in front of it, where the pulpit and the table are placed outside of it [i.e., the area of the congregation]. The lines of vision of the individuals composing it run parallel to each other and meet at infinity. . . . The congregation looks forward, a perspective onto the chancel has been opened, the worshippers 'look into space.'[7]

The basic outlook of Romanticism had invaded the churches of the Reforma-

---

[5] For seventeen illustrations of such early Reformation seating, see Weyres & Bartning, *op. cit.,* pp. 261–263. An especially well-illustrated selection of early churches for Protestant worship, including many seldom-illustrated Huguenot and Scandinavian churches, is to be found in the book by Per Gustaf Hamberg, *Templebygge för Protestanter* (Stockholm: Svenska Kyrkans Diakonistyrelses Bokförlag, 1955).

[6] Senn, *op. cit.,* p. 11.

[7] *Ibid.,* p. 11.

tion and had molded them after the culture of the age. Rationalism was repudiated, and reason was no longer to dominate man (indeed, an overly enthusiastic higher criticism seemed to make the rational content of Christianity suspect in any case). Instead of reason, the age emphasized the importance of man's emotions, and so the whole concern with man's "worship experience" came to the fore. Instead of the architectural expressions of the Reformation which accurately depicted what the church was, the architecture of the Romantic movement in its pseudo-historicalism created emotional settings for worship experiences. In England and America this movement is still enshrined, and repeated day by day, in the building of English Gothic churches with worship arrangements patterned after Medieval Roman Catholic lines. Just as in the liturgical movements of the nineteenth century "the historical and the theological began to mean less and less as the demands of the psychological and the aesthetic loomed larger,"[8] so too in the field of architecture. The Romantic movement engulfed both, to the detriment of both. And thus, because people so readily affirm the architecture (and the liturgy) of their own experience as the way to do things, it is again necessary to state the obvious, that the "emotional experience" of looking forward into space (and backward into a Medieval form of worship) where one gazes upon the ritual of worship being performed beyond the chancel arch, is not worship reformed according to the Word of God. Rather, we are called together by God's Word and Sacraments, and together are God's called-out people.

André Biéler, speaking to the problem of the present location of God's holy place on earth, makes it plain that it is not beyond the chancel arch within the vista where we see the special priesthood performing acts for us, for:

---

[8] Hageman, *op. cit.*, p. 81.

> After Christ's sojourn on earth, the only visible holy place, the only material point at which the meeting occurs between God and men, is the physical gathering of believers, to whom Christ imparts himself through his Holy Spirit when they hear his Word and celebrate the Sacraments which he has given.
>
> And the only authentic clergy is this gathering, as a whole, which has the privilege of celebrating the whole liturgy. Each member is personally associated through faith with Christ in his role as the only High Priest (as the Epistle to the Hebrews tells us, Hebrews 10:5–10).[9]

This Reformed concept of the role of the congregation had already found written definition as early as 1526:

> But all the faithful are admonished to be present at public prayer and the reading of the Gospel, as also at the Last Supper of Our Lord. Morever, these rites shall from now on be no longer celebrated in the choir but shall be performed with due decorum in the midst of the church so that all people of both sexes may learn to sing in harmony and with one heart and may glorify God's name, for all have become priests in Christ.[10]

The biblical truth concerning the Church as the gathered people of God must once again find architectural expression in our church buildings. The criteria for a Reformed expression of the office of the congregation would be as follows:

THE CONGREGATION IS GATHERED BY CHRIST AND IS BUILT AROUND THE WORD AND SACRAMENTS. CHURCH ARCHITECTURE SHOULD FOLLOW THIS PATTERN BY MAKING PULPIT, FONT, AND TABLE OF FIRST CONCERN, AND GATHERING THE CONGREGATION ABOUT THEM.

---

[9] André Biéler, "Liturgy and Architecture," *Lucerne International Joint Conference on Church Architecture and Church Building*, p. 54.

[10] From the *Reformatio Ecclesiarum Hassiae*, quoted by Senn, op. cit., p. 5.

THE CONGREGATION IS THE CHURCH, THE CALLED-OUT PEOPLE OF GOD, GOD'S FAMILY, BROTHERS OF CHRIST AND OF ONE ANOTHER IN CHRIST, MEMBERS OF THE BODY OF CHRIST. ARCHITECTURALLY, THE PEOPLE OF GOD MUST BE TREATED NOT AS SPECTATORS, BUT AS MEMBERS OF A FAMILY.

Before trying to effect a working relationship between these two criteria, which essentially concerns the front-to-back relationship of seating the congregation, cognizance should be given to the somewhat easier problem of its side-to-side relationships. For if the attempt is to be made architecturally to give expression to the people of God as family, rather than spectators, then this architectural concern should be in all directions, side to side as well as front to back. Thus consideration must be given to the relative merits of the common pew and individual seating.

Everyone who has spent a hot summer morning in a pew into which some enthusiastic usher has put too many people, is keenly aware of the disadvantages of the pew. But is it not precisely this quality of a pew, its very lack of separation, that makes it much more suitable to symbolize the oneness, the unity, the familial relations of Christians? It is true that occasionally at crowded services one feels oneself being compressed into an almost literal oneness with one's neighbor, but while this discomfort is to be regretted, the willingness to accept one's fellow Christian, less than perfect though he may be (especially in his judgment of space), as also a part of the family of Christ is admirable. Individual seating, whether it be chairs or divided pews, gives a certain sense of possession, of "this is mine," "so far you may come and no farther," "this is what I as an individual have reserved for myself." It is quite true that proper chairs, or pews with separating arms, or separate seats, offer the greatest opportunities for comfort. But just as our oneness as members of the Body of Christ opens the possibility of discomfort and service in the care of the members of that Body, so the pew should from week to week by its openness reflect the openness and the unity of the members of Christ's Body.

Returning to the larger problem of reconciling the two criteria, one finds the most suitable form to use in fulfilling the second criterion to be that of a circle (e.g., the common phrase "the family circle"). Architecturally, to fulfill the second criterion with a circle demands that the first criterion be fulfilled by putting Word and Sacraments at the center of the circle.[11] The biblical necessity of the proclamation of the Word, however, makes this "perfect" solution imperfect, for the greater the degree of arc to which the minister must address himself, the less direct, and less effective, his communication. Thus to preach from the center of a circle would require an address to an arc of 360°, when at any one time the minister can effectively address directly an arc of only about 60°. The importance of this "direct communication," in which the minister can look at the people and address them face-to-face, can be tested in any conversation or on any television screen. In conversation, the forceful person is generally the person who looks at you—looks you in the eye—when he talks. On television, people giving speeches or making addresses are viewed not from the back of their heads, or even from the side, but from the front, so that they can "look at" their audience. If forceful communication is important in a conversation or on television, it is far more important in proclaiming the gospel. Thus to put a minister in the center of a circle means that while he can effectively address any 60° of the arc, the other 300° are receiving far less effective communication.[12]

---

[11] Precisely this was done in the Hedvig Elsonora Kyrka in Stockholm, 1665. Hamberg, *op. cit.*, pp. 198ff.

[12] It is interesting to note that when Leonhardt Christoph Sturm worked on this problem (1669–1729), while he experimented with the square, triangle, octagon, and circle, he always placed the pulpit close to the wall and so arranged his seating that

It must be further acknowledged that distance from the speaker also plays an important part in communication. Given a long, narrow nave, the minister may have 95% of his congregation within his arc of 60°, but it is questionable whether his communication with the people in the fortieth row of pews is as effective as it might be with people just four rows behind his back. The whole problem, which must be the province of the architect in relation to the desires and habits of the congregation, can be stated as follows:[13]

THE EFFECTIVENESS OF THE COMMUNICATION OF THE MINISTER DECREASES WITH THE INCREASE OF HIS ARC OF ADDRESS. IT ALSO DECREASES WITH THE INCREASE OF DISTANCE OF THE CONGREGATION FROM THE PULPIT.

In resolving these tensions, in which one can never have both/and, the architect of Christ Chapel at Episcopal Academy in Philadelphia chose the Greek-cross plan, similar to that of Christ Church in Düren, only on a very different scale. The relative strengths and weaknesses of the plan become very apparent. In each arm of the cross there are only eight rows of pews, but these are adequate for 600 young boys. The weakness, however, is that while there are never more than eight rows of pews in any direction, the liturgical space at the center adds considerably to the distance between pulpit and worshipper for all except those seated in the left arm of the cross. Even allowing for the fact that the minister's back is constantly toward the choir, he must still address himself to an arc of 180°. Nonetheless, there is an intimacy seldom found in a church seating 600.

---

the minister addressed himself to almost all of the congregation in an arc of 90° or, in most cases, less. Weyres and Bartning, *op. cit.*, p. 245.

[13] A survey of Reformed attempts to solve this problem (both historical and theoretical) can be found in Weyres and Bartning, *op. cit.*, pp. 240–264, 274–275.

Christ Chapel, Episcopal Academy, Philadelphia
Vincent G. Kling, architect

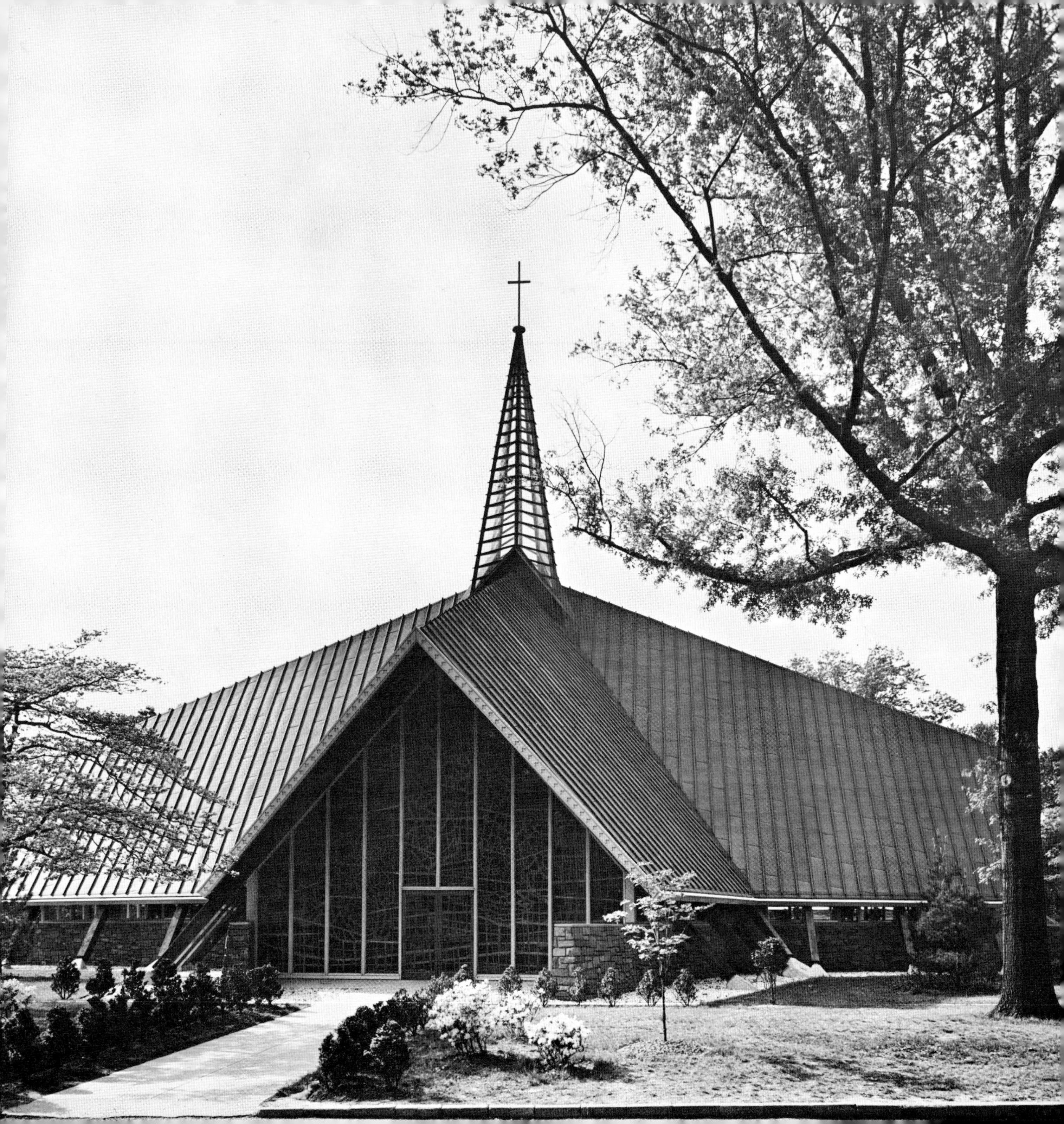

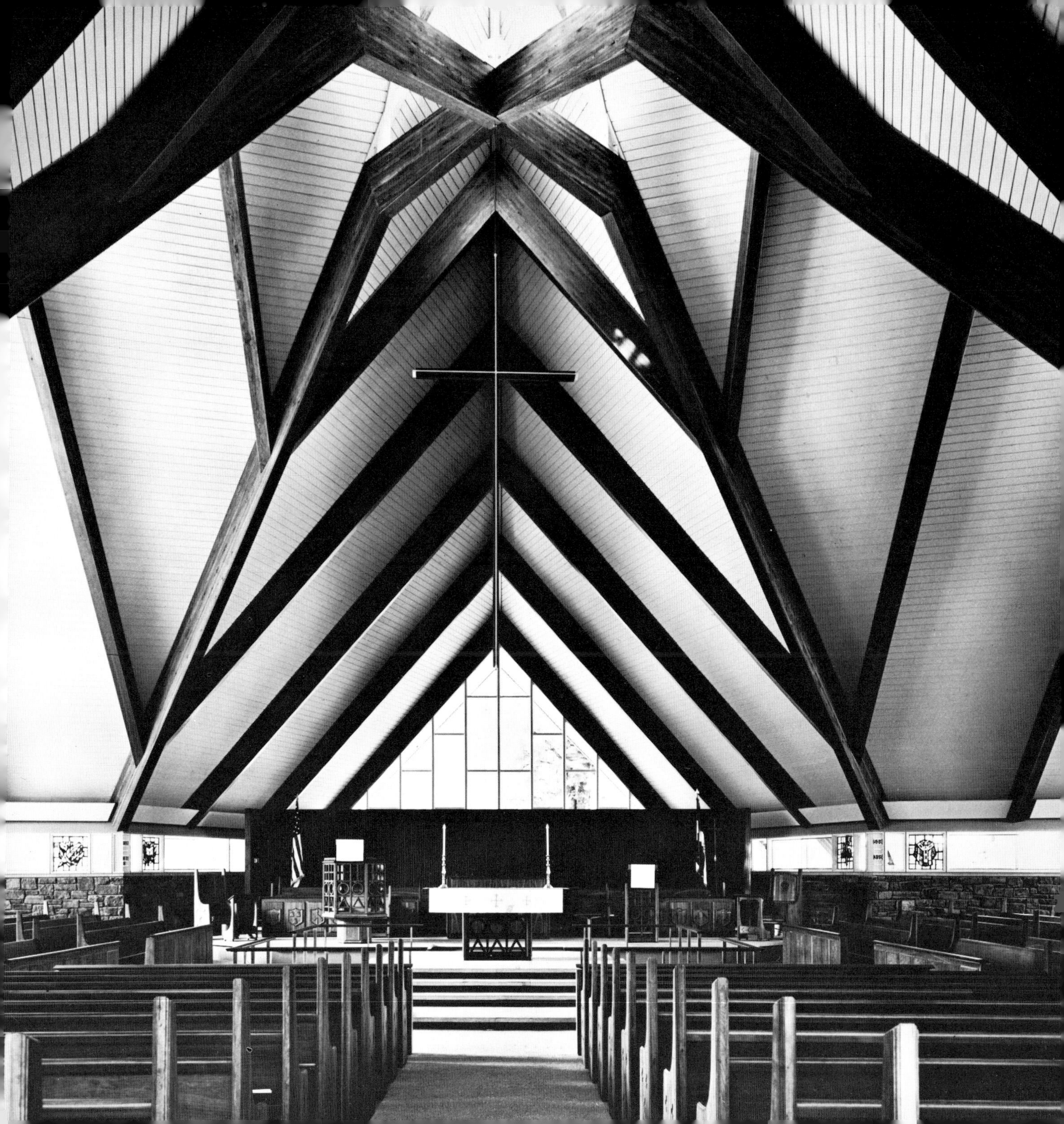

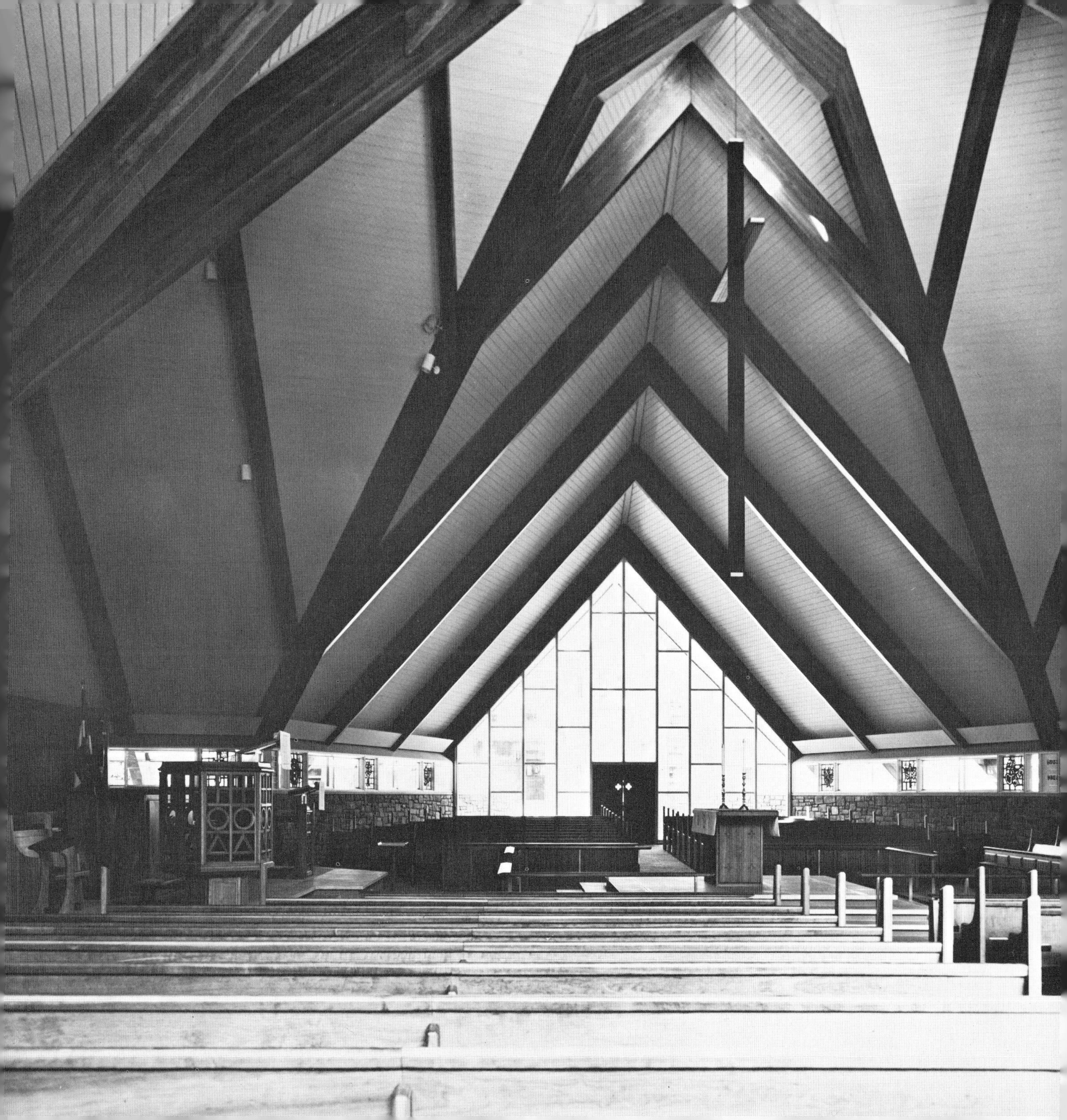

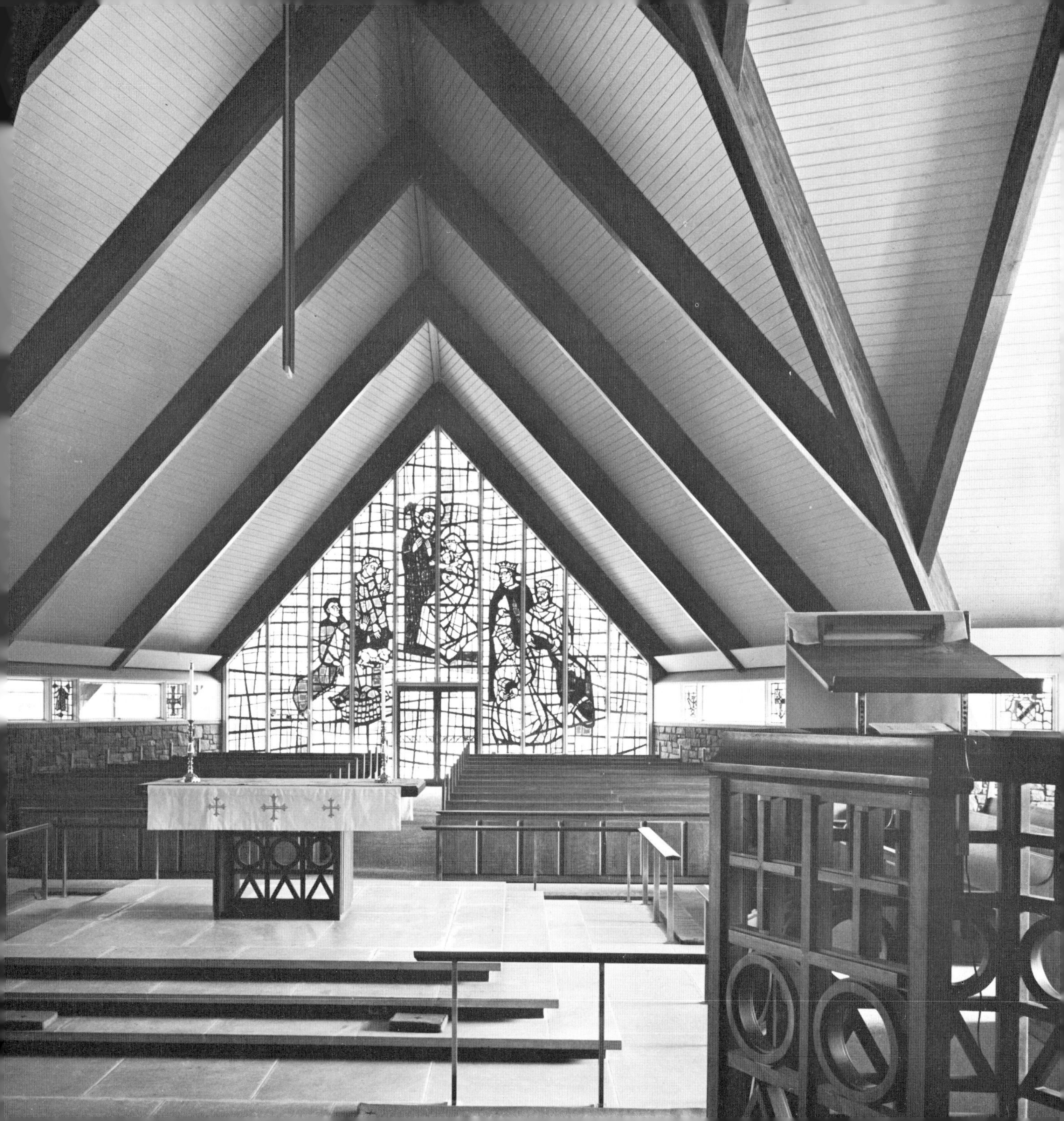

Another architectural statement of the congregation as the gathered people and family of God is found in Bethlehem Church, Bern, Switzerland. While the minister must again preach to an arc of 180°, the pews are much more closely grouped around the pulpit than in Christ Chapel, with the result that 500 adult worshippers can be accommodated with none more than eleven rows away from the pulpit.

Bethlehem Church (Bethlehemkirche), Reformed, Bern, Switzerland
Werner Küenzi, architect

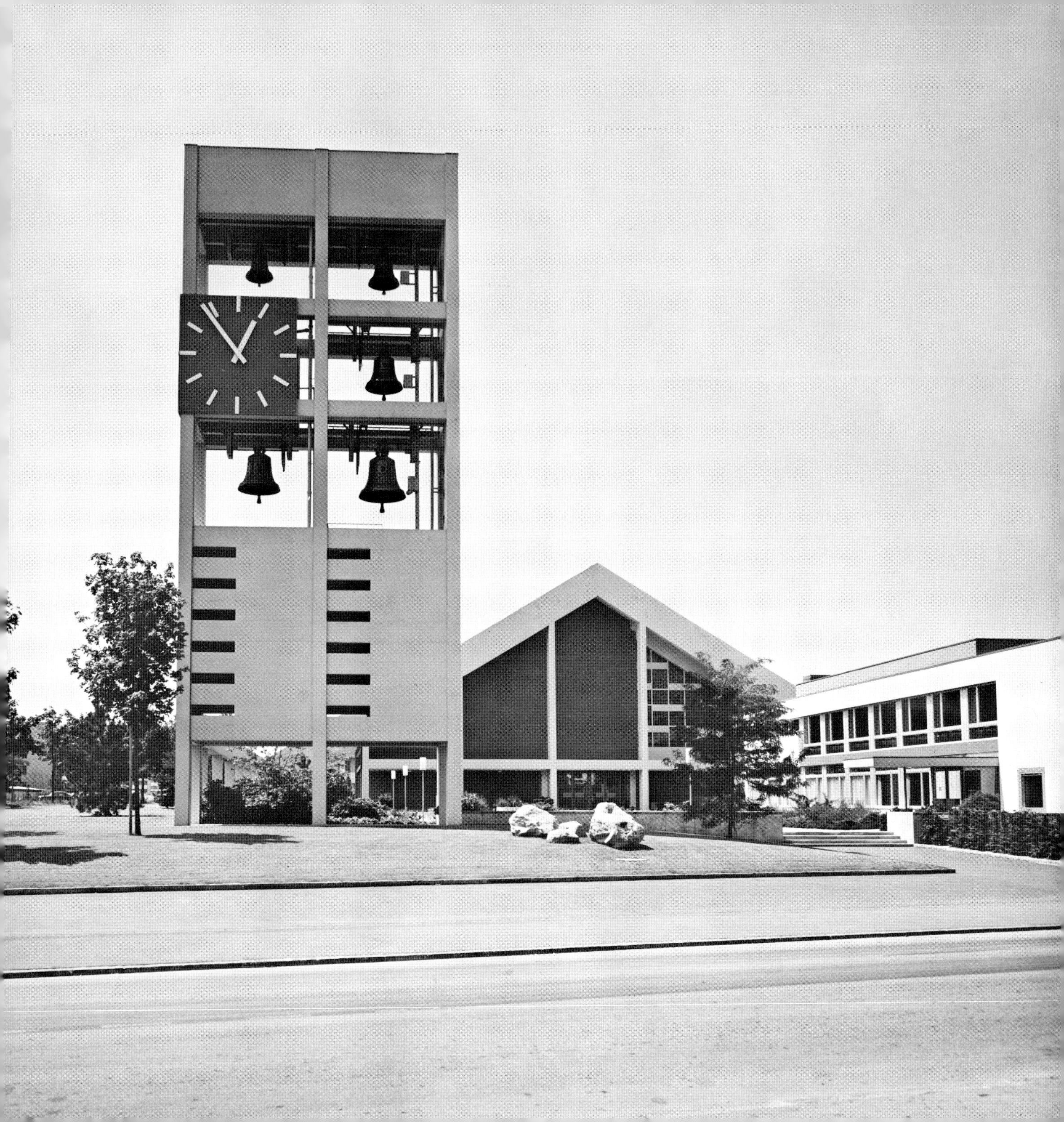

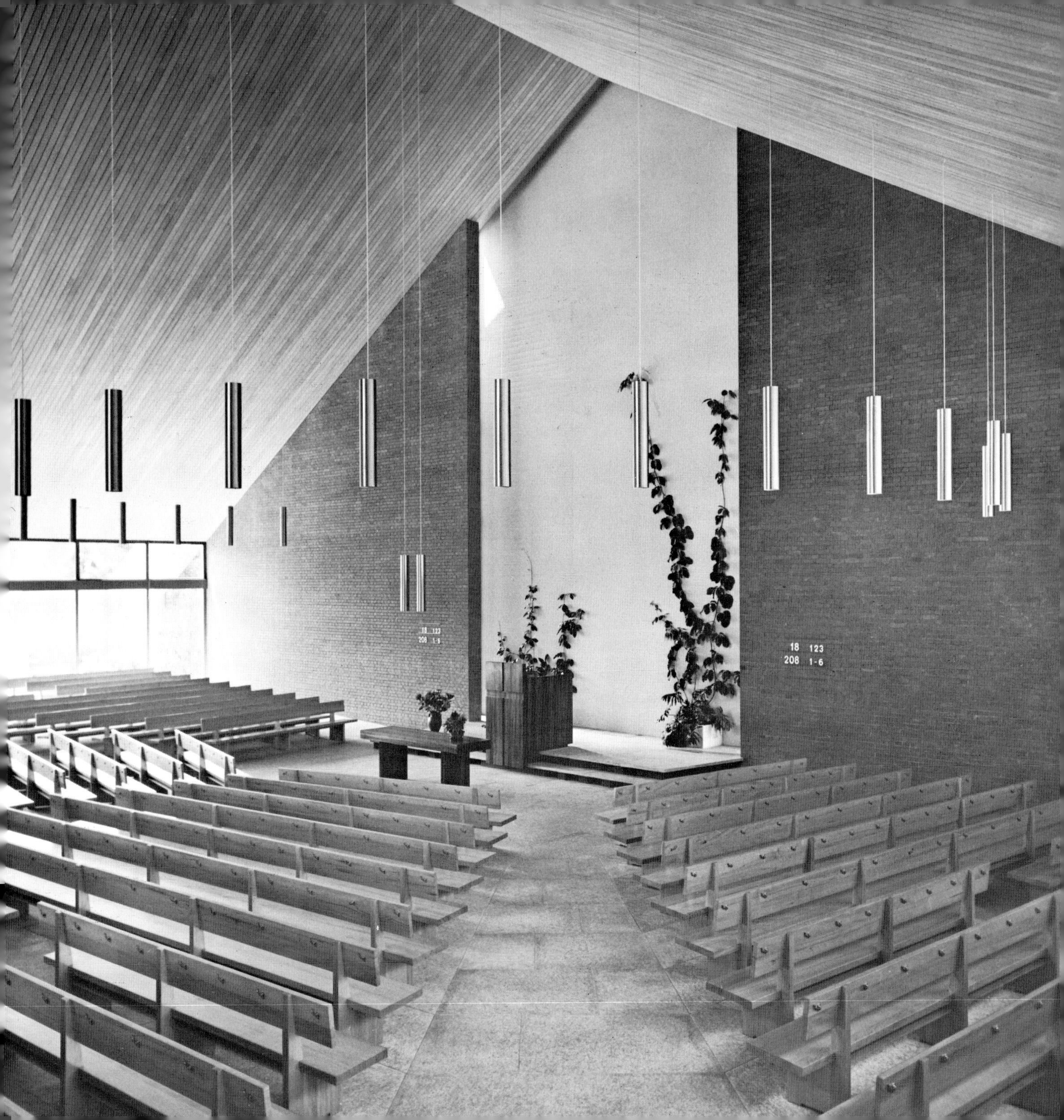
18 123
208 1-6

The position of the lighting fixtures has also been used to increase the implication of the gathered community, the family of God.

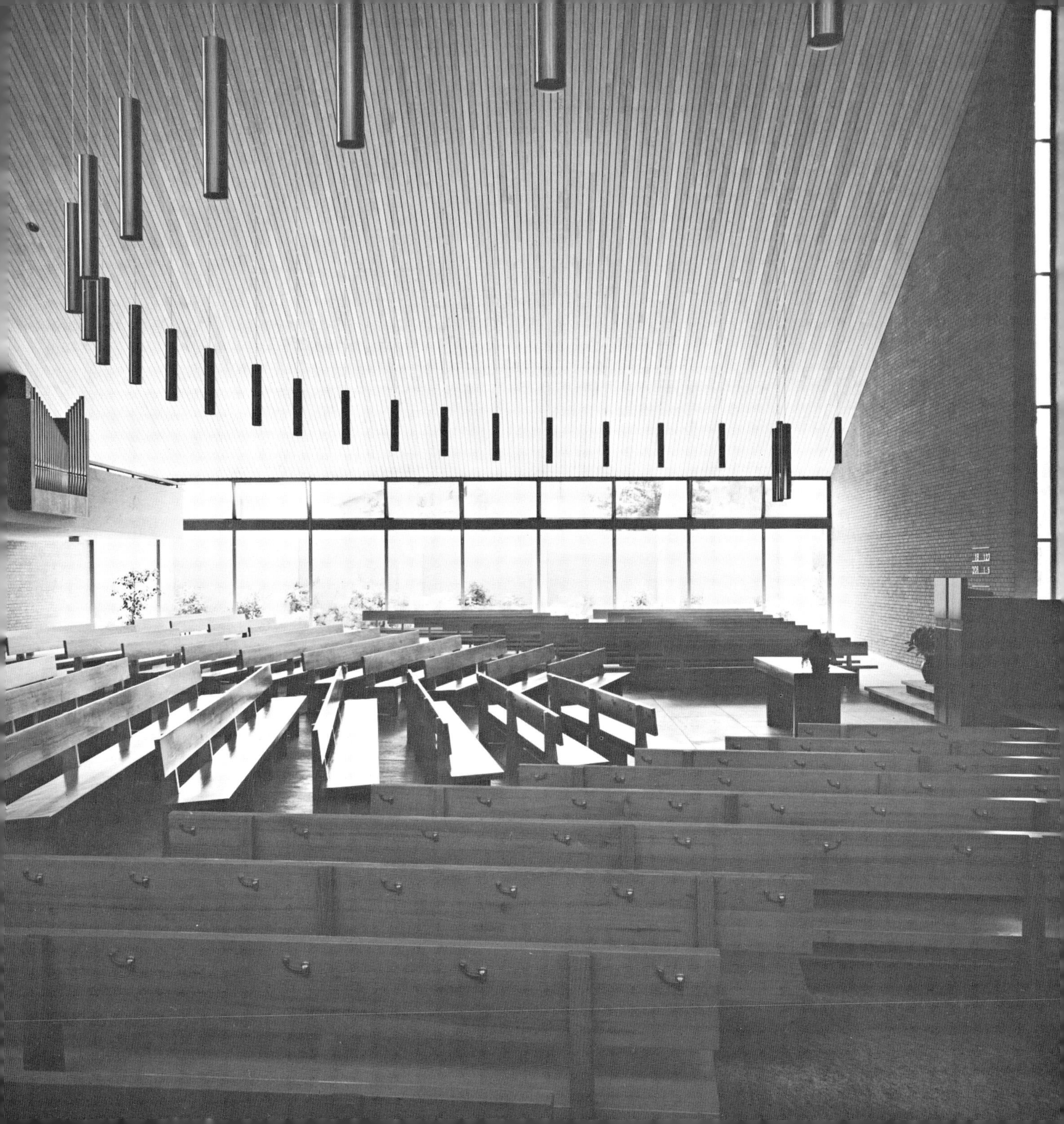

Organ by Orgelbau Genf AG of Geneva

Hauptwerk

Principal	16
Principal	8
Spitzflöte	8
Octave	4
Hohlflöte	4
Superoctave	2
Mixtur 4 ranks	2
Mixtur min. 4 ranks	1
Trompete	8

Oberwerk

Bourdon	16
Suavial	8
Rohrflöte	8
Octave	4
Spitzflöte	4
Nachthorn	2
Quinte	2⅔
Terz	1⅗
Mixtur 4 ranks	1⅓
Zimbel 4 ranks	½
Schalmei	8
Clairon	4

Rückpositiv

Gedackt	8
Quintaton	8
Principal	4
Rohrflöte	4
Flageolet	2
Larigot	1⅓
Sesquialtera	2⅔ & 1⅗
Scharf 4–5 ranks	1
Krummhorn	8

Pedal

Principalbass	16
Subbass	16
Principal	8
Gemshorn	8
Octave	4
Mixtur 4 ranks	2⅔
Fagott	16
Zinke	8
Corno	4

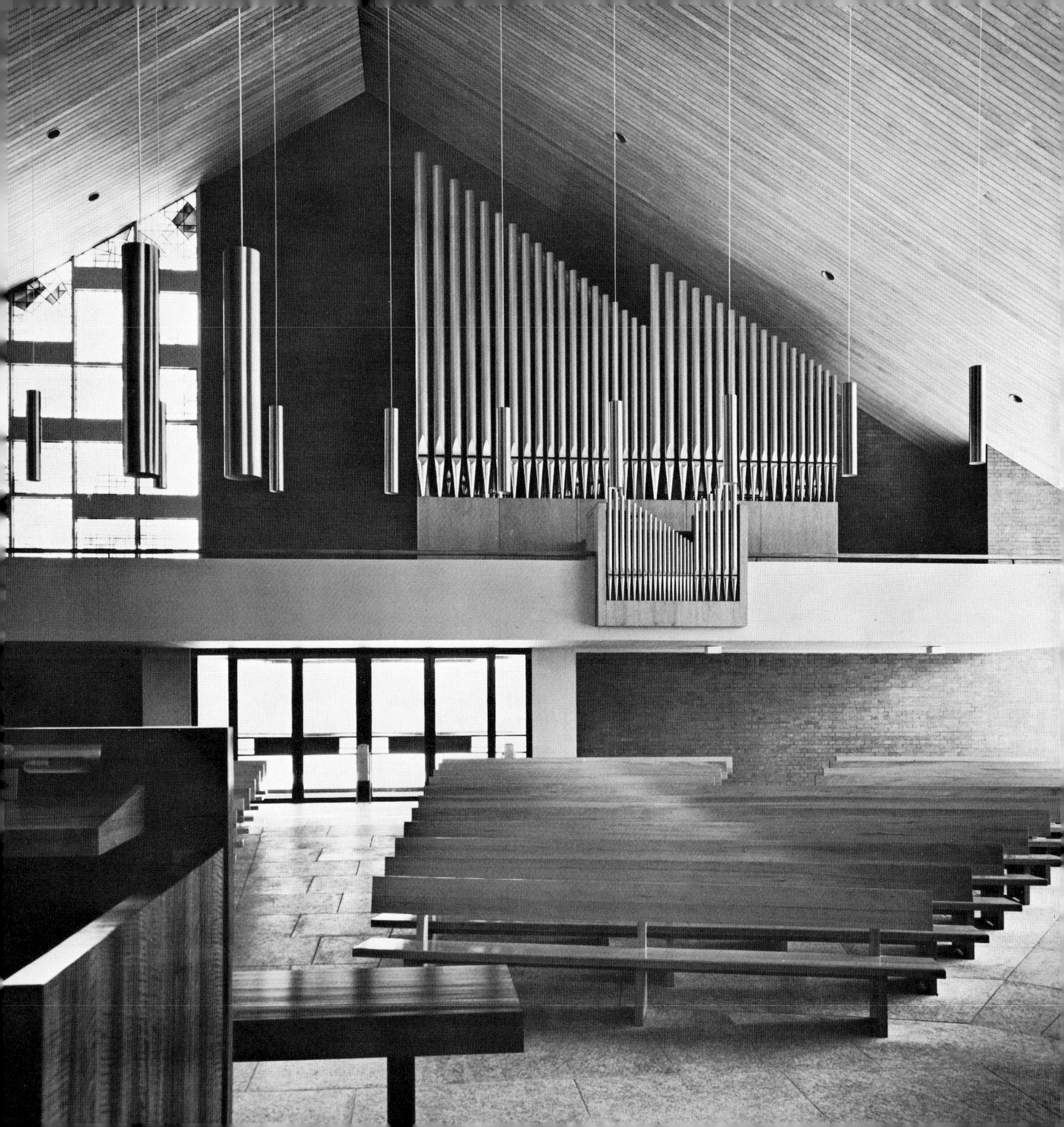

A very different solution in avoiding "spectator seating" is found in the previously pictured Church of the Advent (Adventskerk) in The Hague-Loosduinen (pp. 275, 277). Here the minister addresses an arc of approximately 120°. While the seating is always parallel to the wall lines (showing, undoubtedly, the influence of the seating in the older Dutch churches, e.g., The Grote Kerk, Haarlem [pp. 85, 87]), yet the juxtapositioning of the groups of seats produces the effect of a group gathered about the pulpit and font. A similar effect is achieved by the seating in the Church of the Advent (Adventskerk) in Aerdenhout, the Netherlands (pp. 605, 607). In churches laid out on the more familiar rectangular plan, the Church of the Cross at Amstelveen achieves a seating capacity of 616 (plus 194 with chairs), within 21 rows of pews and an arc of 60° from the pulpit (pp. 95, 97, 107).

A less familiar plan is that of the octagonal Maranatha Church in Amsterdam-South. By placing the pulpit against one wall of the octagon, the arc to which the minister must preach is reduced to approximately 100° with the bulk of the congregation of 560 not more than 13 pews away, although there are four rows beyond the back aisle. The overflow seating of 170 is a great distance from the pulpit and creates a spectator effect. Within the main body of the church, however, there is a strong feeling of the gathered community.

Maranatha Church (Maranathakerk), Hervormd, Amsterdam-South, The Netherlands. Joh. H. Groenewegen & H. Mieras, architects

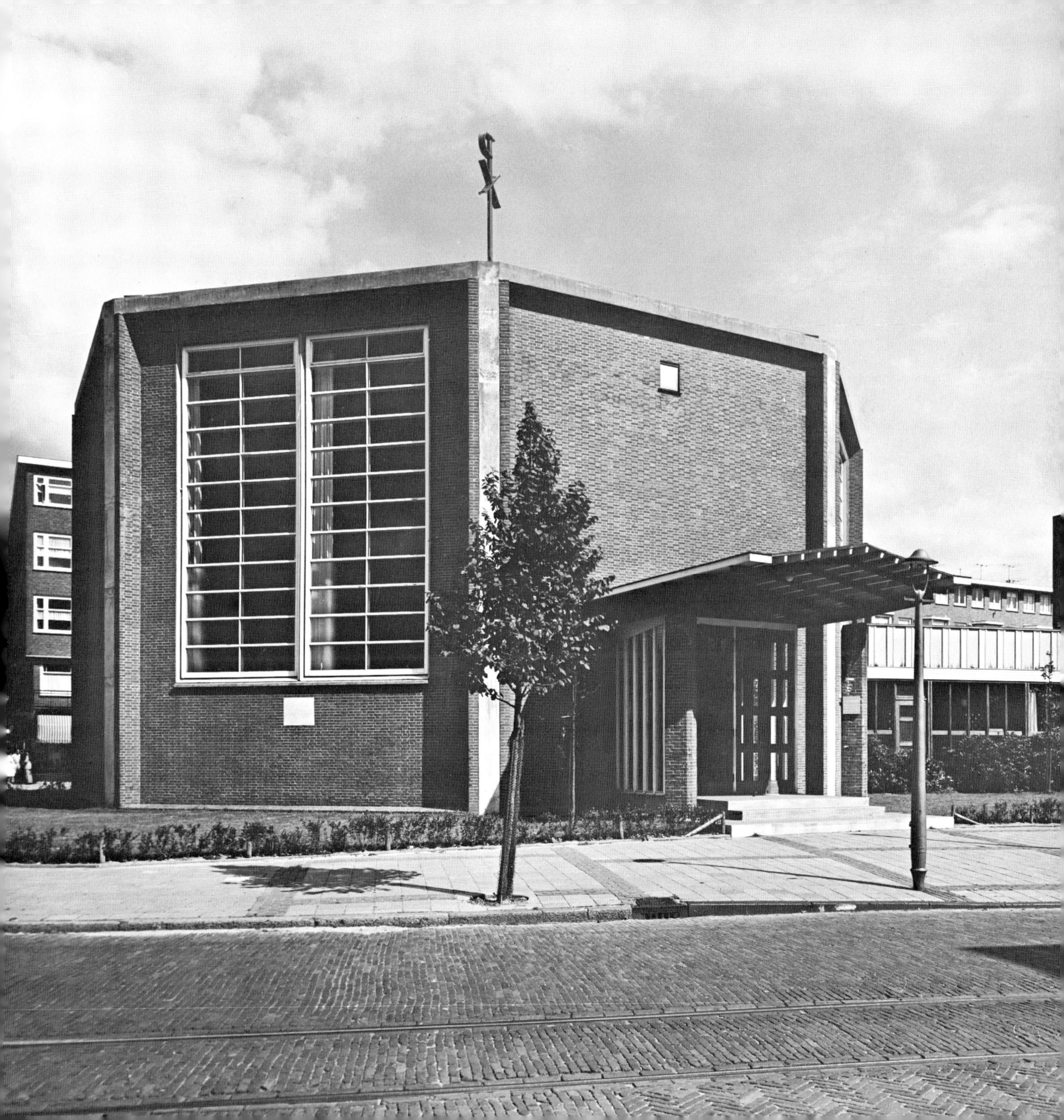

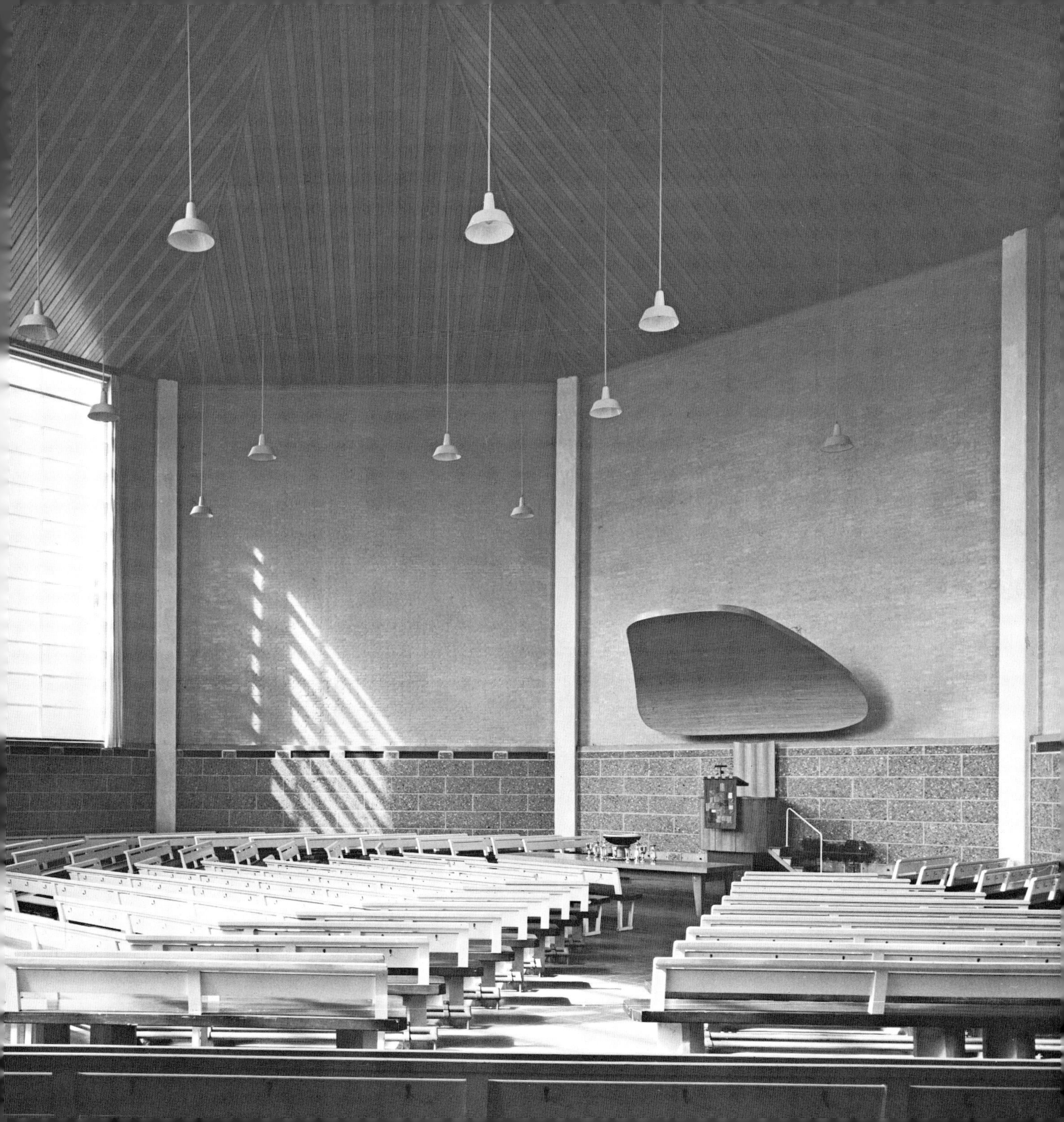

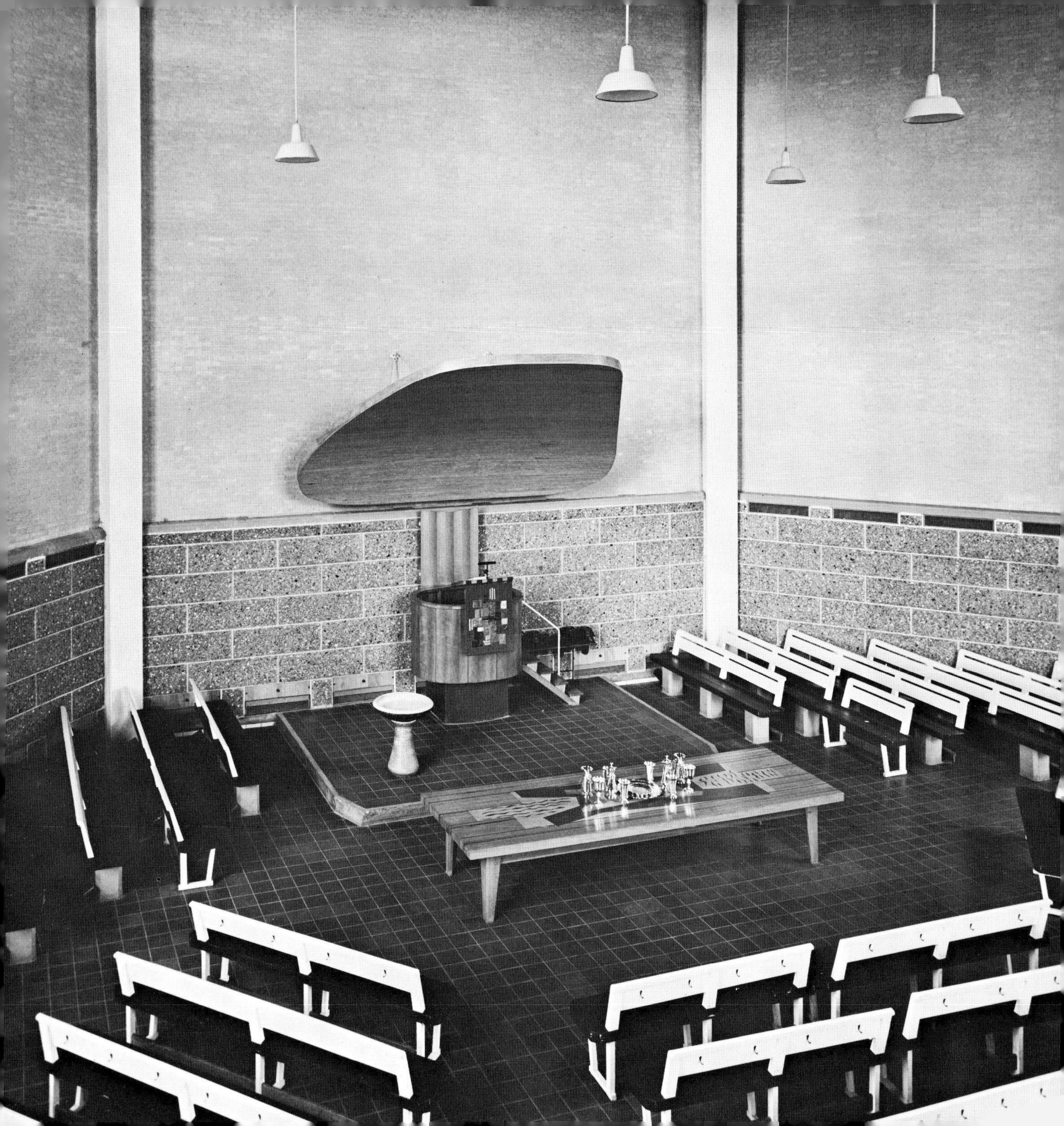

Organ by D. A. Flentrop of Zaandam

Hoofdwerk

Praestant	8
Roerfluit	8
Spitsgamba	8
Octaaf	4
Spitsfluit	4
Nasard	2⅔
Superoctaaf	2
Mixtuur 4–5 ranks	
Trompet	8

Rugwerk

Holpijp	8
Praestant	4
Roerfluit	4
Vlakfluit	2
Quint	1⅓
Sesquialtera 2 ranks	
Scherp 4 ranks	
Dulciaan	16

Borstwerk

Gedekt	8
Quintadeen	4
Praestant	2
Cymbel 2 ranks	
Sifflet	1
Vox Humana	8
Cymbelster	

Pedaal

Subbas	16
Praestantbas	8
Bourdon	8
Octaafbas	4
Ruispijp 4 ranks	
Bazuin	16
Schalmei	4

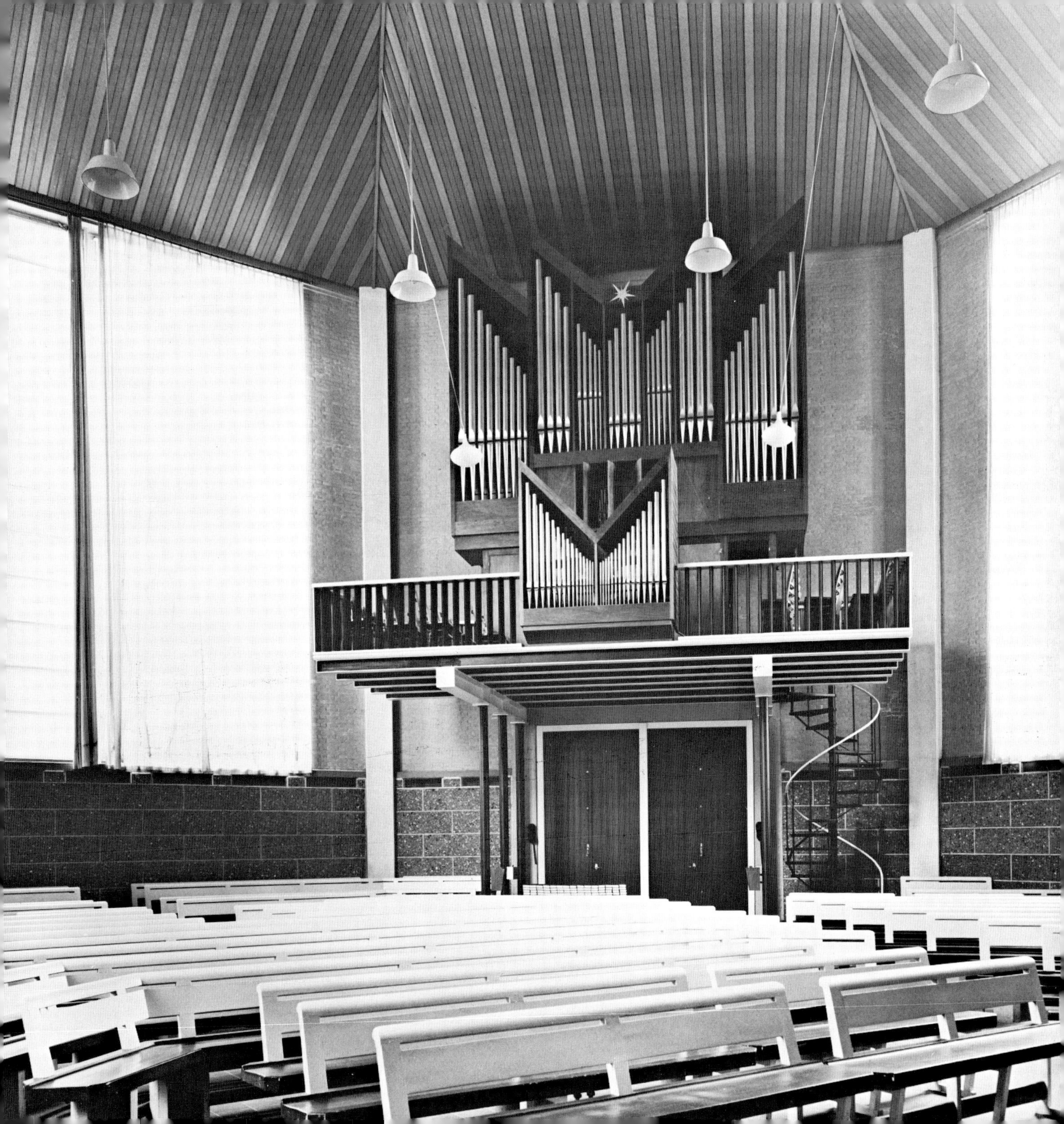

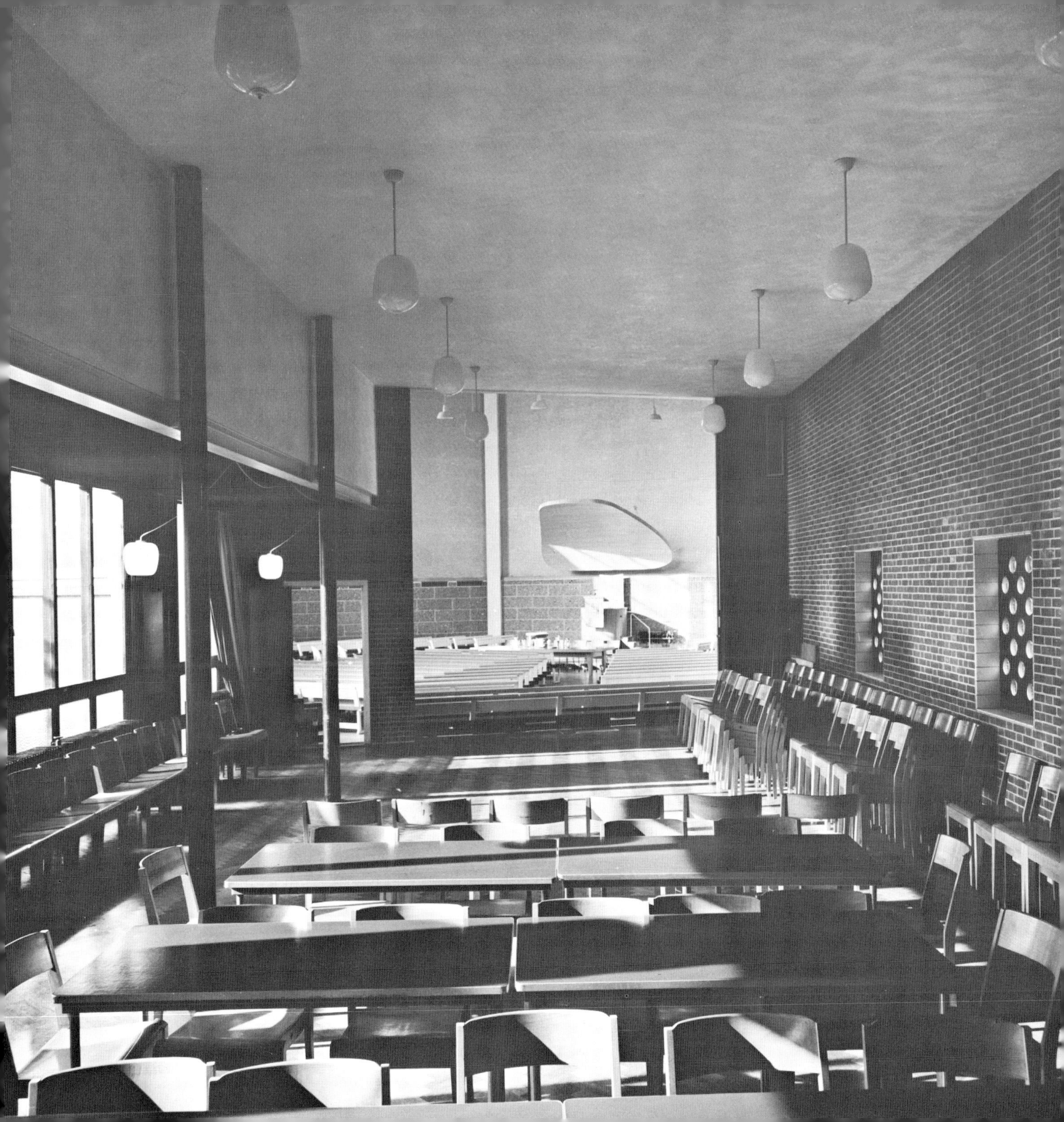

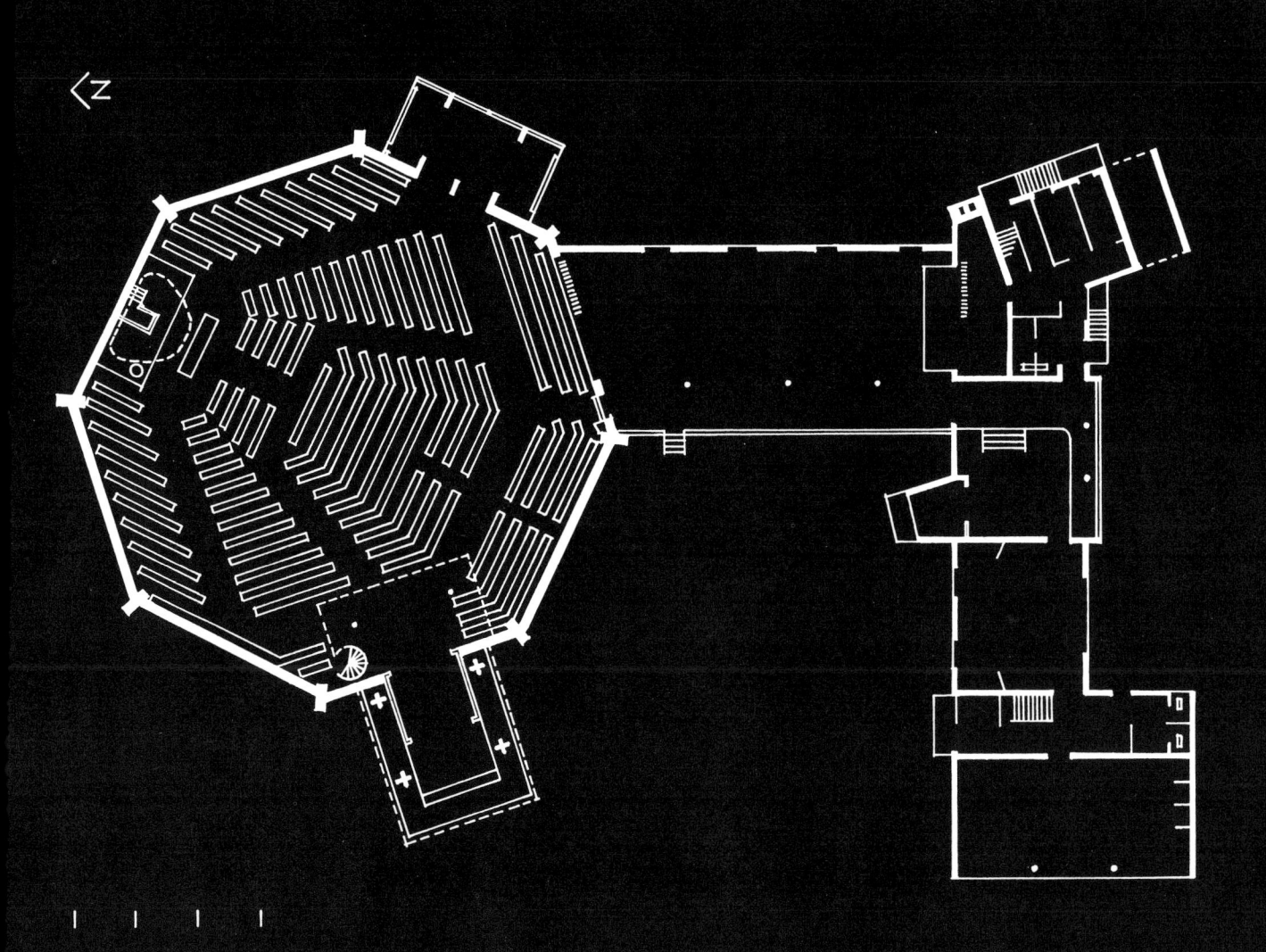

N

In expressing the community of the people of God, an entirely different form has been attempted by W. van der Kuilen of Amsterdam in the Reformed Church at Nagele, N.O.P., and J. Kruger of Voorburg in the Reformed Church, "The Cornerstone," (De Hoeksteen) in Santpoort, both in the Netherlands. In the church in Nagele the entire congregation sits together in a lower level comprising the whole center of the church, with a raised ledge running around the perimeter. One enters the church on this higher level. The pulpit, font, table, organ, and overflow room are also on this level, but three steps below it, together, sits the congregation. It should be noted that the angular features of this church are in conformity with the entire community of Nagele, where the typical polder architecture of sharply pitched, red-tiled roofs has been ordered abandoned for a complete change of pace. There is not a pitched roof nor piece of red tile in the entire community. The angularity of these prescribed town lines has been repeated not only on the exterior of the church, but also within the church, yet by the subtle depression the feeling of community has been achieved in spite of this angularity of line.

The Reformed Church (Hervormd), Nagele, N. O. P., The Netherlands
W. van der Kuilen, architect

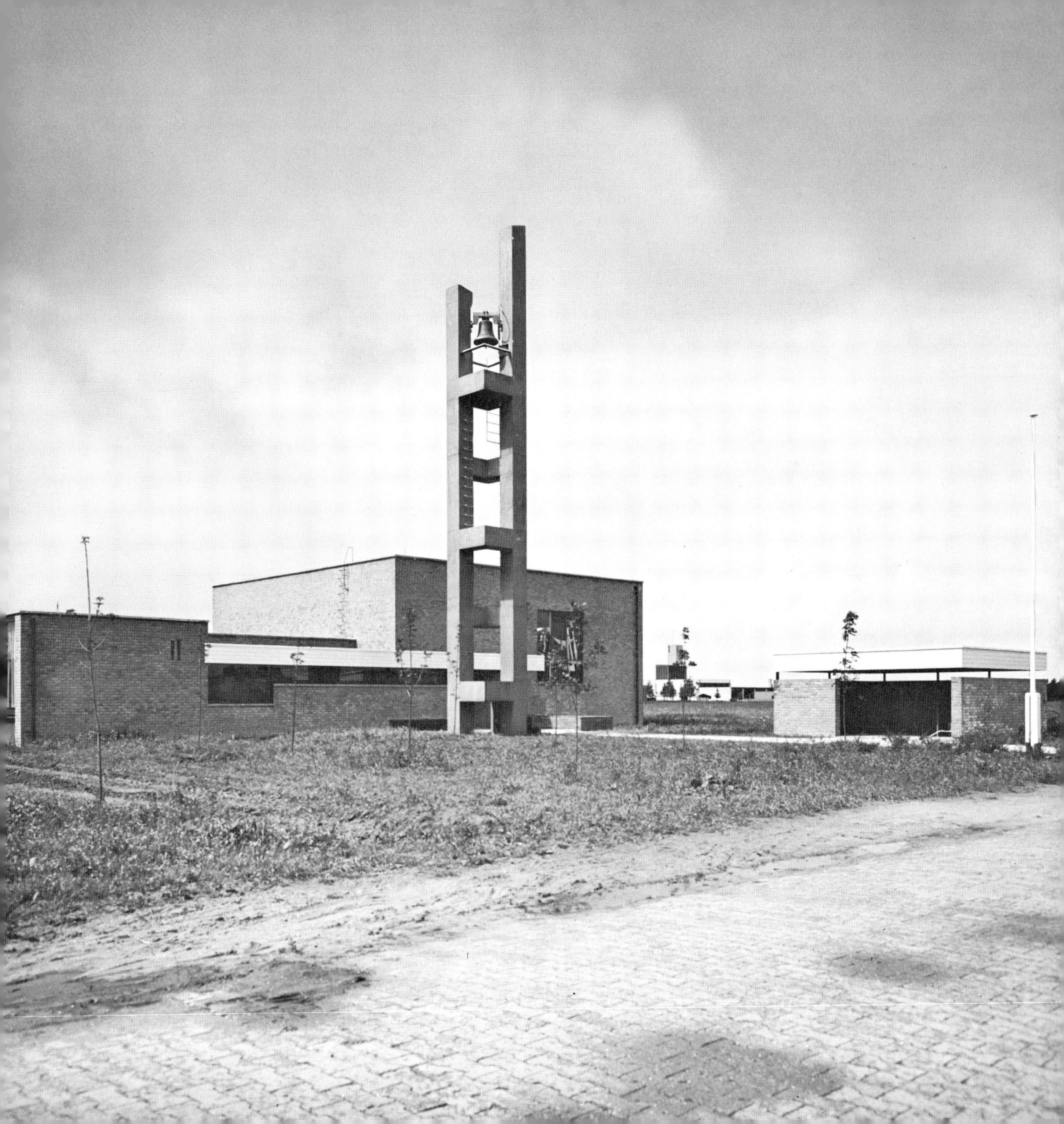

Positiv by Marcussen of Aabenraa

Gedeckt	8
Praestant	4
Roerfluit	4
Octaaf	2
Scherp 2–3 ranks	

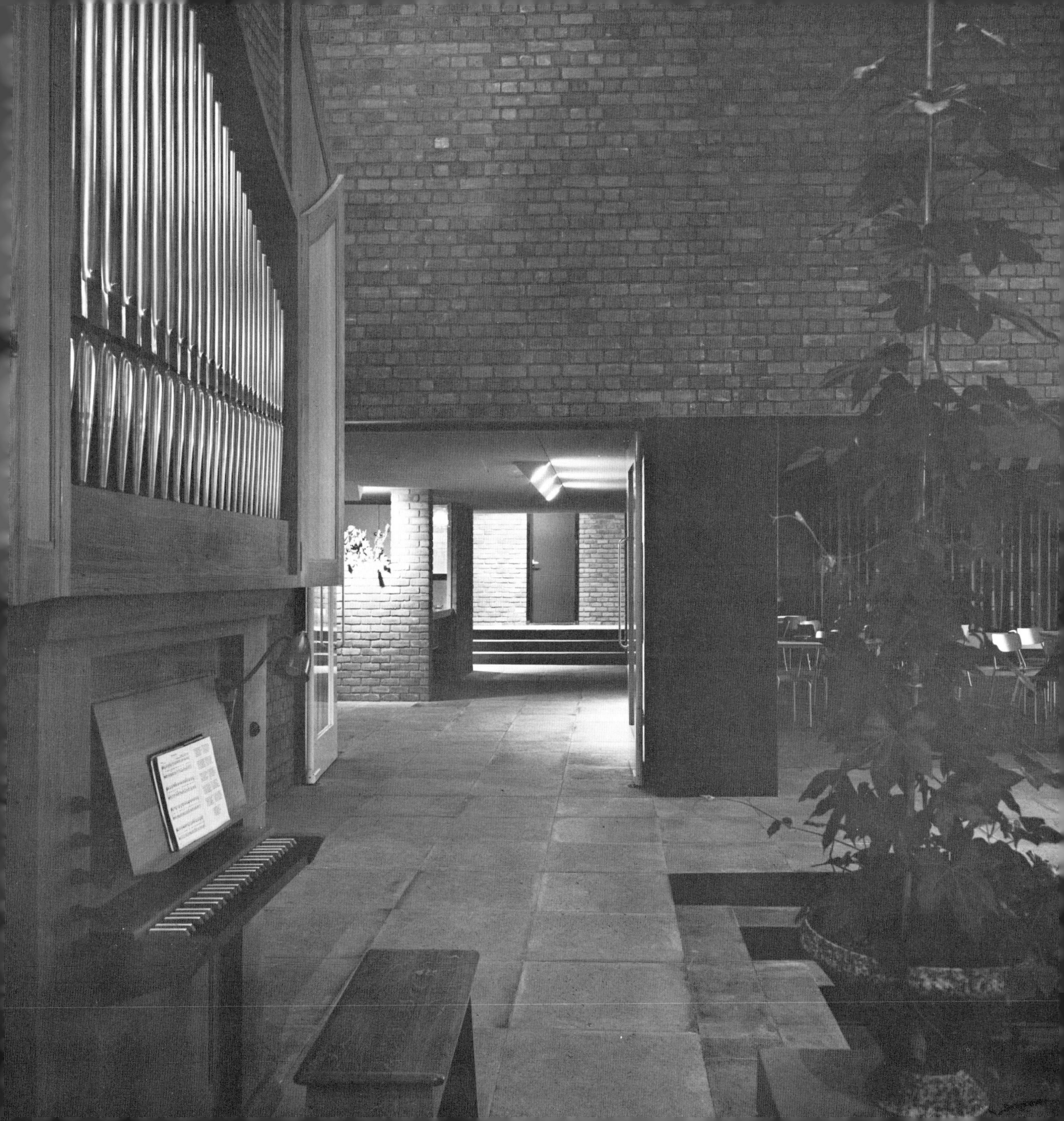

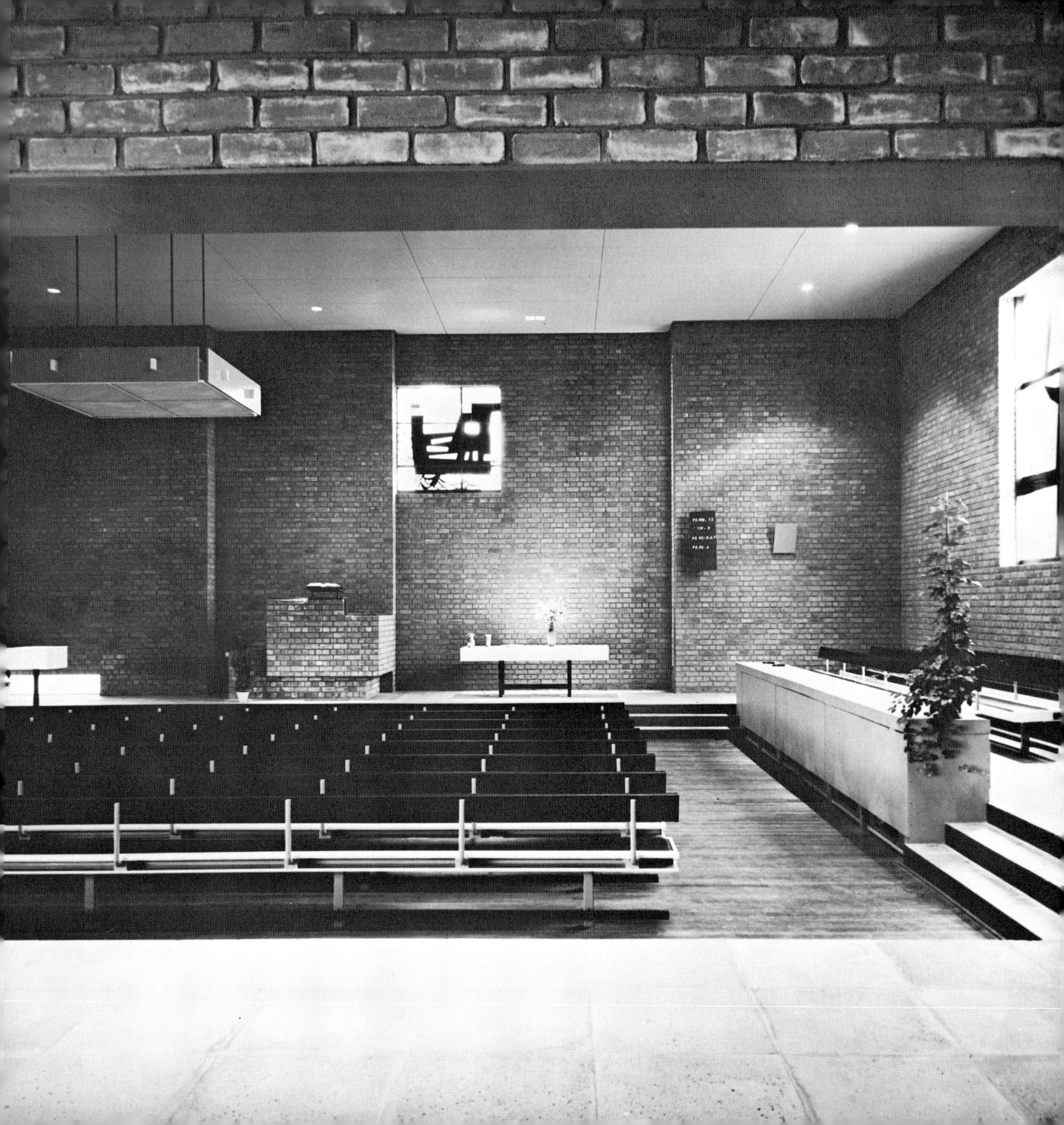

Here, as always, the overflow room does double duty. Standing between a room that can be used as a stage on the left, and the sanctuary on the right, it can be used for seating space for either, or as a room in its own right. The architect has wisely precluded the use of the sanctuary for entertainment purposes, however, for by placing the congregation in the sanctuary at a lower level, and in fixed pews, there can be no temptation to use the sanctuary for purposes other than worship.

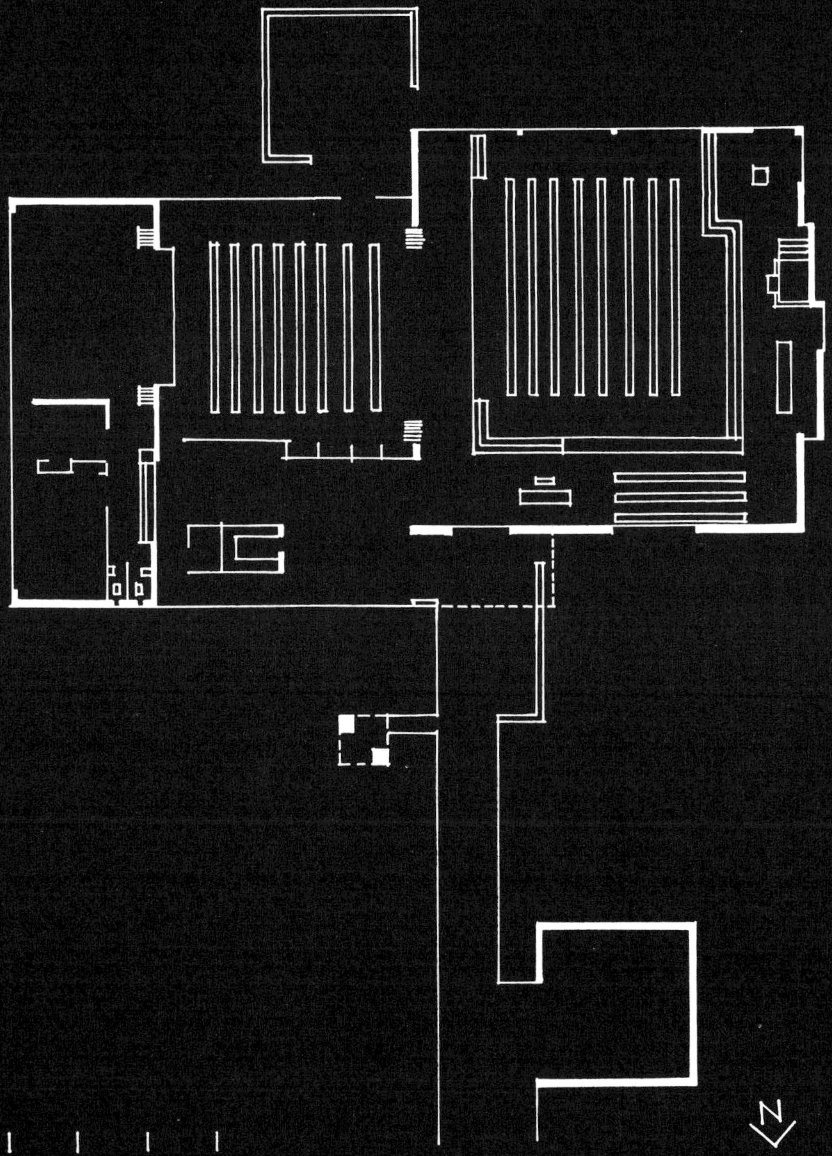
N

In "The Cornerstone" at Santpoort the problem is less severe, for name and form conspire together to remind us that we have our life in Christ, who is the cornerstone, chosen and precious (I Peter 2:6–8). Thus, Mr. Kruger already has his congregation "in Christ" before he gets to the problem of seating. The problem is also less severe than in Nagele because there is no compulsion to be bound by right angles, and so the seating gathers around the pulpit in an arc of 180°. Nonetheless, the architect has put the entire congregation, already "in Christ" and gathered about the Word and Sacraments, together in a depression three steps down from the entrance level to add still a further sense of relatedness to the members of the body of Christ.

"The Cornerstone" (De Hoeksteen), Hervormd, Santpoort, The Netherlands
Ir. J. Kruger, architect

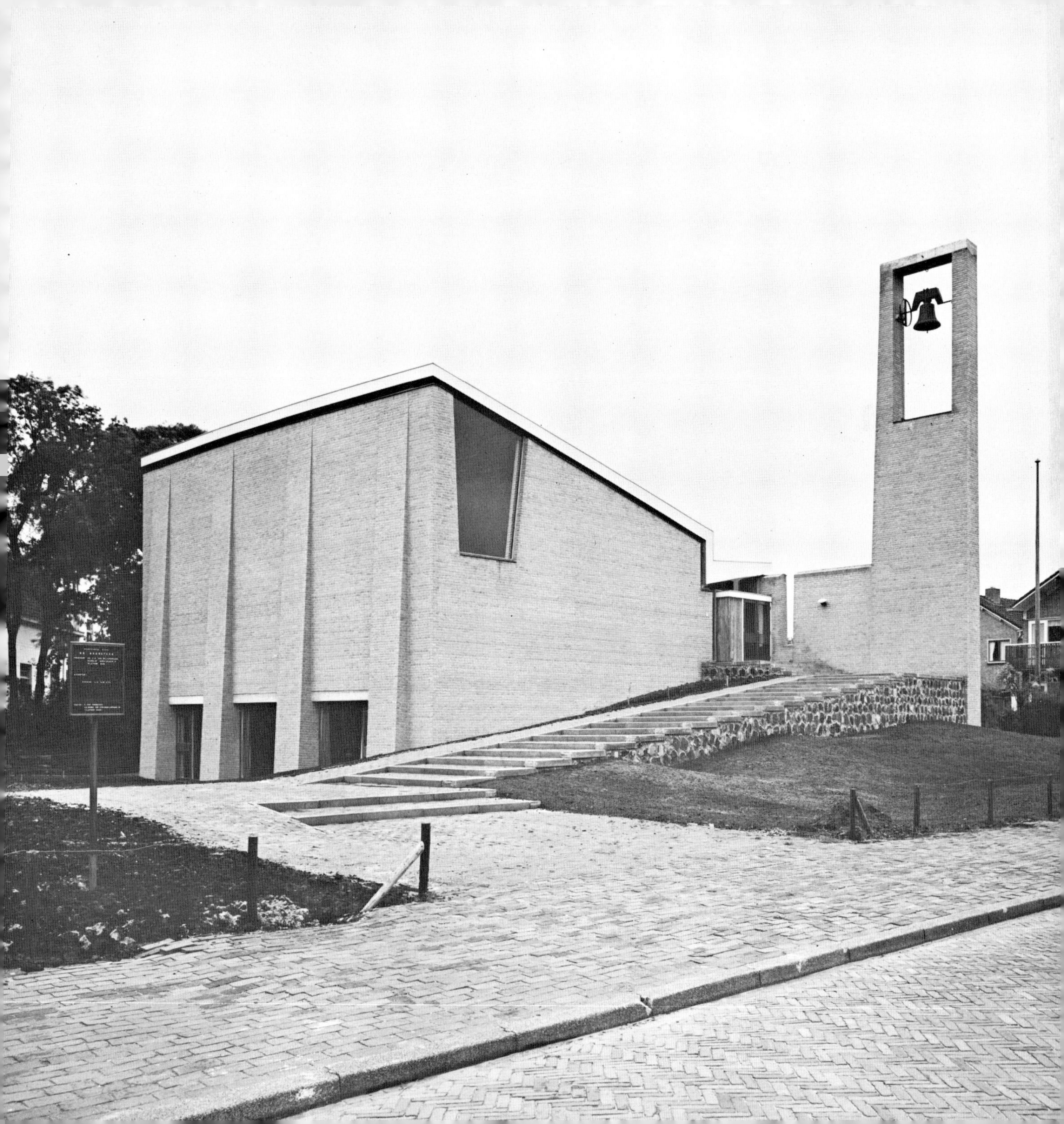

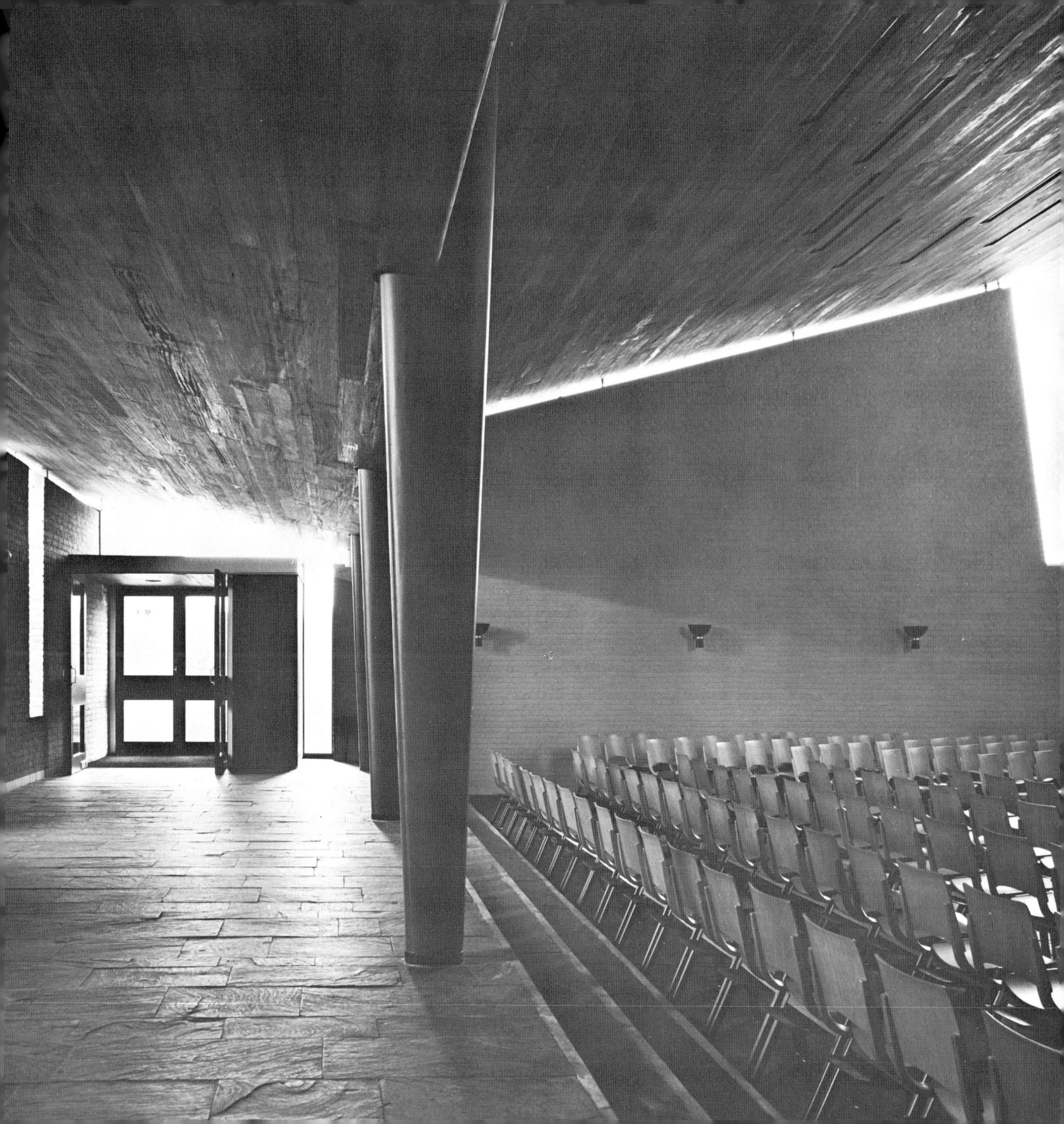

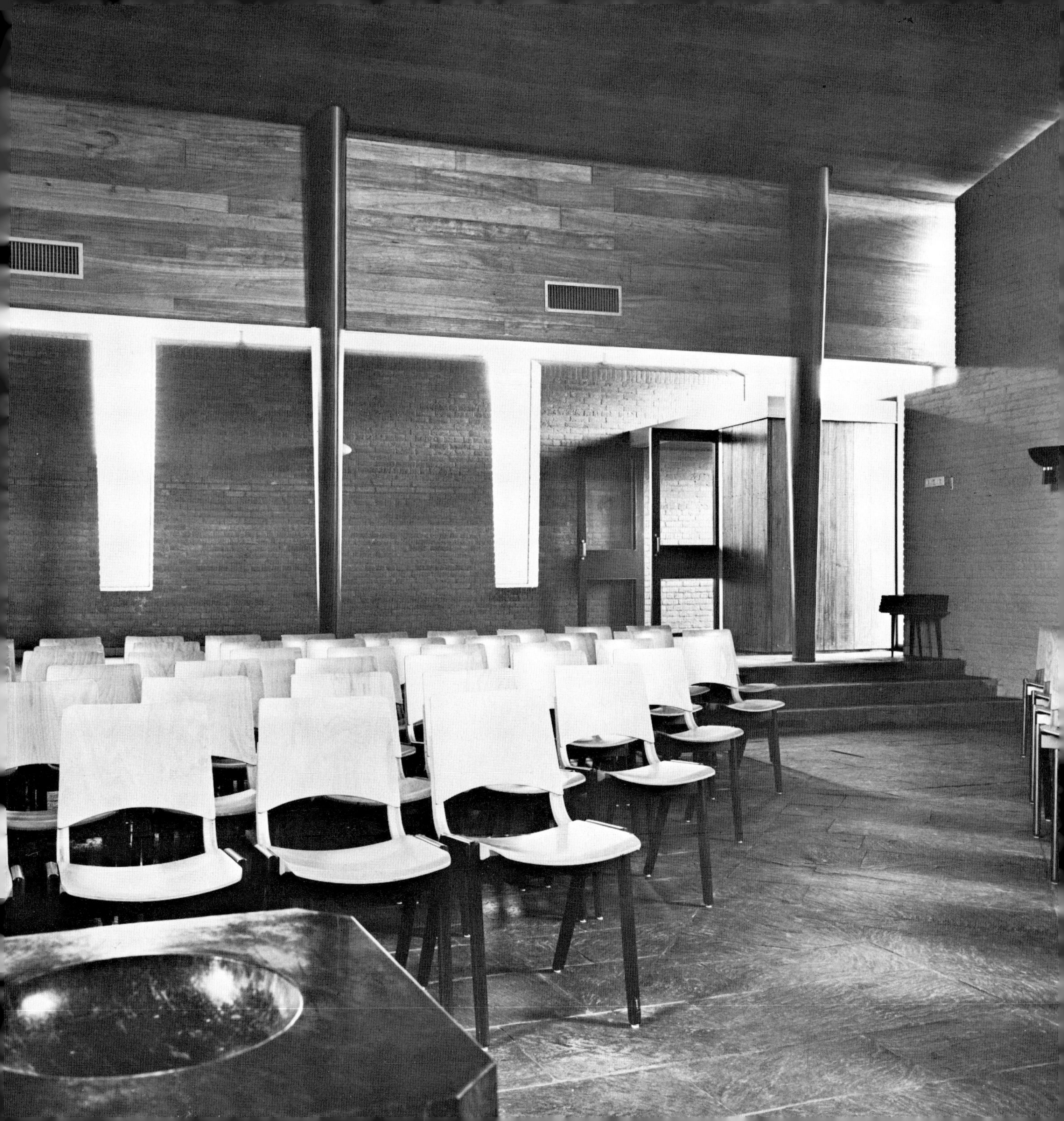

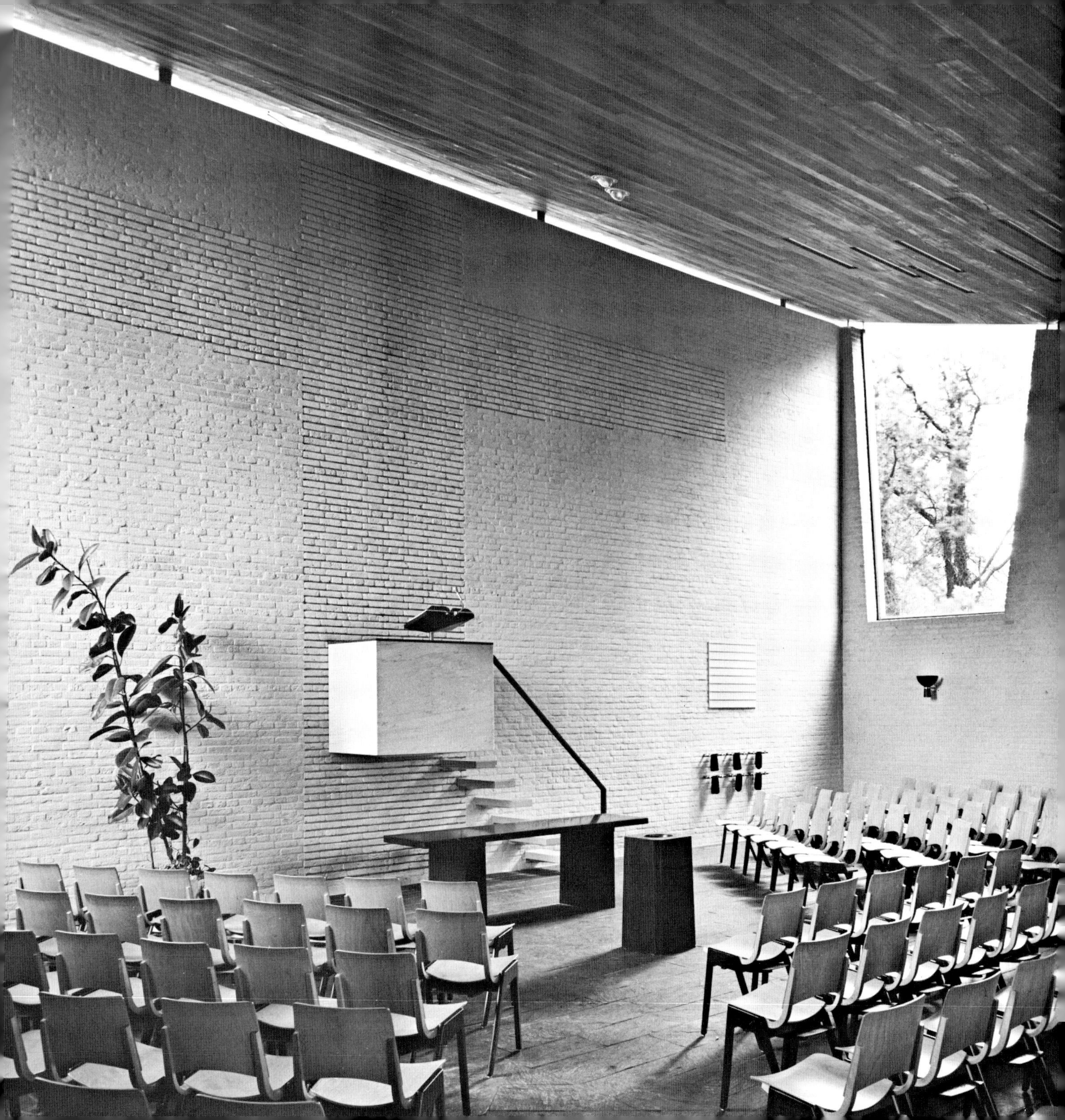

The Ministry

> Now we must speak of the order by which the Lord willed his church to be governed. He alone should rule and reign in the church as well as have authority or pre-eminence in it, and this authority should be exercised and administered by his Word alone. Nevertheless, because he does not dwell among us in visible presence (Matt. 26:11), we have said that he used the ministry of men to declare openly his will to us by mouth, as a sort of delegated work, not by transferring to them his right and honor, but only that through their mouths he may do his own work—just as a workman uses a tool to do his work.[14]

The people of God, the Church, the body of Christ, is composed of all of Christ's people, and not just of the ordained clergy. Every Christian is a member of the body of Christ. For the good ordering of this body "grace was given to each of us according to the measure of Christ's gift. . . . And his gifts were that some should be evangelists, some pastors and teachers, for the equipment of the saints, for the work of ministry, for building up the body of Christ" (Ephesians 4:7, 11–12; cf. I Corinthians 12).

It was one of the achievements of the Reformation that it allowed itself to be so governed by God's Word that it returned to this understanding of the Church. While for the good ordering of the body of Christ various gifts are given to some that the several functions of the body may be fulfilled, the Reformed saw clearly that this did not elevate these brethren to some privileged status with God, but rather constituted a call to duty and function within the priesthood of all believers.

While the gifts are given by Christ, and the call to the office comes by the Holy Spirit, Calvin is explicit concerning the necessity for human agency in the calling to the ministry, observing that no sober person will deny this.[15]

---

[14] *Institutes*, 4:3:1, p. 1053.
[15] *Ibid.*, 4:3:14, p. 1064.

He further returns to Scripture to point out that this is the work of the Church as a whole, for "Luke relates that presbyters were appointed through the churches by Paul and Barnabas; but at the same time he notes the manner, or means, when he says that it was done by votes—'presbyters elected by show of hands in every church' (Acts 14:23)."[16] This point is worth noting insofar as it puts theology into action and makes unmistakable the fact that the ministry had been returned to its proper position as a part of the body of Christ. The separation of the clergy from the laity finds its expression in Roman Catholic worship with the juxtaposition of priest and people, sanctuary (apse) and nave, and for this reason the Bishops of Germany expressed disapproval of the circular form as the solution for Roman worship.[17] If architectural expression of the separation of clergy and people is desired by Rome, then is it not imperative that the Reformed theology of the ministry, with its message concerning the unity of the people of Christ, be given statement in Presbyterian architecture?

The Minister

The minister derives his importance for the Church by virtue of his responsibility to preach the Word and administer the Sacraments. While any minister is keenly aware that these duties carry him beyond pulpit, font, and table into the world and involve him in all manner of other activities, they are nonetheless his foremost duties and find their principal expression in the midst of Christ's people. The architectural expression of Word and Sacraments is thus identical with that of the office of the minister. The architectural statement of the office of the minister must not exalt him as a person, but rather his activity through the Dominical means of bringing Christ to

---

[16] *Ibid.*, 4:3:15, p. 1066.
[17] *Documents for Sacred Architecture,* Directive 6, p. 18.

men. As an individual, the minister is simply another member of God's gathered people, but by virtue of his call, gifts, and ordination, he has a special office to perform. This office does not involve elevating himself, or providing the congregation with his opinions, but rather involves the preaching of God's Word and the administration of Baptism and the Lord's Supper. When proper architectural expression has been given to Word and Sacraments, it has also been given to the office of the ministry.

Thus, while Reformed doctrine allows no separation between the clergy and the rest of God's people, this truth has already found expression in the criterion that the people are in no way to be separated from the liturgical center. There must be no fence, no rail, no visual implication that the congregation is cut off from the means of grace, as if these means were the exclusive prerogative of the clergy. Failure to give expression to Word and Sacraments inevitably involves failure to state properly the doctrine of the ministry. For example, when the Sacrament of the Lord's Supper has been poorly stated by the adoption of a pseudo Medieval Gothic chancel with an altar against the east wall, then there all too frequently goes with it the ceremony of the minister standing at the steps of the chancel and receiving the offering plates from the deacons, bearing them alone into the chancel and placing them on the altar. Think of this. Even the deacons are kept out of the chancel while the minister alone bears the gifts to the altar—a symbolism diametrically opposed to the presbyterian concept of church government and ministry! But, on the other hand, when the communion table is used as a table, and the people may come to that table and use it as such, then there can be no opportunity for a false concept of the ministry as some privileged group who are separated from the rest of God's people and who alone may approach the Lord's table.

ARCHITECTURE WHICH IS FAITHFUL TO THE REFORMED DOCTRINE OF

WORD AND SACRAMENTS IS AT ONCE FAITHFUL TO THE PRESBYTERIAN DOCTRINE OF THE MINISTRY.

The Elders

The special offices do not stop with those of the minister, but include those of the elders and deacons as well.[18] Nor is it any small responsibility that has been given to these men chosen from the midst of the congregation, for the elder has been given responsibility for the right proclamation of the Word of God and the proper use of the Sacraments, in which his field of activity goes out into the lives of the congregation, and thus into the community as well.

By the work of the Holy Spirit, and the appointment of men (usually, as in Acts 14:23, by the vote of the congregation), elders are taken from the midst of the congregation and given these high duties. While the Episcopal Church says, in effect, to the men of the congregation, "We appreciate your help and interest in the church, but you must leave matters of theology and doctrine to the trained clergy," the Reformed have said to the elder, "The right preaching of God's Word is your responsibility."

> The Elders shall have regard to the teaching and conduct of the Ministers of the Word and of their fellow officers and shall prevent the sacraments from being profaned.[19]

Truly, no church order has elevated the elder to a higher plane of responsibility than the Presbyterian. Where else has the elder been given the respon-

---

[18] *Institutes*, 4:3:8, pp. 1060f.

[19] *The Constitution of the Reformed Church in America* (New York: Board of Education, RCA, Revised to June, 1961), p. 17. This constitution stands as a direct descendant of the Rules of Church Order as formulated at Dort in 1619.

sibility of oversight, not only of the conduct of the members of the Church, including fellow officers and ministers, but also of the preaching of the Word? Where else does one find such responsibility vested in members of the congregation? The Church is not at the whim of the minister; he is not allowed to teach and preach as he alone wishes. No, the elders, reading their Bibles and studying their Doctrinal Standards, are given the responsibility for the right proclamation of the Word. They are always there as a safeguard, as part of a system of checks and balances, that the teaching of God's Word may not rest upon a single individual. In Reformed theology the importance of the preaching of God's Word is recognized in church government, where not only the minister but also the elders are responsible for its right proclamation.

Anything so important to the life of the Church as the elder necessitates architectural expression. In many old churches in the Netherlands one finds special elders' benches (e.g., p. 85). There, propped up on the "pew desk," stands a Bible for each elder, and often a copy of the Doctrinal Standards as well. Here the elders are to sit, with their Bibles and their Standards, exercising their responsibility for the right preaching of the Word. The same responsibilty was exercised in other Reformed churches on the Continent. In Scotland throughout the sixteenth and seventeenth centuries the pulpit itself was "flanked by elders' seats." In 1581, St. Giles', Edinburgh, had a pulpit with a "lettroun and saitts about the same."[20] In the "hie Kirk" in 1649 arrangements were made for the "re-erection of the pulpit on a new site . . . with seatts for the ministrie and the Reader ane pairt for baptisme and marriage and ane uther pairt for the elderis and deakens . . . ."[21]

Fortunately, however, this concept of the elders' pew is not a relic of

---

[20] Hay, *op. cit.,* p. 184.
[21] *Ibid.,* pp. 195–96.

the past. In the industrial city of Schiedam, the Netherlands, The Church of the Resurrection, with angular lines of concrete, glass, and steel, has pews for the elders close to the pulpit, equipped with individual fluorescent reading lights that the books may be carefully perused.

The Church of the Resurrection (Opstandingskerk), Hervormd, Schiedam, The Netherlands. Van den Broek & Bakema, architects

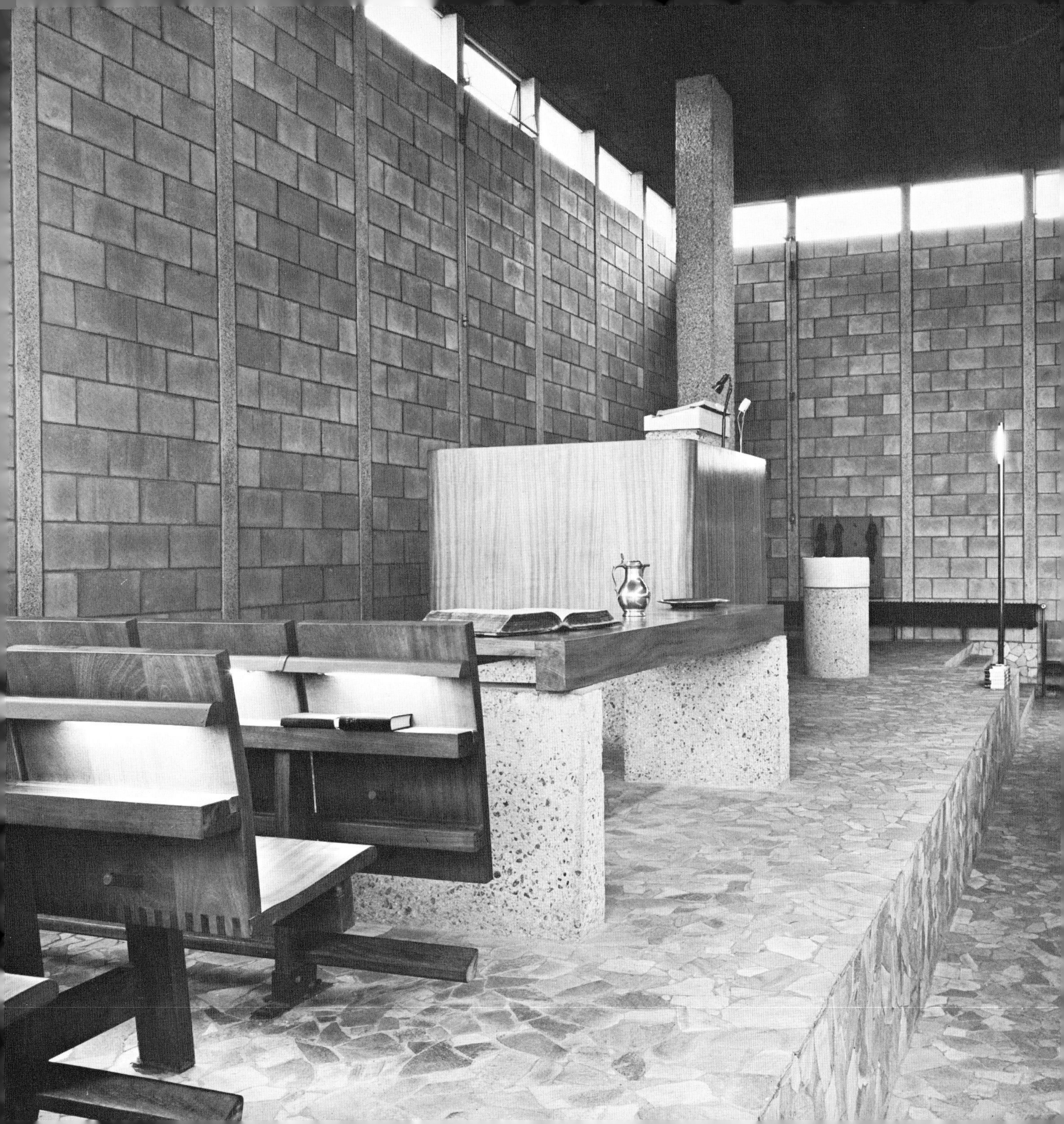

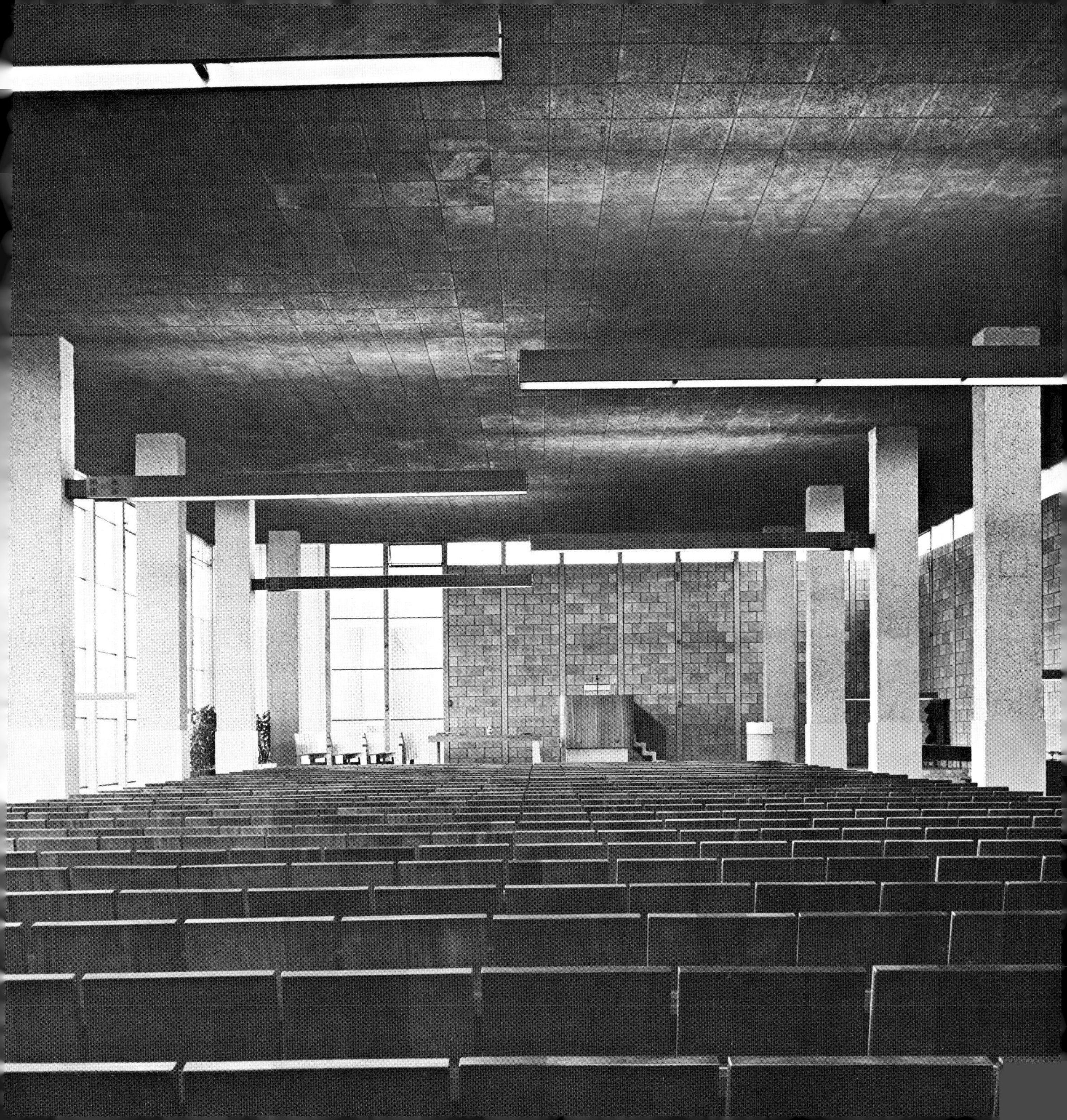

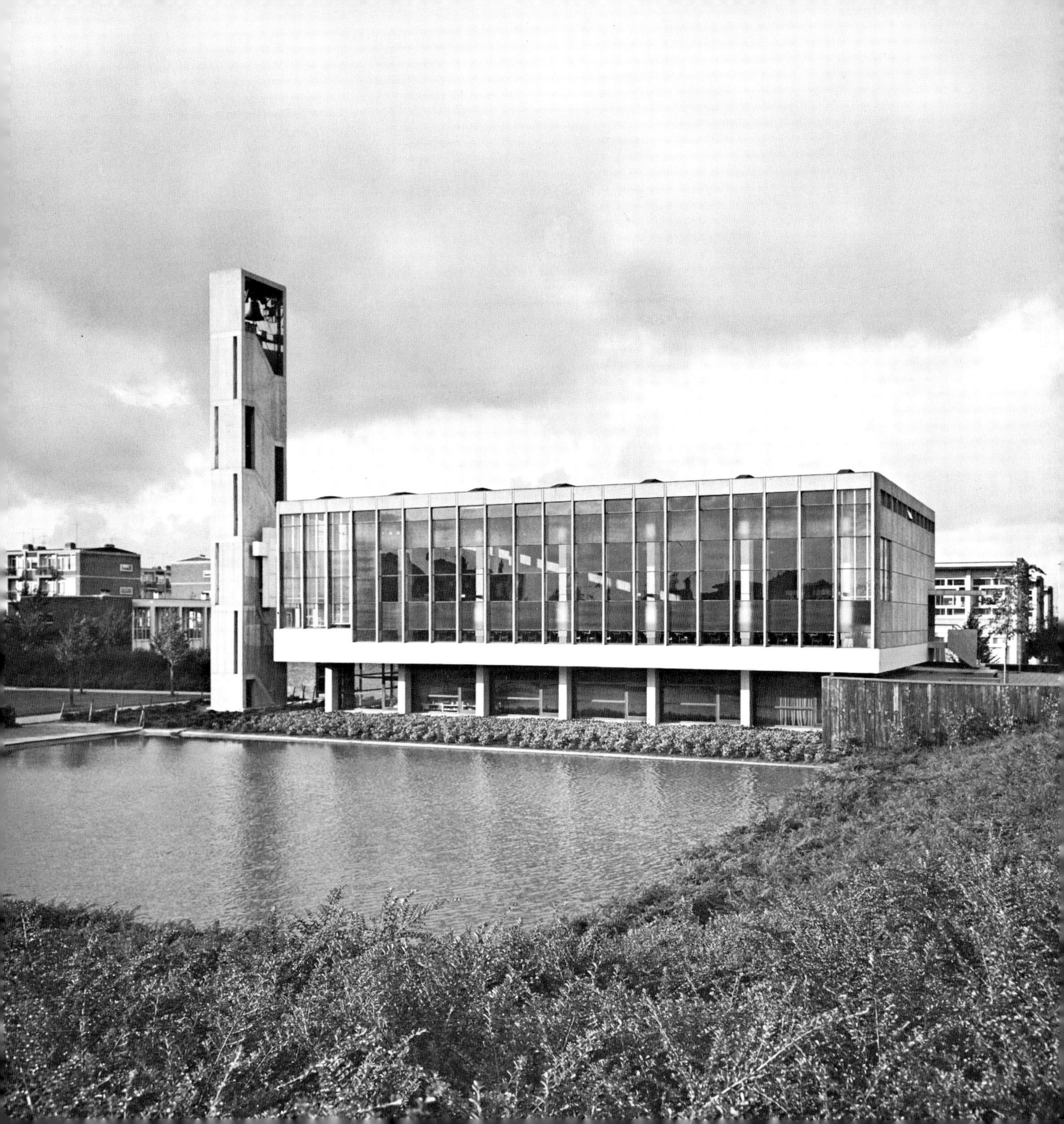

But what has happened to these elders' pews in recent American churches? There are some in older Presbyterian and Reformed churches, but why are they not being built into churches today? Is it because all too often the elders have become simply the men who have oversight of the finances and the church buildings, rather than oversight of the Word and Sacraments? Perhaps it is time that every possible device be used, including architecture, to remind both elders and congregation that the elder stands as a precious gift of God's Word, ordained to the high responsibility of providing for the right preaching of that Word. Should not every building committee interested in a church Reformed in theology and Presbyterian in government include pews for the elders in the front of the church, and racks or desks upon which can be placed Bibles and the Doctrinal Standards? And perhaps with this architectural feature one might even add the custom still widely practiced in the Netherlands, where, as the minister descends from the pulpit at the end of the service, an elder waits at the bottom of the steps, either to commend or to rebuke him for his sermon.

In addition to his responsibilities in respect to the Word of God, the elder is also charged with the duty of church discipline. Into the eighteenth century, the elder in Scotland wielded such disciplinary authority that offenders might on Sunday be placed in the jougs in the kirkyard before entering the church and taking their place on the stool of repentance.

> The jougs consisted of an iron collar, into which the unfortunate's neck was padlocked, secured by chain to the wall of the kirk or kirkyard . . . . An even less pleasant implement, whose use was not confined to Scotland, was the branks or scold's bridle, an uncomfortable steel bridle which made speech impossible for the wearer. It appears to have been largely, if not solely, an adornment for over eloquent females.[22]

---

[22] *Ibid.,* p. 240.

Discipline of this type disappeared later in the eighteenth century. It is doubtful whether it ever constituted an adornment to the Church, and its demise need not be mourned.

Nevertheless, the elder is still charged with Christian discipline and this must be seen in relation to both Word and Sacraments. When sin appears within the covenant community and becomes a stumbling block to others, then the elder, in obedience to the injunctions of the Lord in Matthew 18, must go to the offender in the exercise of his office. But the elder does not possess an authority in and of himself with which he may act as a magistrate, but he goes in the place of his Lord, and it is the authority of the Word of Christ which he bears. The elder approaches the sinner not to punish, but as a bearer of the Word, which while sharper than a two-edged sword, as it convicts of sin, also speaks of forgiveness and reconciliation with God and man. It is only after the Church has duly exercised the discipline of the Word as its elders, with prayer and humility, have sought to apply that Word to specific occasions of sin within the covenant community, and that Word has nonetheless been rejected, that the elders must proceed to the discipline of the Sacraments. Only when the Word has been rejected are the elders to forbid the signs and seals of participation in Christ to the sinner, further to make manifest that by his unrepented sin he has rejected Christ and his Church.

It therefore becomes clear that a graphic display of the elder's true function in discipline is not in the "jougs" or "scold's bridle," but rather in placing him close to the source of his authority as it is both received and exercised. The elders should be seated near pulpit, font and table. There both congregation and elders may be reminded that these men have their authority only as they represent Christ, and that this authority is exercised on behalf of the Christ who comes to his people in Word and Sacraments.

In the exercise of his office the elder is quite obviously not confined to the sanctuary. As Dr. E. P. Heideman so ably points out, while the elder stands in relation to Word and Sacraments both in teaching and discipline, he is also charged with carrying the sanctifying power of the gospel out into the community, for as he is concerned with the lives of the people of the Church—"marriage and home life, relation of parents to children, ways of recreation and modes of entertainment, relationships between neighbors, and temperate living"—he is involved in the life of the community.[23] Nevertheless, the authority for this involvement comes from Christ, and graphic expression of this relationship comes by placing the elder in close proximity to both Word and Sacraments.

THE RESPONSIBILITY OF THE ELDER FOR THE PURE PREACHING OF THE WORD, THE WORTHY PARTICIPATION IN THE SACRAMENTS, AND THE LIVES OF THE MEMBERS OF THE CHURCH CAN BEST BE ARCHITECTURALLY DISPLAYED BY PUTTING THE ELDER IN A SPECIFIC PLACE IN CLOSE PROXIMITY TO THE WORD AND SACRAMENTS, AND BY PROVIDING HIM WITH THE GUIDES OF HIS OFFICE, THE HOLY SCRIPTURES AND THE DOCTRINAL STANDARDS.

---

[23] *The Constitution of the Church* (monograph), p. 156.

The Reformed Church (Hervormd), Rutten, N. O. P., The Netherlands
J. Schipper Jr., architect

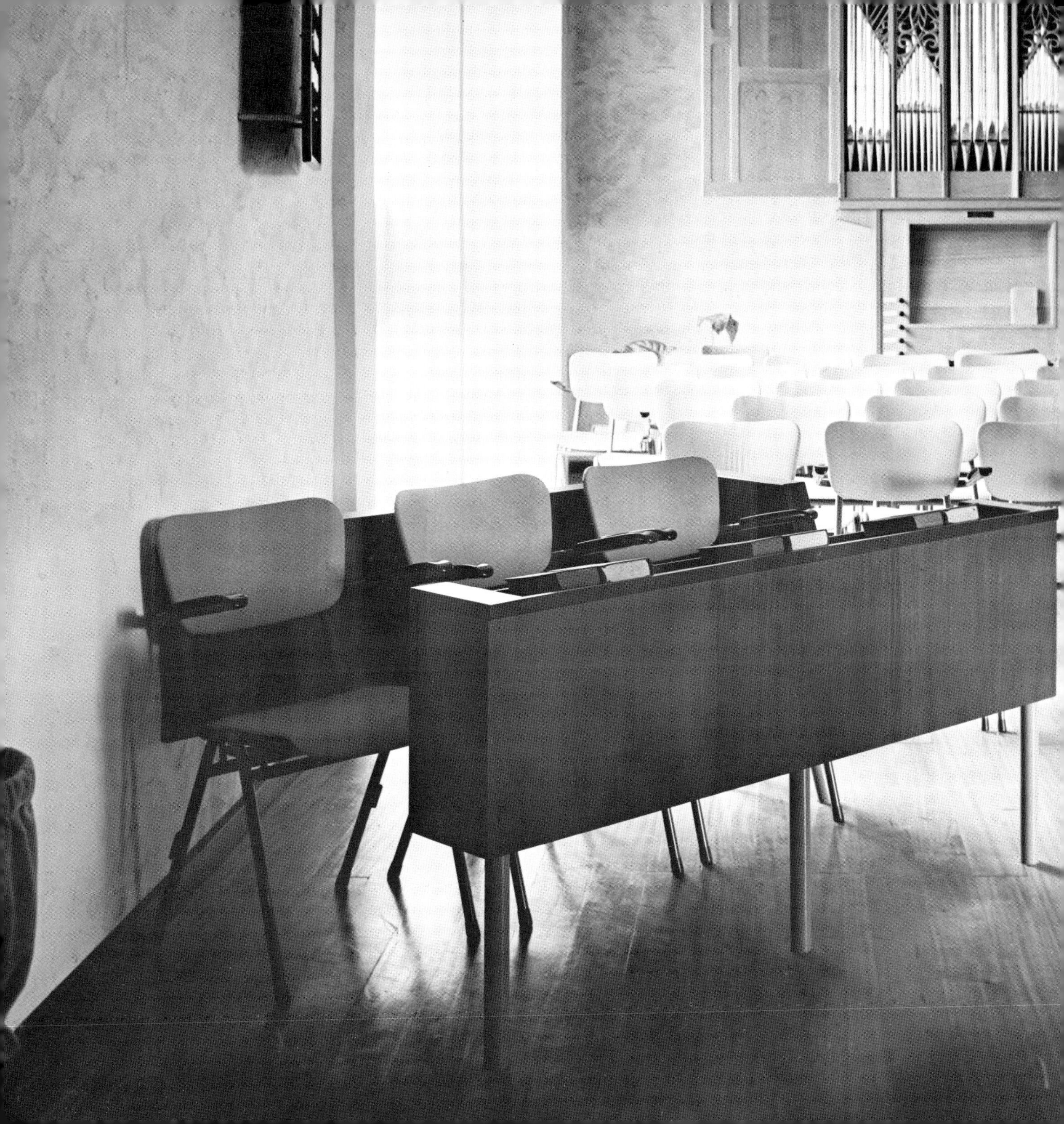

The Reformed Church at Rutten has more to commend it than even its splendid elders' desks. It is a fine example of working within the architectural genre of the polder, yet in such a way as to produce a distinctive, practical place of worship.

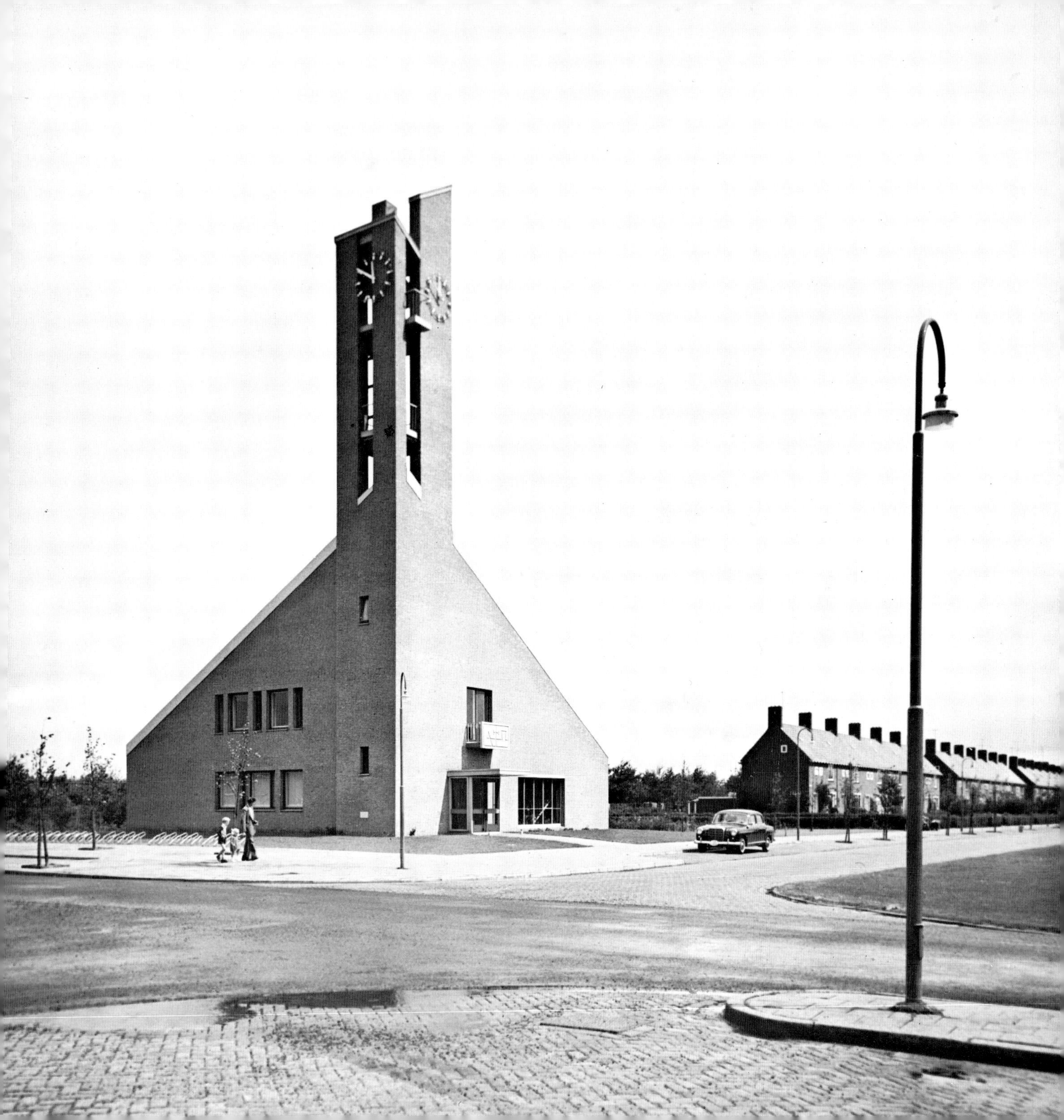

The narthex is generously proportioned for a church of this size.

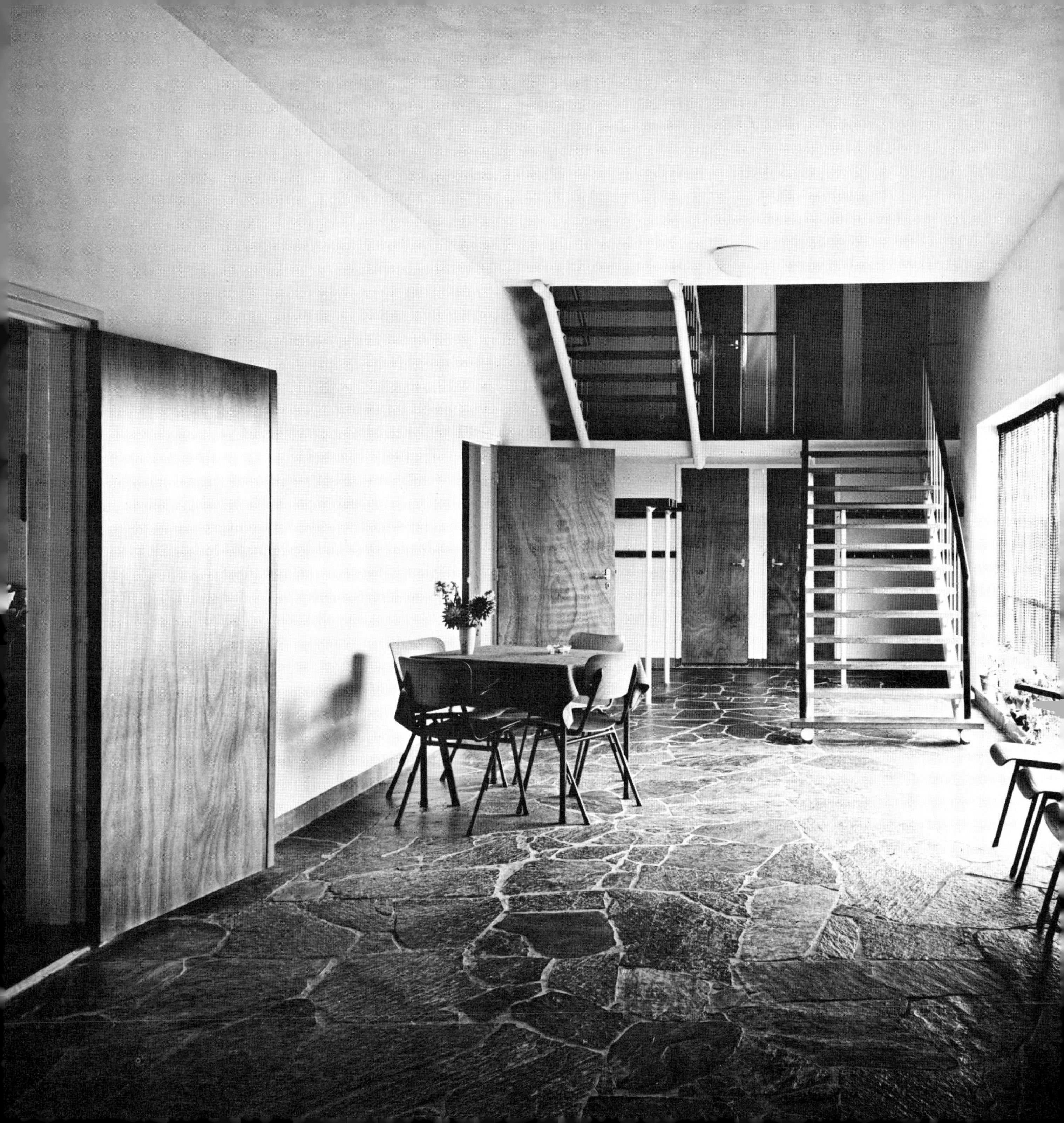

Within the context of this relatively small sanctuary, the table and font (which are perhaps the weakest element of the church) have the virtue of being in the midst of the congregation, which is grouped around them. There is seating for 200 plus room for an additional 30 in the balcony.

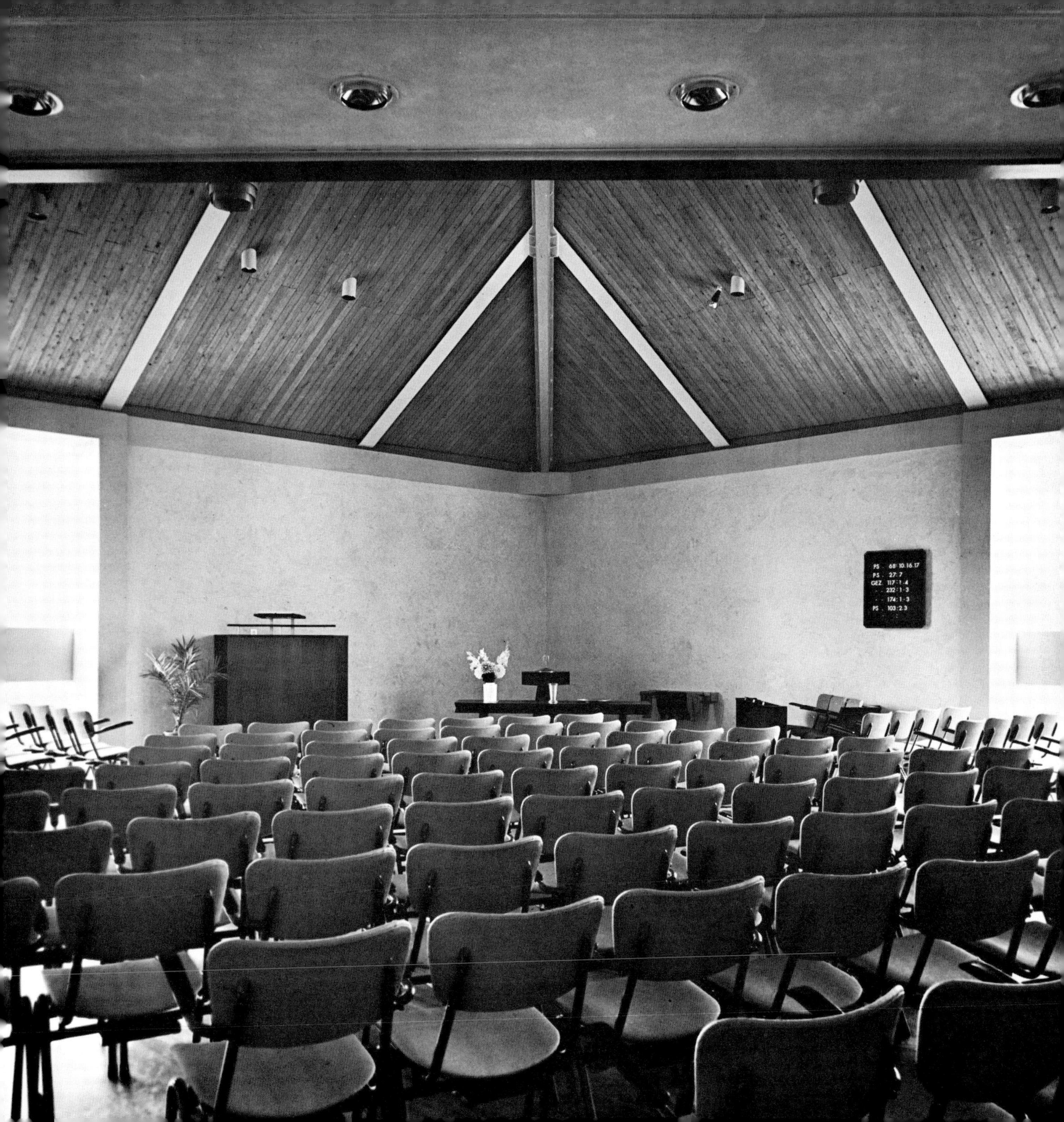
PS . 68:10.16.17
PS . 27:7
GEZ. 117:1-4
232:1-3
174:1-3
PS . 103:2.3

Positiv by Ahrend and Brunzema of Loga by Leer (Ostfriesland)

Gedackt   *8*
Praestant   *4*
Octave   *2*
Spitzgedackt   *4*
Scharf 2 ranks

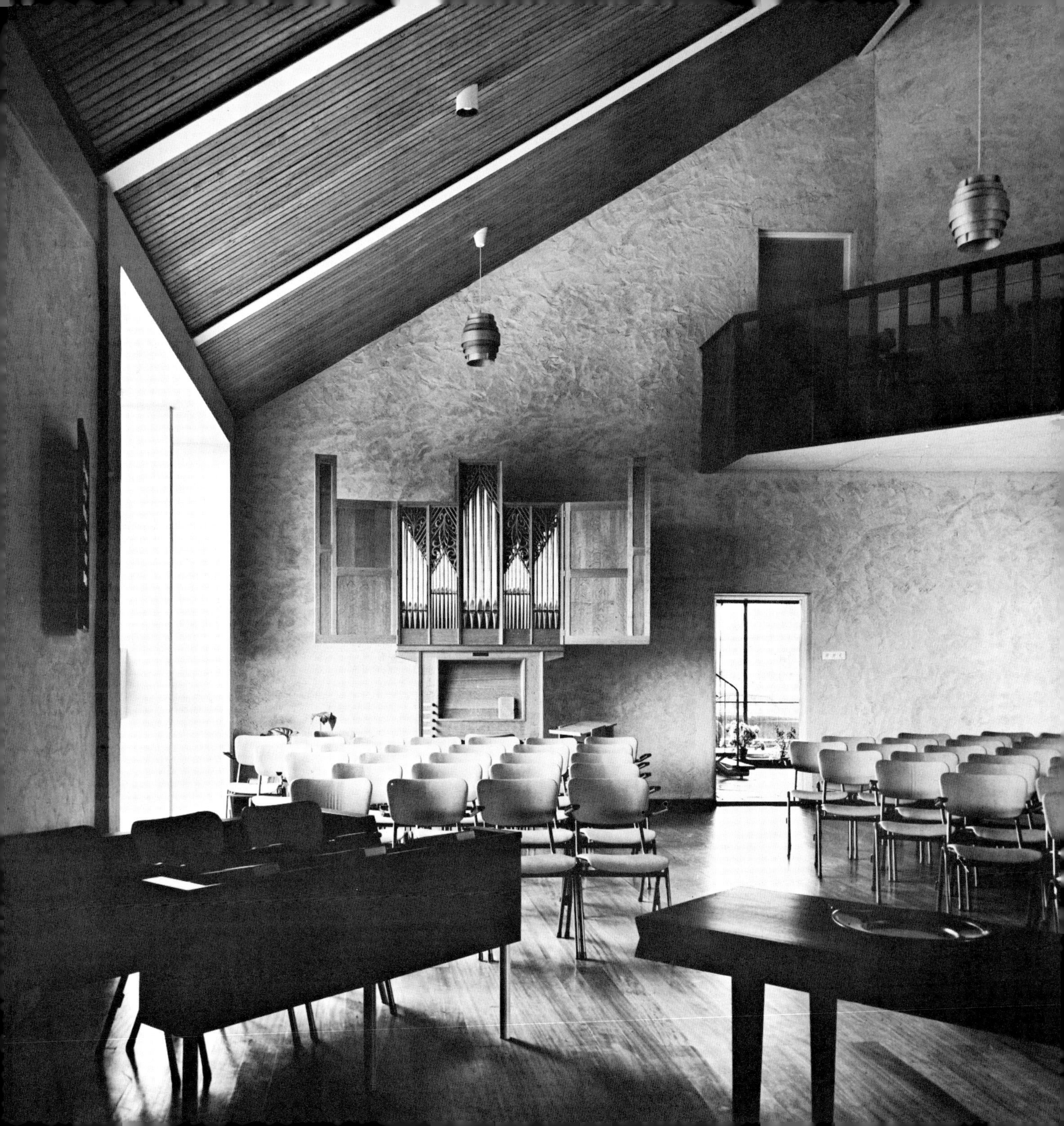

Based upon Numbers 13, this window, so appropriate for this church serving a polder village, was executed by the Rev. P. H. G. C. Kok.

DIT LAND
ZAL IK U
GEVEN

The Deacons

A great deal of confusion has attended the office of deacon throughout the history of the Church. Perhaps this is because in New Testament times the office shows an extremely diffuse growth. The meaning of the Greek, διακονία, is "service" and can include the ideas of aid, support, and distribution. The deacons of the New Testament were first appointed to serve the tables of the poor widows of the Greek-speaking element in the Church at Jerusalem, whom some felt were being neglected. The chapters immediately following, however, find the deacons baptizing, preaching, and suffering martyrdom for their bold proclamation of the Faith.

Since then the office of deacon has suffered many vicissitudes. At one point in the early history of the Church the deacon was regarded with more honor than was the elder. In later years the Roman Church made him but a liturgical helper in the services. Much the same has happened in the Church of England and in the Methodist Church. In these communions also the deacon is but a liturgical figure, and little more. It was Calvin, however, who took the deacon away from the altar and sent him back into a poor and needy world.[24]

Calvin restored the office of deacon to its original New Testament function, which he then divided into two sections: the administration of the alms, and the care of the poor and the sick. But with changing social conditions, in which the state increasingly takes care of poor and sick, what is now the role of the deacon? Perhaps it would be most helpful to acknowledge again that the specific role of the deacon has never been rigidly defined. Calvin, while offering the two classes of deacons (on the basis of a somewhat tenuous exegesis of Romans 12:8), nonetheless admits that "the term diakonia itself

---

[24] *Ibid.*, p. 177.

has a wider application . . . ."[25] As to this wider application, Dr. E. P. Heideman has offered a brilliant interpretation of the office of deacon in terms of God's righteousness, seeing the concern for the poor and needy as a concern of God's righteousness in defending the widows, orphans, and poor against oppression and exploitation. When the concern of the deacon is with righteousness, his office is seen to open into the whole realm of social justice. It is really the deacons who should comprise the social action commissions and deal with the vexing questions of Christianity in modern society.

This emphasis is good, and it is desperately needed. In this area which the Church has often left so empty, the deacon should enter and serve with the freedom for service which he possessed in New Testament times. Nonetheless, the work of the deacon cannot be confined within the bounds of justice, any more than God's justice stands by itself. For if the New Testament concept of the office of deacon is probed in depth, it becomes apparent that whatever else it might have been, the office of the deacon is the proleptic office of love! The office of the deacon is even more than justice; it moves beyond justice under the Lordship of Christ. Into the world of the first century A.D., a world that was cynical and commercial, hardened by war, rebellion and foreign rule, a world of monumental self-concern in which social agencies, private or public, were unknown—into this world of self-interest came the Church with its deacons. The first deacons were appointed to serve the destitute widows. This was more than justice, for these widows had no claim, no legal right, by which they could demand food. They had not been oppressed or defrauded by the Church that they might claim the return of what belonged to them. No, the office of the deacon goes beyond justice, and expresses itself in love. The office of deacon extends food and aid to those who can give absolutely nothing in return. It is the office of love.

---

[25] *Institutes*, 4:3:9, p. 1061.

But this office of deacon is also a proleptic office, for it reaches forward into the time of Christ's Second Coming, into the Parousia. At that time when there shall be a new heaven and a new earth, when the powers of evil have been put down, then we shall all live in righteousness and love. The office of the deacon is to reach forward toward this time, and, as it were, to pull down into our own sinful, selfish, grasping age, some of the selfless service and love of the new heaven and the new earth, when former things will have passed away.

But it is part of the glory of the office of deacon that its substance shall never pass away. There will be a time when the task of the minister is finished, for he proclaims the Christ, and when we see Him face to face the task of the preacher is done. There will be a time when the office of the elder who oversees the preaching of the Word and the Sacraments shall be finished, for when Christ, to whom the Sacraments point us and join us, is here, then Sacraments will be no more. But love, which is the very substance of the office of the deacon, will never pass away.

> . . . as for prophecy, it will pass away; as for tongues, they will cease; as for knowledge, it will pass away. For our knowledge is imperfect and our prophecy is imperfect; but when the perfect comes, the imperfect will pass away. . . . For now we see in a mirror dimly, but then face to face. Now I know in part; then I shall understand fully, even as I have been fully understood. So faith, hope, love abide, these three; but the greatest of these is love.
>
> I Corinthians 13:8-10, 12-13.

But is there any way in which the office of the deacon can be given significant architectural expression? The problems of giving structural form to righteousness and love are immediately apparent. A starting point, however, might be to place the deacon in proper relation to the source of the love which his office must express. It is not an office of general humanism or idealism; the mandate of love comes from the Christ who loved us while we were yet his enemies. Thus the deacon should be placed near the pulpit and table where, through both Word and Sacraments, he may ever be reminded of his union with Christ who is righteousness and love. The source of the love of the deacon, which he in turn must carry from the center of the Church out into the world, is Jesus Christ. Therefore:

THE OFFICE OF THE DEACON IS THE PROLEPTIC OFFICE OF LOVE. ARCHITECTURALLY, AS WELL AS IN FACT, THE DEACON SHOULD REMAIN CLOSE TO THE SOURCE OF THAT LOVE, CLOSE TO CHRIST, WHO COMES IN WORD AND SACRAMENTS.

Having acknowledged the source of the deacon's righteousness and love, how does one visibly express the means by which that love is put into action? Money! No one in the church assumes that money can buy love. On the other hand, let no one assume a false pietism that regards money as something beneath the Christian. In the earliest days of the New Testament Church the overpowering love that these Christians felt for one another expressed itself in part in terms of money, for they "had all things in common; and they sold their possessions and goods and distributed them to all, as they had need" (Acts 2:44—45).

If the destitute are to be fed, or given clothing, or taught a trade, or educated, it takes money! If the blind are to be helped, if educational information concerning burning civic issues is to be distributed, if people are to be informed or mobilized on any level of society, it takes money. If, in short, any provision of goods and services is to be made—and because we are not angels we must act through goods and services—it takes money. Most effective is direct, personal, Christian love and compassion, but whenever that love and compassion seeks to translate itself into goods or services, these must be paid for. Money is the medium of exchange even when one seeks to transfer love into deeds.

Thus let us have an end to such shallow hyprocrisy as being unwilling to talk about money in church. The deacon's office is the proleptic office of love which will never pass away, but the deacon must also deal with money in expressing that love. Therefore let us give architectural significance to the deacon's responsibility of love through the alms, the money which he collects to incarnate the love of Christ's Church.

THE OFFICE OF THE DEACON IS THE PROLEPTIC OFFICE OF LOVE, AND THE INCARNATE MANIFESTATION OF THIS LOVE IN THE GIFTS OF GOD'S PEOPLE IS TO RECEIVE ARCHITECTURAL DEFINITION IN THE RECEPTACLES FOR THE OFFERINGS.

On the Continent, where a box at the door for offerings is a familiar sight, the box constitutes one symbol of the office of the deacon. Of these offering receptacles at the door, one of the most handsome is to be found in The Bullinger Church (cf. pp. 141, 143).

The Bullinger Church (Bullingerkirche), Reformed, Zurich, Switzerland
Bros. Pfister, architects

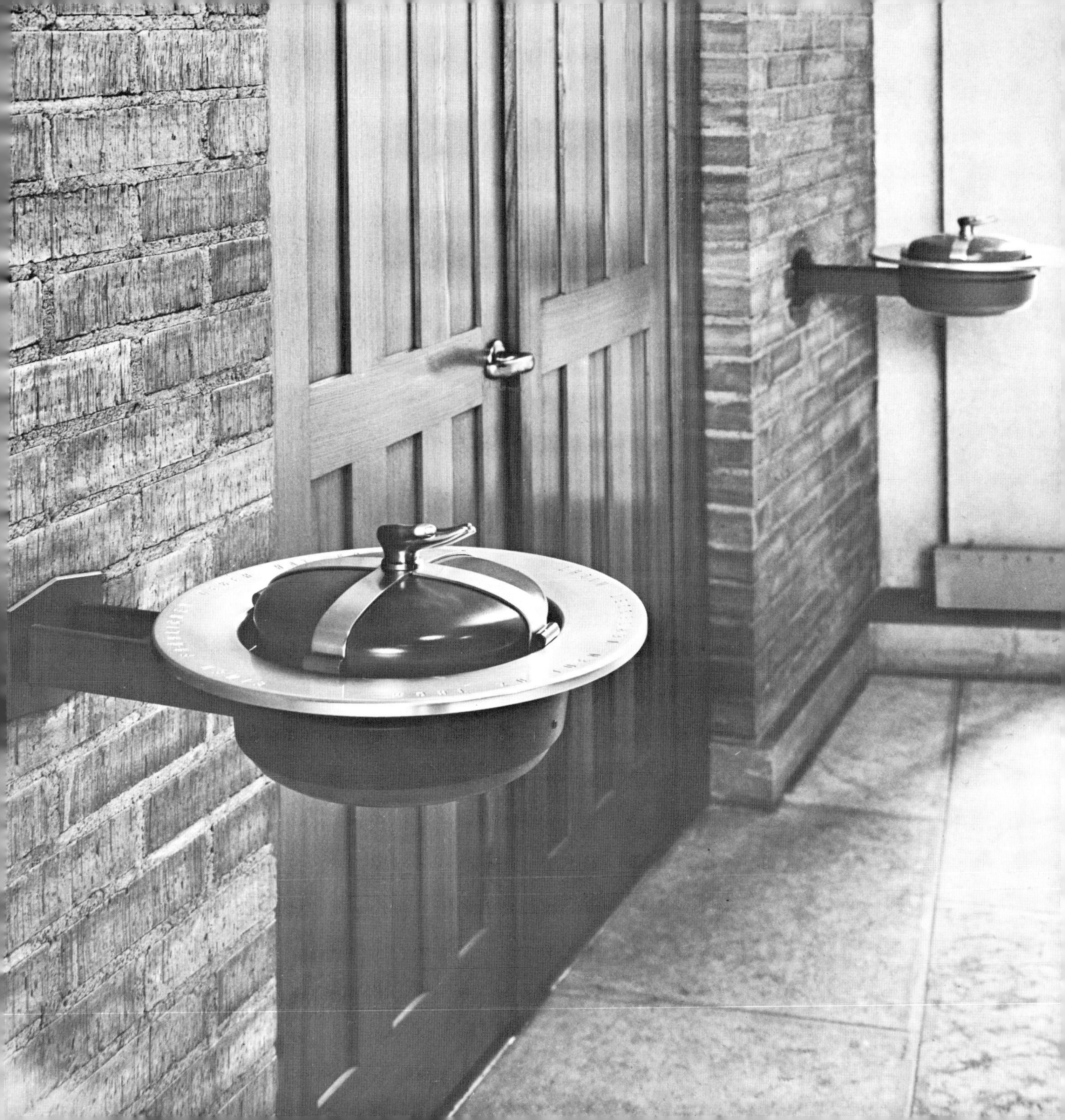

Most Americans will undoubtedly wish to continue the more personal approach to the offering, which gives it as well liturgical recognition as part of our worship and service to God. As such the architect must seek a means of giving visual prominence to the offering receptacles. One means which offers itself to a strong statement of this phase of the deacons office is the Dutch *collectezakje*, or, more popularly *hengelzakje* (a *hengel* being a fishing rod). These *hengelzakjes* are offering bags attached to the ends of long poles. The deacon simply moves the *zakje* in front of the parishioners by means of his pole. However, this is not a job for the amateur, as careless handling can make the long pole quite disruptive. American deacons, and thus also the architects, may not wish to take advantage of the fine visual effects of the office of the deacon as found in the Reformed Church of Ochten.

The Reformed Church (Hervormd), Ochten, The Netherlands
A. Eibink, architect

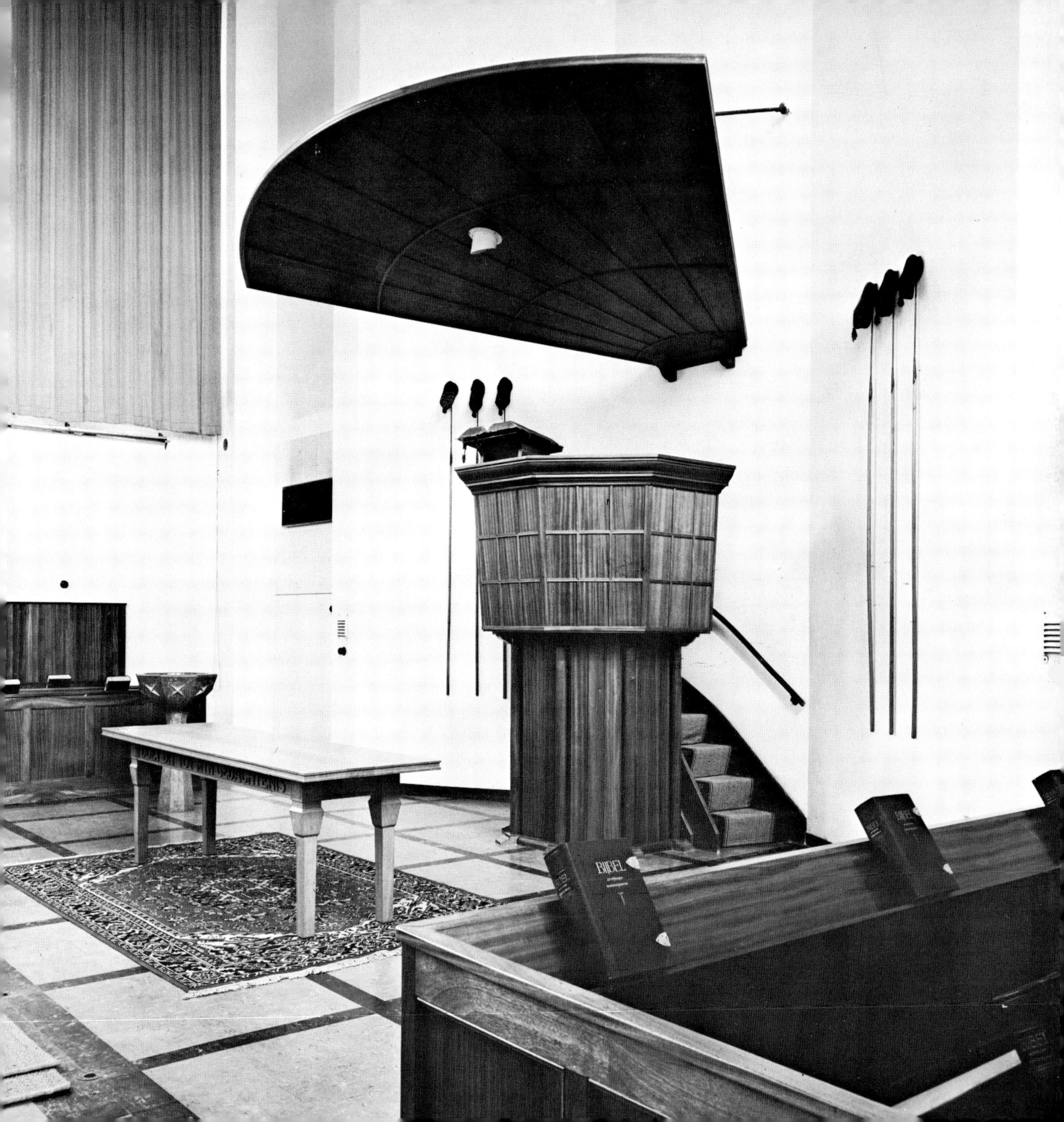
BIJBEL

In addition to the emphatic use of the hengelzakjes, the grouping of the pews and desks for the elders and deacons about the pulpit, font and table should be noted. One might wish that these pews were as "open" as those for the congregation, as a reminder that elders and deacons, despite their added responsibilities, are still members of the congregation.

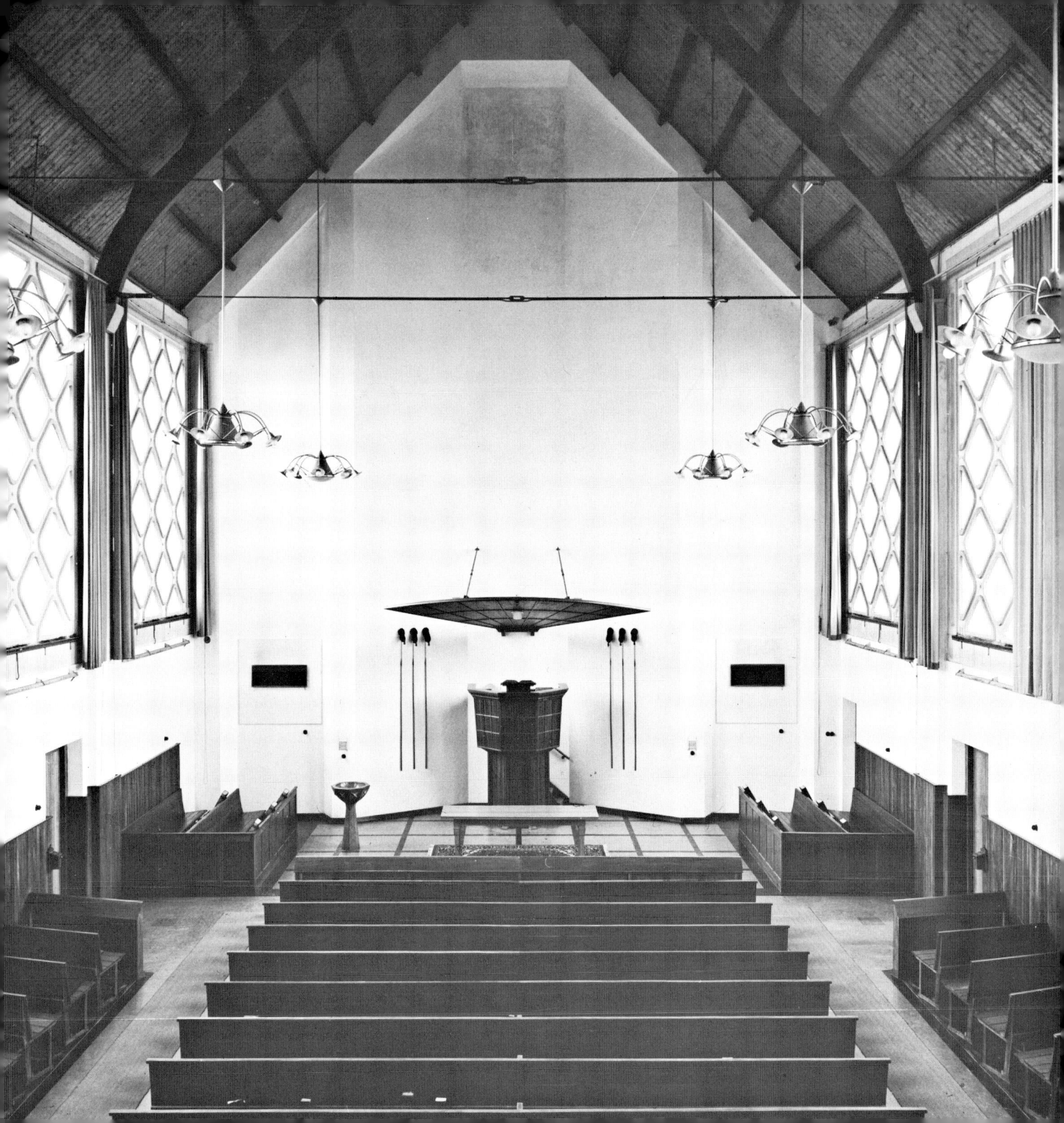

The tower bears the traditional cock which, far from being a secular adornment, is a religious symbol of venerable tradition. Its purpose is to call attention not only to the cock that crowed three times on the morning before the crucifixion, but to remind all who see that, like Peter, they should not be proud of their faithfulness lest they fall, but should instead rely wholly on Christ's strength and thereby stand fast in the Faith.

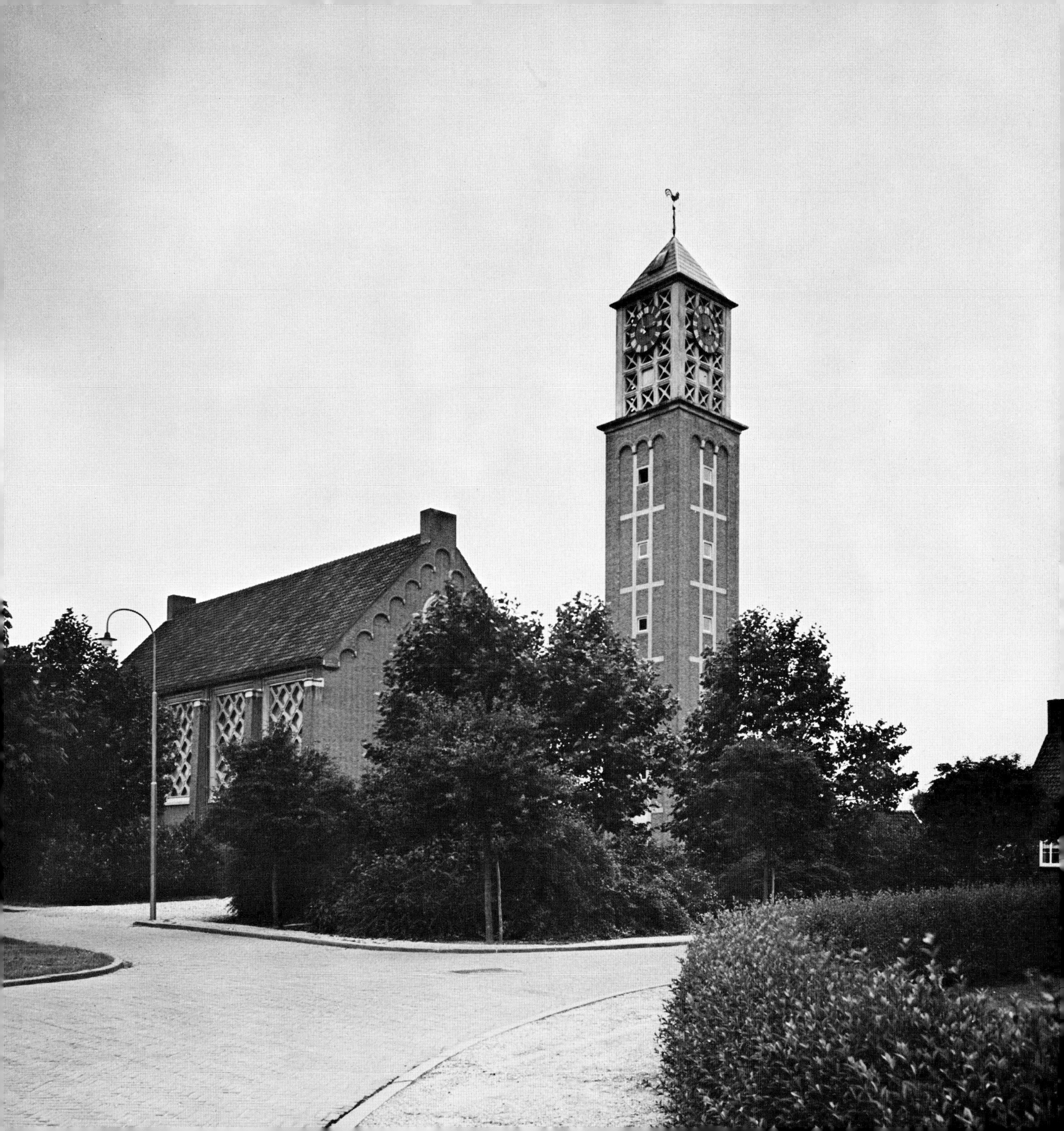

While such *hengelzakjes* are not likely to be used in American churches, there is a lesson in the fact that even in using the smaller *collectezakjes* (or *doorgeefzakjes*, literally, "pass-on bags") special provision has been made for them by the architect! Thus, in such diverse churches as "The Cornerstone" (p. 335), the Reformed Church in Rutten (pp. 351, 357), and the Church of the Advent in The Hague-Loosduinen (p. 273), the architects have in their diversity of treatment nonetheless given positive expression to these means of expressing Christian love.

Is there any other way in which the work of the deacon can be symbolized? It is to be hoped that there is, and that its suggestion will soon come to light. The fact that the Dutch have not done more in this area is evidence of the difficulties. It should be emphasized, however, that much has already been said by positioning the deacons near the source of their love, near the Word and Sacraments of Christ, and a great deal has been done to symbolize their love for men by the prominence given the offering receptacles. And if the love expressed by the deacons can assume the personal form that is beyond the goods or services that money can buy, then it is such a love that cannot readily be symbolized in the regular appointments of the church. Having given expression to both the source and manifestation of the love which the deacon bears on behalf of, and as example to, the whole congregation, one has already gone far in giving architectural expression to his office.

The Church of the Fountain, Voorburg, has many distinctive features of which the pews for the elders and deacons is only one. It will be noted that the architectural mode of the church has been carried into the design of the pews, with their slots in the arm rests for the Bibles and Standards for the elders. Behind these pews are the racks for the zakjes of the deacons. The large number of bags is explained by the large number of offerings—usually four—in most Dutch churches. The offerings are used for different purposes, and the congregation is given the opportunity to contribute to each in such amounts as it desires. The different offerings are identified by different colored bags.

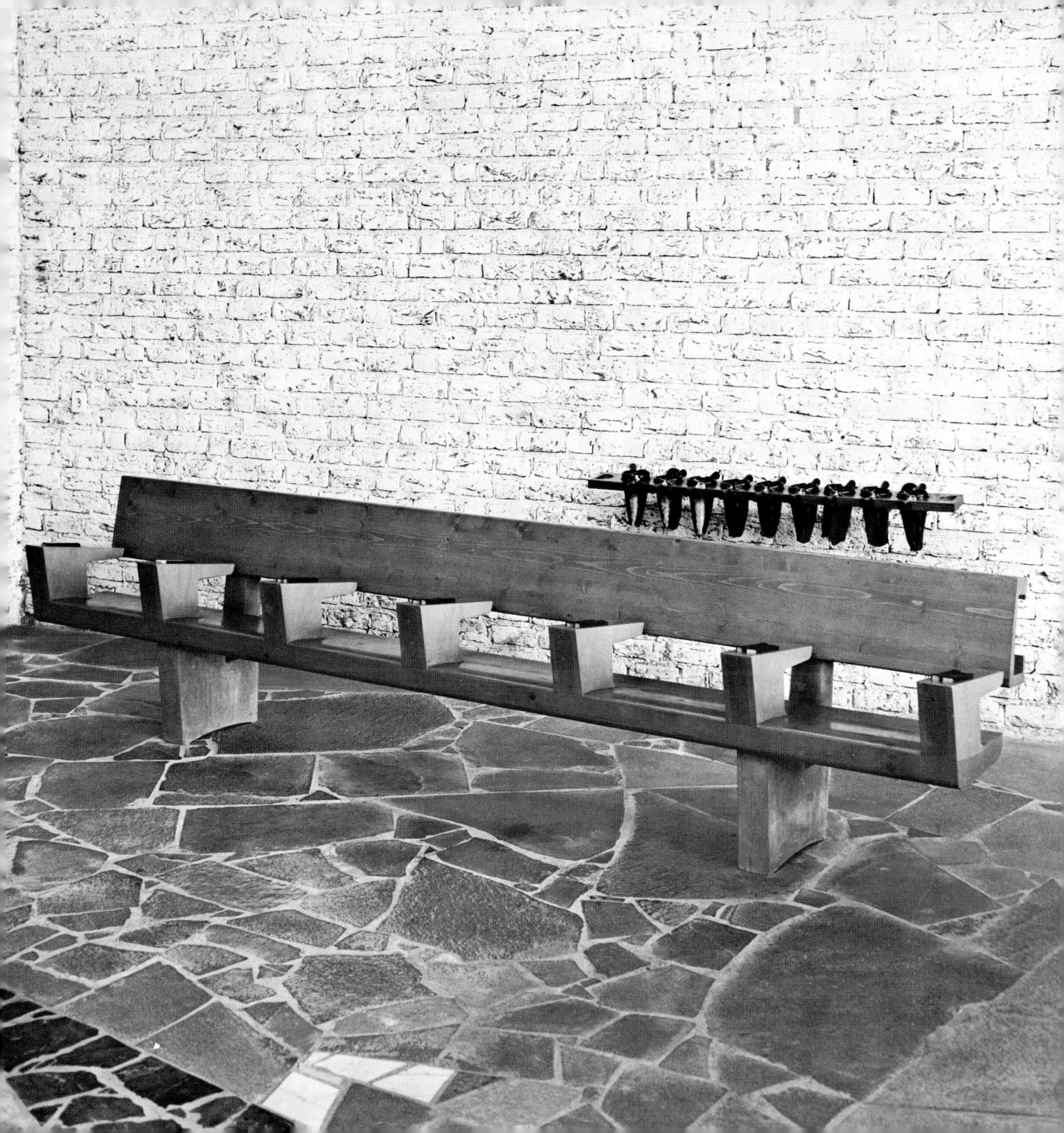

The Church of the Fountain (Fonteinkerk), Gereformeerd, Voorburg, The Netherlands. G. W. van Essen, architect

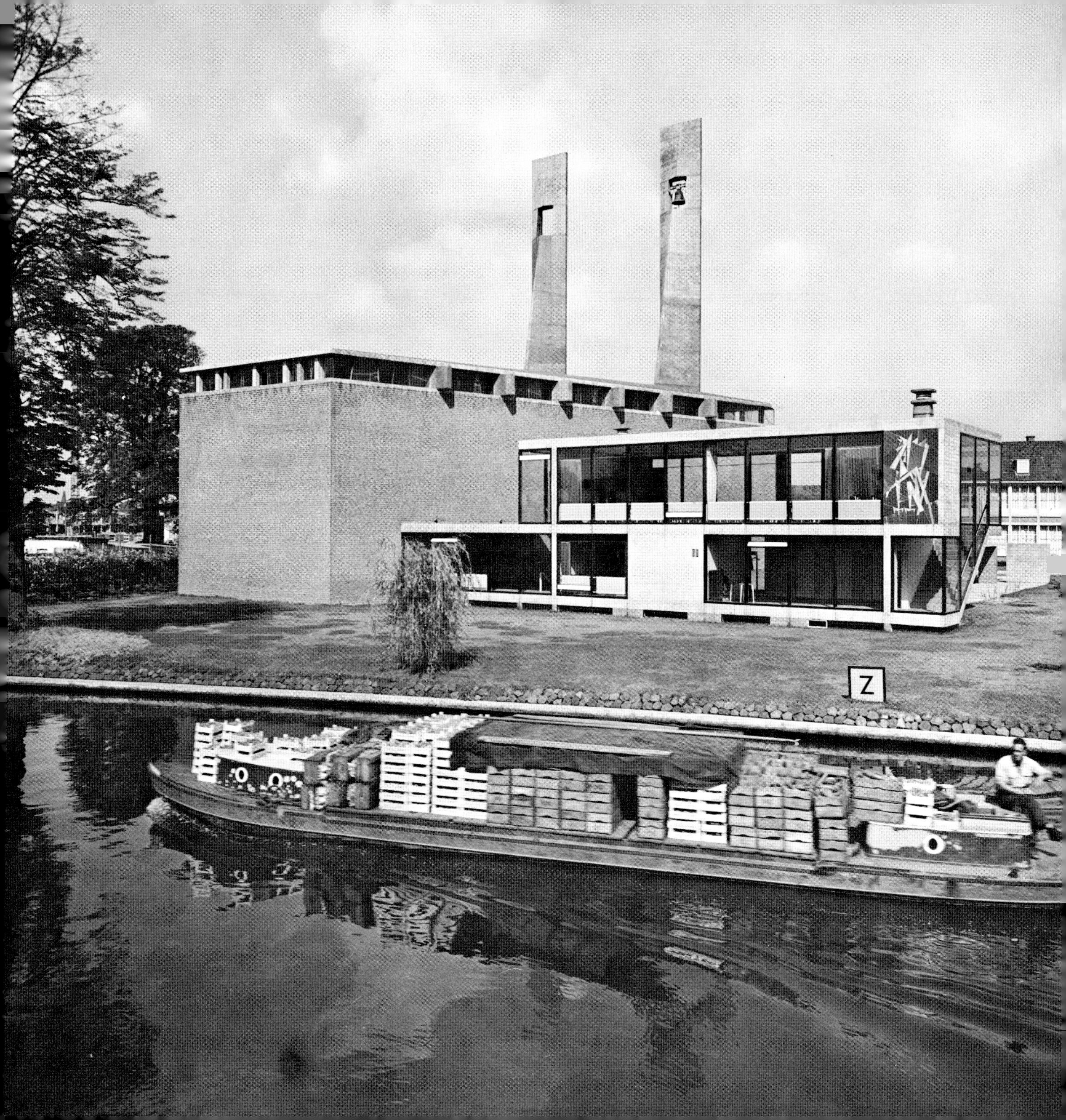
Z

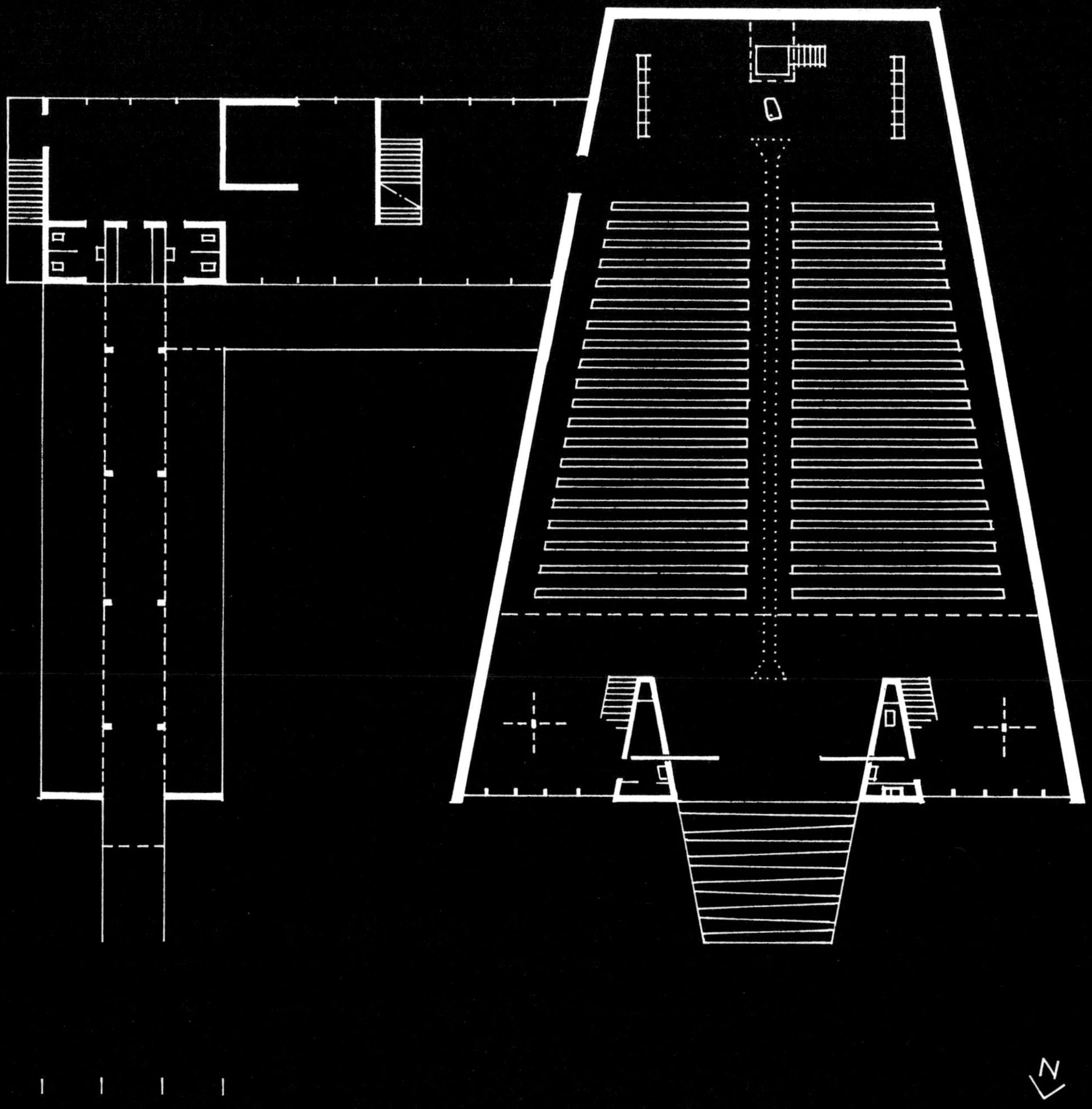
N

As in the early days of the Reformation, the table is set up only for the Lord's Supper, at which time it runs the length of the wide center aisle, with benches on both sides.

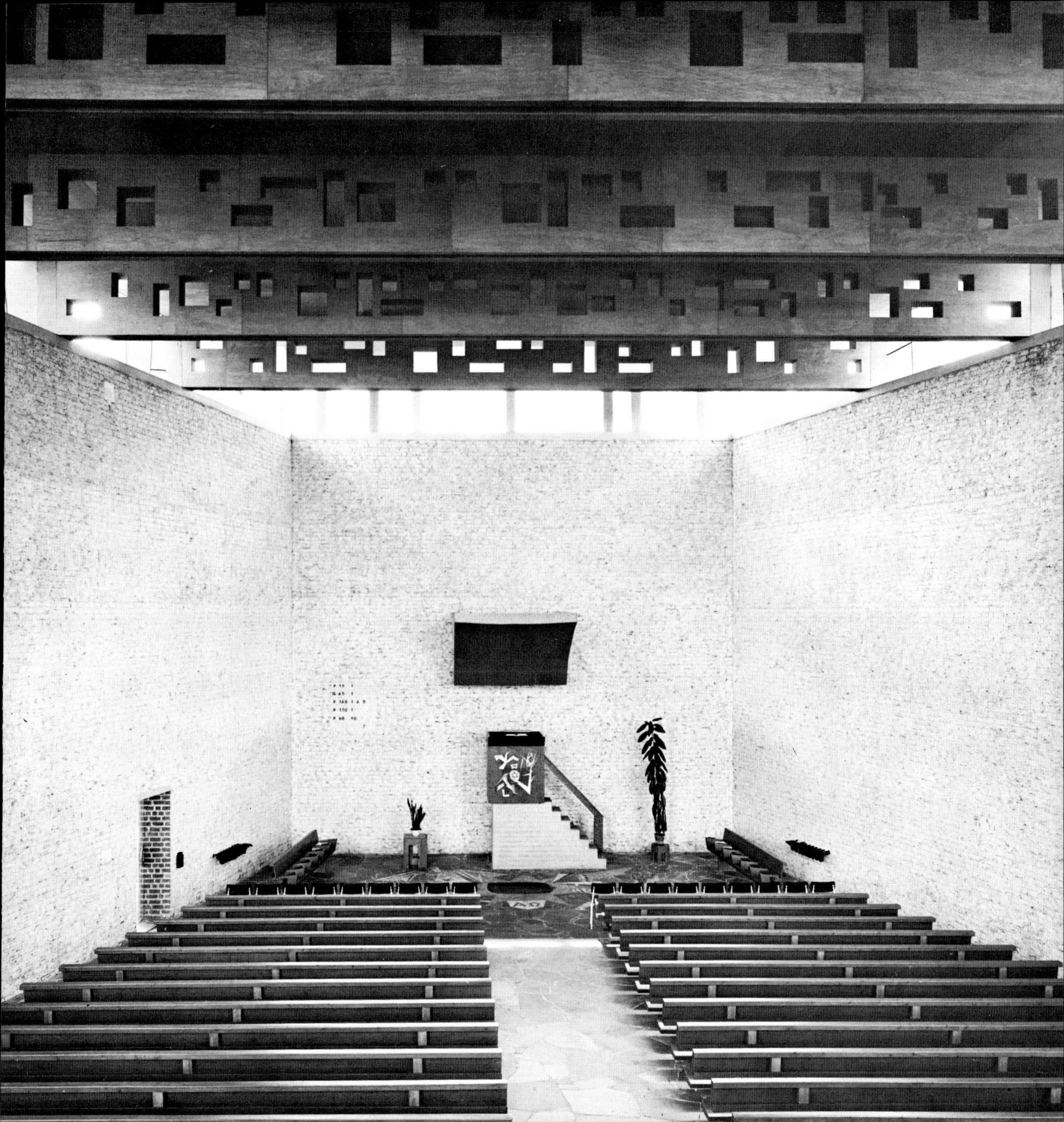

The baptismal font is unique, to say the least. It consists of a black stone, with a shallow indentation, set flush with the floor. A small jet, controlled from an adjoining room, rises from the floor to the desired height. Whether this constitutes baptism by sprinkling or pouring is perhaps debatable.

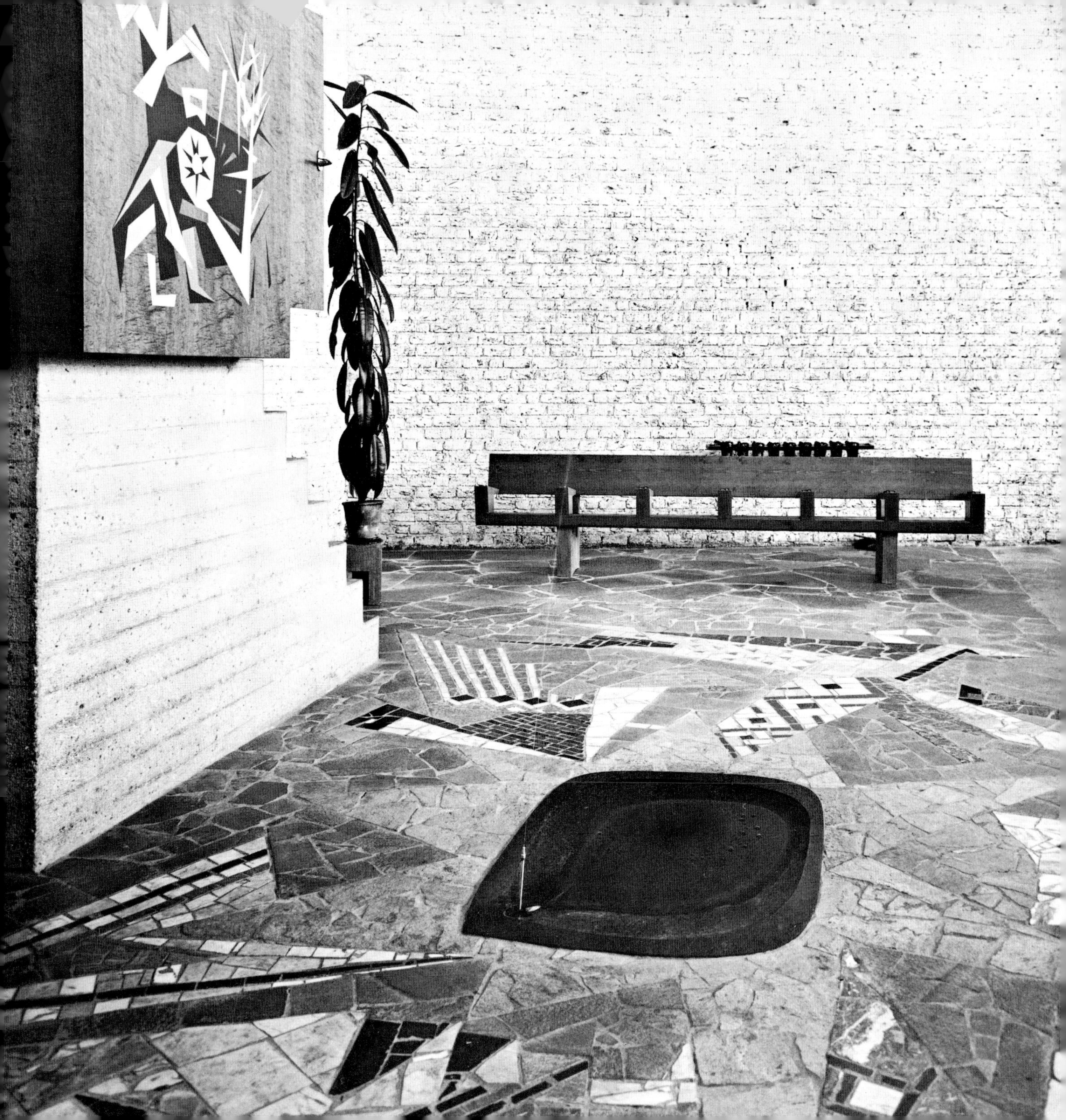

The organ, together with its very unusual casework—which has not impaired its acoustics—is the work of D. A. Flentrop of Zaandam.

Hoofdwerk		*Rugwerk*		*Pedaal*	
Trompet	8	Holpijp	8	Subbas	16
Prestant	8	Prestant	4	Prestant	8
Roerfluit	8	Roerfluit	4	Gedekt	8
Spitsgamba	8	Octaaf	2	Octaaf	4
Octaaf	4	Scherp 4 ranks		Ruispijp 3 ranks	
Spitsfluit	4	Sesquialter 2 ranks		Fagot	16
Quint	2⅔	Dulciaan	8		
Vlakfluit	2				
Mixtuur 5 ranks					

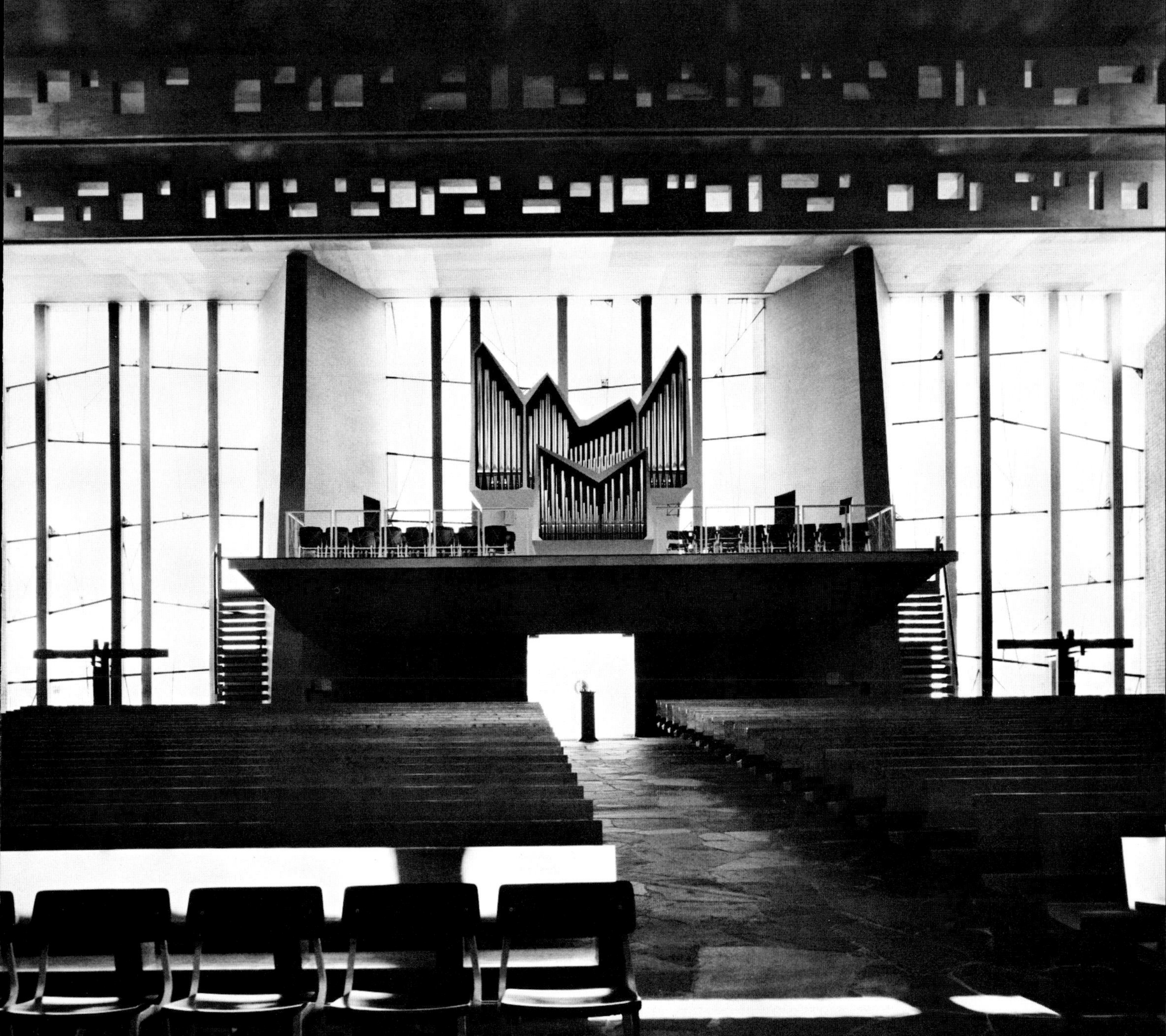

5

Choirolatry

Through the preaching of the Word and the administration of the Sacraments Christ's people are gathered together. Serving these people are those whose gifts have resulted in their choice by the congregation as ministers, elders, and deacons. To all of this, ways have been found to give architectural expression, that in churches reformed according to the Word of God the theology of the Church may be clearly stated.

But where is the choir? In most American churches the answer to this question is terribly obvious, but where is the choir in a properly reformed church? As one looks back over the examples of Reformed churches in the first four chapters of this volume one simply does not find a place for the choir in the east end of the church! Contemplating these churches and their clear visual proclamation of the Reformed faith, one is always confronted with the question, "Could this be done if room had to be made in the front of the church for the choir?" The answer is obviously "No!" One simply cannot make room for from four to forty people in the "chancel" of the church and expect to be able to do anything very meaningful in an architectural statement of the Faith.

Perhaps as many of 90% of all choirs in the United States are seated either in raised tiers behind the minister, or facing each other in a split chancel. But what are the origins, theology, and practicality of these commonly practiced solutions? Because the split chancel of the Medieval Gothic choir preceded the development of the raised-tier, or theater plan, they will be considered in that order.

The Split Chancel

It should be understood from the very beginning that speaking of the split chancel as the Medieval-Gothic choir does not imply that this is the most ancient and proper method of seating a choir. It was, in fact, a completely new fashion established in 1130 by Anselm at Canterbury. Prior to that time the choirs, whether secular or monastic, were seated in the eastern part of the nave (not the chancel) as in Westminster Abbey today. The church was then divided into the sanctuary for the altar and officiating clergy, and the nave for the faithful and the choir. Anselm's innovation meant that

> "the constructional division which had once severed monks and people alike from the altar areas, now severed the people from the monks; while no structural division now intervened between the choir of the monks and the sanctuary itself."[1]

---

[1] Addleshaw & Etchells, *op. cit.*, pp. 16–17, quoting G. G. Scott. It should be noted that in Roman Catholic terminology, the "sanctuary" usually denotes the area immediately surrounding the altar, while in Protestantism the term is usually used to designate the entire room for worship. The theological implications are obvious.

The resulting expansion of the eastern arm of English churches "constituted the greatest innovation made by medieval ecclesiology."[2]

It should be noted that these choir stalls were for the clergy, not a lay choir:

> The most typical feature of an English medieval church is the long chancel, often half or two-thirds the length of the nave. The size of these long chancels is due not only to ceremonial needs; they were also built to provide a place where the parochial clergy and those attached to the chantry altars of a church could say their offices together. . . . they were not intended to provide a place for a choir of lay singers.[3]

This in no way implies, however, that this position of the choir was retained at the time of the Reformation. Quite the opposite! The monks or other clergy who filled the stalls and sang the offices were gone. The altar at the east end of the long choir was torn down, and a table was set up, either in the choir, or in the nave at the crossing. When retained in the choir, the people sat in the stalls during the service of the Lord's Supper. The choir was transferred in most cases to a singing loft in the west gallery. "When there was no singing-loft the singers had a special place in the body of the church, either at the back or side, called a singing pew."[4] It should be noted that after the Reformation the choir did not use the position between the people and altar. That Medieval usage returned only with the return of the pseudo-Gothic of the Tractarians, or Cambridge Ecclesiologists, in the middle of the nineteenth century. This is not the occasion to consider the origins of the Oxford Movement, the Cambridge Camden Society (founded in 1839 by John Mason Neale and Benjamin Webb) or the Tractarians, led in the field of ecclesiology by

---

[2] *Ibid.,* pp. 16–17.
[3] *Ibid.,* p. 16.
[4] *Ibid.,* p. 99.

John Jebb and Theodore Farquhar Hook.[5] It is enough for our purposes to note that the movement was Romantic, pseudo-historical, and very inclined toward Romanism. It should be noted further that this return to Medieval Gothic architecture with all of its Medieval Roman accouterments occured after a lapse of 200 years during which time no Anglican church had been built in Gothic style in England![6]

While the Church had suffered theologically during the period of Rationalism, church architecture had remained faithful to the principles laid down at the time of the Reformation. But in the age of Romanticism which followed Rationalism, the desire was for mystery and awe in worship, for "feeling" and "experience" rather than reason. It was this desire for a "supernatural setting" for worship which led the Tractarians to Medieval Gothic, to the architecture of the "age of faith." Romanticism also affected church music, for

> while Neale and his friends romanticized the Middle Ages, Jebb . . . romanticized cathedral choirs.[7]
>
> Jebb felt that it was far more important to have a service well sung rather than one in which the congregation could join; and he dismisses the idea of congregational singing as a 'mistaken and modern notion'. . . . Corporate liturgical worship is set aside in favour of a beautifully sung service.[8]

The effect of this attitude is still felt in many high Anglican churches today, where the service is beautifully sung by the choir while congregational singing can most kindly be described as "weak."

---

[5] *Ibid.*, Chapter VII, "The Victorian Age," pp. 203ff., and Horton Davies, *Worship and Theology in England, 1690–1850* (Princeton: University Press, 1961), pp. 243–282.
[6] Martin S. Briggs, *Puritan Architecture* (London: Lutterworth Press, 1946), p. 32.
[7] Addleshaw & Etchells; *op. cit.*, p. 213.
[8] *Ibid.*, p. 219.

The success of the Cambridge Ecclesiologists was such that they established as "traditional" an architecture and liturgical arrangement unknown in Protestant churches before the middle of the last century. Romanticism aided their efforts. Even in Scotland an Ecclesiological Society was formed (in 1903, incorporating previous movements of 1886 and 1893) whose aim it was to diffuse throughout Scotland "sound views" and "truer taste," by which was meant "Gothic churches with deep chancels, cluttered up with choir stalls, eagle lecterns, and prayer desks of the type standardized by the Oxford Movement."[9] On the Continent as well the Romantic movement was having a devastating effect upon church architecture as people sought a setting for worship. Instead of the Reformed concept of worship in which "the congregation is inside the place of ministry," that is, the congregation as God's people, gathered about the preaching of the Word, seated about the Lord's table, with their ministers, elders, and deacons in their midst—instead of this an entirely new concept of worship came into vogue:

> The congregation looks into space. It is concentrated on what is in front of and outside of it. The focus of attention of the individual lies beyond the assembly. The decisive factor is the emotional appeal of the building. The church is the visible frame opening on a beyond which is the spiritual place of the holy office [i.e., the place of the altar and the choir where the service is transacted for the people].[10]

---

[9] Drummond, *op. cit.,* pp. 85–87.

[10] Compare these words of the Swiss architect, Otto H. Senn (*Lucerne Papers, op. cit.,* p. 7) with the following, which is so typical of the thinking surrounding church architecture in the United States: "One good result in the past few years has been the tendency of Presbyterian, Baptist, and Methodist churches to adopt the formal architectural plan which calls for a chancel and an altar. This not only makes for a better looking church interior, but results in a more formal and more dignified service *format*." Katharine Morrison McClinton, *The Changing Church* (New York: Morehouse-Gorham Co., 1957), p. 132. Italics mine.

The tragedy of the situation is that today, in the United States, the warmed-over medievalisms of the Romantic era are still often put forward as the best that church architecture has to offer.

Theologically, the Gothic choir between altar and people is intolerable at all points. It puts the altar in the focal point of attention in such a way that it is almost impossible properly to establish the importance and indispensability of the preaching of the Word. This position of the choir is not only unsatisfactory for the Reformed, but for men of the Anglican liturgical movement as well, for it separates the Lord's table from his people:

> One of the peculiar difficulties which stand in the way of the reform of the architectural setting of worship in the Church of England is the persistence of the idea —which dates only from the middle of the nineteenth century—that the one appropriate place for the choir is in a chancel between the altar and the congregation. Such an arrangement makes it almost impossible to achieve a satisfactory relationship between the ministers at the altar and the whole body of the faithful .... the placing of the singers between the congregation and the altar involves a most undesirable element of separation between nave and sanctuary ....[11]

While the people are separated from the table, the choir is also separated from the people, giving to them implied clerical status and function. This was immediately recognized by the Ecclesiologists of a century ago, who, led by Jebb, argued "that parochial choirs should be seated as near the clergy as possible, on the ground that they too had a special, even if subordinate, part, in the offering of the parochial worship."[12] Jebb further insisted that it was the "sacred duty" of the choir "to help the clergy in their work of leading

---

[11] Hammond, *op. cit.*, p. 44.
[12] Addleshaw & Etchells, *op. cit.*, p. 217.

public worship; and because the choir especially attend on this work they occupy a place near the altar higher than that of the laity."[13]

Among the Reformed, the choir was never a part of the clergy. In Reformed architecture and theology neither the minister nor the elders were "chanceled off" from the congregation. How incongruous that at this late date we should begin to "chancel off" our choirs at the very time when Roman Catholics and Anglicans are insisting that the place for the choir is not in the chancel because it "tends to set the singers apart from the rest of the laity and to obscure their true liturgical function."[14] Despite the fact that there is still a good deal of status connected with building "traditional English Gothic" and that it still fits in well with those who are trying to create a "mood for worship" or design a well-balanced setting in which worship can take place, nonetheless it is totally unsuited for Reformed worship. As has been made plain in prior chapters, the setting of the table is wrong, the setting of the pulpit is wrong, and the separation of the chancel itself is wrong in its implied denial of the priesthood of all believers through its separation of both choir and table from the rest of the people of God.

Having considered the total theological unsuitability of the split chancel, it is perhaps unnecessary to add this practical consideration: the divided chancel was never intended for the type of role played by a Protestant church choir. The choir is primarily to assist the congregation in its singing. It cannot do this effectively in a divided chancel. The secondary role which the choir usually performs is that of singing an anthem. This was also outside of the purview of the original chancel stalls. For the whole purpose of the divided chancel was for the sung services of the Medieval clergy. They were singing not to a congregation, nor even to each other, for they were engaged in devo-

---

[13] *Ibid.*, p. 219.
[14] Hammond, *op. cit.*, p. 44.

tions that were at once private, yet corporate, offered directly to the glory of God. It is to be hoped that the work of the choir is still offered to the glory of God, but if their singing is also for the congregation, then a split chancel is simply not the arrangement productive of the best singing. The practical considerations against the attempt to use a split chancel for Protestant choirs are neatly summarized by W. D. Maxwell:

> Such a disposition of the singers overcrowds the normal chancel, provides distraction where there should be tranquility, and tends also to make the leadership of the singers less effective because they are not so well heard. Sometimes an effort is made to overcome this defect by having the singers turn towards the congregation when singing. This looks merely gawkish, prevents the leaders from effectively leading the choir, and gives the impression of the singers singing to the people as in a concert hall, rather than to the glory of God. It should, at all costs, be inhibited.[15]

The cogency of Maxwell's criticisms was apparent in one church where the choir would march out between the stalls in front of the "altar," and sing facing the congregation from the center of the chancel. The skill of the choir was such that it was only in this way that they could effectively sing together. Then there are the many other churches of similar design where the congregation is "treated" to the uninspiring sight of the conductor waving his choir through their performance from the front corner of one of the stalls.

The Theater Plan

If objections can be made on both theological and practical grounds to the Gothic choir plan, these objections can be multiplied in respect to the

---

[15] Maxwell, *Concerning Worship*, p. 108.

theater plan.[16] Throughout the first four chapters of this book the concern has been to build with theological responsibility, using architecture as an ally of the gospel, to define visually the way in which Christ comes to his people in Word and Sacraments, gathering them as his people, serving them through ministers, elders and deacons. But it is in the use of the theater plan of seating the choir that the charge of "choirolatry" may justly be made. For when provision for seating must be made in the east end of the church, and the choir is ranged in tiers above and behind the minister, then the choir (if it is of any size at all) inevitably becomes the most significant visual element in the front of the church, offered competition perhaps only by rows of organ pipes towering behind it. The theology in architecture of the churches already pictured in these pages would be quite impossible if somehow the choir had to be seated in the front and on risers so as to be able to face the congregation. But while this theater plan arrangement of the choir has become so commonplace that for many congregations it is the only thinkable place for their choir, it is less than a century old! Throughout the prior nineteen centuries of Christ's Church the choir was placed in almost every position throughout the church room except above and behind the pulpit! Where did this innovation begin, and what allowed it to take such tenacious hold in American church life?

How the choir attained this position of eminence, where visibly more mighty than pulpit, font, or table it reigns throughout the service, is a story too recent to have been thoroughly chronicled by the historians. However, the difficulties in adapting the Medieval Gothic choir to the needs of Protestantism give us several clues as to how the theater plan got its start. One

---

[16] Is it indicative that books were written drawing "an interesting analogy between Worship and Drama"? E.g., T. L. Harris, *Christian Public Worship: Its History, Development, and Ritual for Today* (London: Williams & Norgate, 1928), quoted by Drummond, *op. cit.,* pp. 233ff.

of the theological difficulties was that it resulted in a "popish" altar rather than a Protestant table. At the same time, the divided choir made both conducting and singing more difficult, while its only virtue seemed to be to afford a properly aesthetic view of the altar. The shortest possible move to rectify both of these difficulties was to swing the sections of the choir about to face the congregation, rather than each other, and thus their presence across the front of the chancel blocked any view of an east wall altar. The chastened communion table was then placed in its familiar position on the floor in front of the pulpit. While the choir might have been kept "on the flat" behind the pulpit, the same desire for drama in worship which had originally led the Cambridge Ecclesiologists less than fifty years before to build churches with an aura of awe and mystery, led low-church Protestants to seek their drama in worship through a choir whose performance could be seen as well as heard, together with a broad platform on which the minister could also perform—this was the period of the very active preaching of Dwight L. Moody and, just a bit later, Billy Sunday.

Stylistic stature and impetus was given to just such a plan by H. H. Richardson's Trinity Church, Boston (1874). The Romanesque revival was sparked by the tremendous attention given to this church, which was built for the popular broad-church evangelical Anglican preacher, Phillip Brooks. The result was a veritable plague of inept imitations of the plan and style of Trinity Church all over America. The effect is described by A. L. Drummond:

> In new Romanesque churches, grotesque adaptations of Trinity, the choir and organ pipes usurped the dominating position, the pulpit was reduced to a low, open platform with a desk and three chairs, and the Communion table (if there happened to be one) quite obscured on the floor of the auditorium, hemmed in by a solid range of pews.[17]

---

[17] Drummond, op. cit., p. 95.

The pervasiveness of this Romanesque enthusiasm can perhaps best be judged when we compare the remaining species of this style with the somewhat fuller description of T. E. Tallmadge:

> Almost every town in the land has one of these Romanesque Revival churches. . . . Its material is red brick and its trimming red sandstone with the familiar Romanesque detail. In place of the thin, narrow, pointed arches of the preceding era, the windows and portals are broad and squat, and have round arched heads. . . .
>
> The interior was as startlingly unlike its elder brother [Gothic Revival] as the outside. Instead of being long and narrow, it was short, almost square, and the pulpit, organ, and choir—hardly a chancel under the circumstances—were tucked into one corner. The floor was sharply bowled, and the pews were all curved, which was inevitable in a cat-a-cornered church. The windows were picture windows—Biblical scenes done with startling realism on a grandiose scale. The woodwork was golden oak, the organ pipes much in evidence, and, like the walls and ceiling, highly decorated. One wall, however, seemed to be a huge gate or portcullis, and so it was, for by some mysterious means it would rise or fall out of sight, disclosing the whole of the Sunday School, built on the celebrated Akron Plan.[18]

As quickly as the Romanesque Revival came, it—fortunately—disappeared, succumbing in the face of the classicism of McKim, Mead & White in the Chicago World's Fair of 1893. But this church plan left an indelible mark, for in the period of eclecticism which followed, despite the style, those churches not using a Medieval Gothic chancel seemed almost inevitably to retain the suggestion of a chancel which was filled with a choir, raised in tiers, and facing the congregation.

The continued popularity of this position was not solely one of stylistic suggestion, for the ecclesiastical dominance of the Romanesque revival lasted

---

[18] *The Story of Architecture in America* (New York: W. W. Norton & Co., 1927), p. 193, quoted by Drummond, *op. cit.*, p. 96.

barely two decades! It is true, of course, that the practical difficulties associated with the Medieval chancel also helped account for the change, for Drummond cites an architect of the Gothic revival period in England who, between 1870 and 1892, designed Gothic churches with choir seats facing the congregation.[19] But to explain the continued popularity of the theater plan for the choir some further reason must be sought, and Joseph Edwin Blanton appears to have found it:

> It is the . . . desire of congregations to be entertained, I believe, which has fixed, more or less, the location of the choir in the chancel.[20]

Coming from a man of such wide architectural and musical erudition as Blanton, this is indeed weighty testimony. If true, it means that the architect and building committee will be faced with stiff opposition if they seek to eradicate choirolatry.

In considering the theological implications of this position, some things have already become obvious: The position assumed by the choir is part of the same Romantic movement which saw high churchmen seeking for a dramatic worship experience, performed in the awe and mystery of the deep Medieval chancel. In low-church Protestantism, the pulpit may be central, but the parishioner, like his high-church counterpart, goes to church with the expectancy of the drama of the service, except that his drama is not one of ecclesiastical awe and mystery but of a performance by choir and minister in which the personalities involved are given the opportunity to play a larger part in relation to their function in the service. Through almost nineteen centuries Christian choirs had been content to sing praise to God unobserved by the congregation, while ministers had preached the gospel from ambos

---

[19] *Ibid.,* p. 77.
[20] *The Organ in Church Design* (Albany, Texas: Venture Press, 1957), p. 88.

or pulpits which generally took visual precedence over the minister. In the late nineteenth century, however, choirs began to be displayed in full view, and ministers were given an entire stage from which to deliver their messages. With this emphasis upon the "performance" and the "performers" the visual place of Word and Sacraments was decreased until the pulpit became but a small reading desk on a platform, while the table and font were delegated to the floor in front of the pews. Is there a relationship between the loyalty of so many Protestant congregations to a particular preacher (allowing people to move from church to church in search of a minister) and this nineteenth-century attitude which put personalities to the forefront?

The late Ray Berry sought to determine the place of a choir in any given church on the basis of three theological questions:

> 1) is the choir a part of the clergy and related closely to this facet; 2) is the choir basically a part of the congregation, therefore most logically placed with this element; 3) is the organ-choir segment an independent unit whose participation is a thing apart in all ways?[21]

Obviously, the Medieval Gothic plan places the choir with the clergy, giving it a very special place in the services. But how is the choir to be considered when it is ranged in tiers in a shallow chancel behind the pulpit? It is no longer near the altar—or the table, from which it is now separated by the pulpit and platform. However, neither is the choir near the congregation, but physically separated from it, and facing it, as does the minister. The position of the choir marks them as closely related to the clergy (which must be denied by the Reformed), while Reformed theology would dictate that they are a part of the congregation (which is denied by the architecture of their position). The result has been that the choir has often become "an independent

---

[21] *The American Organist,* Feb. 1957, quoted by Blanton, *op. cit.,* p. 85.

unit whose participation is a thing apart in all ways" (thus we have "special music"). And indeed it is in many cases an independent entity with which not even the elders or ministers dare interfere, an independent group willing to share their pleasure in performing with the congregation which serves as its regular audience.

Within the Reformed church, however, the choir must always be recognized as basically a part of the congregation. Its sole purpose is to assist the congregation in worship, not to perform for them. It assists the congregation by leading in the singing of the hymns and with discretion uses its anthems for the purposes of worship. In Reformed worship the congregation has its opportunity to respond to God and express itself in praise through its singing. Worship in the Reformed faith finds overt expression as a corporate act chiefly through its singing, which is of all the greater importance because of the infrequent use of the Lord's Supper with its corporate nature. For Calvin, singing was the response of the congregation.[22] Howard Hageman asks:

> How much better off is the congregation that listens to a liturgical performance almost completely dominated by minister and choir than a medieval congregation which watched a liturgical performance almost completely dominated by priest and singers?[23]

The role of the choir within Reformed worship is to assist the rest of the congregation in their singing. The choir is not to sing for the congregation in the sense of either singing in their place or singing to entertain them.[24] In brief, there is no theological reason why the choir should be arranged behind the minister in a theater plan. There are definite theological reasons why it

---

[22] Hageman, *op. cit.*, pp. 64–65.
[23] *Ibid.*, p. 120.
[24] The excellent article by Dr. Howard G. Hageman, "Can Church Music Be Reformed?" which considers the place of the choir within Reformed worship should be consulted in *The Reformed Review,* Vol. 14, No. 2 (Dec. 1960), pp. 19–28.

should not: the members are not a part of the clergy, but of the congregation; their presence too often makes them of such visual significance that it is virtually impossible to put either the Word or Sacraments in proper perspective. In short, in the theater plan the choir gives the visual implication of choirolatry, for the symbols of Christ's presence fade in visual comparison.

Along with the theological, there are also practical considerations which militate against the theater plan for the choir. Few ministers would be foolhardy enough to try to deliver their sermons while a motion picture was projected on a screen behind them. Yet Sunday after Sunday minister after minister competes with between four and forty faces behind him—some intent in devout worship, others animated, some asleep, others beautiful in their symmetry with well-placed noses, eyes, and mouths, topped with lustrous hair, indeed a joy to behold. One is tempted to suspect that this positioning of the choir represents an unspoken conspiracy entered into between choir and congregation for their mutual entertainment on such Sundays as the sermon fails to stimulate attention. In Reformed worship, however, the answer to unsatisfactory sermons is not the entertainment provided by an easily visible choir, but rather the elder, whose office it is to be responsible for the lively preaching of the Word, and who must use his position to guide the minister to such preaching.

The purpose of the choir is to assist the other members of the congregation as they praise God in song. They are not there to entertain the rest of the congregation, either musically or visually. The choir is there for the purpose of praise, just as the songs of the congregation constitute praise. But how is this function of the choir to be described theologically? Is it their function to communicate Christ to his people? There is no such word of description or command from the lips of Christ, or to be found anywhere in the New Testament. Therefore, it cannot be pointed out too forcefully that the role of the choir is not to communicate Christ to the people! The choir does not have a role similar to that of Word and Sacraments. It is not there in the Christ-ordained role of joining him to his people.

But then what is the theological role of the choir? The role of the choir, like that of the congregation, is one of response! The hymns of the choir, like those of the congregation, are a response of grateful praise to God's grace. One must not confuse the response from God's people with that which comes from God, for this is to confuse the word of men with the Word of God. But in either the Medieval Gothic choir or the theater-plan choir these roles are confused. The choir is placed where God's message comes to man—in fact, in the latter plan the choir, which is man's grateful and joyous response to God, is put in a position of constant competition with the Word and Sacraments, both symbolically and through the inevitable distraction of a fully visible choir facing the congregation. If the concept can be kept clearly in focus that the choir is a part of man's response to God's grace, rather than a means of God's grace,[25] then criteria can be formulated which will give the choir architectural definition commensurate with its true role within the worship of the church.

THE CHOIR DOES NOT COMMUNICATE GOD'S GRACE, BUT THE PEOPLE'S GRATITUDE.

---

[25] The term "means of grace" has had such a varied theological history that it is perhaps necessary to define the way in which it is here used. Grace is God's unmerited favor in his act of redemptive love in Jesus Christ. The "means" are the preaching of the Word and the administration of the Sacraments through which the Holy Spirit works in joining us to Christ and all his benefits. This is not to deny that the Holy Spirit in his freedom uses other ways to bring men to Christ, but the appointed means given by Christ to his Church are the Word and Sacraments. Sometimes it is true that God blesses our response of gratitude, prayer (Heidelberg Catechism, Q. 116) and songs of praise, to draw us closer to himself. But in the sense that the term is used above, these should not be described as "means of grace," for they have more of their origin in us, rather than in him, and therefore have none of the faithfulness and certainty that Christ has given his Sacraments and Word.

THE ROLE OF THE CHOIR (LIKE THAT OF THE REST OF THE CONGREGATION) IS TO RESPOND TO GOD IN PRAISE. IT IS NOT TO BE CONFUSED WITH THE MEANS OF GOD'S GRACE—WORD AND SACRAMENTS—AND THEREFORE MUST NOT BE PLACED WITH THEM. ARCHITECTURALLY THE CHOIR MUST BE PLACED WITH THE REST OF THE CONGREGATION WHICH IT ASSISTS IN ITS RESPONSE OF PRAISE TO GOD.

With these criteria, where does one place the choir? In conjunction with the prior discussion, they rule out both the Medieval Gothic choir and the theater-plan choir, and in ruling out those two possibilities, the place for the choir, as experienced by the overwhelming majority of American Protestants, has been eliminated. These criteria also eliminate a number of compromise plans for the choir which keep it undivided and eliminate the constant face-to-face encounter of choir and people but retain a place for it in or alongside of the chancel area. A number of such plans are found in newer American and Canadian churches. Victor Fiddes shows three plans[26] where the choir is placed on the side of the chancel area (it should be noted that there is no room for a pipe organ in any of those plans). In two plans the choir is still definitely within the chancel area, thus confusing the means of grace with the response to grace, while in the Applewood United Church, Port Credit, Ontario, the choir is placed very much to the side in a manner reminiscent of the famous Reformed Church in Zürich-Alstetten. While this church was one of the first Reformed churches to make a clean break with the Romantic movement and return to Reformed principles of church architecture, its unfortunate experimentation in putting the organ and choir in the east end of the church, albeit completely to one side, indicates how it is virtually impossible to give proper visual emphasis to Word and Sacraments when they stand in competition with choir and organ.

---

[26] *Op. cit.*, pp. 88, 89, 90.

404

The Reformed Church, Zürich-Alstetten, Switzerland
Werner Moser, architect

T EUER MEISTER
RISTUS
BER SEID

Organ by Rudolf Ziegler-Heberlein of Uetikon am See (Zürich)

Hauptwerk		Schwellwerk	
Quintatön	16	Gedeckt	16
Principal	8	Principal	8
Flauto maior	8	Rohrflöte	8
Gemshorn	8	Salicional	8
Octave	4	Unda maris	8
Nachthorn	4	Octave	4
Superoctave	2	Hohlflöte	4
Mixtur maior	2	Quinte	2⅔
Mixtur minor	1	Flageolet	2
Zinke	8	Plein jeu 4–5 ranks	1⅓
		Terzian 2–3 ranks	1
		Zimbel 3–4 ranks	½
		Trompete	8
		Schalmei	8
		Clairon	4

Positiv		Pedal	
Gedeckt	8	Principal	16
Quintatön	8	Subbass	16
Principal	4	Gedeckt	16 Tr.
Rohrflöte	4	Principal	8
Sesquialtera 2 ranks		Spillflöte	8 & 4
Principal	2	Octave	4
Spitzquinte	1⅓	Rauschbass 2 ranks	
Super-Octave	1	Mixtur 3–5 ranks	2
Scharf 4 ranks	⅔	Bombarde	16
Krummhorn	8	Trompete	8
		Clarine	4

The Scriptural inscription on the wooden plaque has antecedents from Reformation times (cf. pp. 9, 11).

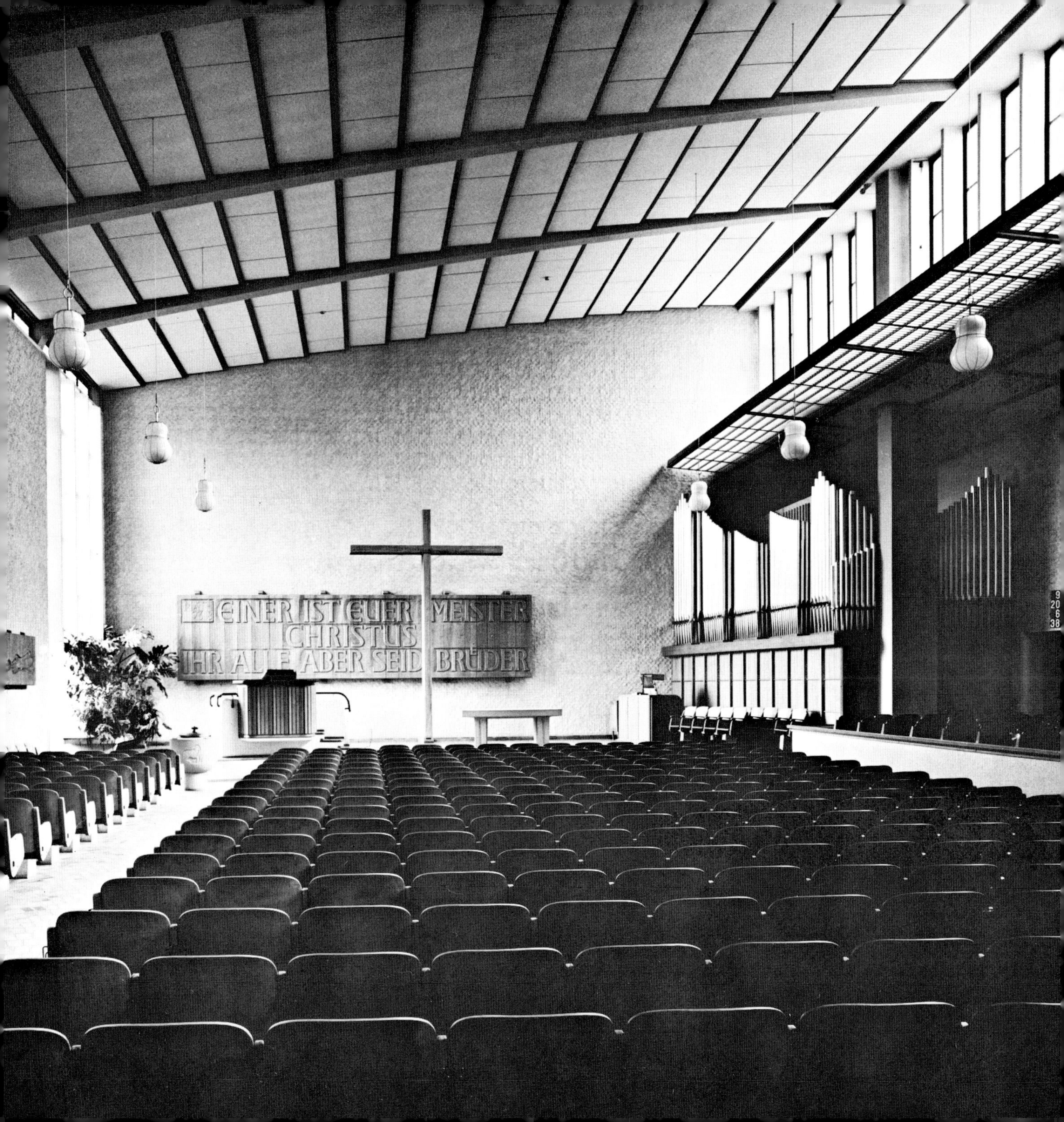
EINER IST EUER MEISTER
CHRISTUS
IHR ALLE ABER SEID BRÜDER

Another possible solution is to place the choir behind the table, separating them visually from the congregation either by a screen, or by placing them at or below floor level so that they are virtually hidden by the table. In the former method, there is no distraction from the choir during the service, providing the screen is high enough. Theologically, however, the choir is still in the wrong place, terribly separated from the congregation and, practically, they suffer from a single view of the minister—his back—or at best a rear-quarter view.

To place the choir on floor level behind the table or altar can be given a certain amount of theological defense if the church is in a circular or Greek cross plan in which the congregation surrounds the table (although because the choir faces in the same direction as the clergy there is still the possibility of theological confusion at this point).[27] But here practical difficulties also persist. The choir must try to support the congregation in its singing from in front, rather than from behind. And, as with any east-end arrangement, it makes positioning of the organ difficult, especially if it is of the tracker-action type, so much favored in Europe. Once any position behind the pulpit or table has been eliminated, however, it becomes almost inevitable that the choir must then be located either in the east end of the church, but with the people rather than the clergy, or in the west end of the church with the people. These positions are almost inevitable because in most cases the organ will have to be located at either one or the other extremity of the church.

As far as present practice among Reformed congregations is concerned, it is in the Church of Scotland that one most frequently finds the choir seated with the people at the east end of the church. This position has good historical precedent. The tremendous ambo, or pulpit, in the great Sancta Sophia

---

[27] Examples of such a plan may be found in Hammond, *op. cit.,* pp. 120f., or in Christ Chapel, Philadelphia (pp. 393–99) or Christ Church, Düren (p. 227).

in Istanbul had a circular enclosure about its base "forming a space for singers."[28] In St. Clement's in Rome, with one of the oldest basilican plans extant, the place for the singers was on the floor, near the ambone. In England, while the usual place for the choir was the west end of the church, when it was in the east end, near the pulpit, the singers were seated near the reading desk and do not seem to have been at all obtrusive.

> With the spread of the choir movement from the northeast during the late eighteenth century, special seating had also to be set aside for the singers or 'band' as they were then called. This was provided for either in a box pew or in a loft.[29]

In Scotland, while some Scottish choirs are found in a west-end gallery, the greater number are found in the east end of the church.

The east end, or "Scottish" position, is simple in its execution. The choir simply sits in the east end of the church on floor level in front of the pulpit. The choir (like the rest of the congregation) faces the minister when seated. When leading the singing, or presenting an anthem, they rise and turn toward the congregation while remaining in their pews. Theologically, this has the great advantage of accurately stating the place of the choir. They are placed with the congregation where they can participate in worship with them, but when they sing they alter their direction to better aid the congregation. This avoids the theological confusion of appearing to make the choir a means of grace along with the Word and Sacraments. And on the practical level, it eliminates the endless competition and distraction of the "stare in the face" position. Not only is the choir unobtrusive during the service, but the choir members have the advantage of being full participants along with the rest of the congregation. Visually as well as actually they are a part of the congre-

---

[28] Addleshaw & Etchells, *op. cit.*, p. 83.
[29] Hay, *op. cit.*, p. 196.

gation which has met together not to entertain or perform but to respond to God's grace in worship and praise.

On this continent, an example of such a plan for the choir can be seen in the chapel of the Lundy's Lane United Church, Niagara Falls, Ontario.[30] In a larger church, it is sometimes necessary to raise the choir a step or two so that their voices may carry properly when facing the congregation (as is the case in St. George's West, Edinburgh). In such large churches, however, this small elevation generally does not detract from either Word or Sacraments.

However, this plan is far from perfect. The primary disadvantage concerns the placement of the organ. Even when an organ with electric-pneumatic action is used, there is still the problem of the console. It can be discreetly screened, and sunk a bit into the floor, as in the Chapel of the Lundy's Lane United Church, but it is still obviously there. Wherever the console is hidden in the front of the church, it is inevitable that the more thoroughly it is hidden, the more difficult will be the task of direction, especially if that direction must come from the console.

But is all of this effort to screen and hide the console just to keep the choir near the east end of the church really worthwhile, especially when one considers that the choir cannot most effectively lead the congregation from this position? For the inherent weakness in the east-end position is that a congregation is best led in praise not when it is sung at, but when it is sung with. A choir, while certainly useful to a congregation when singing at it from in front, is nevertheless far more effective in assisting good congregational singing when adding its support from behind.

THEOLOGICALLY, THE CHOIR CAN BE POSITIONED AMONG THE PEOPLE

---

[30] A floor plan and a picture can be found in the book by Victor Fiddes, *op. cit.*, pp. 91, 115.

AT THE EAST END OF THE CHURCH AS WELL AS AT THE WEST END. FUNCTIONALLY, THE CHOIR IS BEST ABLE TO SERVE ITS PURPOSE OF ASSISTING THE CONGREGATION IN SONG NOT WHEN IT SINGS AT THEM FROM IN FRONT, BUT WHEN IT SINGS WITH THEM FROM BEHIND.

As has been the case so frequently with these criteria, the period of the Reformation gave them their natural expression. In England the "most usual place" of the choir "was a singingloft or gallery generally, though not always, at the west end, which was in many cases a converted rood-loft taken down and reerected at the back of the church."[31] In the flurry of new church building that followed the great London fire, one finds that Sir Christopher Wren's parish churches had "the choir and organ placed at the west end over the vestibule, according to the continental custom."[32] This was also the arrangement in the Colonial churches in America,[33] and "throughout the eighteenth century the rear choir-gallery was an architectural feature common to churches of all denominations."[34] This was the typical position for the choir throughout Protestantism until the period of Romanticism witnessed the wholesale abandonment of Reformed principles of worship.

In examining the Reformed churches of Europe, both old and new, one finds that with rare exception the choir has been placed in the west balcony, or, in some very small churches, simply in the rear of the congregation near the organ. The few exceptions to this rule are not particularly happy ones. Of the Reformed churches pictured in this book, with only four exceptions every choir and organ is placed in the west end of the church!

---

[31] Addleshaw & Etchells, op. cit., p. 98.
[32] Drummond, op. cit., p. 37.
[33] Ibid., p. 95.
[34] Leonard Ellinwood, The History of American Church Music (New York: Morehouse-Gorham Company, 1953), p. 19.

Theologically, the west-end position gives proper architectural expression to the role of the choir in responding to God's grace with praise. It allows no confusion as to whether the choir is a means of communicating Christ to his people. The choir does not bestow God's grace but sings forth the gratitude of the people. When the west balcony is for the organ and choir alone, then it may be regretted that there is this physical separation from the rest of God's people, but because the west end of the church, whether main floor or gallery, has always been the province of the people, there is no opportunity to confuse the role of the choir with that of God's grace. The choir is a part of the response of praise of God's people.

From the standpoint of practical function, the choir is also at its best in this position, for from behind and above, as from nowhere else, the choir can be of assistance to the congregation in its singing. From this position, as from no other, it is possible for the choir to avoid calling attention to itself while also through its anthems it sings God's praises from the congregation.

> There can be no doubt that the best position for the singers and organ . . . is in a low gallery at the west end of the nave. The singers are then among the people, as they should be; and as they are not seen they can be directed and controlled by the organist from his console without distracting the worshippers. The voices are heard clearly. It need hardly be said that this is the traditional place for singers and organ, so excellently is it suited to its purpose . . .[35]

It is heartening to see that this point of view is once again being emphasized in America, and in official church planning boards. James L. Doom, Secretary of the Department of Church Architecture of the Presbyterian Church in the United States, emphasizes that

> the Reformers placed their choirs in the gallery over the entrance with the

---

[35] Maxwell, *Concerning Worship*, p. 107.

organ exposed on the wall above the choir. For three centuries this was the standard arrangement for musicians. It is still the most satisfactory. The director has complete freedom to lead his singers without distracting the congregation. The choir members can see the pastor's face throughout the sermon and the sacraments. The voices of the choir reinforce the singing of the hymns by the whole congregation, especially those timid people who choose to sit on the last pews. The high gallery location gives the choir the best resonance from the ceiling of the sanctuary.[36]

In the author's discussions on the position of the choir, those involved in a possible change have almost invariably been convinced that not only objection, but rejection, would meet any plan that would not leave the choir in an elevated position at the east end of the church. If that objection is simply the result of custom which is uninformed concerning the traditional place of the Reformed choir, then it can be dispelled by a presentation of the facts: historical, theological, and practical. If the objection arises specifically from the choir, then the real source of the objection must be sought. Is it simply a matter of lack of understanding concerning the traditional place and role of the choir? If so, information and patience should eliminate the objections. Or does the change of position represent a threat to the role in which the choir sees itself? Does the change represent a threat to their real purpose in singing—the opportunity to enjoy singing while assured of an audience, or perhaps the opportunity to entertain in the center of attention for at least a part of the morning? Is it possible that there would be members who would leave, or that the choir would be wrecked if the ego-building opportunity of performing in front of the congregation were removed? If such is indeed the case, then a choir playing such a role should have no part in a Reformed

---

[36] James L. Doom, "Reformed Sanctuaries" p. 7. Mimeographed publication of the Department of Church Architecture, Presbyterian Church in the United States, Atlanta, Georgia.

service of worship, and the service would be much safer for the glory of God without such a choir, no matter how technically proficient. When the Church is served by those who seek the glory of self rather than the glory of God, the Church fares better without such "service."

Or is it perhaps from the congregation that the greatest objection will come? If objection persists despite the information that an elevated east-end position is neither traditional, nor theologically correct, nor the most practical, then one can only assume that the congregation is determined to have the choir in front because that is where they can be seen, and because, call it what you will, there they can provide the desired visual entertainment. It can be called choirolatry, or some other name can be found for it, but no matter what term is used, this much remains: there is the desire for something to stand along with God and the symbols of Christ's presence at the center of worship. If the feeling of the congregation is strong in its desire, then perhaps it is all the more indicative that there is real danger and that it has become imperative for the choir to assume its proper theological place, not where it can entertain, but where it can offer praise with the congregation.

Were this a matter of no importance it would certainly be advisable to drop it without causing any disturbance in choir or congregation. But this is a matter of great import both theologically and practically, and the choir, together with the organ, are of such size that once a building is completed, it is highly unlikely that their position will ever be changed. The building committee determines for all practical—or impractical—purposes the position of the choir for the life of that church building. To put the choir in an elevated position in the east end of the church is to perpetrate and perpetuate continuous theological confusion as to the role of the choir, and in the midst of this confusion the choir is usually left to carve out a separate domain for itself where it exists as a largely independent entity within the church. To put the choir in the west end is to give it a proper place, theologically, and also to give the members their finest opportunity to do their real job effectively. The considered opinion of Ray Berry is that

> when the choir-organ unit is considered a part of the congregation what better placement could there be than the rear gallery? From this vantage point, choir and organ can bolster the congregation. The fluidity of arrangement here possible, with movable chairs and/or risers for the singers, who are backed by the organ itself, is from many standpoints the most ideal to be found for the projection of worship music . . . .[37]

The message of Holy Scripture is that Christ communicates himself to us in Word and Sacraments, and nothing should be allowed to becloud this truth by detracting from the symbols of Christ's presence with his people. The choir must not be architecturally confused with these means of God's grace, but instead should be helped both symbolically and practically to play its proper role, which is to lead the people in their sung response of gratitude to Almighty God.

---

[37] Quoted by Blanton, *op. cit.*, p. 85.

6

The King of Instruments

Little can the tongue sing the praises of the king of instruments, the pipe organ. Those who have no ears for its beauty will hardly be impressed by words, while for those whose ears are sensitive to the low power of the bass, the airy lightness of the flutes, the snarl of the reeds, the brilliance of its trumpets—such ears need no words to sing the praises of the pipe organ. Born before Christ, this king of instruments has nonetheless been nurtured by the Church, and in those centuries when the music of the Church rose to great heights, the organ shared those heights as it sang to God's glory.

And indeed the organ is an ideal instrument for the Church. For at the hands and feet of a single individual it can send forth music soft and unobtrusive, appropriate for worshipful meditation, or music powerful and gladsome, appropriate for the joyful praise of the congregation. The organ is ideal for the Church because at the command of an individual stands the reflection of every mood of which the human soul is capable. Even as the Psalms cover the complete gamut of human experience in words, so the organ can cover this experience in its music.

If this description of the organ sounds strange to some ears, it should be added quickly that the description is intended only of a pipe organ, not an electronic instrument. The relative merits of the two, together with the matter of costs, are discussed in an appendix: "The Choice of an Organ."

However, no matter how great one's enthusiasm may be for the glories of the king of instruments, it must be stated firmly that like the choir, the pipe organ is not a means of grace! It has not been given the task of communicating Christ to his people.

THE ORGAN DOES NOT COMMUNICATE GOD'S GRACE, BUT THE GRATITUDE OF THE CHURCH.

Granting this principle, the organ must not be placed in the east end of the church. Whether fronted by rows of false pipes, or by ranks of genuine pipes, the organ in the front of the church constitutes too much competition for the Word and Sacraments. This was observed long ago by Dr. Wotherspoon, who in 1889 noted his displeasure:

> We Scots are always in extremes. . . . One day we will have no organ on any terms, and the next we build a chancel to our preaching-place and fill it with an organ—we have paid hundreds of pounds for it, and we mean to have the worth of our money—so the machinery is set up, like Dagon in the sanctuary, that we may worship towards it, and a pulpit is bracketed above the keyboard.[1]

---

[1] Drummond, *op. cit.,* p. 203. Excellent line drawings of just the sort of arrangement Dr. Wotherspoon was describing can be found in Peter F. Anson's *Fashions in Church Furnishings 1840–1940* (London: The Faith Press, 1960), pp. 341, 358.

It was A. L. Drummond who remarked that it was the "evil genius of the 19th century" that decorated "the blank wall behind the pulpit with gilded organ pipes."[2]

Within the past few decades there has been a growing embarrassment about these tremendous masses of false organ pipes in the front of the church.[3] Generally, the more intelligent treatment of the distractions afforded by such pipes has been the same accorded to the entire interior of these churches. Just as skilled decorators have been willing to paint out such garish decorations of the Romanesque revival churches as had no artistic merit, so the same skilled decorators have often eased the strident appearance of inartistic pipes by painting them a single color. In a similar fashion, the great gilded pipes in many a Gothic revival church have been painted a light color, just as dark and gloomy walls have received the same treatment. For such redecoration a person of artistic knowledgeability is needed lest some real artistic merit (and when there is real merit, it is not to be obliterated just because it is out of fashion!) or the artistic balance of the church be destroyed.

Less fortunate solutions to oppressive organ pipes have generally taken the form of a wholesale remodeling in which the existing organ is thrown out, and an entirely new one installed, still in the front of the church, but this time hidden off somewhere in an organ chamber. Since these organs are already under expression in a swell box, and these boxes are in turn in chambers—and sometimes chambers behind chambers—the result is that

---

[2] *Ibid.,* p. 55.

[3] The visible pipes of the last half of the nineteenth century are almost always false, for the bad taste of the era was unfailing, and having put the entire organ under expression there were no working pipes outside the box, with the result that false pipes of the most unnatural shapes and sizes were erected, an offense to good taste and the principles of organ building alike. See Blanton, *op. cit.,* pp. 69ff., p. 83.

such sound as does escape lacks the brilliance and presence of a properly cased organ. Acoustically, it is rather like spending a great deal of money for a stereophonic hi-fi, and then putting the whole instrument behind some draperies and going into the next room to listen to it. It is also very questionable whether the screens of the organ chambers are any great contribution to the beauty of the church. At best they look like honest screens meant to do an honest job of hiding something. At worst they are covered with decorative motifs of musical symbols or have undergone some attempt at hiding their true nature, in which case it is a matter of trying to hide the fact that something is being hidden!

But the organ is not an instrument whose sound should be muffled, nor is it an ugly thing that needs to be hidden. The opposite is true. But even a thing of beauty must not be allowed to compete with the symbols of Christ's presence, with the Word and Sacraments. The organ must not be allowed to assume the place of the means of grace, any more than the choir. And indeed, if the choir can more advantageously take its position at the rear of the church, the same is true of the organ. For the organ, like the choir, is a part of the response of gratitude to God's grace. The organ, like the choir, is an aid to the congregation in expressing its praise, and, like the choir, it must be placed with the congregation.

THE FUNCTION OF THE ORGAN IS TO RESPOND TO GOD'S GRACE WITH PRAISE. IT IS NOT TO BE CONFUSED WITH THE MEANS OF GOD'S GRACE, AND THEREFORE MUST NOT BE PLACED WITH THE SYMBOLS OF WORD AND SACRAMENT. ARCHITECTURALLY, THE ORGAN MUST BE PLACED WITH THE CONGREGATION WHICH IT ASSISTS IN ITS RESPONSE OF PRAISE TO GOD.

ACOUSTICALLY, THE ORGAN CAN BEST ASSIST THE CONGREGATION WHEN IT IS BEHIND, AND SLIGHTLY ABOVE THEM.

The above criteria certainly represent nothing new, for they plainly point to the west gallery as the place for the organ, and it is precisely this spot which in western Europe has for six and a half centuries been the traditional place for the organ.[4]

---

[4] *Ibid.*, p. 91.

Organ by Ahrend & Brunzema of Loga by Leer (Ostfriesland)

Hauptwerk		Brustwerk	
Praestant	8	Spitzgedackt	8
Gedackt	8	Flöte	4
Oktave	4	Prinzipal	2
Octave	2	Oktave	1
Mixtur		Rankett	16
Spanische Trompete	8	Regal	8

Rückpositiv		Pedal	
Gedackt	8	Bourdon	16
Praestant	4	Oktave	8
Hohlflöte	4	Nachthorn	4
Waldflöte	2	Flöte	2
Nasat	1 1/3	Posaune	16
Scharf		Schalmey	4
Sesquialtera			
Krummhorn	8		

Zorgvliet Church (Zorgvlietkerk), Hervormd, The Hague. M. Kuyper & ir. C. Westerduin, architects

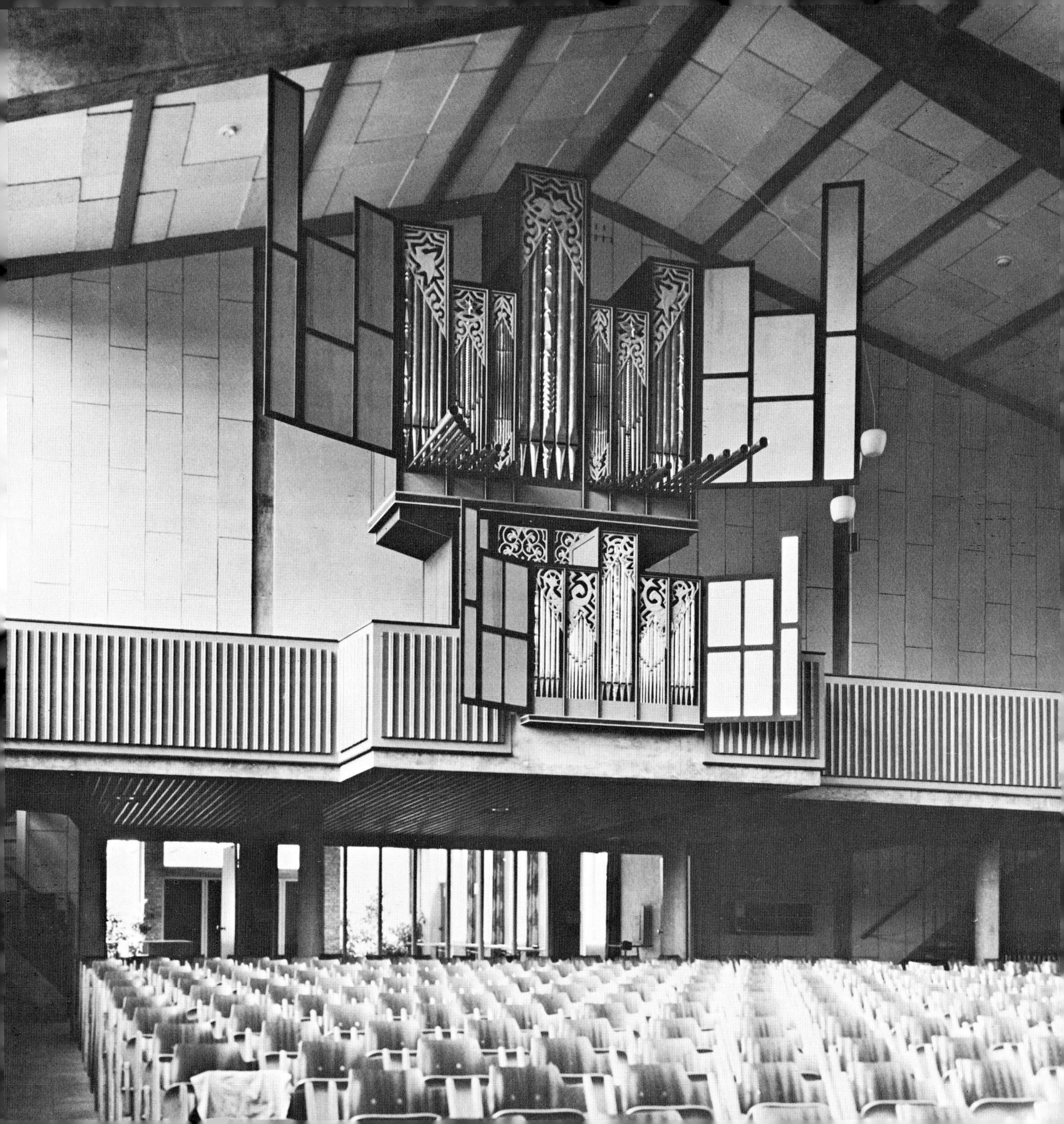

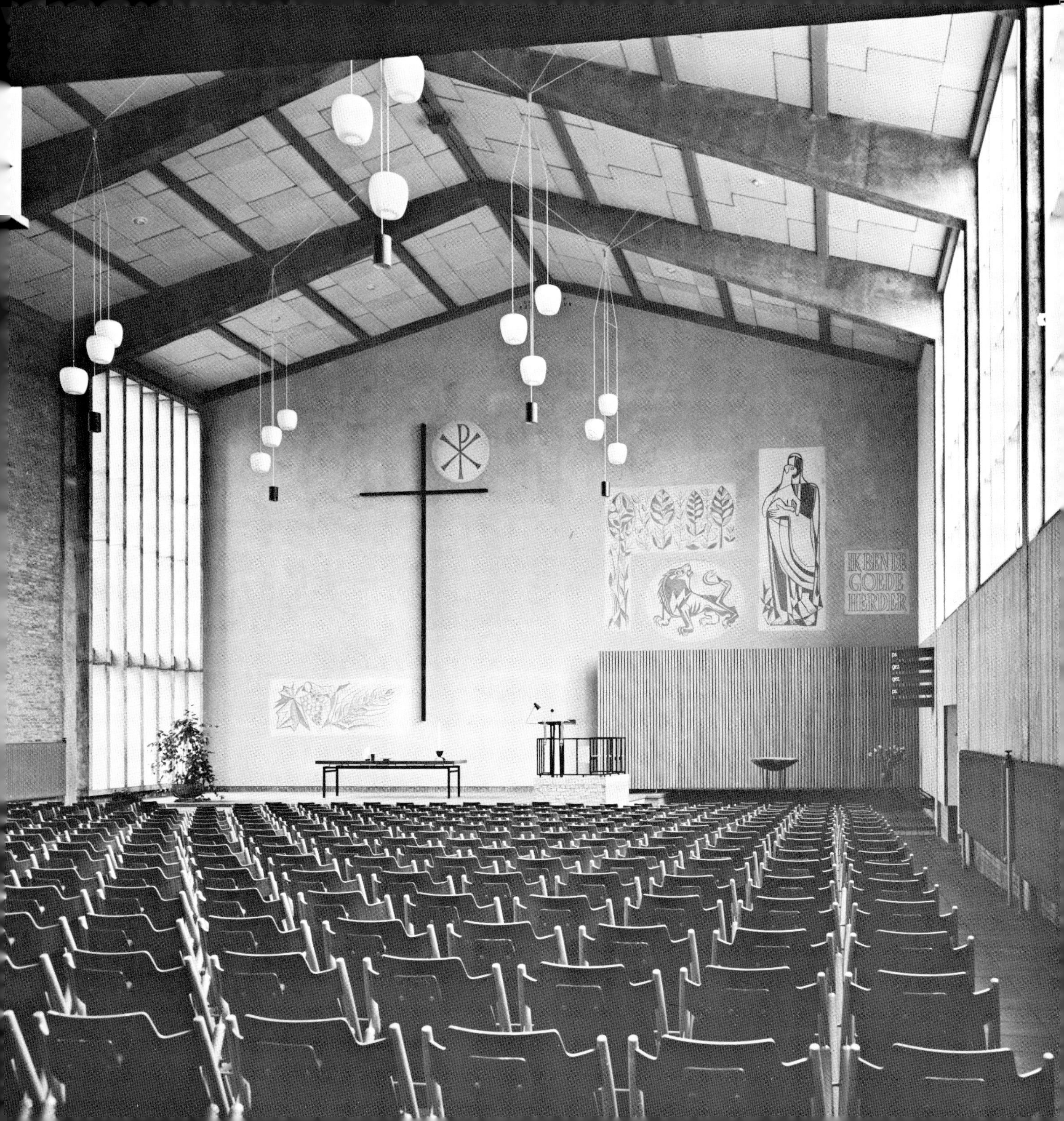
IK BEN DE
GOEDE
HERDER

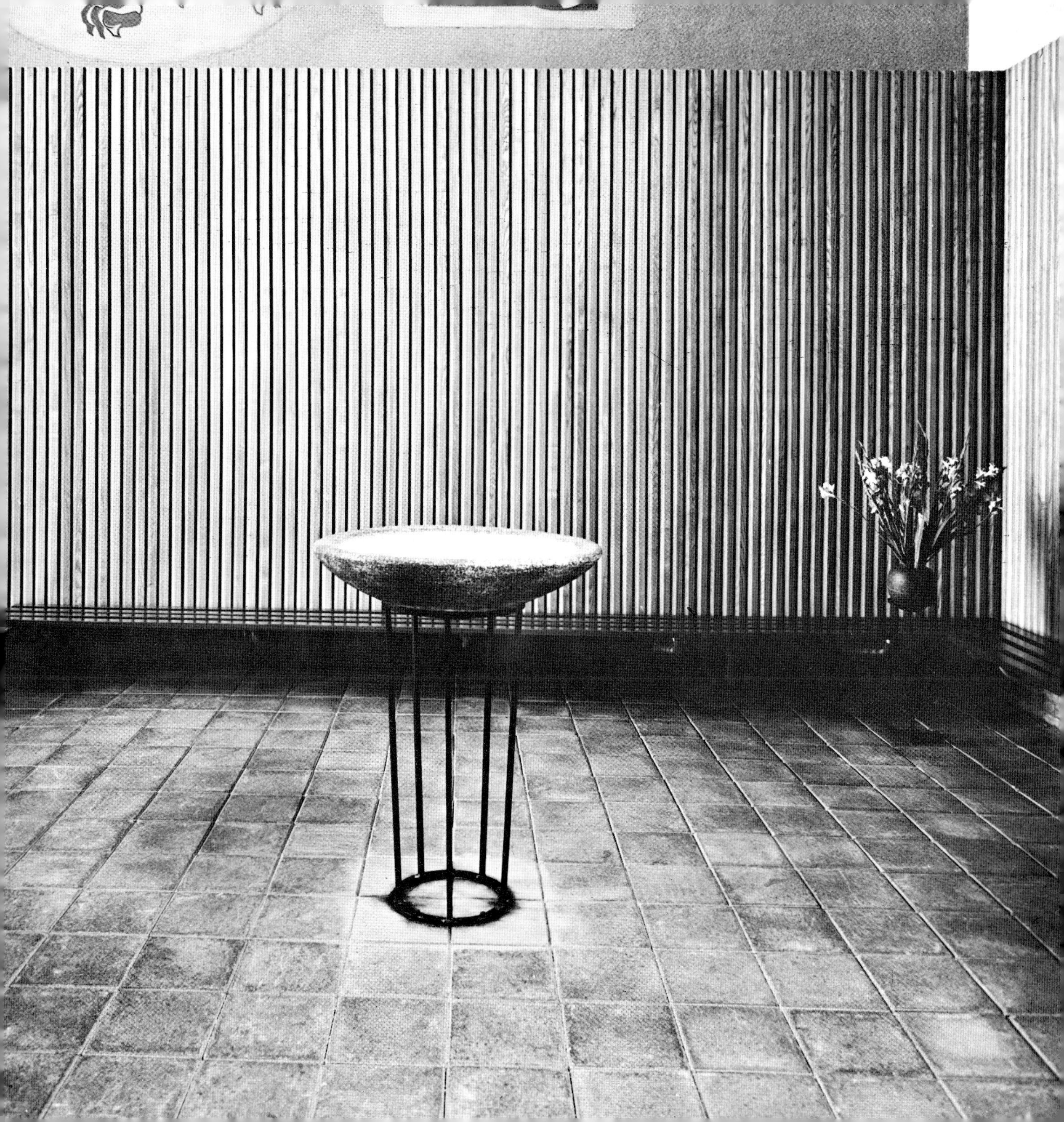

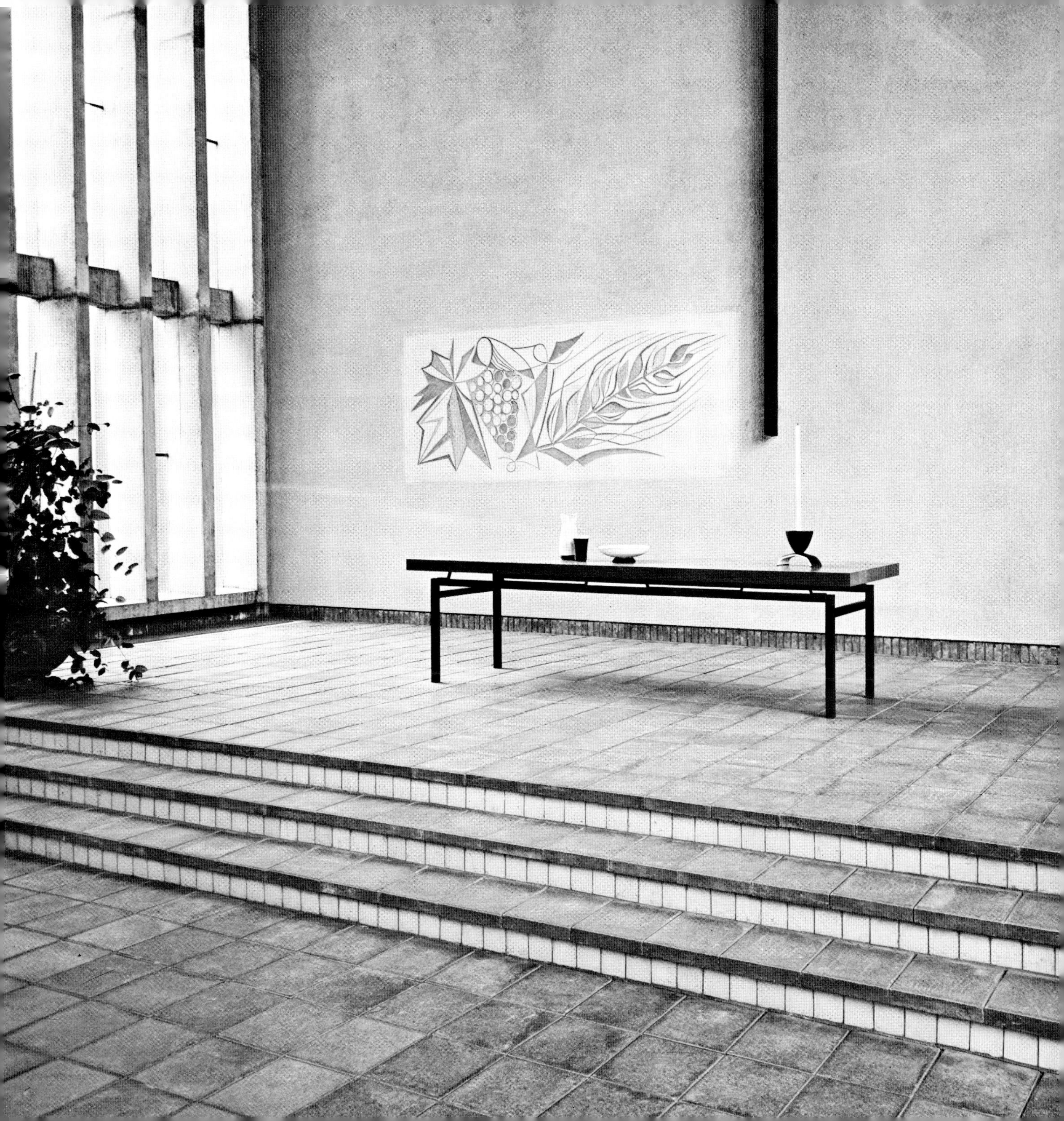

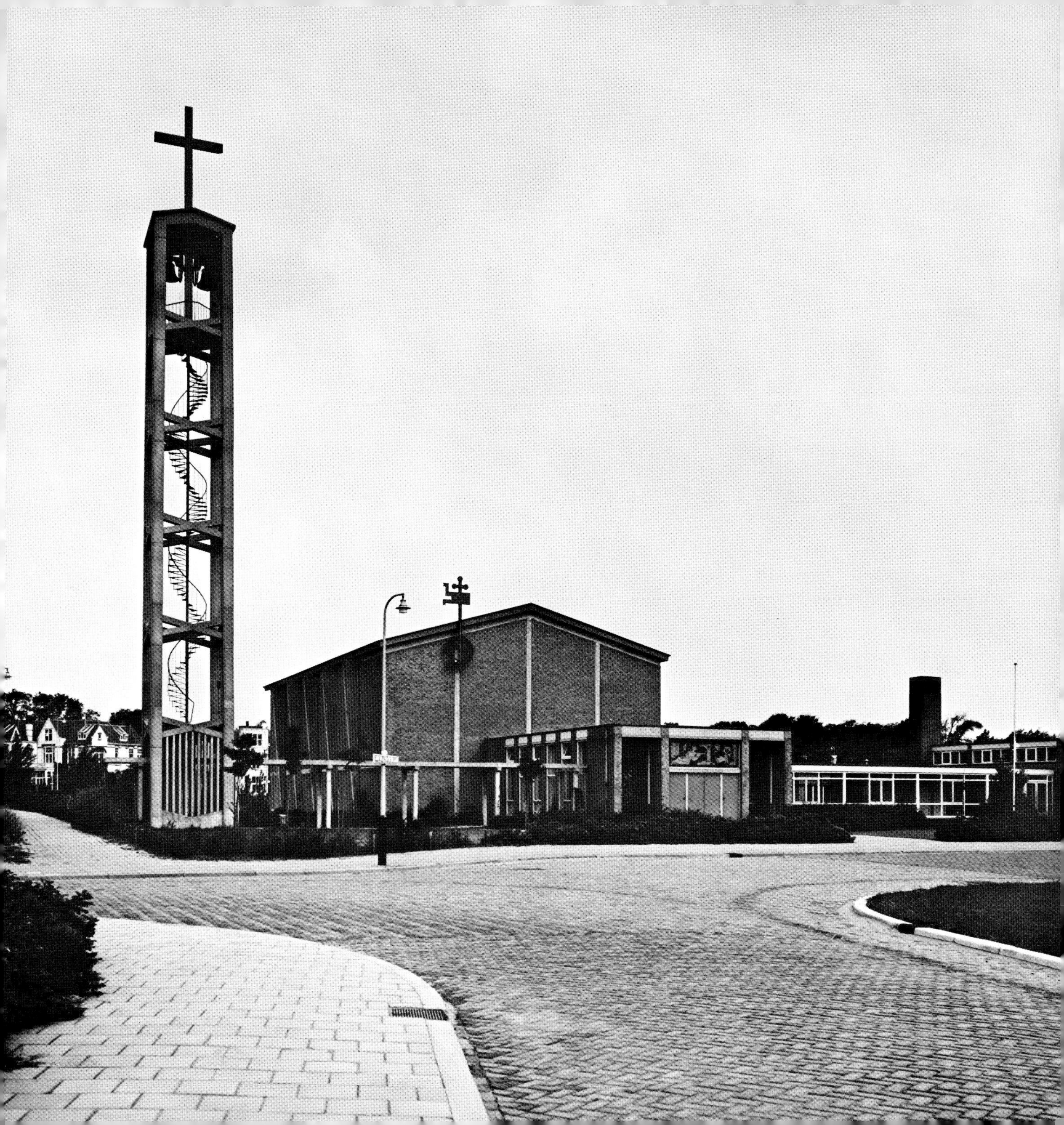

While it is true that all sorts of other locations have been tried for the organ, these are really "deviations from the custom."[5] Certainly there is little doubt as to why this position for the organ should have been so popular throughout the centuries, for the organ could find its place in the rear gallery on either theological or practical grounds. Theologically, it is a part of the congregation's response of praise. Practically, it is from the rear that the organ can be of greatest assistance to the congregation in its praise. The west balcony "is from many standpoints the most ideal to be found for the projection of worship music, provided that floor, walls, and ceiling of the choir-organ area are of hard surfaced, highly reflective materials."[6] Those who have sung with the assistance of the organ behind them know the power of the organ to aid in the worship service. With the assistance of the organ behind them people are given the encouragement and help that they so often need to give themselves fully in songs of praise.

Once the organ has assumed its proper theological position, the architect is once again free to use its wonderful architectural possibilities as a symbol of the congregation's response in joyful love to God's grace in Christ. This leads to a further criterion:

AS BEFITS THE PRAISE OF GOD, THE ORGAN SHOULD BE HONEST. IT SHOULD NOT ATTEMPT TO HIDE, OR TO BE SOMETHING IT IS NOT; IT

---

[5] *Ibid.* If there is any doubt about the rear gallery as the traditional place of the organ, a number of works will remove that doubt: A. Bouman, *Orgels in Nederland* (Amsterdam: Van Mantgem & De Does, 1949), Arthur George Hill, *The Organs and Organ Cases of the Middle Ages and Renaissance, Vols. I & II,* (London: D. Bogue, 1883, 1891), Georges Servieres, *La Decoration Artistique des Buffets d'Orgues* (Paris & Bruxelles: G. van Oest, 1928), and Floris van der Mueren, *Het Orgel in de Nederlanden* (Brussels and Amsterdam: Leuven, 1931), Blanton, *op. cit.*, p. 95.

[6] Berry, quoted by Blanton, *op. cit.*, p. 85.

SHOULD NOT PRESENT A FALSE FACADE. IT SHOULD NOT BE IN A CHAMBER, BUT OUT IN THE OPEN WHERE IT MAY EXPRESS ITSELF IN A MANNER CONSONANT WITH ITS INTRINSIC NATURE. IT NEED NOT MASQUERADE BEHIND FALSE PIPES, BUT SHOULD HONESTLY EXPRESS THE BEAUTY OF ITS NATURE IN PRESENTING ITS WORKING PIPES.

The unmitigated bad taste of the late nineteenth century led to the ridiculous expedient of hiding organs in chambers (an action similar in effect to putting the proverbial light under a bushel). But once the organ is again recognized as a fitting symbol, albeit of man's thanksgiving, rather than of God's grace (which the poorly proportioned ranks of fake pipes were especially ill-suited to do), then one can forget about hiding the pipes, whether in chambers or behind some kind of screen and hanging, and can bring them out into the open.

Nor is there any need to hide most of the organ pipes by putting them "under expression" in a swell box (i.e., a box containing entire ranks of pipes, fitted with louvered shutters that can be opened or closed to control the amount of sound that can get out, and thus changing the volume that reaches the listener's ear, although in no way changing the volume at its source, the pipe lip). Since any given pipe within a pipe organ gives but one note at one level of volume, the only real way to change the volume is by adding or reducing the number of pipes used. This is the method of volume control inherent in the nature of a pipe organ, and is a key factor in the wonderful variety of the instrument.

How, then, has it happened that the swell box has engulfed almost all the organs of our land in its stifling embrace? The most basic answer involves an illusory ease of playing. It enables one to seem to be controlling volume by the use of a pedal, rather than by the more exacting musical discipline of knowing how to add and subtract the proper organ ranks as needed. Thus, to the local pianist, pressed into service without any formal training to play the church organ, the swell pedal was, and still is, a tremendous boon. But in such a situation it must honestly be asked whether there is really any point in making an expenditure for an organ. Rather than have a costly instrument upon which the stops are from year to year set always the same, while the total range of expression is limited to the use of the swell pedal, would it not be better to have a well-played piano? On the other hand, is it not possible for the church that can afford a fine pipe organ also to have a trained organist?

The use of the swell box to control volume may best be compared to the owner of a stereo hi-fi set who finds his volume control broken, and rather than have it fixed puts the whole instrument into a closet, controlling his volume by the extent to which he opens or closes the closet door. If this procedure sounds hopelessly foolish, remember that this is precisely the principle upon which the swell box works. Irony is added by the fact that so to stifle an organ in a swell box is technically known as putting it "under expression." If your stereo hi-fi has everything else, and you want something new, you can put it "under expression" by placing it in the closet and controlling its expression with the closet door.

It must be freely acknowledged, however, that at one point the illustration is inadequate. For the stereo hi-fi incarcerated in a closet is nonetheless at least producing its full range of tone at its source (no matter how this tone may sound once it gets through or around the closet door). A good organist can use a full range and variety of stops, even when they are in a swell box. But the analogy breaks down at the point where the untrained organist fails to use the potentialities of the various ranks of pipes, and, content with the swell pedal for "variety," allows the organ stops to remain unchanged from hymn to hymn. In such a situation, the intrinsic range and variety of the pipe organ is going unused, even at its source.

Thus the temptations of the swell box are understandable in terms of the untrained organist who prefers a pedal rather than the necessity of knowing something about the possibilities of the pipe organ inherent in its ranks. But how could the swell box have been accepted by accomplished musicians? At this point it must be recognized that the swell box is a relatively recent innovation which came into vogue only after the organ began a period of degradation from which it is only now emerging. The swell box was simply one aspect of a period of monumental bad taste. John Challis tartly describes the situation: "The accent was taken out of the pipes by nicking the windway. Out oozed gobs of tone, jellyfishlike. Having lost the accent, the music was expressionless. So part of the organ was put into a box with shutters to control the rate of ooze."[7]

The question may be legitimately raised, however, as to whether the traditional method of volume control—the adding and subtracting ranks of pipes—is really adequate. The answer should be indicated by the fact that the composers of the greatest music that has ever been written for the pipe organ (Sweelinck, Pachelbel, Buxtehude, Bach, Mozart) wrote long before the swell box unfortunately came into existence! But once having encompassed the organ, does the swell box now represent a musical necessity? The answer will somewhat depend upon whether the organ is considered a concert instrument or whether it is to serve the musical needs of a church. It is true that the music of some of the 19th- and 20th-century French organists presumes the effects of a swell box. But it is also true that this music is certainly not a musical necessity in a service of Reformed worship. The musical gain achieved in taking the organ out of its closet where volume is controlled by the opening and shutting of doors would be much greater

---

[7] "The Slider-and-Pallet Wind Chest," *Organ Institute Quarterly,* Summer, 1953, pp. 5f., quoted by Blanton, *op. cit.,* p. 52.

than any loss which might be sustained through a slight limitation in the concert repertoire.[8]

Is the traditional method of volume control adequate? Not only the fact that the greatest church music was written for organs without swell boxes, but also the contemporary church organs of Europe are evidence of its complete adequacy for services of Reformed worship. Of the organs pictured in this volume only three are even partly under expression. It should be added that this is the result not of deliberate discrimination, but simply represents the organs being used in the churches of architectural significance which were photographed for this volume. The organs, like the churches, are honest.

Once having gotten rid of the swell box, the entire organ is free for use as an honest symbol of joy and praise. In the use of the pipe organ as symbol, the old adage about honesty being the best policy seems to be borne out architecturally. During the period of the fake organ pipe, used purely as a façade with no musical function to perform, one might have expected that the architect would use the pipe to its greatest advantage for decorative purposes. Quite the opposite was the result. Uncontrolled by intrinsic necessities concerning shape and size, the undisciplined fake organ pipes finally became so ugly that they stimulated the movement which in shame hid the whole organ in chambers, where even the sound had to slip out as best it could. Even when not hideous, the fake pipe was at best sterile, visually as well as acoustically, as has been well illustrated by Blanton.[9] Compare the sterility of these fake pipes with the working pipes of the organs in this volume (again, without discriminate selection, every organ photographed uses working pipes in its façade), and the difference is unmistakable! Nor is

---

[8] Joseph E. Blanton asserts that the polyphonic, or classic organ (without a swell box) is "ideally suited to the performance of 99 percent of the organ literature worthy of being brought into the Church." *Op. cit.*, pp. 64–65.

[9] Blanton, *op. cit.*, offers fifteen excellent examples, p. 83.

the designer confined to a limited choice of expression. The little positiv in the Church of the Resurrection, Amsterdam-West (p. 121), the respectively stately, straightforward, and audacious organs of the Church of the Cross, Amstelveen (p. 107), the Maranatha Church, Amsterdam-South (p. 315), and the Church of the Fountain, Voorburg (p. 385), as well as the unassuming organ of the Church of Easter, Zaandam (p. 439), were all built under the direction of D. A. Flentrop. Yet the variety of form is seemingly endless, and all of it is exciting because it is disciplined by working within the limitations imposed by intrinsic necessities of the tracker organ.[10]

When one puts together these various factors: the release of the instrument from the prison of the organ chamber, the elimination of the swell boxes that once encompassed almost the entire organ, the elimination of the fake pipes, and the intelligent use of the working pipes by a master builder, then one has the type of instrument pictured in this volume, an instrument that serves as a fit and noble symbol of the praise due God from the congregation in response to his grace. Then the organ as architectural symbol, as well as musical instrument, stands in its proper place, fulfilling its task in the finest possible way, praising the God who in his love joins us to Christ through the means of Word and Sacraments.

---

[10] Joseph Edwin Blanton presents an excellent case for the tracker-action organ in *The Organ in Church Design*. On records, E. Power Biggs has done much to promote the tracker-action organ. On this subject one should not overlook an article by Josef von Glatter-Götz, owner-director of Rieger Organs, Austria, entitled "Observations on Physiological and Physical Aspects of Mechanical Action," *The American Organist*, May, 1960, pp. 13ff.

Organ by D. A. Flentrop of Zaandam

Manuaal		Pedaal	
Holpijp	8 bas en disc.	Bourdon	16
Prestant	4	Quintadeen	8
Roerfluit	4 bas en disc.	Fluit	4
Gemshoorn	2		
Sesquialter 2 ranks			
Mixtuur 3 ranks			

The Church of Easter (Paaskerk), Hervormd, Zaandam, The Netherlands
K. L. Sijmons Dzn, architect

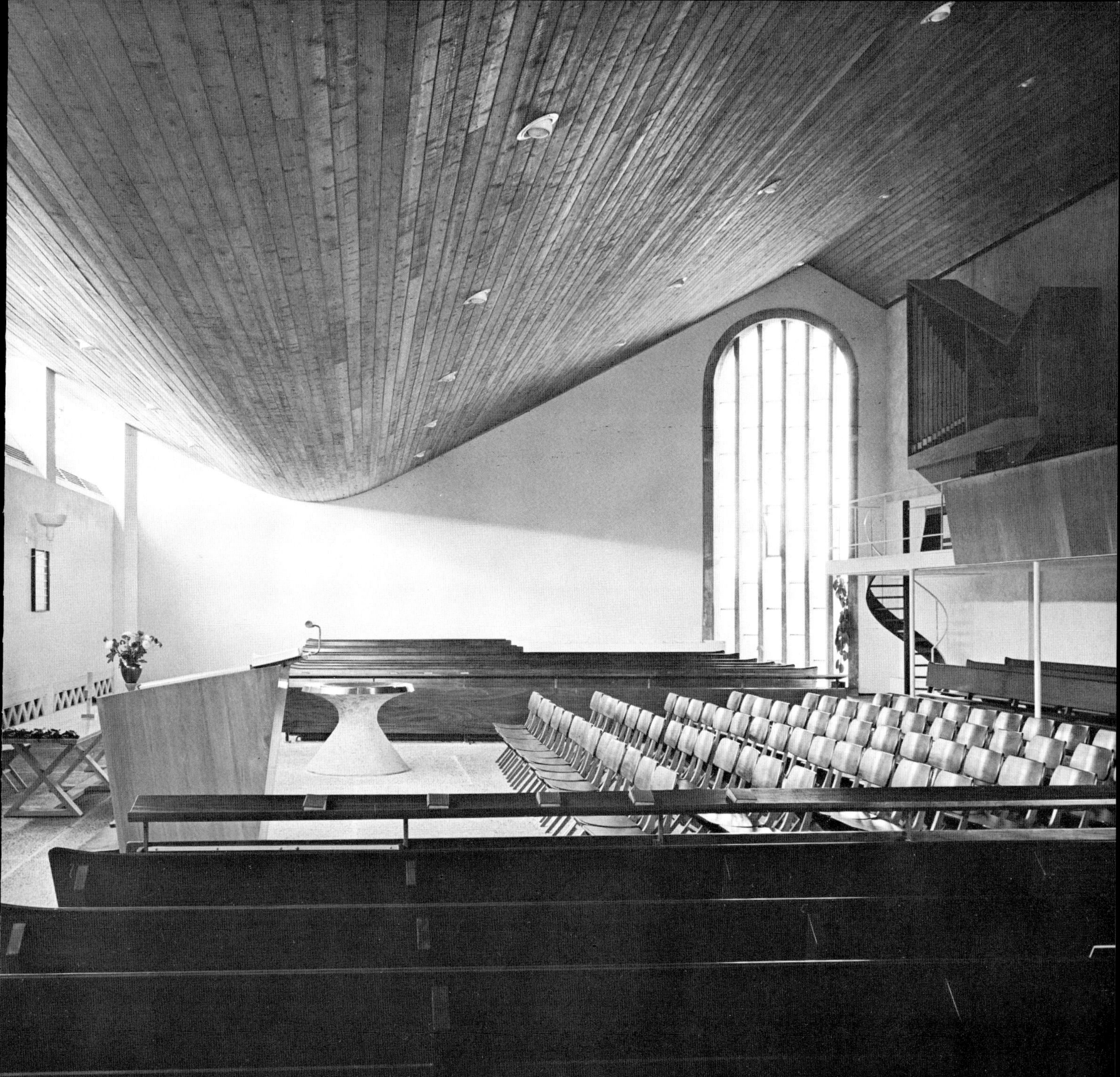

The large block of individual chairs in the center of the church are easy to remove to make an area in which the large tables for the Lord's Supper may be placed. The chairs can then be used around the tables.

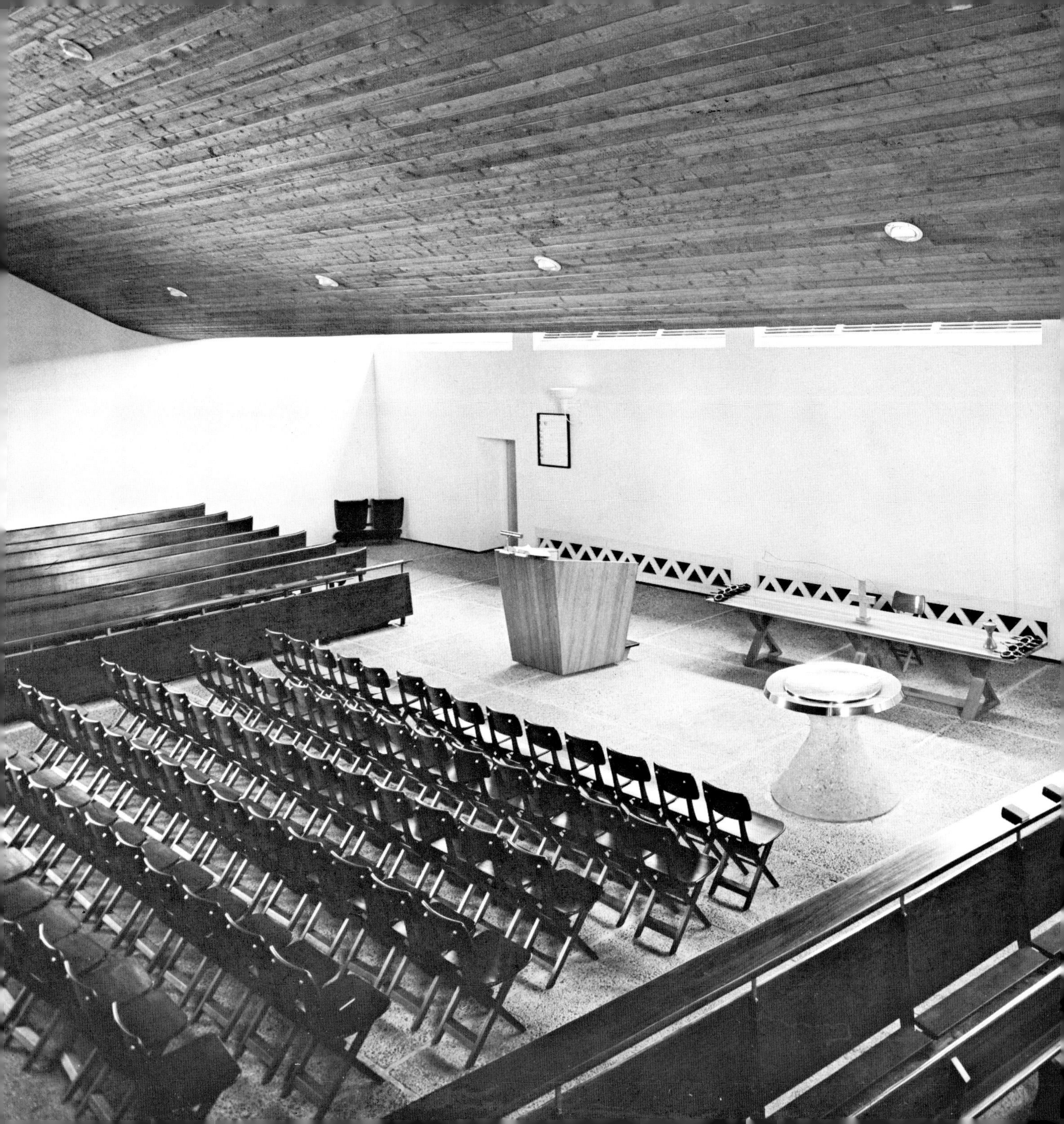

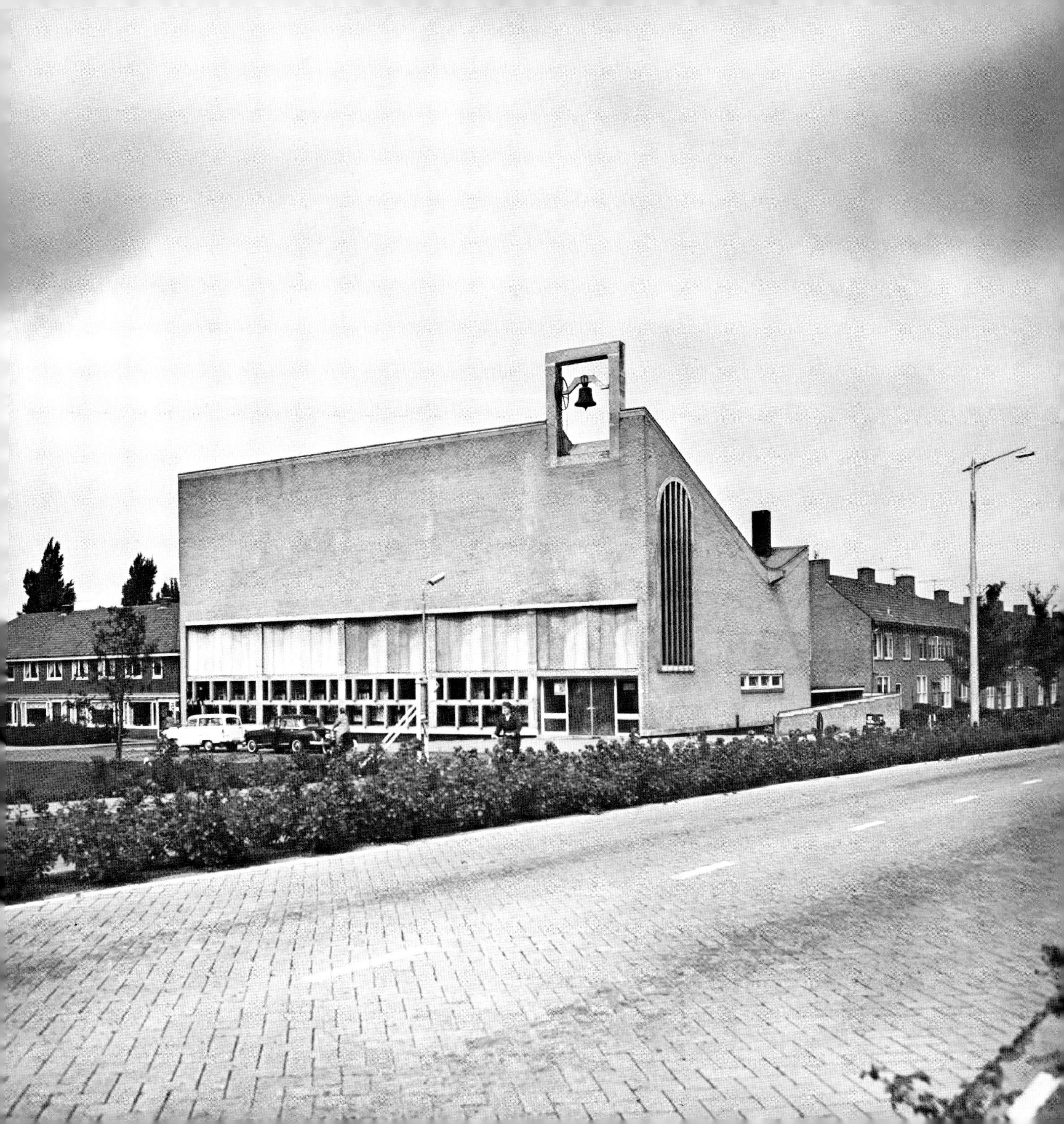

7

Heresy in the Sanctuary

The marks of a true Church were defined at the time of the Reformation as the pure preaching of the Word and the right administration of the Sacraments. Without these there could be no true Church, and rightly so, for it is by these means that Christ binds his people to himself. These are the means of God's grace in Jesus Christ. It was because of their importance that the Reformers were concerned with heresy, with false belief that would cloud, distort, and finally destroy the message of God's love in Christ Jesus. Thus they emphasized that the Word must be "purely preached and heard, and the sacraments administered according to Christ's institution."[1]

In seeking to establish the guidelines for architecture for Reformed churches, these two essential marks of the true Church have been empha-

---

[1] Calvin, *Institutes*, 4:1:9, p. 1023.

sized in the place of prominence given the pulpit, font, and table. But just as the garbled preaching of the Word and a wrong use of the Sacraments are to be avoided because they fail to proclaim clearly God's love, so too a garbled architecture in which the clear statement of Word and Sacraments is lost in a jumble of other things is to be avoided for the same important reason. Because of this the choir and the organ have been moved to a suitable place, for to confuse them with the means of grace is really quite heretical. But there are a good many other "heresies" which have entered our sanctuaries until in many cases they visually obscure both Word and Sacraments. One of the chief of these heresies in our American churches is busyness—or is it better described as clutter?

Pick up any American Protestant church magazine (or Roman Catholic one, for that matter), and look at the pictures of the church interiors. With but few exceptions they are busy, cluttered interiors. Everywhere there is some new material, or some decorative device, or some object of furniture. There is no ease, no repose, no serenity. Everything is busy. The interior gives the feeling of anxiety and nervousness (could it be the result of the uncertainty as to what the church interior should be?), as if the church believed in a doctrine of salvation by works and was frantically trying to save itself by the busyness of its architectural adornment.

Too Many Materials

All too often the church seems so insecure about what it is doing, so anxious, so desirous of proving that it is trying to do something, that one finds all kinds of different materials in the sanctuary. In the east wall of one small Protestant church were two different kinds of wood, plus natural fieldstone, plus brick, plus plaster! These five different materials were used in the structure of the building alone! This list includes neither the materials of the floor or ceiling, nor the pulpit furniture (which was in any case rather insignificant), nor the font, table, organ screens, piano, flags, and exit signs! Not only does one find a multiplicity of materials, but often a multiplicity in the ways they are used: wooden beams both straight and curved in the same sanctuary, or wood, sometimes of the same kind, but used both horizontally and vertically, in addition to a plethora of other materials and devices. One is at a loss to explain how such inordinate busyness should have come about, and it is perhaps more kind not to speculate. Let it simply be said that here so many things are being visually stated, that pulpit, table, and font have little opportunity to say visually much of anything. By using a multiplicity of building materials only the insecurity and ineptness of building committee and architect are proved, for the more materials used, the less effective will be the visual statement of Word and Sacraments, and the less serenity and repose there will be in this sanctuary of God. Architects designing churches should reconsider the wisdom found in the dictum of Mies van de Rohe: "Less is more."

With the confidence that what one is doing is right, that what one is attempting to say through a pulpit and table is the thing which should be said, there need be no fear to construct the entire east wall of a very large church entirely of brick, with but a bit of stone (The Bullinger Church, Zurich, p. 143), or to make every interior wall of the church of white plaster with no decoration other than the fall of natural light (The Church of the Resurrection, Amsterdam-West, pp. 111, 119), or to cover all but the west wall of the church in plain plaster broken neither by window nor symbol (The Ark, Slotervaart, pp. 159–63). These are churches that know what they are saying. Their message is too important to be lost in displaying a multiplicity of building materials. They are churches that are saying something desperately important about Jesus Christ and his coming to men.

IN CHRIST WE HAVE PEACE WITH GOD AND WITH MEN. THIS PEACE

SHOULD BE REFLECTED IN THE ARCHITECTURE OF THE CHURCH. TOO MANY MATERIALS, USED IN TOO MANY WAYS, WITH TOO MANY THINGS, PRODUCE CLUTTER AND BUSYNESS WHICH MAKE VISUAL PEACE IMPOSSIBLE. THE ARCHITECTURE OF THE CHURCH SHOULD BE AT PEACE, REFLECTING THE PEACE WITH GOD AND MAN THAT WE HAVE IN CHRIST.

Too Many Things

But not only are too many materials used, making busy what should be peaceful, there are also too many things. The symbols of Christ's presence are all but lost in the welter of things. What additional things does one find in the east end of many churches? Seating for the choir, an organ console, several apertures in the walls behind which are hidden either pipes or amplifiers (or maybe there are pipes visible and screened amplifiers as well), a piano, two flags, substantial flower stands (even when the flowers end up on the communion table), three chairs or a long bench (seldom occupied except by the minister), perhaps a door or two with the inevitable exit signs, perhaps a cross on the wall and another on the pulpit and another on the table and another on the font. Does this sound like an exaggeration? In four out of five Reformed churches in America for every item not in this list a substitute item not mentioned (such as an illuminated cross hanging from the chancel arch, or extra candelabra on or off the table) can be found.

The criticisms are the same. Like a poorly organized sermon with too many points, no message is conveyed. So too, in the welter of materials and things, the basic symbols of the reason for the presence of the congregation are lost. Is it any wonder that the Church sometimes seems to lose its reason for being, to lose its way? When in the basic architecture of the church, when in the message that need be built only once, the effort is not made to achieve a clear statement of faith, then is it any wonder that the men's or women's or youth groups occasionally lose sight of the purpose of the church?

But what about some of these things which would detract from the clarity of architectural statement? The choir, the organ, the piano are part of the response of the congregation. And what need is there for a piano if there is an organ? The church is not a place for instrumental duets, for entertainment! The church is a place of worship! With good acoustics and a good sounding board, no loudspeakers need be hidden behind screens or grates. Surely the flower stands need not be permanent fixtures, and certainly they should not be of such size that they cannot easily be carried out whenever not in use. In a proper pulpit, rather than a reader's desk on a large platform, there need be room for only one person. If provision need be made for extraordinary occasions when others must be seated at the east end of the church, the architect should be asked to design some special, portable chairs, as well as to suggest room for their placement. But since the church is for worship, and not for impressing people with a number of visiting dignitaries, cannot the pews be utilized for such occasions? If there must be doors, let them be as inconspicuous as possible. Let everything that is not absolutely essential to the use of the means of grace be eliminated from the east end of the church. Only then can architect and artist state with impact the essence of the faith, the purpose of assembling each week: Christ is there, to join his people to himself through Word and Sacraments.

CHRIST OUR PEACE COMES TO US IN WORD AND SACRAMENTS. WHEN WE ALLOW EITHER A DIVERSITY OF MATERIALS, SHAPES, OR THINGS TO DETRACT FROM THE FORCEFUL PRESENTATION OF WORD AND SACRAMENTS, WE SIMILARLY DETRACT FROM OUR MESSAGE OF CHRIST.

Too Many Flags

To get rid of a half-dozen different building materials, a few unused chairs, the ugly flower stands, and even the piano, that may not be too hard.

But what about the flags? There one becomes involved with one's relationship to his country. This is a matter to which extended and careful discussion must be given.

It is extraordinary how one can become accustomed to seeing things that shock and puzzle people who come upon them for the first time. Flags in churches belong in this category. Usually, the very fact that one is thoroughly accustomed to a thing means it will not be changed, no matter how shocked the newcomer, but in the building of something as costly as a new church, and even more important, a structure dedicated to the worship of God, it becomes imperative to try to look at some of these things through new eyes.

Let us imagine a sanctuary which is architecturally designed to express our Reformed worship. There is the pulpit, of ample size and goodly construction, making clear at the very outset that here is a church that takes the proclamation of the gospel of Jesus Christ with great seriousness. And there stands the baptismal font, speaking to us of the baptism into Christ through which we are cleansed of our sins and born into newness of life. And there is the communion table, reminding us of the bread and wine which are to assure us that as certainly as we eat and drink thereof in faith we have part in Christ's sacrifice on the cross. But what of these flags? The pulpit, the font, the table, all point to Christ, but what of these flags? The flags speak not of Christ but of the nation. Are they to tell us that this church is subject to the nation? Are they to tell us that the Word of God may be proclaimed in this church only as long as it does not conflict with the will of the nation? Are they to tell us that we would do well to take Caiaphas as our example when he said "you do not understand that it is expedient for you that one man should die for the people, and that the whole nation should not perish" (John 11:50). Or do they mean that the nation is also a means of God's grace? No, certainly these flags must not proclaim such messages! But then what are they doing there along with the God-given means of grace? Is not the national flag in this position really heresy?[2]

Now please understand, as a good citizen I stand at attention when the flag goes by, I rise for the National Anthem, I know the Pledge of Allegiance and say it earnestly. I also pay the government the taxes due it, and as a Christian do all I can to make this a strong country under God. But having said this, the question must still be raised as to whether putting the national flag on the same visual level with Word and Sacraments is not a visual heresy?

At the time of the Reformation our forefathers were extremely zealous to rid themselves of visual heresy, for they knew that it was often more dangerous than the doctrinal heresies they were fighting. Therefore they eradicated from their churches the statues of the saints, of Jesus, and of Mary. In our own day and age the danger is not from the heresy of idolatry, but that of an extreme nationalism which places country before God. Our times have witnessed the dangerous swiftness with which a nation can call upon patriotism and usurp God's place. One example is Nazi Germany, where even the church was all too often caught up in this monstrous idolatry of nation. A continuing example is that of communism, where ideology and nation together seek to displace God from his throne. Nor is our own country—where children are still taught to admire Stephen Decatur's "Our Country, right or wrong"— immune from a nationalistic heresy, especially in these times when it is engaged in the struggle with communism.

Even at the time of the Reformation Rome insisted that her statues were not really idols—merely aids to prayer and devotion. The Reformers, recognizing the dangers inherent in such "aids," banned them not because they were idols, per se, but because of the dangers involved. In a similar way,

---

[2] It should be noted that in none of the Continental churches pictured does one find a flag near the pulpit or table.

many may rightly insist that a national flag in a church does not necessarily mean the heresy of nation before God. But symbols are significant, and there is an inherent danger in this close identification of Church and nation. In our age of inescapable propaganda, where an objective opinion or independent decision is hard enough to come by, we do the Church a disservice by tying it too closely to the nation. The Church of Christ best serves this great nation not in being an obsequious servant of its policies (a role in which the Church in Russia has suffered under czar and commissar alike), but rather by playing its God-given role of prophet to the nation, speaking as best it can in obedience to Christ.

And if the role of the Church as prophet is taken seriously, perhaps there is a place in the church for a flag. But to put it with the means of grace, Word and Sacraments, is to invite confusion. To place it near the west wall of the church, where it too receives the preaching of the Word, is to give it a proper place. For, really, is not this exactly what Christians believe? The Christian loves his country, not only for its bounty, but also for the freedom it has given him to worship God. Love of country, yes, that should be true for all of us. We are proud of our nation, proud of our heritage and the religious principles that have been a part of our nation. Not only are we alarmed by the seeming breakdown of those religious principles, but it is our desire as well that the Christian message of redemption in Christ be proclaimed to the entire nation. For this reason we have taken many dollars out of our pockets and given them to the denominational agencies responsible for establishing and maintaining churches in all areas of America, for it is our concern that the gospel be proclaimed throughout the land.

Now all of the above is precisely what is expressed when the national flag is put at the west end of the church. This signifies that we believe that it is the hearing of the Word of God that has made America strong in the past, and that our country must continue to hear the Word of God if it is to remain great. Perhaps the flag should not be in the midst of the congregation, for the nation, per se, is not a member of the body of Christ. But it can quite properly be placed at the rear of the nave, either in the middle, or to the side, as the arrangement of the church may dictate. Another, and perhaps preferable solution, would be to have the flag mounted in a bracket, extending from the balcony.

The true Christian patriot is one who wishes to keep this country free and strong, under God. This cannot be done by attaching the church as a caboose to the train of national policy. The true Christian patriot is the one who through the Church helps guide his nation in paths of righteousness. The true patriot is interested in freeing the Church to be true to Christ its King, and in that obedience ministering to the nation. Those who are reformed according to the Word of God, must accept the words of Peter when he told the leaders of his nation, "We must obey God rather than men" (Acts 5:29). If the two are ever in conflict, then God must come before nation.

Since there is no dispute over our love of country and love of God, let us render to both God and Caesar their due, and take the opportunity of building a new church to symbolize properly what we believe. The symbol of the nation does not belong with God's means of grace, the Word and the Sacraments. They alone belong at the front of our churches, for it is God alone who deserves to be worshiped. Instead, the symbol of the nation must be in such a position that it is visually clear to all that the nation must also hear the Word, that it too needs the prophetic and redemptive message of God.

It is to be hoped also that once the need for symmetry in the front of the church is gone, the "Christian flag" may go with it. Of recent manufacture, the "Christian flag" has no official sanction, an exceedingly doubtful purpose, and origins that can most kindly be described as "extemporaneous." The "Christian flag" was given birth at a Sunday school rally at Brighton Chapel in Coney Island in 1897. The prominent speaker scheduled for the occasion failed to appear, and so Mr. Charles Carlton Overton, superintendent of the Brighton school, got up to give the address. Speaking without preparation, he began talking about the American flag draped over the pulpit. The flag makers suggest that what came next was "an inspired idea," but be that as it may, Mr. Overton asserted that since there was an American flag, there should also be a Christian flag to remind all men of their allegiance to God. In this same extempore speech he also worked out the design of the flag: a field of white,

> for, ever since the white-robed heavenly throng sang "Peace on Earth" at the first Christmas, white has been the color of peace and purity and innocence. And, on the battlefields of any war, all guns are silenced at the sign of white, the international flag of truce. In the corner of his white flag, Mr. Overton proposed a union of deep blue—color of the unclouded sky, symbol of faith and trust and devotion; and, on this, the cross on which the Savior died—emblazoned in the color red.[3]

While there is opportunity for dissatisfaction in the above, one must in charity remember that this was a completely extempore speech. Mr. Overton immediately had such a flag made, but it remained within his own church until in 1907 he and Dr. Ralph E. Diffendorfer, secretary of the Methodist Young People's Missionary Movement, arranged for its mass manufacture.[4]

The fact that this flag has found acceptance in so many churches is hardly a convincing argument for its continuance, any more than the wide acceptance of little plastic statues to put on automobile dashboards is an argument for their effectiveness. What is the usual argument for a flag in the church?—that it is a symbol which speaks of Christianity and love, and which

---

[3] "The Christian Flag," a pamphlet distributed by Annin & Co., Flag Makers, New York, New York.

[4] "The Flag in the Church," mimeographed material distributed by Annin & Co., Flag Makers, New York, New York, p. 1.

can be saluted (putting Christianity on a parity with the nation?). But the Church of Christ does not need a flag to display, it has a pulpit, table, and font to impress visually upon its followers the way of God's revelation. A "Christian flag" in the front of the church is not only superfluous, it is distracting from the real, God-given symbols of the faith! Nor is there any point to placing it anywhere else, for if this questionable symbol really represents anything, it is the people of God, and they are to be actually present in the pews, and not there by way of symbol.

Even as the Reformers rid themselves of statues detrimental to the true faith, let this generation continue to be reformed according to the Word of God and end the confusion of the grace of God and the power of nations. Let it perform the task God has given it—the proclamation of his prophetic and redemptive Word to the nation. Let this awareness of our task be illustrated by placing the symbol of the nation where the proclamation of the Word of God may be directed toward it. At the same time, let the congregation look toward the God-given symbols of his grace: Word and Sacraments.

THE NATION IS NOT A MEANS OF GRACE, BUT IS A RECIPIENT OF GRACE AS CHRISTIANS GO FORTH TO LIVE MEANINGFUL CHRISTIAN LIVES AS CITIZENS OF THE NATION. THEREFORE THE FLAG OF THE NATION SHOULD NOT BE CONFUSED WITH THE MEANS OF GRACE, BUT SHOULD STAND AT THE WEST END OF THE CHURCH, SYMBOLIZING THAT THE NATION MUST ALSO HEAR GOD'S WORD.

Too Many Decorations

Or should the phrase be "too many symbols"? One would hardly have expected to find too many of either in Protestant churches—and Reformed churches at that! Unfortunately, the distinction between symbolism and decoration is often far too slight, and the multiplicity of symbols makes them but decorations. And perhaps the symbol that is most overworked—to the point of making that which is central and essential to the Faith a banality—is the cross! This must be made clear: the validity of the cross as a Christian symbol is not being questioned. It is a legitimate symbol that speaks of the Christ who was crucified for the sin of the world, who died and rose again from the dead and sits at the right hand of God the Father Almighty. But just because it stands at the center of the Faith, and speaks of the utmost agony of God's Son, it must be used and respected as a Christian symbol, and not thrown around as a decorative design.

What is one to think, for example, of a church Reformed in theology that uses a cross the height of the east wall (thus far there is no real quarrel) as its primary symbol within the sanctuary, but then goes on to add forty-three more crosses throughout the sanctuary as decorative features? One must suppose that either the cross has been reduced to a decorative motif (which is certainly an indignity), or else that some strange doctrine has crept in which has attributed some sort of merit to the symbol, and has thus encouraged its multiple use. Nichols and Trinterud comment that the development among Protestants of

> "worship centers," little shrines, "eternal lights", etc., witness eloquently to the utter lack of any genuine symbolism, or any theological integrity in these architectural arrangements. Theologically the altar, the pyx, the lights, are among the most sacred symbols of the Roman faith. When they are used as mere "decorations", rather than as true symbols, neither art nor religion are advanced.[5]

This is especially true of the careless use of the cross. If it is used as a symbol, the cross on the east wall need not be repeated on the pulpit, found in brass on the Lord's table, and endlessly repeated on the pew ends and in the light fixtures. If it is used as symbol, and not as decoration, one cross will suffice for any sanctuary.

---

[5] Nichols & Trinterud, *op. cit.*, pp. 16–17.

This matter raises the question as to the validity of other symbols for Reformed worship. If symbols are used at all, they should be readily understandable to the congregation, or else they degenerate into decoration. They should also be symbols that have to do with the business at hand: the coming of the Holy Spirit to make effective Word and Sacraments, or perhaps the bread and the wine. An example of readily understandable Christian symbolism is found in Zorgvliet Church (Zorgvlietkerk), The Hague (pp. 425, 429). However, symbolism can so easily get out of hand, can so easily be trite, or self-conscious, or just downright atrocious art, that one would do well to attempt its use only with the aid of a knowledgeable architect and artist.

When it comes to symbolism it would be well for almost every church to concentrate its attention on the primary symbols of Christ's Church, the Word and Sacraments. Because we preach and celebrate the Sacraments at the command of our Lord, the furniture which we use to obey his command inevitably becomes a reminder, a symbol, of that Christ-commanded action. The preaching and the use of the Sacraments have been commanded by Christ; the use of even the cross as a symbol has not. This is not said in an attempt to take the cross out of Christianity—that is impossible—but to assert that the Christ-ordained Sacraments remind us in a way both more graphic and more accurate of our relationship to the cross than the cross itself. Because of the richness of the Christ-given Sacraments, and his command to preach, let the concern of the Church be for pulpits, tables, and fonts that by their quality show an awareness of the importance of Word and Sacraments.

CHRIST'S COMMANDS CONCERNING THE WORD AND THE SACRAMENTS INEVITABLY INVOLVES PULPITS, FONTS, AND TABLES WHICH BECOME SYMBOLS OF THOSE FUNCTIONS. PULPIT, FONT, AND TABLE ARE THUS THE BASIC SYMBOLS OF THE CHRISTIAN FAITH.

THE CROSS AS A VENERABLE SYMBOL OF THE FAITH SHOULD BE USED WITH RESPECT AS A SYMBOL AND NEVER BE DEGRADED TO THE ROLE OF A DECORATIVE MOTIF. THEREFORE IF THE CROSS IS USED, ONE IS ENOUGH.

Too Many Windows

There is little that can be more disruptive to the proper hearing of the Word than too many windows. One should hasten to add that it is not the number of windows per se, but their placement that makes them a cause of concern. Windows of clear glass, and windows in the east wall, can be especially disconcerting. The problem is of such import that the Bishops of Germany in their "Directives for the Building of a Church" insist that "the terminal wall of the sanctuary (the east wall) should not be pierced by windows, lest the clear vision of the altar be obscured."[6] And there is good reason for the concern of the bishops, for unless the building committee is acting with deliberate malice, there seems to be no good purpose served in building a church so that anyone trying to look in the direction of minister, font, or table, is forced to be uncomfortable by looking directly into strong light.

Stained glass may be very pretty, and a view of God's creation is excellent in its place, but to put it in active competition with the very purpose for which the church is constructed represents a clear victory of sentiment over reason. Everyone has experienced the uncomfortable situation of visiting with a friend who sits framed by a bright window. Looking at a source of light more intense than that with which the room is illuminated is naturally uncomfortable. The pupils of the eyes expand to let in enough light to see the person within the room, and in so doing let in so much of the extra light from the window that discomfort is the inevitable result.

---

[6] *Documents for Sacred Architecture,* Directive 10, p. 19.

Every minister knows the importance of contact with the congregation, but visual contact disappears if the congregation must squint into the blinding light of a window in order to try to see the minister. It is possible, of course, to have windows in the front of the church which are not blinding. If the architect has carefully figured the angle of the sun's rays throughout the year so that they never come through the window directly into the eyes of the congregation, then one danger is avoided. If the architect carefully chooses his glass so that it is of such color and density that it will not be difficult to look at **even** on the brightest days, still another danger is overcome. If the architect provides sufficient interior illumination effectively to balance the light coming in at the windows, so that the pulpit, font, and table may be seen as well as the window, still another danger is removed. But a remaining question must be asked: "Will the window be distracting, drawing attention away from the Word and Sacraments and to itself?" This question is much more difficult than the former, for if the window has any real artistic merit it will call attention to itself, and away from the symbols of union with Christ. A window is not a means of grace. On the other hand, any window in the east wall which is so artistically sterile that it does not lead one's eye toward it seems a rather bad investment. One is caught on the horns of a dilemma, with either a worthy window that is therefore heretical because it competes with Word and Sacraments, or an unworthy window that is as ineffective as it is inoffensive. Is not the simplest solution to place any windows in one of the other three walls of the church?

With reference to stained glass windows, it should be emphasized that they are in no way necessary for a proper church. The many churches illustrated in this volume indicate how many are built without the use of stained glass and with the obvious intention of never installing stained glass. Nor is ours the only age since the invention of stained glass that has done without it. St. Bernard of Clairvaux stipulated that the Cistercian churches were to be as simple as possible, without pretentiousness, and that the windows were to be of "unadorned clear glass.'" In eighteenth-century English churches

> the windows are filled normally with clear glass, making the churches lightsome, to use a favourite adjective of the period. On the whole, the eighteenth century believed that light churches showed an absence of superstition, and witnessed to the Church's escape from what Warburton [the Bishop of Gloucester] called the benighted days of monkish owl-light.[8]

Our own day can afford to look upon the stained glass window as a matter dictated solely by the design of the church. In any case, the possibility of the use of stained glass should be discussed from the beginning with the architect, even if money is not immediately available. The architect should be allowed to choose, or at least help choose the artist, and be given an important voice, and perhaps veto power, when it comes to the final choice of the window. There should obviously be no consideration of buying "stock items" out of religious-goods catalogs. It cannot be emphasized too strongly that any stained glass must be considered as an integral part of the church building and must be considered from the very beginning of the design. Colored glass of any kind is just too visually percussive to be added at random at the whim of donor or committee. Stained glass is the province of the architect and such specialized associates as he may need to do a suitable job.

A new possibility in stained glass arising within the last few decades is beton glass. The glass is not really beton, or concrete, but is set into concrete to form a portion of the wall of the church. The most notable example of such glass in this country is the First Presbyterian Church of Stamford, Connecticut,

---

[7] Hay, *op. cit.*, p. 6.
[8] Addleshaw & Etchells, *op. cit.*, pp. 61–62.

Wallace K. Harrison, architect. In Europe there is a widespread use being made of beton glass, some of it very poor, some very good. One of the finer uses of such glass is in the Church of the Trinity (Trinitatiskirche), in Mannheim (see pp. 589–95). A more typical, but nonetheless striking, use of this glass is in the portrayal of scenes from the Book of Revelation in The Church of the King (Koningskerk).

The Church of the King (Koningskerk), Gereformeerd, Amsterdam-Watergraafsmeer, The Netherlands. Van der Kuilen & Trappenberg, architects

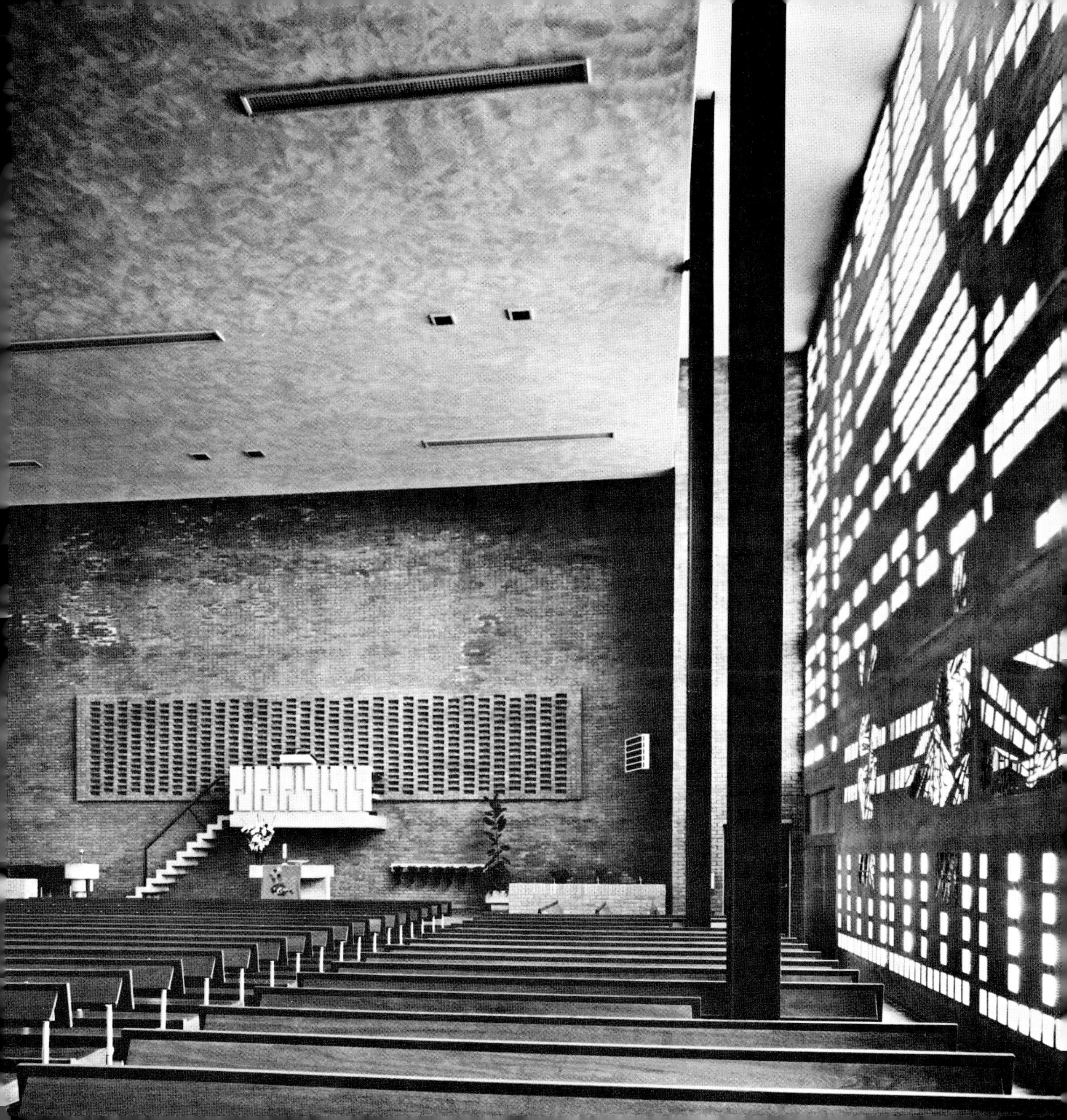

Organ by A. Mense Ruiter of Groningen

Hoofdwerk

Prestant	8
Octaaf	4
Octaaf	2
Mixtuur 3–5 ranks	
Roerfluit	8
Speelfluit	4
Quint	2⅔
Salicionaal	8
Dulciaan	16
Trompet	8

Rugwerk

Holpijp	8
Prestant	4
Quint	1⅓
Scherp 4 st.	
Quintadeen	8
Roerfluit	4
Gemshoorn	2
Sesquialter 2 ranks	
Kromhoorn	8

Pedaal

Prestant	16
Prestant	8
Octaaf	4
Mixtuur 5 ranks	
Bourdon	16
Bourdon	8
Bazuin	16
Cornet	4

The window, depicting the conquest by Christ the King over the powers of evil, represented by the great dragon (Revelation 19), was designed by Berend Hendriks.

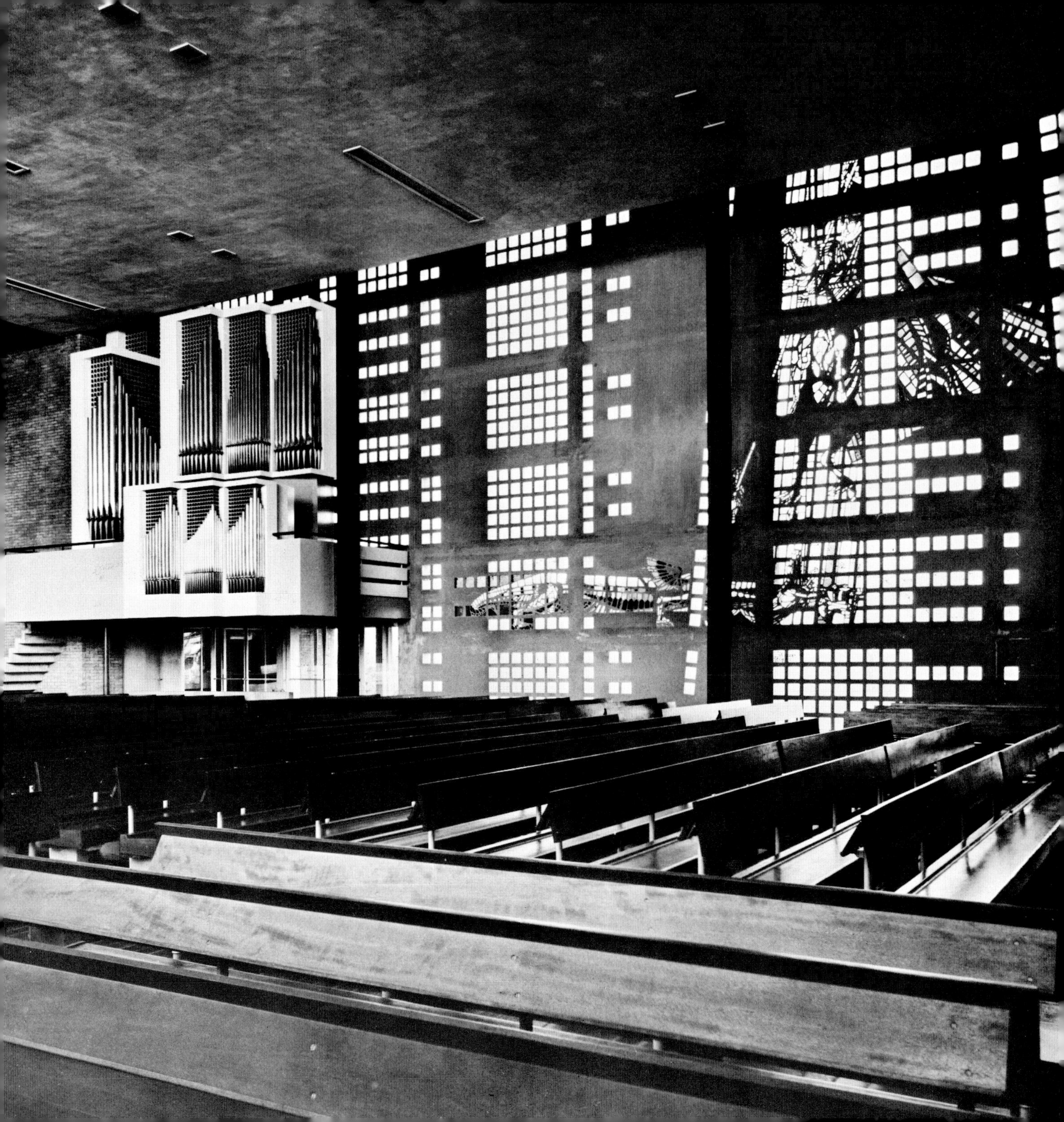

It is also possible to have too many of the clear-glass picture windows in vogue in so many churches. Oftentimes, for lack of better guidance in the proper and essential symbols of the church, the architect or building committee is trying to say something about the church being open to the world, or that its task is to go out into the world, or some such equally valid sentiment. The effectiveness of this device is highly questionable, simply because it is open to so many different interpretations. Conrad H. Massa observes that "just using glass walls may simply do away with the valid and necessary distinction between God and his creation."[9] "Church architecture which accentuates the natural world by using clear glass or plants accentuates not God, but nature which with humanity is fallen. The use of nature may have a place in design, but not as a symbol of God."[10]

At the same time the very mundane matter of distraction should not be overlooked. The Church ministers to people, not angels, and when the church walls are open to outside activity, that activity can easily become a distraction. In the little town of Mittelheim/Rheingau in Germany there is a very nice village church with a good liturgical center (although the pulpit could have received more emphasis), with panels of stained glass set in a floor-to-ceiling glass wall that gives this little church a joyousness that cannot be captured in black and white photographs. But the glass wall looks out over the Rhine with its constant procession of tugs, barges, excursion boats, and a miscellany of others. No minister could compete with a passing scene like that, and so at eye level the clear glass has received a wide band of frosting, which, while it looks like the afterthought that it was, was nevertheless abso-

---

[9] *Op. cit.,* p. 52.

[10] Paul Chapman & Charles Lake, "Toward a Theology of Architecture," *Motive,* May 1959, p. 28. Here it should be said that it is also possible to have *too many plants.* In all too many Dutch churches the plants grow in such profusion they seem often to threaten to engulf the liturgical center of the church.

lutely necessary to the "hearing" of the Word (which Calvin rightly insisted was as essential as the preaching).[11]

---

[11] *Institutes*, 4:1:9, p. 1023.

The Reformed Church, Mittelheim/Rheingau, Germany
H. G. Hofmann, architect

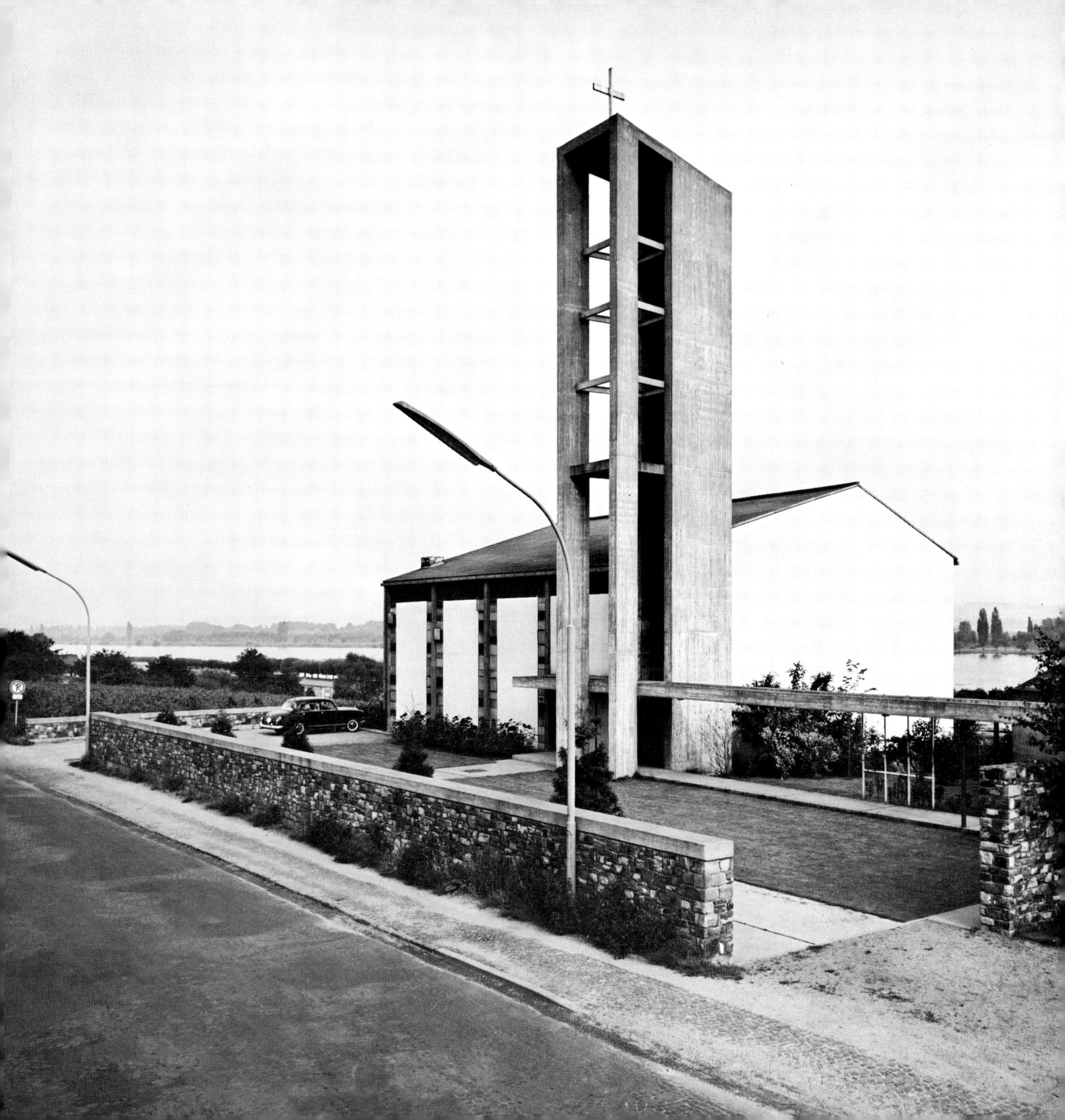

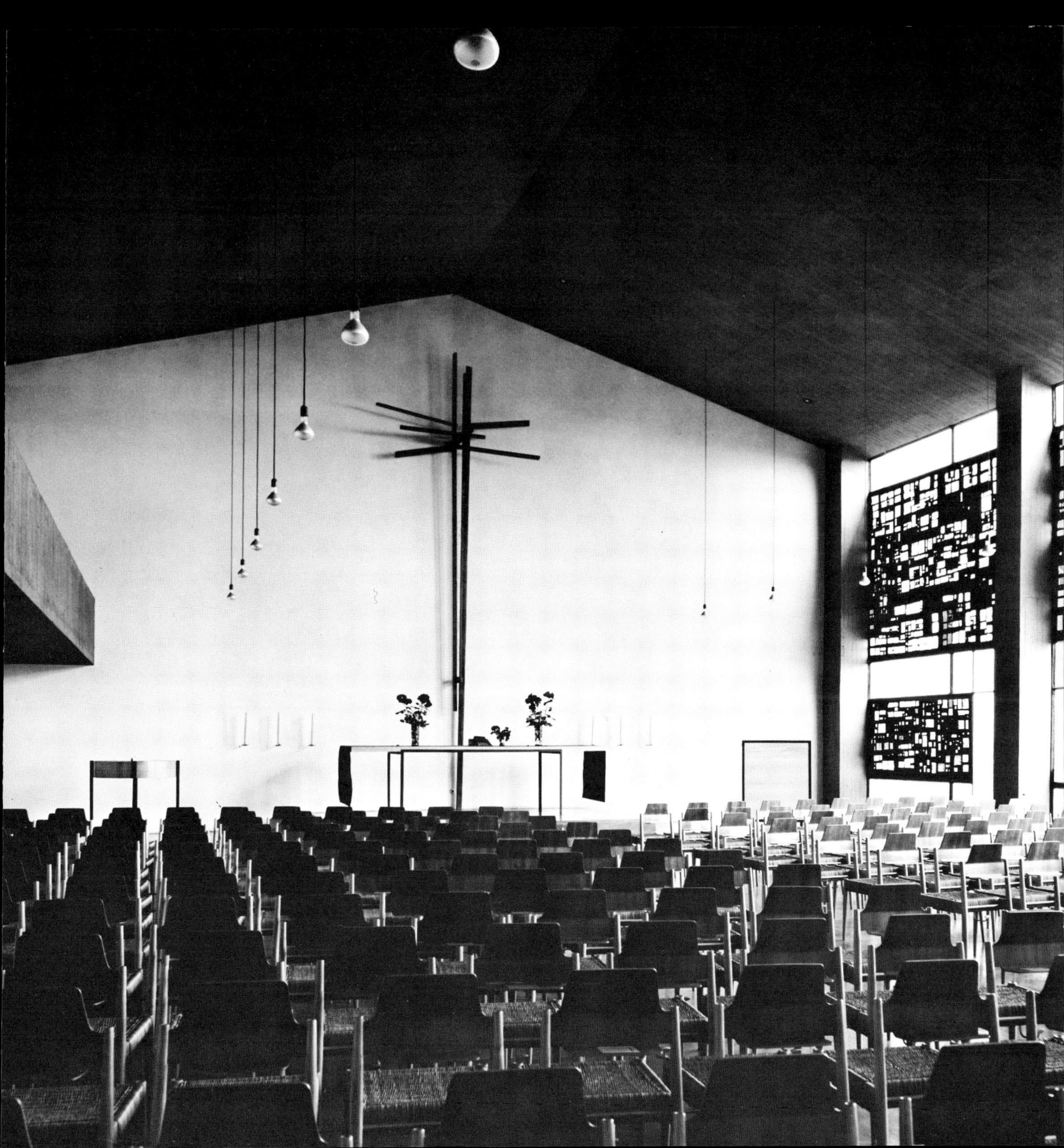

A good example of achieving visual balance between the table and the font.

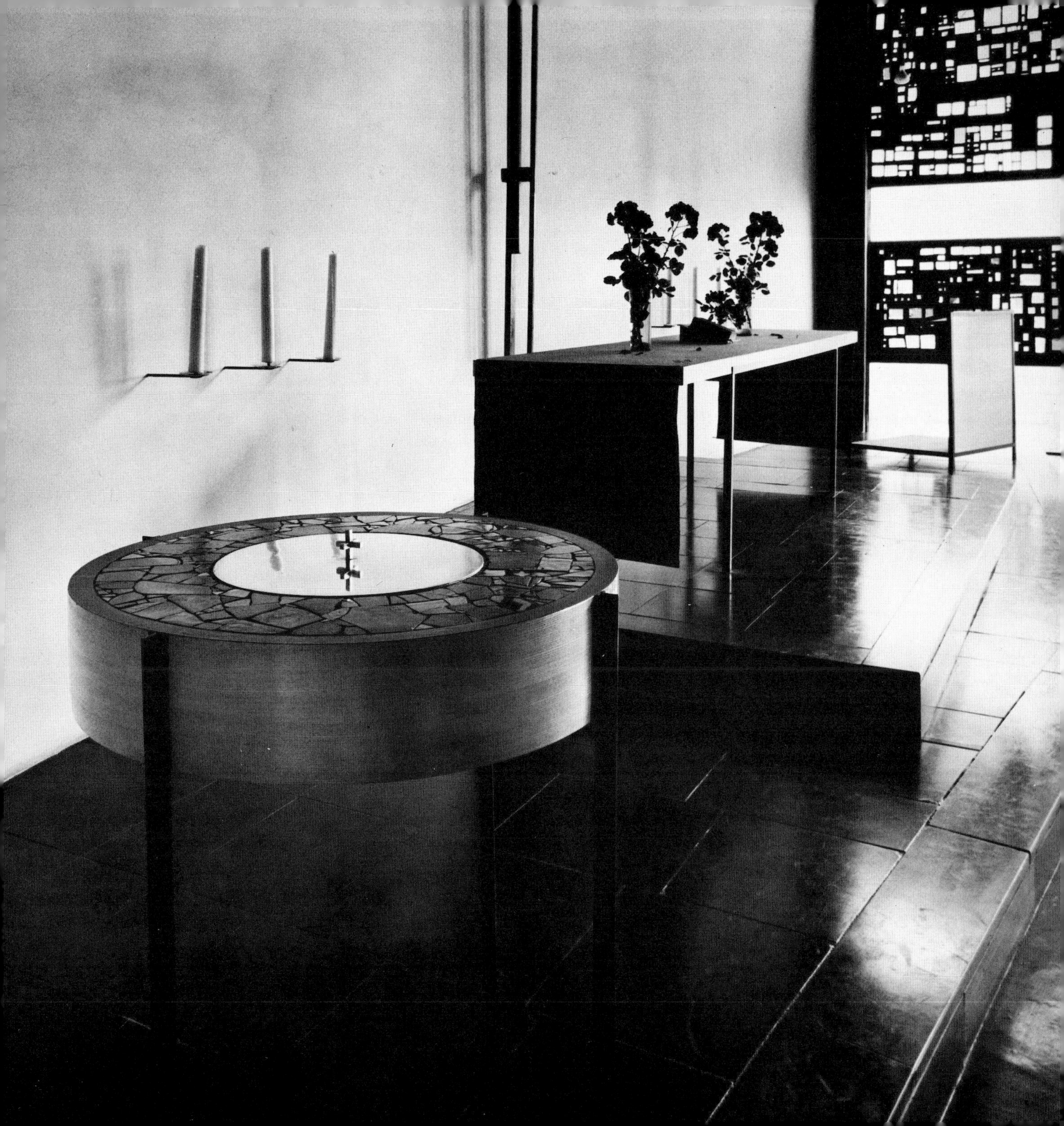

Nature is God's creation, given to man for his use and dominion; it is a part of God's bounty, but it is neither a means of grace nor something to be worshiped. If one wall must be of glass, then let it be the west wall, so that strangers may see in from the outside, so that they may see what is going on without committing themselves to the unknown by going into a strange place. Let them find such assurance in a knowledge of its interior without distraction to the congregation. If one wishes to use clear glass in a way that will help bring people in to hear the preaching of the gospel, then it is the west wall that should be of glass.[12]

WINDOWS ARE NOT A MEANS OF GRACE AND SHOULD THEREFORE NOT IN ANY WAY DETRACT FROM OR COMPETE WITH THE SYMBOLS OF WORD AND SACRAMENTS.

Having established this negative criterion in which windows are treated as a possible enemy of the gospel, it must immediately be acknowledged that natural light can and should be treated as a valuable ally. The pulpit, table, and font all need illumination if they are to be seen, and if they are to be the focal point of the sanctuary it would be well if light were used to help focus attention on them. This light can of course be man-made, and thus have the advantage of constancy. This same dependability of illumination, however, also results in a certain monotony. On the other hand, an intelligent use of natural light can contribute a wonderful variety and liveliness to a place of worship. The variety contributed by natural light has its source both in the weather and the movement of the sun. The former influences the quality of light—from direct sunlight to what is left after filtering through a heavy rain—while

---

[12] An excellent example of such a church is St. Stephen's Episcopal Church on the edge of the Ohio State University campus in Columbus, Ohio. Brooks & Coddington, architects. *Architectural Forum*, Dec. 1958, pp. 39–40.

the latter results in ever-changing patterns in illumination. And it is precisely because the angle of the sun's rays varies from hour to hour, and at the same hour from day to day, while yet following a fixed and inexorable yearly pattern, that it is necessary for the architect to give careful consideration to the sun's total course in relationship to the possibilities of the site and the nature of the building. Thus, what is done in any given situation to use the natural fall of light to accentuate the means of grace is completely dependent upon the opportunities and limitations of that specific situation. At this point one must rely upon the competence of the architect, being limited in criteria to the following:

NATURAL LIGHT SHOULD BE USED AS AN ALLY OF THE GOSPEL TO EMPHASIZE THE SYMBOLS OF CHRIST'S COMING TO HIS PEOPLE.

A few examples of the way in which the fall of natural light adds both emphasis and variety to the symbols of Word and Sacraments are found in the Church of the Advent, Den Haag-Loosduinen (pp. 269–81), the Church of the Resurrection, Amsterdam-West (pp. 111, 119), and the Parma Park Reformed Church, Cleveland, Ohio (pp. 197–203).

Too Many Memorial Gifts

Many churches may dispute the fact that it is possible to have too many memorial gifts, but as the discussion of this chapter has involved decorations, flags, and stained glass windows, some very unwise memorial gifts have no doubt come to mind. The single broadly pictographic window in the midst of a church that otherwise has rather good glass, some piece of furniture completely out of keeping with the rest—but there is no need to go on. The fact that memorial gifts inevitably have emotional associations with the deceased often make them rather delicate subjects. The refusal of a memorial gift by a church board is sometimes interpreted in terms of rejection of the deceased. Because of the strongly emotional context, compliant boards all too often accept memorial gifts that turn out to be extremely unwise when placed within the architectural context of a particular church.

The proper time to prepare for memorials, or any special gifts, is when the church is first planned, before it is built. One of the wisest rules a consistory could pass concerning a church that is being carefully planned to be a Reformed church is the stipulation that the architect be sole judge and jury as to what is to be allowed in the building or on the grounds as a memorial gift. This law, like that of the biblical Medes and Persians, should be unbreakable and unalterable. Its advantages are manifold. The architect, trained in taste, whose loving care has gone into the building, who knows its proportions and intentions much better than anyone else, is by far the best equipped to judge whether an intended memorial will be an asset or a liability. Having been associated with the planning of the church from the beginning, he will know just those desirable, but not essential additions that were left out when the church was built. But best of all, the architect is not subject to the same pressures from members of the congregation under which both consistory and minister suffer. The architect can be impartial; he can be objective; he can be an impervious safeguard of the beauty and visual proclamation of the church. With expert advice of this nature mandatory, the church should often find its donors happily planning their intended memorial in co-operation with the architect.

Memorials can be very detrimental, or greatly beneficial. The wise church board will insure that memorials will be beneficial by insisting, when their building is still in the planning stage, that throughout the life of the church the architect be the arbiter and guide in the acceptance of memorials. With such wise planning, the congregation will have the beauty of its church protected, while the donors of memorials will have the expert advice necessary to prevent the expenditure of sums upon such things as would give neither the congregation, nor ultimately even the donor, satisfaction.

THAT THE THEOLOGICAL STATEMENT OF THE CHURCH IN ITS ARCHITECTURE MAY CONTINUE UNIMPAIRED, AND THAT MEMORIAL GIFTS MAY BE OF LASTING SATISFACTION TO BOTH DONOR AND CONGREGATION, THE ARCHITECT SHOULD BE MADE SOLE ARBITER AS TO THE USE AND INSTALLATION OF SUCH GIFTS BY THE CHURCH.

Too Many Lecterns

In considering the superfluous items that clutter the east end of the church and confuse the architectural statement, one piece of furniture which must receive consideration is the lectern, for the lectern may or may not have a valid place, depending upon its use. There may be situations in which a lectern is essential, or it may be that to have one is to have too many.

The lectern as it is positioned in most of our churches today dates back no further than the Gothic revival of the Cambridge Ecclesiologists. But first, let us consider the uses of a lectern, or reading desk, since the Reformation. At the time of the Reformation there was generally a great shortage of ministers. In Scotland, for example, there had been an inadequate number of priests prior to the Reformation, and many of these were illiterate, uneducated men who even if so inclined were often incapable of preaching from the Scriptures for Reformed worship. Churches could not be left without services, however, and as a temporary expedient

> lay readers were appointed "to read the Commoune Prayeris and the Scriptures" and usually as precentors they led the singing. These offices were normally performed by the parish schoolmaster.[13]

---

[13] Hay, *op. cit.*, p. 184.

Thus the reader's desk, or "lattron" was until about the middle of the nineteenth century an "invariable adjunct to the pulpit."[14] It was a place for a lay reader who, because he was not ordained to the ministry, was not allowed into the pulpit to preach the Word. Much the same situation prevailed in other Reformed countries. In the Netherlands as well, the lectern or reading desk was installed for an unordained reader of the Scriptures. When ordained ministers were unavailable, the people were at least fed by the reading of the Word of God. Evidently, however, the lay reader was not always dropped when ordained ministers did become available, for in the middle of the eighteenth century the reader's service was still extant. Organs were not in general use in Reformed churches at that time, and so while the people were gathering, instead of a musical prelude the lay reader stationed at his reader's desk or lectern provided a verbal prelude.[15] It should be carefully noted that in Reformed worship the reader's desk or lectern is a place where a lay person reads the Scriptures. Since the minister also reads the Scriptures prior to his sermon, it must not be imagined that the Scriptures were read only from the reader's desk.

The Anglican usage of the reader's desk was rather different. The Prayer Book worship of the Church of England in its Morning and Evening Prayer is derived from the monastic "Hours" and is essentially that service set in the vernacular that all may understand and participate in the worship.[16] The various elements of this worship were taken from different positions. The concern of the Reformers was to move the reading of the service out of the chancel and into the nave where the people could hear. Thus in the Elizabethan Settlement the bishops are soon found using their powers to

---

[14] *Ibid.*, p. 184.
[15] Hageman, *Pulpit and Table*, p. 55.
[16] Drummond, *op. cit.*, p. 209.

transfer the minister from the chancel into the nave of the church where the saying of his offices could be heard by the people.[17] In Canon LXXXII of 1604 the reading pew (for the saying of Morning and Evening Prayer) is given synodical authority, and the canon orders " 'that a convenient seat be made for the minister to read service in.' "[18] Addleshaw observes:

> It is commonly supposed that loyalty to the Prayer Book rubrics means that the priest reads the prayers at Matins and Evensong from a stall in the chancel, the lessons in the nave facing the people, the Litany at a special desk in the central alley, and Altar Prayers at the altar. But throughout this period [Elizabethan] it was very rare for the prayers to be said from a seat in the chancel; the minister's usual place, both for the prayers as well as the lessons, was the reading pew in the nave.[19]

Thus, when the Eucharist was not celebrated, the entire service was taken from the reading pew and pulpit. Sometimes the location of this reading pew was opposite the pulpit, either attached to the first pillar west of the table (in an auditory church), or at one side of the chancel arch. More and more frequently, however, it was combined with the pulpit, being on a level just below it. When room was also needed for the clerk (who read the marriage banns, etc.), he was placed at the bottom, the reading desk on the next level, and above that the pulpit, surmounting all. This was popularly known as a "three-decker."[20] But with the rise of the Romantic movement and the Roman inclinations of the Cambridge Ecclesiologists, both reading pew and especially the three-storied pulpit came into disrepute because of

---

[17] Addleshaw & Etchells, *op. cit.*, pp. 30ff., 69.
[18] *Ibid.*, p. 69.
[19] *Ibid.*, pp. 70–71.
[20] A beautiful three-decker can be seen in this country in Trinity Church, Newport, Rhode Island.

the "belief that the chancel was the proper and traditional place for the minister when taking the offices."[21]

> The ecclesiologists therefore suggested that the minister should read the lessons from a lectern in the nave, placed at one side of the chancel arch opposite the pulpit. The lectern they had in mind was the kind which the Middle Ages had used either for the Gospel at Mass, or for the cantors during the singing of the divine office. The eagle variety was recommended as being the most useful as well as the most beautiful.[22]

While the lectern was the place for the lessons, the reading of the litany was to take place at a special litany desk standing at the entrance to the chancel just above or below the chancel steps. Even this brief description of the principles of the Cambridge Ecclesiologists makes it plain, however, that these are not the necessary accounterments for Reformed worship. If the pulpit is deemed unsatisfactory as a place of prayer, then the proper place is, as Calvin indicated, the Lord's table.

For Reformed worship, is there any theological reason why the Word read and the Word proclaimed should be separated? No. Preaching is not to be separated from the Word. Preaching has its validity only as it is informed by the Word. In the liturgies of Zwingli, Bucer and Calvin the sermon always followed immediately upon the reading of the Word. Theologically, there is no cause for separation. As Conrad Massa points out, "There is an unfortunate psychological impact from this physical separation of the written Word of God and its reading, from the place where that Word is to be expounded in its preaching."[23] Visually, it is impossible to have as much

---

[21] Addleshaw & Etchells, *op. cit.*, p. 208.
[22] *Ibid.*
[23] Massa, *op. cit.*, p. 55.

impact if attention has to be divided between a number of items. In this regard Addleshaw and Etchells note that

> the modern practice of a separate lectern, litany desk, and pulpit means that each detracts from the other; the nave has no one object of special significance, only a number of obtrusive and distracting pieces of furniture.[24]

Therefore, Canon Addleshaw wishes to combine the functions of the reading pew with the litany desk and once again join it to the pulpit. Peter Hammond, also an Anglican, feels that "the ideal would seem to be a single ambo or pulpit from which the word of God is proclaimed in the lessons and expounded in the sermon."[25] How incongruous that while there are movements in various camps within the Anglican communion to consolidate the functions of litany desk, lectern, and pulpit, churchmen of Presbyterian/Reformed background should unthinkingly be cluttering their churches with extra pieces of furniture.

This is not to say that the lectern has no place in a house of worship. Nonetheless we must remember that for the Reformed it was limited to the lay reader. If a lay person is to take a part in the service, now as at the time of the Reformation, he should do so at a reader's desk and not in the pulpit. The very fact that it is necessary for ministers to be called of God, extensively educated, ordained, and called by their churches, is ample evidence of the high value affixed to the special office of the ministry of proclamation. Visually, the special office of the minister is set forth in closing the pulpit to all without such calling, training and ordination. If there is a place in the service for the layman, it should be the lectern. When the service is taken by the minister, the lectern again becomes superfluous furniture. If laymen from time to time participate in the services of worship, would not the best

---

[24] *Op. cit.,* p. 81.
[25] *Op. cit.,* p. 40.

solution be to inform the architect of this need so that a portable reader's desk, or lectern, could be built? A suitable place could be reserved for it; it could be of handsome design, suitable to the rest of the church; and it could be removed when not needed. Exactly such a lectern is found in The Ark, Amsterdam-Slotervaart (p. 163).

Let lecterns be used for their proper purposes within the context of Reformed liturgy on those occasions when a non-ordained member of God's people assists in the leading of worship, but when worship is wholly led by those members of God's people who have been called and ordained to that task, then the lectern should not separate Word written from Word proclaimed, nor present two foci when one is more effective. It is God's Word which must sound forth alike in reading and proclamation.

THE LECTERN IS FOR THE USE OF A LAY READER, AND APART FROM A LAY READER HAS NO PLACE WITHIN A SERVICE OF REFORMED WORSHIP (THE MINISTER SHOULD TAKE ALL PARTS OF THE SERVICE EITHER FROM THE PULPIT OR THE LORD'S TABLE). IF A LECTERN IS TO BE USED FOR A LAY READER, IT SHOULD BE OF SUCH DESIGN AS TO BE COMPATIBLE WITH THE ARCHITECTURE OF THE CHURCH, AND SHOULD BE PORTABLE, SO THAT IN THOSE SERVICES WHEN IT IS NOT USED IT WILL NOT DETRACT FROM THE WORD, WRITTEN AND PROCLAIMED, AS SYMBOLIZED IN THE PULPIT.

Too Many Interruptions

The burden of this volume has been that church architecture is primarily a matter of theology, not a matter of style. Because Christ gathers his Church and nourishes it through Word and Sacraments—indeed through them communicates himself to his people—emphasis has constantly been upon the necessity for a strong architectural statement of Word and Sacraments, removing all things superfluous from these means of grace.

It has not been intended in any way to imply that a clear architectural statement can take the place of clear preaching of the gospel. But because of the permanent impact of architecture, its message should be in agreement with the verbal proclamation of the gospel, and at its best it can act as a powerful ally in reinforcing that message, reformed according to the Word of God. Nonetheless, it must also be remembered that without a clear preaching of the Word, architecture can, like even the Sacraments themselves, become but a dumb symbol.

There is yet another important way in which architecture can contribute directly to the preaching of the Word: through the placement of the minister's study! All too often there is already a study in the manse, and the building committee feels it unnecessary to provide another in the church. At other times they may feel that it will be a great convenience for the minister to have his study in his home. One building committee placed the study in the manse next to the kitchen, and then cut a hole in the wall so that the pastor and his wife could communicate freely and share the same telephone! Few members of that congregation have probably ever guessed how much that hole in the wall has cost them in lost ministerial efficiency.

In the days when the manse was a huge, rambling, two- or three-storied structure, it was conceivably possible to isolate a room from the everyday living that goes on in a home. The modern home makes such separation almost impossible. Even those ministers who lock their studies are still not separated from crying babies, children in real or imagined distress, the television set, the delivery man who has to be paid, the automatic washer that doesn't seem to be going just right, and a hundred more completely reasonable demands upon his time that living in a home makes.

Of the talented and able ministers with whom this subject has been discussed, the pattern is much the same: only after moving out of a study in the manse and into one in the church has there been a sense of satisfaction with the amount of work accomplished. These men, all of whom are hard-working, able, and in command of their own homes, nevertheless testify to the disrupting effects of a study in the manse and the great loss in terms of productive work.

No detailed analyses have been made of the actual work loss resulting from such distracting surroundings, but a conservative estimate would be that those men who are especially strong-willed and efficient may suffer only a 10 to 20% loss in efficiency (although their own expressed feelings on the matter would indicate that the loss is much greater), while those who are easily distracted may well suffer a 50% loss. When one figures the total dollar cost of a minister to a congregation for a year, and then computes lost productivity in terms of dollar value, the results are shocking. Strictly from the point of view of economy and protecting the investment every congregation makes in its minister, a study should be provided in the church. And the same desire for economy should also dictate the planning of sufficient office space for the secretarial assistance that is rapidly becoming a necessity in so many churches.

But apart from the monetary considerations, there are other benefits of no small importance which accrue from putting the study in the church. From the perspective of the minister, he and his wife can live a more normal family life, working apart, and experiencing the joys of return. The minister may work hard and efficiently while at the church, but then return home to a bit of rest and relaxation with his family, without the temptation to return to more interrupted and inefficient work. From the viewpoint of the congregation, a major benefit of a study in the church will be that many members will feel at greater liberty to come to the pastor with their personal problems if they do not have to approach him in his home.

In a church reformed according to the Word of God, where place has been made for the elders and deacons, where the baptismal font and the Lord's table stand out forcefully, speaking silently but eloquently week after week of the Christ of the Sacraments, and where the pulpit is given the prominence that God's written and proclaimed Word deserves, the congregation will also want a minister who as he enters his pulpit has been able with the utmost efficiency to pursue his studies, his prayers, and the production of his sermons with which he must feed the flock entrusted to him. Thus equipped, his preaching may be like the architecture of his surroundings, reformed according to the Word of God.

PREPARATION FOR THE LIVELY PREACHING OF THE WORD SHOULD BE DONE UNDER OPTIMUM CONDITIONS, WHICH FIRST OF ALL MUST MEAN TAKING THE MINISTER OUT OF THE STUDY IN THE HOME AND INTO A STUDY IN THE CHURCH, FOR THE LIVELY PREACHING OF THE WORD IS INDISPENSABLE TO THE LIFE OF THE BODY OF CHRIST.

Foreword to Part II

In an attempt to build a bridge between the theology of the Church and the architect who must give expression to this theology, a number of criteria have now been established. It might seem that at this point the task of this book is finished, that the discussion of theology and the architecture of the Church—of Christ and architecture—has come to an end. In a sense it has, but if the volume is to be true to its subtitle, Building Presbyterian/Reformed Churches, then this second part is absolutely essential, for there will be no such architecture unless the architect can play his proper role.

In many churches there is not a single member who has worked with an architect in the role of a client. When this is true, it means that not only for the congregation as a whole, but for every member in the congregation, working with an architect is a completely new experience. This unfamiliarity is all too often the fertile ground of gross misunderstanding which makes a really fruitful relationship with an architect almost impossible, and equally impossible the context in which a valid architecture for Presbyterian/Reformed churches can be created.

Just as a good architect will be intensely interested in the criteria the committee establishes for the building of a church, and just as he will strive to understand what it is they wish to express, in this same manner, if there is to be a really fruitful relationship, it is also well for the building committee to understand the role of the architect and strive to see the situation from his point of view.

Theologians by themselves cannot build churches; they can only help formulate the criteria to tell the architect what the Church is attempting to say in its building. If ever architecture for Presbyterian/Reformed churches is to take form in wood, stone, brick, concrete and glass, then the church through its building committee must be able to establish a meaningful relationship with its architect. Having begun with the theologian and the architectural criteria, it is now time to turn to the architect and consider something of his role and outlook.

What is the role of an architect? Where does it begin, where does it end, how much does it cost? The architect can work most effectively when the ethical standards upon which his profession is based are maintained. To this end it is well for the building committee to be aware of the services rendered by the architect and the remuneration he rightfully requires for those services.

How does an architect look at his work? The good architect is interested in true economy—economy which will give maximum value in relation to expenditure and expected use. The architect's work is to give expression to ideas within both the limitations and possibilities of structure and shape. But the expectations and hopes of the building committee will be most satisfactorily fulfilled if, as a client, it has clarified its ideas by preparing an adequate program.

The work of the architect is the subject matter of the rest of this volume. Having considered the theological criteria of church architecture, it is now time to consider architecture from the point of view of the architect, that the building committee, being familiar with both the science of theology and the art of architecture, may be the successful intermediary in the building of Reformed churches with an architecture worthy of their theology.

8

Teamwork in Church Building

The Building Committee

At the beginning of an architectural project there is often great confusion about the duties of the building committee. It is charged with the responsibility of building the new church but usually with no strict delineation of its duties. Naturally, being made up of conscientious people, the committee assumes all the duties suggested for it and finds itself completely swamped. None of the work can be done properly, and none of the duties are given adequate consideration. The committee needs organization.

The first thing to do is to limit the size of the building committee. Two people who have the confidence of the congregation along with the minister are an adequate committee, provided the congregation is willing to put forth effort in other ways. The congregation should meet in study groups to consider their beliefs and their form of worship, make written statements of their conclusions, and submit them to the building committee. They must state objectives, not solutions. They must understand worship reformed according to the Word and describe their needs. They must state their educational objectives. To do this requires much thought, writing, and organizing. When the objectives are clear they can be presented to the building committee, which can then act as a clearinghouse of ideas and actually formulate the criteria, or program, for the building. The writing of a clear program is the chief task of the building committee, for it is this program which describes the criteria, objectives, and needs of the church in words, which the architect will translate into brick and stone. The building committee is cautioned to work with the ideas presented, as these will create a building reformed according to the Word if the work of the study groups has been done carefully. Too often committee members want to bring in ideas from a former church or the church of their youth, which frequently brings nostalgic memories but never brings good architecture. A combination of such ideas can only result in chaos. Too many of our church buildings look like just such a compromise or combination of ideas.

Having formulated the criteria, the building committee should make sure they are stating objectives and not room sizes, dimensions, and specific locations. Taking their clue from the objectives stated in Chapter 13, they should implement these objectives in the light of their particular program and situation. The committee must assume the responsibility for objectives and directions to the architect since out of these criteria will come a church reformed according to the Word. They must accept and reject ideas as the criteria for the building are determined, making it clear to the congregation that only the best ideas compatible with the program can be used.

It is not the duty of the building committee to do the actual planning of the church. Here they must look to the architect for guidance. Neither is it the duty of the building committee to raise the funds for the building of the church—they must stay within the budget worked out in co-operation with the finance committee. It is the duty of the building committee to determine the criteria for the building and act as liaison between the architect, the other committees, and the congregation. In establishing the criteria for the building, the building committee often forgets to call on the person who can be of greatest help to them—the architect. He has established the criteria for many buildings and welcomes the opportunity of being of assistance at this point. It is the duty of the building committee to select the architect and meet with him as the planning develops.

The Architect

Selection of an architect must be on the basis of his potential service to you. The best architect is often not the best salesman. The best architect prefers creating buildings to creating speeches. The architect best suited to create your church building is no more expensive than the one who creates other types of buildings. Ethical standards have set the architect's fee, therefore the wise building committee selects the architect with care. Often the building committee looks for an architect who has designed many other churches and then examines these churches. If they are outstanding church buildings, he may be well-suited for the job; if they are all mediocre, the committee had better consider another.

Sometimes the building committee creates a competition in which various architectural offices are invited to enter. If the competition is written and conducted by the American Institute of Architects, some of the offices invited may participate. Others may feel the cost of the competition to be too great, or find they have too much work in the office to risk spending time on work that may prove to be nonproductive. A competition is more feasible for a very large church or as a device to acquaint architects better with the planning principles of a church reformed according to the Word.

Occasionally a building committee thinks it can request free sketches from the architects it is interested in and use the sketches as a method of selection. The building committee usually has in mind a sketch of the church building in perspective. If the committee would think about this request they would realize that they are asking the architect to make a site plan and the plans of the building and the elevations in order to make a perspective that has meaning. In essence they are asking him to develop the whole concept of the church and then make a sketch. Needless to say, the architect is unable to achieve this. He can only make an artist's conception that has no meaning but might amaze the building committee by being such a "pretty picture." The expense involved in developing the whole concept of the building in a preliminary way to make a sketch would require weeks of office work by the architect or his most skilled associates. Thus it is readily seen why the architect will not submit free sketches. He will not submit free sketches because he is doing disservice to you, disservice in not carefully planning the building, disservice in submitting a sketch that has very little chance of looking like the finished building, disservice in presenting a false, "pretty picture." To ask for free sketches is the same as asking for free consultation with a doctor or lawyer or free labor from a carpenter or bricklayer. That "a man is worthy of his hire" should be understood by the building committee.

Sometimes the building committee selects a "designer" or other person who is not a registered architect because his fee may be lower, only to find that he gives partial service and is not responsible for his work. Only architects registered by the state are permitted to practice architecture. If you are hiring an architect, check the telephone book to see if he is listed under registered architects or ask to see his state registration. In almost all cases state registration means the architect has completed a course in architecture to receive his Bachelor of Architecture degree. This is a professional degree and requires a full five years of work instead of the normal four years of university work for a Bachelor's degree. In addition, he has also served three years of apprenticeship in a registered architect's office. Only after this point is he eligible to take the state board examinations which consist of planning; engineering in wood, steel, and concrete; construction; mechanical engineering in heating, sanitation, and lighting; architectural history; architectural design; architectural specifications; architectural practice and supervision; and other phases of architectural training. Having passed his state board examinations he is eligible to open his own office. If his first job is in an adjoining state he is required to obtain a reciprocal state registration or to apply for a national registration which enables him to obtain registration in another state with greater ease.

Hire a registered architect; get complete plans and specifications. This cannot be stressed enough. To do otherwise and hope to get something for nothing is just wishful thinking. No one can draw plans and write specifications for nothing. These take time, study, conferences, and revisions. The builder, designer, or prefabricator can offer only partial services. It is impossible to build a church that is reformed according to the Word without receiving full services at the full architectural fee.

Selection of an architect should be on the basis of complete services. Inquiry should be made into the architect's understanding or desire to know the theology of your church. Selection should be made after seeing the best work—not necessarily church work—which he has done and comparing that with the work of other architects. Preference might be given to the conscientious architect who is doing his first church, simply because he must study harder, work harder, and think harder than the architect who has done ten churches. Find out how many churches the architect has in his office at the time. Too many may indicate he cannot do justice to all of them. Choose the architect for his intensity of interest, not for glib talk but for the carefully done brochure, the carefully drawn working drawings, the carefully written specifications and documents—these are the instruments of service from which you build. Consider the architect's ability to do detailed work in programming, planning, detailing and specifying, and his ability to do comprehensive planning (site, stage developments). Select an architect who wants freedom in planning and avoid the architect of adaptation who can give you a Colonial, Gothic, or modern front on your church building—he is simply hanging a style, the rags of another generation, on your building. He is not thinking and thus cannot express the church reformed according to the Word. Fortunately there are few architects of adaptation, but their place has been taken by the builder, designer, and prefabricator who are not paid enough to be creative but see the opportunity of making a quick dollar on the unsuspecting church member.

Surveys

Call in your architect as early as possible, preferably before you buy the church property. If you wish, he can make a survey of desirable sites for you. His services can include land studies, population studies, zoning studies, climate studies, circulation studies, space studies, and site studies, all of which are worked out with a variety of consultants. What do such services cost? Often most of them are performed to a limited extent by the architect under his regular fee, but for the special site or condition, the architect may recommend that additional information be obtained. For the church, this is most often the population study, and the architect puts such a study on an hourly basis with a percentage for profit and overhead. The building committee sometimes sets a limit on the amount to be spent for such a survey.

CHURCH NEIGHBORHOOD SURVEYS

DISTANCE CONSIDERATIONS

locate on a street with public transportation in an unchurched area
keep walking distance within   keep riding distance within

1 mile
20 minutes

10 miles
20 minutes

BOUNDARY CONSIDERATIONS

locate the church building in relation to natural and artificial boundaries
avoid being isolated by   avoid being confined by

rivers, lakes
topography
green belts

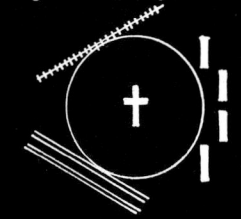

railroads, airports
commerce, industry
turnpikes, thruways

LOCATION CONSIDERATIONS

locate near a public school for children, near a shopping center for parking
advertise your church by   provide easy access with

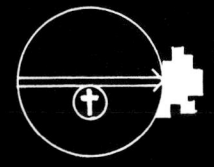

its location on
a main road

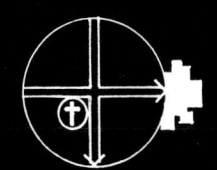

cross roads
right turns

DWELLING CONSIDERATIONS

locate to serve desired dwelling type whether detached or multi-family
apartments may have   lots 80 × 100 feet have

10–15 families
per acre
limited canvassing

5 families
per acre
easily canvassed

COMMUNITY CONSIDERATIONS

locate in a community with the ability or potential to support a church
look for a potential of   look for a grade school of

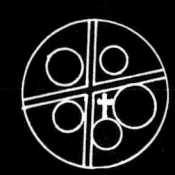

500–700 families
1,800–2,500 persons

6–8 classrooms
180–250 pupils

As co-ordinator of the work, the architect collaborates with city planners, site engineers, the landscape architect, and other specialists that may be needed for the job. He is also interested in the success of your financial campaign and can be valuable in preparing sketches, study models, renderings, and perspectives that can be used in your church brochure and literature to show how the building fund will be spent. If commissioned to do so, he can prepare the brochure—layout, drawings, photos, and type faces. In this field he has a broad range of consultants including architectural photographers, commercial designers, artists, and craftsmen with whom he works daily. He knows what to ask for to achieve a certain end result, and the information he needs from you. The same sort of planning that goes into the organization of a building can be used in the organization of your brochure. Although the organization of a building requires three-dimensional planning, its parts (floors, walls, partitions) require the two-dimensional planning necessary to a brochure.

For surveys the importance of obtaining the right information must be stressed. In many site surveys which churches have prepared, the entire survey must be repeated for the architect. On the accompanying sketch note the various items that a survey may require, and consult the architect about his needs in the survey. The architect may be requested to hire a surveyor and have the land survey completed at the church's expense. Here is a typical place where the architect can be of service. Service is the commodity the architect sells. He does not sell drawings, specifications, documents or models—these are just the results of service. He does not sell "blueprints." You can buy all the blueprints you want at the local blueprinting company. This is just a simple process of reproducing drawings.

SITE SELECTION PRINCIPLES

look for well-drained building site with good soil-bearing capacity, topsoil, easy access

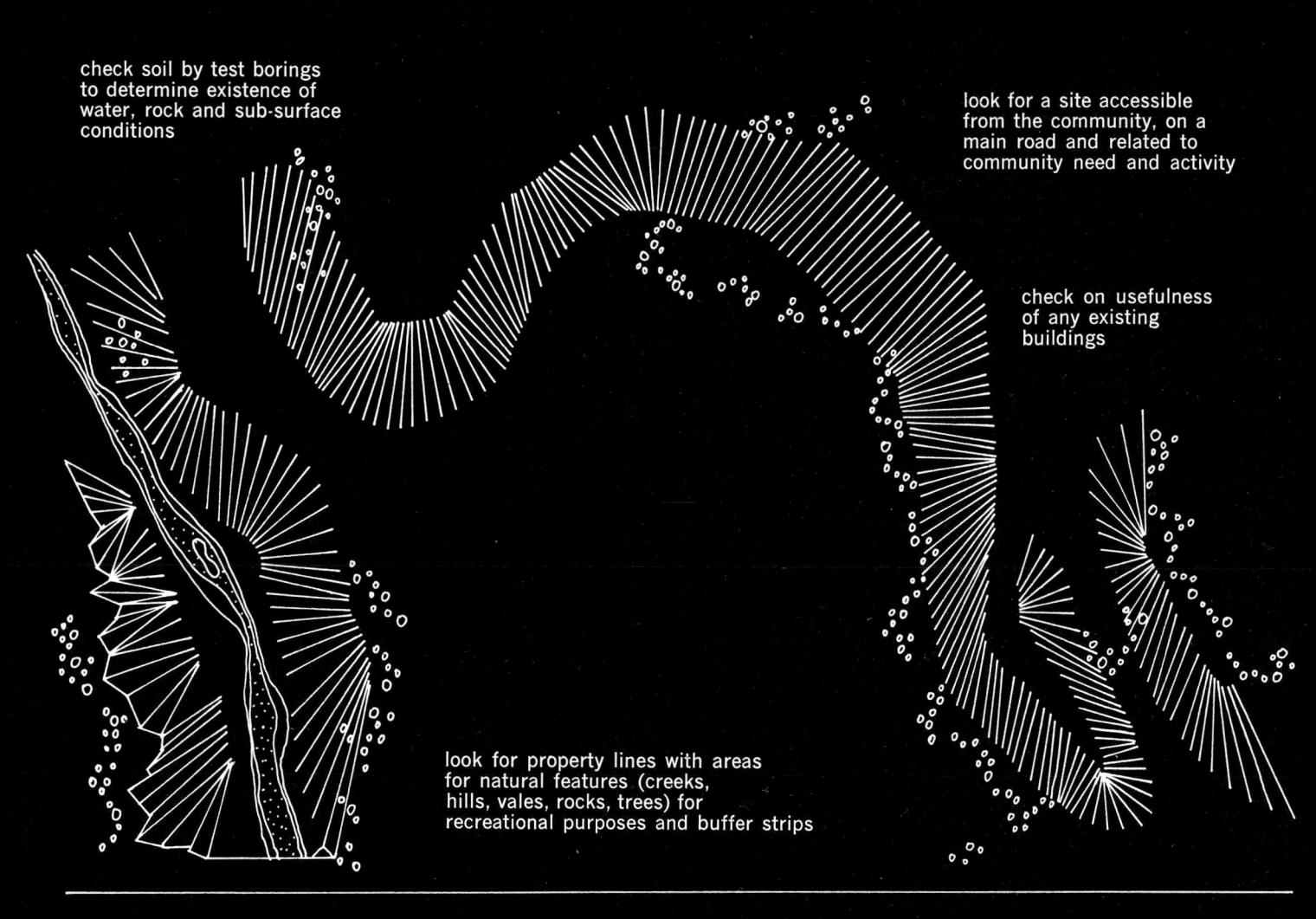

check soil by test borings to determine existence of water, rock and sub-surface conditions

look for a site accessible from the community, on a main road and related to community need and activity

check on usefulness of any existing buildings

look for property lines with areas for natural features (creeks, hills, vales, rocks, trees) for recreational purposes and buffer strips

---

look for utilities: water, sanitary sewer, storm sewer, gas, electricity, phone, roads

check area for hazards: noise, dust, smoke, odor, objectionable business or industry

Services

The more conventional services the architect provides center around drawings, specifications, documents, and supervisory services during construction. The exact nature of his services can best be explained by outlining a typical building procedure. It is assumed that the architect has been selected.

The client and architect have preliminary conferences to reach a verbal understanding of the project. Ethical practices require that the architect does not make a single sketch or drawing until the contract between client and architect has been completed. To determine the fee, the church can request a "Schedule of Minimum Fees for Architectural Work" from their architect. This is often published by the regional society of architects of the state. Typical of these is the "Statement of Architectural Service and Schedule of Proper Minimum Fees by The Architects Society of Ohio of the American Institute of Architects." Under Schedule C, which includes churches, the following building cost and its minimum fee rate have been determined:

Building Cost	Fee Rate
50,000	8.00%
100,000	7.00%
200,000	6.75%
300,000	6.50%
500,000	6.25%
1,000,000	6.00%
2,000,000	6.00%
5,000,000	6.00%

The fee is for normal services which include the preliminaries, working drawings, specifications and services during construction, and the engineering services that are customarily required. The fee for work let under additional separate contracts should be increased by five percent of such contracts. If the construction involves alterations to existing buildings, the fee is increased by fifty per cent; if it involves special services, the fee for these should be agreed upon prior to the performance of the services. It should be noted that the above fees are minimums and higher fees are to be expected where the project is more complex. A fee of 12% is not unusual. Fees are based on a bid or a reasonable estimated cost until the time construction costs are determined. The Standard Form of Agreement Between Owner and Architect on a Basis of a Percentage of Construction Cost of the American Institute of Architects now requires that "a minimum primary payment of 5 per cent of the compensation for basic services, payable upon the execution of the Agreement, is the minimum payment under the Agreement. Subsequent payments shall be made monthly in proportion to services performed to increase the compensation for basic services to the following percentages at the completion of each phase of the work . . .

Schematic Design Phase	15%
Design Development Phase	35%
Construction Documents Phase	75%
Receipt of Bids	80%
Construction Phase	100%"

Continuing with the nature of the architect's services, the client and the architect write a building program and establish due dates for the drawings. The architect analyzes the building program and draws schematic plans on which he seeks the approval of the client. With the completion of the Schematic Design Phase 15% of the fee is due the architect. The architect then makes the preliminary drawings, writes the preliminary specifications, and obtains the preliminary estimate. The client reviews this preliminary work and the architect makes any necessary revisions. After approving the preliminary work, the client authorizes the final work and the retaining of any special consultants. In the case of a church building an acoustical engineer or a theological consultant might be desired.

At this point the Design Development Phase has been completed and the client pays the architect 35% of the fee. The architect finishes the working drawings and specifications and obtains the final estimates. The work to date is reviewed with the client and a construction schedule is determined. Final revisions are made by the architect and reviewed by various authorities. The client approves the final work, pays the architect 75% of the fee, and with the architect makes the selection of contractors for bidding. The architect issues the bidding documents, which are returned to the client at a specified time. Together they approve the contractor. The client makes the contract awards and pays the architect 80% of the fee. The architect guides the contract fulfillment, but it is the client that enforces the fulfillment. The architect approves the bonds and insurance and gives the contractor the order to start building. Together, the client and architect see construction begin. At this time the architect hires a clerk-of-the-works to supervise construction if the client so requests and is willing to pay the extra cost; otherwise the architect makes periodic supervisions and writes these up as inspection reports. In the meantime the architect is approving shop drawings and samples and preparing the monthly certificates while the client is paying the monthly construction costs. Together they review the construction reports and sign the change orders. The client now pays the architect the remaining amount of the fee. The architect receives the guarantees and bonds and makes the final report. The client receives the lien releases, makes last payment for construction, and accepts the finished building.

Supervision

The architect's supervision of a job is seldom understood. Why hire the architect to supervise work he has clearly shown on the drawings and written in the specifications? Why pay a percentage of the fee for supervision? In fact, these very questions are posed to suggest that this is a method of reducing building costs. Some architects even encourage this saving, since this is rather a neat method of avoiding responsibility on the part of the architect. If anything goes wrong during the construction period, and there never has been a building project without problems, the architect can claim improper construction or noncompliance with the drawings and specifications. This leaves the owner in the undesirable position of trying to correct a problem about which he knows very little.

To do a proper job of supervision requires knowledge of construction, codes and standards. Who can supervise construction of a building better than the architect who created it to conform to these restrictions?

To do a proper job of supervision requires anticipation. How is the carpenter going to fit the trim at a corner? He can butt, miter, or form it in a variety of ways, but the architect knows that the over-all appearance requires one of these. What happens when two dissimilar metals are used together? The architect must anticipate the corrosion of one of these and change the metals accordingly.

To do a proper job of supervision requires time. During the supervision period the work of the architect appears to be the easiest part of the job, but ask any architect about the period that takes the most time with the least remuneration and he will say the supervision period.

Why then does the architect insist on doing the supervision? Simply because it is the last opportunity of making the building the finest he can make. First he designed the building and with drawings determined the proper proportions. Next he checked those proportions by designing the building for the second time with a perspective or a model. The last check on the building comes during supervision, when he designs the building in actuality and improves it once more. This is why the architect is so desirous of supervising the building.

Note who the architect sends out to the job to do the supervision. It is not one of his draftsmen but his most capable man and most often the architect himself! Does he consider supervision important? The answer is obvious.

Why not permit the contractor to supervise his own work? Most contractors don't want the responsibility. Good contractors even have architects supervising buildings they do for themselves. A good contractor will tell you that lack of supervision can make him into a thief. His continual problem without supervision is whether to use a better product or make more profit. Supervision by an unbiased party solves these problems on a basis of what is right, not what is more profitable.

Contracts

The problem of making owner-architect or owner-contractor agreements has been greatly simplified by the American Institute of Architects, which has produced standard forms of agreement for use under a variety of conditions. These agreements have withstood the test of time, are revised when improvements can be incorporated, are understood by the building trades, and are fair to all parties. Special circumstances may require additions to such contracts and the advice of an attorney. The owner-architect contract can be arranged on a variety of bases to suit the particular circumstances outlined below:

PERCENTAGE BASIS: The fee is a percentage of the total construction cost of the work, computed on a preliminary bid basis or a cost estimate until the total construction cost is established. This method of payment keeps the fee proportionate to the work done, and the client receives exactly what he pays for. The client may feel that the architect is increasing the construction cost in order to receive a larger fee. While the client does not know the total fee in advance, he does have a good estimate.

COST PLUS A FEE: The fee is the total of the architect's direct expenses plus a proportionate amount of overhead and a percentage of office cost or a fixed fee as agreed upon. This method of payment overcomes the fear that the construction cost is being increased to increase the fee. Usually paid on a monthly basis, it puts the client at the disadvantage of not having a good idea of the total fee in advance.

LUMP-SUM BASIS: The fee is a lump sum not subject to change through variation between the estimated cost and actual cost of construction. Used where the work is clearly established, this method of payment gives the client an exact amount to use in his budget. If the services are less than anticipated, the client suffers; if the services are more than anticipated, the architect suffers.

PER-DIEM BASIS: The architect is reimbursed the cost of travel and other expenses, the rate varying according to the individual. If the client knows exactly what he wants and the architect can translate these ideas into drawings and specifications with very few conferences, this can be a good method of payment. Here again, the client does not know the total cost for budgeting.

If the client trusts his architect, and this is the basis on which mutual agreements should be made, any of the above owner-architect contracts can be used. In the majority of cases the PERCENTAGE BASIS is used and seems to be the most acceptable to the client.

Models

One of the best methods of understanding a building is to have your architect construct a model. This is a method of visualizing that everyone can understand. Often the drawings and specifications are not understood by the congregation, and the members are not willing to show their ignorance by saying they do not understand them. Such situations result in many surprises in the completed building which are totally unnecessary. A study model to understand the general mass of the building in a solid form is the most economical method of producing a model. A finished model is more exacting and produces a model with much more detail. Either method of model-making will pay for itself in clear understanding. Some architects prefer to make a study model rather than the customary perspective drawing of the building. Such models enable the architect to present a series of colored slides of the model that visualize all sides of the building rather than two sides as shown in the perspective drawings.

A model such as this is useful to help the congregation not only to understand the exterior of the church, but also such interior features as a table that extends across the width of the nave. A portable reading desk on the table holds the Bible for the proclamation of the Word. On one end of the table rests a large bowl for baptism, and on the other end the utensils for the Lord's Supper. In this way the fact that both Word and Sacraments have their unity and reality in Christ is forcefully emphasized. For services of Communion the table is cleared except for the accouterments of the Supper. The congregation comes forward to celebrate.

St. Paul's African Methodist Episcopal Church, Cleveland, Ohio
Raymond P. Chaty & Carl H. Droppers, architects; Donald J. Bruggink, theological consultant

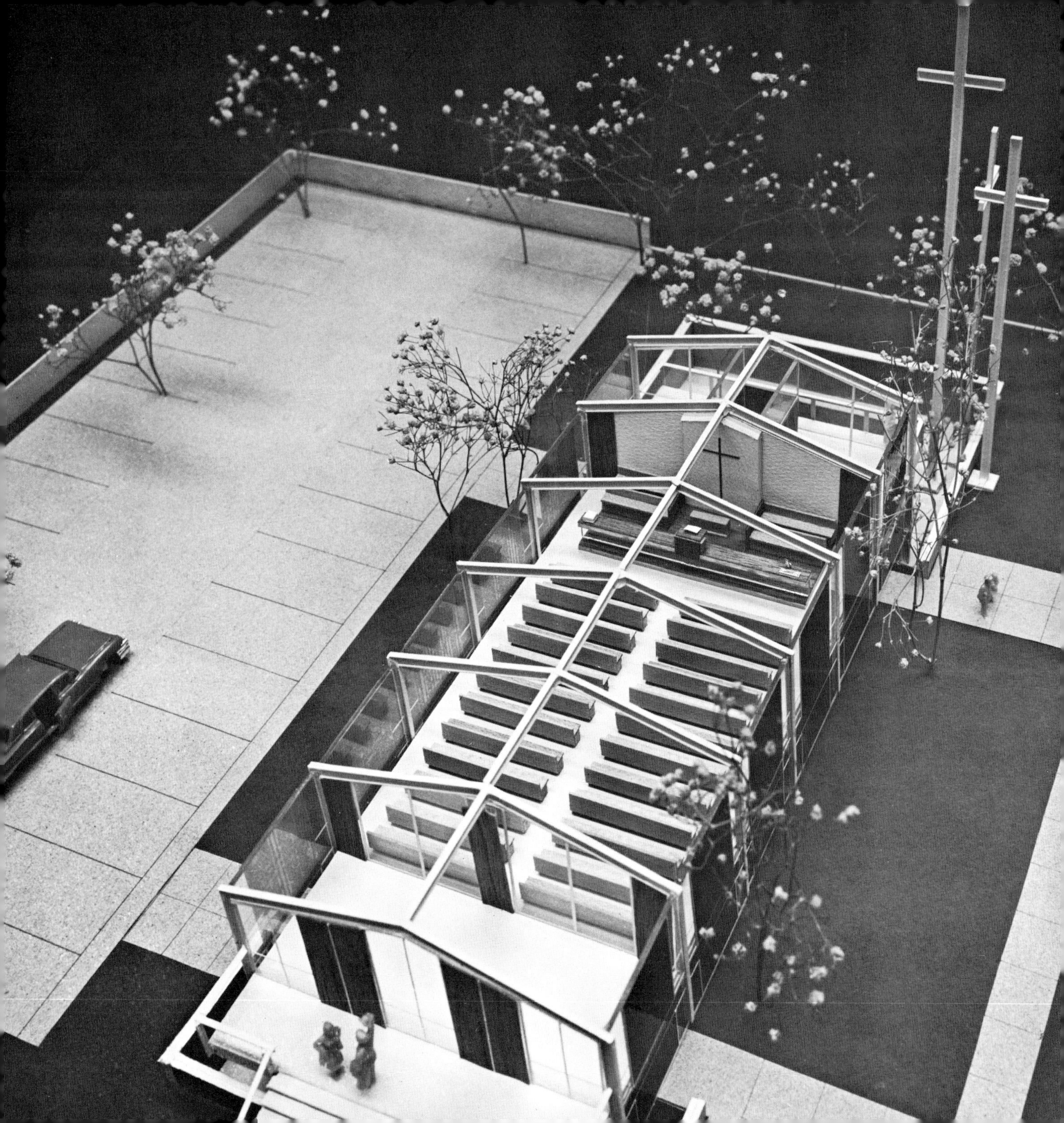

Naturally the architect must be compensated for the extra time involved in constructing a model, as this is not a normal part of his fee. If the client wishes to retain ownership of such models, it should be so stated in the contract for the making of the model. The fee for a finished model is about one-half of one percent based on the estimated cost of the building. Study models done along with the preliminary drawings and sketches help to visualize various ideas and establish the one-eighth inch to the foot preliminary plans and elevations.

Documents

Certain documents constitute the legal means of representing a building and include:

WORKING DRAWINGS are the interpretation of the preliminary plans and elevations in a construction drawing. The working drawings for a small church may consist of twenty sheets of drawings on tracing paper from which the blueprints are made. The working drawings cover plans, elevations, sections, plot plans, and mechanical drawings.

DETAILED DRAWINGS illustrate at large scale how stairs, cabinets, windows and doors go together. They are used to show construction joints, corners, connections, and any typical details that are repeated. Careful detailing creates the finished building.

SPECIFICATIONS are the written description of the manufactured items, materials, methods of construction, jurisdiction and requirements of workmanship. The specifications for a small church building may constitute a book of 50 pages.

CORRESPONDENCE includes the contracts plus addenda, bulletins, change orders, forms, inspection reports, minor changes made by the architect on the job, certificates of payment, letters on fire insurance, bonds, guarantees, samples, and shop drawings.

GENERAL CONDITIONS include many items common to all construction work such as: ownership, samples, materials, royalties, surveys, laws, protection, inspection, supervision, changes, claims, deductions, extensions, corrections, rights, payments, insurance, bonds, assignment, subcontractors, allowances, and arbitration. Other items not common to all construction jobs are added in the Supplementary General Conditions.

Contractor

The teamwork of client and architect establishes the program and drawings that can create a church reformed according to the Word, but it is the contractor that changes these words and drawings into reality. To achieve good teamwork with this man it is to your advantage to have a skilled contractor, one who knows how to organize and expedite and also knows good craftsmanship in the trades. The best method of checking a contractor is to inspect a previous job or jobs which he has done. Ask the owner if the work flowed along smoothly. If there were delays, check to see whether they were the fault of the contractor or whether strikes, bad weather, or "acts of God" created a situation over which he had no control. Check the quality of the work. Is the masonry laid carefully; is the trim carefully fitted; is the quality what you want in your church building?

Having checked your contractors, judge whether the lowest bidder is the best expediter, organizer, and whether his work exhibits the best craftsmanship. If so, select him as the contractor. If not, then seriously consider whether several thousand dollars more for the better contractor might not be advantageous. One church chose the second lowest bidder after careful investigation because he was a much more qualified contractor. Finer workmanship will more than compensate for the higher contract award. The architect will gladly outline the qualifications of the contractors he knows in order to assist in a wise selection.

Expect to pay the contractor a profit. One of the most important reasons for going into business is the profit motive, and without this incentive very few would dare to risk a hundred thousand dollars or more. Expect the profit to be ten percent. Does this sound high? Consider that this same contractor can place his money in a bank and receive five percent without doing a single thing. Do you expect him to have thirty or forty thousand dollars outstanding and not receive more than five percent? There is a lot of risk involved in building, and this is where the ability to do the job rapidly and efficiently serves the contractor best. Outside of wanting to keep his crew together in slack periods or having too many jobs, there is very little reason for his not wanting to finish a job as rapidly as possible. It is his ability to do this that enables him to stay in business. In spite of their abilities, the number of contractors who go bankrupt each year is high.

In addition to profit, the contractor charges overhead. This varies a great deal among contractors, and you may find that the small contractor operating out of his own building and using his family in many capacities can keep overhead to a minimum. This is fine if he remains efficient and has a core of subcontractors he can call on that regularly work with him. The larger contractor tries to handle more of the work with his own people and therefore he has an advantage in not having to use as many subcontractors and reduces his overhead in this manner.

Along with profit and overhead, the contractor sometimes thinks he is entitled to ten percent on each of his subcontractors' bids. It is at this point that confusion exists. The client can readily understand a basic ten percent profit, but taking an additional ten percent profit on the subcontractors' bid he regards as unfair. Fortunately our competitive bidding system keeps such profits to a minimum. In the same category is the subcontractor who charges ten percent profit but also buys his products at a reduced percentage. In this case as well, competitive bidding keeps such profits to a minimum.

Because the risk in contracting is very great, many safeguards have been set up by the architect to protect the client. Starting with the bid, the architect spells out the rules in the Invitation to Bid and the Instructions to Bidders. He follows this with the Form of Proposal and a Request for the Names of Principal Subcontractors, as well as a List of Substitutions that the contractor might propose with the amount each item adds to or deducts from the cost. A Bid Bond may be required to assure the client that the contractor will sign the contract and furnish a Performance and Payment Bond after he has been awarded the contract. All too often the contractor discovers an error in his bid and realizes he would be unable to perform the contract under its conditions. Rather than take such a risk he forfeits the Bid Bond (a percentage of the amount of the bid, or the difference between his bid and that of the higher bidder with whom the client can make a contract).

The next safeguards are The Contract between Contractor and Owner, the carefully written specifications, the contract documents, and the exact drawings. All of these are carefully done, but the client should not be so naïve as to think that hundreds of decisions made by the architect in the plans and specifications can be made without some necessary changes. This is humanly impossible. The effort of the architect is to keep such changes to a minimum. When necessary, he therefore issues Change Orders, written descriptions of changes in the work involving additions or reductions in cost.

The Application for Payment and the Certificate of Payment are additional safeguards. The Application for Payment endeavors to keep a running account of the job, advising the client of the contract amount for each subcontractor, the amount requested monthly, the work completed, and the balance needed to finish the job. The Certificate of Payment is issued by the architect and accounts for the amount due the contractor each month less the customary ten percent that is retained and paid one month after substantial completion of the work.

Other safeguards may be required. A Joint Check Request may be used as a method of assuring the client that the contractor is paying his subcontractors and suppliers. With this method the contractor submits a monthly list of subcontractors and suppliers and the amount due each. The client in turn issues a check made out to the contractor and the subcontractor or supplier. After being endorsed by the contractor, these are sent to the subcontractors or suppliers as their payment. This method helps to eliminate liens against the building during the building operation, but it requires at the completion of the job the safeguard of a Release of Lien from the subcontractors and suppliers and an Affidavit of Contractor stating that all bills are paid in full.

The architect also uses additional safeguards in his own office during the building operation. Letters of Transmittal, Notification of Contract Awards, Reminders to the Owner, Schedules of the Work, Reminders and Submissions Due from the Contractor, and Inspection Reports are being issued in a steady stream. But in spite of these safeguards, the ways in which contractors can go bankrupt are legion. If the contractor bids too low, if his accounting system is incorrect, if he lacks capital, if he loses his bank credit, if he is disabled, if he overextends himself financially, if he loses his key men, if he pyramids his losses by taking another job to pay for the last, if he lacks adequate insurance protection, if he has labor troubles, if he has strikes, or if he has unexpected price raises—he may still default on the contract. Under any of these conditions, the safeguards are the Performance Bond which guarantees that the contractor will fulfill the Contract and the Payment Bond which guarantees that the contractor will pay the subcontractors and suppliers. The Performance Bond and the Payment Bond can be thought of as the client's insurance against default by the contractor. The insurance is for one hundred per cent of the contract price and usually costs one per cent of the contract amount for the first hundred thousand dollars.

Along with the above safeguards, the community requires the building inspector, the plumbing inspector, the heating inspector, the electrical inspector, and a host of other inspectors to check on the building. Sometimes it seems a wonder that with all of these restrictions buildings get built at all. In comparison, the restrictions on the building of an automobile or a house trailer are almost nonexistent.

Consultants

There are a number of team members the client never sees, yet who are so closely associated with the work, and play such an important role in the building of the church, that they are included on the sign at the construction site. These consultants are sometimes hired directly by the church, but more often the architect pays for their services out of his fee. The church member is informed that the architect for their one-hundred-thousand-dollar church building has been hired for a fee of seven percent. He quickly figures the fee to be seven thousand dollars and imagines what the church could buy for this amount of money if the services of the architect were eliminated. As he is investigating this idea he finds that even without the architect there is a need for a structural engineer to satisfy the community of the structural soundness of his church building. This engineering service the architect provides out of his fee. Further investigation reveals the need of a mechanical engineer to determine the heating and plumbing requirements for serviceability, economy, and code compliance. This service is also paid out of the architect's fee. The church member also wants the electrical system to comply with the local code and to be engineered by a competent electrical engineer for electrical loads of motors, fans, heating equipment, lighting, and future air conditioning. Here is another service that comes from the architect's fee. Why is this the preferred method? It simply enables the architect to co-ordinate the work of the engineers with the construction of the building and provide the client with an organized building.

By this time the fee of the architect has diminished to five thousand dollars without a single expenditure towards the architect's own work. In spite of this, the architect believes in the services provided by these engineers to the point where he would not think of doing without them. He considers it a necessity to have these people checking and co-ordinating the work in order to give the client the finest building he can possibly create.

In a similar manner the church has a responsibility to build the finest church possible, reformed according to the Word. The committee should hire a consultant in this field to guide them. The responsibility of the church for competent advice on theological matters pertaining to church building is no different from the responsibility of the architect to secure competent advice on engineering matters. The real difficulty comes from the parishioner who says, "The church never needed a theological consultant in the past, why do we need one now?" The same thing could have been said a century ago of many doctors, specialists, and consultants whom we now feel are necessities and imperative to retain.

What can such a theological specialist do? Using the phrase which is the foundation of this book, he can direct the committee toward creating a church reformed according to the Word. He can bring the latest thinking in theology concerning church building, compile a list of definitive writings on the subject, and illustrate with visual aids the best church buildings being built from a theological point of view. Enumerating the pitfalls to be avoided, he can bring to the committee the experiences of other churches. He is able to review the particular situation and guide the client toward a church building that truly expresses the theology of the Reformation Church. Speaking freely and to the point on theology and church building matters where your minister cannot, often he can unify the thinking of the church people. After all, when the consultant leaves he can be the person blamed for everything, giving the members of the congregation the opportunity to "save face." The consultant comes in as an authority who can solve differences of opinion with factual information before they arise. By the single expedient of channeling the efforts of the congregation in one direction he can more than pay for his fee in time and effort otherwise wasted by the congregation.

What are the charges for such consultation? Travel expenses, room and board and a fee per diem are standard. With such an arrangement the congregation can afford to have a consultant in for a series of meetings or just one meeting. They can tailor their consultation to what they can afford. The congregation that employs a consultant in theological matters will gain information, unity, and direction of purpose that will far outweigh the small amount spent on consultation. To enable a congregation to grow rapidly in building a church reformed according to the Word, the building program should start with the theological consultant. He should set the tenor of the thinking, the direction, and the teamwork of the approach to church building. The scope of the church building operation requires participation on the part of the people and an intensity of interest that is only apparent when they are a vital part of the church building program.

9

Economy in Church Building

One must not confuse economy, frugality in expenditure, with cheapness, with things of little value. There is an old adage that says "you get what you pay for." This would make the most expensive item the one to purchase. The choice of materials would then be very simple. Such is not the case, however. There are a host of agencies that cater to the consumer in the choice of materials and equipment. Witness the various reports, tests, seals, guarantees and listings of equipment in almost any magazine. For any given set of conditions one piece of equipment fits the conditions just a little better than the others. A certain camera, vacuum cleaner, washer, or automobile is chosen because it fits a particular set of conditions a little better than all the rest. The same thing is true of building materials. There are a host of agencies that cater to the architect, engineer, and contractor. Almost every material is represented by an institute, whether this be brick, cork, gypsum, lead, metal lath, steel joists, or asphalt shingles. Almost every component or assembly of materials is represented by an association: witness the wood window, steel window, metal door, sliding door, or curtain-wall associations. In addition there are independent agencies that test materials and combinations of materials such as the American Society of Testing Materials, Underwriters Laboratories, and various universities. A certain material is picked because it fits your set of conditions a little better than all the rest and not because it costs more or even less than another material. Church economy starts with selecting materials for your set of conditions, your site, your finances, your needs and your aspirations. A careful check of the following items can enable you to get "more than what you pay for."

Property

If at all possible, purchase property well in advance of building and get "more than what you pay for." Land always has value and generally increases in value. Therefore, it is a wise investment for any church. Be generous in your acquisition of land: 5 acres for the church with 300 communicants, 10 acres for the church with 600 communicants. Five to ten years from now it will be discovered that the church has made the greatest saving it could make by using foresight in land purchase. During those five to ten years a business recession may present a desire for money, but the wise congregation has faith and confidence in the future and retains the land. To determine the minimum amount of land that should be purchased follow the diagram on Church Property Planning.

CHURCH PROPERTY PLANNING

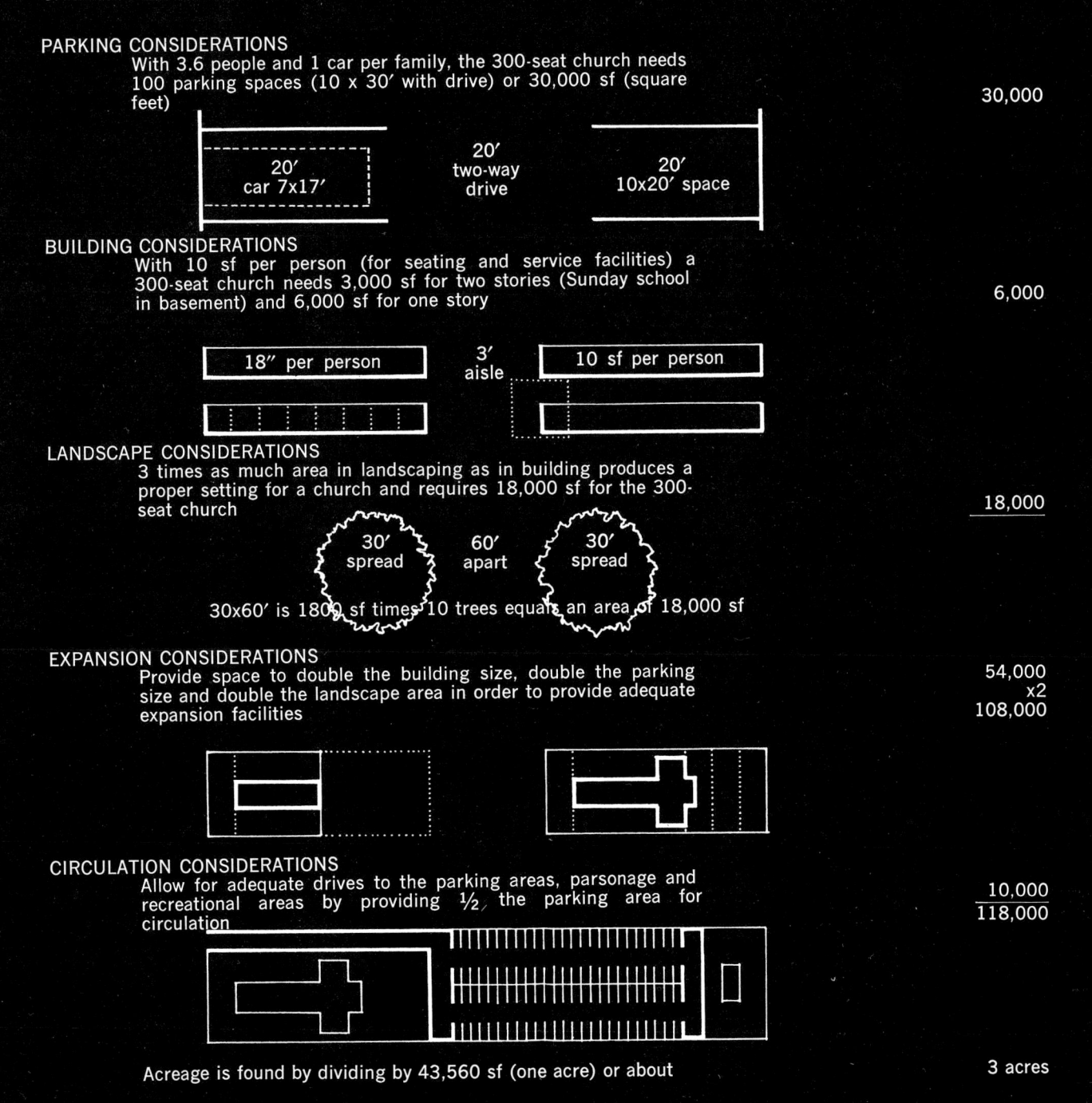

PARKING CONSIDERATIONS
With 3.6 people and 1 car per family, the 300-seat church needs 100 parking spaces (10 x 30' with drive) or 30,000 sf (square feet)   30,000

- 20' car 7x17'
- 20' two-way drive
- 20' 10x20' space

BUILDING CONSIDERATIONS
With 10 sf per person (for seating and service facilities) a 300-seat church needs 3,000 sf for two stories (Sunday school in basement) and 6,000 sf for one story   6,000

- 18" per person
- 3' aisle
- 10 sf per person

LANDSCAPE CONSIDERATIONS
3 times as much area in landscaping as in building produces a proper setting for a church and requires 18,000 sf for the 300-seat church   18,000

30' spread   60' apart   30' spread

30x60' is 1800 sf times 10 trees equals an area of 18,000 sf

EXPANSION CONSIDERATIONS
Provide space to double the building size, double the parking size and double the landscape area in order to provide adequate expansion facilities

54,000
x2
108,000

CIRCULATION CONSIDERATIONS
Allow for adequate drives to the parking areas, parsonage and recreational areas by providing ½ the parking area for circulation

10,000
118,000

Acreage is found by dividing by 43,560 sf (one acre) or about   3 acres

When purchasing the land, have it surveyed in the usual manner with metal pins set at the corners. But at the same time have a surveyor make a topographical survey to determine the hills and vales, and have trees over six inches in diameter and existing utility lines marked. Such surveys enable the church to begin planning at any time, for it provides the information the architect needs to begin his work.

Have engineer draw survey to an architectural scale 1/16" = 1'–0" or 1/32" = 1'–0"

Check subsoil by two or more test borings to depth below footings, located thus ⊕

Establish topography on one foot intervals for the building site, two foot intervals for property

294
292
290
288

wooded

N

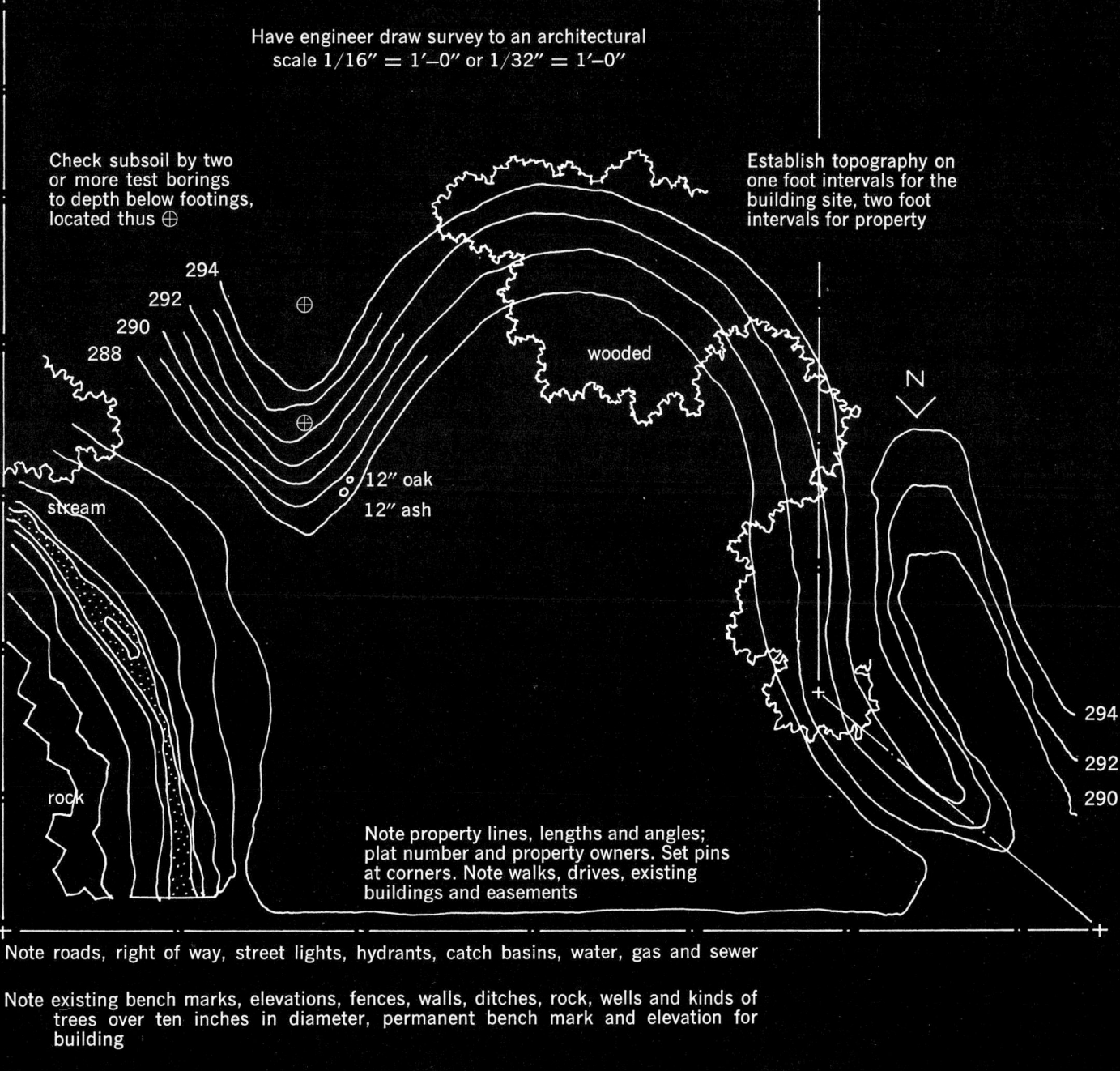

stream

12" oak
12" ash

rock

294
292
290

Note property lines, lengths and angles; plat number and property owners. Set pins at corners. Note walks, drives, existing buildings and easements

Note roads, right of way, street lights, hydrants, catch basins, water, gas and sewer

Note existing bench marks, elevations, fences, walls, ditches, rock, wells and kinds of trees over ten inches in diameter, permanent bench mark and elevation for building

Note street name, community and location; property owners names on survey

Subsurface

Watch subsurface expenditures. Compare the true purchase price of developed and undeveloped land, then determine which property is actually the least expensive.

An accurate survey will determine the water supply to be expected from a well or other source, the depth of the well, drilling, casing, pump, and storage tank. In the same manner a public water supply should be checked for adequate pressure, metering, piping required, trenching needed, service charges, and rates. The accompanying sketch illustrates the basic concerns in the selection of a water supply system.

WATER SUPPLY PRINCIPLES

GUSTATORY CONSIDERATIONS
pure water supply is essential from lakes, wells, springs, cisterns or streams
check for taste of iron, sulphur or silt   check location for bacteria, sewerage

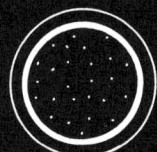

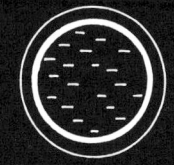

GEOLOGICAL CONSIDERATIONS
lime makes water hard and clogs pipes; water with acid causes corrosion of pipes
sodium compound is water softener   neutralize acid with alkali

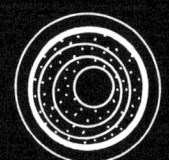

BIOLOGICAL CONSIDERATIONS
impure water carries the germs of many diseases, and poisons from manufacturing
check for purity, provide chlorination   stop pollution, filter and aerate

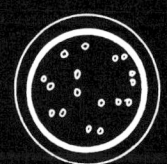

PHYSICAL CONSIDERATIONS
warm metals create heat loss, cold cause condensate; water under pressure surges
insulate pipe, place below frost   use air chambers, pressure-relief valve

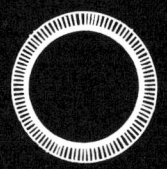

CHEMICAL CONSIDERATIONS
metals are subject to corrosion by other metals, fatigue by expansion and contraction

electrolytic scale — relate metals
greater corrosion occurs to metals numbered
lower on scale by higher number

aluminum	– 1	nickel	– 5
zinc	– 2	tin	– 6
steel	– 3	lead	– 7
iron	– 4	copper	– 8

provide expansion sleeves and loops:
expansion of pipe in inches per 100
feet with change of 100° F.

cast iron .787 or 13/16″ –
steel pipe .898 or 14/16″ –
w.i. pipe .939 or 15/16″ –
Copper   1.338 or 1 5/16″ –

Public sewerage systems require piping, clean-outs, connections, service charges, and carry a charge for service over the life of the building. Private sewerage disposal systems require checking for soil absorption and porosity, and the cost of septic tank, filter bed, or other method of disposal.

In addition, it is important to weigh the cost of gas from a public utility against the cost of oil, LP gas, or electricity.

Subsurface exploration will give valuable knowledge of conditions of rock, water, and soils below the surface. Borings by a testing laboratory to determine subsoil conditions would be one way of obtaining this information. Another method that may be used for preliminary investigation is to drill three or four holes with a post hole digger to the depth of the footings, at least six feet, and check the subsoil in this manner prior to purchasing.

Supply and demand tends to keep the true cost of developed and undeveloped land about equal. Differing subsurface conditions, however, often make them very unequal. The opportunity for reducing subsurface expenditures is available to any church willing to do a little preliminary investigation.

Climate

Look at the land. Look at the sun. Look at nature. In a cold climate sunlight for seeing and heating is gained by inviting the sun into the building during the winter. In a warm climate glare is reduced and heat eliminated by excluding the sun. One can often select better climate on the same piece of property. The southern slope of a hill in a cold climate will create a climate comparable to a warm climate hundreds of miles to the south, and the same thing is true of a northern exposure in a warm climate. An area sheltered from the wind can raise the temperature in a cold climate. Inviting a breeze can make an uncomfortably warm space comfortable. Take advantage of the climate by observing the suggestions on the accompanying sketch on Climate Principles. Real savings can be made by using the climate and making it serve your purposes.

CLIMATE PRINCIPLES

for comfort range of 70° to 80° F.

SITE: FOR WINTER HEAT AND LIGHT GAIN
choose a warm southern slope
second choice — east slope

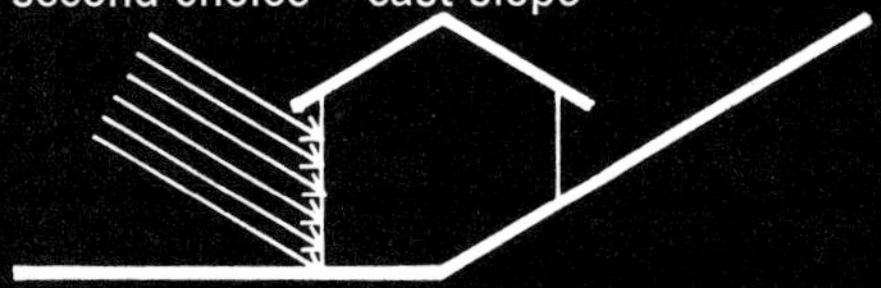

avoid a cold northern slope

HEAT: IN WINTER, DOUBLE GLASS FOR DAY, DRAPES AT NIGHT
invite low, warm winter sun and light

stop hot summer sun and glare

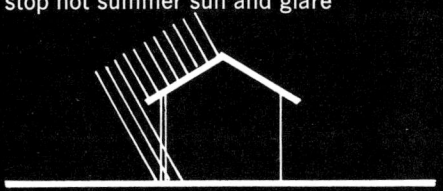

COOL: IN SUMMER, SHADE GLASS DURING DAY
stop sun before it reaches building
consider cool rooms below grade

at night invite cool ground air

WIND: CONTROL WITH WIND BREAKS (TREES, FENCES, WALLS)
invite southwest winds for cooling

stop cold northwest winds for warmth

RAIN: NORTHERN PROBLEM (FREEZE AND THAW)
dark surfaces absorb heat and melt snow
avoid slush by paving and draining

SOUTHERN PROBLEM (MILDEW AND RAIN)
light surfaces reflect heat, are cooler
avoid mud by paving and draining

Resources

To build economically the church must use the finances of today. The church may have limited resources but these could be almost unlimited. Let us take a close look at how funds are raised. Much of the world is on a "pay as you go" basis. This comes as a surprise to many with outstanding debts, but look at a typical pay check: it has social security, federal income tax, hospitalization, and annuity or pension payments already removed. At the same time the employer is providing a share of insurance, hospitalization, retirement insurance, life insurance, sickness and accident insurance, surgical-medical insurance and other fringe benefits for you, all on a "pay as you go" basis. In addition charge-account payments (department stores, gas, restaurants, travel), house payments, car payments, utility payments and appliance payments are paid monthly. Tithing, which is the original "pay as you go" method for supporting the work of the church, has all too often been superseded by other more demanding payments. The company takes over the responsibility of making payments to the government, hospital, and insurance company in order to make sure it is done. It is about time that the church provided a checkbook to each member in which the first check of each month or week enabled him to lay aside 10% or more as God has prospered him. The church does not have limited resources, it has limited payments!

Interest

Collect as much of the money for your church building as possible before you build and save the interest rates. Some churches have purchased two buildings by the time they have paid the interest on their mortgage. Many churches pay more interest than is necessary because they are not good stewards of their money. A church which builds a $200,000 building at 5% interest on a 20-year loan pays an average of 5% on $100,000, or $5,000 for 20 years, making the interest payment equal to $100,000. Therefore the building actually costs $300,000. If the church can pay back the loan in 10 years it will save $50,000 in interest. If the church can negotiate a loan for 4% (1% less) it will save an extra $20,000 in interest on a 20-year loan or an extra $10,000 in interest on a 10-year loan. If the churches of a denomination pool their resources—whether savings, endowments, or investments—and invest in themselves through a revolving loan fund they can do a great deal more with their money while showing real concern for others.

Revenue

All materials have taxes on them, whether federal, state, or local. If the church is required to pay these, then by all means do so. Some taxes, however, the church is not required to pay, and here savings can be made. Some states exclude houses of worship from sales taxes on materials that are incorporated into the church building. Check this with your local tax authority.

Progress

By far the greatest savings can be made by being progressive in your thinking. Congregations must recognize that they are building for today and not for the Colonial or Gothic periods. Many new framing systems have come into being in the last fifty years that can be used to frame churches. These systems have been too frequently ignored or carefully hidden under more "acceptable" materials like wood and stone. The steel frame is loaded with the stone it must carry to be "acceptable," and this sort of acceptance is expensive. New steel framing systems cannot be used because they do not look Gothic. New wood framing systems cannot be used because they do not look Colonial. Then there is the compromise that tries to make the steel or wood look like Gothic or Colonial and fails because Gothic and Colonial were the outgrowth of a time and age that is no more. Their validity is gone forever.

The only thing the Gothic or Colonial styles can add to our buildings is expense—expense out of all proportion to the so-called "acceptance" people think it engenders. The necessity of "acceptance" comes from being conservative in thought and narrow in outlook, playing it safe by following the crowd. People admire Chartres Cathedral but ignore its greatest contribution—one of its towers is Romanesque and the other tower is Gothic. Built 400 years apart, they were each built for their own time and age.

The church can build contemporary framing systems more economically than those which are outmoded. To saddle the architect with a Gothic or Colonial style and then expect to get anything more than a fake and dishonest building is plain wishful thinking. In most cases the congregation is the loser.

Simplification

Review your requirements. Can service space be made smaller? Can several functions be housed in the same room at different times? Can corridors be incorporated into classrooms? Can furniture, dividers, lockers, or storage cabinets be used as partitions? What happens in that Sunday school space? Do separate classrooms really make sense or are they the result of Sunday school classes that are too large to begin with? Should a teacher and a class of five students need any more than an area in a large room? The most difficult thing to do in planning is to simplify, yet it looks so effortless when the job is done. Here is where your architect can be of immeasurable help—he knows how to make an open plan or a shut plan, how to combine elements and how to simplify, but he must have a sympathetic client—one who wants to simplify, one who is willing to change, one who wants to economize. Review the diagram on Plan Simplification Principles for methods of simplifying a plan.

SINGLE-CORE CONSIDERATIONS

note how service areas (lavatories, furnace room, storage, kitchen, etc.) can act like buffer strips to divide space and create rooms with the use of a minimum amount of construction

open plan

DOUBLE-CORE CONSIDERATIONS

note how combining rooms increases their flexibility so they can be used in a variety of ways (large or small rooms, rooms lighted and heated from one or two sides) with minimum construction

shut plan

OFFSET-CORE CONSIDERATIONS

note how a variety of room sizes can be achieved through the astute placement of a core element (stairs, lavatories, corridor) in a non-symmetrical planning arrangement

open plan

UPWARD-CORE CONSIDERATIONS

note how the moving of a vertical element (chimney, stairs, tower, mechanical core) to the outside of the building simplifies the planning within the building and between the various levels

shut plan

HOLLOW-CORE CONSIDERATIONS

note how an interior court opens all rooms to daylight with the use of a minimum amount of construction and at the same time creates a private outdoor area

shut plan

Combination

Consider combinations of rooms and flexibility of use as a method of economizing. Avoid giving one specific name to a room and establishing ownership, as the occupants will refuse to move even though the room is much too big for the activity. Here are some suggested combinations:

1. Pastor's study and office with possible classroom use.
2. Parlor, guild, consistory and classroom.
3. Young people's and beginners room.
4. Sanctuary and classrooms.
5. Choir room and classrooms.
6. Sunday school space, recreational space, and banquet space.
7. Kitchen and nursery.
8. Entry and classroom.
9. Entry and coatroom or Sunday school office.
10. Entry and lounge.

Investigation by the architect will reveal other combinations that are not listed here. This is a method of making considerable savings on church building costs.

Postponement

Temporary savings can be made by postponement. Acoustical tile in classrooms can be applied later, walls and ceilings painted later, resilient tile laid later. Part of the plumbing might be "roughed in." Part of the electrical system may be installed with only the conduit in. Part of the landscaping can be postponed. Cabinet work and ceramic tile can be omitted. Electrical floodlights, spots, panel boards, and special lighting are not immediately necessary. Furniture, folding doors, incinerator, and kitchen equipment can be omitted. Window drapes, shades, and blinds are easily reduced in number. Paved areas can be reduced. The number of toilet stalls can be reduced. Gutters can be left off generous overhangs. Parts of the building can even be omitted. Using alternatives for the surety bond also cuts down expenses.

In addition to these items there are many others that might be temporarily postponed. If postponement means that you are able to proceed with an essential building at once, then by all means temporarily postpone these items. But if you can afford these items you will save by including them in the original contract for the church building.

Insurance

The first conclusion arrived at from a review of the diagram on Building Insurance Rate Basis is to insist on fireproof construction and thereby reduce the insurance rate. This generality does not recognize the many variations that can occur in the insurance ratings of buildings. For example, if a frame church were equipped with a sprinkler system it might be thought of as more in the category of Fire Resistive Construction. Likewise a light frame metal building would be placed in the category of Frame Construction. In addition the details of construction have to be recognized. Fire doors, openings, heating, lighting, occupancy, fire alarm and sprinkler systems, all have an influence on the building insurance rate. The diagram only gives a general idea of the possible types of construction, and your church building will need detailed analysis along these lines by a competent insurance agent.

In practice, costs of construction and the need for a definite amount of space often dictate the choice of construction for the church building. Often rooms or additional spaces are more important than a lower fire rating. How are such problems solved? The answer is found in trying to obtain the best fire rating under a given set of conditions and a careful check on construction details to keep the building in the preferred construction class for its type.

Sometimes fire safety is confused with fire rating. Fire safety is related to the protection of the occupants of the building and providing them with sufficient and direct exits plus protection from suffocation, whereas fire rating is concerned with the protection of the building.

Savings in insurance rates can be made by obtaining the best fire rating for the building. Since such savings are for the life of the building, a true picture of the most economical building, insurance wise, must be balanced against lower initial construction costs.

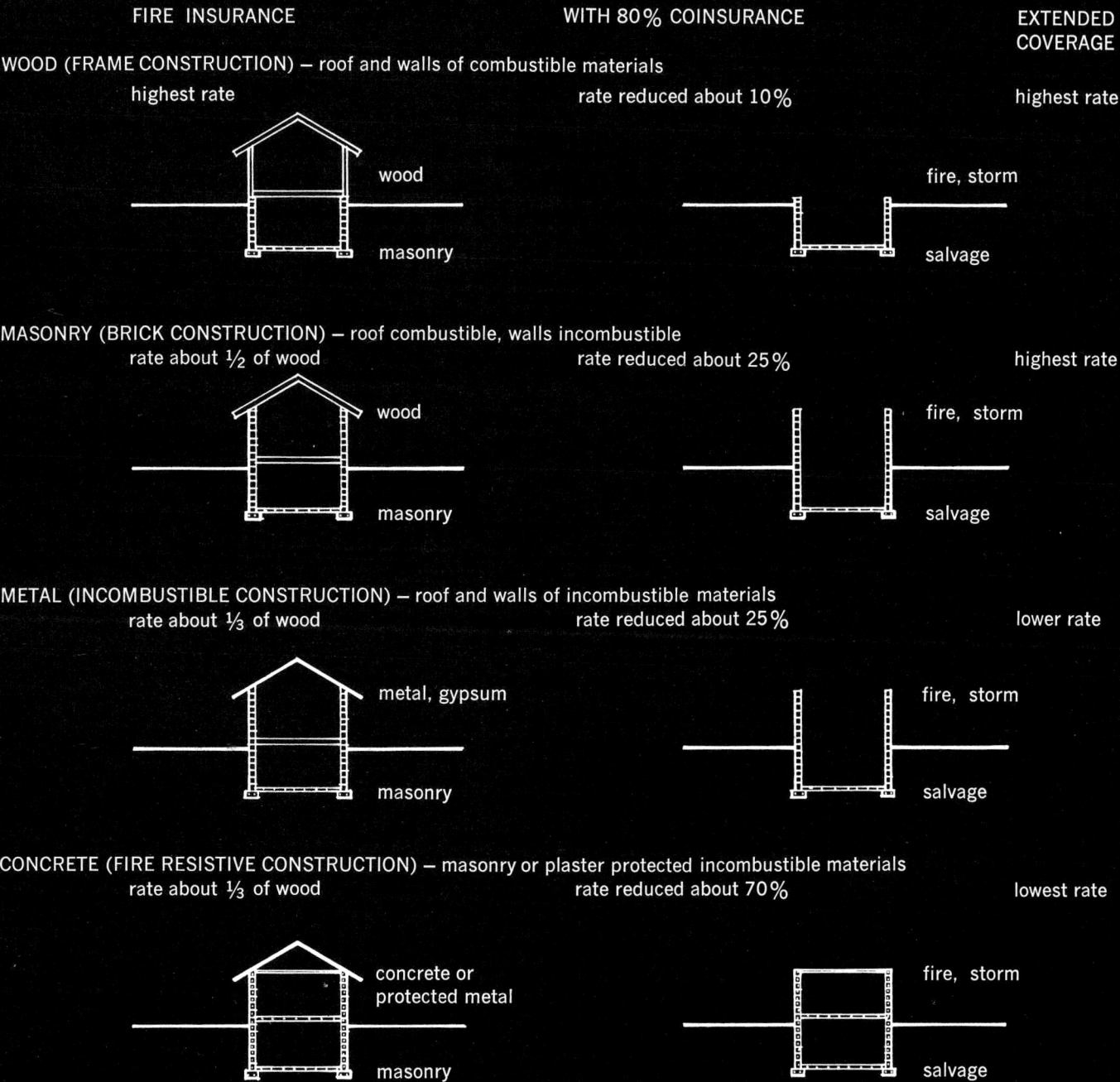

FIRE INSURANCE	WITH 80% COINSURANCE	EXTENDED COVERAGE

WOOD (FRAME CONSTRUCTION) – roof and walls of combustible materials

highest rate	rate reduced about 10%	highest rate

wood
masonry
fire, storm
salvage

MASONRY (BRICK CONSTRUCTION) – roof combustible, walls incombustible

rate about ½ of wood	rate reduced about 25%	highest rate

wood
masonry
fire, storm
salvage

METAL (INCOMBUSTIBLE CONSTRUCTION) – roof and walls of incombustible materials

rate about ⅓ of wood	rate reduced about 25%	lower rate

metal, gypsum
masonry
fire, storm
salvage

CONCRETE (FIRE RESISTIVE CONSTRUCTION) – masonry or plaster protected incombustible materials

rate about ⅓ of wood	rate reduced about 70%	lowest rate

concrete or protected metal
masonry
fire, storm
salvage

Stock Plans

Why not buy stock plans or a prefabricated church building and make a saving by eliminating the architect, the general contractor, and many of the subcontractors and suppliers? Here are the items that should be considered.

Is the site a flat piece of ground that will accomodate such a building? Does the local building code permit this type of building without alterations? Don't be careless on this point. The code may require double flooring, for example. Sounds simple, does it not? This "simple" requirement cost one church over two thousand dollars. First the flooring had to be purchased and installed. Second, ten doors had to be cut one inch shorter and two fire doors had to be replaced. Third, all radiators had to be raised one inch so that they projected one inch above the window sill, not a desirable condition but one that had to be accepted. Lastly, the base trim had to be reinstalled and the floor finished.

Will the needs of the church be met exactly without a single change in the stock drawings or prefabricated building? The architect hears over and over again these words from the client: "This is the plan I want except for a few changes." Then the client proceeds to itemize a dozen changes that completely change the plan, structure, and the building. As an analogy think of the housewife baking a cake and someone saying to her, "I like your cake except for a few changes," and then suggesting another teaspoon of baking soda and several other ingredients. The only possible end result is something unfit to eat. The design of a good cake is governed by careful planning and control of the ingredients. The design of a good church will also be so governed.

Does anyone in the church know a good plan from a poor one, good specifications from poor ones? Can anyone tell whether the specifications and drawings conform to local conditions? Can a church reformed according to the Word be created out of an empty shell? Do local zoning regulations permit this type of construction?

Is a prefabricated church really less expensive than a custom-built one? Great care must be exercised in avoiding the "come on." This consists of an empty shell with a very attractive price. Very soon, however, this "inexpensive" shell needs excavations, footings, drain tile, a concrete slab on grade, vapor barriers, water supply, sewage disposal, gutters, downspouts, drains, furnace, chimney, radiators, water closets, sinks, piping, venting, stacks, lights, conduit, electrical service, and so on and on.

Can competitive bidding and selection of a competent contractor be done by the church, or is it obliged to take the captive contractor that the prefabricator requires? Can all the proper safeguards for the building operation be arranged: bid bonds, guarantees, insurance, applications for payment, certificates for payment, change orders, and a host of others?

Can the most economical materials available be used? The costs of materials vary. As an example, the costs of the basic structural materials—wood, steel, and concrete, vary from year to year. A prefab concrete frame might be less expensive than the custom-built concrete frame, but is it less expensive than the steel or wood frame? Only a careful analysis can determine this. Investigation by one church revealed that a concrete frame would cost five thousand dollars more than a comparable steel frame. A year later the prices were approximately the same, and the following year the concrete frame was less expensive than the steel. With the structure representing one-fourth of the building cost, this sort of analysis is important.

Is the church itself willing to supervise the job and make sure it is being built according to plans and specifications? Does it know what is written in the several hundred detailed specifications or standards of materials published by the American Society for Testing Materials, the American Concrete Institute, the American Institute of Steel Construction, the American Standards Association, and scores of other agencies?

Does anyone know the various types of contracts that can be made with the contractor and the advantages and disadvantages of each?

Who knows how to have concrete, steel, welds, bolts, rivets, connectors, wood, block, brick and other products tested to see if they meet specifications?

Do any members know soils, how to determine soil capacities and how to meet unexpected conditions of rock, quicksand, soft spots, abandoned gas wells, hardpan and water? An abandoned gas well required the relocation of a section of one church when the only safe expedient was to vent the gas well high above the roof. Rock might eliminate an entire basement. Water can make a septic system with filter bed an impossibility.

Does anyone know materials? Different kinds of woods, paints, and metals are difficult to recognize. Different grades of fixtures—electrical and mechanical—need careful checking.

Who can judge workmanship and quality well enough to know when a wall needs to be redone, or if the steel connections are properly made?

Does anyone understand shop drawings? These instruct the shop to shape each piece of stone, cut each piece of steel, erect each toilet partition, fabricate each piece of cabinet work, build each stair, and form each piece of precast concrete. Who has the time and knowledge to check and approve these shop drawings?

Are there any special requirements such as built-in furniture, custom pews, a pulpit, communion table, baptismal font, choir and organ equipment?

Can a better loan be negotiated than can be obtained through the local combination of bank-architect-contractor?

True economy results from meticulous review of every phase and every detail of the building and relating this review to the desired quality of the building. Keep all of these things in mind when considering any standardized plans or structures.

Height

The question of whether to build a church with a basement or a church building on grade is a question of economy which only investigation can solve. Generally a church with a basement needs fireproof stairs, heavier beams for the floor above and possibly additional sanitary facilities. But a church with a basement has less foundation, less roof area, and therefore reduced heat and maintenance cost. It is more compact on the property. Where sites are small and costly, the church with a basement may be a necessity.

A church building on grade must spread out, use more wall, roof, and slab surface. Extra space is obtained by the elimination of stairway space and its enclosure. Construction can be less expensive since the floor is a slab on grade and the roof can be of lighter construction. Fire rating of the construction can be reduced since the occupants can easily escape from the building. Poorer soils can be used because loads are less. Maintenance is easier for one-story buildings. If the land is relatively flat and the site generous in size, consideration must be given to the church building on grade. With your needs and land in mind, investigate at what elevation you should place your building as illustrated on the diagram, Selection of Floor Elevation.

SELECTION OF FLOOR ELEVATION

ON-GRADE BUILDING CONSIDERATIONS

note how a slab on grade minimizes the amount of foundation needed below grade, reduces cost of floor construction and can make use of economical fill

BASEMENT BUILDING CONSIDERATIONS

note how below-grade spaces make the maximum use of foundation walls and how these spaces can be improved with natural light by means of economical grading

ELEVATED BUILDING CONSIDERATIONS

note how raising the building on short stilts above grade creates the minimum amount of foundation and fits conditions of unusual terrain

TWO-STORY BUILDING CONSIDERATIONS

note how raising the building a full story above grade provides economical first floor space which can be related to the land by economical berming

CANTILEVER BUILDING CONSIDERATIONS

note how cantilevers or overhangs increase space without appreciably increasing structural members and how the cantilever can relate to unusual terrain

Expansion

Plan for future expansion. Allow space for additions to the building. Allow space for an additional heating plant, electrical service, and plumbing connections. Consider a stage development, a master plan or a comprehensive plan to set your goals and thereby avoid the pitfalls of periodic planning. A good architect can make a comprehensive plan that will include the sanctuary, chapel, educational unit, parsonage, garage, parking lot, landscaping, outdoor amphitheater, and any other facilities as a guide to building the first of these units, which might be the church or chapel.

The building units might be zoned for the mechanical trades. Several units might be heated with one furnace, or if the units are large they might each have their own heating equipment. Considerations such as these enable the church to build in stages without oversizing the existing mechanical equipment and increasing operating expenses.

Materials

It is difficult to say which materials to use and which not to use. Availability and economy vary from season to season and place to place. In general, try to simplify: that is, use one material where two are often used. Why not expose brick instead of covering it with lath, plaster and paint? Why cover a finished wood floor with carpet? Why have colored glass if plain glass will do? Economy in materials is using the right material in the right place. A more expensive material may be the most economical in the long run. Use stock materials and especially stock sizes whenever possible. An architect can reduce material cost if the parts slip together without elaborate cutting and fitting on the job. If a church really wants him to reduce building costs, it must permit him to use building elements like doors, windows, panels, beams, and cabinets over and over again in the same size. This will enable the building elements to be built economically in a shop or on the production line, the contractor to give you a better bid, the architect to design a few elements well rather than many elements hurriedly. Let your architect choose the materials for a given set of conditions. Let him choose components to fit these materials.

*The Ascent (De Opgang), Hervormd, Beverwijk-West, The Netherlands
S. van Woerden, architect*

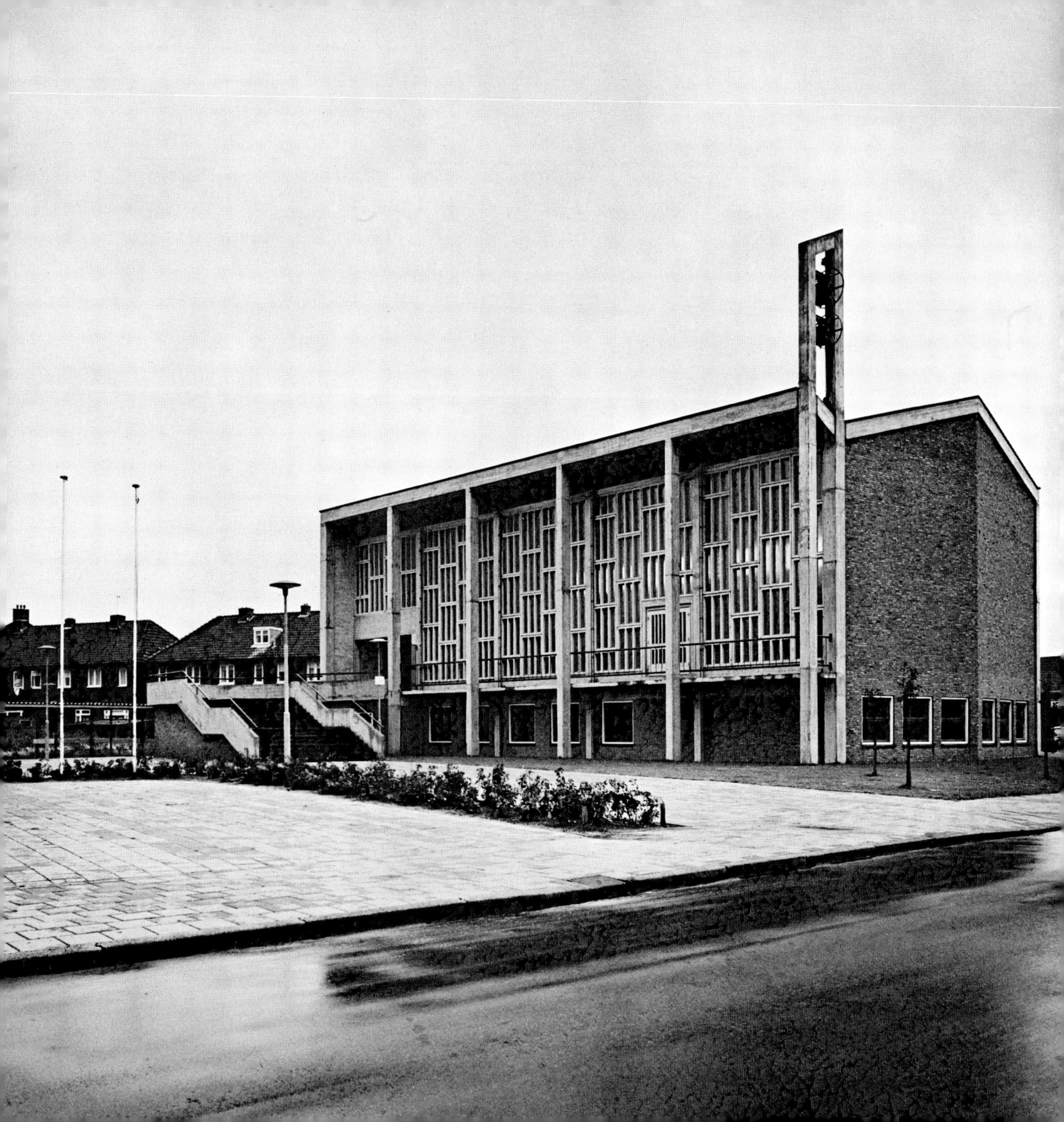

Note the simple materials and the adequate worship center of De Opgang

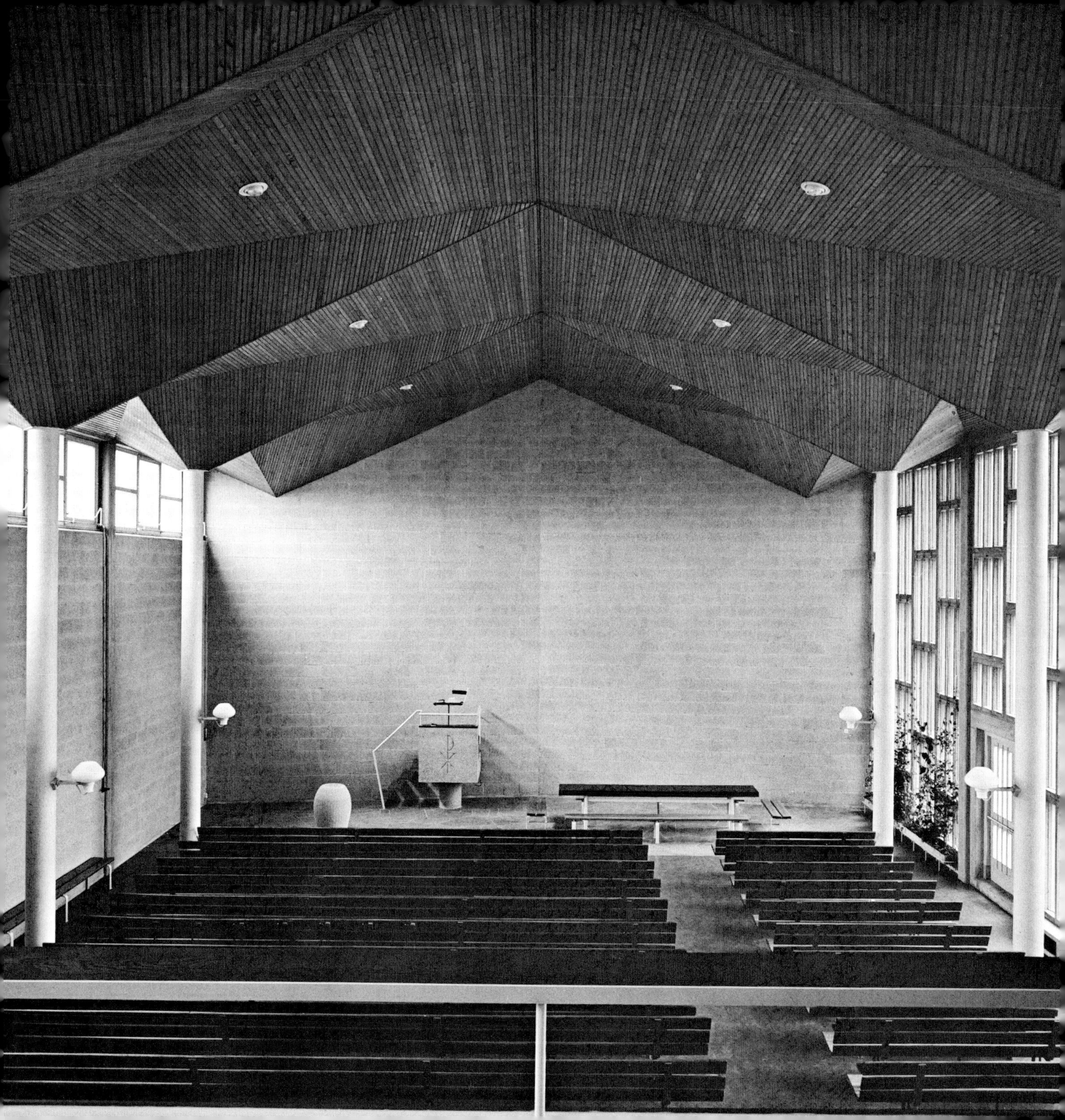

The most difficult component to choose is the window. If it is a non-operating window the problem is easy, but for operating windows the variety of windows available makes the choice a very important one. Basically the type of operation must be determined. On the accompanying sketch, Window Operation Principles, the four basic types of window operations are shown with the advantages and disadvantages noted below:

SLIDING   The double-hung window is a vertical sliding window. It can provide only 50% of its opening for ventilation. It is easily screened, storm sashed and curtained. The same is true for the horizontally sliding or gliding window.

HINGING   The casement window is a hinging window. It can open in or open out and provides 100% of its opening for ventilation. Out-opening casements or out-opening awning windows present some difficulty in order to be screened or storm sashed. In-opening casements or hopper windows are more difficult to curtain.

PIVOTING   The horizontal pivoting window provides 100% ventilation and 100% ability to direct a breeze up or down. It is difficult to screen except with "belly screens" and difficult to curtain. The vertical pivoting window has 100% ability to direct a breeze from side to side.

PROJECTING   The projecting window differs from the hinging window in that it is not stationary at the hinge point but moves by sliding in a groove of the window frame. It provides through ventilation as well as directed ventilation. Screen, storm sash and curtain problems are the same as for hinging windows.

All four types of windows present some problems in washing, which have been solved in greater or less degree by the manufacturer. Your architect will make recommendations along this line. Hopper windows must be given

WINDOW OPERATION PRINCIPLES

SLIDING

left — right — up — down

HINGING

left — right — top — bottom

PIVOTING

horizontal — vertical — top — bottom

PROJECTING

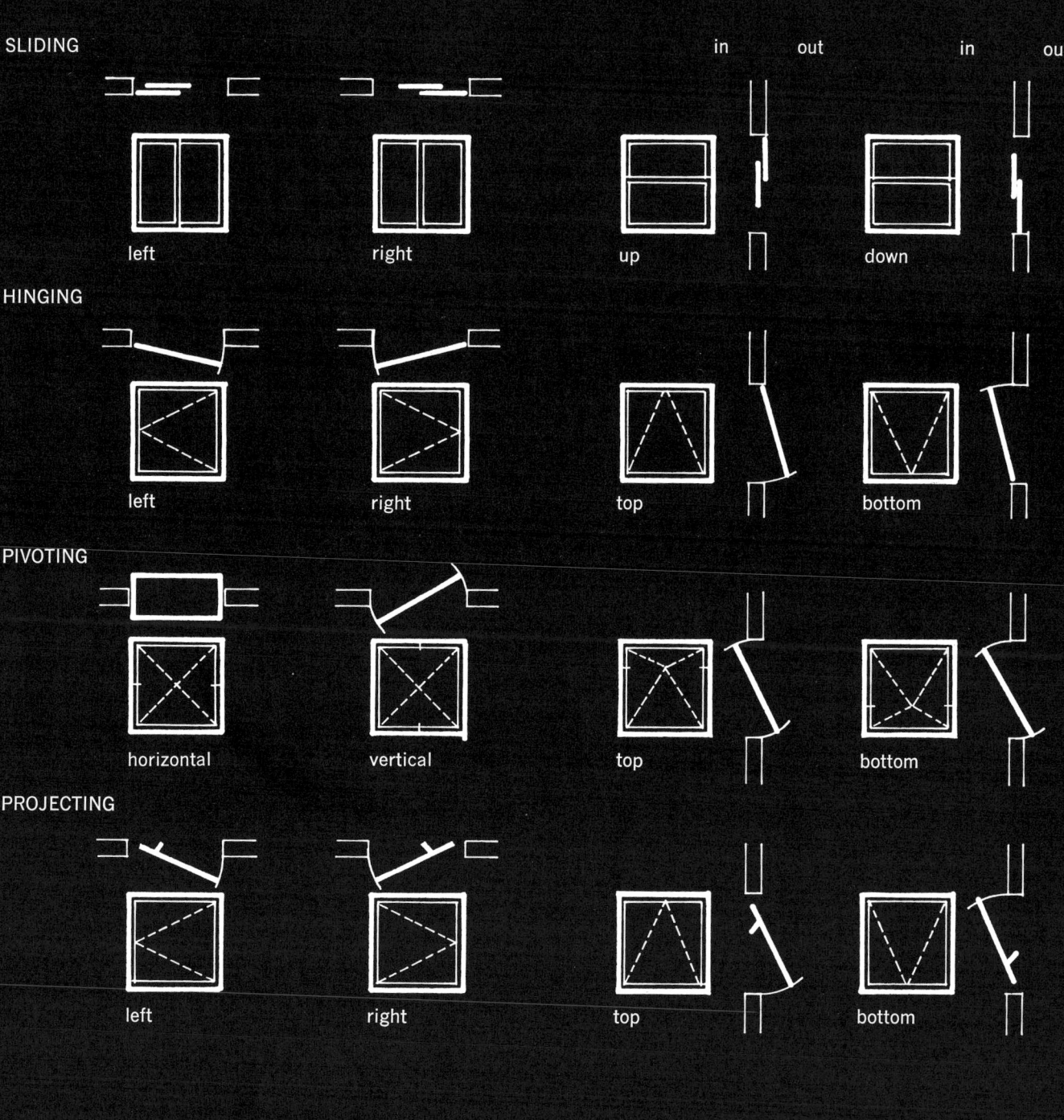

left — right — top — bottom

special consideration during installation to make sure they shed rain rather than invite it into a building.

Maintenance

Look for materials that require the least maintenance. Look for materials that need not be painted. Look for materials that people respect—natural finished woods, exposed brick, aluminum, and stone. Look for materials that need only be dusted, washed, vacuumed, waxed, or scrubbed. These are the things the members of the congregation or custodial staff can do easily and do well; these are the things they can do in the limited time they have to work on the church building. Architects know a great deal about materials and their maintenance. They go back to old jobs to see how materials have held up and to see what sort of maintenance they have received in actual practice. Architects make it a practice to put new materials through a series of tests before they use them. They experiment with abrasion tests, heat and cold tests, flexing tests, and other tests the product might receive in actual practice. Architects are acquainted with the tests these products are given in various laboratories and testing bureaus, and are accustomed to selecting materials on the basis of performance and ease of maintenance.

Depreciation

Depreciation is an important economic consideration. What is the life expectancy of your church? In Europe it might be 100 to 200 years. In the United States it might be 50 years in the city and 100 years in the small town. When you build for a life expectancy of 50 years or more you need good materials. Look at an old dump site for an example of enduring materials. Bits of glass, brick, copper, stone, and tile attest to the permanency of these materials. Big pieces of steel, wood, and concrete attest to the need for bulk for permanency in these materials. The architect wants an enduring building; he takes pride in a well-built structure. Yes, he is even accused of building monuments to himself. But if you do not have an architect who is trying to do a good job and build an enduring building, a so-called monument to himself, you had better hire another man.

When depreciation is taken into consideration a church builds differently. Materials are chosen for their lasting qualities, materials that are both lasting and economical. Then a church begins to create rather than choose a style. A site and location are chosen where there is the expectancy of a minimum of depreciation.

Equipment

With the mechanical and electrical equipment requiring over one-fourth or more of the budget, it is wise to check on economies that can be found in this part of the building operation. The plumbing fixtures can be institutional or in many cases even residential type fixtures. The lighting fixtures might be standardized for fluorescent lamp length or for incandescent lamp size. To reduce maintenance costs it might be wise to use either fluorescent or incandescent but not a mixture of both. The heating plant and radiation units should be simple. The boiler might be a package unit. The possibility of exposing equipment for easy access and maintenance should be considered. Careful examination of the churches illustrated in this book will reveal many examples of exposed equipment that have resulted in both attractive and economical solutions to problems of exposing mechanical equipment.

The exposed heating pipes illustrate a very practical application of exposed equipment. As manufacturers house their equipment in better-looking packages more and more equipment can be economically and aesthetically exposed.

Maranathakerk (Hervormd), Amsterdam-South, The Netherlands
Joh. H. Groenewegen & H. Mieras, architects

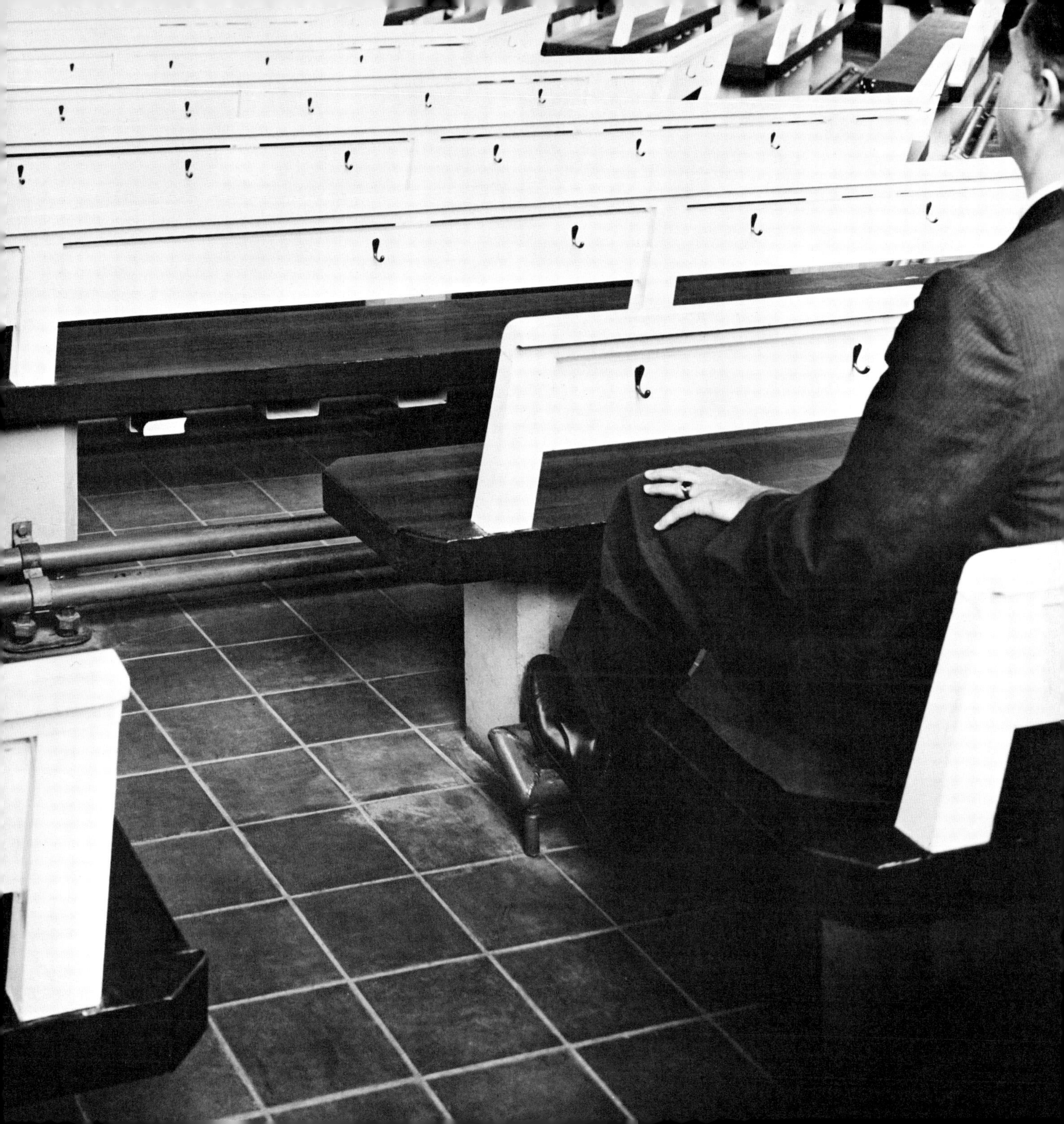

HEATING PRINCIPLES

for 70° – 75° F., relative humidity of 30 or 35%

COMFORT CONSIDERATIONS

reducing the temperature makes the occupants cold and restless
increasing the temperature makes the occupants hot and languid

reducing humidity irritates nose and throat, warps and cracks wood
increasing humidity creates condensation on windows and some walls

heat moves to bodies of lower temperature by convection, conduction, radiation

CONVECTION CONSIDERATIONS

cool air falls, warm air rises—place heaters at windows to stop downdrafts
heat flow can be increased by pumps or fans

CONDUCTION CONSIDERATIONS

heat is transmitted by close contact—place heaters for maximum contact
avoid cold floors as they conduct heat from the feet

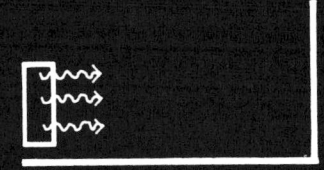

RADIATION CONSIDERATIONS

heat rays warm colder objects—the sun warms a person outside on a cold day
rays of heat flow in a straight line, so create radiant floors or ceilings

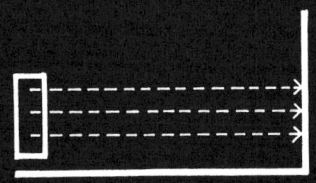

HEAT LOSS CONSIDERATIONS

by transmission (loss of heat through materials)
    choose insulation, materials construction resistant to heat loss

by infiltration (leakage of outside air into a building)
    choose careful workmanship, weatherstripping

by evaporation (people are heaters with skin pores to control heat loss)
    in summer, cool walls provide absorption of body heat
    in winter, warm walls prevent loss of body heat
    air movement compensates for high humidity and temperature
    lower temperature and humidity reduce perspiration

Planning

Have complete plans and specifications so contractors can bid intelligently. When drawings are incomplete, when specifications are not clear, the contractor protects himself by quoting a higher price for the work involved. As the work progresses, the contractor can substitute a great many materials and still be within the requirements of an incomplete set of drawings and specifications. Complete plans and specifications reduce the number of changes on the job and therefore materially reduce the cost of the building. Complete plans and specifications assure real competitive bidding. The contractor can make a "take off" that actually represents the quantity of materials in the building, then through skill, organization, and ability he competes to make the lowest bid. A good architect will insure the preparation of complete plans and specifications. The savings made on complete plans and specifications alone will pay the architect's fee. The savings made by keeping the work flowing smoothly, with each workman doing his part, and by the reduction of mistakes will show in the quality of the building, the earlier completion date, and the earlier occupancy of the building.

Contracts

Make the building contracts at the most opportune time. Fall is a good time for bidding since contractors are looking for work to tide them over the winter. Winter is also a good season for bidding since less building is being done and the contractor has extra time on his hands. A contractor's need for a job and the need to keep his crew together will enable a church to get a bid for a job that is closely figured and often just over cost. Some contractors can give a better bid because they are more efficient, better expediters, or know better and faster ways of construction. Other contractors can give a better bid because they are geared to church construction or to the structure that is being built, whether of masonry, wood, or metal. It is recommended that competency be rewarded by giving the contract to the most efficient contractor. One wonders if church people know how difficult it is for an architect or contractor to get church jobs when he belongs to a different faith. Jobs should be awarded on the basis of merit alone.

Workmen

High pay may be the most economical. One good and higher-paid carpenter can hang a door in half the time it takes a semi-skilled and less expensive carpenter. The skilled carpenter will hang it right the first time, another will have to be called back to correct the job. One plumber never has to be called back to the job while another leaves scores of unfinished items. One contractor anticipates the work of each of his trades and how they will have to collaborate, while another just blunders along accepting halfhearted collaboration and less than quality work. One contractor keeps a core of key men on his payroll while another has to scrounge for workmen when a certain job has to be done. There is real economy in hiring the right man for the job in spite of the higher bid. The low bidder is not always the most competent. Rely on your architect to help choose the contractor for the job; he has had experience with contractors, their work and their workmen.

Participation

Every church should count on its people being involved in some way in the building project. If they would assume only the planting, landscaping, or final cleaning of the church building, the building project would mean more to them. If the people of God give of their time as well as their money they will take greater pride in their church. It is only when you put something of yourself in a building that you are concerned about that building. The people of the church will be concerned about the house of God because they have shared in its building, and at the same time they will be making a saving on the cost of the church building.

10

Expression in Church Building

Honesty

Christianity demands honesty. Architectural form can be honest or dishonest. This is a strange subject to be writing about, and it would seem unnecessary to tell people in church work about honesty in architecture. Church members can be deceived, and may be unable to recognize basic honesty or dishonesty in architecture because they lack experience in this field. Our buildings express the dishonesty of our times and do this indelibly. Several thousand years from now the archaeologists will dig up our churches, reconstruct them, and wonder if our civilization was simultaneous with that of the Renaissance or Gothic, only to discover that the buildings are imitations, the mere styles of an artistically decadent society, because their form and material had so little to do with the structure.

Honesty has disappeared in church building. Look at many of our present church buildings. The Gothic tower is not of masonry but of steel columns from which the masonry is hung like a string of dirty clothes, attempting to give the appearance of the old Gothic churches of Europe. This is dishonest! A church cannot afford an authentic Colonial tower, so steel frames are erected and covered with metal in attempted imitation. Even the mouldings are made out of sheet metal and painted to simulate wood. This is dishonest! Why this dishonesty? Why this fakery in, of all places, the church? It stems from the fact that the church member does not have experience in this field; he does not know what to look for, and perhaps he does not have faith in contemporary materials. He has had little or no experience to help him decide what is architecturally honest or dishonest. But once the issue of honesty has been raised, a whole new method of judgment is open to him, and he will be able to determine for himself what is honest or dishonest in architecture.

Do not allow inner dishonesty. Do not allow fake towers, painted tin in place of wood, Colonial whale oil lamps, electrified Gothic lighting fixtures that do not produce sufficient illumination, colored glass as an imitation of stained glass, "authentic" Gothic pews (the people often stood or used chairs in the Gothic period), good walls on only one side (stone in the front, brick in the back, or now it's brick in front and block in the back and sides). Do not be influenced by well-intentioned but erring people who argue that everybody does Gothic or Colonial and therefore it might be right. Do not be influenced by one member with money who wishes to foist his personal desires onto the congregation. It would be better for the congregation to build the church without his help than to corrupt succeeding generations with a dishonest building.

It is a common experience to sit in a church trying to read a hymnbook or the Scriptures and be unable to do so because a little of God's sunlight cannot penetrate the gloom (is ours a religion of darkness and despair?). Sitting in certain seats, it is often difficult to hear; one wishes something could also be done about the acoustics. And then one must try to concentrate while sitting in the draft from the windows. These problems are all too frequent when trying to worship and participate in our churches. In the old cathedrals the people looked on while others read, sang, and conducted the service—in fact most could not read! Consider that this was 400 years ago, and then consider that some are still in this generation constructing buildings designed for people who cannot read, sing, or participate in the service! We sometimes forget that Gutenberg, Luther and Calvin changed all that. We cannot look elsewhere; we must find an expression that fits our time and age, a building that expresses the Church reformed according to the Word.

The Church reformed according to the Word will have the congregation participate in worship (it is not the audience, for there is only one in the audience: God). It will enable the congregation to receive the Word, to share in the breaking of the bread, to witness Baptism, and to respond with the choir in joyous praise of God. It will express the principles determined by the Reformation:

    a. The indispensability of the Word
    b. The Sacraments as assurance of full salvation in Christ
    c. The congregation as the people of God
    d. A Presbyterian form of church government

The Church reformed according to the Word will express itself in the spirit of the Reformation. It will express itself clearly, not in the confusion of one Reformed church which, in copying a "style," copied as well the confessional booths, and so applied its decoration to suggest the stations of the cross. Symbols that say one thing while the opposite is being said by the minister cannot be used. The Church must stop using warmed-over architectural styles that do not express its concept of worship. Rather, the Church must plan with the specific intention of expressing its faith, reformed according to the Word. When this is the motivation, great churches will be built and great architecture created. When motives are weak and aspirations low, mere buildings in which members meet will be constructed and labeled churches.

PLANNING ELEMENTS FOR REFORMED CHURCHES

word		elder's		seats	
font		deacon's	○ ○ ○ ○	plates	
table		level	– – – – –	change	

Materials must be honest. If brick is a worthy material for the front of the church building, then it is also a worthy material for not only the sides but also the insides. Plaster, paneling, or other covering need not be used on the inside of our buildings to cover a fine material like brick. Take a careful look at many of the church interiors illustrated in this book and you will discover brick interior walls, brick exterior walls, and even pulpits made of brick or other masonry. The same is true of concrete block. Used correctly, not as something to be hidden at the rear of the church building, it has an honest expression all its own.

The Reformed Church (De Gereformeerde Kerk), Nagele, N. O. P., The Netherlands. J. H. van den Broek & J. B. Bakema, architects

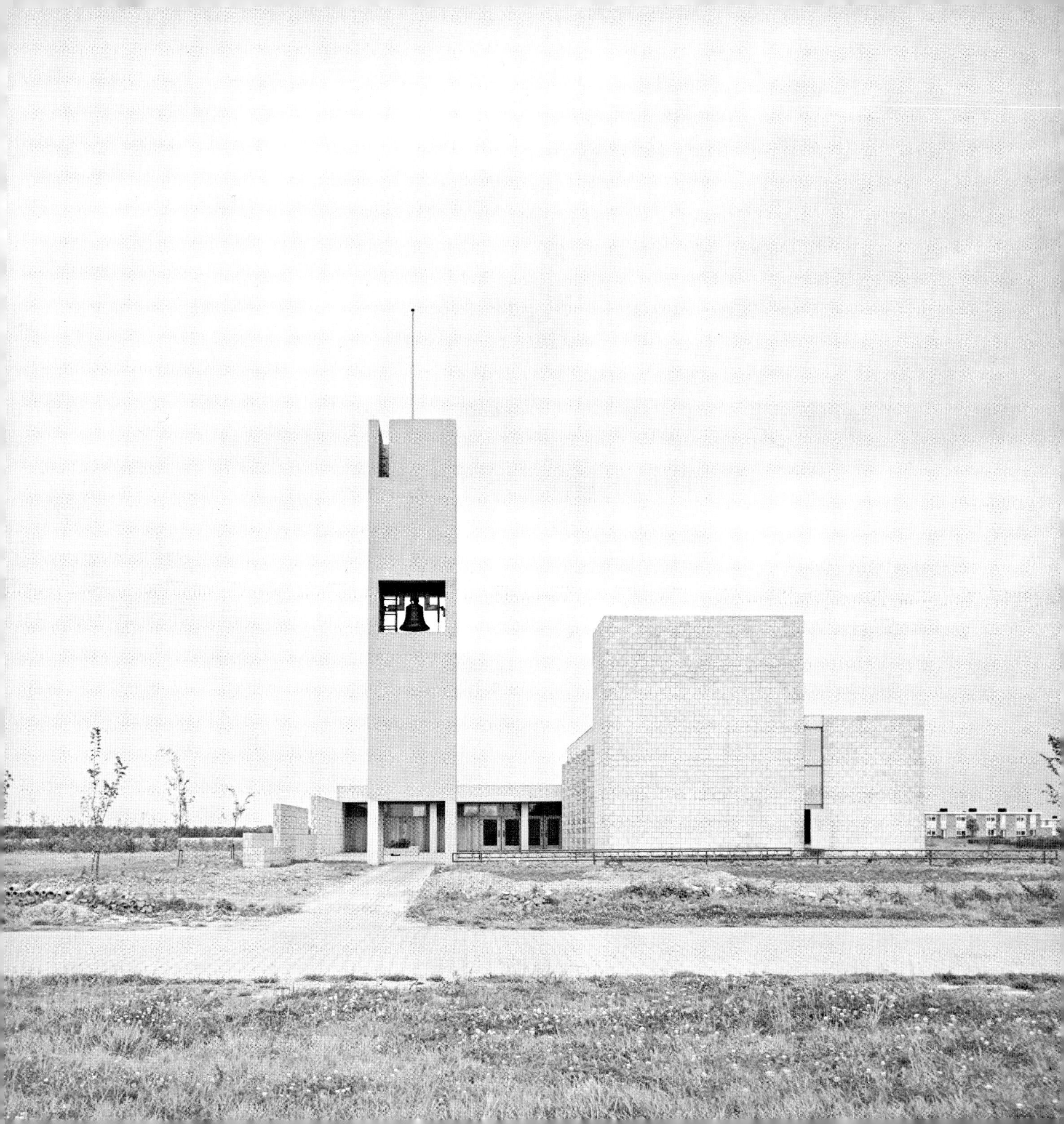

While coat racks are a necessity, unfortunately they often present a jumbled sight when full of coats of every description. Here the architect has organized the jumble by placing a rack for both children and adults behind a neat bulletin board. Note the identification symbols by the hooks for the children's wraps.

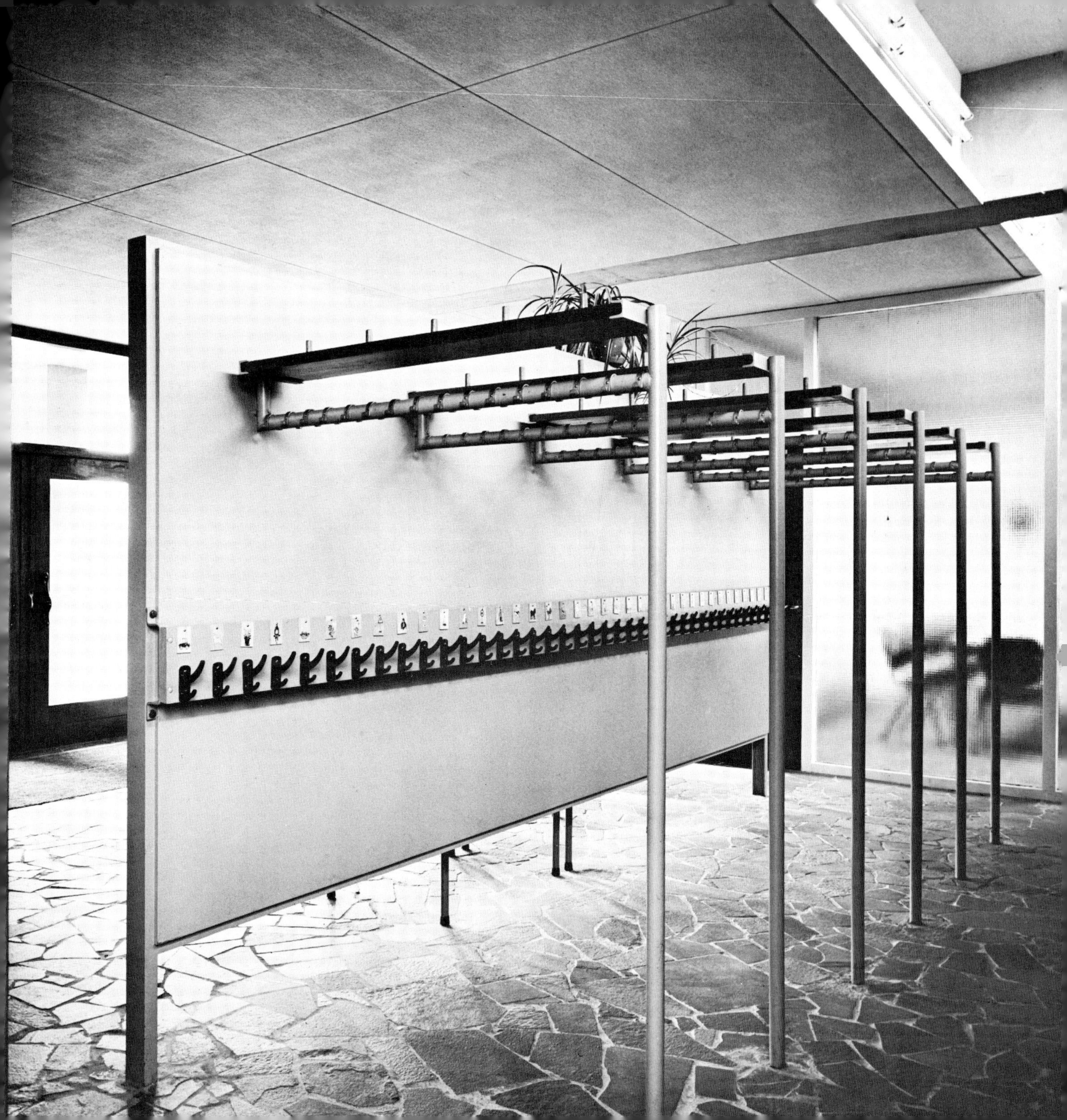

Organ by Fonteyn & Gaal of Amsterdam

Manuaal I

Prestant	8
Holpijp	8
Mixtuur 3 ranks	2

Manuaal II

Holpijp	8
Gemshoorn	4
Flakfluit	2

Pedaal

Subbas	16

Note the honest use of concrete block as the interior surfacing, the honest use of precast beams and precast slabs of the roof. There is no attempt here to cover this basic material with older, more acceptable, materials. The materials are honest. At the same time note the use of concrete for pulpit, font and organ support. There is no pretense; these materials are doing the job well without camouflage of any sort.

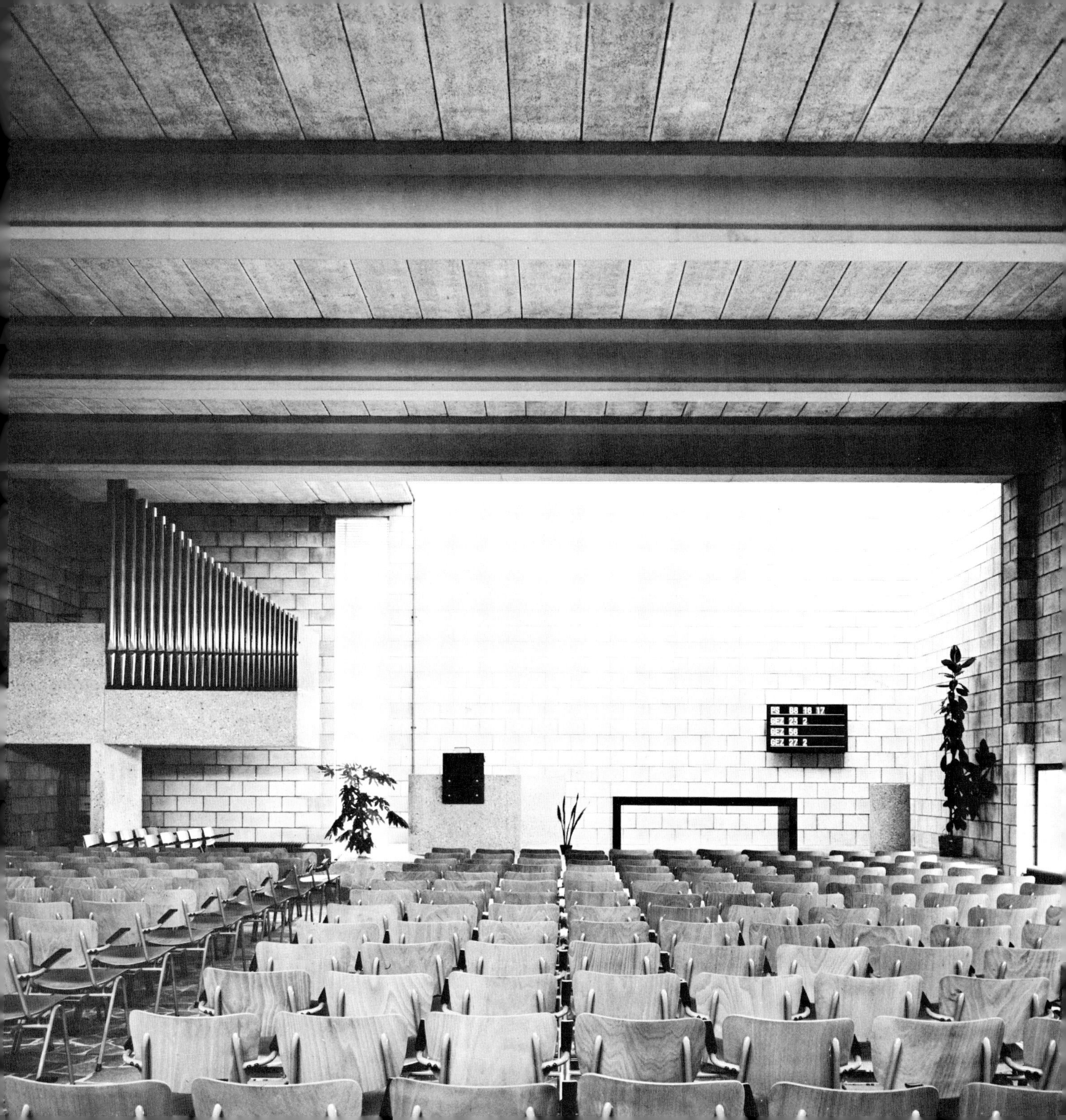
GEZ 23 2
GEZ 27 2

For many years, the manufacturers of concrete block pretended it was stone. The surface was made rough and uneven to simulate stone; the edges were tooled and hammered like stone. It was a great revelation when they realized that concrete block could be concrete block in its own right, that it need not look like stone or any other material. At that moment it became an honest material. That particular sham has disappeared, but a host of new ones are taking its place. Laminates that simulate oak, walnut, teak, maple and mahogany are a good example. They are dishonest. Yet these same laminates in colors and patterns of their own become very honest surfaces for counter and sink tops. Metal cabinets painted to simulate wood are dishonest.

If we accept honest materials, why not put up a church building with steel or concrete as the structural material? Why not erect a tower of steel? For the tower, can some ideas be gathered from the masts of the radio and TV stations? If a tower is used for height, it can be a beacon to the world and can house the bell to call the community together. The tone of the bell once identified the church, tolled the hour, informed the community of death, told the age of the deceased, warned of approaching enemies, called together the people, and was the communication system of the people. But even the tower has fallen into dishonest use as the structural material is camouflaged, the bell is removed, and it is frequently not built to a sufficient height to even exceed the peak of the church roof.

Unfortunately, a dishonest use of materials reflects the culture that so uses them. A change must occur in the people before a change can occur in their architecture. The people must decide to have honest buildings and to use honest materials if they wish to represent themselves as honest people.

Order

Nature is beautiful because it is not whimsical. The beauty of a flower comes from a structure, an inner character of simplicity and honesty. Beauty comes from an inner order. The more man studies nature, the more order he perceives. The molecule has order. The laws of the universe have order. Our church buildings must have order. Trying to create a beautiful building from the outside is false. It must be created from an inner order, an inner clarity, an inner character. It must be honest in its function, like a flower. These are the principles. Whimsy or the outer trappings of so-called styles are not principles and cannot produce good architecture. The inner impulses of honesty, character, and order result in architecture. The architect must try to create a church building with integrity; he must stand on principles so that when the moment of inspiration comes he can make a beautiful church building. Only then can he produce architecture; only then is he producing an architecture for the church reformed acording to the Word that manifests honesty, character and order.

Clarity

Clarity should be found in the structure or frame of church buildings, an orderly arrangement of columns and beams, walls and slabs. Clarity should be found in materials: a single material for walls, a single component for roofs, a single component for floors, and a single material for openings. Clarity should be found in planning: fewer rooms with greater versatility and greater flexibility. Clarity and simplicity should be found in furnishings, in pews, pulpit, font, and table. Clarity and simplicity should be found in the bell tower: a tower of height, honestly constructed, a silhouette against the sky. The more clearly and simply we can do things, the more we can simplify materials, surfaces, and spaces, and the closer we come to an expression of clarity and honesty. Clarity should be found in a generous area of paving, in a plateau or podium for our church building. Clarity should be found in landscaping, with trees fulfilling their function of providing shade, humidity, cooling, and beauty.

TREE SELECTION PRINCIPLES

HEIGHT CONSIDERATIONS
conditions of space, light, soil and the species determine the tree height
horizontal lines show the tree height in feet for a ten-year growth period

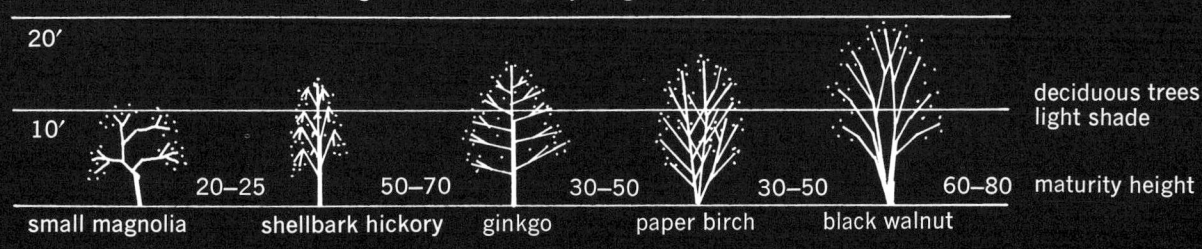

20'
10'

small magnolia	shellbark hickory	ginkgo	paper birch	black walnut
20–25	50–70	30–50	30–50	60–80

deciduous trees
light shade

maturity height

VISUAL CONSIDERATIONS
the structure of a tree determines its shape and its characteristics of growth
choose small trees for city lots and limited spaces, forest trees for open spaces

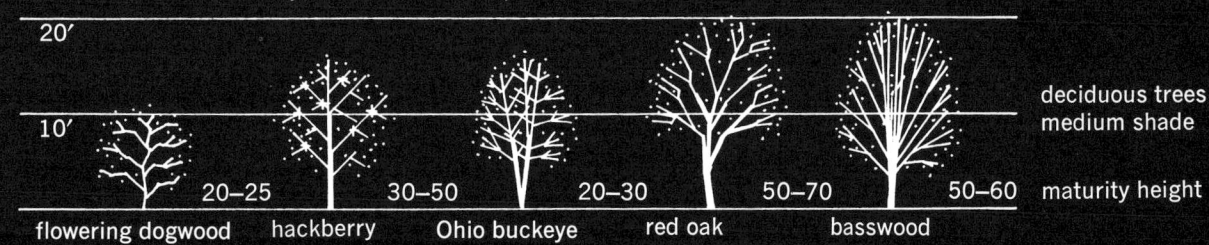

20'
10'

flowering dogwood	hackberry	Ohio buckeye	red oak	basswood
20–25	30–50	20–30	50–70	50–60

deciduous trees
medium shade

maturity height

GROWTH CONSIDERATIONS
check color, foliage, flowers, bark, seed, roots, rate of growth, wind break
avoid weak growth, shedding bark, fruit stains, seed pods, extensive root systems

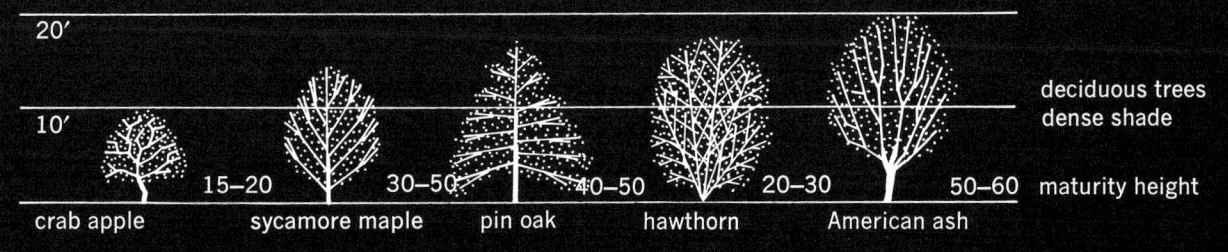

20'
10'

crab apple	sycamore maple	pin oak	hawthorn	American ash
15–20	30–50	40–50	20–30	50–60

deciduous trees
dense shade

maturity height

SHADOW CONSIDERATIONS
for shade and cooling, plant a tree to the southwest of a terrace or glass area
choose light shade trees for lawns and play areas, dense trees for shading rooms

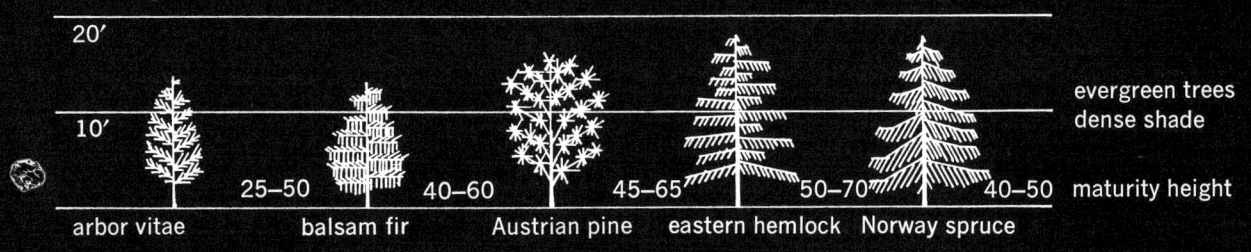

20'
10'

arbor vitae	balsam fir	Austrian pine	eastern hemlock	Norway spruce
25–50	40–60	45–65	50–70	40–50

evergreen trees
dense shade

maturity height

Clarity, honesty, simplicity, the removal of all distractions, are expressions of Reformed worship. The architect says simplicity is the keynote of design. The simple and the clear are the most difficult to achieve. To add meaningless ornament and decoration is easy. Adding mouldings and bric-a-brac is done with facility. To use restraint is difficult, yet when this is done the building looks very effortless when finished. Achieving simplicity and clarity when the characteristics of our age are change, variety, and novelty is not easy, but clarity must be a symbol of our form of worship. A striving for simplicity and clarity means that the church must be able to consider, to analyze, to accept the results of study and to make a building program from the information it has gleaned. This takes courage of a high order, for the church will not be following the crowd; it will be doing its own thinking and its own creating.

Lightness

The expression of our age is openness and lightness as compared to the solidity and heaviness of masonry in previous ages. It is an expression of our ability to span greater distances than ever before. In wood structure, it means greater distances between supports by using laminated beams, bents, or frames. In metal structures, greater spans are achieved, and with cables, tentlike structures are being built. In reinforced concrete, shell structures are being created. All of these structures tend to be light and open. The architect can also now provide large areas of glass, making the building even lighter and more open. He combines rooms to achieve flexibility and versatility, again emphasizing openness and lightness. Church buildings tend to become lightsome: lighted, luminous, bright. Light, both natural and artificial, becomes a primary planning element.

In the past, natural light was handled with great dexterity. The architect plotted the shades and shadows upon his massive masonry buildings and etched his building into sunlight and dark shadow. The building had depth and texture, it was alive with the play of sunlight and shadows across its face. In our age the massive wall has disappeared, in its place is a light, transparent wall. This wall mirrors the sky, landscape, or city of its environment. The play of sunlight and shadows has changed to a reflection of the surroundings. The buildings of our age have become lightsome: lighted, luminous and bright. The effort of the architect and lighting engineer is to create an environment that is lighted artificially in the same manner as the building is lighted naturally. Sources of light remain constant in this way, so that classroom and office equipment need not be shifted to comply with a new light source.

In *Hervormde Kerkbouw na 1945*, published under the auspices of the Bouw- en Restauratie-Commissie van de Nederlandse Hervormde Kerk, there are listed three items of consideration for determining the interior of the church (p. 219):

1. the arrangement of the seats
2. the arrangement of the furniture of the church in the center of attention (liturgical center),
3. the fall of the light, which is decisive for spacial perspective

The last item, "the fall of the light," is very important in our churches. Naturally it is desirable to control glare and direct sun in the church building and especially the sanctuary, but it is of equal importance to use sunlight to advantage.

LIGHTING PRINCIPLES

OPTICAL CONSIDERATIONS
light is invisible; use surfaces to reflect the effect of light to the eye

dark colors absorb light

light colors reflect light

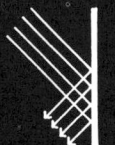

BRIGHTNESS CONSIDERATIONS
objective: control glare and brightness of the surroundings

uniform brightness from above

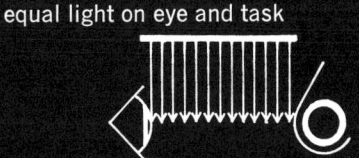

equal light on eye and task

REFLECTION CONSIDERATIONS
law: the angle of reflection is equal to the angle of incidence

reflect with smooth surfaces

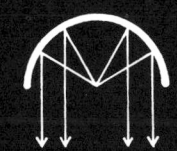

scatter with rough surfaces

REFRACTION CONSIDERATIONS
deflection of light in passing obliquely from a medium of one velocity to another

a lens can concentrate light

a lens can diverge light

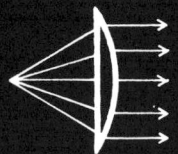

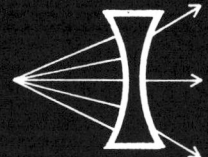

TRANSMISSION CONSIDERATIONS
at night glass becomes a mirror; for transparency light from both sides

clear glass transmits most light

colored glass absorbs certain colors

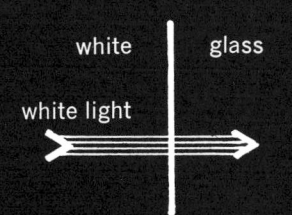

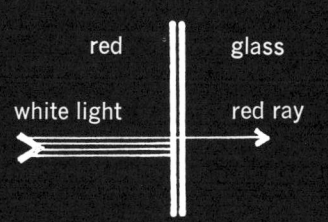

white   glass

white light

red   glass

white light   red ray

Organ by *Valckx & Van Kouteren of Rotterdam*

Fluit	4
Octaaf	4
Roerfluit	8
Prestant	8
Gamba	8
Celeste	8
Bourdon	16

Pedaal

| Subbas | 16 |

Observe the honest use of materials where brick is used for the walls, wood for the ceiling and stone for the floor. Equally important is the emphasis the natural light puts on the pulpit, table and baptismal font.

The Church of the Cross (Kruiskerk), Hervormd, Woltheze, The Netherlands
G. Bruins, architect

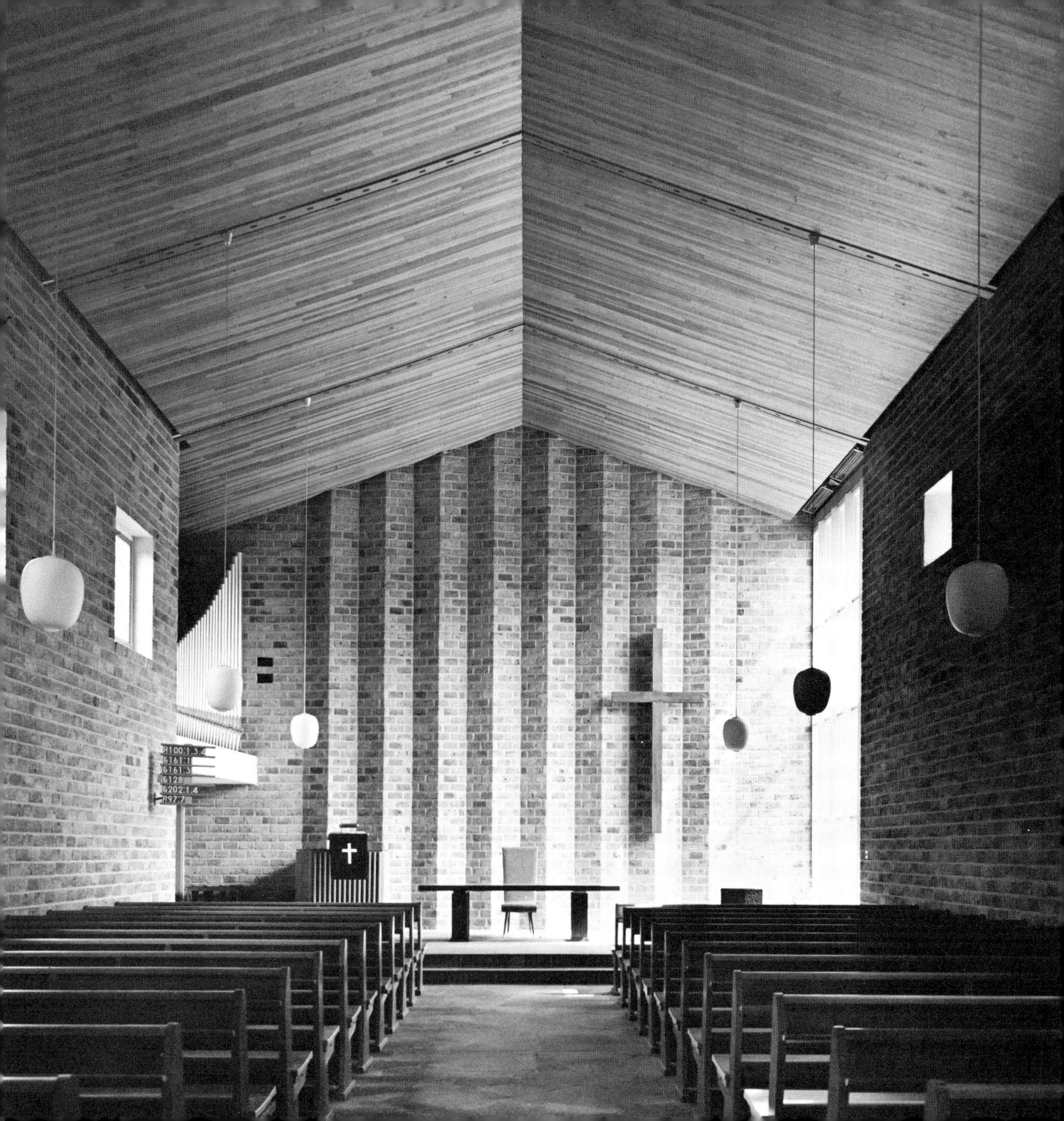
R100:1.3.4
G161:1
G161:3
G128
G202:1.4
R97:7

The exterior of this small church reformed according to the Word has a simple brick wall with piers located in a clear and orderly manner to receive the weight of the roof tiles transferred by rafters and beams to these points. Exterior location of the window puts emphasis on the liturgical center.

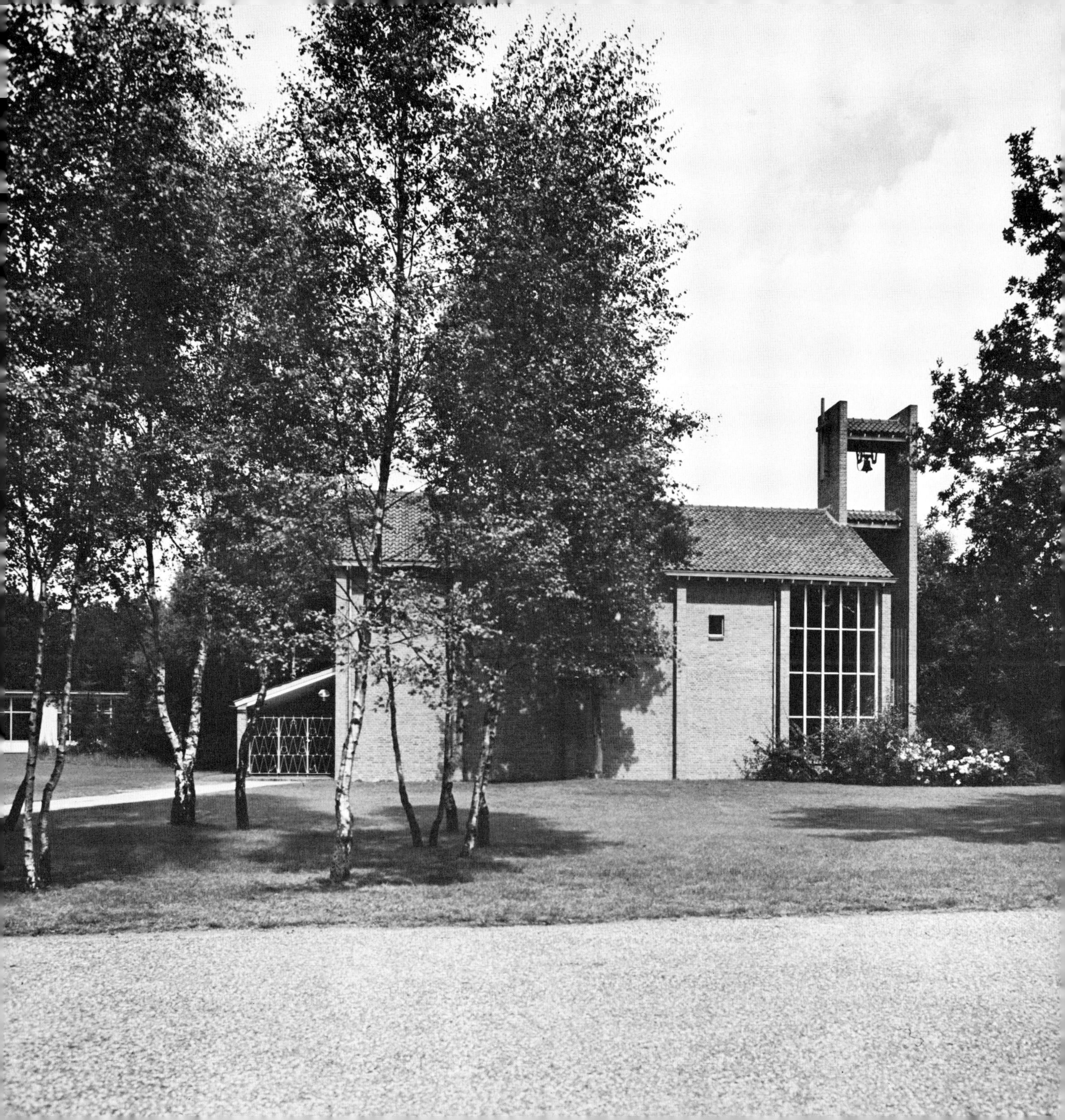

Without pretense, the church entry is shielded against the weather and a story told in the symbols on the gate.

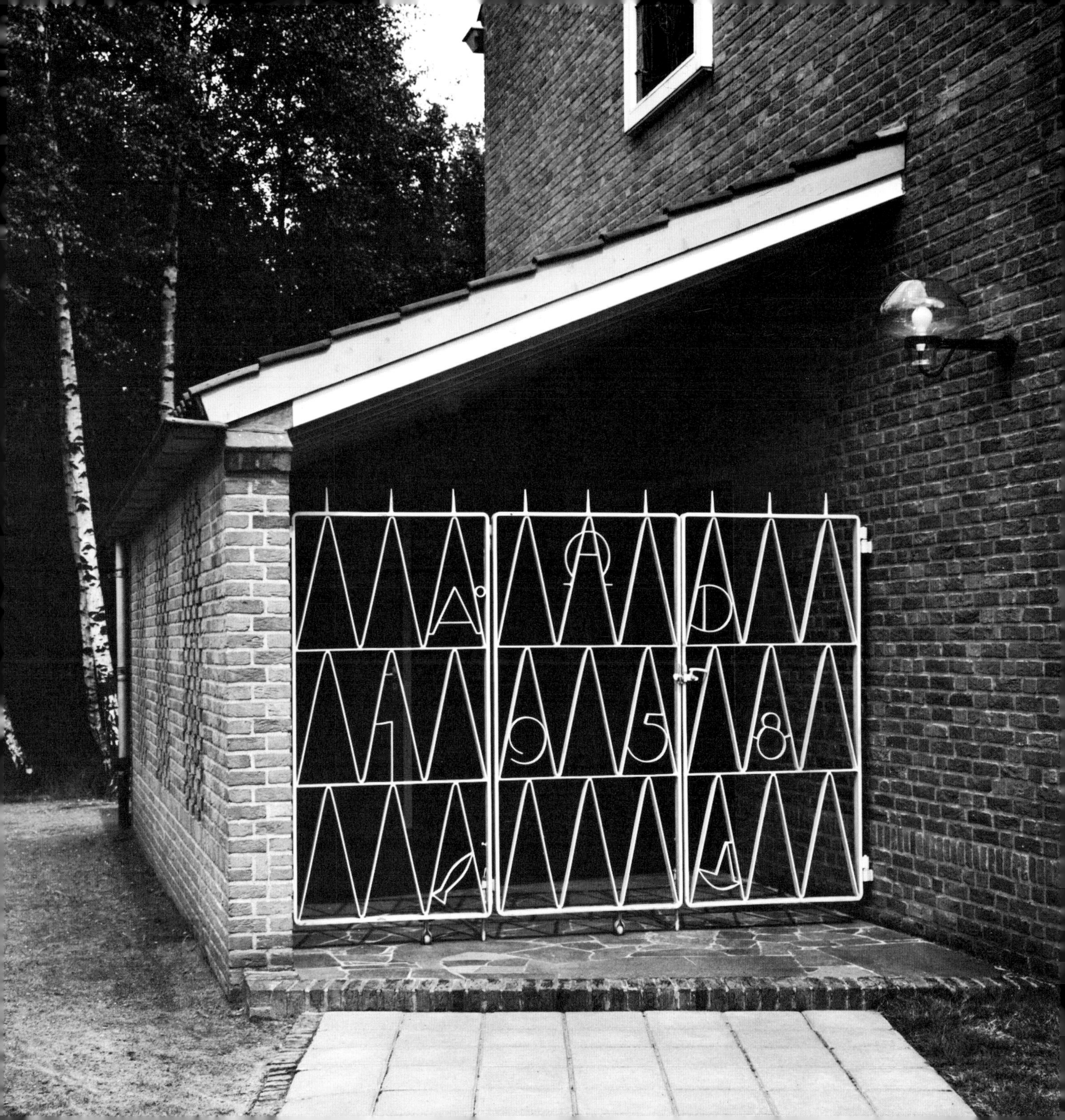
1958

For over-all lighting, natural light coming through a strip skylight or ridge skylight can enhance the building and make it lightsome. Lights mounted in these same skylights will simulate the effect after dark. For emphasis, natural light from a small skylight can create a shaft of sunlight to highlight the baptismal font. Once the basic principles of lighting are understood, they can be used as tools to put emphasis on the architecture of the church and even create that architecture.

Emphasis is placed on the altar by a shaft of sunlight cutting across the east wall.

The Church of Brother Klaus (Bruderklausenkirche), Roman Catholic, Liestal, Switzerland. Fritz Metzger, architect

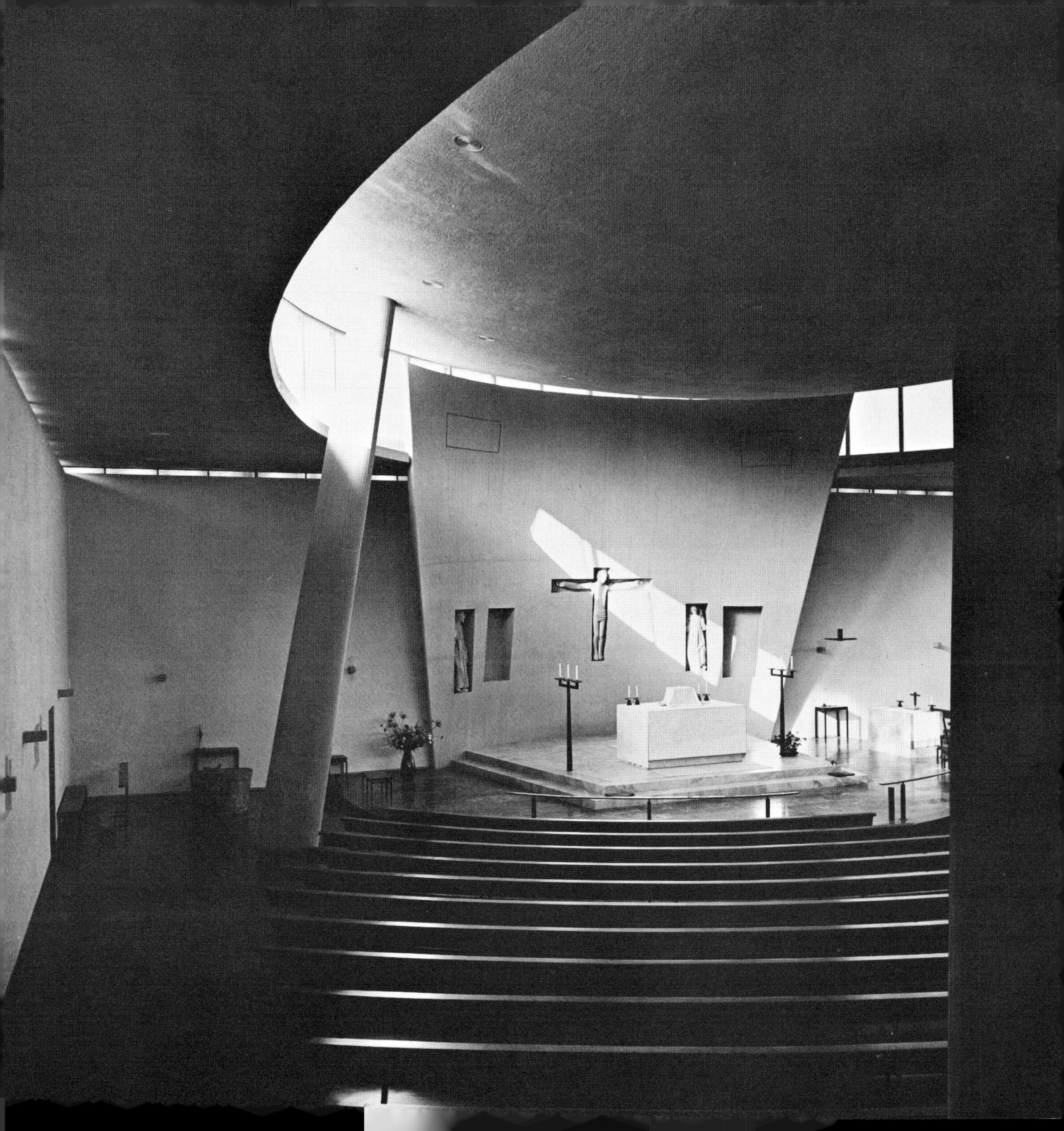

Natural light can also be used to express lightness and openness by locating the windows above or especially below eye level to "float" the building with light. In a sanctuary this eliminates the window as a viewing device but enhances it as a lighting device. The interiors of such spaces must be experienced to be understood.

This little Reformed church invites direct sunlight into the lower portions of its glassed areas, diffuses the light with thin drapes in the upper portions.

Kirche Bottmingen, near Basel, Switzerland
Walter Wurster, architect

Beundenstrasse

In the interior a translucent glass is used to invite the sunlight but exclude the view. A thin band of transparent windows serve as ventilators. The overhang and drapes control the direct rays of the sun.

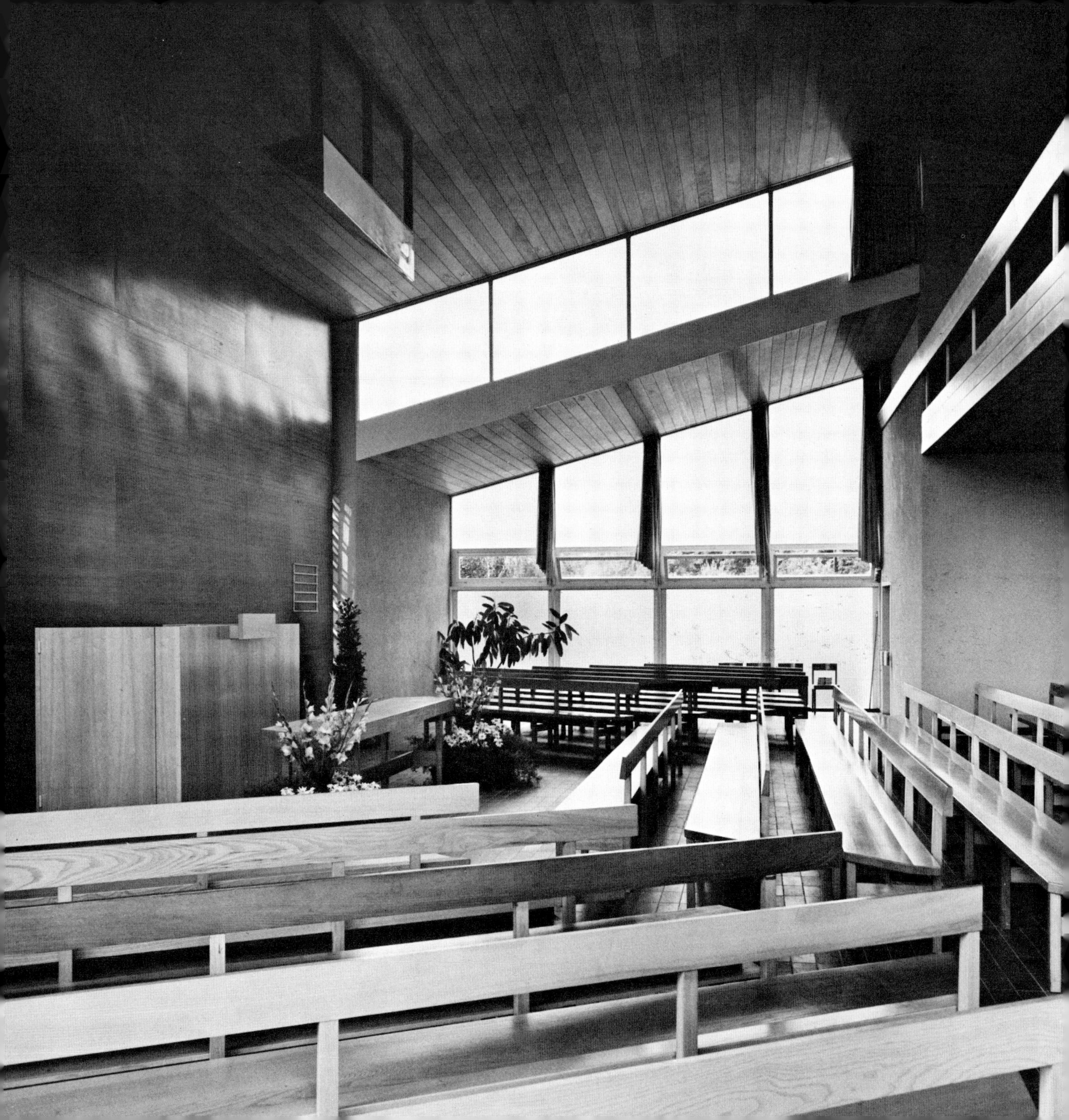

The use of direct sunlight must be carefully considered. The architect can plot the path of the sun through a given opening for a particular location as far as latitude is concerned. He will be able to determine the location of sunlight when the sun is at its greatest height during the summer and when the sun is lowest in the sky during the winter. For a particular hour, such as that of the morning service, it might be desirable to have sunlight fall on the baptismal font or the communion table for a few minutes and then serve to light some portion of the wall or roof, avoiding glare but still retaining the reflected light.

The fall of light by no means has to be direct sunlight. Light reflected from a bright north sky vault can give a luminous quality to a sanctuary. It is an ideal light for general illumination with the absence of harsh shadows and great contrasts. Artists prefer it for their studios for this reason. North light can be captured like direct sunlight with skylights of various sorts. The amount of skylight needed for a building as compared with wall light is surprisingly small, and the tendency is to provide too much skylight. It should be understood that a skylight permits direct penetration of light from the sky vault or from the sun into the deepest recesses of the building. A wall window limits the penetration of light to portions of the floor and is not nearly as effective as the skylight. It is therefore wise to limit the amount of skylight or control it with shading devices.

The skylight can provide another experience in the sanctuary by attesting to God's sovereignty, authority, dominion—his glory. In the old cathedrals of Europe the worshipper enters a tremendous space: it is dark, shafts of light sprinkling sunlight on the floor, as he looks up to vaulting that disappears in the shadows. The expression of awe, the unlimited space and the quiet of these spaces serve to speak of the sovereignty of God. In a different manner, a skylight overhead permits the worshipper to experience infinity overhead, an experience similar to the unlimited space in the old cathedrals of Europe but with one marked difference: it is a lightsome space rather than a darksome space.

One other moving experience can be gained from the skylight. During the evening service, at dusk, or at times during the year when artificial light is not needed, the night sky vault of stars can bespeak the glory of God in a most direct way. If the skylights can be opened and the reflection of the glazing eliminated, the experience is further enhanced.

The heavens are telling the glory of God;
and the firmament proclaims his handiwork.

Psalm 19:1.

The glory of God can also be expressed in a way very similar to the method used in the old cathedrals of Europe. Witness The Church of the Trinity (Trinitatiskirche), Mannheim, Germany, by Helmut Striffler, architect. In this city church the surroundings did not permit a view, nor did the noise of the city suggest thin walls of glass and the attendant transmission of sound, so the architect had heavy chunks of colored glass fabricated into concrete panels for the windows. Upon entering through a door shielded from the light, the worshipper is immediately silenced by the darkness. As he quietly takes his pew and sits in this darksome space, which is at the same time filled with brilliant color, his eyes accustom themselves to the available light. The first time the worshipper enters this space it is a tremendous experience. Subsequent visits do not lessen the experience but make the worshipper more aware of this period for devotion, meditation and worship. The glory of God is experienced in a different manner than in the lightsome church building, but is experienced nonetheless.

The Church of the Trinity (Trinitatiskirche), Reformed, Mannheim, Germany
Helmut Striffler, architect

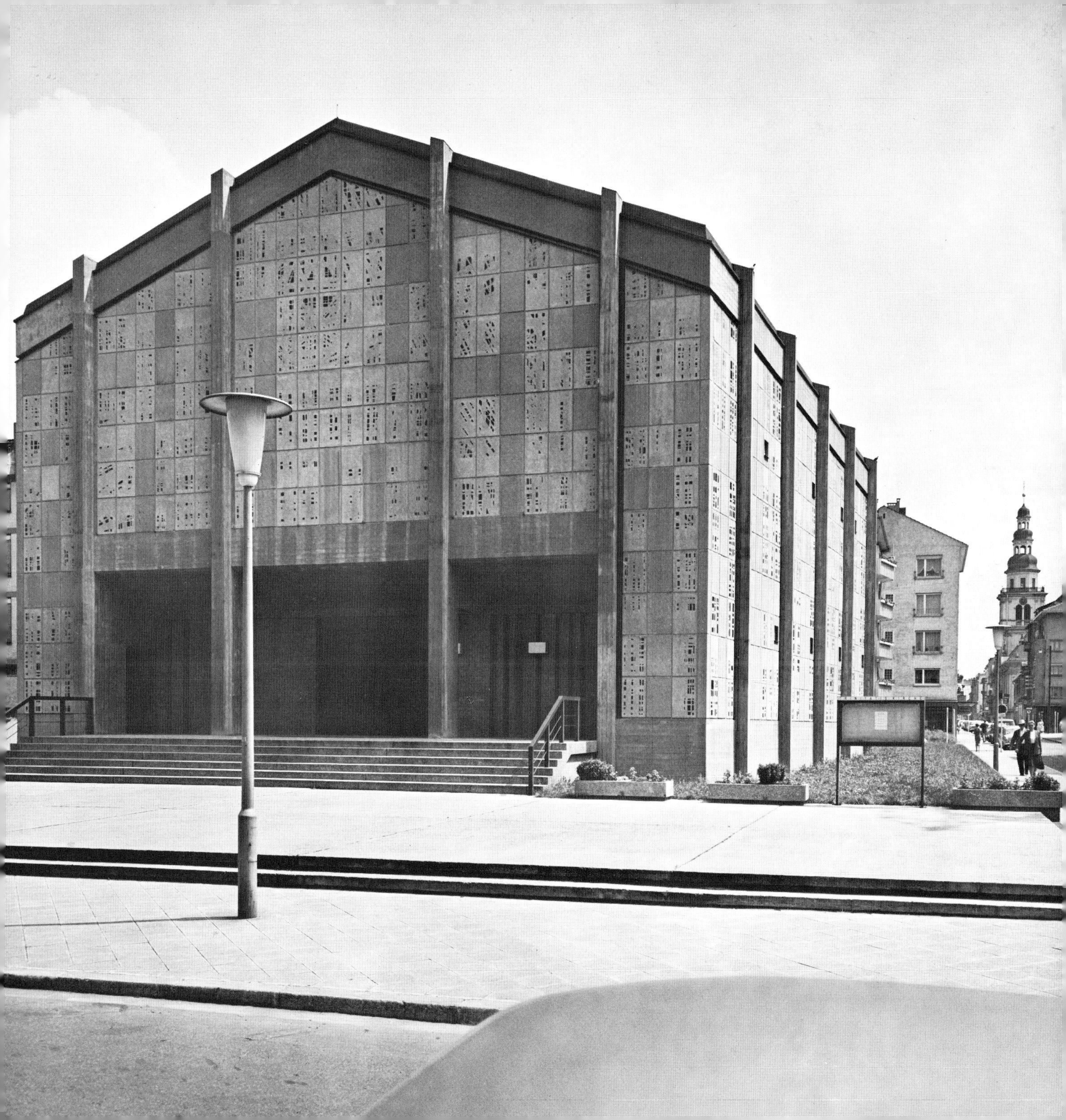

It is only after having been in this sanctuary for several minutes that one's eyes are able to adjust themselves and distinguish the details observable in this photo (4-minute exposure, f. 22, Panatomic-X—A.S.A. 64).

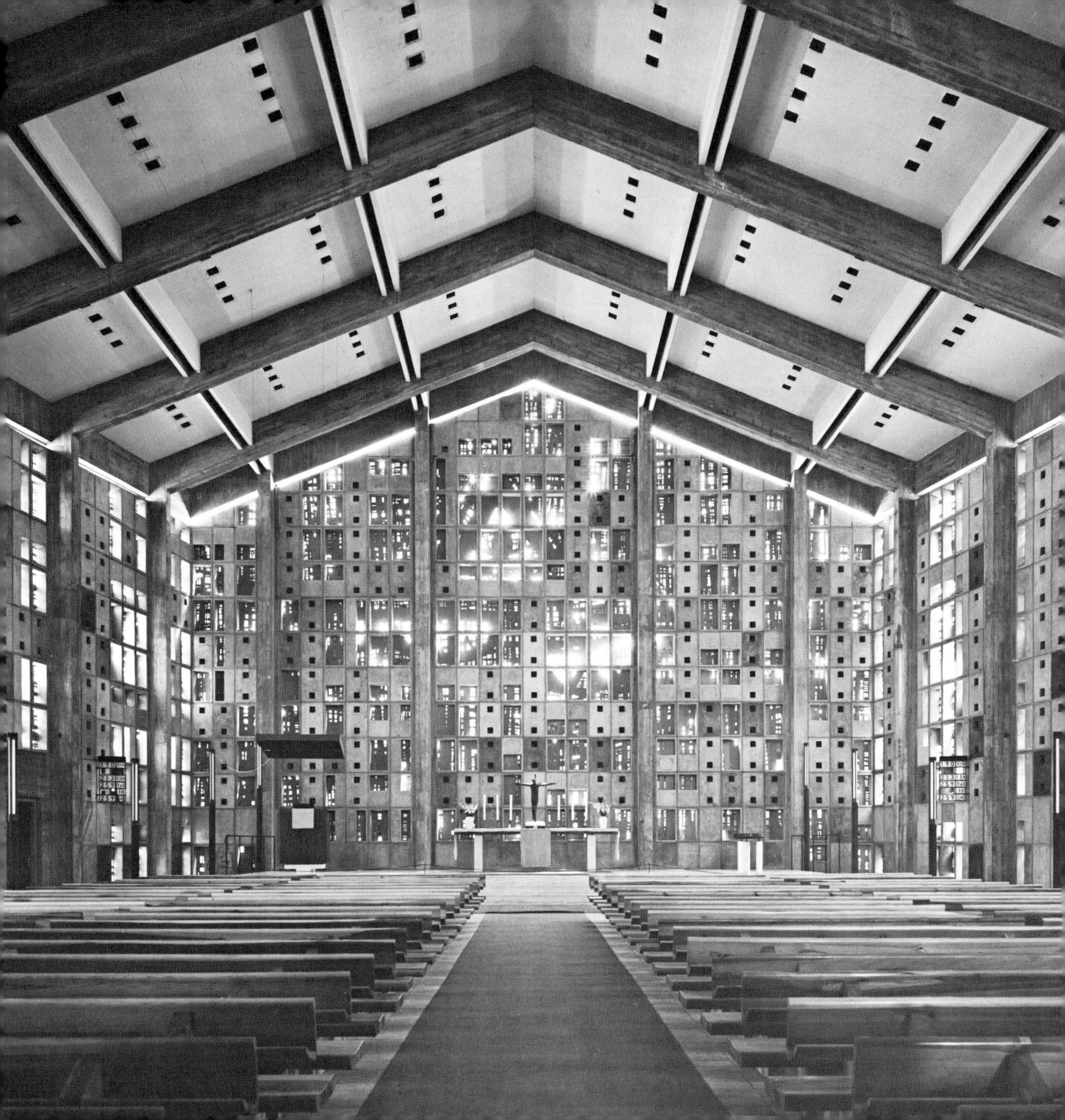

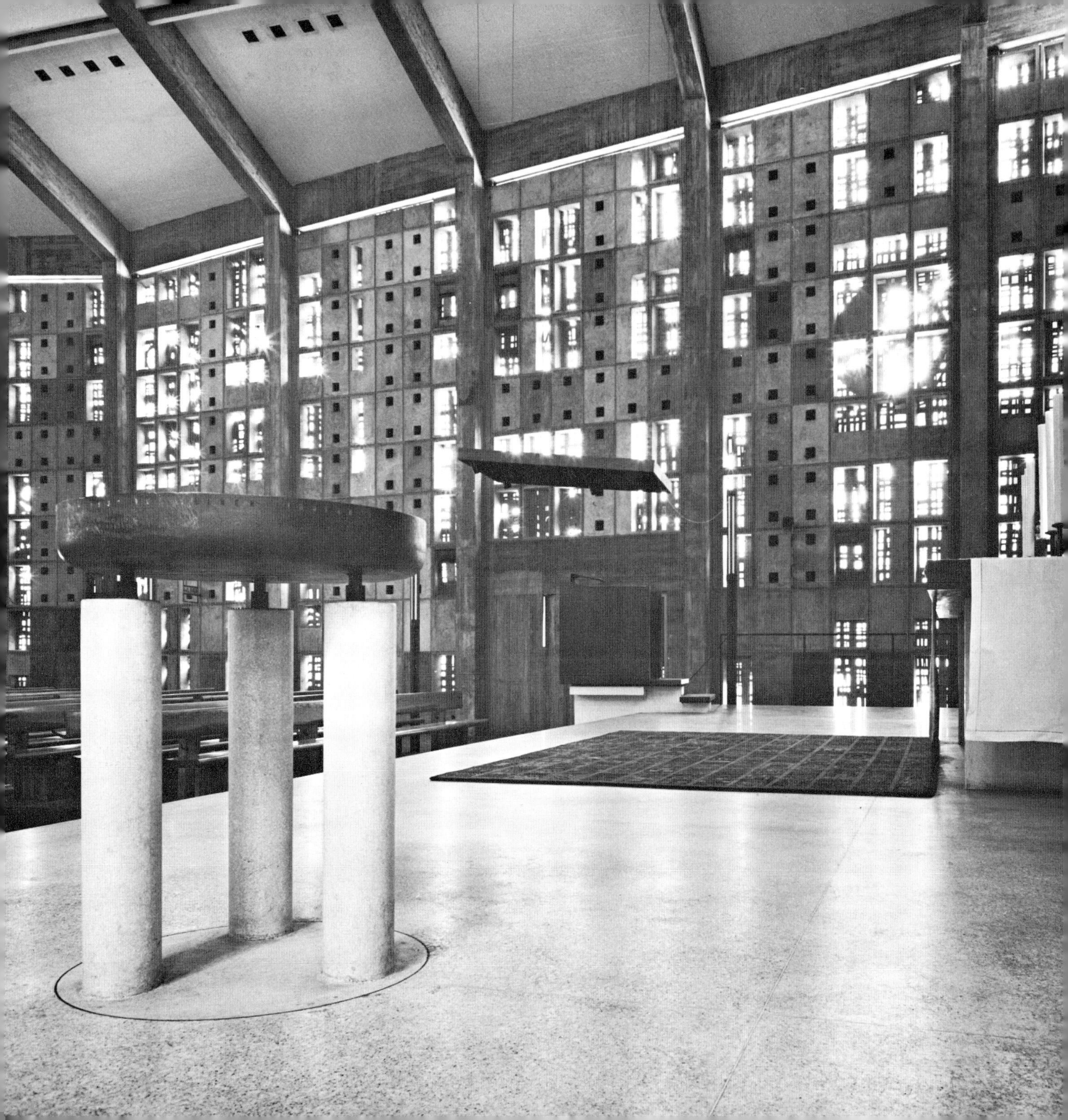

Organ by G. F. Steinmeyer of Oettingen/Bayern

Hauptwerk		Schwellwerk	
Quintade	16	Nachthorngedackt	16
Prinzipal	8	Flötprinzipal	8
Spillflöte	8	Rohrflöte	8
Grobgedackt	8	Weidenpfeife	8
Oktave	4	Weitprinzipal	4
Rohrflöte	4	Spitzgambe	4
Oktave	2	Schwiegel	2
Quinte	2⅔	Blockflöte	1
Grossmixtur 5–6 r.	2	Nasat	1⅓
Terzzimbel 3 ranks	⅘	Kornett 3–5 ranks	4
Fagott	16	Plein jeu 4 ranks	1⅓
Trompete	8	Sordun	16
Clarine	4	Echotrompete	8
		Schalmei	4

Positiv		Pedal	
Liebl. Gedeckt	8	Prinzipalbass	16
Soloquintade	8	Subbass	16
Singend Praestant	4	Gedacktpommer	16
Koppelflöte	4	Oktavbass	8
Kleinprinzipal	2	Gedackflöte	8
Sifflöte	1	Dolkan	4
Sesquialtera 2 ranks	2⅔ + 1⅗	Bauernpfeife	2
Scharfmixtur 4–5 r.	⅔	Rauschpfeife 2 ranks	5⅓ + 4
Rankett	16	Hintersatz 4 ranks	2⅔
Krummhorn	8	Bombarde	32
		Posaune	16
		Trompete	8
		Clairon	4

The photo was taken while the organ was in the process of construction.

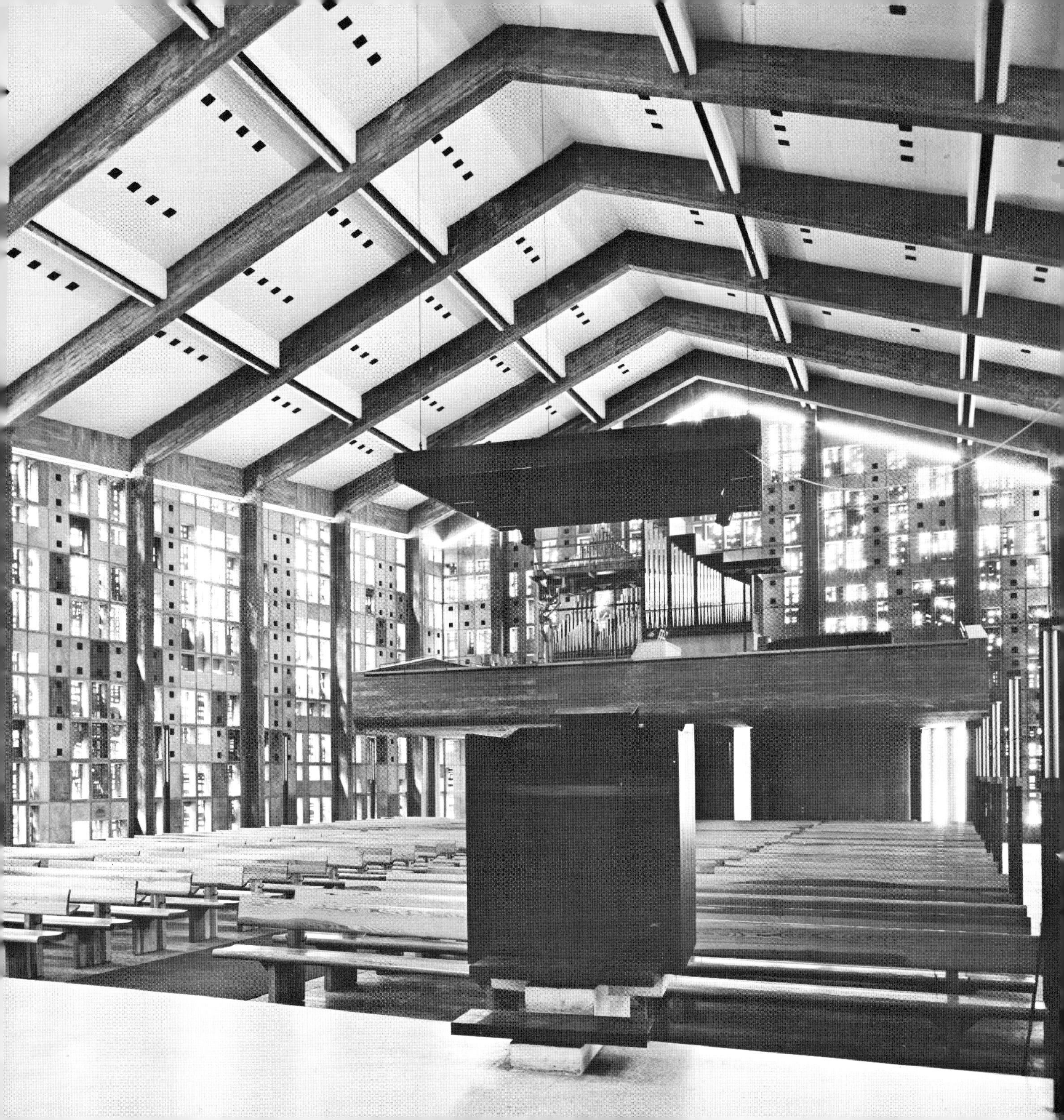

Perhaps the finest example of a lightsome religious building is Beth Sholom Synagogue, Elkins Park, Pennsylvania, by Frank Lloyd Wright. A tripod of steel and aluminum rises to an apex one hundred feet above the floor, carrying a double wall of translucent panels—white corrugated wired glass outside and cream-white corrugated plastic inside. The sky makes the interior alive and glowing. Dark skies catch the somber mood. The bright sky vault is reflected in a thousand exterior ripples. The building is indeed lightsome.

Beth Sholom Synagogue, Elkins Park, Pennsylvania
Frank Lloyd Wright, architect, and Rabbi Mortimer J. Cohen

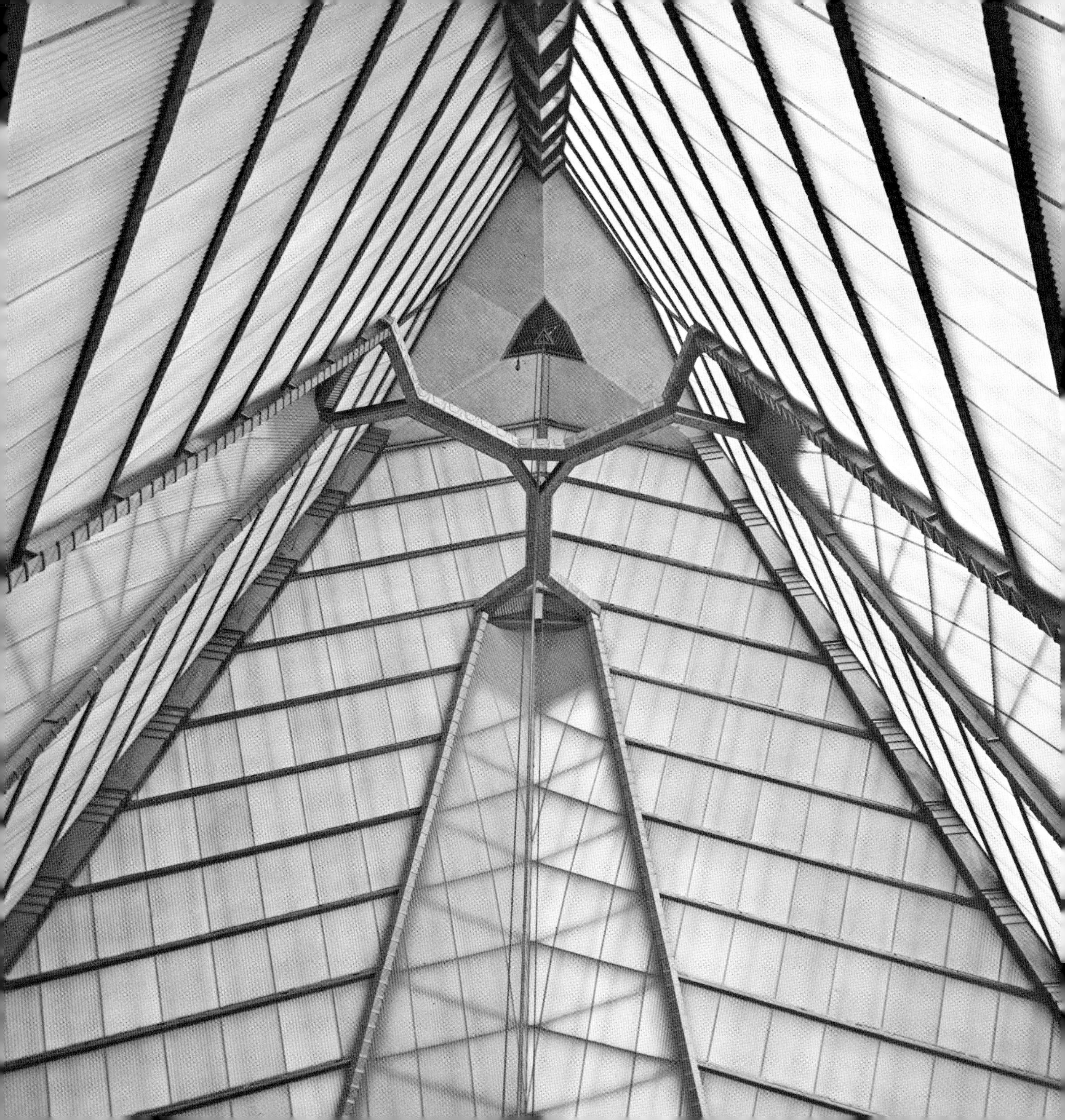

Beth Sholom is in no sense an arbitrary building, but is governed by the faith of its congregation. Its form speaks of Mt. Sinai, where God gave Israel the Torah. Its use of light addresses itself to this same revealing act of God. At night, when the synagogue glows from within, it is an eloquent reminder of Sinai, where God revealed himself amidst lightning and fire. During the day, the exterior glitters with light, while the lightsome interior reminds one of Psalm 89:16, "They shall walk, O Lord, in the light of thy countenance."

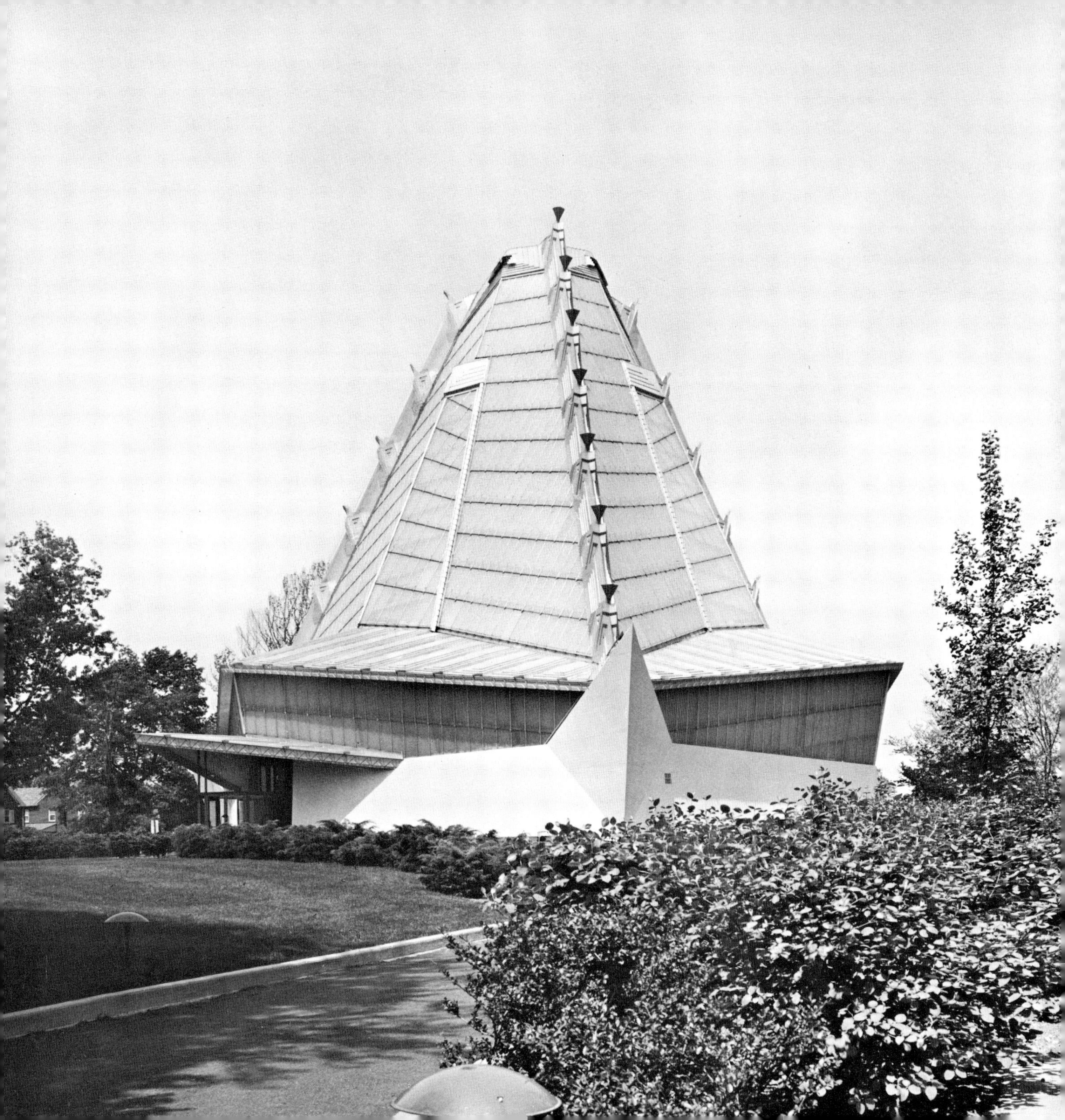

The affinities between Judaism and Christianity are apparent in the theological precision of this sanctuary. The Congregation of Israel has been gathered together by God, who reveals himself by his Word. The shape of the monolithic block behind the pulpit suggests the tables of the Law, while imbedded in it is the Ark, containing the Torah. The doors of the Ark are never completely shut, and from the interior streams forth light, reminding one that the light of the Torah should stream out into the world. Because it is in the Torah that God reveals himself to man, pulpit and Ark stand in the midst of gathered Israel.

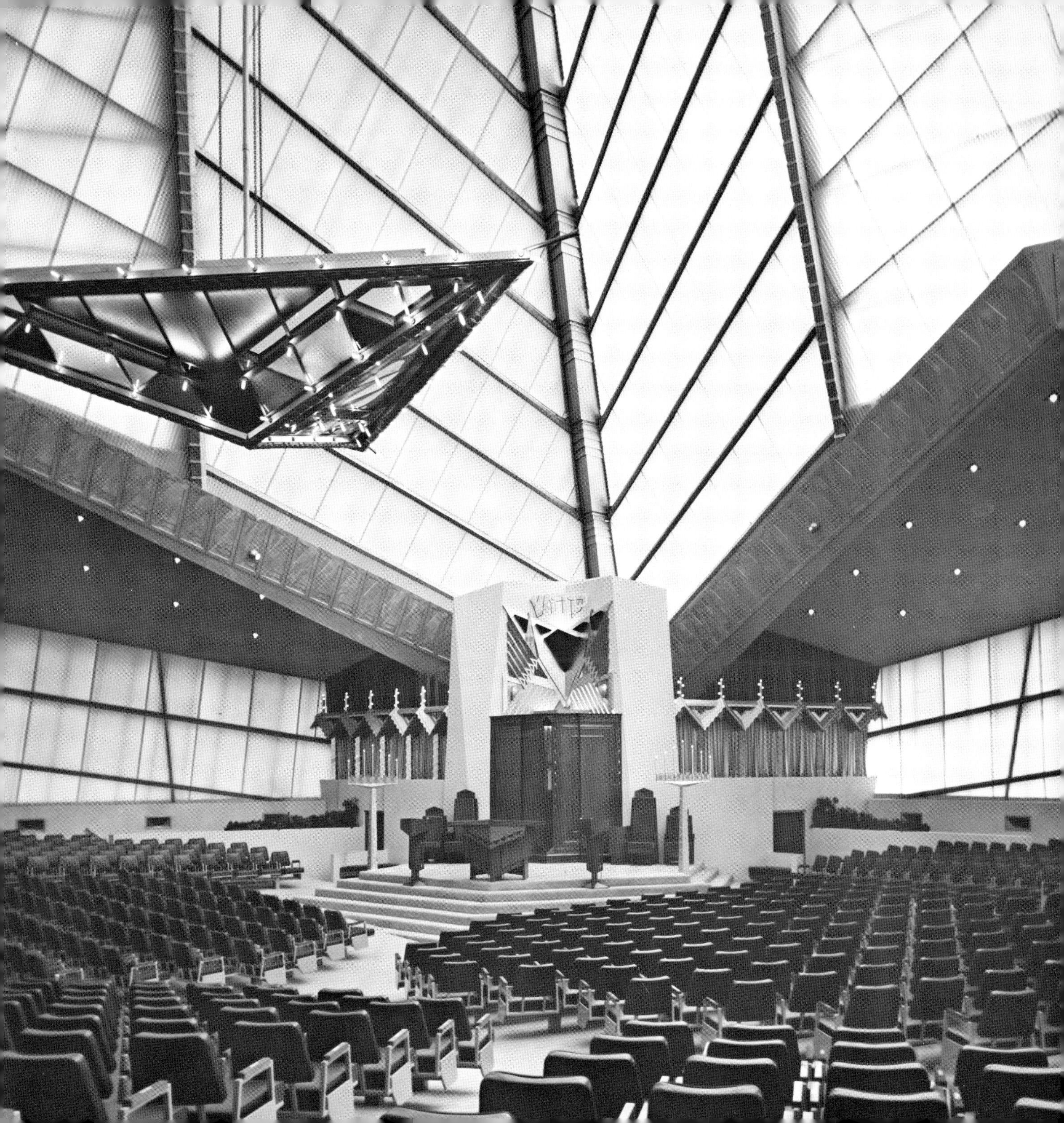

Even as the large ornament above the Ark reminds us of the splendor of God in coming to man, as in Isaiah's vision, so too the Torah declares God's holiness, and insists, " 'You shall be holy; for I the Lord your God am holy' " (Leviticus 19:2).

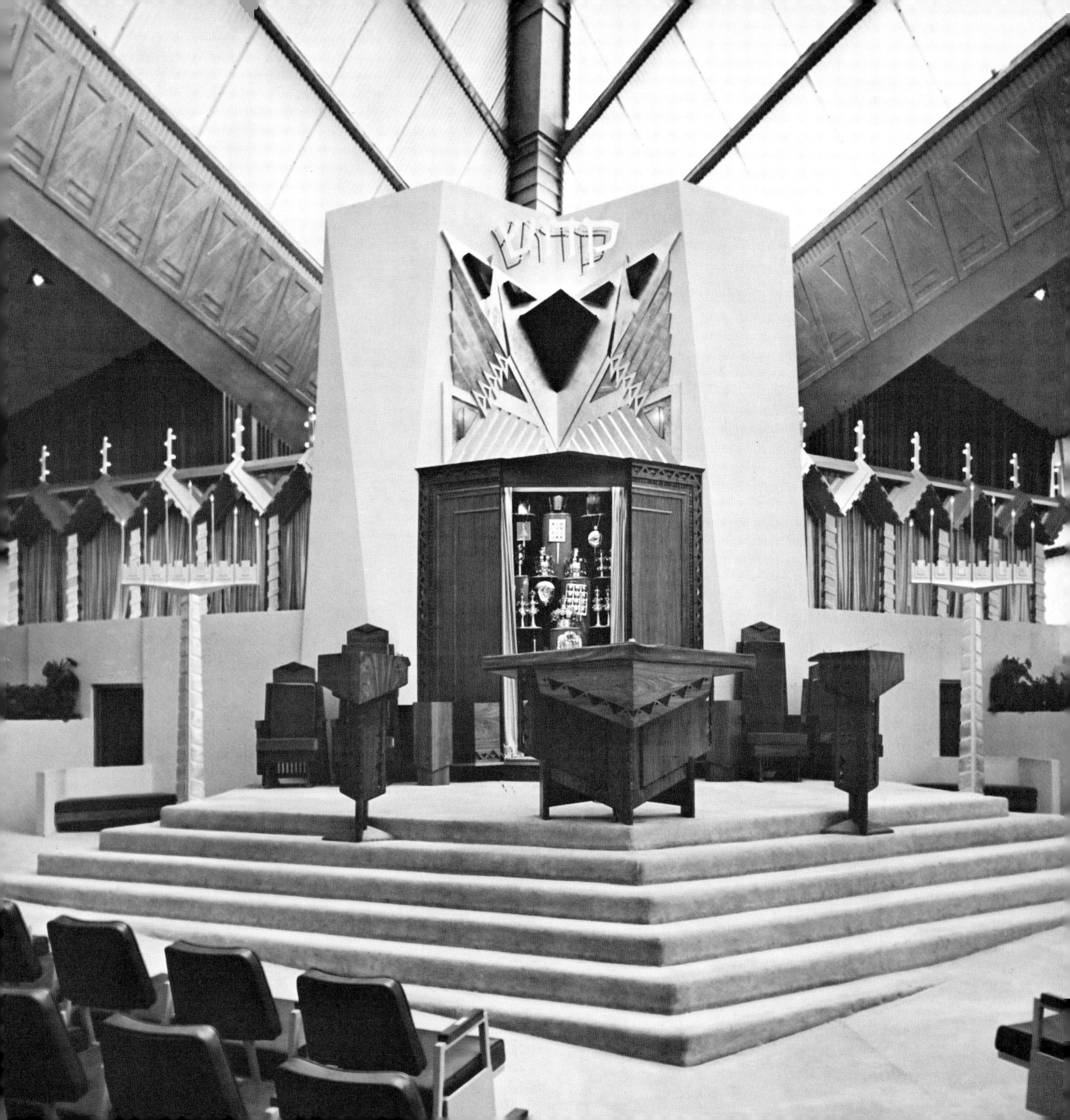

Another striking use of light is found in The Church of the Advent (Adventskerk), Aerdenhout, the Netherlands. The sanctuary is lighted by windows with fixed panes of plain and colored glass. The barrel vaults of the high roof permit the light to penetrate the sanctuary deeply, creating a lightsome space. Significantly, this lightsome space contains the baptismal font which is placed among the people. At the front of the church is the communion table. The low ceiling over the communion table suggests the upper room, and even more significantly it is without windows. The space is a darksome space. Both spaces tend to put the worshipper in the frame of mind conducive to the celebration of each sacrament in the desired atmosphere. Light, or the absence of light, creates the architecture.

The Church of the Advent (Adventskerk), Hervormd, Aerdenhout, The Netherlands. K. L. Sijmons Dzn, architect

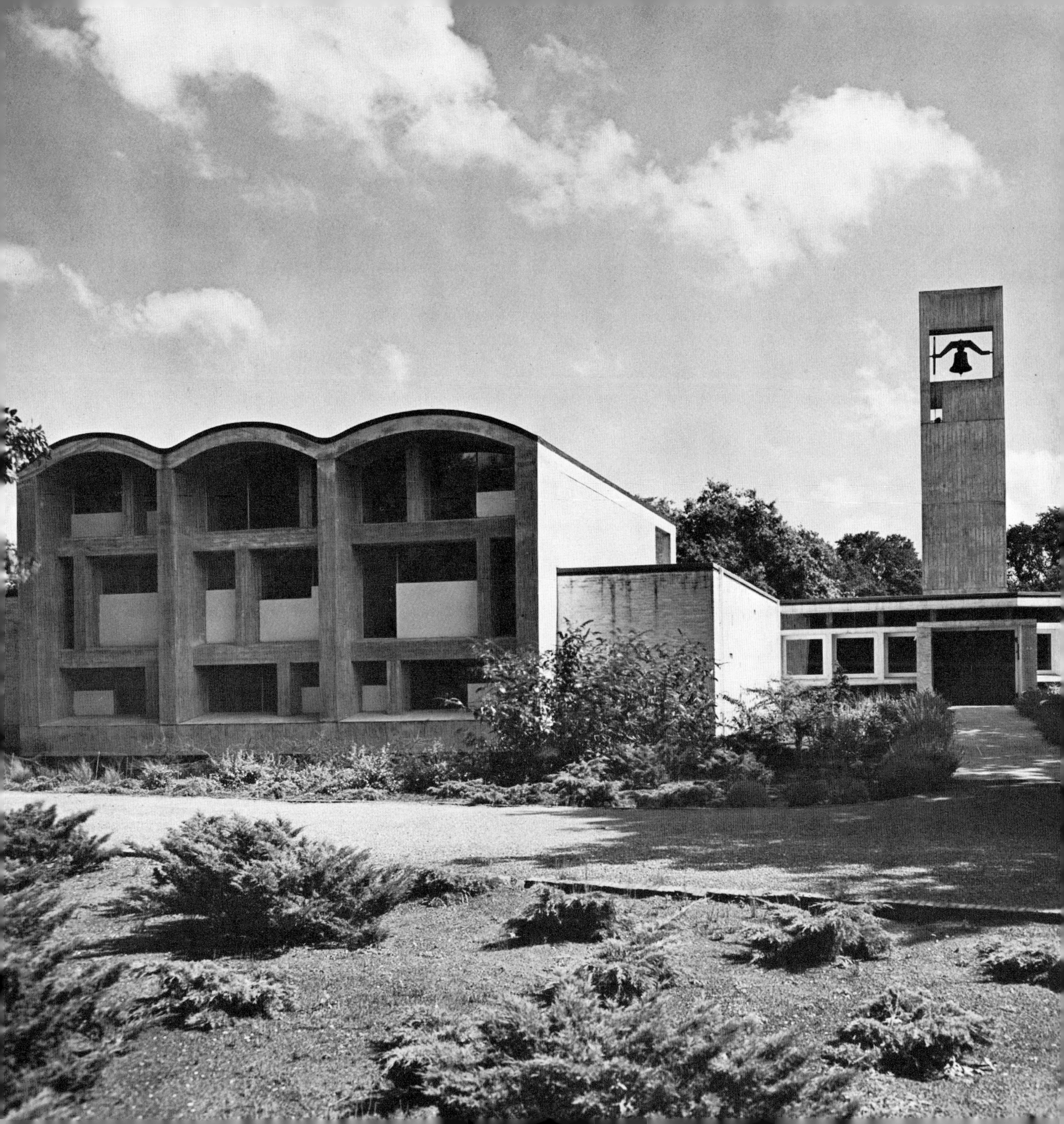

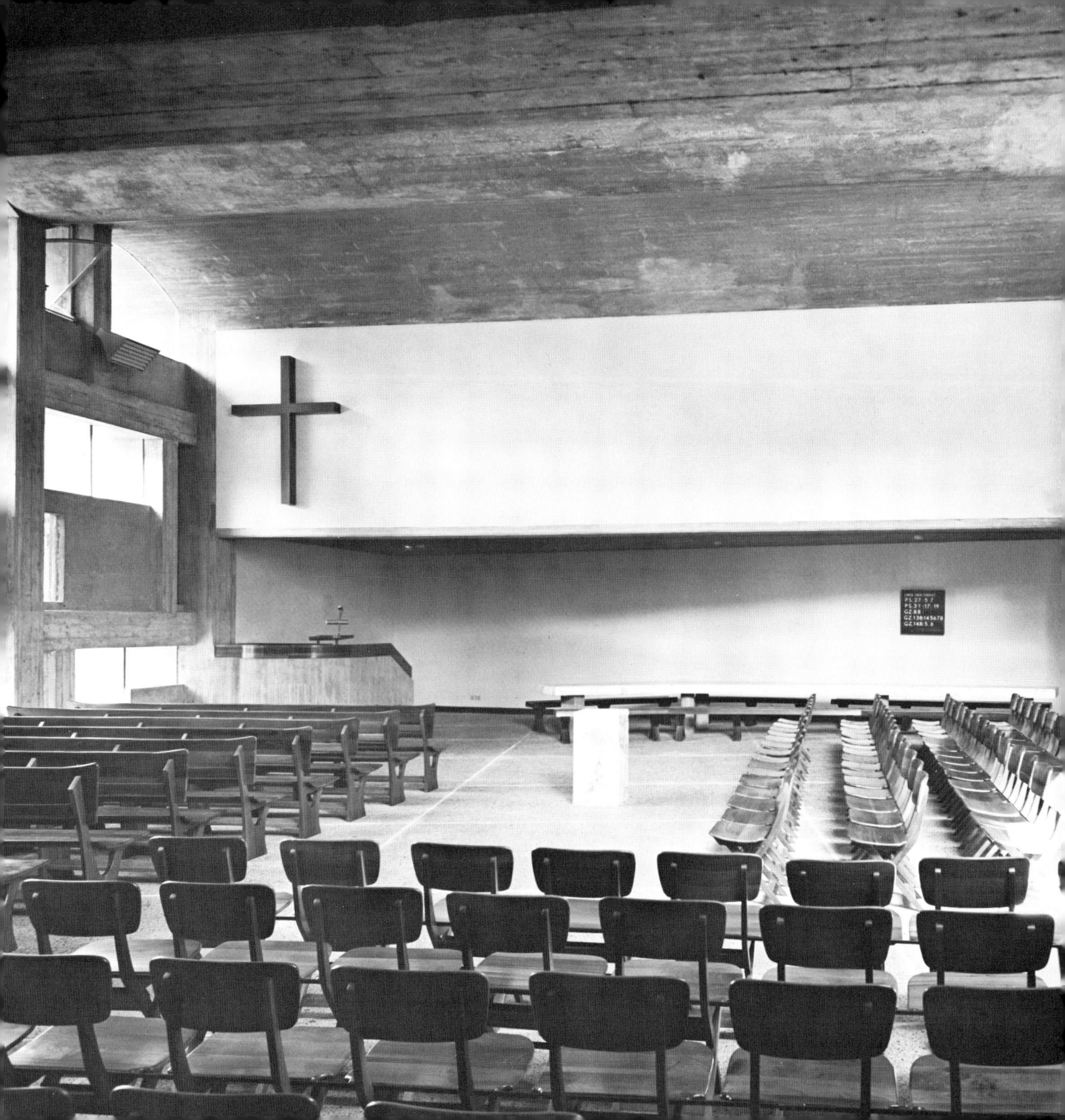

The rich oiled wood of the benches, the luxurious marble of the table, the shining silver of the communion vessels, and the whole illumined by the window panels of rich primary colors, constitute a use of material things that enables this Church of the Advent to say something of the glory of the Second Advent of our Lord to which the Supper bears witness: "For as often as you eat this bread and drink the cup, you proclaim the Lord's death until he comes" (I Corinthians 11:26).

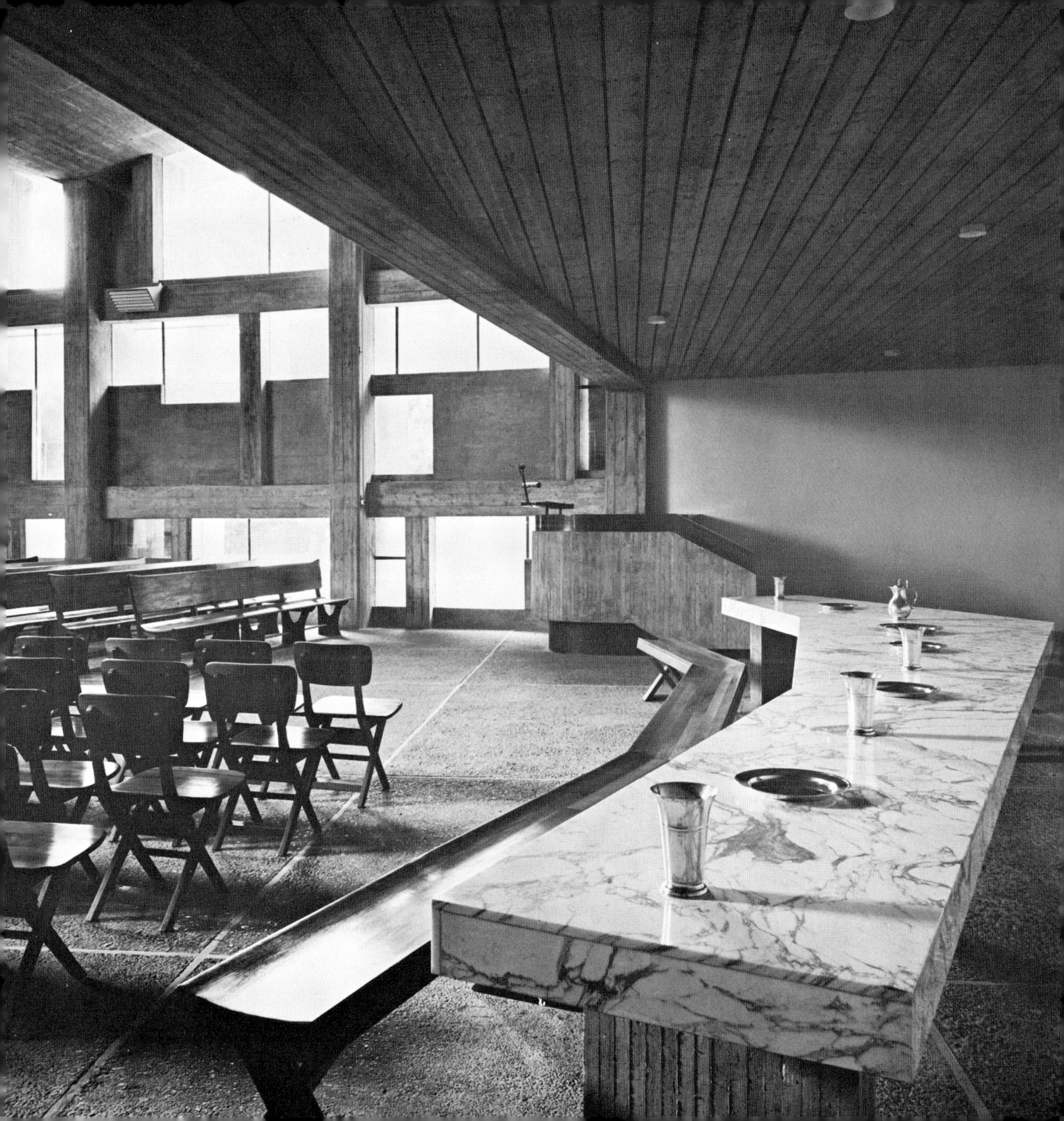

The Book of Genesis speaks of the world as being without form and void. Form and void are two words in the architect's vocabulary that have a great deal to do with the comprehension of space. The form or exterior of the space has received a great deal of consideration, but just as important is the void or the interior of the space. Neither the form nor the void, however, have any meaning without light. God in his sovereignty over all things said: " 'Let there be light'; and there was light." If the form of the church is to be fully utilized then God's light must also be used to its fullest advantage. Although the Church through the ages has used light to heighten the effect of its architecture, modern technology opens a bewildering array of new possibilities for its use. The use of light can do much to remind the worshipper of the creative power and sovereignty of God, but the use of the fall of light is also to bring into focus God's means of grace: Word and Sacraments.

> The heavens declare Thy glory, Lord;
> In every star Thy wisdom shines;
> But when our eyes behold Thy Word,
> We read Thy name in fairer lines.
>
> Isaac Watts

Rhythm

Because the architect uses an orderly structure or frame, his buildings begin to have a rhythm or sequence. When he adds to this the rhythm of bands of windows, he accentuates this pattern. When he standardizes the windows and other components, it can be understood why one of the expressions of our time and age is rhythm or sequence. It is an expression of our technology, our ability to fabricate, our methods of building with the assembly line. The new craftsman is the man in the shop who is producing windows, doors, panels, and mechanical equipment on a production line; he is the one who encourages economy through repetition and sequence. Parts are no longer repaired, they are replaced. Already some windows and frames are replaced rather than repaired. Many electric motors for pumps of various sorts run continuously until replaced. In the field of equipment nearly all parts are replaced rather than repaired. Certainly in the automotive field this is the most common practice. Our economy is closely related to the production in the shop and our ability to mass-produce an item at very low cost. The repetitive unit will be a symbol of our age as it is a logical outcome of our economy.

Thus, the buildings of our time and age should be logical. They start with an orderly frame or structure. Using the materials of our age, they should honestly express the inner character of the building. The logical use of our building materials and techniques should result in simplicity, clarity, and order. There is a consistency, a finesse, a precision, a reasonableness in our structures that comes from a logical approach to the problem of building.

Elegance

Elegance is a result and not a principle of architecture. It is a result of selecting and choosing. It is a result of discernment, taste, and character. To many people, the common and ordinary are good enough, and to think of elegance is to be aligned with the snob, the "better than thou" fellow—at least this is sometimes associated with elegance. Real elegance is something altogether different; it stems from an inner character, an inner refinement that can be aspired to. Indicating a concern for others and a desire to do something fine, above the ordinary, elegance is the mark of a tasteful, refined, and handsome building. It would be a comely thing if the church building could express elegance. The road to elegance is paved with honesty, clarity, simplicity and order.

CHURCH EXPRESSION PRINCIPLES

CONTEMPORARY CONSIDERATIONS
the architecture must be of our age; it must speak through our technology
expect to see more: expect to see less:

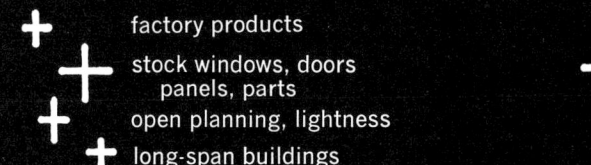

✛   factory products   —   handcraft products
✛   stock windows, doors   —   custom-made mouldings,
     panels, parts   carving, ornament
✛   open planning, lightness   —   closed planning, heaviness
✛   long-span buildings   —   use of short spans

INTEGRITY CONSIDERATIONS
the architecture must be honest for a church reformed according to the Word
expect to see: avoid distractions:

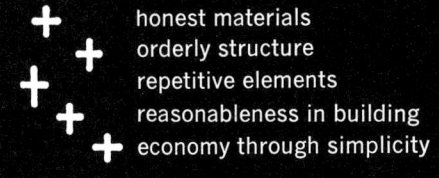

✛   honest materials   —   novelty, variety
✛   orderly structure   —   fake, imitation
✛   repetitive elements   —   gimmicks, bric-a-brack
✛   reasonableness in building   —   the bizarre, the jazzy
✛   economy through simplicity   —   the sensational, the clever

THEOLOGICAL CONSIDERATIONS
the architecture is for the people of God, to aid in the worship of God
try to express: avoid suggesting:

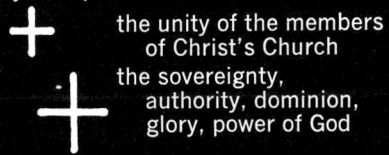

✛   the unity of the members   —   the separation of minister and
     of Christ's Church   layman
✛   the sovereignty,   —   that God is weak, feminine,
     authority, dominion,   old, paternal, permissive,
     glory, power of God   absent

LITURGICAL CONSIDERATIONS
the architecture must show the worshipping together of a corporate body,
worshipping requires space for

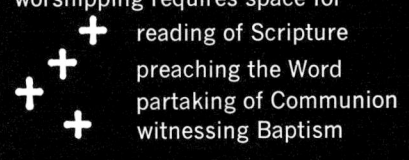

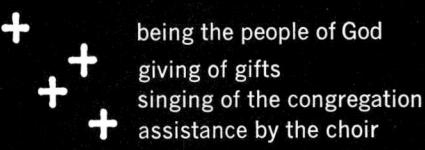

✛   reading of Scripture   ✛   being the people of God
✛   preaching the Word   ✛   giving of gifts
✛   partaking of Communion   ✛   singing of the congregation
✛   witnessing Baptism   ✛   assistance by the choir

DISCIPLINE CONSIDERATIONS
the architecture must show concern for man
it should express:

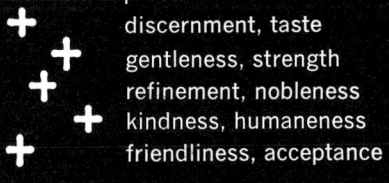

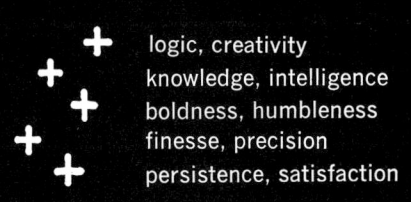

✛   discernment, taste   ✛   logic, creativity
✛   gentleness, strength   ✛   knowledge, intelligence
✛   refinement, nobleness   ✛   boldness, humbleness
✛   kindness, humaneness   ✛   finesse, precision
✛   friendliness, acceptance   ✛   persistence, satisfaction

II

The Structure of the Church Building

  The shape and space of a building is determined by the structure. Structure consists of the structural supports or the distribution of forces within a building, room, tree, plant, or even molecule. If an axiom were to be established, it would be STRUCTURE DETERMINES SPACE. Whether the structure is a canopy of rock that encloses a cave, a masonry-walled building that encloses a room, or a Gothic cathedral where the structural forces are frozen into stone, all these structures determine space. Another element, transparency, can extend that space in reference to the structure. Rooms disappear and space begins to flow. Walls disappear and space is extended. The perimeter wall of the building disappears and the space is extended into the landscape. Raise this building and the space flows on to infinity—but always in relation to a point of reference, the structure. Raise the building and the space seems endless like the edge of a cliff or the rim of the Grand Canyon.

Space has to be experienced to be understood; the accompanying diagram on Space Selection Principles can only give you an idea of what to look for.

Perhaps the "glass box" has done more for our understanding of space than any other structure. The glass box is not significant for the glass but for the space it envelops. It is not significant for its flexibility in allowing drapes to be closed or opened but for its ability to control time and space, its ability to reach for the sun and heat, its ability to close off the dark and the cold. The glass box is not significant as a box but as one or two planes suspended in space extending the view as far as the eye can see. In the glass box the forces of structure have been made into visible action.

SPACE SELECTION PRINCIPLES

VISUAL CONSIDERATIONS
space is defined by light and color on an object
objects recede without background contrast

objects advance with contrast

SENSORY CONSIDERATIONS
space is appraised by the perception of the individual
provide space sequence — near and far

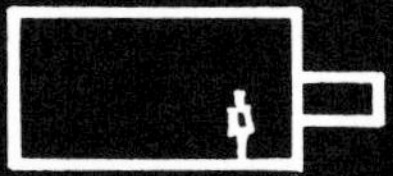

space contrast — wide and narrow

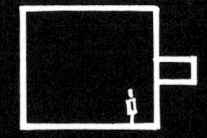

MENTAL CONSIDERATIONS
space is conditioned by the mind and experience
create infinity by endless space,
mirrors, illusion, perspective

create awe by height, contrast
of high and low, near and far

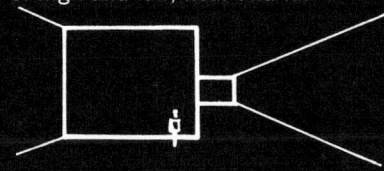

BODILY CONSIDERATIONS
space is related to the human being in action
provide volume by motion analysis

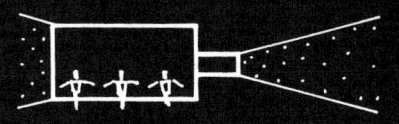

circulation by space pattern analysis

VOLUME CONSIDERATIONS
space is governed by enclosure and transparency
the closed plan, contained and unit space

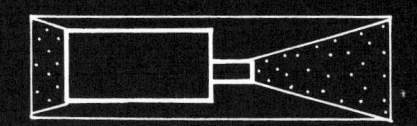

open plan, continuity, implied space

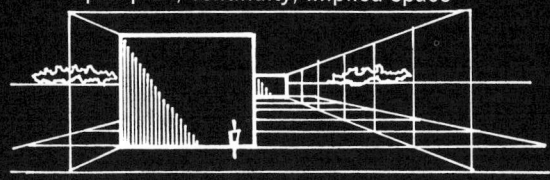

In each time and age certain structural principles determine the space. Among the Greeks the stone post and lintel determined the space. For the Romans, the masonry arch, vault, and dome determined the space. In the Gothic age the ribbed vaulting determined the space. In our own age steel and reinforced-concrete structures are determining the space. In each age the character of the building is expressed through different but valid structural principles. The structure, like the bones of the body, has functional integrity. To conceive of a body with misplaced bones is to conceive of a freak or a monster. Buildings that violate structural principles, that lack structural integrity, are often either freakish or monstrous.

Our own problems of structure stem from having an abundance of systems to choose from, the old as well as the new. The old structural systems have a history of use behind them that readily enables the architect to build correctly with them. The new structural systems have no heritage of use that can be reviewed to help determine proper usage. Trial and error and careful consideration of the structural system appropriate for the use must determine the structure.

In the stone cathedrals the piers, arches, and vaults were thinned until the maximum span and height for a particular set of conditions was reached. The architect took advantage of compression, with stone on stone distributing the loads of the building into the earth. In the bearing-wall building of today is seen a similar but continuous distribution of loads, with brick on brick or block on block. Our church buildings began by using bearing walls with punched openings and were improved with the substitution of piers that permitted greater openings. But even greater openings were made possible when the skeleton and skin each began to perform their individual functions. The skeleton received and distributed the loads to the earth while the skin or wall protected and kept out the weather. With this clear distribution of functions, the skeleton was born, and a whole new group of structural systems became available to the architect. Post and beam, column and girder, rigid frames, arch frames, truss frames, and space frames are all expressions of the skeletal system. But the bearing wall and vault had not been forgotten. It was discovered that when a piece of paper was bent in the form of a vault it immediately became stronger and could support a greater load. Why not take one new material, reinforced concrete, and bend it into the vault shape? In fact, why stop at this point? Why not take that piece of paper and see what other folds or bends would increase its strength? With this investigation was born another group of structural systems. Thin shells, folded planes, warped planes, undulating hyperbolic paraboloids, and a host of other planar systems gave expression to these structural principles.

A new element had entered these structures—tension. By adding steel to stone or steel to concrete (manufactured stone) the best qualities of each material are combined, the steel for tension and the stone for compression. Stone had been used mostly in compression. Could a structure be built using a majority of tension members? Ropes, cables and wires indicate that such is the case. The possibility of working with tension members, alone or combined with other materials, has arrived so recently that the principle of building with tension members has had very little application to church buildings. Great bridges have been built that give us some idea of the potential of structures that have a majority of tension members. Just as surely, great churches will be built that will also realize the potential of tension structures. The tension structure is one of the great contributions of our day and our architecture will mirror it. It will mirror our day because of the economy of building with tension structures. The tent shape is an appropriate one for the church building, and it can be a fine tension structure. The bubble shape is also an appropriate one for the church building, which can be achieved with the air structure, another fine tension structure. Shell shapes are also fine tension structures which are appropriate for the church.

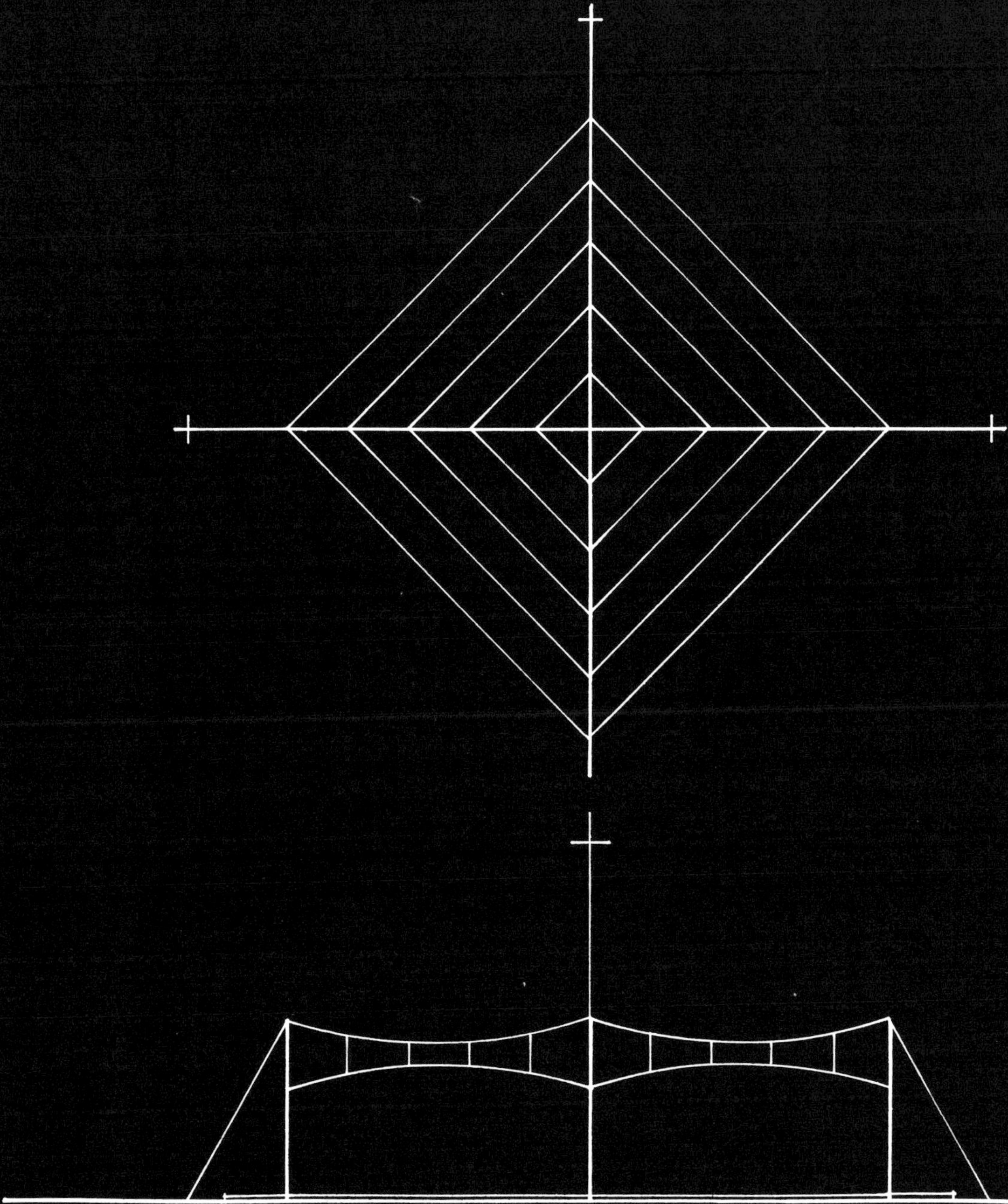

When building a church the immediate concern is with structure. How wide must the church be, how high must it rise to enclose a given area or volume? Because the church building is a unit space for the act of worship, it is also an ideal one for the expression of structure. The clarity of the structure of the great cathedrals of Europe is apparent. The clarity of the timber structures of the early meetinghouses in this country is evident. Structures since that time have become progressively more amorphous. With so many structural materials available, our church structures have become complicated—they mirror the complication of our times. The church has been disorderly and wasteful long enough; now is the time to simplify our church buildings. The orderliness of our structural system is reflected in the cost of our church buildings. It is the skeleton or structure of the building that should organize the location of walls, windows, partitions, and of course bearing walls and columns. To create a jumbled structural system just because it can be done is not good planning or good architecture. Good planning permeates all phases of building from beginning to end. It begins with an organized structure. Good planning demands cubic thinking, the kind of thinking that is required in a simultaneous equation. Each portion has to be correctly solved in relation to the whole before an answer is forthcoming. Anyone can enclose space by adding enough rooms, sheds, shanties, lean-tos, and pieces of building, but to organize it with a structural system is a different matter. A wide range of structural systems must be investigated to select the correct one. With the structural system costing one fourth or more of the building, this selection is an important one.

Structural material might be the first consideration. Available are wood, metal, and masonry, which can be reinforced with tension or compression material to create many structural members or forms. Basically any one of these materials can be used to produce bearing walls, arches, and vaults by placing one block on another, but the economy of such structures would be in question. So the thin shells, folded planes, warped planes, and undulating planes are used. Or the skeletal systems can be investigated. Closely spaced vertical and horizontal members provide a joist system in each material. Increasing the span between members creates beams and columns in each material. If the span is increased beyond this, trusses and frames are the expression in each material. Many of these structural materials are prefabricated and available for church building. Witness the use of just one masonry material, reinforced concrete. It is preformed in beams, channels, slabs, columns, and wall panels. Reinforced-concrete units of eight hundred square feet are being trucked to the site. The church member must be prepared to use these structural materials.

The Church of St. Peter (Petruskirche), Leverkusen-Burig, Germany
Hentrich & Petschnigg, architects

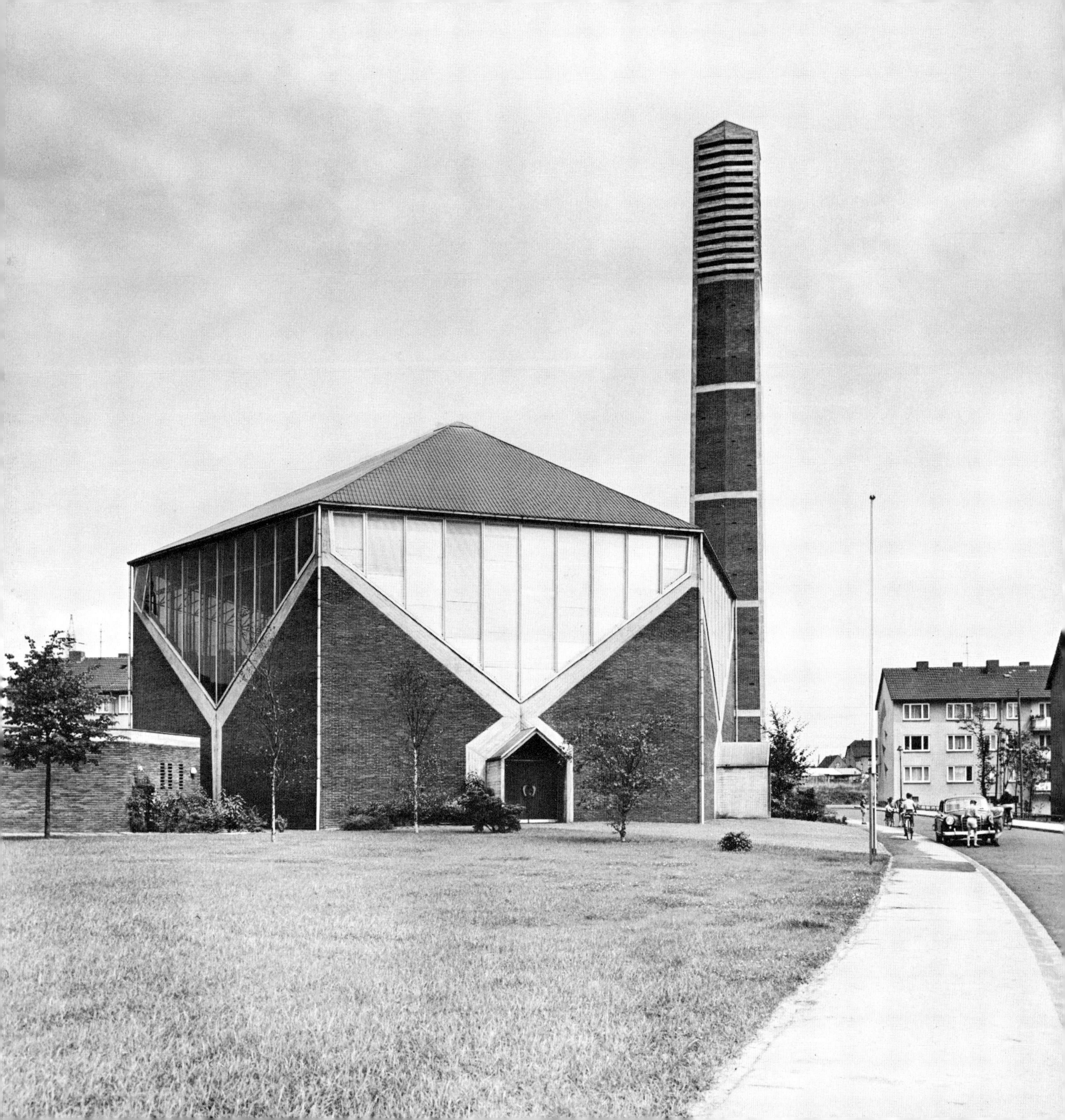

The supporting concrete frame is honestly used, and is as apparent as the fish doorhandles which remind one that this is the house of Jesus Christ, God's Son, Savior.

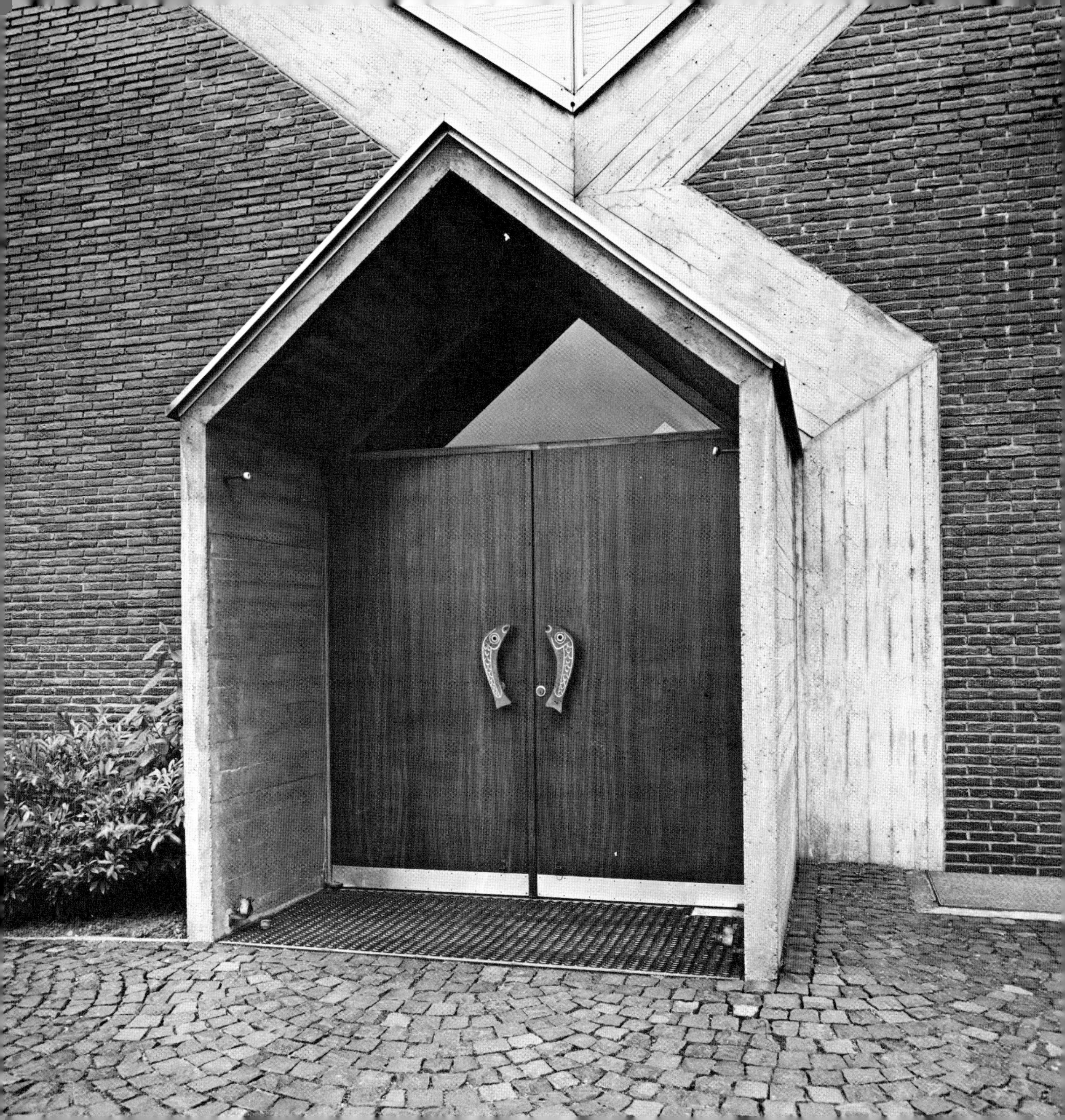

The tetrahedron space frame provides a large space without columns, enabling the congregation to be gathered together around the liturgical center. The lightness and openness of the system suggests the possibility of using it as a wall or roof that might be clad with various glazing materials. It is a lightsome framing material.

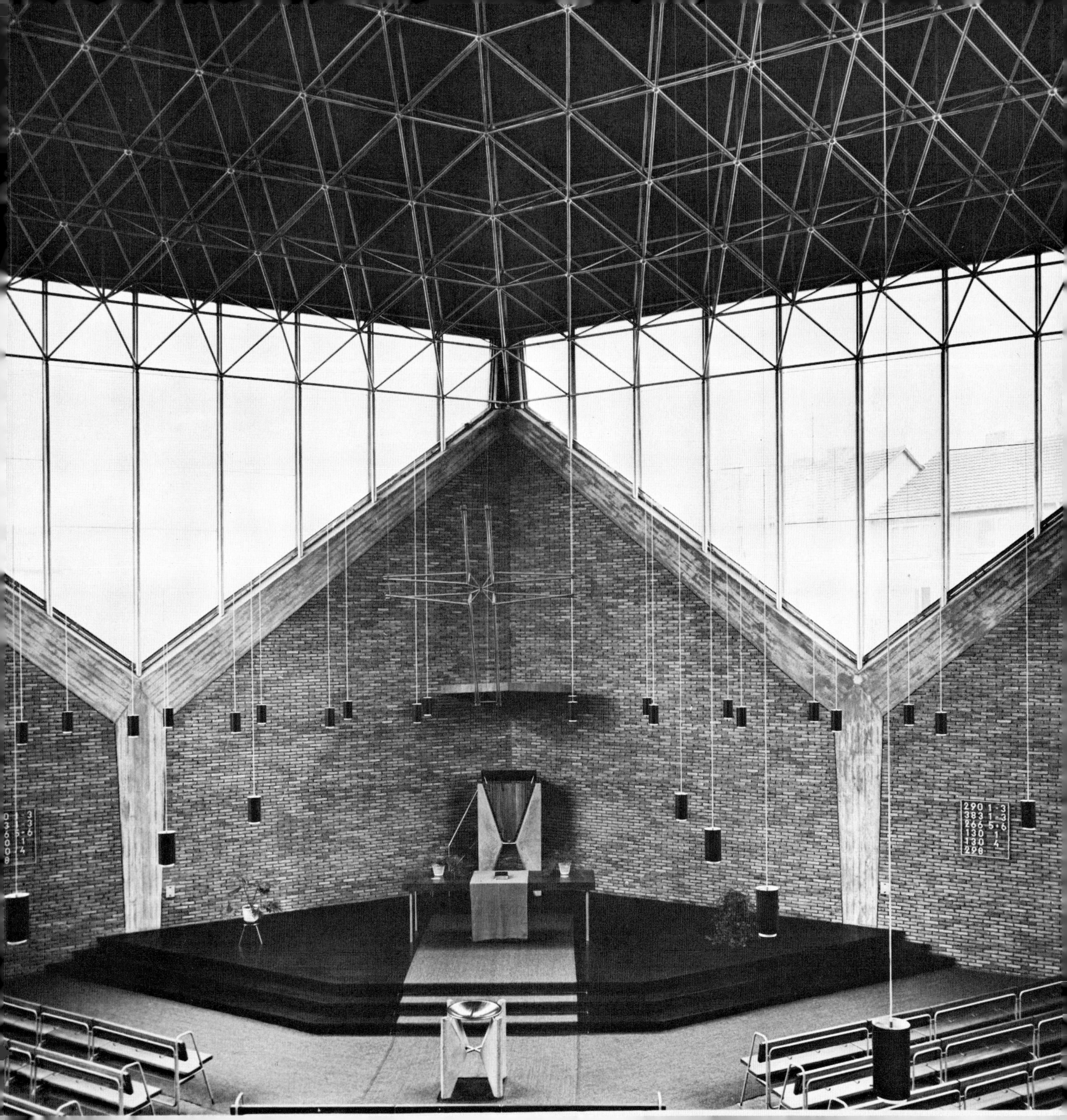
290 1-3
383 1-3
266 5-6
130 1
130 4
298

Positiv (temporary) by Willi Peter of Cologne-Mülheim

Gedackt	*8*
Rohrflöte	*4*
Prinzipal	*2*

The new organ of 22 ranks will be built by the firm of Willi Peter

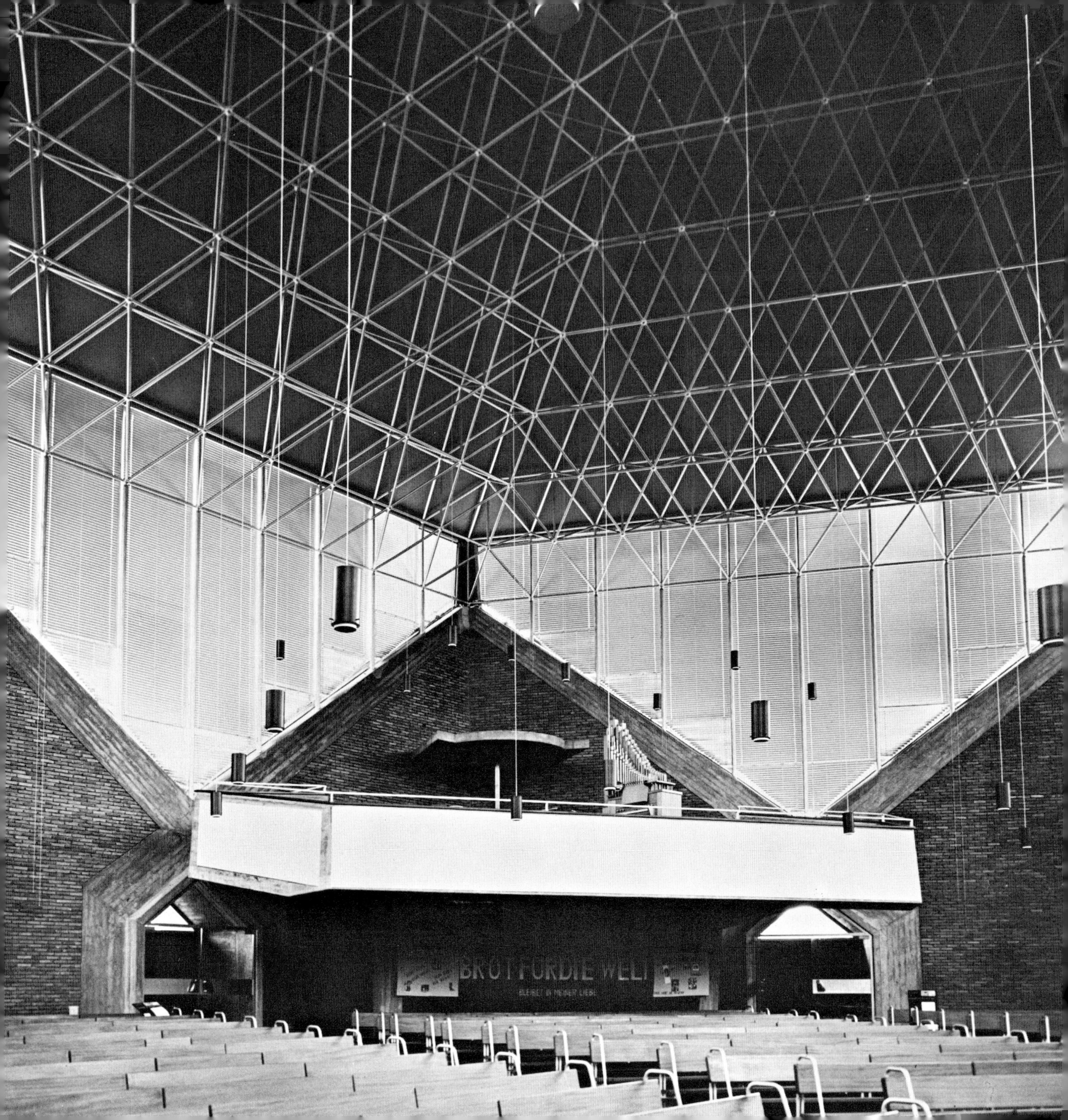
BROT FUR DIE WELT

Note how the expression of the framing system is carried out in the pulpit furniture, pews, cross, and lighting system. Honest use is made of brick for the exterior and interior walls as an infill material.

290	1-3
383	1-3
266	5-6
130	1
130	4
298	

The liturgical center—reformed according to the Word

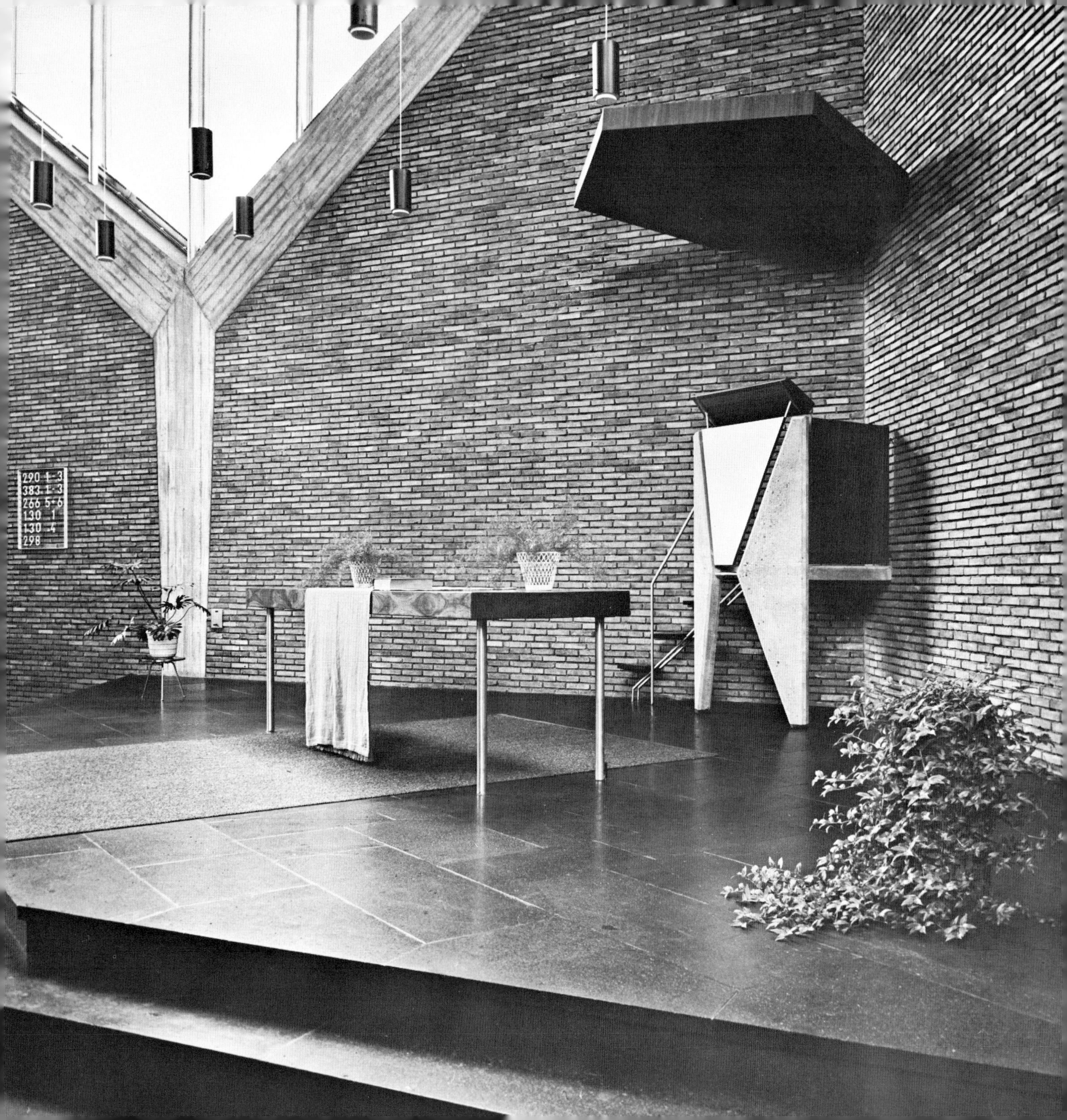
290 1-3
383 1-3
266 5+6
130 1
130 4
298

12

The Shape of the Church Building

The shape of the church building is exclusively the preserve and the responsibility of the architect, but so much advice is given by the parishioner in this area that it would be helpful to the architect if the advisor was well-informed. To ask for an economical building but insist on a cathedral-type building in the same breath forces the architect to give either the economical building, a more expensive cathedral-type building, or a combination of both. All of the resulting buildings may be poor architecture, with the cathedral-type building the poorest architecture of them all because it dictates an end result rather than the development of a building.

Several considerations should be well thought out by the parishioner. The primary consideration is the structure. The building must have a logical structure. The structure must be clarified first in order to think of shape. The structure can only be clarified in relation to the space and how it is used, but once this is determined the structural system should be rigidly adhered to with no deviations permitted. When this procedure is followed by the architect and the planning of the spaces studied and restudied to work with the requirements and structure of the building, fine architecture can result. The architecture will "belong," it will look effortless, but the time spent to organize such an effortless building by the architect will be astounding. The resulting architecture will be creative in the sense that it will be truly a work of art, an outgrowth of needs, structure and economy. It will express its structure and its requirements. The shape will manifest itself. It will arrive rather than being contrived.

It would be well if the parishioner understood something of space and structure and the resulting shape created by these spaces and structures. Actually, space can be enclosed in many different forms, each with its own advantages. Some are easier to build, others are more economical to build, and still others are easier to enlarge. In addition to these advantages, some lend themselves better than others to express a church reformed according to the Word.

The box, prism, and cylinder all put emphasis on an axis. The cube and pyramid can be used in this manner if the axis runs from one corner to the opposite corner. The sphere creates a center focus. The accompanying sketch shows the decided effect the selection of the basic solid has upon the shape of the building. These are just the very basic solids; many other forms can be achieved by variation of the roof-spanning members, or combinations of solids. If a comparative study is made of the church-building shapes using solids with equal floor areas of 3,000 square feet, some very interesting statistics are revealed.

	VOLUME in cubic feet	PERIMETER in lineal feet	WALL-ROOF SURFACE in square feet
BOX	90,000	230	9,900
CUBE	90,750	220	9,625
PRISM	60,000	230	7,284
SPHERE	61,965	195	6,035
PYRAMID	54,000	240	7,200
CYLINDER	76,800	230	7,138

VOLUME SELECTION PRINCIPLES

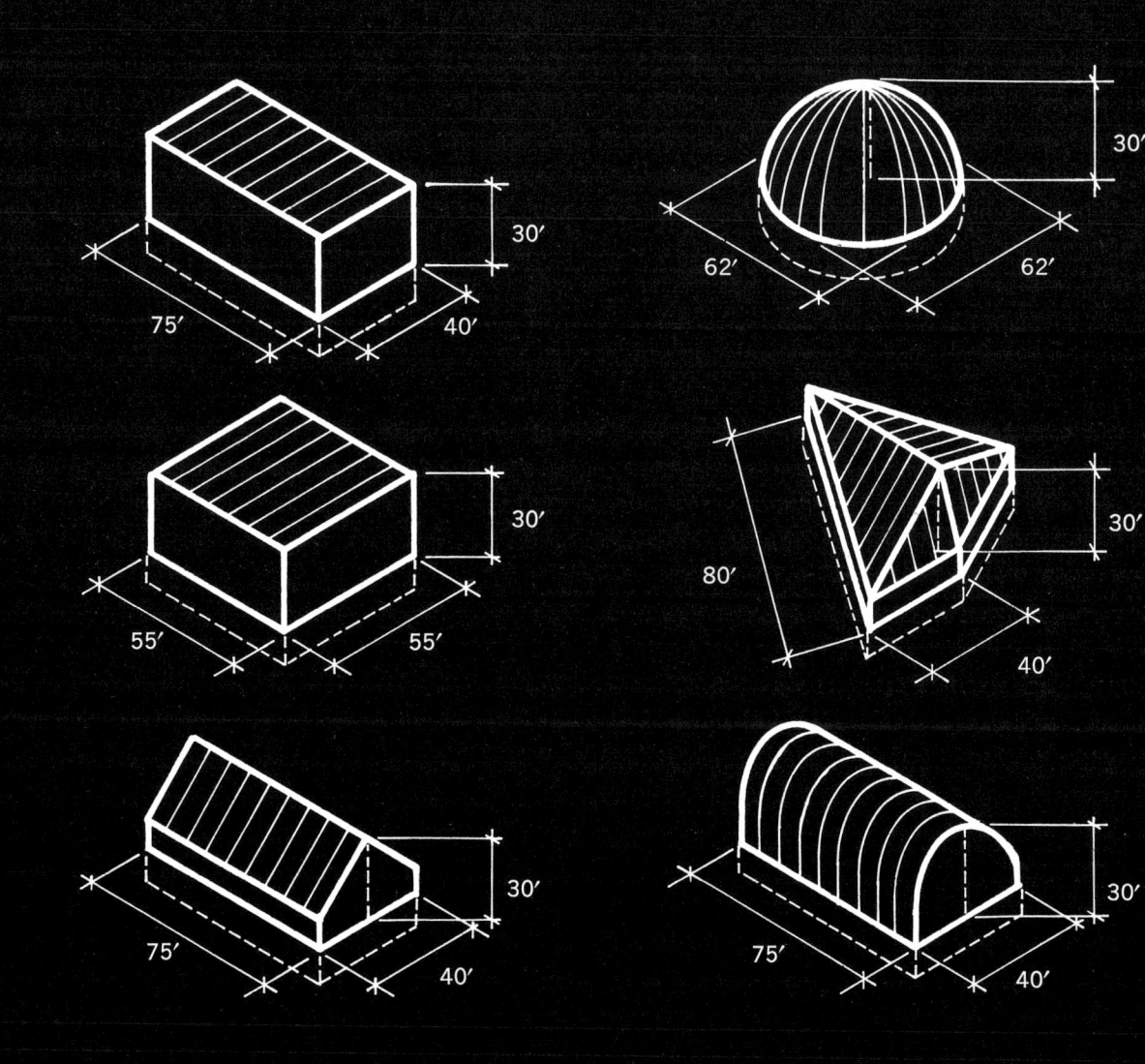

comparative analysis of church building shapes using solids with
3,000 square foot floor areas

Obviously, if a square-foot cost were applied to buildings made in these forms, all of the buildings would be the same price because they have the same number of square feet in floor area. If a cubic-foot cost were applied, the buildings would range from 54,000 cubic feet to 90,750 cubic feet. This is why a square-foot or cubic-foot cost method of figuring a building can only be an estimate. This is why a contractor or professional estimator is called on to make a quantity take-off of the materials in a building and submit a quote on buying materials and erecting the building. It is the only accurate way of determining the cost of a building.

In addition to the variation in cost, each shape has advantages and disadvantages, as outlined below:

BOX: The box has short spans, can be easily built with materials available. It can be enlarged easily but creates a church that is long, with the congregation farther away from the minister. The worship center can be placed on the long wall to bring the congregation close to the minister.

CUBE: The cube has fewer but longer and relatively more expensive members for spanning. It can be easily enlarged to form a box. It has the advantage of placing the congregation near the minister. It uses 275 square feet less surface material than the box.

PRISM: The prism has the shortest spanning members, which meet at the ridge, and creates one of the most common methods of building with its pitched roof. It can be easily enlarged and has 2,616 square feet less surface material to build than the box.

SPHERE: The hemisphere has 28,035 cubic feet less to heat than the box. It has 35 lineal feet less perimeter and 3,865 square feet less surface to build than the box. It is difficult to enlarge at the present time and must be built of specially shaped materials.

PYRAMID: The pyramid has 36,000 cubic feet less to heat than the box and 2,700 square feet less surface material to build and maintain. It uses many lengths of structural members which could be economically built with wood members.

CYLINDER: The half-cylinder has 13,200 cubic feet less to heat than the box and 2,762 square feet less surface to build and maintain than the box. It requires special framing members and surface materials which are available at the present time only in some materials.

The size of the solids are based on 30 feet to the highest point. This may be desirable in the prism, sphere, pyramid and cylinder but may not be necessary in the box and cube where a 25-foot height could be considered the equivalent of 30 feet in the other solids. Here the inner space, the inner character desired in the building, must dictate; the building solid can only provide a comparison of volume.

The Church of the Redeemer (Verlosserkerk), Hervormd, Bussum, The Netherlands. Nielsen, Spruit, & Van der Kuilen, architects

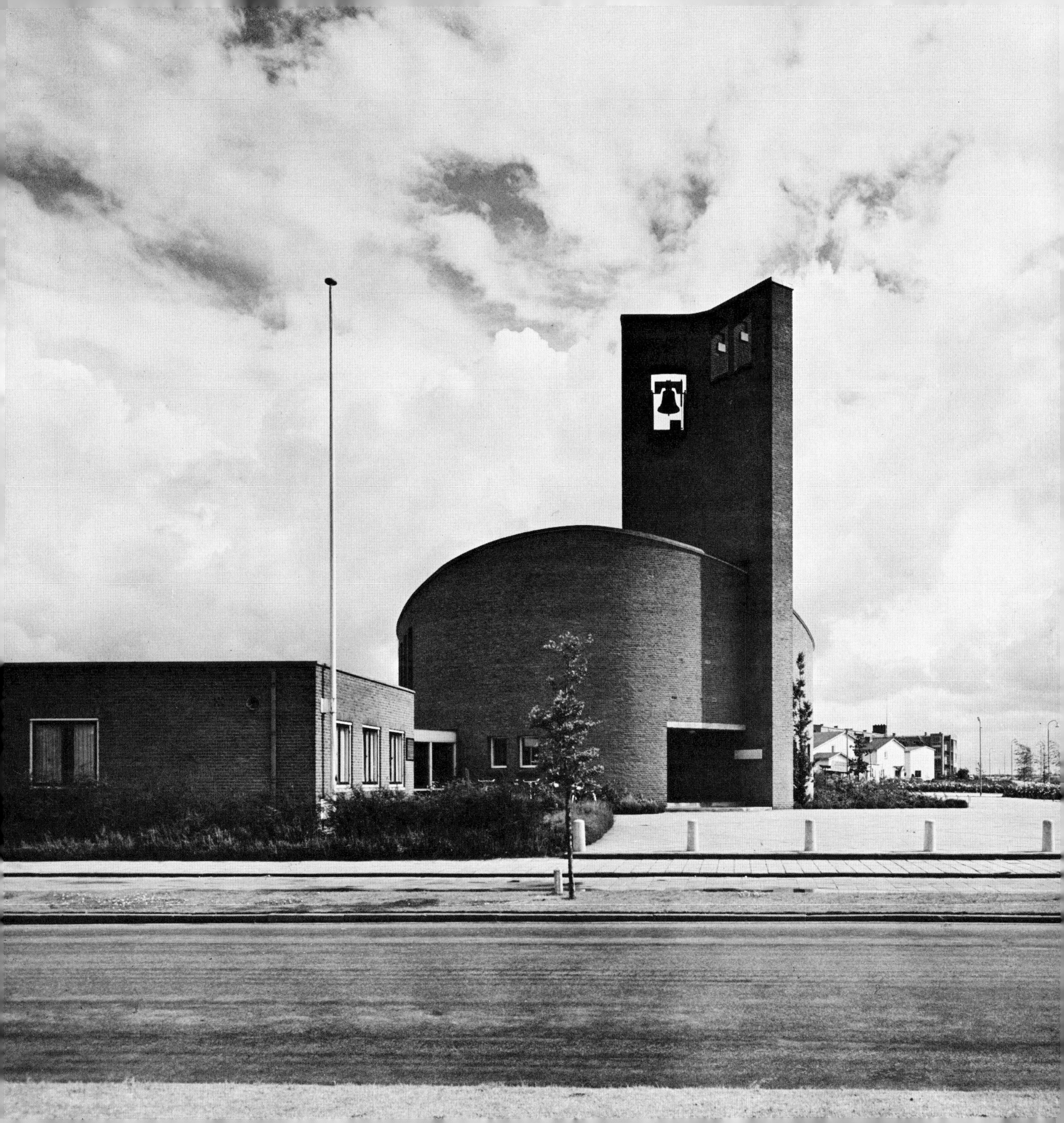

By elongating the sphere the architect has created a simple ellipsoidal shape with an axis that is not found in the sphere.

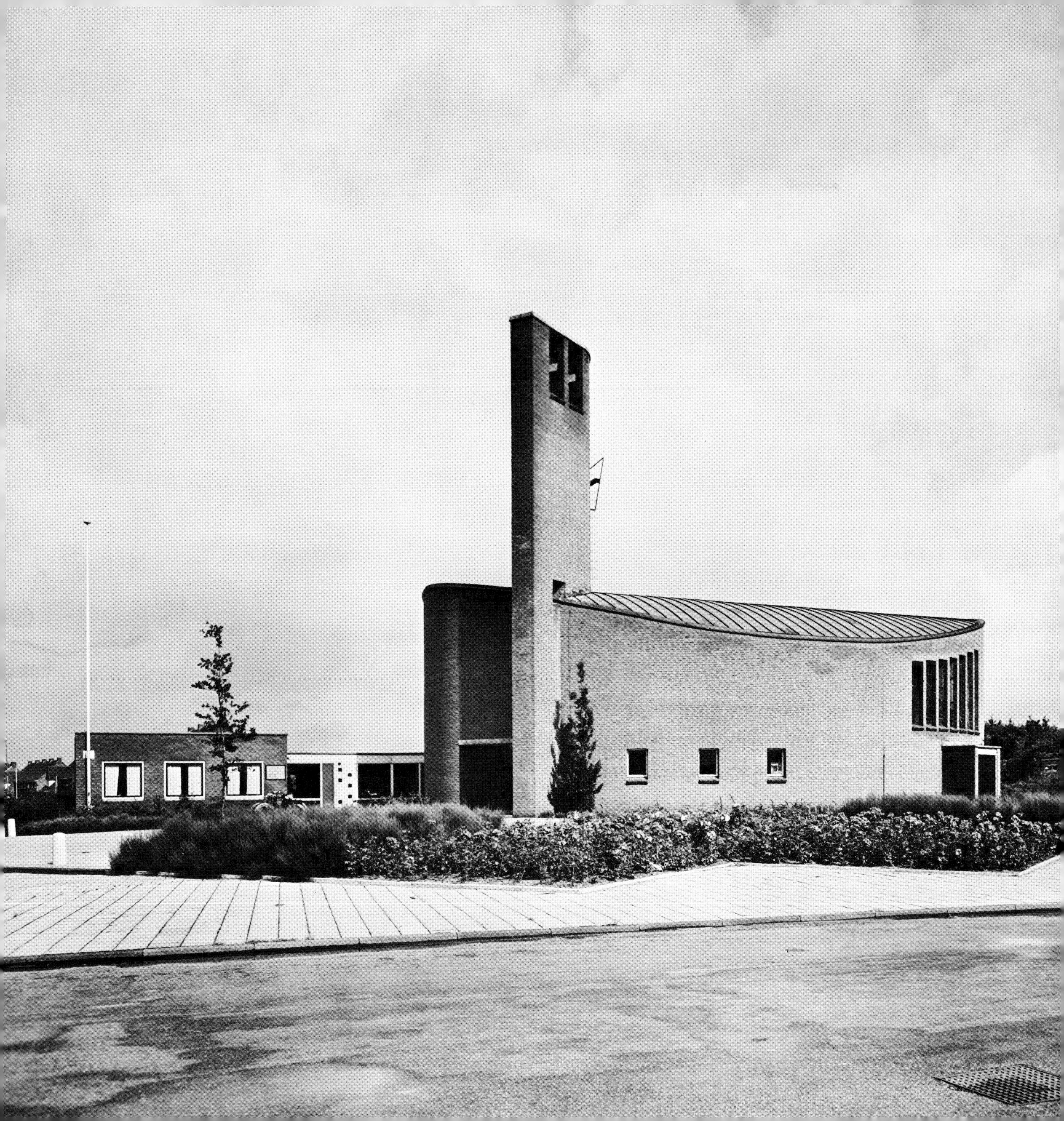

The widest part of the ellipse accommodates the seating, while the tapering ends nicely accommodate the liturgical area at one end and the organ and choir in a balcony at the opposite end.

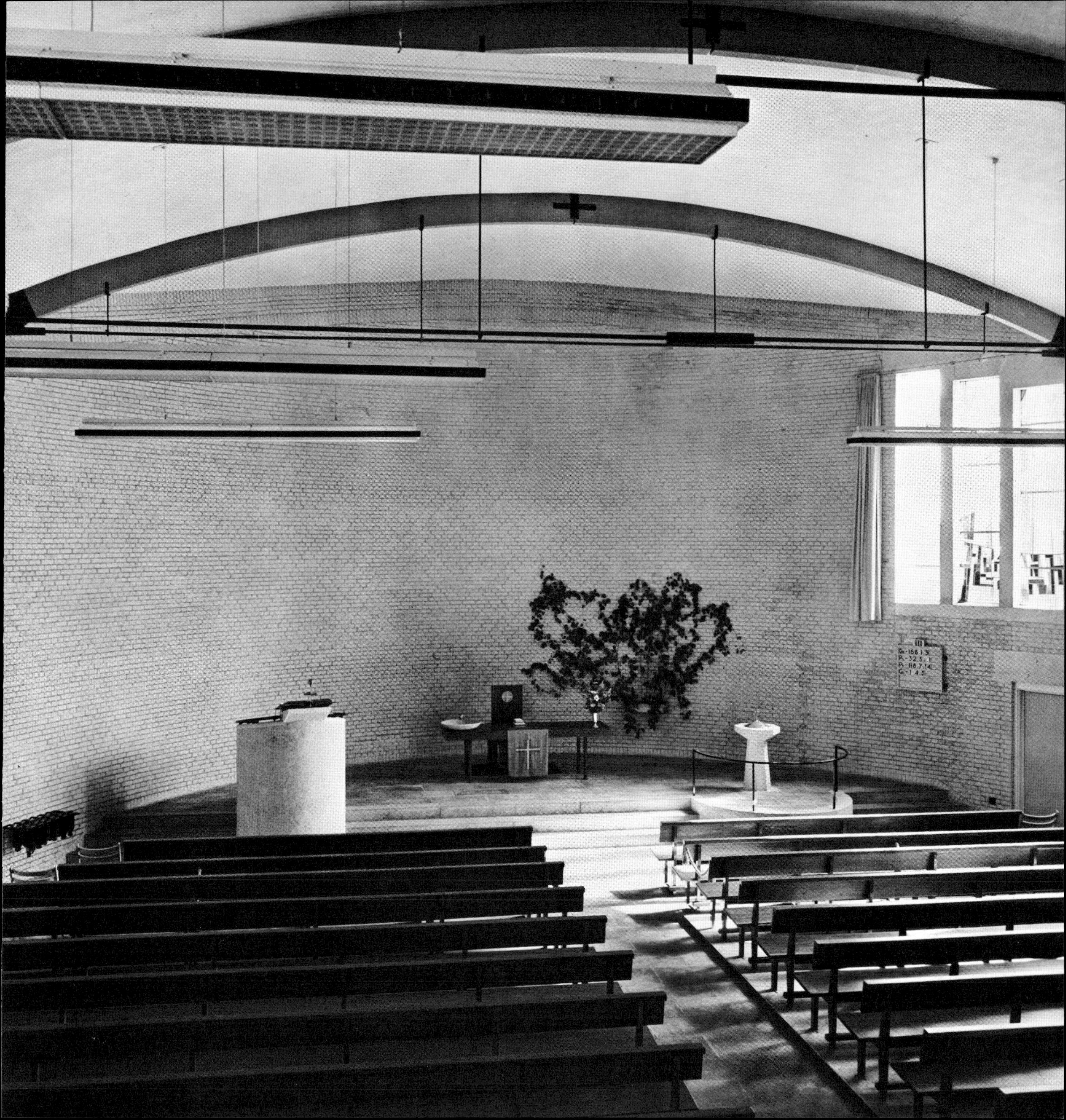

From the earliest times the Church has accepted many shapes as proper to places of worship. These have included shapes developed from the rectalinear plan to shapes developed from the circular plan. The Church reformed according to the Word, with its emphasis on hearing the Word, seeing the Baptism, and partaking of the Lord's Supper, has required the shape of a church that brings the people as close as possible to the liturgical center. In Europe this has been achieved in many churches by using the rectangular plan with the liturgical center on the long wall. In colonial times in the United States it was achieved by a rectangular, almost square, plan with the worship center at one end and with a balcony on three sides to increase the seating capacity while keeping the people near the liturgical center. In the early part of this century the churches that showed some understanding of the problem used a square plan with the liturgical center in one corner and the congregation grouped about it, seated in great arcs around this focal point. Any of these shapes are still valid today both from a theological and an architectural point of view. New shapes, however, have come into being that need to be tried for churches reformed according to the Word. There are many shapes that can be created by imagining a curved or bent wire held at both ends being revolved in space in a variety of ways. As indicated by the accompanying sketch, all of these create a circular-type plan. With the advent of reinforced concrete and new frames in wood and steel, these shapes are becoming easier and more economical to build. It behooves the church to give these shapes careful consideration. The liturgical center can be placed on a perimeter wall, rather than at the center, to create the desired corporate worship. Admittedly the arc of address becomes greater than desirable, but the arc could be reduced by allowing room to the sides of the liturgical center for overflow, entrances, and circulation requirements. Architecturally the interiors of such circular shapes are difficult to handle when divided into smaller spaces with walls. The best architects permit the circular shapes to

CIRCULAR PLAN CONSIDERATIONS

comparison of shapes with circular plans using a variety of structural framing systems

serve as unit spaces without dividing them with walls. They permit the circular shape and volume to express its completeness, its over-all sense of oneness, without subdivisions. If additional units are added to the circular-shaped buildings, the architect can retain the completeness of the circular shape by creating a neck to make the necessary link between buildings. He must raise the circular portion, as he would do with a dome, if he desires to increase the seating capacity beyond the perimeter in order to express the circular shape and volume.

Shape is the result of planned structure and planned space. Shape is a three-dimensional representation. Shape cannot be divorced from structure or space. When the architect is required to have a pitched roof because it "looks like a church," the shape of the building is no longer an end result. Such a request forces the architect to abandon many ideas that fit a church reformed according to the Word, or clumsily add pieces of roof to cover the space. To improve appearances he must add other "interesting" features to the building. The situation might be compared to buying an automobile, when the customer gets so involved in the "interesting" details, such as tail fins, fancy chrome, stamped grills, false air scoops, and fake ornament, that he forgets about buying quality transportation. In architecture, the client can buy fake dormers, empty gables, pseudo columns, and spurious windows rather than a fine piece of architecture, if he looks for outward appearances rather than at the heart, which is fine church architecture.

Since the range of shapes is so unlimited, the client is his own worst enemy when he establishes the shape of the building. He eliminates many sound and reasonable possibilities. Take the circular plan of a church as an example. Such a plan would seldom be considered by a building committee. There is no precedent to point to. The shape is foreign. How can one worship in such a church building? Immediately, the circular plan is controversial.

But let us examine the circular plan from the architect's point of view.

He knows that the circular plan encloses the greatest amount of usable space with the least amount of wall area. He knows that the roof and floor area are minimal. Economically this seems an ideal way to enclose a building, but there are also difficulties. To build circular walls with present materials is often more expensive. To structure the roof of a circular building may be more difficult. However, the time is at hand when these difficulties will be overcome. At that time the architect can offer a circular plan as an economical method of building, but will the client refuse the circular plan because it is not in his range of shape solutions?

We must be prepared to accept the architecture that is the outgrowth and expression of our day and age. The farmer readily accepts circular silos, circular storage bins, and circular grain elevators when they perform the task or operation more efficiently than another shape. Is he as willing to accept a circular church if it is likewise as efficient? The urban dweller readily accepts the circular water storage tank, the circular apartment tower, and the circular parking ramp, but is he as willing to accept the circular church?

The mast and guy wires are fine in a circus tent, but will the parishioner shudder when someone suggests these things for shaping a church? It is not in his range of shape solutions to the building of a church. Yet the possibilities of using masts and guy wires for a church are very real. From the point of view of the architect such space can be enclosed easily and, within our generation, economically. Will such a building be acceptable? The architect knows that guy wires and masts can take tremendous loads with a minimum amount of material. The architect looks at television masts and the towers for high-tension wires and sees the structures of the near future being used today. He would like to incorporate the economies of such structures into the church buildings of tomorrow. He believes that with skillful handling these structures can become fine church buildings. If demands by the parishioner for the same amount of space with no increase in cost continue, our age and time will dictate new solutions to the building of churches, and among these are the mast and guy-wire structures which the parishioner should include in his range of shape solutions for a church.

This chapter has one main purpose: it is intended to extend the thinking of those who would build churches that are reformed according to the Word. With some understanding of why the architect is forced by the economies of his time and age to build in certain ways, the parishioner will be more understanding of the role the architect must play. The parishioner must see the necessity of working with the architect in finding the shape solutions that our times force upon us. Since shape is a spatial image of a three-dimensional structure and an end result of space and structure, it remains the architect's responsibility to determine it.

Admittedly there are many shapes the church can take, but whatever the shape of the church building, it must express the beliefs of her people.

13

Programming the Church Building

Ultimately, whether or not we will have an architecture for Presbyterian/Reformed churches will depend upon whether or not the building committee is able to establish a program for the architect. This is the function of the building committee. Its function is not to raise the funds for the church—that is the job of the finance committee (and the finance committee should carefully survey all resources and establish a figure that will actually be available so that the architect does not design two buildings: one that the church would have liked to have had, and a second that it could actually afford). Nor is it the job of the building committee to plan the church—that is the job of the architect. The single and crucial job of the building committee is to establish the program, the careful description of the functions that the church building must perform.

How does the building committee go about programming? The committee will wish to start with that which is most important: with Word and Sacraments. More will be said later about the use of the criteria given in the first seven chapters as a guide to programming. It may be helpful to engage a theological/architectural consultant. He can be a source of education to the whole congregation, so that they may understand the theological foundations upon which the committee is building, and be able to concur enthusiastically in their efforts. Such advance efforts to educate and inform the congregation long before the architect puts pencil to paper pays rich dividends in understanding and co-operation throughout the program. The consultant can also engage in dialogue with the committee, stimulating them, helping them to formulate new insights, and guiding them into the program. The consultant can also be helpful as an impartial observer, helping to clarify and evaluate different points of view: trying to help the committee avoid the inevitable pitfalls of attempting to offer solutions, rather than clear statements of needs and, on the other hand, guiding the committee in its writing of a full and adequate program with which the architect can work.

But two things must be recognized: first, neither the consultant nor the architect should be forced to write the program for the church. This is the job of the building committee. They represent the congregation, and ultimately, in the writing of the program, theirs will be the responsibility of decision. Secondly, the building committee must give the congregation an opportunity to participate in the programming for the church. They should meet with the various societies and departments of the church and try to find out what their functions and needs really are—and make a distinction between real needs and enthusiastic desires. The building committee should also make clear to all that they are ready to accept written suggestions from the congregation. When insisting that the suggestions be in writing, they should also make it clear that only the best ideas that are compatible with the total program can be used. They should also point out that ideas are stimulating and although an idea may not fill a direct need it will often suggest new and better solutions.

Let us briefly consider this matter of programming in three realms of church activity as yet untouched in these pages: Christian education, the church kitchen, and recreational facilities.

Architectural Programming for the Church School

The Church reformed according to the Word of God has always believed in both an educated clergy and laity. Theologically, the faith through which we receive God's grace has always been seen by the Reformed to consist at least in part of a certain knowledge of the promises of the gospel. So that men might have that knowledge, the education of the laity through preaching, catechism, discussion, and Sunday or day schools, is a continuous part of our heritage. If we continue to believe in justification by faith, and if faith is in part knowledge, then we must continue to educate, both that we may have saving faith, and that we may be educated in the expression of the thankfulness that we desire to show God. Thus as a basic criterion:

CHRISTIAN EDUCATION IS NECESSARY THAT WE MAY KNOW OUR NEED OF A SAVIOR, THAT WE MAY HAVE THAT KNOWLEDGE WHICH IS A PART OF SAVING FAITH, SO THAT WE MAY LEARN FROM GOD'S WORD HOW TO EXPRESS OUR GRATITUDE TO HIM.

As anyone conversant with the Heidelberg Catechism knows, that knowledge which is a part of saving faith comes from the gospel, which is ever to be the proclamation heard from the pulpit, and which is also stated in sign in the Holy Sacraments. All that has been said thus far about the sanctuary and its focal point in the liturgical center where pulpit, font, and table play their part in the Christ-ordained means of grace has been to the end of

Christian education. The concern of this book as a whole is with the important role played by architecture in the education of the Christian. Once it is made clear, however, that the sanctuary and the worship of the people of God occupy a major role in Christian education, it is possible to proceed to the other important area of this education: the church school. The criterion remains the same, but for architectural programming for the church school it needs to be elaborated. The question must be raised as to what method we intend to use to educate. There are several methods available.

First, there is the one-room schoolhouse method. One relied on the schoolmaster to teach all grades much as one relied on the minister to teach all catechism classes. With an outstanding schoolmaster or minister the method was effective, or with a brilliant student and an ordinary teacher it often was equally effective. But the system worked best with a small group and plenty of individual attention. Each student proceeded at his own pace, much as the "Major Work" pupils do today. The advantages are obvious and the results are attested to by the many men and women of ability it produced.

Second, there is the graded-school method. Here we have a series of classes graded from the very young to the adult. The student periodically meets with a new teacher, usually on a yearly basis. The lesson material becomes progressively more difficult and the content ever greater in depth. The student receives less individual attention but the orderly procedure and lessons compensate for this deficiency.

Third, there is the consolidated-school method. The object of this plan is to change classes and teachers and benefit from the special field of endeavor of each teacher. It gives the student a chance to consider special fields of endeavor and experience different methods of instruction. He also has the opportunity for more rapid growth and comprehension.

And last, there is a combination of these methods, taking advantage of the best parts of each. General instruction is given in a carefully prepared lecture by a gifted instructor and speaker. The group is then dismissed to individual classes for discussion and research. In the classrooms are provided individual study areas for advanced work of the gifted student on individual assignments, or the slow student for special instruction.

How does one best educate? Any of these four methods might be used, but to direct the architect in the physical planning of the Sunday school some decisions need to be made. Will there be an assembly and then dismissal to classrooms for individual study and discussion? Will there be departmental assemblies or will classes meet only individually? Will there be a general lecture and then research of the topic? Perhaps there will be study and then assembly for discussion? What age groups comprise the Sunday school? Is there adequate provision for adult education? What should the class size be?

At this point it becomes obvious that decisions will also have to be made concerning the curriculum to be used. Here the denominations can usually be helpful in offering material which sets forth the ideal space and equipment requirements for the use of their curriculums. It is to be hoped that the church will always use the very finest curriculum which it is capable of using. And it is also to be hoped that it will be a curriculum that gives an adequate and imaginative place to the education of adults.

In programming for the church school the method of education should be known, and that involves knowing the curriculum to be used. But if these answers are to be realistic several other factors must be taken into consideration. The number of students to be educated is a matter of prime importance, as is the number of teachers and their level of competence. These factors might well alter the intended method and curriculum. Also to be considered is the maximum amount of money that will be available. There is no point in talking about a Christian education plant that will cost $300,000 when the greatest amount of money that can be made available is $50,000. Thus, if the building committee is to do realistic programming, it must enter into earnest conversation with the Christian education department of the church, as well as with the finance committee, and obtain their thinking concerning these matters. Then, with an over-all view of the total needs and resources of the church, it will do its programming for Christian education with these elements in mind:

1) WHAT METHOD AND CURRICULUM WILL BE USED TO EDUCATE?
2) HOW MANY STUDENTS WILL NEED TO BE EDUCATED?
3) HOW MANY TEACHERS WILL THERE BE TO EDUCATE?
4) HOW MUCH MONEY CAN BE DEVOTED TO BUILDING FOR CHRISTIAN EDUCATION?

The wise building committee will of course devote every dollar it can to providing good space for Christian education—pleasant space, comfortable space, space in which it is a joy to study. But having thoroughly worked out these four factors to provide the additional criteria for the programming of Christian education, the building committee must remember that the function of designing the space belongs not to itself but to the architect.

Architectural Programming for the Church Kitchen

The men of the building committee may well approach the problem of the church kitchen with considerable fear and trepidation. Certainly they would do well to listen quietly and politely to the plans of the women for the church kitchen. Having heard the complete plans, however, they would do well to ask four basic questions which are usually never asked when the church kitchen planning is done. If there is to be intelligent programming, these questions must be asked: 1) Theologically, why do you cook? 2) How do you cook? 3) How often do you cook? 4) Will there be anyone to cook?

Theologically, why do you cook? Is there any sophistry by which the entree of the church into the restaurant business can be theologically defended? If so, it should be brought forward, for all over the country churches are abandoning this occupation of an easier age as the church settles down to its real task. If, however, one cooks in the church to contribute to the fellowship of the saints, to provide the occasion where in social fellowship the relationships may grow that will later become true Christian fellowship, then a more enthusiastic view of the church kitchen might well be taken. But this theological decision has already gravely affected the kitchen, for the needs of ministering to the congregation, and those of serving dinner to a large and paying crowd, are very different.

How do you cook? For most churches the answer is surprisingly simple: Just as we do at home except that we need more of the same equipment. Restaurant equipment is strictly for people who know how to use it and use it daily; it is not for the church kitchen. Steam tables, baking ovens, soup kettles, and short-order cooking equipment are strangers to most housewives, and rightly so, because they have no need for them in their homes. What the church needs are two or more ranges, sinks, counters, pass-throughs, and serving carts to make the job easy for the group. Beyond a refrigerator, coffee maker, drinking fountain with cold-water filler, and plenty of storage space, there are no other needs. To provide equipment beyond this is unnecessary. In a good many cases the equipment might even be less.

How often do you cook? For the church of virtually unlimited resources the answer is one of good stewardship. For the church of limited resources it concerns how money will be distributed in the church building program. If the church, by actual count, only cooks for four fellowship suppers a year, does it then really make sense to deprive the Christian education department of an extra room for fifty-two Sundays of the year? It might also be good to review whether the number of church suppers now being served is more or less than it was ten years ago. If the church has a fellowship supper only three or four times a year, but it is still felt that kitchen facilities are needed, would it not be the better part of wisdom and Christian grace to establish kitchen facilities in a room basically designed for perhaps a Christian education function (since its use ratio will be 52 to 4)? All of the equipment could be placed along an ample wall, with provision for folding or sliding doors to both protect the equipment and keep it out of sight when not in use.

Will there be anyone to cook? This question is not as foolish as it first appears. Older women in the church must often look askance at the younger generation as they experience increasing difficulty in staffing the church suppers (at least in urban and suburban areas). But a fact of American life is the increasing number of women who have a salaried occupation. These women already have their families, homes, jobs, and probably a part in the choir or Christian education program of the church. Often they do not look forward with enthusiasm to serving church suppers. They would prefer to have the meal catered. In a recently constructed urban church several thousand sorely needed dollars in a heavily mortgaged building program were devoted to the church kitchen which was, of course, an absolute necessity. Three years after dedication the older women of the church no longer found it possible to carry the burden of the church suppers, and now all church suppers are catered! The building committee in its programming of the church kitchen would do well to find the percentage of women under fifty who are working, the percentage remaining who would actually be free and willing to participate in providing church suppers, to project the trend for the future, and to plan accordingly. Needless to say, these problems, while nonexistent in many rural areas, become increasingly acute as one moves closer to the urban scene. To provide the architect with the kind of information with which he can intelligently plan and provide for the needs of the church kitchen, this criterion must be acknowledged and these questions must be answered honestly:

COOKING IN THE CHURCH IS JUSTIFIABLE FOR FELLOWSHIP, NOT FOR PROFIT.
1) HOW DO YOU COOK?
2) HOW OFTEN DO YOU COOK?
3) WILL THERE BE ANYONE TO COOK?

Architectural Programming for Church Recreation

A new building program, especially for an established church, is often the occasion for enthusiastic planning for recreation in the church. This enthusiasm is usually based upon the premise that the church must do something for its youth—and who could disagree with such a basically Christian sentiment? But for good programming, and wise use of the money of the church so that it will indeed help the youth, some additional questions need to be asked: 1) Theologically, what is the goal of church recreation? 2) What funds are available to build, maintain, and staff such facilities? 3) What volunteer personnel are available? and 4) What is being done at present?

Theologically, what is the goal of church recreation? Is it to be a means of evangelism? If so, this presents some very pointed questions, both in terms of basic integrity of approach and in terms of available skilled personnel. Or is it to provide recreation for the young people of the church, the children of the covenant? If so, do they really need additional recreation? Or would existing organized athletic programs preclude the success of a church program? Young people have a way of claiming in almost the same breath that they have nothing to do and that they haven't a free evening for the next month. The truth of the matter should first be established.

If there is a real need for recreational facilities, the matter of funds, both for building and staff, must be carefully considered. Even if there is ample money to build the facilities, the necessities of maintenance and staff must not be forgotten. Experience has indicated that it is impossible to have an unguided recreational program. The finest facilities tend to disintegrate with unsupervised use. A certain New York church has two bowling alleys and a basketball court, as well as two ping pong tables and three pool tables. They are seldom used by the church for the simple reason that funds are not available for a supervisory staff. Or is it the intention to run such facilities with a volunteer staff? If so, the building committee should be sure that such plans are not centered around one or two enthusiastic men whose departure might mean the simultaneous departure of the program. The possibilities of a future program may often be judged by the present program. For the church without the enthusiasm, personnel, or staff to organize a good softball team, there is no point in spending thousands of dollars in the vain hope that a basketball team might be more popular. For responsible stewardship and intelligent planning, the building committee, regardless of the amount of money available, must insist upon rigorously thought-out answers to the following questions concerning its program for church recreation:

1) THEOLOGICALLY, WHAT IS THE GOAL OF CHURCH RECREATION? IS IT NEEDED AND/OR PRACTICAL?
2) WHAT FUNDS ARE AVAILABLE FOR BUILDING, MAINTENANCE, AND PERMANENT STAFF?
3) WILL VOLUNTEER PERSONNEL BE AVAILABLE ON A CONTINUING BASIS?
4) DOES THE PRESENT PROGRAM INDICATE BOTH THE NEED AND THE SUCCESS OF THE PROJECTED PROGRAM?

Architectural Programming for the Church Sanctuary

In its enthusiastic acceptance of the crucial task of programming, the building committee must avoid two pitfalls. The first is the temptation to assume the function of the architect. It must not present architectural solutions. The building committee must furnish the program detailing the needs of the church, but good architecture will result only if the architect is given the freedom to work out the solution to these needs. Do not stifle the architect by trying to make architectural decisions for him.

The second pitfall to be avoided is that of getting so wrapped up in programming for the peripheral functions of the church (for example, recreation and cooking) that the more important matters of Christian education, and above all the worship of Almighty God in his sanctuary, are neglected. The early Church did not come together for recreation. Nor did it grow rich in serving church dinners. It did grow strong in the weekly celebration of the Lord's Supper. And with that Supper it was nourished as well with God's Word. Christ's means of grace have not been altered. It is still his pleasure to come to us through his own appointed means: the preaching of the Word and the celebration of the Sacraments. Above all, it is important to program for this, because it is the heart of the church where Christ comes to speak and to communicate himself to his people.

It is because of a lack of programming in the most important of all places, the sanctuary, that many architects are forced to rely almost entirely upon their good intentions and their own religious experience, hoping to do their best to interpret what their client wants. The architect should not be forced to design the sanctuary by guesswork. If we are to have an architecture that is commensurate with our beliefs then we must start from within. This means that one must question and analyze his faith. The first part of this volume, as it has specifically considered the architectural implications of Reformed theology, has established certain criteria which are precisely the sort of concise information the architect must find in the church's program. Let us briefly consider these criteria and the kind of questions they would raise for the architect as he attempts to allow the program to govern the design of the church in order to create architecture reformed according to the Word of God.

The Pulpit

TO SET FORTH THE GOD-ORDAINED MEANS BY WHICH CHRIST COMES TO HIS PEOPLE, THE REFORMED MUST GIVE VISUAL EXPRESSION TO THE IMPORTANCE OF BOTH WORD AND SACRAMENTS.

BECAUSE THE WORD IS INDISPENSABLE, THE PULPIT, AS THE ARCHITECTURAL MANIFESTATION OF THE WORD, MUST MAKE ITS INDISPENSABILITY ARCHITECTURALLY CLEAR.

BECAUSE THE PULPIT DERIVES ITS IMPORTANCE FROM THE PREACHING OF THE WORD, THE BIBLE SHOULD BE VISIBLE IN THE PULPIT.

Does the church make the pulpit architecturally clear? Could the clarity of the pulpit be improved by raising it? Could it be improved by making it of more noble proportions? Could its location be improved? Would a sounding board improve the acoustics as well as make more obvious the importance of the Word? Does the pulpit speak of a church reformed according to the Word? Can the Bible be seen by the congregation? Does the architectural message agree with the message from the pulpit?

The Font

AS THE SIGN AND SEAL OF BEING BAPTIZED INTO CHRIST, BAPTISM IS TO BE PERFORMED IN THE PRESENCE OF THE CONGREGATION, WHERE THEY, THE BODY OF CHRIST, MAY BOTH SEE AND HEAR.

BAPTISM INVOLVES CONTINUING PARTICIPATION IN THE ATONING WORK OF CHRIST; THEREFORE THE FONT SHOULD STAND EMPHATICALLY BEFORE THE CONGREGATION AS A CONTINUING REMINDER OF THIS REDEMPTIVE RELATIONSHIP TO CHRIST.

BAPTISM CONSTITUTES CONTINUING PARTICIPATION IN THE RESURRECTED CHRIST; THEREFORE THE FONT SHOULD STAND EMPHATICALLY BEFORE THE CONGREGATION AS A CONTINUING REMINDER THAT THEY HAVE BEEN RAISED TO NEWNESS OF LIFE IN CHRIST.

Is the baptismal font in a location where it can be seen by all? Can it be seen during the service? Is it of noble proportions, or is it a little item off in some corner? Does its design make a bold statement or a half-hearted, middle-of-the-road compromise? Is the font a continuing reminder Sunday after Sunday that the Christian is baptized into the Lord? Does it help recall the works of the Lord? Will the children ask why the font is placed here? Will they ask why it is made of certain materials? Will they ask what it represents? If not, then the font is not teaching a lesson and a change is in order.

The Table

FOR THE CELEBRATION OF THE LORD'S SUPPER, THE TABLE SHOULD LOOK LIKE A TABLE.

ONLY THOSE ARTICLES WHICH ARE COMMENSURATE WITH THE CELEBRATION OF THE LORD'S SUPPER SHOULD BE PLACED UPON THE TABLE.

Do the articles on the communion table symbolize the Lord's Supper, or are they extraneous and not related to that great event? Will children ask the meaning of these things? Will it be necessary to invent an answer for the articles that happen to be on the table each Sunday? How should the Lord's Supper be commemorated? How should the bread and the wine be symbolized? How can that expression be kept before the people every Sunday, in fact, every day of the year? Does the table look enough like a table so that anyone will think of Christ eating with his disciples?

THE LORD'S TABLE SHOULD BE ACCESSIBLE AND VISIBLE.

Is the table ready for a supper, or does it have to be pulled out from the wall, and will some chairs, a cloth, and vessels have to be found to give a hint that it is a table? Is it visible? Is it placed so it can be seen over the heads of the congregation? Will the congregation feel that it participates at the table? How can each member be made to feel that he or she is a participant? In what ways can the people of God gather around the table?

THE LORD'S TABLE SHOULD BE DESIGNED TO BE ACTUALLY USED AS A TABLE WITH THE COMMUNICANTS SEATED AROUND IT.

Have chairs, stools, or benches been considered as a part of the communion table? What are the possibilities of all communicants being seated around the table? Could the pews become an extension of the Lord's table? Could wide aisles accommodate the communion table? Could a generous chancel accommodate an enlarged communion table? What is the possibility of an overflow and upper room combination? What are the possibilities of gathering around the table as a family, the people of God? Should some of the seating be folding chairs which can be arranged around the communion table? Could a depression for seating create a table at the perimeter or sides? Does the design of the communion table really express the church reformed according to the Word? These are all possibilities the architect should consider, but because the present practices of celebrating the Lord's Supper have often strayed far from biblical and Reformed prototypes, it would be well to have the building committee and congregation agree on how the Supper is to be celebrated before asking the architect to start planning.

combined

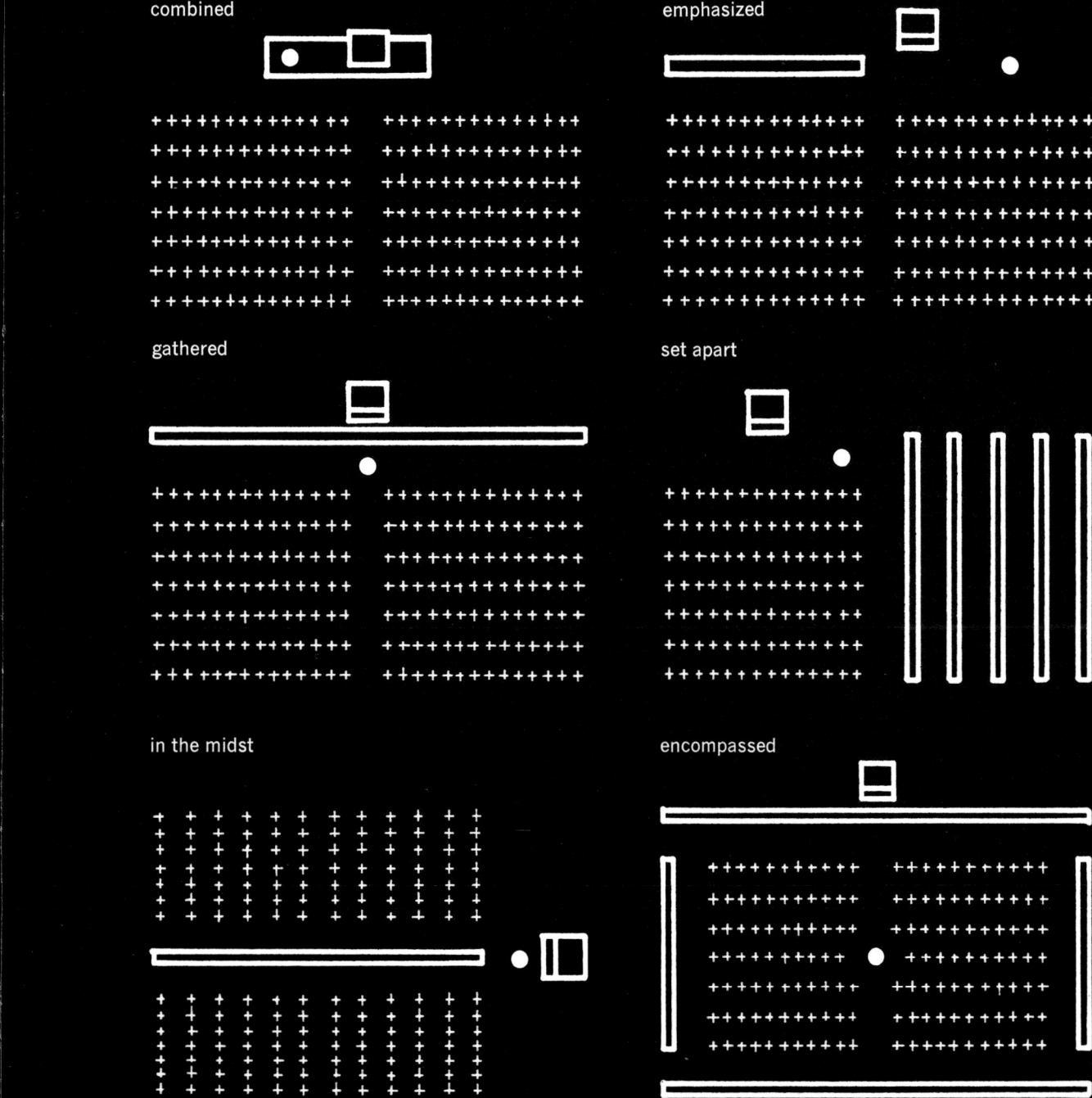

emphasized

gathered

set apart

in the midst

encompassed

The Pews

THE CONGREGATION IS GATHERED BY CHRIST AND IS BUILT AROUND THE WORD AND SACRAMENTS. CHURCH ARCHITECTURE SHOULD FOLLOW THIS PATTERN BY MAKING PULPIT, FONT, AND TABLE OF FIRST CONCERN, AND GATHERING THE CONGREGATION ABOUT THEM.

THE CONGREGATION IS THE CHURCH, THE CALLED-OUT PEOPLE OF GOD, GOD'S FAMILY, BROTHERS OF CHRIST AND OF ONE ANOTHER IN CHRIST, MEMBERS OF THE BODY OF CHRIST. ARCHITECTURALLY, THE PEOPLE OF GOD MUST BE TREATED NOT AS SPECTATORS, BUT AS MEMBERS OF A FAMILY.

Perhaps the pew is the one piece of furniture always associated with the church. The phrases, "church pew," "common pew," "front pew," "empty pew," "pew for saints and sinners," "family pew," tell a story in themselves. The family of man is welcome here. The equality of man was never better expressed. The questions about pews should be concerned with visibility, comfort, and appearance. The pew provides excellent visibility. In auditoriums you will find the seats staggered to permit visibility—how much simpler to slide over six to nine inches for exactly the same result in the church pew. This leaves only the raising of the pulpit, font, and communion table to bring them into the vision of everyone. But one should also be concerned with comfort. Do the pews permit standing with comfort? Do they permit the stout person to enter between the pew ends without embarrassment? Are pew ends necessary, or might the idea of "members of a family" be better expressed without pew ends—which are but choice elbow rests for the few? Are the pew ends nothing but "climb over places" for those entering the pew? Consider the increased family feeling in All Saints Church (p. 35), a church without pew ends, in contrast to The Church of St. Antony (p. 29), a church with pew ends. Pew ends have much the same effect today as boxed-in or "boughten" pews had a century ago.

Do the hymn racks and cup holders of the pews provide a perfect spot to hit knees? Would a shelf under the seat for hymn books and holes for cups provide fewer knee hazards and a neat and uncluttered look (pp. 199, 673)? How are the pews selected? This is the task of the architect, but he should have the assistance of a committee; however, not one composed of lithe young ladies and gentlemen. This is hardly appropriate. The real problem is in seating a six-foot, two-hundred-pound gentleman (he will not be embarrassed if appointed to the pew committee). If he can sit in comfort in a half-hour test then the pew is comfortable. With a generous back and seat width, the seat height then becomes critical in accommodating people with short or long legs. For comfort serious thought should be given to the "open back" pew. Perhaps no other item sets up the appearance of a church more than the pews. The material, color, and finish of the pews must be a part of the plans of the architect even though the pews may be the last item purchased. The kind of pew can determine whether a church will express the family of God, Sunday after Sunday and year after year. When children ask why the pews do or do not have pew ends, when they ask why there are pews in place of chairs or seats, then it will be apparent that the pews have spoken. It is to be hoped that they say what they were intended to say.

PEW A

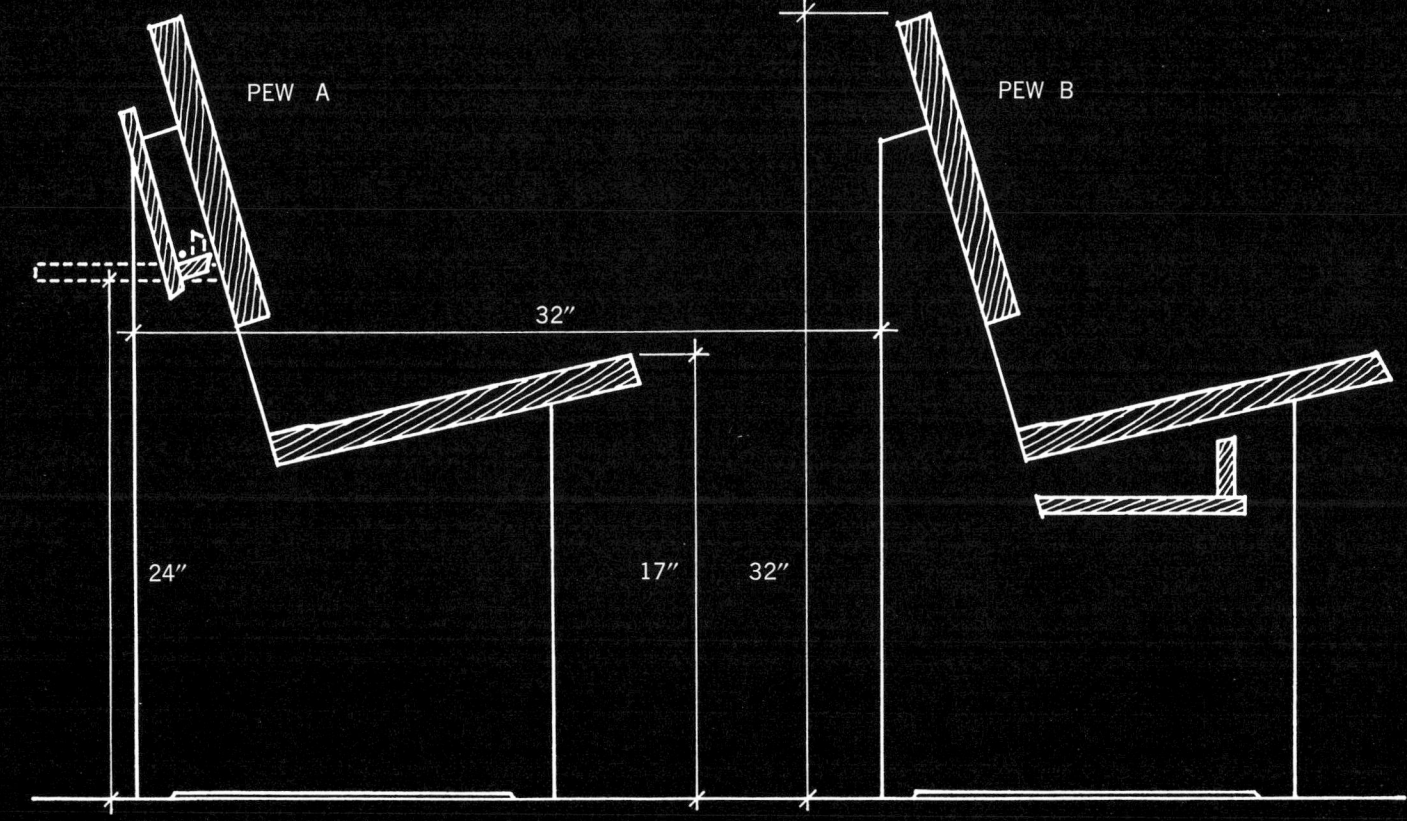

PEW B

32"

24"   17"   32"

ESTHETIC CONSIDERATIONS

note absence of clutter on back of pew B and the spaciousness of churches illustrated in this book using pews without the pew ends

LITURGICAL CONSIDERATIONS

note continuous underseat rack in pew B for bibles, hymnbooks and cups; note how pew A provides an extension of the communion table

THE EFFECTIVENESS OF MINISTERIAL COMMUNICATION DECREASES WITH THE INCREASE OF HIS ARC OF ADDRESS. IT ALSO DECREASES WITH THE INCREASE OF DISTANCE OF THE CONGREGATION FROM THE PULPIT.

This statement establishes the relation between pulpit and pew, but it is one of either/or, and the building committee must decide if it will offer the architect some guidance as to which of the alternatives it prefers. It should decide whether it wishes to gather the people close to the pulpit even though that means increasing the arc of address, or whether it desires a strong axis with the pulpit at one end. There is, however, no better way of architecturally expressing the family of God in church than through the seating. There is no better way to improve the communication between minister and congregation than by reducing the distance between them.

Communications are also influenced by auditorium acoustics. The accompanying diagrams illustrate some basic considerations to be investigated when a church is in the planning stages. Diagrams of this sort must be interpreted with great care as they point out problems of a general nature. At first, in reading the diagrams, it might appear that an auditorium with a one-to-one proportion should be avoided. Yet this auditorium with proper acoustical material on the rear wall could be satisfactory and at the same time decrease the distance from the congregation to the pulpit. The architect's consultation with an acoustical engineer might reveal that the acoustics could be further improved by changing one dimension a few feet or by using another material for the rear wall.

PROPORTION CONSIDERATIONS

consider a plan of one to one and three quarters (for 300–600 seat churches):
if greater, too many reverberations   if less, too many rear wall reflections

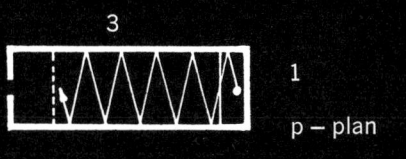

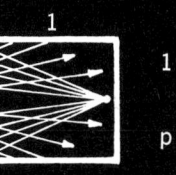

p – plan

DISTRIBUTION CONSIDERATIONS

keep travel distance of reflected sound within 50' of direct sound—adjust ceiling height
for high ceilings reflection is slow   low ceilings reduce sound toward rear

s – section

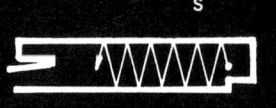

DISPERSION CONSIDERATIONS

consider non parallel surfaces, recesses and projections to break up sound waves:
rear balconies break sound waves   non parallel walls, sloped ceilings

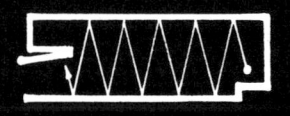

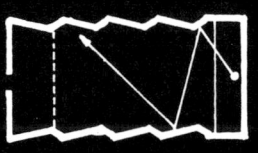

REFLECTION CONSIDERATIONS

sound waves are reflected at angle equal and opposite to angle of incidence:
sounding boards, nearby walls reflect   concave reflections create echoes

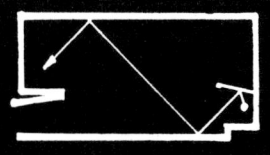

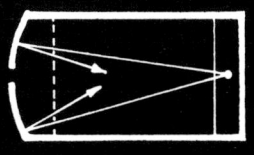

CORRECTION CONSIDERATIONS

add necessary absorbing material to areas that produce delayed reflections:
consider rear wall areas   consider high ceiling areas

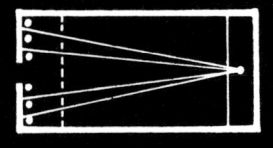

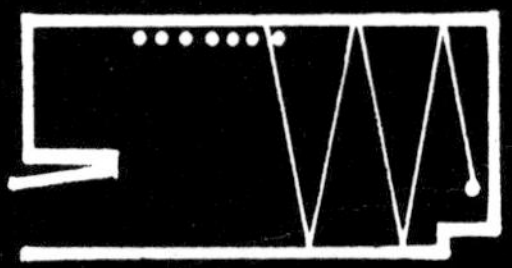

The Minister

ARCHITECTURE WHICH IS FAITHFUL TO THE REFORMED DOCTRINE OF WORD AND SACRAMENTS IS AT ONCE FAITHFUL TO THE PRESBYTERIAN DOCTRINE OF THE MINISTER.

Does the church give expression to the office of the minister? Does it separate the laity and clergy or does it unite them? Do the chairs, lecterns, and platform suggest a performance rather than a preaching?

The Elders

THE RESPONSIBILITY OF THE ELDER FOR THE PURE PREACHING OF THE WORD, THE WORTHY PARTICIPATION IN THE SACRAMENTS, AND THE LIVES OF THE MEMBERS OF THE CHURCH CAN BEST BE ARCHITECTURALLY DISPLAYED BY PUTTING THE ELDER IN CLOSE PROXIMITY TO THE WORD AND SACRAMENTS AND BY PROVIDING HIM WITH THE GUIDES OF HIS OFFICE, THE HOLY SCRIPTURES AND THE DOCTRINAL STANDARDS.

Does the church give expression to the office of the elder? Are the elders' pews related to the Word and Sacraments? Are the Word and Standards given proper recognition? Are changes necessary to give proper expression to the office of the elder?

The Deacons

THE OFFICE OF THE DEACON IS THE PROLEPTIC OFFICE OF LOVE. ARCHITECTURALLY, AS WELL AS IN FACT, THE DEACON SHOULD REMAIN CLOSE TO THE SOURCE OF THAT LOVE, CLOSE TO CHRIST, WHO COMES TO US IN WORD AND SACRAMENTS.

THE OFFICE OF THE DEACON IS THE PROLEPTIC OFFICE OF LOVE, AND THE INCARNATE MANIFESTATION OF THIS LOVE IN THE GIFTS OF GOD'S PEOPLE IS TO RECEIVE ARCHITECTURAL DEFINITION IN THE RECEPTACLES FOR THE OFFERING.

Could the office of the deacon be better expressed with offering bags and racks? Would a special shelf be more appropriate for the collection plates? Can they be placed close to the Word and Sacraments? How are love and concern expressed? Can its expressions invade the community? Do the entire church building and its surroundings express this concern? Does second best in design and materials indicate a lack of pride? Does lack of maintenance show a different kind of concern?

The Choir

THE CHOIR DOES NOT COMMUNICATE GOD'S GRACE, BUT THE PEOPLE'S GRATITUDE.

THE ROLE OF THE CHOIR (LIKE THAT OF THE REST OF THE CONGREGATION) IS TO RESPOND TO GOD IN PRAISE. IT IS NOT TO BE CONFUSED WITH THE MEANS OF GOD'S GRACE—WORD AND SACRAMENTS—AND THEREFORE MUST NOT BE PLACED WITH THEM. ARCHITECTURALLY THE CHOIR MUST BE PLACED WITH THE REST OF THE CONGREGATION, WHICH IT ASSISTS IN ITS RESPONSE OF PRAISE TO GOD.

Does the position of the choir clearly indicate that its function is one of thankful response to God's grace? Is it clear that it is not as important as Word or Sacraments, or related to them as another means of grace? Is it a part of the congregation and not the liturgical center?

THEOLOGICALLY, THE CHOIR CAN BE PLACED AMONG THE PEOPLE AT THE EAST END OF THE CHURCH AS WELL AS AT THE WEST. FUNCTIONALLY, THE CHOIR IS BEST ABLE TO SERVE ITS PURPOSE OF ASSISTING THE CONGREGATION IN SONG NOT WHEN IT SINGS AT THEM IN FRONT, BUT WHEN IT ASSISTS THEM FROM BEHIND.

Does the location of the choir speak of a performance for the people, or of assisting them in worship? Is the choir so placed that functionally it can best serve the congregation?

The Organ

THE ORGAN DOES NOT COMMUNICATE GOD'S GRACE, BUT THE GRATITUDE OF THE CHURCH.

THE FUNCTION OF THE ORGAN IS TO RESPOND TO GOD'S GRACE WITH PRAISE. IT IS NOT TO BE CONFUSED WITH THE MEANS OF GOD'S GRACE, AND THEREFORE MUST NOT BE PLACED WITH THE SYMBOLS OF WORD AND SACRAMENT. ARCHITECTURALLY, THE ORGAN MUST BE PLACED WITH THE CONGREGATION WHICH IT ASSISTS IN ITS RESPONSE OF PRAISE TO GOD.

ACOUSTICALLY, THE ORGAN CAN BEST ASSIST THE CONGREGATION WHEN IT IS BEHIND, AND SLIGHTLY ABOVE.

AS BEFITS THE PRAISE OF GOD, THE ORGAN SHOULD BE HONEST! IT SHOULD NOT ATTEMPT TO HIDE, OR TO BE SOMETHING IT IS NOT; IT SHOULD NOT PRESENT A FALSE FAÇADE. IT SHOULD NOT BE IN A CHAMBER, BUT OUT IN THE OPEN WHERE IT MAY EXPRESS ITSELF IN A MANNER CONSONANT WITH ITS INTRINSIC NATURE. IT NEED NOT

MASQUERADE BEHIND FALSE PIPES, BUT SHOULD HONESTLY EXPRESS THE BEAUTY OF ITS NATURE IN PRESENTING ITS WORKING PIPES.

The choir and organ should be so closely associated that questions concerning the one apply to the other also. The chief concern then is the kind of instrument. While the electronic instrument is adequate for the roller rink, dance hall and cocktail lounge, one would hope that Christ's people would demand the best, insisting upon the pipe organ as the proper instrument for the church. The visual sculpture of the pipe organ probably speaks as loudly as its music. Churches should not deny themselves this bold statement that says without pealing a single note, "Make a joyful noise unto the Lord." Churches should let the sculpture of the pipe organ speak. The temptation may be to get along with an inferior instrument, or to delay a decision, but the architect must know the congregation's plans early if he is to work with the organ builder in the planning of the church. He must know the answers to these questions: How much may be spent for music when the church is built? Will this be a temporary instrument or will it be permanent? If a larger organ is to be added later, how big an organ will it be?

The above are indicative of the type of questions which must be asked by the architect in response to the criteria which the building committee has written into its program. (Further criteria are found on pp. 447–85.) It cannot be emphasized too strongly, however, that it is not the task of the committee to present architectural answers to such questions. This is not to say that individually the solutions of the committee might not be good, but that separate answers can seldom be combined to form a workable building—let alone one that will be great architecture. When the building committee has formulated the criteria of its building program, it would be well to share the program with the congregation and ask them to vote an explicit assent. With the agreement of the congregation to the program, the architect can begin his job of seeking an architectural solution, directing his skill toward the harmonious solution of the multitude of requirements for a church that is faithful to the intentions of the congregation.

The finished building should be one of honesty, order, clarity, lightness, rhythm, and elegance, but as a building built for the purpose of the worship of God it will truly fulfill the desires of the congregation only if it is also a clear statement of their faith. If the Faith has been clearly understood and carefully transformed into criteria for the architect by a building committee that is also knowledgeable in the problems and opportunities of architecture, and thus able to use the skill of their architect, then there is the possibility of a clear and handsome statement of that faith that will continue year after year to point to Word and Sacraments, through which the people of God are gathered and nourished by Christ.

Appendix
The Choice of an Organ

What are the relative merits of the pipe organ and its electronic counterpart? And what is the comparative cost? There is no real question as to which instrument offers superior quality of tone. The very fact that the makers of electronic instruments seek to praise their products by describing them as sounding like a real organ, a pipe organ, or having true pipe organ tone, is evidence enough of where the real superiority lies. No advertisements in the field ever claim that "our instrument sounds like a real electronic organ."

The trained musician will need no arguments to establish the superiority of the pipe organ. Should a building committee have any doubts in the matter it would be best to seek counsel not from a salesman, but from an impartial expert in the field. A nearby college or university, or an institution of one's denomination, would be a good place to seek advice. The professors of music who teach organ and have devoted their lives to this field can be an excellent source of impartial judgment. The advice of these musicians should convince any building or music committee of the desirability of the organ over an electronic instrument.

While the tone of even the Romantic church organ is to be preferred to the sound of the electronic, nonetheless the sympathy of the authors is entirely with the classic organ (sometimes called polyphonic or baroque) of low wind pressure, unnicked lips, and voicing that produces a pipe speech and tone of unsurpassed quality. This is the type of organ which reached its apogee in the organs of Arp Schnitger in the early 17th century, the principles of which were recovered by such early champions as Albert Schweitzer and D. A. Flentrop, and promoted in our own country by E. Power Biggs and Joseph E. Blanton, to mention just a few. The works of both Schweitzer and Blanton will prove rewarding for anyone wishing a proper understanding of the classic organ.

The first criterion upon which consideration of a church instrument should begin is that

THE PIPE ORGAN IS TO BE PREFERRED BECAUSE OF ITS SUPERIORITY OF TONE.

All except the most avid promoters of the electronic instrument are willing to grant the first criterion. However, it is on the question of costs that many committees immediately dismiss the possibility of a real pipe organ, despite its acknowledged desirabilty, and settle instead for the second best. This is the result of the well-promoted myth that the pipe organ is vastly more expensive than the electronic. But the matter is not so simple. Before the cost of an electronic instrument or pipe organ can be compared, careful consideration must be given to the size of the organ, which also means a consideration of its purpose.

How big an organ does a specific church need? All too often a committee makes a decision in terms of the specific offer of an electronic organ for four to twelve thousand dollars over against the memory of Old First Church whose pipe organ cost fifty thousand dollars. This is very much like deciding that a one-bedroom frame house is a better buy than a five-bedroom brick house simply because it costs less. Everyone is sufficiently familiar with housing to realize that in such an instance one is dealing with such different items that comparison is difficult. A lack of familiarity with organs means that an equally great dissimilarity is not so readily apparent. Therefore, if a rational decision is to be made, the question must first be both asked and answered: How big an organ does a specific church need? And to answer this, one must determine the purpose of the organ.

Is the purpose of the organ to serve the congregation in its praise of God, or is it also to be used as a concert instrument? Undoubtedly many organists would desire a large concert instrument with a variety of ranks to be used for every possible need that the literature for the organ might demand. But over against such desires one must place the actual musical needs of the church. Does the church require an elaborate instrument upon which a highly accomplished organist is to give regular concert recitals as an integral part of the program of the church? Or is the organ to be used to provide the necessary music for the church service—the preludes, offertories, responses, postludes and hymns? "Churches whose members attend for truly religious reasons can do very well with a surprisingly modest organ."[1]

How large must an organ be in terms of ranks to provide the religious music necessary for a service of worship? The amount of fine church music which can be adequately played on a pipe organ of four or five ranks is so

---

[1] Joseph Edwin Blanton, *The Organ in Church Design* (Albany, Texas: Venture Press, 1957), p. 64.

abundant that no church having even such a modest instrument needs to fear an inadequate amount of organ literature! This is what is basically necessary for the worship service of the church. For those churches which can afford a larger pipe organ, more ranks to give additional variety would certainly be desirable. However, it should be noted that it is usually totally irrelevant to the religious music of the church to buy an organ just because it can boast many stops. The electronic organ is often purchased because it offers an electronic imitation of twenty or thirty stops for six or eight thousand dollars, while a pipe organ of similar size would cost thirty or forty thousand. However, for the average church to buy an organ just because it has twenty or thirty stops is rather like the local florist buying a huge semitrailer in which to make his deliveries. Twenty or thirty stops are simply unneeded for the music of worship. Unless a church has a highly trained organist it is unlikely that the potentiality of such a large number of stops would even be used. And an organist of real musical skill and insight will prefer a small pipe organ of pure tone over a much larger electronic instrument of lesser quality. It is far better to have a pipe organ of real quality with the basic stops than to suffer the inferior tone of an electronic instrument, even though it has a multiplicity of stops.

IF THE PURPOSE OF THE ORGAN IS TO PROVIDE MUSIC FOR SERVICES OF WORSHIP, A PURCHASE SHOULD BE MADE IN TERMS OF QUALITY RATHER THAN QUANTITY.

The many small and middle-sized churches of the United States where music is a valued part of the praise of the congregation to God would do well to consider the example of their counterparts in Europe. As can be noted in the churches illustrated in this volume, the choice of the small European church is invariably for a small pipe organ of from four to eight stops. Examples of five- and six-stop positivs are found in the churches of Bant (p. 239), Nagele (p. 323), and Rutten (p. 359). The cost of these five- and six-rank positivs, built by Europe's finest organ builders, varies from $5,000 to $6,000.

Another factor which affects the size of an organ, this one architectural, is the size and acoustics of the church. Any organ pipe has a given volume which cannot be increased. To increase the volume of an organ, ranks are added so that the same note may be played on more than one pipe. Thus, in a large church, a four-rank organ would be unsuitable, not because it is insufficient to play the music needed for worship, but because of inadequate volume. However, the size of organ needed will be determined by the acoustics of the church even more than by its size. One should look again at the small positivs used in such large churches as the Wilhelmina Church in The Hague (p. 241) and the Church of the Resurrection in Amsterdam-West (p. 121). In both of these churches the organ, including its blower, is entirely contained in the little box in the west balcony. Both churches plan, when finances allow, to purchase more elaborate pipe organs. In the meantime, these positivs aid with pure and precise tone the worship of God. But are they adequate to support the worship of a singing congregation of five or six hundred? The secret is in the acoustical properties of the buildings. In both cases the pews are of wood, and without cushions, the floor is of stone or tile, the walls of the Wilhelmina Church are of brick, while those of the Church of the Resurrection are of plaster. None of these materials absorb or muffle the pure tones of the pipe organ, thus making these exquisite minimal organs nevertheless adequate for sacred worship. The situation in the United States is quite different. Blanton, in addition to offering helpful tables of "Sound Absorption Coefficients" and "Optimum Reverberation Times,"[2] also has the following trenchant observations concerning acoustical practices in American churches:

---

[2] *Ibid.*, pp. 113 and 115.

The current extensive and indiscriminate use of sound-absorbing materials in churches is one of the most deplorable developments in contemporary church practice. It is a common experience today for a church group to spend several thousand dollars for sound-absorbing materials which render the interior of their new church acoustically dead. This in turn calls for the spending of hundreds of dollars more for an amplifying system to enable the congregation to hear the preacher and many more thousands of dollars for additional ranks of pipes for the organ which would be wholly unnecessary if they had not spent the money for the acoustical materials in the first place. This is a vicious sequence of expenditures which ends up with the church having put out a lot of extra money for an inferior result; in some cases of very large projects these ill-advised expenditures reach prodigious sums.[3]

SOLID, REFLECTIVE MATERIALS IN THE CHURCH SANCTUARY WILL BOTH ENHANCE THE BRILLIANCE OF THE ORGAN AND REDUCE ITS NECESSARY SIZE.

How does one obtain an answer as to what will be an organ of adequate size? The architect and organ builder should be in consultation from the very beginning to insure the proper placement of the organ and the use of the proper materials to allow an organ of minimum size to do an adequate job. The Associated Pipe Organ Builders of America advertise regularly that a church should consult a qualified member before plans for a new church or remodeling program are completed and that valuable and necessary information will be given without obligation. Any organ builder that is unconcerned in the early planning stages with all those aspects of the building which will affect the acoustics is probably one with which the church should also be unconcerned.

Both the volume of the church sanctuary and its acoustical properties will affect the size of the organ that is needed. As has already been pointed

---

[3] *Ibid.*, p. 111.

out, even large churches can, with the proper acoustics, use very small organs. But it should further be noted that proper acoustics may themselves constitute money saved: proper acoustics for an organ require the use of hard, reflective surfaces—the surfaces which are often a natural part of building structure: brick, plaster, concrete, and tile. The acoustical materials are usually those which must be added to the basic structure, and thus represent additional costs: acoustical panels, draperies, carpeting. Thus, musically "alive" interiors are usually far less expensive than "dead" interiors. In brief, through building a church acoustically suitable for a pipe organ, the savings may go far in paying for the organ.

When considering the comparative costs of a pipe organ or an electronic instrument the matter of installation must also be given careful consideration on the basis of specific instruments, rather than upon generalizations. One manufacturer publishes a brochure picturing on one page a church full of scaffolding, being torn apart by workmen in order to install a pipe organ, while on the opposite page is a picture of a hand putting an electric plug into a socket. That picture must sell dozens of organs to harried building committees. However, the comparison is largely an illusion created by comparing a hypothetically large pipe organ with a small electronic, whereas the installation of a comparably small pipe organ is as easy as the picture showing the plug being put into the socket. While the small positiv is a real pipe organ, it is built as a self-contained unit, with everything except its own source of electricity. If comparisons are to be made honestly, they must not be made on the basis of illusory generalizations, but upon the basis of a specific building with a specific musical need. In such instances, a pipe organ adequate for the worship needs of many churches can be installed with no more difficulty or cost than an electronic instrument.

Other considerations in the relative costs of these two varied instruments are the matters of maintenance, depreciation, and obsolescence. With reference to maintenance, it will be the rare committee that does not have at least one member who is keenly aware of a church which has been put to great expense in repairing a large pipe organ. It is all too easily assumed that pipe organs have great repair costs, while electronic instruments have none. This is not the case. Experience indicates that a maintenance contract for a small pipe organ costs no more than one for a small church-model electronic organ. Even the best electronic manufacturers provide maintenance contracts that cost approximately one per cent of the cost of the instrument per year.

When the question of depreciation and obsolescence enters in, the purchaser of an electronic instrument faces little more than a question mark. Many electronic instruments that twenty years ago were the best in the field and sold for several thousand dollars are today virtually worthless—so worthless that even in a trade-in on a new electronic they are worth only one or two hundred dollars. In twenty years they have become virtually obsolete, and so subject to breakdown that they are uneconomical to keep. And what of new electronic instruments? This is a risk the purchaser must assume.

And what is the obsolescence of a pipe organ? One builder has a standard fifty-year guarantee on all of his pipe organs. If properly maintained, a pipe organ will often outlast the building housing it. An organ built by Arp Schnitger, the master German organ builder, in 1695, and now housed in Cappel, near Hamburg, is not only still in use, but is such an excellent organ that it is used by recording companies to record Bach's organ works. An organ over two and a half centuries old, sought out for recording purposes not because it is a novelty, but because of its unimpaired artistic excellence!

In reference to questions of maintenance, depreciation, and obsolescence, it must be emphatically noted that pipe organs do not "wear out." It is true that the leathers of a pipe organ, essential to the pneumatics, are the weak point of every pipe organ, and must be replaced every two or three decades (which is not too bad when one considers that many electronic organs become totally obsolete in that time). It is true of course that an organ can be ruined. Despite the fact that pipes, boards, console and racks are all virtually permanent, the pipes can be ruined in the course of two or three centuries of careless cone-tuning. Water from a constantly leaking pipe or roof could cause warping of the boards and racks, and rats could conceivably damage not only leathers but wooden elements as well. But except for such monumental bad care, and the exception of the leathers, the organ is virtually permanent.

It is simply false to suggest that a pipe organ wears out. A pipe organ is not a piece of statuary, it needs regular tuning and adjustment—which is also true of an electronic instrument—and in the time that many electronic instruments have become obsolete, it will have to have its leathers replaced. But when it is suggested that a pipe organ is worn out, further inquiry must be made into such a highly suspicious statement. It does not make sense to discard a pipe organ as worn out simply because it needs new leathers. Pipe organs can be neglected until they sound terrible. Rotted leathers may make some stops unusable, but unless fire, rats, or water have seriously demolished the organ proper, it can still be repaired to sound forth with its original brilliance. Thus, in comparing the relative costs of maintenance, the pipe organ and electronic instrument cost approximately the same. The rate of both obsolescence and depreciation of current electronic models is unknown. On the other hand, pipe organs can last for literally centuries, and often do. The superior long-range economy of the pipe organ is obvious.

The fact that we seek the very finest that we have with which to worship God should lead us first to consider the pipe organ with all of its musical superiority. When factors of cost seem to limit the choice, then it must be remembered that an organ of very few ranks will often be adequate for the worship music of the church, and that quality is to be preferred to quantity. By careful building for maximum musical expression, a church may often find itself making savings in building costs, as well as savings through the possibility of a smaller organ doing an adequate job. In the areas of maintenance, depreciation, and obsolescence, the pipe organ appears to be the superior long-term investment from a financial point of view. From the aspect of music, and the joyous praise of God, the pipe organ is not without reason called the king of instruments.

Select Bibliography

PRIMARILY ARCHITECTURAL

Aspecten van Kerkbouw. Aalten: N. V. Uitgeversmaatschappij de Graafschap, n.d.
Addleshaw, G. W. O. and Etchells, Frederick. *The Architectural Setting of Anglican Worship.* London: Faber & Faber Ltd., 1948.
Bakhuizen van den Brink, J. N. *Protestantsche Kerkbouw.* Arnhem: S. Gouda Quint–D. Brouwer en Zoon, 1946.
Biedrzynski, Richard. *Kirchen unserer Zeit.* München: Hirmer Verlag, 1958.
Biéler, André. *Liturgie et Architecture.* Geneva: Labor et Fides, 1961.
———. "Liturgy and Architecture," *Lucerne International Joint Conference on Church Architecture and Church Building.* New York: Department of Church Building and Architecture, N.C.C.C., 1962.
Blanton, Joseph Edwin. *The Organ in Church Design.* Albany, Texas: Venture Press, 1957.
Briggs, Martin S. *Puritan Architecture.* London: Lutterworth Press, 1946.
Christ-Janer, Albert and Foley, Mary Mix. *Modern Church Architecture.* New York: McGraw-Hill Book Co., 1962.
Doom, James L. "Reformed Sanctuaries." Atlanta: Department of Church Architecture, Presbyterian Church in the United States, mimeographed, n.d.
———. *Church Architecture for Christian Education.* Richmond: Board of Christian Education, Presbyterian Church in the United States, n.d.

Drummond, A. L. *The Church Architecture of Protestantism*. Edinburgh: T. & T. Clark, 1934.
Documents for Sacred Architecture. Collegeville, Minnesota: The Liturgical Press, 1957.
Ellinwood, Leonard. *The History of American Church Music*. New York: Morehouse-Gorham Co., 1953.
Fiddes, Victor. *The Architectural Requirements of Protestant Worship*. Toronto: Ryerson Press, 1961.
Hamberg, Per Gustaf. *Templebygge för Protestanter*. Stockholm: Svenska Kyrkans Diakonistyrelses Bokförlag, 1955.
Hammond, Peter. *Liturgy and Architecture*. London: Barrie and Rockliff, 1960.
———— (ed). *Toward a Church Architecture*. London: Architectural Press, 1962.
Hay, George. *The Architecture of Scottish Post-Reformation Churches, 1560–1843*. Oxford: Clarendon Press, 1957.
Massa, Conrad H. "Architectural Implications of Recent Trends in Reformed Liturgy," *The Princeton Seminary Bulletin*, LIV, 3 (Feb. 1961).
Nichols, James H. and Trinterud, Leonard J. *The Architectural Setting for Reformed Worship*. Chicago: Presbytery of Chicago, 1960.
Pfammatter, Ferdinand, *Betonkirchen*. Zurich: Benziger Verlag, 1948.
Pichard, Joseph. *Les églises nouvelles à travers le monde*. Paris: Deux-Mondes, 1960.
Senn, Otto H. "Church Building and Liturgy in the Protestant Church," *Lucerne International Joint Conference on Church Architecture and Church Building*. New York: Dept. of Church Building & Architecture, N.C.C.C., 1962.
Schwarz, Rudolf. *The Church Incarnate*. Chicago: Henry Regnery Co., 1958.
————. *Kirchenbau*. Heidelberg: F. H. Kerle Verlag, 1960.
Thiry, Paul, Bennett, Richard M., and Kamphoefer, Henry L. *Churches and Temples*. New York: Reinhold Publishing Corp., 1954.
Van Mourik, W. J. G. *Hervormde Kerkbouw na 1945*. The Hague: Boekencentrum N. V., 1957.
Weyres, Willy and Bartning, Otto. *Kirchen Handbuch für den Kirchenbau*. Münich: Callwey, 1959.

PRIMARILY THEOLOGICAL

Benoit, J. D. *Liturgical Renewal, Studies in Catholic and Protestant Developments on the Continent*. London: SCM Press Ltd., 1958.
Calvin, John. *Institutes of the Christian Religion*, Vol. 1, Library of Christian Classics. Translated and edited by Ford Lewis Battles. Philadelphia: Westminster Press, 1960.
Connell, Francis J. *New Baltimore Catechism No. 3, Official Revised Edition*, 1949. Boston: Benzinger Brothers, Inc.
Cullmann, Oscar. *Early Christian Worship*. London: SCM Press Ltd., 1953.
Davies, Horton. *Worship and Theology in England, 1690–1850*. Princeton: University Press, 1961.

Dix, Dom Gregory. *The Shape of the Liturgy*. Westminster: Dacre Press, 1945.
Dowey, Edward A., Jr. *The Knowledge of God in Calvin's Theology*. New York: Columbia University Press, 1952.
Hageman, Howard G. "Can Church Music Be Reformed?" *The Reformed Review*, Vol. 14, No. 2 (Dec. 1960).
———. *Pulpit and Table*. Richmond: John Knox Press, 1962.
Heidelberg Catechism, 400th Anniversary Edition, 1563-1963. Translated by Allen O. Miller and M. Eugene Osterhaven. New York: Board of Education, Reformed Church of America, 1963.
Jungmann, Josef A. *The Mass of the Roman Rite*. Translated by Francis A. Brunner. New York: Benziger, 1951–55.
Maxwell, W. D. *Concerning Worship*. London: Oxford University Press, 1948.
———. *John Knox's Genevan Service Book 1556*. Edinburgh: Oliver & Boyd, 1931.
McEwen, James S. *The Faith of John Knox*. Richmond: John Knox Press, 1961.
Michell, G. A. *Landmarks in Liturgy*. London: Darton, Longman & Todd, 1961.
O'Brien, John A. *Understanding the Catholic Faith, An Official Edition of the Revised Baltimore Catechism No. 3*. Notre Dame: Ave Maria Press, 1955.
Parker, T. H. L. *The Oracles of God*. London: Lutterworth Press, 1947.
Thompson, Bard (ed.). *Liturgies of the Western Church*. Cleveland: The World Publishing Co. [Living Age Books], 1961.
Torrance, T. F. *Conflict and Agreement in the Church*, Vol. 2, *The Ministry and the Sacraments of the Gospel*. London: Lutterworth Press, 1960.
Van Buren, Paul. *Christ in Our Place*. Grand Rapids: Wm. B. Eerdmans Publishing Co., 1957.
Wallace, Ronald S. *Calvin's Doctrine of Word and Sacrament*. Grand Rapids: Wm. B. Eerdmans Publishing Co., 1953.
———. *Calvin's Doctrine of the Christian Life*. Grand Rapids: Wm. B. Eerdmans Publishing Co., 1959.

Index of Churches

(Entries are arranged by cities. Italicized numbers indicate pages with illustrations.)

Aerdenhout, The Netherlands. The Church of the Advent (Adventskerk), Hervormd, 308, 604, *605–07*

Amstelveen, The Netherlands. The Church of the Cross (Kruiskerk), Hervormd, 94, *95–107*, 110, 134, *135,* 170, 228, 231, 308, 437

Amsterdam-Slotervaart, The Netherlands. The Ark (De Ark), Hervormd, 149f., *151–167,* 231, 447, 482

Amsterdam-South, The Netherlands. Maranatha Church (Maranathakerk), Hervormd, 308, *309–15,* 437, 548, *549*

Amsterdam-Watergraafsmeer, The Netherlands. The Church of the King (Koningskerk), Gereformeerd, 461–62, *463–65*

Amsterdam-West, The Netherlands. The Church of the Resurrection (Opstandingskerk), Hervormd, 110, *111–23,* 228, 437, 447, 475, 687

Bant, N. O. P., The Netherlands. The Reformed Church, Hervormd, 231f., *233–39,* 687

Barisal, Eastern Bengal, India. Church of the Oxford Mission in Calcutta, 137

Basel, Switzerland. All Saints Church (Alleheiligenkirche), Roman Catholic, 32, *33,* 670

Basel, Switzerland. Munster, Reformed, 81

Basel, Switzerland. The Church of St. Antony (St. Antoniuskirche), Roman Catholic, 27, *28,* 670

Basel-Birsfelden, Switzerland. The Church of Brother Klaus (Bruderklausenkirche), Roman Catholic, 36, *37–40*

Bern, Switzerland. Bethlehem Church (Bethlehemkirche), Reformed, 300, *301–07*
Bern, Switzerland. The Church of St. Mark (St. Markuskirche), Reformed, 172, *173–79,* 228
Beverwijk-West, The Netherlands. The Ascent (De Opgang), Hervormd, 540, *541–43*
Bonigen near Interlaken, Switzerland. Kirche Bonigen, Reformed, 144, *145–47,* 228
Boston, Massachusetts. Trinity Church, Episcopal, 396
Bottmingen near Basel, Switzerland. Kirche Bottmingen, Reformed, 582, *583–85*
Bussum, The Netherlands. The Church of the Redeemer (Verlosserkerk), Hervormd, 644, *645–49*
Charlotte Amalie, St. Thomas, The Virgin Islands. St. Thomas Reformed Church, 230
Chartres, France. Chartres Cathedral, Roman Catholic, 526
Cleveland, Ohio. Parma Park Reformed Church, *189–203,* 475
Cleveland, Ohio. St. Paul's African Methodist Episcopal Church, 139, 504, *505*
Columbus, Ohio. St. Stephen's Episcopal Church, 474
Crownhill, England. The Church of the Ascension, Church of England, 81
Delft, The Netherlands. Immanuelkerk, Gereformeerd, 170, 250, 252, *253–63*
Düren, Germany. The Church of Christ (Christuskirche), Reformed, 222, *223–27,* 291, 408
Dunfermline, Fife, Scotland. North Kirk, Church of Scotland, 230
Edinburgh, Scotland. St. George's West, Church of Scotland, 410
Elkins Park, Pennsylvania. Beth Sholom Synagogue, 4, *5,* 596, *597–603*
Frankfurt am Main, Germany. The Church of St. Michael (St. Michaelskirche), 43f., *45–57*
Frankfurt am Main, Germany. Grace Church (Gnadenkirche), 6, 14, *15–17,* 228
Geneva, Switzerland. Saint-Pierre, Reformed, 81, 90, 209, 210
Gumligen near Bern, Switzerland. Kirche Gumligen, Reformed, 182, *183–87,* 228
Haarlem, The Netherlands. St. Bavo Church (Grote Kerk), Hervormd, 82, *83–89,* 90, 250, 308
The Hague, The Netherlands. Nieuwe Kerk, Hervormd, 90
The Hague, The Netherlands. The Wilhelmina Church (Wilhelminakerk), Hervormd, 240, *241–49,* 250, 687
The Hague, The Netherlands. The Zorgvliet Church (Zorgvlietkerk), Hervormd, 218, *219,* 422, *423–31,* 457
The Hague-Loosduinen, The Netherlands. The Church of the Advent (Adventskerk), Hervormd, 264, *265–81,* 308, 374, 475
Istanbul, Turkey. Sancta Sophia, Greek Orthodox, 408f.
Kirchenthurnen, Switzerland. The Church, Reformed, 6, *7–13,* 144, 228
Leverkusen-Burig, Germany. The Church of St. Peter (Petruskirche), Reformed, 624, *625–35*
Liestal, Switzerland. The Church of Brother Klaus (Bruderklausenkirche), Roman Catholic, 580, *581*
Litchfield, Connecticut. Congregational Church, 18f.
London, England. Westminster Abbey, Church of England, 388

Mannheim, Germany. The Church of the Trinity (Trinitatiskirche), Reformed, 461, 587–88, *589–95*
Mittelheim/Rheingau, Germany. The Reformed Church, 466, 468, *469–71*
Nagele, N. O. P., The Netherlands. The Reformed Church, Gereformeerd, 560, *561–65,* 687
Nagele, N. O. P., The Netherlands. The Reformed Church, Hervormd, 320, *321–27*
Newport, Rhode Island. Trinity Church, Episcopal, 479
Niagara Falls, Ontario, Canada. Lundy's Lane United Church, 410
Ochten, The Netherlands. The Reformed Church, Hervormd, 368, *369–73*
Paris, France. Notre-Dame du Raincy, Roman Catholic, 30
Philadelphia, Pennsylvania. Christ Chapel, Episcopal Academy, 291f., *293–99,* 408
Port Credit, Ontario, Canada. Applewood United Church, 403
Rome, Italy. St. Clement's, Roman Catholic, 409
Rutten, N. O. P., The Netherlands. The Reformed Church, Hervormd, 350, *351–61,* 687
Santpoort, The Netherlands. The Cornerstone (De Hoeksteen), Hervormd, 320, 328, *329–35,* 374
Schiedam, The Netherlands. The Church of the Resurrection (Opstandingskerk), Hervormd, 342, *343–47*
Stamford, Connecticut. First Presbyterian Church, 460
Stockholm, Sweden. The Hedvig Elsonora Kyrka, Lutheran, 290
Tingwall, Zetland, Scotland. Church of Scotland, 230
Torphichen, West Lothian, Scotland. Church of Scotland, 230
Voorburg, The Netherlands. The Church of the Fountain (Fonteinkerk), Gereformeerd, 374, *375–85,* 437
Wolfheze, The Netherlands. The Church of the Cross (Kruiskerk), Hervormd, 574, *575–79*
Zaandam, The Netherlands. The Church of Easter (Paaskerk), Hervormd, 437–38, *439–43*
Zeist, The Netherlands. Thomaskerk, Hervormd, 139
Zurich, Switzerland. The Bullinger Church (Bullingerkirche), Reformed, 139f., *141–43,* 228, 366, *367,* 447
Zurich-Alstetten, Switzerland. The Reformed Church, 403, 404, *405–07*

Index of Persons

(Italicized numbers indicate pages with illustrations.)

Addleshaw, G. W. O. and Etchells, Frederick, 76f., 90f., 137, 213, 218, 221f., 388ff., 392f., 409, 411, 460, 479f.
Ahrend and Brunzema, 238, *239*, 358, *359*, 422, *423*
Anselm, St., 388f.
Anson, Peter F., 418
Arndt, W. F. and Gingrich, F. W., 284
Augustine, St., 78

Bach, Johann Sebastian, 435, 690
Barth, Karl, 139
Baur, Hermann, 32, *33–35*, 36, *37–39*
Baxter, Richard, 71
Beauduin, Lambert, 30
Bennett, Richard M., Thiry, Paul, and Kamphoefer, Henry L., 21
Benoit, Jean Daniel, 41f., 74, 79
Bernard of Clairvaux, St., 459f.
Berry, Ray, 399, 415, 432

Biéler, André, 81f., 287f.
Biggs, E. Power, 437, 684
Blanton, Joseph Edwin, 398f., 415, 419, 432, 435ff., 684f., 687f.
Bohm, Max, 182, *183–187*
Bouman, A., 432
Bouyer, Louis, 79
Briggs, Martin S., 390
Broek, J. H. van den, and Bakema, J. B., 343, *343–47*, 560, *561–65*
Brooks and Coddington, 474
Brooks, Phillip, 396
Bruggink, Donald J., 188, *189–203*, 504, *505*
Bruins, G., 574, *575–79*
Bucer, Martin, 222, 480
Buxtehude, Diderik, 435

Calvin, John, 23f., 58ff., 68, 70, 73, 75, 78ff., 80, 127ff., 168f., 180, 196, 207, 209, 211f., 336f., 339, 362f., 445, 467, 480
Challis, John, 435

Chapman, Paul, and Lake, Charles, 466
Chaty, Raymond P., and Droppers, Carl H., 139, *189–203,* 504, *505*
Cohen, Rabbi Mortimer, J., 4, *5,* 596, *597–603*
Connell, Francis J., 26f., 58, 64, 168
Conover, Elbert M., 148
Cranmer, Thomas, 216
Cullmann, Oscar, 129ff.

Davies, Horton, 390
Decatur, Stephen, 451
Diffendorfer, Ralph E., 454
Dix, Gregory, 62, 77
Doom, James L., 412f.
Dowey, Edward A., Jr., 70
Droppers, Carl H., 139, *189–203,* 264, 504, *505*
Drummond, A. L., 92, 391, 395ff., 411, 418f., 478
Duintjer, M. F., 94, *95–107,* 110, *111–123,* 134, *135,* 139

Eibink, A., 368, *369–73*
Ellinwood, Leonard, 411
Eschauzier, F. A., Eschauzier, Frits; Berg, Fons van den; and Vletter, Paul de, 252, *253–63*
Essen, G. W. van, 374, *375–85*

Fiddes, Victor, 92, 403, 410
Fierens, Jan, 86, *87*
Flentrop, D. A., 106, *107,* 120, *121,* 314, *315,* 384, *385,* 437–38, *439,* 684
Flue, Niklaus von, 38
Fonteyn and Gaal, 564, *565*
Forster and Nicolaus, 50, *51*
Fueter, Max, 172, *173,* 186, *187*

Glatter-Gotz, Josef von, 437
Goll and Cie, 178, *179*

Groenewegen, Joh. H., and Mieras, H., 308, *309–15,* 548, *549*
Guntenaar, Ben, 134, *135*

Hageman, Howard, G., 18, 77, 126, 218, 287, 400, 478
Hamberg, Gustaf, 286
Hammond, Peter, 21, 23, 30, 40, 43, 81, 110, 137, 392f., 408, 480
Harris, T. L., 395
Harrison, Wallace K., 461
Hay, George, 90, 108, 138, 148, 229f., 340, 348, 409, 460, 477f.
Heideman, E. P., 350, 363
Hendriks, Berend, *463,* 464, *465*
Hentrich, and Heuser, Hans, 222, *223–27*
Hentrich and Petschnigg, 624, *625–35*
Hill, Arthur George, 432
Hofmann, H. G., 468, *469–71*
Hook, Theodore Farquhar, 390
Hooper, John, 213
Hubers, Dirk, 280, *281*
Huston, Harry M., 188, *189–203*

Indermuhle, Ernst and Ulrich, 144, *145–47*

Jebb, John, 390, 392

Keusa, Benedicht, 8, *9,* 13
Kittel, Gerhard, 71
Kling, Vincent G., 292, *293–99*
Knox, John, 22, 208
Kok, P. H. G. C., 360, *361*
Kruger, J., 328, *329–35*
Küenzi, Werner, 300, *301–07*
Kuhn, Th., 12, *13*
Kuilen, W. van der, 320, *321–27*
Kuilen, W. van der, and Trappenberg, C., 462, *463–65*
Kuyper, M., and Westerduin, C., 218, *219,* 422, *423–31*

Laud, William, 76f.
Leeuwen, W. van, 268, *269*
Luther, Martin, 58ff., 78

McClinton, Katherine Morrison, 391
McEwen, James S., 208
McKim, Mead, and White, 397
Marcussen and Søn, 84, *85,* 322, *323*
Massa, Conrad H., 23, 221, 285, 466, 480f.
Mauriac, Francois, 59
Maxwell, W. D., 138, 220, 264, 394, 412
Metzger, Fritz, 580, *581*
Michell, G. A., 216
Moody, Dwight L., 396
Moser, Karl, 27, *28*
Moser, Werner, 404, *405–07*
Mozart, Wolfgang Amadeus, 435
Mueren, Floris van der, 432
Muller, Christian, 84, *85*
Muller, Karl, and Daxelhofer, Henry, 172, *173–179*

Neale, John Mason, 389f.
Nichols, James H., and Trinterud, Leonard J., 18, 212, 217, 230, 456
Nielsen, Spruit, and Van der Kuilen, 320, *321–27,* 644, *645–49*

O'Brien, John A., 26, 74
Overbosch, W. G., 164
Overton, Charles Carlton, 454

Pachelbel, Johann, 435
Paquier, Richard, 221, 285
Parker, T. H. L., 210
Parsch, Pius, 30
Perret, Auguste, 30
Peter, Willi, 226, *227,* 630, *631*
Pfammatter, Ferdinand, 30
Pfister Bros., 139f., *141–143,* 366, *367*

Pius XII, Pope, 41f., 74

Richardson, H. H., 396
Ridley, Nicholas, 213
Ritenour, Scott T., 19
Roguet, A. M., 79
Ruiter, A. Mense, 464, *465*
Ruskin, John, 92

Scherrer, Samson, 12, *13*
Schilling, Albert, 32, *33–35*
Schipper, J., Jr., 350, *351–61*
Schnitger, Arp, 684, 690
Schwarz, Rudolf, 31, 43f. *45–57,* 222
Schweitzer, Albert, 684
Scott, G. G., 388
Senn, Otto H., 91, 286, 288, 391
Servieres, Georges, 432
Sijmons, K. L., Dzn., 264, *265–81,* 438, *439–43,* 604, *605–07*
Sleeswijk, C. Wegener, and Wichers, S. J. S., 232, *233–39*
Steinmeyer, G. F., 594, *595*
Striffler, Helmut, 587–88, *589–95*
Sturm, Leonhardt Christoph, 290
Sunday, Billy, 396
Sweelinck, Jan Peterszoon, 435

Tallmadge, T. E., 397
Thompson, Bard, 229
Torrance, T. F., 205

Valckx and Van Kouteren, 574, *575*
Van Buren, Paul, 71
Van Vulpen, 240, *241*
Verschueren, L., 162, *163*

Wallace, Ronald S., 68, 72
Warburton, William, 460
Watts, Isaac, 610
Webb, Benjamin, 389f.

Westcott, Brooke Foss, 71
Weyres, Willy, and Bartning, Otto, 90, 286, 291
Woerden, S. van, 540, *541–43*
Wotherspoon, H. J., 418
Wren, Sir Christopher, 90, 411
Wright, Frank Lloyd, 4, *5,* 596, *597–603*

Wurster, Walter, 582, *583–85*

Zanstra, Giesen, and Sijmons, 264, *265–81*
Zanstra, P., 150, *151–167*
Ziegler-Heberlein, Rudolf, *405,* 406, *407*
Zwiers, H. T., 240, *241–49*
Zwingli, Ulrich, 209, 218, 229, 480

Index of Scripture

Genesis		Psalms		Amos	
1:3	64	19:1	587	5:21	60
2:16	59	89:15	598	5:24	60
3:9	59				
12:1–2	60	Isaiah		Matthew	
		6:8	78	9:1ff.	66
Exodus		25:6–9	206	11:4–6	129
6:7	60			12:39–40	134
14:28	186	Jeremiah		13:16	61
17:6	186	1:4–5	60	15:10	61
		1:9	60	24:27	22
Leviticus		5:14	60	26:26ff.	62
19:2	602	31:34	61	27:66	130
		32:10–11	131		
		32:14	131	Mark	
Numbers		32:44	131	14:22ff.	62
13	360				
		Daniel		Luke	
Esther		6:17	130	1:23	22
8:8	131	9:24	131	14:15–24	206
8:10	131	12:4	131	14:23	204
		12:9	131	17:5	128

22:15ff.	62	10:17	61	4:11–12	336
24:13–53	205	12:1	211	4:30	131
24:45	68	12:5	230	5:26	132
		12:8	362	5:30	70
		15:28	130		

John
- 1:1–4 65
- 1:14 65
- 1:18 65
- 2:6 129
- 2:11 129
- 3:5 132
- 4:10–15 132
- 4:13–14 186
- 6 129
- 6:1ff. 66
- 6:27 131
- 6:35 66, 207
- 7:37–38 132, 186
- 7:38 132
- 11:4 66
- 11:25 66, 67
- 11:43–44 66
- 11:50 450
- 14:16–17 68
- 14:21 68
- 19:34 132

Acts
- 2:44–45 365
- 5:29 453
- 10:47 132
- 14:23 337, 339

Romans
- 4:11 131
- 6:2–4 180
- 6:3–4 134
- 8:14–15 230
- 10:13–14 61

I Corinthians
- 2:12–13 68
- 6:15 72
- 10:1–4 202
- 10:1–5 186
- 10:4 186
- 10:5 202
- 10:16ff. 62
- 10:17 207
- 11:20–34 62
- 12 336
- 13:8–10 364
- 13:12–13 364
- 14:13–19 62
- 15:12 72
- 15:15–16 72
- 15:20 72
- 16:20–22 62

II Corinthians
- 1:22 131

Ephesians
- 1:3 70
- 1:4 70
- 1:7 70
- 1:12 71
- 1:13 70, 131
- 2:4–6 73
- 2:5 70
- 2:10 72
- 2:12–13 70
- 4:7 336

Colossians
- 2:6–7 76
- 3:3 73
- 3:3–4 76

Philippians
- 2:17 22

I Timothy
- 2:7 285

Hebrews
- 9:21 22
- 9:26 75

I Peter
- 2:6–8 328
- 2:9 284
- 3:18–21 150, 156, 186
- 3:20 132

I John
- 3:14 68
- 3:24 71
- 4:12–13 69
- 5:6–8 132
- 5:20 71

Revelation
- 7:17 132
- 19.9 464
- 21:6 132
- 22:1 132
- 22:17 132

Index of Subjects

Acoustics, church auditorium, diagram, 675
Aesthetics, 2, 287, 611f.
Akron Plan, 397
Altars, 338, 396
    as focal point, 26ff., 43
    coffin form, 212, 214, 217
    ornamentation, 36
    single altar in each room, 40
    stone, 2, 213
    table form, 211ff.
Architects, 491ff., 655ff., 664ff.
    fees of, 491, 498ff.
    registration of, 492f.
    selection of, 491
    services of, 498ff.
        consultants, 511ff.
        contracts, 502ff.
        contractors, 507ff.
        documents and drawings, 506f.
        models, 503ff.
        plans, 552
        supervision, 500ff.
Associated Pipe Organ Builders of America, 688
Auditory churches, 90f.

Baptism, 132, 134ff., 205, 221, 666f.
    baptismal regeneration, 132, 137
    Christ, as entrance into, 136ff.
        continuing participation in atoning work, 168ff.
        continuing participation in resurrection to newness of life, 180f.
Baptismal fonts, 126, 138ff., 169f., 666f.
    basin on Lord's table, 138ff., 148, 168f.
    bracketed on pulpit, 148, 168f.
    font/table, 144f.
    forms, sizes and materials, 170
Basements, 535ff., diagram, 537
Basilicas, 91ff.
Belgic Confession, 136
Bouw- en Restauratie-Commissie van de Nederlandse Hervormde Kerk, 20, 571
Building Committees, 489ff., 655ff., 664ff.

Cambridge Camden Society, 389
Cambridge Ecclesiologists, 137, 214, 287, 389ff., 392, 396
Candles, 214, 216ff.
Candlesticks, 36, 40
Choir, 387ff., 677
   historical considerations:
      lay membership, 389
      Medieval Gothic, 388ff., 395, 403
      monks, choir of, 388f.
      Reformation, at, 389f., 393, 400
   plan:
      facing congregation, 398
      Scottish practice, 408ff.
      separated from congregation, 408
      singing loft or pew, 389
      split chancel, 388ff.
      theater plan, 388, 394ff., 401f., 403
   practical considerations, 393ff., 408, 412f., 414
   theological considerations:
      choirolatry, 395, 414
      clergy, relation to, 388f., 392f., 399
      congregation, as part of, 399, 408
      independent unit, 399f.
      theological role, 402f., 412ff.
Christ:
   second coming of, 210, 364
   union with, 67ff., 180f., 205, 207f., 221
Church:
   body of Christ, 138, 148, 208, 230, 328, 336f., 453
   congregation, 148ff., 391, 670f.
   definition of, 283ff.
   family of God, 211
   unity of, 208f.
Church Architectural Guild of America, 21
Church of England, 218, 390, 392
Church of Scotland, 22, 207f., 229f., 391, 408ff.
Church school, 657ff.

Clarity, 567
Classical revival, 19, 397
Climate, 522, diagram, 523
Cock on tower, 372f.
Collectezakjes, 368, 374
Colonial architecture, 18f., 556f.
Communication, 291, 674f.
Communion, 204ff.
   frequency of, 209f.
   rails, 221
   room, 250ff., 264ff.
   see also Lord's table
Competitions, conducted by American Institute of Architects, 491
Confessions of Reformation, 23f.
Consultants, 511ff., 656f.
Contracts, 502f., 552f.
   safeguards in building, 509ff.
Contractors, 507ff.
   workmen, 553
Covenant, 138ff., 164
Criteria, 24
   baptism, 138, 169, 181, 666–67
   choir, 402f., 410f., 677f.
   Christian education, 657
   church kitchens, 663
   communication, 291, 674
   congregation, 288, 289, 670
   cross, 458
   deacon, office of, 365f., 676f.
   elder, office of, 350, 676
   flags, 455
   lectern, 482
   Lord's Supper, 212, 214, 220, 229, 667–68
   materials, 447f.
   memorial gifts, 477
   minister, office of, 338f., 676
   natural light, 475
   organ, 418, 420, 432–33, 678, 684, 686, 688

pulpit Bible, 109
study, 485
symbols, 457f.
things, 449
windows, 474
Word, 80, 666
Crosses, 40, 214, 216ff.
Crucifixes, 36, 217

Deacons, 338, 362ff., 676f.
architectural symbol of, 366ff.
office of, 284, 362ff., 374
pews for, 84
Deaconesses, 152
Decorations, 455ff.
Deism, 133
Department of Church Building and Architecture of the National Council of Churches of Christ, U.S.A., 21
Depreciation, 546f.
Deutsche Evangelisch-Reformierte Gemeinde, 14
Diagrams
Building Insurance Rate Basis, 531
Church Auditorium Acoustics, 675
Church Expression Principles, 613
Church Neighborhood Surveys, 495
Church Property Planning, 517
Circular Plan Considerations, 651
Climate Principles, 523
Heating Principles, 551
Lighting Principles, 573
Pew Selection Principles, 673
Plan Simplification Principles, 527
Planning Principles, 559
Selection of Floor Elevation, 537
Site Selection Principles, 497
Space Selection Principles, 617
Survey Requirements, 519
Toward a Corporate Worship, 669
Tree Selection Principles, 569

Volume Selection Principles, 641
Water Supply Principles, 521
Window Operation Principles, 545
Documents and drawings, 506f.
Doorgeefzakjes, 374

Eucharist, 59, 222
sacrifice and meal, 41f., 211
see also Communion
Elders, 339ff., 362, 676
architectural symbol of, 340ff.
office of, 284, 339ff.
pews for, 84f., 340, 348ff.
Elegance, 611f.
English nonconformists, 229
Equipment, 547ff.
Expansion, 538
Expression, church, diagram, 613

Financial resources, 524
First Congress for Protestant Church Architecture, Berlin, 1898, 20
Flags:
national, 449ff.
"Christian," 453ff.
Flowers, 214f., 449
Fonts—see Baptismal fonts
Fourth Lateran Council, 73

Gothic, 82, 556f.
revival, 18f., 397f., 419
Romantic movement, 137, 213, 287
choir, 392, 403
medieval chancel, 338, 390, 397
Grace, means of, 402

Heating principles, diagram, 551
Heidelberg Catechism, 128, 136, 211, 402
Hengelzakjes, 368, 374
Heresy, 445ff.

Holy Spirit, 67ff., 205f., 210, 221, 336f., 339, 402
Honesty, 555ff.
Huguenots, 208, 286

Insurance, 529, diagram, 531
Interdenominational Bureau of Church Architecture of the National Council of Churches, 19
Interest, 524

Jougs, 348f.

Kitchens, church, 660ff.
Klosterneuburg, 30

Laity, 283ff.
   lay readers, 477f.
   separation from clergy, 337
Lecterns, 477ff.
   Cambride Ecclesiologists, use of, 478ff.
   Reformed use of, 477ff.
Light, natural, 474f., diagram, 573, 586ff.
Lightness, 570ff.
Liturgical movement, 30ff., 211, 217, 392
Liturgy, 22f.
Lord's Supper—*see* Communion, Eucharist, Lord's table
Lord's table, 81ff., 125, 210ff., 338, 396, 667ff.
   architectural considerations:
     accessible and visible, 220ff.
     accouterments, 214ff.
       carpet on, 218
       wooden vessels, 212, 218
     communicants seated at table, 81f., 88f., 229ff.
     liturgical use during worship service, 220f.
       prayers at, 221
     separate room for Lord's table, 82, 88f., 250ff., 264ff.
     should look like a table, 212ff.
     temporary table, 81f., 88f., 380, 440f.
   theological considerations:
     Last Supper, 204
     Messianic Meal, 206f., 210f., 230
     present Lord, 204ff.
     united family, 207ff.
Lucerne International Joint Conference on Church Architecture and Church Building, 21

Maintenance, 546
Maria Laach, Benedictine abbey, 30
Martyrs, tombs of, 212
Mass, 2, 26ff., 41ff., 73ff., 211
Materials, 538f., 622ff.
   excessive variety of, 446ff.
Mediator Dei et Hominum, 41f., 74
Memorial gifts, 475ff.
Messianic Meal, 206f., 210f., 230; *see also* Lord's Supper
Minister, office of, 284, 336ff., 481, 676
Minister's study, 482ff.
Models, 503ff.
Murals, ceramic, 280f.

Narthex, 137
Nederlandse Hervormde Kerk, 20, 571

Offering plates, 214ff.
   receptacles, 374
   shelves for, 270ff.
Offertory, 215
Order, architectural, 566
Organs, 417ff., 678f., 683ff.
   acoustics, 687ff.
   chambers, 419f., 433ff.
   cost, 684
   depreciation and obsolescence, 690ff.
   false pipes, 436f.

maintenance, 690ff.
position, 408, 410, 420f., 432ff.
purpose, 684ff.
size, 684ff.
superiority of pipe tone, 683ff.
swell boxes, 419f., 433ff.
tracker action, 408
volume, 433ff., 686ff.
Orgelbouw Genf, A. G., 306f.
Orthodox Christendom, 40, 59
Overflow room, 268f., 326f.
Oxford Movement, 389, 391

Participation, 553f.
Pews, 198, 670ff.
elders' pews, 340ff., 348ff.
folding communion pew, 229, 289f.
pew desk, 340
pew selection principles, diagram, 673
Pianos, 449
Pietism, 126
Plan simplification, diagram, 527
Planning principles, diagram, 559
Plans:
circular, 222, 290, 408, diagram, 651
Greek cross, 222ff., 291, 408
long nave, 291
octagon, 290, 308
triangle, 290
Plants, 466
Prayer chapel, 164f.
Prefabricated church buildings, 532ff.
Presbyterian:
government, 22, 339
history, 22
presbyters, 337
Presbyterian Church in the United States, 412f.
Priesthood of all believers, 284ff., 336
Prof. Dr. G. van der Leeuw-Stichting, 20, 139

Programming, 24, 110, 490, 655ff., 664ff.
Property, church, 516ff., diagram, 517
subsurface expenditures, 520, diagram, 521
Pulpit, 80ff., 286, 666
Bible on, 109
central position of, 92ff.
three-decker, 479f.

"Quickborn" R.C. Youth movement, 30

Rationalism, 69, 125, 133, 287
Recreation, church, 663ff.
Redemption, 70ff.
Reformation, 63, 81ff.
alteration of churches, 2, 218ff.
choir, position of, 389f., 399f., 411
priesthood of all believers, 284ff., 288
special offices, 284ff., 336
Resurrection, 70ff.
Rhythm, 610f.
Roman Catholic building directives, 31, 40, 136, 337
Romanesque revival, 19, 396f., 419
Romanticism, 12, 91, 137, 213, 286f., 390ff., 398, 403, 411, 479f.

Sacraments, 58ff., 125ff., 285, 337, 339ff., 409f.
discipline, 349f.
seals, 128, 130ff., 204f.
signs, 128ff., 204f.
St. John's, Benedictine abbey, 31
Sanctification, 70ff.
Sanctuary, 388, 664ff.
Scandinavian churches, 286
Scholastic orthodoxy, 69, 71
Scold's bridle, 348f.
Scriptural inscriptions on walls, 9ff., 406f.
Shape of church building, 637ff., diagram, 641

Site selection, diagram, 497
Sounding board, 82, 94ff., 108f.
Space selection principles, diagram, 617
Stained glass, 458ff.
Stock plans, 532ff.
Strasbourg liturgy, 220
Structure, 615ff.
Style, 2, 6, 212, 251
Surveys, 494ff., diagrams, 495, 519
Symbols, 455ff.
   chi rho, 250
   cross, 456ff.
   eternal lights, 456
   fish, 250
   pyx, 456
   worship centers, 456

Taxes, 525
Theology, 22f.
Things, excessive number of, 448f.
Torah, 598ff.
Transubstantiation, 41f., 73ff.
Tree selection principles, diagram, 569

Unitarians, 133

Volume selection principles, diagram, 641

Westminster Confession, 138
   Larger Catechism, 128
Windows, 458ff., 544ff., diagram, 545
   beton glass, 460ff.
   clear glass, 458, 466ff., 474
   stained glass, 458ff.
Word, 58ff., 221, 285, 337, 339ff., 409f.
   discipline in, 349f.
   Holy Spirit and union with Christ, 67ff.
   made flesh, 65ff.
   power of, 64f.
   preaching of, 482ff.
Worship, corporate, 148ff., 400, diagram, 669
"Worship experience," 287f.
Workmen, 553